Contracting with
the Federal Government

Fourth Edition

Margaret M. Worthington
Partner, Price Waterhouse LLP
Washington, D.C.

Louis P. Goldsman
Partner, Price Waterhouse LLP
Costa Mesa, California

JOHN WILEY & SONS, INC.

New York • Chichester • Weinheim • Brisbane • Singapore • Toronto

Copyright ©1984, 1988, 1992, 1998 by John Wiley & Sons, Inc.

Published simultaneously in Canada.

This publication is designed to provide accurate and authoritative information in regard to the subject matter covered. It is sold with the understanding that the publisher is not engaged in rendering legal, accounting, or other professional services. If legal advice or other expert assistance is required, the services of a competent professional person should be sought.

Library of Congress Cataloging-in-Publication Data:
Worthington, Margaret M.
    Contracting with the federal government / Margaret M. Worthington,
Louis P. Goldsman. — 4th ed.
        p.   cm.
    Rev. ed. of: Contracting with the federal government / Frank M.
Alston. 3rd ed. c1992.
    Kept up to date by supplements.
    Includes bibliographical references and index.
    ISBN 0-471-24218-7 (alk. paper)
    1. Public contracts—United States. 2. Government purchasing—Law
and legislation—United States. I. Goldsman, Louis P. II. Alston,
Frank M. Contracting with the federal government.   III. Title.
KF849.C664   1998
346.7302′3 — dc21   97-31547
                                                                                      CIP

Printed in the United States of America.

10 9 8 7 6 5 4 3 2

About the Authors

MARGARET M. WORTHINGTON, CPA, is a partner in the Government Contractor Consulting Services Group at Price Waterhouse LLP. She has extensive experience in developing and reviewing cost estimating and cost accounting systems. She has assisted numerous clients in implementing programs of self-governance. She actively consults with clients and provides expert witness testimony on issues relating to cost allowability, cost accounting standards, defective pricing, contract terminations, and equitable adjustment proposals. Before joining Price Waterhouse, she was employed by the Defense Contract Audit Agency in a variety of positions, including program manager in the Cost Accounting Division of DCAA Headquarters and Special Assistant to the Director of DCAA.

LOUIS P. GOLDSMAN, CPA, is a partner in Price Waterhouse LLP Government Contractor Consulting Services Group with years of experience dealing with almost all types of businesses contracting with the federal government. Mr. Goldsman has extensive experience in assisting clients in resolving defective pricing issues and in preparing and resolving contract claims for equitable price adjustments. Prior to joining Price Waterhouse, he was a technical programs specialist in the Los Angeles Region of the Defense Contract Audit Agency, serving as a cost accounting standards monitor.

Both authors are active lecturers on topics relating to the accounting and administrative requirements of federal contracting.

Preface to the Fourth Edition

"The only constant is change." That's how we started the Preface to our third edition and history has shown this adage to be true in the government contracting environment. But different from the past, change is now being motivated, and in some ways instigated, by the private sector more so than the government. Today the changes are more in the nature of the basic structure of the contracting community as it reacts to the economic environment in which that community operates. The changes in the procurement process are in many ways an attempt by the government to address industry's structural realignment.

The end of the cold war and the reductions in the federal acquisition budgets resulting from the change in the security risk to the United States has eliminated the need for many programs and products. Additionally, products the government intends to continue purchasing, particularly for defense purposes, are being bought in smaller quantities. In some cases there may not be a need for the kind or minimum quantities of items that contractors can economically produce. This creates a dilemma for both buyers and sellers. On one hand, the seller needs to have enough sales to make the recovery of production costs economically viable. On the other hand, the buyer needs to have enough sellers so there will be meaningful competition to control price demands.

For many products there are too few buyers and too many sellers. As a result, many contractors no longer have the luxury of concentrating on the U.S. government as a customer; or to survive they must be the principal source of supply for the reduced government requirements. The result has been mergers and acquisitions on a major scale. These mergers and acquisitions have significantly reduced the number of major government contractors. The government reaction demonstrated that the government contracting environment is still very much a regulated environment. The government has changed some of the procurement rules and regulations as it has sought to protect itself from an environment that did not have sufficient incentives to keep contractors from passing unreasonable merger and acquisition related costs to the government.

At the same time the government recognized that there was and is an economic cost to the procurement regulations. Presumably the cost incurred by contractors complying with the procurement regulations is included in the price paid by the government for the goods and services it procures from the private sector. The government has sought to change the procurement process to reduce this cost. It has sought, to the extent practical, to use commercial practices as the basis for controlling the buyer/seller relationship. In addition, after an approximately two-year effort, the rewrite to streamline and simplify the Federal Acquisition Regulation, Part XV—*Contracting by Negotiation*, was issued on September 30, 1997. Its use became mandatory for solicitations issued on or after January 1, 1998. As we write this Fourth Edition, the competing forces, those seeking to "commercialize" and simplify the procurement process and those seeking greater protections for the government, are creating a more complex environment for those charged with buying and selling goods and services in this marketplace.

Politicians and defense planners must also deal with domestic and geopolitical pressures and risks. Fortunately, the procurement related changes are taking place in a period of strong economic growth and low inflation. As we write this edition the federal deficit is at its lowest level since 1970. Nevertheless, the goal to eliminate the federal deficit, coupled with a reduced security risk, creates political pressure to reduce procurements and the cost of government. Congress has responded by including a provision in the Fiscal Year 1998 Defense Authorization Act to reduce the defense acquisition work force by 25,000 positions in Fiscal Year 1998. It will be interesting to observe how the changes to the Federal Acquisition Regulation, Part 15, which provide more discretion to the contracting officer, will be implemented by a shrinking government acquisition workforce. In one sense the increased flexibility provided by the revised regulations provides a greater opportunity for second-guessing. If the economy does not maintain its current strength, we may relive the government procurement related "horror stories" of the mid-1980s. Only time will tell.

Perhaps it is time for a new adage: the only certainty is uncertainty. As each party seeks to address change, processes evolve; one party takes a step and the other reacts. The mergers and acquisitions by industry, and the changes in the rules and regulations by the government are but examples of this dynamic at work.

We have endeavored to update this book to reflect the changes in the rules and regulations brought about by changes in the economic and political environment that have occurred since our last edition. Our objective for this edition remains the same as prior editions: to provide timely, practical information regarding the rules and regulations that define the federal procurement process. We have attempted to provide the information necessary for both buyers and sellers to operate successfully in the current environment.

Washington, D.C.   MARGARET M. WORTHINGTON
Costa Mesa, California   LOUIS P. GOLDSMAN
January 1998

EDITOR'S NOTE

While we have made every attempt to ensure that the forms included in this book are complete and current, the reader/user should investigate any changes in regulations and forms that may have been issued since the publication of the book.

Preface to the Third Edition

"The only constant is change." While this adage is often used to describe our modern society, it is particularly relevant in the arcane and dynamic world of federal procurement. How the U.S. Government behaves as a customer, especially in meeting the nation's defense needs, is directly influenced by political and economic developments, both international and domestic, which define those needs, determine the available resources to meet them, and shape the acquisition process to be followed by the participants. Certainly, since publishing our second edition, momentous geopolitical and economic changes (e.g., the abrupt end of the Cold War, the Persian Gulf Conflict, the savings and loan debacle) have occurred which will profoundly alter the federal marketplace for the foreseeable future. The challenge for procurement professionals, from both government and industry, is to discern what fundamental changes must be made to the contracting process to ensure continued effectiveness in meeting redefined needs. Equally important, participants in this process must keep in sharp focus what must remain constant. These judgments must be made with a clear and unwavering commitment to what must continue to be the basic objective of a procurement system: to motivate industry to meet government procurement needs by providing quality goods and services, delivered on time, at fair and reasonable prices.

Our objective for the reader of the third edition remains the same as that established for the earlier versions: to provide timely, practical information regarding the rules and regulations that define the federal procurement process. We continue to emphasize that, from industry's perspective, the federal government must be viewed as a unique and complex marketplace. As in any marketplace, a prerequisite for success is a thorough knowledge of its requirements. This edition is intended to update the material to reflect not only the expected changes in regulations and federal procurement organizations, but also to recognize the structural changes that have occurred in this important market and the implications of those changes for those responsible for awarding and performing government contracts.

In the middle 1980s, the government made, what appeared to be, a rather dramatic change in its approach to enforcing compliance with the prescribed procurement process. The emphasis on contractor self-governance; greater inclination in federal agencies to use the judicial process to resolve product pricing and contract administration disputes; and the proliferation of regulations and contract clauses imposing certification requirements and exacting penalties for administrative noncompliances; all point to the need for contractors to reassess their management strategy for assuring that the contractually mandated procurement process is, in fact, followed. The legal and financial risks of dealing with the matter of regulatory compliance on an ad hoc basis had simply become too high. The second edition was intended to assist the contracting community to successfully respond to this development.

We perceive that the changes occurring since our second edition are fundamentally different. Unlike the past developments which required us to reexamine and establish or improve processes within a market structure, these geopolitical and economic events have profoundly and unalterably changed the fundamental structure of the market itself. Managers of industry must now develop, design, and implement new business strategies for entering, staying in, or exiting a marketplace dramatically different and, in many ways, much more complex and demanding that it was just two or three years before.

With astonishing suddenness, the Cold War abruptly ended, rendering virtually obsolete a defense policy of preparing to deter, and if necessary, fight an unthinkable strategic nuclear war. Before we could begin to "beat our swords into plowshares," a full-fledged military conflict erupted in the Persian Gulf, emphasizing the need for a military response materially different from what had been the core of our defense strategy for over 40 years. Added to this was the nation's desire to address pressing social needs and federal budget deficit reduction, with the "peace dividend" ostensibly resulting from the fact that the Soviet Union and the eastern bloc countries were no longer regarded as a serious threat to our national security. Public support for defense spending appeared to diminish even more when the "peace dividend"—if these ever was one—was more than absorbed by the need to bail out of the savings and loan industry using public funds. These events accelerated and intensified the ongoing efforts in the Pentagon to rethink and redefine the nation's defense needs. The outcome of this process is likely to be a marketplace that is structurally different from what we have known.

More so than ever before, the watchword for federal contracting, especially relating to defense procurement, will be *cost-effectiveness*. That is, doing more with less. Dr. Jacques Gansler, a former deputy assistant secretary of defense, accurately described the major concern of the nation's defense planners in this new environment as: how to reduce the cost of defense equipment while maintaining a viable defense base that keeps cost to a minimum and ensures surge capability for future emergencies. Unquestionably, industry will find more intense competition for a smaller, and less predictable market. In commenting on the new defense marketplace, the editors of *Fortune* magazine observed that, "Budget holddowns means that U.S. forces will have to get smaller, smarter, swifter, and stronger. Wise contractors are finding ways to turn this imperative to their advantage."

The authors of our third edition recognize and fully appreciate the challenges facing those involved in the federal procurement process. The pricing, costing, and administration of contracts, already complex, will become even more formidable as government agencies redefine their needs and cope with the realities of severe budgetary constraints. Concurrently, industry will be seeking innovative ways to compete successfully to fulfill federal procurement needs while providing their owners a reasonable return. All parties, those responsible for enforcing as well as those obligated to comply, require a thorough knowledge of the rules and regulations in order to ensure that the process works as intended.

We certainly hope the contents of this text make a meaningful contribution to facilitating this important activity: federal contracting.

Bethesda, Maryland
Newport Beach, California
January 1992

FRANK M. ALSTON
MARGARET M. WORTHINGTON
LOUIS P. GOLDSMAN

Preface to the Second Edition

Since our first edition in 1984, the Federal contracting environment has undergone a rather dramatic and fundamental change. Those who are reasonably knowledgeable about this activity would recognize that government procurement is truly a dynamic process and that a certain amount of change is expected. Even so, we believe there was general surprise at the rapid and extensive change in the procurement culture; that is, change in the basic set of assumptions and ground rules that underline the rules and regulations and define the government–contractor relationship. This cultural change manifested itself in a spate of new and revised regulations as well as a noticeably different approach by the government in its enforcement practices. Unquestionably, these developments materially altered the way contractors must conduct business with the government customers. For this text to continue to fulfill its purpose of not only helping the reader to identify and understand the relevant regulations but also understand the government's attitude toward implementation, an update of the material to reflect this new environment is certainly required. With this revision, we are hopeful that the book will remain a practical guide for all who are involved in this complex activity of pricing, costing, and administering federal contracts.

In its legitimate role of establishing the legal framework for the Federal acquisition process, Congress enacts legislation from time to time that alters the basic structure in which this activity takes place. Since 1984, however, the legislators have uncharacteristically gotten involved directly in managing government contracts. Ostensibly responding to media revelation of alleged excesses in contracting, Congress enacted so-called reform legislation that prescribed detailed changes to specific provisions of the procurement regulations. This unprecedented "micromanagement" by Congress has caused difficulty for contractors and government officials; primarily because the direct involvement by Congress at level previously reserved for implementing agencies introduced yet another variable into the government–contractor relationship, causing even greater uncertainty and complexity.

The new procurement laws are intended to remedy a broad spectrum of alleged contractor abuses such as: billing the government for labor costs mischarged to contracts, requesting reimbursement for unallowable indirect expenses, and inflating negotiated prices by failing to provide government negotiators the required cost and pricing data. Moreover, Congress concluded that these problems were widespread and, in many instances, deliberate. The legislators criticized the federal agencies for being both negligent and inept in discovering these problems and in taking appropriate actions against the guilty contractors. To ensure that agencies became more effective in ferreting out contractor fraud, waste, and abuse, the new laws, among other requirements, (1) made procurement regulations more restrictive, (2) increased the penalties for violating regulations, (3) required contractors to certify under the penalty of perjury that their indirect cost submissions comply with the regulations, (4) directed the contracting agencies to impose tighter control on their suppliers, and (5) mandated an increased level of oversight of the acquisition function. Taken together, these actions had a profound impact on the procurement climate.

Stung by the harsh Congressional criticism that they were lax in their enforcement of the procurement regulations, the executive agencies, especially the Department of Defense, have become more aggressive in performing contract audits and conducting other oversight reviews. As expected, DOD has increased the number of audits and, in many instances, substantially expended the scope of these reviews. Contractors, of course, must respond to this initiative by providing more resources to support this general increase in audit activity. While the increased audit activity certainly adds to the cost of doing business with Uncle Sam, this does not represent the fundamental change in the environment. What does represent change, and is causing considerable trauma among contractors, is the lessening ability to predict how the government will characterize an audit issue or in what forum the government will seek to have the matter resolved. In other words, is the noncompliance a contractual matter or is it to be regarded as an attempt to defraud? It seems that the government is more prone to use criminal rather administrative remedies to resolve problems arising out of the contracting process.

This shift in focus has serious implications for contractors. First, what actions should contractors take to minimize the incidence of noncompliances. Second, when noncompliances are discovered, how can contractors improve their ability to objectively establish that the problem was inadvertent rather than a deliberate attempt to overcharge; and third, what must be done in the way of system design and implementation to demonstrate that adequate safeguards are present to protect the government's interests.

The Department of Defense Inspector General (DODIG) appears to emphasize using the criminal process to deal with contracting problems. Specifically, in its role as overseer of the contract audit function, the DODIG advised auditors and contracting officials *never* to make any assumption about contractor intent or good faith whenever a noncompliance is discovered. Unfortunately, this approach effectively makes every noncompliance a potential crime until a criminal investigator has determined otherwise. This is, without a doubt, a very serious change in the government's approach in resolving alleged noncompliance. Our revised edition discusses, in some detail, how contractors must manage in a business environment that involves considerably more risk as compared to pre-1984. We focus on the imperative for contractors to reevaluate their financial management systems in light of current circumstances for the express purpose of assuring their effectiveness in avoiding, disclosing, and eliminating conditions of noncompliance.

The concept of industry accountability for compliance with federal procurement regulations was given major emphasis by the President's Blue Ribbon Commission on Defense Management (The Packard Commission). Actually, there is nothing new about contractors having an affirmative obligation to comply with the terms and conditions of the contracts they sign. What we believe to be different and significant is the increased emphasis the government will place on evaluating how well contractors are policing themselves for compliance with applicable regulations. The Commission in its final report recognized the limits of even the most effective enforcement and oversight activities as means for bringing about the needed improvements in the procurement process and for ensuring reasonable compliance in the future. Corporate self-governance, the Commission asserted, could redress the current weaknesses in the procurement system and could ultimately lead to a more productive relationship between the government and its suppliers. Fundamentally, self-governance requires the contractor to establish and maintain the necessary system of internal accounting and administrative controls to ensure the integrity of their own contract performance. This book describes the attributes of financial management systems that should meet these objectives.

While much has changed during the past three years, much remains the same. We have described in the preceding paragraphs what we perceive to be material changes in the government's fundamental approach to enforcing compliance with a basic procurement process that has stayed fairly constant. However, we emphasize that successfully providing the product or service only partially fulfills a company's contractual obligation to the government. What truly makes the federal government a different customer is that, unlike a commercial contract, it regards complying with administrative requirements as important as technical performance. Our second edition is intended to reflect changes in the current procurement environment that directly impact a contractor's ability to avoid serious economic loss or legal exposure for failure to fulfill the administrative requirements (i.e., pricing and costing, and settling) of government contracts. Since so much of this process is unchanged since 1984, the Preface for the first edition is still relevant and is included with minor revisions.

Bethesda, Maryland   FRANK M. ALSTON
Newport Beach, California   MARGARET M. WORTHINGTON
January 1988   LOUIS P. GOLDSMAN

Preface to the First Edition

To have any reasonable chance of success in business, the entrepreneur must understand the market in which he or she operates. An effective business strategy results not only from insight regarding how the consumer behaves, but even more importantly, what motivates consumer behavior.

Who are my potential customers?

How does the customer decide what to buy and when to buy?

What process is the customer likely to use in selecting the sources to fulfill his or her perceived needs?

What type of relationship will the customer seek to establish with suppliers?

These questions reflect the technical, economic, and legal characteristics of a marketplace, which determine, to a large extent, consumer behavior. The challenge to managers of business organizations is to be sufficiently knowledgeable about the market to anticipate or, in some cases, even influence the demand for their product. Those who succeed in this effort will be able to take the necessary actions to give their companies a competitive advantage.

While intimate knowledge of the critical factors that influence consumer behavior is important for selling in any market, it is doubly so if the consumers are federal agencies. This is true because doing business with Uncle Sam is certainly a unique experience. For reasons that will be discussed in this book, the U.S. government, as a customer, behaves differently than almost any other customer you will encounter. It follows then that any company planning or proceeding to do business in this market should know the rules that govern this particular customer's behavior and should have some understanding of, and appreciation for, why the rules were written in the first place.

The many regulations that control every step of the federal procurement process account for the major differences between government contracting and doing business in the private sector. Since these regulations determine how the federal government behaves as a customer, it would be foolish indeed to operate in the public market without a reasonable level of knowledge about what the rules and regulations require. While the government is certainly not intent on deliberately putting anyone out of business, it, nevertheless, expects a contractor to know and understand the technical and administrative requirements of the contract that is signed. Accordingly, the procuring agency will not rescue a company from the consequences of bad business judgment made in forming or performing a government contract; neither will the government refrain from penalizing a company for violating an acquisition regulation or failing to fulfill a contractual term or condition simply because the requirements were not known or were misinterpreted. Indeed, in far too many instances, contractors have watched profits on their government work drastically shrink or totally disappear because the applicable regulations were either overlooked, misunderstood, or ignored.

This book is based on the premise that doing business with the U.S. government can be an economically rewarding experience despite the voluminous and complex regulations. Contractors who have and continue to realize reasonable profits on their federal contracts recognize that coping with the unique aspects of government business is much the same as coping with the idiosyncratic behavior of any distinctive market.

This book provides a practical discussion of the rules and regulations that impose special financial and accounting requirements on government contractors. Its purpose is not only to help the reader to identify and understand the relevant regulations but, equally important, to provide significant insight into how the government will go about implementing the requirements. The authors, who are all members of Price Waterhouse's Government and Other Long-Term Contractors Industry Services Group, are uniquely suited for this purpose since they include both former U.S. government officials, who were extensively involved in developing and implementing the regulations affecting procurement, and individuals whose careers in public accounting have been concentrated on matters relating to government contracting. With such backgrounds, the authors are especially capable of providing the reader with practical information to assist in identifying the applicable regulations and establishing a basis for determining what constitutes reasonable compliance. Furthermore, this text represents Price Waterhouse's continuing commitment to provide full financial and accounting services to companies engaged in government business.

The ability to successfully deal with federal regulations is materially enhanced if the contractor has some knowledge and appreciation of the underlying concepts and rationale followed in developing them. Therefore, the text includes a brief historical background for the major regulatory requirements discussed. Included in this coverage are the authors' views of the particular problem the government was attempting to solve. In the experience of the authors, such information has been found to be extremely helpful in identifying alternative approaches to satisfying the regulatory requirements.

This book covers that portion of the federal procurement process involving the practices followed in making the government's needs known to the public to settling a contract at completion. Because the authors are all accountants by profession, the primary focus of this book is on the financial and accounting considerations related to this process. The book is intended to serve as a practical reference for those who are directly responsible for pricing and administering contracts with federal agencies. Those with overall management responsibilities, as well as individuals involved in marketing or providing legal advice, should also find the material useful. Knowledge of the regulations is critical in establishing short- and long-term business objectives, developing marketing plans and strategies, and avoiding or resolving disputes related to government contracts.

Anyone involved in government business must have a working knowledge of such terms as *allowability*, *reasonableness*, *allocability*, and *defective pricing*. Unfortunately, many contractors become acquainted with these concepts, as they apply to their government business, when in the midst of a crisis—too late, for often the damage is already done.

For those who are considering the government contracting market, this book should provide a fairly complete overview of the financial and accounting aspects of your decision. Responsible officials should be able to identify the changes that are necessary in management and control systems and assess the impact of those changes on the overall operation of the business. For existing contractors, the book should serve as an aid in identifying relevant regulations, and providing additional insight on what actions are in company's best interest and which satisfy the requirements of the customer—the U.S. Government.

While compliance with applicable government regulations is certainly important, contractors must be sure that their systems used for estimating, accounting, and billing costs meet management's internal needs. As indicated previously, many contract losses occur not because the contractor experienced unexpected technical difficulty in doing the work, but because its management systems failed to provide the necessary information to effectively price the contract and control the cost incurred during performance. In recognition of this need, the book also has a section on accounting systems and internal control. Additionally, throughout the text, the authors suggest what they believe are good practices to follow in estimating costs for contract negotiation purposes and monitoring and controlling costs incurred during contract performance. Particular emphasis is given to the importance of these systems as they relate to pricing the effect of changes to the contract after the date of award.

Los Angeles, California
Bethesda, Maryland
December 1983

FRANK M. ALSTON
FRANKLIN R. JOHNSON
MARGARET M. WORTHINGTON
LOUIS P. GOLDSMAN
FRANK J. DEVITO

Acknowledgments

The authors are particularly indebted to Charles L. Gardiner, Harry N. Hann, and Francis G. Peiffer for their efforts in updating portions of this text.

We also deeply appreciate the dedication and hard work of Cheryle R. Plater and Elizabeth B. Stedman in typing the manuscript and researching the footnote citations.

Contents

List of Figures, Tables, and Appendices

Chapter One

Historical Perspectives and Background

1-1. EARLY FEDERAL PROCUREMENT STATUTES

According to historians, the U.S. Congress enacted the first law governing the purchase of military goods and services in 1795. That law, the Purveyor of Public Supplies Act,[1] enabled the Army and the Navy to meet their needs by purchasing from private business. The next significant procurement law, passed in 1808, continues to serve as the basis for a clause that is still required in federal contracts issued today—the "Officials Not to Benefit" clause. It expressly prohibits members of Congress from deriving personal benefits from U.S. government procurements.

In an attempt to bring some integrity and fairness into the process of awarding federal contracts, Congress later passed a series of statutes that virtually eliminated negotiated procurement and required, with limited exceptions, competitive bidding. By 1845, the use of sealed bids with public openings dominated the federal procurement process. The 1861 Civil Sundry Appropriations Act,[2] for all practical purposes, continued the principle of advertised procurement until after World War II.

The emphasis on competitive bidding practices during this period reflected a desire to free federal contracting from favoritism, political influence, and profiteering by individuals in power. Despite the well-meaning intent of these practices, shortages of available production facilities and raw materials during World War I produced intense competition between the military branches, which were acquiring available goods and services in the civilian marketplace. The war demonstrated that such shortages produced a seller's market and that the intense competition among buyers drove prices up. In addition, formal advertising was slow and cumbersome and greatly hindered the timely receipt of the goods and services so desperately needed by the military.

Unfortunately, the time between World War I and World War II was spent in recriminations against the manufacturers rather than the development of alternative practices. Congress continued to focus its attention on profit limitations, price controls, and taxes. The unfortunate conflicts between the military departments and Congress interfered with the effort to resolve procurement problems before the start of World War II. Indeed, the military departments were reluctant to give up the protection afforded by the strict provisions of formal advertising procedures. They believed that doing so would make them even more vulnerable to congressional criticism.

Nevertheless, the approach of World War II saw a slow transition to negotiation as a contract selection and award technique. By December 1941, the First War Powers Act[3] removed most restrictions on the military services' procurement functions and authorized advance, progress, and other payments whenever such action would further the prosecution of the war.

The complete turnabout from advertised bidding to negotiation came with Directive 2, issued in 1942 by the War Production Board. This directive required that all contracts be negotiated, and established criteria for selecting a contractor during an armed conflict. This federal contracting environment featured (1) an emphasis on delivery, (2) procurement of complex items from companies possessing the required engineering and managerial capability, and (3) award of contracts to firms that did not require significant new equipment or facilities. The War Department provided for control of profits through proper pricing; as a result, the unfortunate experiences of World War I did not recur. As an additional safeguard, Congress gave the executive branch certain powers to discourage contractors from making unreasonable demands in the wartime seller's market, including the right to inspect plants, conduct audits, establish delivery priorities, allocate raw materials, unilaterally establish reasonable prices if negotiations failed, and so forth. Although these powers were rarely used, their existence, as intended, motivated government contractors to exercise voluntary controls during World War II.

When the conflict ended, the need to rapidly change from a wartime to a peacetime economy was apparent. Congress' effort to meet this challenge culminated in the enactment of the Contract Settlement Act,[4] which established uniform termination procedures and related contract clauses. A new era in government procurement had begun.

1-2. THE FEDERAL PROCUREMENT ENVIRONMENT FROM WORLD WAR II TO TODAY

The statutes and regulations passed during World War II were, for the most part, temporary. To apply the lessons learned from the war, Congress enacted the Armed Services Procurement Act of 1947,[5] which became effective after the emergency legislation expired. The act established sealed bidding, then known as formal advertising, as the preferred procurement method. Exceptions were provided, however, when the circumstances required or justified such action. The Department of Defense (DOD) implemented Title 10 through the Armed Services Procurement Regulation (ASPR). In March 1978, the DOD changed the name of the regulation to the Defense Acquisition Regulation (DAR). The Federal Property and Administrative Services Act of 1949[6] provides the contracting authority for all executive agencies except the DOD, the Coast Guard, the National Aeronautics and Space Administration (NASA), and any other agency that has a separate procurement statute. Uniform policies and procedures for NASA's procurements are established under the National Aeronautics and Space Act,[7] as amended. Until 1984, the Federal Procurement Regulations (FPR), issued by the General Services Administration (GSA) in 1959, governed procurement by civilian agencies other than NASA and were very similar to the acquisition regulations that applied to defense agencies. The DOD took the lead in developing procurement regulations, with NASA and the GSA generally incorporating the DOD's changes in their regulations. However, notable differences existed between the regulations. In April 1984, the DAR, the NASA Procurement Regulation, and the FPR were replaced by the Federal Acquisition Regulation (FAR) and agency FAR supplements. Unfortunately, due to the somewhat controlled development of the FAR supplements, acquisition regulations are still far from uniform. Consequently, companies must still exercise care to ensure that appropriate regulations are applied.

The sheer magnitude of federal purchases and the unique products and services acquired have dictated the need to reassess how the risk inherent in such purchases should be apportioned between buyer and seller. New issues having a direct impact on the very structure of the procurement process have also emerged. Some of the basic concerns involve redefining potential military threats in view of dramatic geopolitical changes and decreasing the overall cost of defense while maintaining a viable military industrial base. Faced with the daunting challenge of doing more with less and "getting more bang for the buck," the need for special procurement procedures (and the accompanying oversight to ensure compliance) must be balanced with the need to provide the nation's defense at the lowest cost.

- In the early 1980s, the DOD budget increased significantly to strengthen military preparedness and to offset what was perceived as years of neglect. But large federal deficits created considerable pressure to reduce budget outlays. The Competition in Contracting Act (CICA),[8] enacted as part of the Deficit Reduction Act of 1984, amended the Armed Services Procurement Act in favor of competitive procurement methods. As a result, the government is required to use competitive procedures for all procurements except under certain specified conditions.

- In the late 1980s, the "Ill Wind" operation, conducted by the Federal Bureau of Investigation and the Naval Investigative Service, investigated alleged bribery and fraud by defense contractors, consultants, and government employees, involving the disclosure of sensitive information during the contract selection and award process. That investigation highlighted the need to separate more clearly the buyer–seller relationship in government procurements. The Office of Federal Procurement Policy Act Amendments of 1988[9] added procurement integrity provisions that prohibit certain marketing activities, particularly with regard to disseminating proprietary or source selection information. The Byrd Amendment,[10] enacted in late 1989, further narrowed the range of acceptable marketing activities to be used by contractors in obtaining federal awards.

- The President's Blue Ribbon Commission on Defense Management, known as the Packard Commission, identified numerous recommendations for improving the defense procurement process. Its report[11] focused on the need for contractors to promulgate and enforce codes of conduct and to develop and implement internal controls to ensure compliance with corporate standards and regulatory requirements. Contractors were also urged to expand the role of internal audits to encompass federal contract compliance and to adopt procedures for voluntary disclosure of violations and corrective actions. The report also urged the DOD to eliminate undesirable duplication of surveillance and oversight.

- In response, the Secretary of Defense submitted the Defense Management Report[12] to the President in June 1989, outlining changes in defense acquisition management and organization, planning, acquisitions, and government–industry accountability.

- In 1981, the Center for Strategic and International Studies (CSIS) explored the challenge of how to reduce the cost of defense equipment while maintaining a viable defense industrial base that keeps cost to a minimum but also ensures a surge of production in any future emergency. The CSIS report[13] concluded, as had the reports of previous task forces and government commissions, that the solution lies in far greater use of "civil/military integration." The report also recommended that the DOD, when appropriate, rely on commercial products, processes, and buying practices, resulting in a far larger industrial base and significantly greater economies of scale and scope. The report focused on four barriers to integrating the commercial and military sectors: cost accounting requirements; military specifications; technical data rights; and DOD contract clauses, which have formed formidable barriers to integrating military and commercial technologies. After discussing the changes needed to remove these barriers, the report concluded that this integration would require a total commitment to change by both Congress and the DOD and a specific legislative and regulatory agenda for implementation.

- Despite the constraints imposed by federal budget deficits, the government has taken numerous actions to address these challenges, including the following:

  - Assisting the defense industry in the transition to nondefense work
  - Preserving unique defense systems that are critical to national security
  - Accelerating development of dual-use technologies
  - Encouraging new manufacturing techniques
  - Eliminating regulatory barriers to commercial/defense integration
  - Strongly encouraging the procurement of commercial, nondevelopment supply items and eliminating regulatory barriers to selling commercial products to the government
  - Largely eliminating long-standing DOD requirements for recoupment of nonrecurring costs for products or technology developed under government contracts
  - Phasing out allowability ceilings on independent research and development and bid and proposal costs
  - Increasing the small purchase threshold (renamed the simplified acquisition threshold) from $25,000 to $100,000
  - Establishing a structured approach to address industry's efforts to consolidate and restructure operations and amortize restructuring costs

Even with these developments, including passage of the monumental Federal Acquisition Streamlining Act of 1984[14] and the Clinger–Cohen Act of 1996,[15] much work remains to achieve true acquisition reform. Government and industry must continue to work together to achieve the common goal of maintaining a viable industrial base that can respond to our national security needs. The process of awarding and administering contracts that require submission of cost or pricing data prior to award remains in dire need of streamlining. Indeed, recent changes in cost principles and cost accounting standards have made that environment more difficult, not easier.

1-3. THE FEDERAL PROCUREMENT PROCESS

The ultimate objective of the procurement process is to acquire supplies and services of the quality required, in a timely manner, and at fair and reasonable prices. An additional responsibility is to ensure that certain socioeconomic goals are met. This segment briefly describes how the federal government goes about determining what it is going to buy, who will be the supplier, and what price will be paid for the work performed.

Government Requirements

Generally, the government has rather formal procedures for determining its procurement needs. These procedures tend to vary from agency to agency and depend on the organizational mission. The process invariably starts with Congress, which sets forth an agency's overall mission and authorizes the purchase of specific products and services. Describing the process of determining what each agency buys is certainly beyond the scope of this book. Nevertheless, the importance of becoming intimately knowledgeable about those agencies that represent a company's market cannot be overemphasized.

A company, through its relationship with an agency, may even assist in determining the agency's needs or at least exert some influence on the process. The extent to which a company is able to anticipate agency needs can be important in making decisions regarding marketing strategies, research and development, and bid and proposal activities. Perhaps the best way to be kept informed about government needs is to have a continuing contracting relationship with officials who decide such matters.

Contract Award

Once the government has identified its needs, the method to be used for acquiring the products or services must be determined. Federal contract awards result from either sealed bidding or negotiation. In a sealed-bid procurement, the solicitation document is an invitations for bid (IFB). The selection is made solely on the basis of the lowest price submitted by a qualified supplier. In a negotiated procurement, the solicitation document is either a request for proposal (RFP) or a request for quotation (RFQ). In this situation, the award is made on the basis of price and other technical factors. RFPs and RFQs are similar, except that the government may unilaterally accept offers made pursuant to an RFP without further negotiations. For an RFQ, a bilateral agreement must be negotiated.

In preparing for negotiations, the government contracting officer may require the assistance of engineers, accountants, and price analysts to determine whether the proposal constitutes an acceptable basis for reaching an agreement. This process of bargaining between buyer and seller is, of course, critical. To effectively serve its stated purpose, each party must come to the negotiation table adequately prepared to vigorously and responsibly pursue its individual interest. When either party fails to do this, the procurement process is weakened. A successful negotiation is one that results in a pricing arrangement that is fair to both parties.

Contract Settlement

Most contract settlements occur as a result of successful completion of the work. For flexibly priced contracts, a firm final price is negotiated according to the allowable cost incurred and adjusted for those items provided for in the contract. To settle cost-reimbursement contracts, the contracting officer must obtain from the government contract auditor a report on the allowability of the total cost claimed. Based on this report, a settlement is usually reached. The contractor will be reimbursed for all acceptable costs incurred, plus an allowance for a fee as determined by contract terms and conditions. If a contract is prematurely terminated for the government's convenience, the contractor is entitled to reimbursement for work performed, adjusted for profit or loss, as appropriate, plus costs incurred in settling the contract. Compensatory damages or anticipatory profits are not permitted. In the unfortunate circumstance that a contract is terminated for default, remuneration is provided only for products delivered and accepted.

Uniform Contract Format

The government uses a uniform contract format as a standard for solicitations and resulting contracts. The format, however, does not apply to certain procurements, such as basic agreements, construction contracts, and architect–engineer contracts.

The uniform contract format consists of four parts: Part I—The Schedule (Sections A–H); Part II—Contract Clauses (Section I); Part III—Lists of Documents, Exhibits, and Other Attachments (Section J); and Part IV—Representation and Instructions (Sections K–M). Each of the contract sections is described briefly below:

- Section A, Solicitation/Contract Form, usually consists of Standard Form (SF) 33, Solicitation, Offer, and Award, or Optional Form (OF) 308, Solicitation and Offer—Negotiated Acquisition. According to 48 C.F.R. Part 1, et al (Part 15 Rewrite of the Federal Acquisition Regulation), effective October 10, 1997, prescribed forms are not required to prepare solicitations. Other forms may be used at the discretion of the contracting officer (CO).

- Section B, Supplies or Services and Prices/Costs include a brief description of the supplies or services to be provided.

- Section C, Description/Specification/Statement of Work, needed in addition to Section B.

- Section D, Packaging and Marking, describes packaging, packing, preservation, and marking requirements, if any.

- Section E, Inspection and Acceptance, describes quality assurance, inspection, acceptance, reliability, and warranty requirements.

- Section F, Deliveries or Performance, establishes the period of time allowed for performance and/or the time, place, and method of delivery.

- Section G, Contract Administration Data, includes accounting and appropriation data and any contract administration information or instructions (such as billing information) in addition to that in Section A.

- Section H, Special Contract Requirements, includes special contract clauses that are unique to the contract and not included in Section I.
- Section I, Contract Clauses, lists contract clauses required by law or regulation, although the full texts of the clauses are not included.
- Section J, List of Attachments, lists the title, date, and number of pages for each attached document or other attachment.
- Section K, Representations, Certifications, and Other Statements of Offerors, contains solicitation provisions that must be acknowledged or completed by the offeror.
- Section L, Instructions, Conditions, and Notices to Offerors, contains solicitation provisions and other instructions to guide prospective offerors in preparing bids, proposals, and quotations.
- Section M, Evaluation Factors for Award, lists the significant factors that will be considered for award. For sealed bidding, only price-related factors can be considered in awarding the contract. For negotiated procurements, nonprice-related factors and subfactors can also be considered. Section M identifies the relative importance the government places on these evaluation factors.

Contract Type

The extent to which the government remains actively involved with a contractor during contract performance is determined by the type of contract awarded. Contract types are discussed in FAR Part 16. There are two broad categories: fixed-price contracts and cost-reimbursable contracts. These pricing arrangements reflect the risk involved in contract performance. Under the firm fixed-price arrangement, the contractor is obligated to perform at the negotiated price, thus accepting 100% of the risk of performing the contract within the negotiated price. Flexibly priced (e.g., cost-reimbursable, incentive) contracts may provide for the final price to be determined either when the work is finished or at some interim point during contract performance. If the flexibly priced contract is cost-reimbursable, the contractor can legally stop work when all contract funds are spent, thus shifting the cost risk to the government. If the flexibly priced contract is fixed-price in nature (e.g., fixed-price incentive), continued performance is required even though contract completion may cause incurrence of a loss. The major types of contracts are briefly described below:

- *Firm-fixed price:* The price is not subject to adjustment by reason of cost of performance. The contractor is obligated to perform the contract at the established price.
- *Fixed-price with economic price adjustment:* The fixed price is adjusted upward or downward based on the occurrence of contractually specified economic contingencies that are clearly outside the contractor's control.
- *Fixed-price incentive:* The profit is adjusted and the final price is established by a formula based on the relationship of final negotiated cost to target cost.
- *Firm-fixed-price, level-of-effort:* A fixed price is established for a specified level of effort over a stated time frame. If the level varies beyond specified thresholds, the price is adjusted.
- *Cost:* Reimbursement consists of allowable cost; there is no fee provision.
- *Cost-sharing:* An agreed portion of allowable cost is reimbursed.
- *Cost-plus-fixed-fee:* Reimbursement is based on allowable cost plus a fixed fee.

- *Cost-plus-incentive-fee:* Reimbursement is based on allowable cost incurred and a fee adjusted by a formula based on the relationship of allowable cost to target cost.

- *Cost-plus-award-fee:* Reimbursement is based on allowable cost incurred and a two-part fee (a base amount which may be zero and an award amount based on an evaluation of the quality of contract performance).

- *Time and material:* Direct labor hours expended are paid at negotiated fixed hourly rates, which usually include direct labor costs, indirect expenses, and profit. Material costs are reimbursed at actual cost plus a material-handling charge, if applicable.

- *Labor hour:* Direct labor hours expended are paid at negotiated fixed hourly rates, usually including all cost and profit.

- *Definite-quantity:* This type of contract provides for delivery of a definite quantity of supplies or services. Deliveries are scheduled upon order.

- *Requirements:* The contract identifies supplies or services, and mutually agreed upon prices, that the government may procure, if the government has a requirement for such supplies or services.

- *Indefinite-quantity:* Delivery or performance of supplies or services are provided based on orders placed by the government; quantities are flexible. Payment is made on some form of a fixed-price basis.

1-4. MAJOR DIFFERENCES BETWEEN PRIVATE AND PUBLIC CONTRACTING

It should be reasonably clear that many of the factors that distinguish public sector contracting from doing business with commercial organizations can be attributed to the statutory framework in which the federal government must operate when it enters the marketplace as a customer. When considered objectively, the unique requirements of federal contracting should not represent an insurmountable barrier to an economically rewarding experience for those companies that elect to do business in this arena. Nonetheless, success is greatly affected by how well a contractor understands and copes with the rules that govern the federal government's behavior when engaged in this important activity.

The government's procedures for selecting, monitoring, and paying its contractors are more complex than those found in the commercial sector. To further compound the problem, the government is not monolithic but is an amalgam of individual agencies and procurement activities using complex procurement rules and regulations to obtain an incredibly diverse variety of goods and services. Whether all the rules and regulations are needed is certainly the subject of considerable debate. However, it is important to recognize that the government can be a good customer only when the seller understands those rules and regulations and the specific actions they require.

The need for the extensive rules and regulations stems from the government's dual role in the marketplace. Acting in its contracting capacity, the government is a vast business organization purchasing a wide variety of goods and services from every segment of the private sector. At the same time, it is a political entity—a sovereignty. In this latter role, its objectives go beyond obtaining goods and services at a stated price. The government must establish and follow practices that not only represent good business judgment but also are fair to all concerned. Therefore, the practices should reasonably ensure that (1) known, responsible suppliers have an equal opportunity to meet the government's needs; (2) the quality of goods and services acquired is acceptable; (3) the prices paid are fair and reasonable; and (4) the government buys only what the public needs.

As a customer, the government must be treated like any other contracting party in order to protect those with whom the government deals. As a sovereign, the government deserves special treatment since it is acting in the public's interest. To achieve an appropriate balance between these two concerns, a more structured and controlled environment is required for government business than that for private industry.

Some of the considerations in government contracting that appear to have no real counterparts in the commercial arena are summarized as follows:

- Procedures to ensure fairness in the award of contracts from the standpoint that all interested, responsible suppliers have an equal opportunity to do all work
- Cost accounting rules that govern the contract pricing, reporting, and billing
- Procedures for the government to unilaterally change its mind after the contract has been signed
- Procedures and techniques for technical and administrative surveillance during contract performance to ensure the reasonableness of prices and the quality of products or services
- Contractual arrangements for the government to stop performance whenever it is in the public interest
- Contractual arrangements for different payment or contract financing methods (discussed further in Chapter 9)
- Miscellaneous social objectives, such as (1) giving a fair share of the work to small, small disadvantaged, and women-owned small business concerns, and (2) preferences to U.S. companies

Some differences between government and commercial contracting as they relate to specific steps in the procurement process are examined next.

Marketing

The government operates on the basic tenet that all responsible suppliers should have an equal opportunity to meet the government's needs. Consistent with this mandate, the government advertises its needs and requires strict compliance with the detailed specifications that it imposes.

In addition to being aware of the published information, effective marketing to government agencies requires maintaining appropriate contacts with those individuals responsible for making the purchasing decisions. However, conduct condoned in the commercial sector may be prohibited by such statutes as the Procurement Integrity provisions of the OFPP Act Amendments of 1988 and the Byrd Amendment.

Contract Award

Government procedures leading to a contract award are detailed and precise. They are directed toward precluding partial or preferential treatment to any responsible bidder. These procedures are also intended to ensure strict compliance with detailed specifications set forth in the requirements data. In most instances, they require actions by the offeror that are unique to government business.

Negotiated procurements generally begin with a proposal that details the price and technical aspects of the work to be done. The proposal serves as the basis for arriving at a contract price and may be subject to technical reviews, cost or price analyses, and, finally, negotiation. The proposal may also have to comply with various requirements covering the following:

- Submission of cost or pricing data provided in support of estimated costs, discussed further in Chapters 3, 5, and 6
- Exclusion of specific costs that are deemed unallowable by the federal cost principles, discussed further in Chapter 7
- Measurement, assignment, and allocation of costs in compliance with cost accounting standards, discussed further in Chapter 8

There are few, if any, circumstances in the private sector in which a company must divulge its cost data to a customer as a prerequisite for negotiating a contract.

Social and Economic Goals

The government uses its buying power to achieve certain social and economic goals. Some of the more notable socioeconomic requirements that are imposed through contract clauses involve the following areas:

- *Equal employment opportunity:* Various statutes and executive orders forbid companies that contract with the federal government to discriminate in their employment policies and practices.
- *Trade restrictions:* The Buy American Act[16] limits the extent to which a product manufactured for public use can contain components or materials from foreign suppliers. The DOD has substantially relaxed its Buy American barriers through the Trade Agreements Act (TAA)[17] and the North American Free Trade Agreement (NAFTA)[18] to permit fair and equal competition among the industries of the participating countries.
- *Wage standards:* Various statutes ensure that employees working on federal contracts are treated fairly in payment and benefits when compared with other workers in the country. These laws include the Service Contract Act,[19] the Contract Work Hours and Safety Standards Act,[20] the Davis–Bacon Act,[21] and the Walsh–Healy Public Contract Act.[22]
- *Occupational Safety and Health Act:*[23] This law requires companies to maintain healthful and safe working conditions.
- *National Environmental Policy Act:*[24] This law, which establishes a national policy for protecting the environment, requires federal agencies to determine the impact a particular project will have on the environment. It directly affects federal agencies and indirectly applies to contractors that may be involved in the projects.
- *Clean Air and Water Acts:*[25] These acts are directed primarily at controlling air pollution caused by industry and motor vehicle emissions. The contracting process may be delayed if it is determined that the proposed work violates the requirement of this law.

- *Small Business Act:*[26] This act establishes a national policy for the government to assist small businesses in obtaining their fair share of the government's business. To achieve this objective, agency officials may set aside certain procurements exclusively for small business. Categories of set-aside contracts are total set-asides for small business and partial set-asides for small business. The 8(a) program also permits awards on a noncompetitive basis to firms owned by economically and socially disadvantaged persons.

Any company electing to do business with the U.S. government must take these requirements seriously and make certain that its business practices ensure reasonable compliance. To do otherwise would contribute unreasonable risk, since failure to conform could result in contract termination.

Contract Administration

Throughout the 1980s, management of the DOD's contract administration activity was disbursed among the Defense Logistics Agency, the Air Force, the Navy, and the Army. Effective October 1, 1990, these activities were consolidated into a single organization, the Defense Contract Management Command, managed by the Defense Logistics Agency. The principal reason for establishing the command was to achieve greater efficiency and to reduce operation cost. The contract administration function encompasses all actions performed at a contractor's facility for the government's benefit that are necessary for contract performance or that support the buying offices' organizations, excluding the contract audit function assigned to the Defense Contract Audit Agency (DCAA). The contract administration function is described in FAR Part 42 and in Part 242 of the DOD FAR Supplement (DFARS).

In 1987, the DOD issued a policy on Contractor Responsibility to Avoid Improper Business Practices, which further emphasized the need for contractors to develop appropriate mechanisms to promote ethics and compliance with federal contracting requirements.

For certain procurements, such as research and development activities, the government closely monitors contract performance. It believes the nature of some of its purchases requires such scrutiny to ensure fair and reasonable pricing, adequate performance of the work, and remuneration to the contractor in a manner consistent with public policy.

The government can unilaterally direct a contract change, including ordering a delay or suspension of work. Recovery of increased costs resulting from contract changes or delays is discussed in Chapter 11.

The government can also terminate a contract for either convenience of the government or default. Financial implications of contract termination are discussed in Chapter 12.

Contract Audit

As the significance of cost as a factor in contract pricing increased, so did the government's need to assure itself of the validity and reasonableness of the costs proposed or charged by contractors. Consequently, government agencies began to audit contractors' books and records to determine how much the government would pay for the work performed. Each of the military agencies (Army, Navy, and Air Force) originally had its own separate audit activity. Effective July 1, 1965, contract audit activities in the military agencies were combined into one independent organization, the DCAA. While the DCAA provides financial and accounting advice to DOD procurement officials, it remains organizationally separate from the procurement activities it supports.

Most civilian agencies also use the DCAA for their contract audit requirements. Others that have established a contract audit capability have, unlike the DOD, incorporated this activity either in their financial management operations or in their offices of the inspector general.

The office of the DOD Inspector General also makes certain audits in carrying out its mission to identify instances of fraud, waste, and abuse in defense procurement. Many of these audits address the same or similar issues covered by the DCAA.

1-5. TAX CONSIDERATIONS

Research and Development Tax Credit

As part of the Economic Recovery Act of 1981[27] and the Tax Payer Relief Act of 1997,[28] Congress enacted the research credit to encourage additional research within the U.S. economy. The research credit is a nonrefundable tax credit for research activities based on the increase in a taxpayer's "qualified research expenses" paid or incurred in carrying on a trade or a business. The credit is currently computed by applying a 20% rate to the difference between the current year's qualified research expenses and a taxpayer-specific base.

The research credit is available for certain costs incident to developing new or improved products, processes, inventions, software, or similar items. The costs of research may generally be treated as qualified research expenses eligible for the credit if the following tests are met:

- Substantially all of the activities undertaken in performing the research involve an experimentation process.
- The experimentation process is undertaken for the purpose of discovering information that is technological in nature.
- The research undertaken relies fundamentally on principles of the physical or biological sciences, engineering, or computer science.

The credit is not available for expenditures incurred to produce individual units of products, to acquire or produce depreciable property or land, or for marketing costs. In addition, costs for research performed outside the United States and for research funded by another person do not qualify. Research performed pursuant to certain government contracts may be credit eligible.

Qualified research costs give rise to a credit only to the extent that they exceed a taxpayer-specific base. Before January 1, 1990, the base was calculated as a moving average of the prior three years' qualified research costs. For years beginning after December 31, 1989, the base computation relies on a "research intensity" concept. This concept begins with a computation of a five-year historic ratio (1984 through 1988) of research costs to sales and then applies this ratio to the average four years' sales to arrive at the base. This base is the amount of research that is assumed to be funded from a taxpayer's sales. Both computations contain a minimum base rule that states that the base cannot be less than 50% of the current year's qualified research expenses. The research credit is effective for costs incurred to June 30, 1998.

In a private ruling arising out of an examination, the IRS ruled that costs incurred pursuant to a firm-fixed-price contract were funded because of the high likelihood that the contractor would be entitled to retain progress payments made during the term of the contract. In a 1994 decision, the Court of Federal Claims concluded that a substantial portion of the costs incurred by Fairchild Industries, Inc., on a fixed-price incentive, full-scale development (FSD) Air Force contract were ineligible for the credit.[29] The disallowed percentage represented the ratio of FSD costs paid to total FSD costs incurred. The court concluded that Fairchild did not incur the research expenditures because Fairchild received progress payments under the contract as work progressed. The Court of Appeals for the Federal Circuit reversed the prior decision because "the contract explicitly placed solely on Fairchild the risk of failure of every line of FSD."[30] The Federal Circuit noted that "[a] progress payment does not commit the agency to accept unsuccessful performance or to make full or partial payment if the product is not successfully produced." Thus, the Court of Federal Claims "erred by not distinguishing between 'funding' as the term as used in Economic Recovery Tax Act and the mechanics of financing."

Accounting for Long-Term Contracts

Before the 1986 Tax Reform Act,[31] a taxpayer could elect to use either the percentage-of-completion or the completed-contract method of accounting for long-term contracts. A taxpayer electing the percentage-of-completion method would include income from the contract in proportion to the percentage of the contract completed during the year, and deducted as incurred expenses on the contract. A taxpayer using the completed-contract method would defer all income recognition and expense deduction until the year in which the contract was completed. In the case of extended-period contracts (contracts requiring three years or more to complete), regulations specified which expenditures had to be allocated to the contract and which could be deducted currently.

The Tax Reform Act generally repealed the completed-contract method of accounting for long-term contracts. For contracts entered into between February 28, 1986, and July 11, 1989, taxpayers were permitted to use the percentage-of-completion capitalized-cost method, a hybrid of the percentage-of-completion method and the completed-contract method. A taxpayer opting for this method accounted for 40% of the income and expenses of the contract items on the percentage-of-completion method and the remaining portion of the contract items on the "normal method" (generally, the completed-contract method). The look-back rule was applied to the percent accounted for under the percentage-of-completion method.

The hybrid method was no longer available for long-term contracts entered into after July 11, 1989. Taxpayers must use the percentage-of-completion method.

1-6. SUMMARY

Unquestionably, the typical relationship between two commercial organizations differs from that between the parties to a federal procurement process. The latter relationship is highly structured and formal. The acquisition system is designed primarily to ensure that the vast number of government employees involved are reasonably uniform and effective in carrying out their responsibilities. It is also hoped that the system provides some assurance that all responsible offerors are treated fairly, that the process has integrity, and that actions are sufficiently documented to ensure that the necessary monitoring and surveillance can occur.

At the same time, government procurement merely represents another market. As in any separate and distinct marketplace, the entrepreneur must understand the process as well as the factors that affect the environment in which he or she operates. For the company that knows the rules of the game, government business is probably no more nor less treacherous than any other market. But without at least a basic knowledge of the rules and regulations, or if the rules and regulations are ignored, the risk of loss or expensive litigation for the supplier is real and can be considerable.

1-7. NOTES

1. Purveyor of Public Supplies Act, 1 Stat. 419, enacted Feb. 23, 1795.
2. 1861 Civil Sundry Appropriations Act, CH 133, 21 Stat. 457, 31 U.S.C. §741, enacted Mar. 1861, Rev. 1874 and Amended 1878 and 1910 (Revised Stat. 3709).
3. First War Powers Act, CH 593, 55 Stat. 838, 12 U.S.C.S. 95a; 50 U.S.C. Appx. 5, enacted Dec. 18, 1941.
4. Contract Settlement Act of 1944, CH 358, 58 Stat. 649, 18 U.S.C. §3287, enacted July 1, 1944.
5. Armed Services Procurement Act, 10 U.S.C., 62 Stat. 21, enacted Feb. 19, 1948 and 70A Stat. 1, enacted Aug. 10, 1956, Pub. L. 84-1028.
6. Federal Property and Administrative Services Act, 41 U.S.C., 63 Stat. 378, enacted June 30, 1949, Pub. L. 81-152.
7. National Aeronautics and Space Act of 1958, 72 Stat. 426, 10 U.S.C. §2302, enacted July 2, 1958, Pub. L. 85-568.
8. Competition in Contracting Act, 10 U.S.C. §2304 and 41 U.S.C. §253, enacted July 18, 1984, Pub. L. 98-369.
9. Office of Federal Procurement Policy Act Amendments of 1988, 41 U.S.C. §422, 97 Stat. 1325, enacted Nov. 17, 1988, Pub. L. 100-679, §27.
10. Byrd Amendment, Department of Interior and Related Agencies Appropriations Act, 103 Stat. 701, 31 U.S.C. §1352, enacted Oct. 13, 1989, Pub. L. 101-121.
11. A Quest for Excellence, a Report to the President by the President's Blue Ribbon Commission on Defense Management, June 1986.
12. Defense Management Report to the President, Secretary of Defense, June 1989.
13. Center for Strategic and International Studies, 1800 K Street, NW, Suite 400, Washington, D.C. 20006. Report of the CSIS Steering Committee on Security and Technology: Co-chairs, Jeff Bingaman, Jacques Gansler, and Robert Kupperman; Project Director, Debra van Opstal.
14. Federal Acquisition Streamlining Act of 1994, 41 U.S.C. §251, enacted Oct. 13, 1995, Pub. L. 103-355.
15. Clinger–Cohen Act of 1996 (formerly known as Federal Acquisition Reform Act of 1996), enacted Feb. 10, 1996, Pub. L. 104-106.
16. Buy American Act, CH 212, 47 Stat. 1520 and 102 Stat. 1545, 41 U.S.C. §10, enacted Mar. 3, 1933 and Aug. 23, 1988.
17. Trade Agreements Act, CH 474, 48 Stat. 943, 19 U.S.C. §1001, 1201, 1351–1354, enacted June 12, 1934, and 5 U.S.C. §5315, 13 U.S.C. §301, enacted July 26, 1979, Pub. L. 96-39.
18. North American Free Trade Agreement Implementation Act, 107 Stat. 2057, 19 U.S.C. §3301, Pub. L. 103-182.
19. Service Contract Act, 79 Stat. 1034, 41 U.S.C. §351–357, enacted Oct. 22, 1965, Pub. L. 89-286.
20. Contract Work Hours and Safety Standards Act, 76 Stat. 357, 42 U.S.C. §401, enacted Aug. 13, 1962, Pub. L. 87-581.
21. Davis–Bacon Act, CH 411, 46 Stat. 1494, 40 U.S.C. §276a, enacted Mar. 3, 1921.
22. Walsh–Healy Public Contract Act, CH 881, 439 Stat. 2036, 29 U.S.C. §557, enacted June 30, 1936.
23. Occupational Safety and Health Act, 84 Stat. 1590, enacted Dec. 29, 1970, Pub. L. 91-596.

24. National Environmental Policy Act, 83 Stat. 852, 42 U.S.C. §4321, enacted Jan. 1, 1970, Pub. L. 91-190.

25. Clean Air Act, 80 Stat. 954, 42 U.S.C.5 §7506, 7571, 1857, enacted Dec. 17, 1963, Pub. L. 88-206, as amended, Oct. 15, 1966, Pub. L. 89-675, and Oct. 9, 1996, Pub. L. 104-264.

26. Small Business Act, CH 282, 67 Stat. 232 and 69 Stat., 15 U.S.C. §631 et seq., enacted July 30, 1953 and June 30, 1955.

27. Economic Recovery Tax Act of 1981, 26 U.S.C. §1, enacted Aug. 31, 1981, Pub. L. 97-34.

28. Tax Payer Relief Act of 1997.

29. Fairchild Industries, Inc., CFC No. 91-1546, March 25, 1994, 30 Fed. Cl. 859 (1994).

30. Fairchild Industries, Inc. v. U.S., CAFC No. 94-5116, Nov. 29, 1995, 71 F.3d 868.

31. Tax Reform Act of 1986, 26 U.S.C. §1, enacted Oct. 22, 1986, Pub. L. 99-514.

Chapter Two

The Organization of the Government's Acquisition Function

2-1. INTRODUCTION

Contrary to a widely held view, the federal procurement function is not mono-lithic. In fact, it is very diverse. Many different government activities procure myriad products and services, each following practices that support the needs of each of the various military and civilian agencies of the federal government. Underlying these practices are federal procurement regulations that define the government–contractor relationship. These regulations are designed to ensure that the government acquires goods and services of acceptable quality, at a fair price, delivered on time, and that a prescribed process is followed in acquiring the required goods and services. The government considers the prescribed acqui-sition process to be just as important as the product being procured. Although the executive branch of the government is responsible for most procurement-related activity, both the legislative and judicial branches play crucial roles. A working understanding of the government's acquisition organization and the roles and responsibilities of the personnel involved is essential for contractors who do business in the government marketplace. This chapter focuses on these two topics.

2-2. ORIGIN OF THE GOVERNMENT'S ACQUISITION AUTHORITY

The United States, as a sovereign entity, has inherent authority to expend public funds in order to fulfill the duties and responsibilities of the federal government. Congress enacts the laws that set forth the acquisition process, and Congress pro-vides the authorization and the funding for projects requested by government agencies. The procurement powers of Congress are expressed in several basic procurement laws. The Armed Services Procurement Act[1] governs all procure-ments of goods and services (except land) made with appropriated funds by the Army, Air Force, Navy, and Coast Guard. Procurements by the National Aeronautics and Space Administration (NASA) are governed by the National Aeronautics and Space Act.[2] The Federal Property and Administrative Services Act[3] applies to procurements of property and services made by government agencies not covered by the Armed Services Procurement Act or the National Aeronautics and Space Act. These acts prescribe the general policies and procedural framework on which government acquisition is based.

2-3. ROLE OF THE LEGISLATIVE BRANCH

Congress

The Constitution gives Congress the exclusive authority to appropriate funds from the Treasury, which, in effect, requires Congress to approve the purpose and use of monies appropriated to fund the operation of the government, including all procurement.

In addition to approving agency procurement outlays, Congress has been quite active in developing procurement-related laws. Some examples include: the Truth in Negotiations Act,[4] which requires disclosure of current, accurate, and complete cost or pricing data during contract negotiation; the Office of Federal Procurement Policy Act Amendments of 1988,[5] which contain provisions designed to promote consistency and uniformity in contractor cost accounting and to safeguard the integrity of the procurement process; and the Federal Acquisition Streamlining Act of 1994[6] and Clinger–Cohen Act of 1996,[7] which made far-reaching changes to the federal procurement process.

The General Accounting Office

Another legislative organization with a major role in the government's acquisition process is the General Accounting Office (GAO), created by the Budget and Accounting Act of 1921.[8] Its charter has been expanded by subsequent legislation. It is a large, independent agency that performs a wide variety of reviews required by various statutes, specifically requested by Congress or self-initiated. The broad range of its examinations is made possible by its almost unlimited charter and the employment of a wide variety of specialists, including accountants, auditors, attorneys, economists, social scientists, actuaries, engineers, and mathematicians.

In the late 1950s and early 1960s, the GAO spent considerable effort in auditing government contractors, but this activity has diminished significantly over time. The GAO, under the control and direction of the Comptroller General, now emphasizes reviews of the effectiveness of government agencies and audits performed by the Defense Contract Audit Agency (DCAA) and other contract audit organizations in federal departments and agencies. Responding to congressional requests and on its own initiative, the GAO reviews and makes recommendations concerning virtually every activity financed by federally appropriated funds. Acquisition policies and procedures constitute an area in which considerable attention has been focused. The GAO also examines profit policies, procurements of major weapon systems, logistics and communications, financial and general management, and international programs. Many of these evaluations cover not only federal departments and agencies but also government contractors. The GAO's activities also include the following:

- Review and settlement of all claims against the United States
- Deciding the validity of protests regarding contract awards
- Audits of federal departments and agencies, including examining financial transactions; testing compliance with laws and regulations; and reviewing the efficiency, economy, and effectiveness of operations
- Assistance to Congress

While the GAO has been the primary forum for resolving protests of contract awards, and has been since the Comptroller General decided the first protest in 1925, the Competition in Contracting Act (CICA)[9] significantly expanded the GAO's role in bid-protest resolution. Congress believed that a strong enforcement mechanism was necessary to ensure that its mandate for competition was enforced. Accordingly, CICA provided, for the first time, an express statutory basis for the GAO to hear bid-protest cases. Regulations implementing the CICA provisions are contained in Title 4 of the Code of Federal Regulations, Part 21, and the Federal Acquisition Regulation, Subpart 33.1. Bid protests are discussed further in Chapter 13.

2-4. ROLE OF THE EXECUTIVE BRANCH

The executive branch is responsible for initiating and managing procurements designed to fulfill specific department or agency needs. In addition, the executive branch serves as the government-wide leader in initiating and monitoring overall procurement policy. These roles, and the government agencies and officials that carry them out, are discussed next.

Policy-Making Organizations

Office of Federal Procurement Policy

The Office of Federal Procurement Policy (OFPP) is an executive-level office with overall responsibility for government-wide procurement policies, regulations, procedures, and forms. The OFPP is charged with leadership in policy making and in developing the acquisition systems to be used by executive agencies. In establishing the OFPP, Congress recognized that an organization was needed to provide overall policy direction to executive agencies and to promote uniformity in the government's acquisition process.

The Federal Acquisition Regulation (FAR) is the vehicle used by the OFPP to implement policy. The stated objective of FAR is to curb the proliferation of redundant and sometimes conflicting regulations issued by the various federal agencies and, to the extent possible, replace the numerous agency rules and regulations with a single, simplified set of acquisition regulations. While that goal has only partially been achieved, the OFPP continues its oversight role to reduce the regulatory inconsistencies among the various executive departments. The mandate for simplification and uniformity can be traced to the OFPP Act Amendments of 1979.[10]

The OFPP's regulatory authority, established by the 1974 act, was withdrawn by the 1979 amendments. Limited regulatory authority was reinstated with the 1983 amendments but was not exercised. Greater authority was given to the OFPP with the 1988 amendments, which established a Federal Acquisition Regulatory Council, chaired by the OFPP Administrator, to assist in directing and coordinating a government-wide procurement policy and regulatory activity. The council's charter is to maintain the FAR and to limit any agency FAR supplements to "(A) regulations essential to implement government-wide policies and procedures within the agency and (B) additional policies and procedures required to satisfy the specific and unique needs of the Agency." The other council members are the lead acquisition officials for the Department of Defense (DOD), NASA, and the General Services Administration (GSA).

The OFPP does not engage in procurement and is discouraged from monitoring or directing the day-to-day operations of departments and agencies. Its focus is on such policy issues as improving contract administration, setting government-wide goals for small business and small disadvantaged business utilization, and revising the cost principles for educational institutions.

Office of Management and Budget

The Office of Management and Budget (OMB) plays a significant role in the procurement process by issuing circulars to be followed by the federal departments and agencies. The circulars cover a broad range of public sector management topics. Active OMB circulars include the following:

- Circulars A-21, A-87, and A-122, which prescribe cost principles for educational institutions, state and local governments, and nonprofit enterprises, respectively

- Circular A-50, which prescribes procedures for follow-up of reports issued by the Inspector General, other executive branch audit organizations, the GAO, and nonfederal auditors

- Circular A-76, which specifies rules, procedures, and cost–benefit tests for government operations

- Circular A-125, which defines and establishes payment policies for government obligations

- Circular A-133, which establishes criteria for audits of institutions of higher learning and other nonprofit institutions

Procurement Organizations within the Executive Branch

Approximately 13 departments and 60 agencies in the executive branch award literally billions of dollars' worth of contracts each year. In addition, these organizations make policy-related decisions, consistent with OFPP mandates, which affect their individual procurement mission. These departments and agencies, along with the specific products or services they procure, are identified in several publications that can be obtained from the U.S. Superintendent of Documents: *Selling to the Military, Selling to the U.S. Government, Doing Business with the Federal Government,* and *U.S. Government Procurement and Sales Directory.* Military contract award statistics are also available from the DOD Office of Public Affairs. Because of its major role in the procurement process, the DOD is discussed in some detail next. Other key agencies and departments that play a role in the procurement process are also briefly mentioned.

Department of Defense

The DOD is so large that it almost defies description. Its assets have been estimated to be twice those of the 100 largest manufacturing corporations in the United States. More importantly, it accounts for about 80% of all federal procurement and, next to the Department of the Interior, is the nation's largest real estate operator.

The Office of the Secretary of Defense is actually limited to purchasing relatively minor housekeeping items. The Army, Navy, Air Force, Defense Logistics Agency, and certain other DOD agencies are responsible for the major DOD acquisitions.

The Undersecretary of Defense for Acquisition and Technology is the senior DOD procurement executive. The Undersecretary's responsibilities include the following:

- Supervising the DOD acquisition process
- Setting policy for acquisition, including defense contractor oversight and contract audit
- Directing policy for maintenance of the defense industrial base
- Directing the military service secretaries and heads of DOD agencies in matters falling within the Undersecretary's responsibility
- Consulting with the DOD Inspector General to prevent duplication of audit and oversight of contractor activities

The Director of Defense Procurement, who reports to the Deputy Undersecretary of Defense for Acquisition and Technology, is responsible for several functions that play an important role in the acquisition process.

- The Directorate for Cost, Pricing, and Finance is responsible for implementing DOD policy on cost accounting standards; independent research and development (IR&D) and bid and proposal (B&P) costs; progress payments; and other areas involving the costing, pricing, and financing of government contracts.
- The Directorate for Defense Acquisition Regulatory System has responsibility for issuing and updating the DOD Federal Acquisition Regulation Supplement (DFARS). The DFARS contains all the regulatory material that is applicable to the DOD agencies.

Army. The principal procurement organization within the Department of the Army is the Army Materiel Command (AMC), located in Alexandria, Virginia. The AMC is responsible for the issuance and management of research and development, production, and maintenance contracts. The AMC manages numerous major subcommands and installations; contracts are issued by those subcommands and installations. Major subcommands of the AMC include the Aviation Systems Command, Communications Electronics Command, and the Tank–Automotive Command.

Other significant Army purchasing organizations include specialized laboratories, the Corps of Engineers (construction), the Army Medical Department (medical supplies), Army Information Systems Command (communication equipment), and the Military Traffic Management Command (military ocean terminals for movement of cargo).

Navy. The major commands within the Navy, which provide material support for the operating forces and to some extent the Marine Corps, include the Naval Air Systems Command, the Space and Naval Warfare Systems Command, the Naval Facilities Engineering Command, the Naval Sea Systems Command, and the Naval Supply Systems Command. The Military Sealift Command also has procurement responsibilities.

Each of these commands is responsible for research and development of the items of equipment they procure, as well as for production and maintenance.

Air Force. The Air Force Material Command, which was formed in 1992 to consolidate approximately 14 different Air Force procurement organizations, is responsible for all procurements—research and development, production and maintenance—within the Air Force.

Defense Agencies. Other significant defense agencies include the Defense Advanced Research Projects Agency (DARPA), the Ballistic Missile Defense Organization, the Defense Commissary Agency, the Defense Logistics Agency (which is the military equivalent to the GSA), the Defense Intelligence Agency, and the Defense Imagery and Mapping Agency.

National Aeronautics and Space Administration

The NASA, a civilian agency of the government, conducts research in various aspects of aeronautics and space technology, including development of space transportation systems. Major NASA acquisitions are made by the various NASA field installations; the procurement system is decentralized; that is, the field installations negotiate, award, and administer their own contracts.

Contracts awarded by NASA are basically for large and continuing research and development contracts for major systems, including aeronautical and communications systems. Procurement is governed by the National Aeronautics and Space Act.

General Services Administration

The GSA was created by the Federal Property and Administrative Services Act of 1949 to consolidate dozens of agencies involved in the executive branch's many housekeeping activities, such as purchasing supplies, providing communications facilities, keeping records, and acting as the federal architect, builder, and landlord. The GSA is the federal government's central supply agency and, as such, is the government's largest purchasing agent. Procurement is accomplished primarily by three groups: the Federal Property Resource Service, the Public Building Service, and the Federal Supply Service. A considerable portion of GSA procurement involves standard items. Procurements by the Federal Supply Service are discussed further in Chapter 6.

The GSA's responsibilities include the administration of the national reserve of defense plant equipment; the stockpiling of strategic materials; records management; transportation, traffic, and communications management; management of the government's Automatic Data Processing (ADP) resources; construction and maintenance of the government's real property; and centralized procurement, storage, and distribution of supplies.

Department of Energy

The Department of Energy (DOE) was established in 1977 by the Department of Energy Organization Act.[11] The DOE's mission is to manage the federal government's energy functions toward meeting and solving our nation's energy problems.

DOE contracts include construction and Architect and Engineer (A&E) services, fuel processing fabrication and recovery services, ADP and related software, and communications equipment.

Most of the contracts awarded by the DOE fall into one of the following categories: atomic energy defense activities, energy conservation, energy supply research and development, fossil energy research and development, and energy production demonstration and distribution. One of the DOE's major challenges of the future will be managing the safety, health, and environmental issues that have surfaced in recent years at the DOE nuclear weapons systems plants.

Department of Health and Human Services

Because of its functional responsibilities in such areas as health care, licensing of food products, and retirement security for the aged, the Department of Health and Human Services touches the lives of most people in the United States. Procurement in the department is carried out by various national, regional, and field offices of the National Institutes of Health, the Public Health Service, the Food and Drug Administration, and the Social Security Administration.

Department of the Interior

The Department of the Interior is responsible for about one-half billion acres of federal land, as well as development and preservation of natural resources. Procurement activities are decentralized within the department's various bureaus, with activity concentrated in the western part of the United States.

Department of Transportation

The Department of Transportation (DOT) includes such diverse entities as the U.S. Coast Guard, the Federal Aviation Administration (FAA), the Federal Highway Administration, the Federal Railroad Administration, and the Urban Mass Transportation Administration. As in the Department of the Interior, procurement activities are decentralized among the various agencies.

The FAA has become a leader in acquisition reform, and has developed, on a trial basis, a very streamlined procurement process. The FAA awards research and development contracts and production contracts that support the air traffic control system as well as ground systems.

Department of Agriculture

The Department of Agriculture was established more than 100 years ago. The department's substantial procurement expenditures are concentrated in three services: Agricultural Stabilization and Conservation, Food Safety and Inspection, and Natural Resources and Environment.

Executive Branch Procurement Personnel

Successful government contracting depends largely on a clear understanding of the authority, responsibility, and limitations of each government official involved in the procurement process. The doctrine of actual authority is well established in legal precedence. As stated by the Armed Services Board of Contract Appeals (ASBCA) in *General Electric Co.*,[12] "It is appropriate that the government cannot be bound by one acting without authority."

Program Manager, Project Manager, and Other Technical Staff

Government officials with technical and management responsibilities play a major role in the procurement process.

- Program managers, found in the DOD, NASA, the DOE, and certain other agencies, are important officials who have overall responsibility for the procurement action. Although they have a key role in acquiring major weapon systems, they may not be widely known to small government contractors. In the DOD, program managers are designated only for systems with anticipated costs in excess of $75 million in research, development, test, and evaluation, or $300 million for the entire program.

- Project managers and other government technical staff are better known to most contractors. Although generally not assigned contracting responsibilities as such, they are responsible for ensuring that goods or services meet the government's technical specifications and requirements.

While various government technical representatives may make suggestions relating to contract performance, their suggestions must be carefully evaluated. If the suggestions are expected to change the contract's scope or to increase costs, the contracting officer must personally authorize the necessary change orders or other contractual authorizations.

The Contracting Officer

The key government official in a contractual relationship with private industry is the contracting officer (CO), who is the only government representative duly authorized to enter into or administer contracts. Only a CO has the authority to obligate the government, and then only to the extent of the authority that has been delegated to him or her. This authorization stems from the agency head and is evidenced by a written delegation of authority, usually defined in a certificate of appointment.

In a case brought before the U.S. Supreme Court approximately 50 years ago (*Federal Crop Insurance Corp. v. Merrill* et al.),[13] Justice Frankfurter's opinion stated that "... anyone entering into an arrangement with the Government takes the risk of having accurately ascertained that he who purports to act for the Government stays within the bounds of his authority ... even though, as here, the agent ... may have been unaware of the limitations upon his authority." It is very important that contractors be sure that whoever issues direction allegedly on behalf of the government has the authority to do so.

Additionally, individuals may be appointed as authorized representatives of the CO, such as the contracting officer's technical representative (COTR), with designated limits of authority. In view of the considerable financial risk of doing work at the direction of unauthorized officials, it is important for contractors to (1) understand the authority that has been delegated to an authorized representative of a CO, and (2) obtain the appropriate CO's approval before proceeding with any work that was not understood by the parties to be an existing contractual requirement.

- An example of a COTR's acting beyond the delegation of authority and thereby causing the contractor a serious problem is apparent in *Amis Construction and Consulting Services, Inc.*,[14] wherein the contractor asserted that work performed beyond the scope of its cost-plus-fixed-fee contract was authorized by the CO's technical representative. However, the contract explicitly stated that the technical representative was a technical advisor and was not empowered to sign contractual documents or to direct any actions that would change the scope, price, terms, or conditions of the contract. In denying the company's claim for reimbursement of its contract overrun, the Department of Labor Board of Contract Appeals observed that "the doctrine of apparent authority is not binding upon the government and accordingly, it is not estopped from denying the authority of its agents."

- In another appeals proceeding, *Abbott W. Thompson Associates*[15] contended that additional design services performed under an architect–engineer contract were compensable because the work had been done at the direction of the DOT regional architect. However, the changes clause in the contract required the CO's prior written approval before services could be rendered or before the government would be responsible for payment of an additional charge. In ruling that the contractor's claim was not compensable, the DOT Contract Appeals Board concluded that "where such written approval [by the contracting officer] is required as a precondition for a compensable change, the failure to obtain that approval bars any recovery on account of the change. . . . Accordingly, any work performed by the appellant under the circumstances is done as a volunteer for which no compensation is due."

- In a decision involving *DOT Systems Inc.*,[16] the DOT Contract Appeals Board ruled that the contracting officer's technical representative had implied authority to direct a contractor to use excess warehouse space to store government property. Here, the contract did not clearly specify the limitations of the technical representative's authority, and the board ruled that in those circumstances, the representative was empowered to direct the contractor to store the government property in a particular manner. Since the requirement to use excess warehouse space constituted a constructive contract change, the government was held liable to reimburse the contractor for additional costs related to the change.

Within the DOD, separate COs are frequently designated for (1) procuring, (2) administering, and (3) negotiating termination settlements. The responsibilities of these various types of COs are discussed next.

Procuring Contracting Officer (PCO). In the DOD and certain other large procurement organizations, contracts are often awarded by one office and administered by a completely different office. The procuring CO, who is usually located in the same area as the systems acquisition manager or project manager, is a key member of the acquisition team and is the only team member authorized to enter into contracts on behalf of the government, but, again, only within the limits of the authority so delegated. The delegation of authority to a CO often limits the authority of the appointee to a particular contract type, and/or to dollar amounts. Contractual actions that exceed such limitations usually require the written approval of the head of the contracting activity.

After contract award, a different office may be assigned the responsibility of administering the contract.

Administrative Contracting Officer (ACO). This official is primarily responsible for monitoring contract performance and negotiating certain contract modifications. The authority of the ACO is derived through the delegation of specific administrative responsibilities from the PCO.

FAR 42.302(a) designates 67 functions as "the normal contract administration functions to be performed by the cognizant [contract administration office]." These designated functions include the following:

- Reviewing contractor compensation and insurance plans
- Negotiating forward pricing rate agreements and advance agreements regarding the treatment of specific costs
- Approval (or disapproval) of contractor's requests for progress payments
- Determining the allowability of costs suspended or disapproved
- Issuing Notices of Intent to Disallow or to Not Recognize Costs
- Establishing final indirect cost rates and billing rates for business units of multidivisional corporations under the cognizance of a corporate administrative contracting officer or business units having resident ACOs
- Determining contractor compliance with the cost principles set forth in FAR Part 31 and the Cost Accounting Standards (CAS)

Other functions designated in FAR 42.302(b), such as negotiating change order proposals, are performed by ACOs when specifically authorized by the PCO. In the case of determining the extent to which a contractor is complying or not complying with any portion of the Cost Accounting Standards, the Armed Services Board of Contract Appeals decided that McDonnell Douglas Corporation's[17] appeal of a CAS noncompliance determination by a PCO should be dismissed without prejudice because the noncompliance determination had not been made by the cognizant ACO. In the Board's view:

> The threshold issue presented by the instant motion goes simply to the PCO's authority under pertinent procurement regulations to perform certain CAS administration functions. ... The T-45 contract was subject to the FAR, a plain reading of which, we have observed, leaves little room for doubt that determination of the "contractor's compliance with Cost Accounting Standards" are "normal contract administrative functions to be performed by the cognizant CAO [Contract Administration Office]" and thus the ACO.

In *World Computer Systems Inc.,*[18] the Department of Transportation Board of Contract Appeals invalidated a final decision by a contracting officer that involved the disallowance of certain indirect costs. The Board concluded that the CO lacked the authority to issue such a decision because a delegation of authority to the CO did not carry with it the authority to issue final decisions under the Contract Disputes Act. In the Board's view, that particular contracting officer was not delegated the "full panoply of contract administration functions that would be tantamount to appointment as an Administrative Contracting Officer."

Within the DOD, the vast majority of contract administration functions are assigned to the Defense Contract Management Command (DCMC), which is a part of the Defense Logistics Agency. That command operates from five district headquarters (Atlanta, Chicago, Philadelphia, Boston, and in Southern California) and these districts collectively manage approximately 90 offices at defense contractor locations or facilities.

When the DCMC determines that a significant level of contractor oversight is necessary, the oversight is usually accomplished on a contractor-wide basis rather than contract by contract. In such circumstances, the contract administration office designates a cost-monitoring coordinator. This individual could be the administrative contracting officer or some other staff member. The coordinator is assisted by auditors from the DCAA and technical personnel. The coordinator's responsibilities include the following:

- Preparing and maintaining review plans with assistance from DCAA and other specialists comprising the cost-monitoring team
- Coordinating the efforts of all team members
- Providing assistance to team members or arranging for assistance when requested
- Advising the contract administration office of deficiencies in contractors' operations, and monitoring the status of recommendations made to the contractor
- Preparing for the ACO's consideration a "Notice of Intent to Disallow or Not Recognize Cost" when recommendations involve a significant cost or an important principle

This DCMC function, which provides important information to the ACO in his or her role of monitoring contractor performance, has contributed to a reduction in the government's oversight program at several contractor facilities.

Termination Contracting Officer (TCO). The TCO is authorized to terminate contracts for the convenience of the government, or for default, "when in the best interests of the government." The TCO is also authorized to negotiate termination settlements, or, if agreements cannot be reached on a mutually agreeable settlement, the TCO is empowered to settle the matter by determination.

Executive Branch Personnel Involved in Procurement Oversight/Enforcement

Audits of Government Contractors

The role of a government auditor in the acquisition process has basically been as an advisor to the CO, but in recent years the government auditor has assumed more of an oversight role in the contracting process. The oversight role has had a significant impact on the acquisition process, often creating conflict between the auditor and the CO.

Most government agencies that do a significant amount of procurement have an audit function or organization. For example, the DCAA, by far the largest government contract audit organization, is authorized by the DOD to audit, examine, or review the books and records of contractors and subcontractors in order to establish the adequacy of internal controls, accounting systems, and general and business practices. In fulfilling these responsibilities, the DCAA is proactive in the establishment of forward pricing, billing, final overhead rates, and contract prices.

The DCAA provides audit services not only for the DOD but also for NASA, the Department of Energy, and for other civilian departments. This is particularly true when contracts are awarded by civilian agencies to companies already engaged in DOD work. A few civilian departments, including the GSA, perform contract audit functions on their own through their inspector general's office.

The DCAA Mission. DOD Directive 5105.36, dated June 9, 1965 (revised June 8, 1978), which established the Defense Contract Audit Agency, defined the agency's mission as follows:

- To perform all necessary contract audits for the DOD, and provide accounting and financial advisory services regarding contracts and subcontracts in connection with the negotiation, administration, and settlement of contracts and subcontracts
- To provide contract audit service to other government agencies as appropriate

As further discussed in Chapter 16, the agency's principal activities are involved in virtually every stage of the procurement process. The services provided by the DCAA to contracting officers include preaward contract audits, postaward audits, and contractor internal control system audits.

DCAA Organization. The DCAA is a separate DOD agency that reports to the Assistant Secretary of Defense (Comptroller), but is subject to oversight by both the DOD Inspector General (DODIG) and the Undersecretary for Acquisition and Technology. The DODIG exercises certain oversight of DCAA operations as a result of its statutory responsibility to:

- Provide policy direction for audits relating to fraud, waste, and abuse.
- Monitor and evaluate the adherence of DOD auditors to contract audit principles, policies, and procedures.
- Develop policy, evaluate program performance, and monitor actions taken by all DOD components in response to contract audits.

As a result, such traditional contract audit activities as defective pricing reviews may be performed by DOD Inspector General auditors, as well as by DCAA auditors. A federal court decision[19] to grant the Inspector General access to internal audit reports has further blurred the contract audit roles of the Inspector General and DCAA. That decision has also increased industry's concern over DCAA's ability to remain independent, because it clearly endorses an intermingling of the oversight and administrative audit functions.

The DCAA consists of six major organizational components, that is, headquarters (located at Fort Belvoir, Virginia) and five geographic regions: Eastern, Northeastern, Central, Western, and Mid-Atlantic, plus a field detachment that focuses on classified work. The agency operates at the field audit office level, with both resident offices and branch offices. Resident offices are established at specific contractor locations where the audit workload warrants a permanent audit staff, and often where the Defense Contract Management Command has established an on-site contract administration activity such as a Defense Plant Representative Office (DPRO). Branch offices are strategically located in each DCAA region to conduct contract audits at other contractor locations in the assigned geographic area. The audit work assigned to branch offices is generally done on a mobile basis, with the auditors responsible for all contractors within a segment of the geographic area covered by the branch office. Also, DCAA procurement liaison offices have been established in various Army, Navy, and Air Force procurement offices to provide for effective communication and coordination between the procurement officials and the field audit activities.

While DCAA headquarters develops overall audit policy, the regional offices and the field detachments are the primary operating units. Regional audit managers (RAMs) are responsible for planning, directing, and evaluating the contract audit mission for an assigned group of field audit offices. They provide regional direction to the branch managers, and to resident auditors, to help resolve complex or controversial contract audit or cost accounting issues. RAMs also are responsible for ensuring that audits are accomplished in a timely and effective manner, and in accordance with agency policy and acquisition regulations.

Audit Follow-Up. For many years, the GAO and Congress have expressed concern that the government may be losing billions of dollars because executive departments are not following audit recommendations. In response to this prodding, federal agencies have placed increased emphasis on tracking audit recommendations.

From its issuance on August 31, 1981, DOD Directive 5000.42, "Policy for Follow-Up on Contract Audit Recommendations," generated considerable interest and controversy. The directive required DOD components to track and report on the resolution of all significant contract audit recommendations if the contracting officer did not concur. To alleviate industry concerns that the directive impaired the contracting officer's independence, the Assistant Deputy Undersecretary of Defense for Acquisition reiterated in a November 1981 memorandum that the contracting officer remained responsible for all final determinations concerning contracts. The memorandum expressed the view that the DOD directive merely formalized review practices that previously existed rather than changed the direction of acquisition policy.

To clarify the meaning of "significant contract audit recommendations" and to reduce the number of audit reports subject to tracking, the directive was reissued as DOD Directive 7640.2, "Policy for Follow-Up on Contract Audit Reports." The directive currently:

- Clarifies the responsibilities of the contracting officer, contract audit function, and the DOD Inspector General
- Identifies specific reports to be tracked and outlines reporting and resolution requirements
- Eliminates the requirement for auditors to request independent reviews of differences
- Clarifies and separates tracking, reporting, and resolution requirements

However, a widespread perception remains, both in industry and in government, that the directive has diminished the contracting officer's authority by making it more difficult for a contracting officer to take a position materially different from an audit recommendation. This de facto shift in power to the contract auditor has complicated and, in some instances, delayed the process of resolving contract pricing and costing issues. In this environment, since the contracting officer may be reluctant to go against the audit recommendation, it becomes even more critical for the contractor to make every reasonable effort to resolve purely accounting issues with the contract audit activity or be prepared to provide the contracting officer with clear and convincing evidence that the contract auditor position is wrong.

Civilian agencies are subject to a similar procedure for audit follow-up pursuant to revised OMB Circular A-50.

Inspectors General

Charter. One of the major congressional responses to rising criticisms of government laxity was the Inspector General Act of 1978.[20] The purposes of the act were to promote economy, efficiency, and effectiveness in government and to prevent and detect fraud and abuse in specific civilian agencies and in the DOD. The act has provided a means for keeping department heads informed about deficiencies in the administration of their operations and the progress of any necessary corrective action.

The act established an office of inspector general in 12 federal departments and agencies. Several inspectors general (IGs) were already in place before the act was passed. The act was amended by the DOD Authorization Act of 1983[21] to establish an IG for the DOD. Each IG is appointed by the President with the advice and consent of the Senate. The act also provided for the removal of an IG from office by the President, provided the President communicates the reasons for such removal to both houses of Congress. The advice and consent of the Senate is not required for an IG's removal.

The act provided broad responsibilities and authority to the IG for conducting audits and inspections relating to policies, practices, and operations of their respective departments. IGs can discharge their responsibilities in any manner they deem appropriate, provided they:

- Comply with the Comptroller General's Standards for Audits of Governmental Organizations, Programs, Activities, and Functions.

- Report promptly to the U.S. Attorney General whenever reasonable grounds exist for belief that a federal criminal law has been violated.

- Submit to the agency or department head a semiannual comprehensive report identifying significant problems, abuses, and deficiencies; recommendations for corrective actions; recommendations previously made for which corrective action has not been completed; matters referred to prosecutive authorities; prosecutions and convictions that have resulted; and audit reports issued during the period. (Within 30 days of submission of the semiannual report, the agency or department head must submit a copy, together with any desired comments, to the appropriate committee or subcommittee of Congress. No later than 60 days after transmitting the semiannual report to Congress, the agency or department head must make copies available to the public upon request and at a reasonable cost.)

- Report immediately to the agency or department head any "particularly serious or flagrant problems, abuses, or deficiencies." (The head of the department or agency has only seven calendar days to forward the report to Congress with any appropriate comments.)

The act grants IGs significant and unusual powers for accessing records, selecting audit and investigative procedures, and obtaining subpoenas. In *U.S. vs. Westinghouse Electric Corp.*,[22] the court took an extremely broad view of the IG's subpoena power.

DOD Inspector General Organization. Four assistant inspectors general and a director report to the IG and are responsible for the following:

- Administration and Information Management
- Policy and Oversight
- Auditing
- Investigations/Defense Criminal Investigative Service
- Department Inquiries

The Deputy IG for Policy and Oversight is responsible for the IG activity related to DOD Directive 7640.2. The Deputy IG for Investigations/Defense Criminal Investigative Service is responsible for conducting procurement-related criminal investigations when required.

Department of Justice

The U.S. Department of Justice is responsible for prosecuting fraud and criminal activity in procurement. Civil actions brought against contractors due to violations of such statutes as the False Claims Act are handled through the Civil Division.

In 1982, the Department of Justice established the Defense Procurement Fraud Unit to investigate fraud allegations in defense programs. Investigations by the fraud unit are closely coordinated with the DOD Assistant IG for Investigation and with the DCAA. Specific investigations are often jointly staffed with Department of Justice and DOD personnel.

The Department of Justice plays a key role in the suspension of contractors who have engaged in, or who have been indicted for, unlawful activities; suspension of contractors from eligibility to be awarded government contracts if often the initial step in the debarment, wherein contractors are precluded from receiving new government contracts for periods up to three years.

2-5. ROLE OF THE JUDICIAL BRANCH

The federal court system plays an important role in the acquisition process. In certain circumstances (claims, for example), government prime contractors may pursue relief in the federal court system, rather than (or, in some cases, in addition to) the various administrative boards of contract appeals in most major procurement agencies. The federal court system, which includes Federal District Courts, the U.S. Court of Appeals for the Federal Circuit, the U.S. Court of Federal Claims, and the U.S. Supreme Court, has played an important role in resolving government contract-related disputes, and in establishing legal precedents.

Contractors may elect to bypass an agency Board of Contract Appeals and file an appeal from an adverse decision of a contracting officer directly with the U.S. Court of Federal Claims. The government is represented in this court by lawyers from the Department of Justice.

The Court of Appeals for the Federal Circuit reviews decisions that have been rendered by the various Boards of Contract Appeals, as well as the decisions of the U.S. Court of Federal Claims. This court is a forum that is available to contractors and to the government; decisions are usually rendered by a board of three judges.

The U.S. Federal District Courts (as well as courts in the various states) also hear and render decisions on cases involving contract disputes. These courts are most frequently involved in deciding cases between prime contractors and their subcontractors and in interpreting specific statutes and regulations that involve the acquisition process.

While the U.S. Supreme Court rarely agrees to review cases involving government contracts that have been decided by lower courts, the Supreme Court has rendered several important decisions that have had a significant impact on the acquisition process—including one far-reaching decision that was rendered over 100 years ago.[23]

2-6. NOTES

1. Armed Services Procurement Act, Title 10, U.S.C., 62 Stat. 21, enacted Feb. 19, 1948 and 70A Stat. 1, enacted August 10, 1956, Pub. L. 84-1028.
2. National Aeronautics and Space Act 72 Stat. 426, 10 U.S.C. §2302, enacted July 2, 1958, Pub. L. 85-568.
3. Federal Property and Administrative Act, 41 U.S.C., 63 Stat. 378, enacted June 30, 1949, Pub. L. 81-152.
4. Truth in Negotiations Act, 10 U.S.C. §2306a, enacted September 10, 1962, Pub. L. 87-653.
5. Office of Federal Procurement Policy Act Amendments of 1988, 41 U.S.C. §423, 97 Stat. 1325, enacted November 17, 1988, Pub. L. 100-679, §§26 and 27.
6. Federal Acquisition Streamlining Act of 1994, 41 U.S.C. §251, enacted October 13, 1994, Pub. L. 103-355.
7. Clinger–Cohen Act of 1996, formerly known as Federal Acquisition Reform Act of 1996, enacted February 10, 1996, Pub. L. 104-106.
8. Budget and Accounting Act of 1921, ch. 18. 42 Stat. 20, 31 U.S.C. §1, 2, 11 . . . , enacted June 10, 1921.
9. Competition in Contracting Act, 31 U.S.C. §3551–3556, enacted July 18, 1984, Pub. L. 98-369.
10. Office of Federal Procurement Policy Act Amendments of 1979, 41 U.S.C. §422, enacted October 10, 1979, Pub. L. 96-83.
11. Department of Energy Organization Act, 42 U.S.C. §2751, et seq., effective October 1, 1977.
12. General Electric Co., ASBCA No. 11990, May 25, 1967, 67-1 BCA 6,377.
13. Federal Crop Insurance Corp. v. Merrill et al., Nov. 10, 1947, 332 U.S. 380, 68 S. Ct. 1.
14. Amis Construction and Consulting Services, Inc., LBCA No. 81-BCA-4, March 11, 1982, 82-1 BCA 15,679.
15. Abbott W. Thompson Associates, DOT CAB No. 1098, January 21, 1981, 81-1 BCA 14,879.
16. DOT Systems, Inc., DOT CAB No. 1208, June 10, 1982, 92-2 BCA 15,817.
17. McDonnell Douglas Corp., ASBCA No. 44637, April 6, 1993, 83-2 BCA 25,700.
18. World Computer Systems, Inc., DOT CAB No. 2802, January 11, 1995, 95-1 BCA 27,399.
19. U.S. v. Westinghouse Electric Corp., Misc. No. 11710, DC WD PA 1985, August 14, 1985, 615 F. Supp. 1163, affirmed CA 3 No. 85-3456, April 14, 1986, 788 F.2d 164.
20. Inspector General Act of 1978, 5 U.S.C. App 2, 9, 11. Pub. L. 96-88.
21. Fiscal Year 1983 National Defense Authorization Act, 96 Stat. 759, 5 U.S.C. §5315, 10 U.S.C. Pub. L. 97-252.
22. U.S. v. Westinghouse Electric Corp., supra, note 19.
23. U.S. v. Corliss Steam Engine Co., (US S. Ct. 1876) 91, US 321.

Chapter Three

Obtaining Government Business

3-1. BACKGROUND

The U.S. government is by far the largest consumer of goods and services in the world. A government agency is likely to have a need for just about any product or service imaginable, and probably in quantities that stretch the imagination. Because of the vast sales potential, it is small wonder that federal procurement is viewed as a major market opportunity.

Understandably, there are many misconceptions about the federal market, both positive and negative. Many believe that selling to the federal government ranks next to finding a pot of gold at the end of the rainbow. Others avoid government orders because the rules, regulations, and contractual terms and conditions are viewed as traps, designed to ensnare the unwary, intrepid company that dares to venture into this market. Of course, both of these views are uninformed and should not be the basis for any company's decision to sell or not to sell to the federal government.

This chapter discusses the process of obtaining government business. It covers how the government communicates what it is interested in buying, how companies interested in fulfilling government needs should respond, and how the contractual relationship and pricing arrangements are ultimately established. The contracting procedures have been fairly well standardized and apply to all companies, whether foreign or domestic.

A company electing to enter this specialized market should recognize that the objective of the procurement process is to acquire necessary supplies and services of the desired quality, in a timely manner, and at fair and reasonable prices. A fair and reasonable price is one that is fair to both parties to the transaction, considering the quality and timeliness of contract performance. As in all other business dealings, the potential seller to the government must decide whether the proposed contractual arrangement serves the company's best interest and is consistent with the company's goals and objectives.

3-2. PRELIMINARIES FOR ENTERING THE GOVERNMENT MARKET

Marketing

Before attempting to enter the government market, a company must determine which of the many government agencies might be interested in the products or services that the company is capable of providing. Federal purchasing activities may provide either a permanent or a one-time marketplace for a company's products. Only after the potential customers are identified can the company determine how best to obtain government business. Because the military and civilian government organizations purchase literally thousands of goods and services, ranging from complex space vehicles to paper clips, as well as food products, medicines, machinery, equipment, ships, airplanes, paper, ink, furniture, clothing, and so forth, a list of all the potential government needs for any specific category would be lengthy indeed. Therefore, the company should develop a sufficient database to identify which agencies should be the targets of its marketing strategy. To assist small business, the Small Business Administration publishes the *U.S. Government Purchasing and Sales Directory,*[1] which identifies federal entities purchasing certain items and services.

No matter what the government is buying, the procurement will use either competitive procedures, which includes sealed bids, competitive negotiations, or procedures excluding a particular source; or other than competitive procedures, which applies in only seven circumstances.

Government Marketing Defined

A common misperception among contractors is that marketing is simply the process of finding opportunities to bid or propose on government contracts. While locating opportunities to bid is an integral part of marketing, the marketing process is much more comprehensive. For example, establishing a good working relationship with a government agency through exemplary contract performance can lead to many bidding opportunities. For the purposes of this discussion, "government marketing" is defined as all activities that contribute to winning government contracts. In the government contract environment, marketing involves two basic activities: (1) identifying and tracking potential contract opportunities, and (2) conveying to the government customer the company's capability to provide specific products and services.

Strategic Marketing Planning

Successful marketing, which represents a significant expenditure of resources, is the result of careful and comprehensive planning, both at the overall business level and at the individual contract level. The purpose of strategic marketing planning is to enhance the decision-making process related to the benefits of entering or remaining in the market (return on investment, profit level, absorption of fixed operating costs, etc.) and the costs associated with entering the market (administrative cost increases, legal liability, etc.). The strategic plan, once developed, requires periodic updating, as appropriate, to assess whether the government is still a viable market. Information on current contracting activity should be considered in making this decision. When the plan is complete, it should answer these questions:

- Are we going to enter the government market?
- What products or services are we going to provide?
- To what customers will we provide our products or services?
- What changes in our organization or methods of doing business must we undertake in order to be successful?
- What portion of the market will we enter?

Listed below are some questions to consider when preparing a strategic marketing plan.

Product
- Does the government currently purchase similar product(s)?
- Are the products purchased by sealed bids or negotiated procurement?
- Is procurement centralized or performed by individual buying activities?
- Is the market potential significant enough to attract us?

Agencies
- Which agencies can be considered potential customers?
- How are these agencies structured in terms of size and responsibility?
- What type of pricing arrangements do these agencies normally include in their contracts?

Profitability
- Does the market offer sufficient long-term profit potential based on analysis of pricing history competition?
- How effective is the competition?
- What new production techniques are required?
- What new or special requirements, such as accounting and quality assurance, are required?
- What investments in technology, labor, and capital are required?

Results
- Which portion of the market should we target for individual contract opportunities?

Prohibited Marketing Activities

Procurement Integrity. The Office of Federal Procurement Policy Act Amendments of 1988 added requirements for procurement integrity.[2] In essence, these provisions prohibit the disclosure of attempts to obtain certain procurement-related information before contract award. The law also restricts contractor employment, or discussions of employment, of former government procurement personnel. The procurement integrity provisions are incorporated into Federal Acquisition Regulation (FAR) 3.104.

The initial implementation of the law resulted in confusion by both contractors and government personnel, since it conflicted with numerous existing statutes concerning government employee ethics and other "revolving door" provisions. As a result, Congress suspended the legislation for one year: November 30, 1989, to December 1, 1990.[3] Congress reinstated the law, effective December

1, 1990,[4] except for provisions that prohibited certain government employees from working for contractors after leaving federal employment. Those revolving-door provisions remained suspended until May 31, 1991, at which time all provisions of the law again became applicable.

The procurement integrity provisions apply to both contractor procurement personnel and government procurement officials on all federal agency procurements for property or services. Contractors are prohibited from obtaining contractor bid or proposal information or source selection information before award of a federal contract to which the information relates. Federal procurement officials are prohibited from disclosing contractor bid or proposal information or source selection information before the award of a federal contract to which the information relates.

Any agency official who is participating personally and substantially in a federal procurement that is expected to exceed the simplified acquisition threshold must promptly report any potential offer of employment by a bidder or offeror and either reject the potential offer or disqualify himself or herself from further participation in the procurement. "Source selection data" are defined as information prepared or developed by the federal agency to conduct a particular procurement that has not previously been made available to the public.

Prior to January 2, 1997, contractors and government procurement officials were required to certify, in writing, compliance with the regulation for all procurements over $100,000. The contractor's representative was required to certify that "to the best of his or her knowledge and belief . . . such officer or employee . . . has no information concerning a violation or possible violation" and that all employees personally and substantially involved in the procurement were familiar with the act. Contractor employees were required to certify that they were familiar with the procurement integrity provisions, would comply with its requirements, and would report any violations. All employees, officers, consultants, and agents involved in the procurement process were required to receive training on all aspects of procurement integrity. The individual employee certifications served as a basis for signing company certifications with each contract and were required to be maintained until six years after cessation of employment or retention as an agent or consultant. The Fiscal Year 1996 National Defense Authorization Act[5] eliminated the certification requirements. Implementing regulations were incorporated into FAR, Subpart 3.104, effective January 2, 1997.

All solicitations and contracts awarded in excess of the simplified acquisition threshold include clauses entitled "Cancellation, Recession, and Recovery of Funds for Illegal or Improper Activity" (FAR 52.203-8) and "Price or Fee Adjustment for Illegal or Improper Activity" (FAR 52.203-10). When a procurement integrity violation is determined before contract award, an offeror may be disqualified or the procurement may be canceled. When a violation is determined after contract award, these clauses define the price and/or fee adjustment parameters, by contract type, for a contract adjustment. The contracting officer may also terminate the contract for default.

Lobbying Activities. The Byrd Amendment[6] amended the Federal Regulation of Lobbying Act[7] by specifically addressing lobbying by federal government contractors. The amendment prohibits recipients of federal grants, contracts, loans, or cooperative agreements from using federally appropriated funds to pay any person to influence or attempt to influence Congress or any executive branch official in connection with the award of a contract, grant, loan, or cooperative agreement. The act also requires those who request or receive federal contracts, grants, loans, or cooperative agreements to report whether they have made or agreed to make any payments from other than appropriated funds and to disclose the names of the lobbyists or consultants paid with those funds.

The Byrd Amendment, incorporated in FAR 3.8, "Limitations on the Payment of Funds to Influence Federal Transactions," covers federal contracts, subcontracts, grants, and cooperative agreements that are awarded as a result of sealed-bid, competitive negotiation, or sole-source negotiation, and federal loans.

Activities covered by the act are face-to-face meetings, letters and other written submissions, telephone conversations, and other verbal communications. Prohibited activities do not include the following:

1. *Bona fide agency and legislative liaison activities:* These activities are performed by officers or employees of the company who must qualify as regular employees receiving reasonable compensation. The following agency and legislative liaison activities, when not related to a specific government solicitation, are permissible by employees anytime:

   - Discussions and presentations to agencies concerning the qualities and characteristics of products or services, conditions or terms of sale, and service capabilities
   - Technical discussions and other activities, including presentations on the application or adaptation of products and services to the agency's use

   Before the government issues a formal solicitation, the following agency and legislative liaison activities are allowed by employees:

   - Providing information not specifically requested but necessary for the agency to make an informed decision on initiating the solicitation
   - Technical discussions regarding preparation of an unsolicited proposal prior to its official submission
   - Capability presentations by persons seeking an award pursuant to the provisions of the Small Business Act

2. *Professional and technical services:* Professional or technical services are limited to advice and/or analysis that directly applies to a professional or technical discipline (e.g., legal, accounting, or engineering). These services should be rendered directly and solely in the preparation, submission, or negotiation of the government procurement. Professional or technical services cannot be paid for with appropriated funds if the purpose is to influence a procurement.

The Office of Management and Budget (OMB) Standard Form LLL, Disclosure of Lobbying Activities (see Appendix 3.1) must be submitted with any offer if any funds other than federally appropriated funds were paid or will be paid to influence a covered federal transaction and that these requirements will be passed down to subcontractors at all tiers.

Contractors should establish internal policies concerning lobbying activities. Meetings, conversations, and presentations should be documented so that allowable interaction with government personnel can be distinguished from prohibited activities.

The Lobbying Disclosure Act[8] established new disclosure rules for lobbyists. Lobbyists who make or plan to make lobbying contacts to members of Congress, congressional staff, White House officials, and federal agencies must register with the Secretary of the Senate and the Clerk of the House if lobbying income exceeds $20,000 semiannually. Separate registrations are required for each client providing income to the lobbyist in excess of $5,000 semiannually. Semiannual reports on the contracts made for each client must be submitted.

Electronic Commerce

The federal acquisition community is rapidly moving into the world of electronic commerce, which is defined in the National Defense Authorization Act for Fiscal Year 1998[9] as "... electronic techniques for accomplishing business transactions, including electronic mail or messaging, World Wide Web technology, electronic bulletin boards, purchase card, electronic funds transfers, and electronic data interchange." The Federal Acquisition Streamlining Act of 1994 (FASA)[10] as implemented in FAR Subpart 4.5, established a program to develop and implement a Federal Acquisition Computer Network (FACNET). The FASA required a government-wide FACNET capability to be fully implemented by January 1, 2000. FACNET was designed to:

- Provide widespread public notice of solicitations for contract opportunities and contract awards (including price)
- Receive responses to solicitations and associated requests for information
- Receive questions regarding solicitations
- Issue orders
- Make payments to contractors
- Archive procurement action data

The requirement to implement FACNET capability was repealed by the National Defense Authorization Act for Fiscal Year 1998. The act requires federal agencies to facilitate access to federal procurement opportunities and provide convenient and universal access to notices of agency requirements or solicitations through a single, government-wide point of entry. The act also requires the Administrator of the Office of Federal Procurement to:

- Issue policies that promote uniform implementation of electronic commerce, where practicable
- Report to Congress annually from 1998 through 2003 on: the strategic plan for implementing a govenment-wide electronic commerce capability; progress made by individual agencies in implementing electronic commerce; the volume and dollar value transactions conducted via electronic commerce methods and possible enhancements to the capability to increase the level of federal contract information available to the private sector.

Getting on the Solicitation Mailing List

An important marketing step is getting on the solicitation mailing list for each agency that represents a potential source of business. Each procuring agency maintains lists of those firms that have expressed an interest in contracting.

To be placed on an agency solicitation mailing list, a company must submit Standard Form 129, Solicitation Mailing List Application. (See Appendix 3.2.) Often, individual departments and agencies have developed supplemental, detailed capability questionnaires that also must be submitted. Using the data in the application forms and questionnaires, the agency places the company on the mailing list only for the items listed.

To ensure complete coverage, a company should submit a Solicitation Mailing List Application listing the items that it is offering to each organization to which it is interested in selling. Firms should not send company catalogs with a request to be placed on the mailing list for all the items shown. The information should be as specific as possible since mailing lists are broken down by major commodity classification, as specified on the agency's forms.

Before placing a firm on its mailing list, an agency will often require additional information, such as the following:

- Production capability
- Description of items normally produced
- Number of employees
- Plant and transportation facilities
- Government contract experience
- Financial position
- Scope of the firm's operations

Being placed on a solicitation mailing list does not necessarily mean that the company will be notified of all agency procurements specified in the application. FAR 14.205-4 requires only that a sufficient number of bidders be solicited to ensure adequate competition. The agencies normally use a rotation system to ensure that each firm has a fair chance of being selected periodically.

Any company that learns about a specific procurement may submit a bid or offer if it is otherwise qualified to do so. Even though a company is included on an agency's solicitation mailing list, it should nevertheless attempt to secure information about bids from other sources to maximize the opportunities to sell to the government.

Where Business Opportunities Are Publicized

Information concerning government business opportunities also is contained in such publications as the *Commerce Business Daily* and *Business America*. General Services Administration (GSA) business service centers are also excellent sources of information on what the government is buying.

Each workday, the Department of Commerce publishes the *Commerce Business Daily*, which lists proposed government procurements, subcontracting leads, contract awards, sales of surplus property, and opportunities for foreign businesses to sell to U.S. government agencies located outside the United States. Virtually every proposed procurement over $25,000 must be published in the *Commerce Business Daily* except those in which (1) such notice could compromise national security, (2) the procurement is made under a requirements contract, or (3) the procurement is for perishable subsistence supplies. An unsolicited research proposal may be an additional exception if the proposal generates a procurement and if notice of such a proposal would disclose its originality or innovativeness or would reveal proprietary information. However, awards of all contracts exceeding $25,000 must be synopsized if they are likely to result in the award of subcontracts. Notice must be published at least 15 days before the solicitation is issued, and at least 30 days is required between the date the solicitation is issued and the bids or proposals are received.

Business America is published biweekly by the Secretary of Commerce. The magazine provides helpful interpretations of government policies and programs that may affect daily business decisions. It gives concise, up-to-date information on worldwide trade and investment and has a special section on business leads.

GSA business service centers are responsible for: (1) issuing bidders' mailing list applications; (2) furnishing invitations for bids and specifications to prospective bidders; (3) maintaining a current display of bidding opportunities; (4) safeguarding bids; (5) providing bid-opening facilities; and (6) furnishing free copies of publications designed to assist business representatives in doing business with the federal government. There are 10 centers nationwide, mostly located in the main lobbies of federal buildings in cities having GSA regional headquarters.

Opportunities for Small Business Concerns

Each federal agency has a Small and Disadvantaged Business Utilization Office to help small business concerns through the maze of government procedures.

Small Purchases

Simplified acquisition procedures for small purchases are contained in FAR, Part 13. Small purchases, previously defined as acquisitions of $25,000 or less, were set aside for award to small business concerns and subject to a reduced set of FAR clauses. The small purchase threshold was renamed "Simplified Acquisition Threshold" by FASA and raised to $100,000. Procurements under the $100,000 threshold are reserved for small business concerns and exempt from numerous FAR clauses, such as Prohibition against Contingent Fees, Examination of Records, and Drug-Free Workforce Act.

The Role of the Small Business Administration

The government uses its buying power to achieve certain social and economic goals. One area that receives a great deal of political attention and contracting dollars is the encouragement of small businesses. The Small Business Act has established the following as a national specified goal for awards to small businesses and small disadvantaged businesses:

> The Government-wide goal for participation by small business concerns shall be established at not less than 20% of the total value of all prime contract awards for each fiscal year. The Government-wide goal for participation by small business concerns owned and controlled by socially and economically disadvantaged individuals shall be established at not less than 5% of the total value of all prime contracts and subcontract awards for each fiscal year.[11]

The Small Business Administration (SBA) was created to aid and assist small businesses in the pursuit of government contracts. It has offices throughout the country to assist small businesses in understanding and obtaining government contracts. In two rare exceptions to the authority of contracting officers, the SBA has the responsibility to make determinations on the competency of small businesses to perform contracts in a satisfactory manner and to determine whether a company is, in fact, a small business.

The criteria for being classified as a small business are set forth in the SBA regulations[12] and have been incorporated in FAR, Part 19. The regulations define a "small business" as a concern, including its affiliates, that is independently owned and operated, is not dominant in the field in which it is bidding on government contracts, and can further qualify under specified size criteria. The SBA establishes industry size standards by number of employees and/or gross annual receipts. These standards determine which businesses merit special government consideration and assistance. The SBA regulations include size standard levels that are either receipt based or employee based. These levels incorporate the entire Standard Industrial Code (SIC) population, which consits of hundreds of different four-digit codes, established by the OMB. In 1994, the SBA reduced the number of different size standards from 30 to nine. The five employee-based levels remain unchanged, but the receipt-based levels were reduced to the four most common receipt-based size standards and then adjusted upward for a 48.2% inflation using the Gross Domestic Product (GDP) Implicit Price Deflator.

To determine whether it qualifies as a small business, a company must first identify its line of business. For companies having more than one business line, it is possible to be a small business when proposing for a particular requirement and not be a small business when pursuing another procurement. Since being a small business offers some advantages in obtaining government contracts, companies should ensure that their classifications have been appropriately determined.

The government has adopted many policies designed to enhance the development of small businesses and to increase their share of federal contracting. The objective of these policies is twofold: to assist in achieving certain social and economic goals and to broaden the United States' industrial base. Keeping abreast of these emerging policies is critical to both large and small business concerns. To market its products/services to the federal government, a small business should exploit these policies to the fullest extent possible. Additionally, a large government contractor needs to be aware of its subcontracting responsibilities to use small and small disadvantaged businesses in its federal programs.

Certificate of Competency. If an offer from a small business concern is rejected solely on the grounds of insufficient capacity or inadequate credit, the contracting officer (CO) must notify the SBA. If a subsequent SBA investigation reveals that the firm is able to perform the contract, the SBA will issue a certificate of competency. Normally, the CO must then award the contract to that firm. The National Defense Authorization Act for Fiscal Year 1993[13] significantly changed the certificate of competency requirements. The CO previously was required to notify the SBA if a small business was not selected for contract award because it was determined nonresponsible. Now, the CO must notify the small business in writing of the nonresponsibility determination and must advise the business of its right to request an SBA determination of responsibility. A small business wishing to request an SBA determination must inform the CO in writing within 14 days of the CO's notice of nonresponsibility determination. Upon receipt of the request, the CO transmits the notice, along with pertinent documents, to the SBA for its review and determination. This change is noteworthy because it could delay contract awards, as more small businesses request SBA determinations. The act also requires COs to justify and document nonresponsibility determinations more thoroughly.

Set-Asides. The SBA works closely with federal purchasing agencies to ensure that a fair proportion of the total purchases in contracts or subcontracts for property and services is given to small business concerns.

Traditionally, small business set-asides have been utilized to achieve that objective. However, in October 1995, FAR, Part 20, was revised to eliminate set-asides for small businesses located in labor surplus areas (LSAs). The elimination of the LSA set-aside program was directed by FASA.[14]

In October 1995, DFARS, Part 19, was amended to suspend set-asides of acquisitions for small disadvantaged businesses. An interagency government-wide review of affirmative action programs is underway as a result of the Supreme Court's decision in *Adarand Constructors Inc. v Pena*[15] to significantly limit the federal government's authority to implement programs that favor racial minorities. After losing a construction project to a minority-owned contractor despite being the lowest bidder, Adarand filed a reverse discrimination suit claiming that the minority preference provision violated the equal protection component of the Fifth Amendment's due process clause. The Supreme Court held that federal racial preference programs must be subject to the same strict scrutiny that applies to state and local government programs. Under the "strict scrutiny" standard, racial preference programs must serve a compelling governmental interest and must be narrowly tailored. Justice Sandra Day O'Connor wrote the majority opinion, which states:

> The Fifth and Fourteenth Amendments to the Constitution protect persons, not groups. It follows that all governmental action based on race should be subjected to detailed judicial inquiry to ensure that the personal right to equal protection of the laws has not been infringed.

Section 8(a) Program. Under Section 8(a) of the Small Business Act, federal departments and agencies are authorized to award selected contracts to the SBA, which then subcontracts, on a noncompetitive basis, with eligible firms for the work required by the government buying offices. Along with the contracts, the SBA provides management, technical, marketing, and financial aid. In 1969, the eligibility criteria were revised to limit participation to firms owned or controlled by both socially and economically disadvantaged persons. The 8(a) program strives to promote the competitive viability of such firms by providing contract, financial, technical, and management assistance.[16]

Section 8(a) defines social disadvantage as follows:

> Socially disadvantaged individuals are those who have been subjected to racial or ethnic prejudice or cultural bias because of their identities as members of groups without regard to their individual qualities. The social disadvantage must stem from circumstances beyond their control.[17]

A company wishing to participate in the program must establish to the SBA's satisfaction that socially and economically disadvantaged persons operate the business and have at least a 51% ownership share. The program's objective is to make the small disadvantaged business self-sustaining through this controlled market. When that objective is achieved—that is, when the company appears capable of competing in the general marketplace—it is then graduated from the program. Participation in the program is limited to nine years.[18]

A number of minority/racial groups are considered to be socially disadvantaged. In the absence of evidence to the contrary, individuals who are members of these designated groups are presumed to be socially disadvantaged. The *Adarand* decision is having enormous implications for 8(a) and Small Disadvantaged Business (SDB) programs, which are historically race-based. In *Cortez III Service Corp. v NASA*, the U.S. District Court for the District of Columbia[19] granted a preliminary injunction to enjoin NASA from procuring the Management and Operations Contract 1 (MOC-1) as an 8(a) set-aside. The court found that neither NASA nor the SBA performed any analysis before making MOC-1 an 8(a) program. Furthermore, the court noted that the predecessor contract to the MOC-1 was considered too large for a small business program and was thus awarded on the basis of full and open competition; yet MOC-1, which would be even larger than the predecessor contract, was designated 8(a).

Other Programs for Small Business

Pilot Mentor–Protégé Program. The National Defense Authorization Act of Fiscal Year 1991[20] established the Pilot Mentor–Protégé Program to encourage prime contractors (mentors) to provide developmental assistance to small disadvantaged businesses (protégés). Such assistance, including general business management, engineering and technical expertise, and other capability-enhancing support, is intended to increase the protégé's federal contracting opportunities. To promote this assistance, the government provides incentives to the mentor in the form of cash or credit toward its subcontracting goals. The program is voluntary, but the mentor must be approved by the Department of Defense (DOD), and both the mentor and the protégé must meet eligibility requirements. Program participation is for a term up to five years and can be extended for another four years, thereby creating a long-term business relationship between the two companies. The Policy and Procedures for the DOD's Mentor–Protégé Program policy are contained in the DOD FAR Supplement (DFARS), Appendix I.

Goals for Small Disadvantaged Businesses. Section 804 of the National Defense Authorization Act for Fiscal Year 1993 extended through fiscal year 2000 the annual goal that 5% of contract dollars be spent on contracts to small disadvantaged businesses, historically Black colleges, and other minority institutions. To reach the 5% goal, the contract price may include a price preference not to exceed the anticipated fair market price by more than 10%. Small disadvantaged businesses are defined in a fashion similar to 8(a) firms. Implementing regulations ensure that potential contractors submitting sealed bids or competitive proposals to the DOD comply with applicable subcontracting plan requirements of the Small Business Act, and the subcontracting plan is considered in evaluating bids or proposals.

In addition to the SBA's contracting goals, the Department of Transportation (DOT) established a goal that 10% of the contract dollars flowing down to state and local governments be spent on contracts to small disadvantaged businesses.[21] In keeping with this philosophy, the National Aeronautics and Space Administration (NASA) FAR Supplement 18-19.7001 established a NASA goal of 8% of contract dollars to be spent with such businesses. Both of these agencies include female-owned and -operated businesses in their definition of a small disadvantaged business, which, prior to enactment of FASA, was an exception from the definition in the SBA regulations and FAR, Subsection 19.001.

The FASA, Section 7106, amended the Small Business Act to establish an annual government-wide goal of 5% of contract dollars and reporting requirements for participation by small business concerns owned and controlled by women.

Small Business Modernization. The Defense Production Act Amendments of 1992[22] specify that a strong preference be shown to small business concerns when providing assistance under this act. To the maximum extent practicable, preference is to be shown to small businesses located in areas of high unemployment (i.e., labor surplus areas). Title III of the act authorizes the use of funds to guarantee the purchase or lease of advanced manufacturing equipment and related services, and Section 108 emphasizes that a strong preference is to be shown to proposals for Title III funds submitted by small business suppliers. This creates a way for a small business concern to modernize its manufacturing process capabilities with government financial assistance.

Small Business Innovation Research Program. An important federal marketing avenue for small businesses is the Small Business Innovation Research (SBIR) program. This is a three-phase research and development (R&D) program with funding to $100,000 in phase I, funding to $750,000 in phase II, and commercialization of the product/service in phase III. Successfully winning SBIR contracts establishes credibility for the small business in the government market and gets the company involved on the ground floor of research projects, which will assist it in moving with the projects through development and into production. It is difficult to become involved in projects after the R&D stages because of the costs of qualifying new suppliers.

The Small Business Research and Development Enhancement Act of 1992[23] extended the SBIR program until October 1, 2000. Any federal agency with an extramural R&D budget of $100 million or more must allocate to the SBIR program at least 1.5% in fiscal years 1993 and 1994, 2% in 1995 and 1996, and 2.5% thereafter. Federal agencies with SBIR programs are required under Title III of the act to provide small businesses with technical assistance services, such as introductions to scientists and engineers with pertinent experience and access to technical literature. The small business firm retains the rights to data generated under the program for a period of not less than four years and continued use of government property in the third phase of the program for a period of not less than two years.

Cooperative Research and Development. The Small Business Technology Transfer Act of 1992 incorporated in the Small Business Research and Development Enhancement Act of 1992, established a pilot program under which a portion (0.05% in fiscal year 1994 to 0.15% in fiscal year 1996) of a federal agency's budget with over $1 billion in extramural R&D funds was reserved for award to small business concerns for cooperative research and development. "Cooperative R&D" is defined as a joint R&D project in which not less than 40% of the work is done by the small business and not less than 30% of the work is done by a nonprofit research institution. A "nonprofit research institution" is defined as an organization owned and operated exclusively for scientific or educational purposes, no part of the net earnings of which insures to the benefit of any private shareholder or individual.[24] Through this program, small businesses can obtain access to highly specialized individuals and research facilities to assist in their research efforts without the expense of employment or capitalization.

Government Investment Funding. The Small Business Credit and Business Opportunity Enhancement Act of 1992[25] was enacted to encourage increased investments in small business concerns. The act increased government-backed funding for small business investment companies to $90 million and authorized the SBA to guarantee payment of redemption price and prioritized payments on participating securities, such as preferred stock.

Opportunities for Foreign Suppliers

The U.S. government represents a significant market opportunity for foreign companies. As a result of memoranda of understanding and other international agreements, the DOD and NASA have determined that it is inconsistent with the public interest to apply restrictions of the Buy American Act/Balance of Payments Program to the acquisition of equipment that is mined, produced, or manufactured in qualifying countries.

Certain items of defense equipment have been placed on a restricted list; that is, they may not be acquired from foreign sources. To avoid wasting resources in trying to sell such products to the U.S. government, every foreign company interested in doing business in this market should obtain a list of the restricted items from the DOD. In addition to the DOD restricted list, Congress, through the annual appropriations act, invariably prohibits government agencies from buying certain items from foreign sources. Therefore, foreign suppliers also need to know what items have been restricted by the Defense Appropriations Acts.

The acquisition regulations provide a framework for free and open competition among foreign and domestic suppliers for DOD work. It was never intended that the memoranda of understanding would guarantee any business to foreign sources. Non-U.S. companies, like domestic companies, must aggressively market their products and seek contracting opportunities with DOD and must comply with the same procurement regulations that apply to U.S. contractors. Considerable pressure has been and continues to be exerted by participating European governments and their industrialists to exempt non-U.S. contractors from the FAR and allow them to apply their own procurement regulations. They are not likely to succeed in achieving this exemption because many of the acquisition regulations and contractual terms and conditions are based on statute. Consequently, it would require an act of Congress to remove these requirements from a contract. Another point that argues against such an exemption is that the memoranda's fundamental objective is to provide foreign sources an opportunity to compete on a fair and equal basis, which could not occur if competing companies were subject to different procurement regulations.

The Bid/No-Bid Decision

Since a significant commitment of both financial resources and staffing is required for successful proposals, proposal activities should be adequately planned. Fundamentally, the first step of proposal planning is determining whether to submit a bid on a given business opportunity. Although a portion of this decision may be made long before the government issues a solicitation, a detailed review must be made after receipt of the solicitation to ensure that all major provisions are understood. Most companies believe that they approach the bid/no-bid decision scientifically when, in fact, many approach it in a highly emotional manner and, as a result, may make poor bidding decisions based on "pet interests," preservation of an empire, or a desperate grabbing at straws when business is slow.

A number of factors must be considered in making the bid/no-bid decision. These factors, while usually recognized intuitively by contractors, are nevertheless often disregarded in the quest for new business.

- The government opportunity should be a real, funded program, or, in the case of a potential subcontractor, the prime contractor should have made the decision to buy.

- The technical homework should be done so that a concrete solution exists.
- Prior customer contact pertinent to the program should have been significant.
- A marketing pursuit plan should be prepared.
- Staffing should be available for a maximum proposal effort and for the performance of the program.
- The company should have a positive feeling that it can win the bid.
- There should be compelling reasons why the company can unseat any competitors that may be there first.
- Profit/risk possibilities should be attractive.

As part of the bid/no-bid decision, the solicitation should be thoroughly reviewed. A single individual, who will have overall responsibility for the review (and the proposal preparation as well), should head the effort with participation by all appropriate company resources (technical, financial, etc.). This review effort should have two basic results.

- Identification of inconsistencies between the solicitation and the information on which the bid/no-bid decision was based. If these inconsistencies are significant, the decision to bid should be reconsidered.
- Development of a plan to establish a schedule for the proposal preparation and identification of the individuals who will be involved in its preparation and their responsibilities.

A list of any unique requirements imposed by the solicitation should be developed, as well as a "wish list" of factors that would optimize performance under a resulting contract. This information should be issued during the proposal's preparation.

3-3. THE GOVERNMENT PROCUREMENT PROCESS

Competition in Contracting Act

The Competition in Contracting Act (CICA)[26] of 1984 revised substantial portions of the Armed Services Procurement Act of 1947[27] and the Federal Property and Administrative Services Act of 1949.[28] The CICA applies to any solicitation issued after March 31, 1985. The basic objective of the act is for each agency to obtain full and open competition by specifying procurement needs, developing appropriate specific actions, and narrowing the circumstances for use of other than competitive procedures. The basic requirements of CICA are implemented in FAR, Parts 6, 14, and 15.

Competitive Procurement Procedures

The CICA replaced the two categories of procurement procedures previously recognized by statute (formal advertising and negotiation) with competitive procedures and other than competitive procedures. Competitive procedures include the sealed bidding process and the solicitation of competitive proposals. Using either of these methods satisfies the requirement for full and open competition if two or more responsible sources submit bids or proposals.

Sealed Bidding. Sealed bidding is the government's preferred procurement method for all government departments and must be used under these conditions:

- Time constraints permit solicitation, submission, and evaluation of sealed bids.
- Award can be made on the basis of price and other price-related factors.
- Discussions will not be necessary.
- It is reasonably expected that more than one bid will be received.

Sealed bidding is appropriate when the requirements have been clearly established and are well known by the prospective suppliers. Sealed bids are submitted in response to an invitation for bids (IFB) which must clearly, accurately, and completely describe the government's requirements. The IFB includes bid preparation instructions; details concerning inspections, delivery, and payment; technical data and specifications; and any other pertinent information concerning the purchase. The sealed bids are submitted by prospective contractors to the contracting officer at the time and place indicated in the IFB. A public bid opening is held, and the contract is awarded to the responsible bidder whose bid is most advantageous to the United States, considering only price and other price-related factors included in the solicitation.

When the technical specifications are not defined sufficiently to enable the government to clearly, accurately, and completely describe the requirements, FAR, Subpart 14.5, allows COs to use a two-step sealed-bidding procedure. Step one requires prospective contractors to submit only technical proposals without price data. The CO then determines which offerors are proposing technically acceptable supplies or services. In step two, offerors whose technical proposals were acceptable submit sealed bids, and the lowest responsible offeror receives the award. For the two-step procedure to be effective, the CO must work very closely with technical personnel to establish reasonable and valid criteria to evaluate the technical proposals and, even more importantly, to judge how well they measure up.

Competitive Proposals. The competitive proposal method generally entails holding discussions with the potential contractors, unless the solicitation notified offerors of the government's intent to evaluate proposals and make award without discussion.

The competitive range is determined by considering price and other factors included in the solicitation. Award is made to the source whose proposal is most advantageous to the United States, considering price and other factors included in the solicitation. The FAR Part 15 rewrite, that was effective October 10, 1997, addresses "the competitive range," as well as discussions with offerors.

Sealed bids are distinguished from competitive proposals in that award under sealed bidding must be made on the basis of price and price-related factors, while award under competitive proposals may be made on the basis of price and other factors.

The Statutory Exceptions to Competitive Procurement

In contrast to the numerous exceptions to using formal advertising that were cited in the predecessor statutes,[29] CICA, as implemented in FAR 6.302, provides only six specific exceptions to contracting without full and open competition and a seventh broad, public interest exception authorized by the agency head.

- *Exception 1:* The supplies or services are available from only one responsible source, and no other type of supplies or services will satisfy the agency's needs. Use of this exception requires publication and consideration of any bids received in the *Commerce Business Daily.* This exception permits:

  - Award of a follow-on contract for continued development or production of a major system or highly specialized equipment to the original source when award to any other source is expected to result in (1) substantial duplication of cost that is not expected to be recovered through competition or (2) unacceptable delays in fulfilling the agency's needs; such systems or equipment may be deemed to be available only from the original source and may be procured through other than competitive procedures

  - Award of a contract based on an unsolicited research proposal that (1) demonstrates a unique or innovative concept or a unique capability, (2) offers a concept or service not otherwise available to the government, and (3) does not resemble the substance of a pending competitive action

- *Exception 2:* The agency's need for the property or services is of such an unusual and compelling urgency that the government would be seriously injured unless the agency is permitted to limit the number of potential bidders or offerors. The exception does not ordinarily permit sole-source procurement, since agencies must request offers from as many potential sources as practicable.

- *Exception 3:* It is necessary to award the contract to a particular source or sources to (1) maintain a facility, producer, manufacturer, or other supplier available for furnishing property or services in case of a national emergency or to achieve industrial mobilization; or (2) establish or maintain an essential engineering, research, or development capability to be provided by an educational or other nonprofit institution or by a federally funded research and development center.

- *Exception 4:* The terms of an international agreement or treaty between the United States and a foreign government or international organization, or the written directions of a foreign government reimbursing the executive agency for the cost of the property or services for such government, require the use of other than competitive procedures. This exception relates primarily to memoranda of understanding between the United States and foreign governments and to foreign military sales.

- *Exception 5:* A statute expressly authorizes or requires that the procurement be made through another executive agency or from a specified source, or the agency's need is for a brand-name commercial item for authorized resale.

  This exception may be used for (1) acquisitions from Federal Prison Industries, (2) acquisitions from qualified nonprofit agencies for the blind or other severely handicapped, (3) government printing and binding, (4) sole-source awards under the 8(a) Program, and (5) disaster relief and emergency assistance.

- *Exception 6:* The disclosure of the executive agency's needs would compromise the national security unless the agency is permitted to limit the number of sources from which it solicits bids or proposals. This exception parallels the prior negotiation exception. However, when using this exception, the agency must request offers from as many potential sources as practicable. The standard of "compromise the national security" requires a factual showing of the potential harm to the national security.

- *Exception 7:* The head of the agency, on a nondelegable basis, determines that it is necessary in the public interest and notifies Congress in writing at least 30 days in advance of the award. This waiver can be exercised only on a case-by-case basis, not on a class basis.

The Source Selection Solicitation and the Proposal Process

Competitive proposals are sought when the supplies or services to be purchased cannot be so clearly, accurately, and completely described as to make price the sole determinant. In such cases, the government normally issues a request for proposal (RFP) wherein the government states its minimum requirements, the time and place for the receipt of proposals, and any other information necessary for prospective contractors to prepare and submit proposals or quotations.

RFQs are sometimes used when the government does not intend to award a contract on the basis of the solicitation without further discussions but requires the data for planning purposes. A quotation is not an offer, and consequently cannot be accepted by the government to form a binding contract. An RFP is used when a contract award is contemplated by the government. A proposal submitted in response to an RFP is a legal contract offer that can be accepted as is by the contracting officer, and thereby the proposal, if accepted by the government, becomes a binding contract. Contracting officers are instructed to provide all prospective contractors with identical information and to not knowingly give any advantage to one offeror at the expense of another.

There are two basic forms used by the government in requesting a proposal. Standard Form 33, Solicitation, Offer, and Award (see Appendix 3.3), is often used for RFPs where the government's written acceptance would create a binding contract. The government generally accepts the proposal within the time specified unless it is withdrawn in writing before acceptance. Standard Form 33 is used as the solicitation document for both invitations for bids and requests for proposals. FAR Part 15, as revised on October 10, 1997, introduced Optional Form (OF) 308, Solicitation and Offer—Negotiated Acquisition. This form is only to be used when a negotiated procurement is anticipated (see Appendix 3.4).

The government's formal source selection process applies to high-dollar-value acquisitions and major system procurements. The process is characterized by a specific evaluation group structure, which generally includes an evaluation board, an advisory council, and a source selection authority. Also, a source selection plan, which formalizes the evaluation process, is prepared by the government. In large system acquisitions, the source selection plan is extremely detailed and very specific. The key element in a formal source selection is the authority of the source selection authority, often other than the contracting officer, to determine which competitor is to be awarded the contract. The source selection process and criteria being used will be identified in the solicitation. The October 1997 FAR Part 15 rewrite substantially revised the formal source selection process.

Purpose of the Proposal

A proposal is an offer to supply a product or perform a service, or a combination of the two. In some cases, the products or services are simple tasks and have been done before. In other cases, they are unique R&D efforts with a number of substantial state-of-the-art problems to be solved. Nonetheless, the proposal is needed because the product specifications or a description of the services to be performed are not definite enough to justify the use of sealed bidding.

From the government's perspective, the proposal is the primary vehicle by which a contractor will be selected to provide the goods or services needed. From the company's perspective, the proposal's function is to sell its managerial and technical capabilities to carry out the required work at a reasonable cost. The proposal is the point of sale; it should be considered the company's most important selling tool. Therefore, it must convince the CO that the company is offering an acceptable solution to the government's problem for a reasonable price. It must also communicate that the company has an adequate organization and sufficient personnel and facilities to perform the required effort within the time specified. The offeror has considerable latitude in conveying these messages to the government; the proposal may be just a few pages or many volumes in length.

Types of Proposals

The government requests companies to submit proposals under various circumstances, and the proposals are usually categorized based on these circumstances. For example, if new work is involved, the proposal is considered an initial price proposal. If the government requests the contractor to submit a proposal to continue work begun under an existing contract, such a proposal is normally referred to as a follow-on proposal. Often, the government will add or delete work in either a sealed-bid contract or a negotiated contract. When this occurs, a contract change proposal reflecting the effect of the contract modification is required.

The type of pricing arrangement contemplated by the offeror is also indicated in the proposal. Accordingly, proposals are categorized based on the type of contract that is expected to be negotiated, such as a firm-fixed-price proposal, cost-plus-fixed-fee proposal, or fixed-price-incentive-fee proposal.

Notwithstanding how the proposals are classified, they must communicate to the soliciting government agency how the company intends to perform and manage the effort required by the contract. Additionally, they must state the price and provide supporting data in sufficient detail for the government to satisfy itself that the amount it will ultimately pay is fair and reasonable.

Proposal Format

The proposal must adequately cover three broad areas: (1) the technical solution to the problem as defined by the government's solicitation, (2) how the offeror will manage contract performance, and (3) the price of the proposed work. All of these areas should be directed toward one common goal: selling the contractor's product or services while complying with the applicable laws and regulations.

Technical Proposal

The technical proposal should demonstrate the company's understanding of the problem and the proposed method of solving it. The data should be organized and presented in a manner that is compatible with the government's request for proposal/quotation, the statement of work, and the company's organizational structure and accounting system. The technical section must be responsive to the needs of the government and convince the government that the company offers the most cost-effective approach to solving the problem.

Management Proposal

The purpose of the management proposal is to explain how the company intends to manage the effort required under the proposed contract. Therefore, it should reflect whether the company intends to set up a separate management organization for the specific contract contemplated or to incorporate the effort into the existing structure. It should also explain how program management fits within the overall company organizational structure and point out any limits of authority or responsibility. If no specific management group is to be formed, the method of operation within the overall company management structure should be described.

Specifically, the management section should explain the organizational structure, management capability, management controls, and the assignment of key personnel with experience directly related to the work required by the contract. This section must also be tailored to the circumstances described by the government. Therefore, it should reflect the management structure the company intends to have in place to manage not only the proposed contract but also the overall company operations.

Price Proposal

The price proposal should indicate the proposed price of the work to be performed under the anticipated contract. It should be compatible with, and provide sufficient information and detail to support, the technical and managerial aspects of the proposal. Because the proposed amount is the point from which negotiations begin, the price proposal should be an integral part of the proposal's overall use as a sales tool.

Submittal of Cost or Pricing Data. When cost or pricing data are required by a RFP, the offeror has little latitude in the amount detail and format of the proposal. Table 15-2 of FAR 15.408 provides detailed instructions for submitting cost or pricing data and prescribes requirements for separate supporting schedules, detailing various cost elements, for each proposed contract line item. Those requirements are outlined in Appendix 3.5. In addition to submitting the required detailed cost data, the company's cost proposal should include any information reasonably required to explain the estimating process used, including judgmental factors applied, the methods used in the estimates (including projections), and the nature and amounts of any contingencies included in the proposed price. As stated in FAR 15.403-5(b), the CO may permit submission of cost or pricing data in the contractor's format. The use of Standard Form (SF) 1411 has been discontinued.

In addition, the proposal must be consistent and in accord with the cost-accounting system that the contractor anticipates using to measure and accumulate costs during contract performance. To comply with government requirements for most contracts, the cost-accounting system must be able to produce information on the specific cost elements and in the same detail as proposed.

As a final point, accurate, current, and complete information must be provided to the CO before contract negotiations are completed. The contractor should carefully maintain a record of all data provided and the date and to whom the data were provided; copies of all data provided to the CO and/or the auditor should be maintained by the contractor.

Information Other Than Cost or Pricing Data

When information other than cost or pricing data are requested, the contractor's format for submitting such information may be used unless the CO determines that a special format is essential. Such data are not subject to certification.

Evaluation Criteria

Federal agencies are required to evaluate competitive proposals in accordance with the evaluation criteria in Section M of the solicitation notice. FAR 15.203(a)(4) and 15.304(d) require the solicitation notice to identify all factors and any significant subfactors that will be considered in awarding the contract, and to state whether all evaluation factors, other than cost or price, when combined, are significantly more important, equal to, or less important, than cost or price.

While COs have broad discretion to select relevant evaluation factors and establish their relative importance, the agency head is responsible for ensuring that proposals are evaluated based solely on the factors and subfactors set forth in the solicitation.

FAR 15.304 states that proposal evaluation factors and significant subfactors are to:

- Define key areas of importance to be considered in the source selection decision
- Provide for a meaningful comparison between and among competing offers

Those factors, and their relative importance, are within the broad discretion of the contracting agency, subject to the following requirements:

- Price or cost to the government must be evaluated in every source selection (excluding Architect–Engineer contracts; see FAR Part 36).
- Product or service quality must be considered through noncost evaluation factors, such as past performance, technical excellence, management capability, personnel qualifications, and responsiveness to the requirements of the solicitation. Past performance must be evaluated in all source selections for negotiated competitive acquisitions expected to exceed $1 million. The past performance evaluation threshold falls to $100,000 on January 1, 1999.

Past Performance

Office of Federal Procurement Policy (OFPP) Policy Letter 92-5, Past Performance Information, requires executive agencies to prepare evaluations of contractor performance on all contracts over $100,000 and to specify past performance as an evaluation factor in solicitations for offers for all competitively negotiated contracts expected to exceed $100,000. Past performance information, as defined in the Policy Letter, includes relevant information concerning a contractor's actions under previously awarded contracts. Areas considered are: (1) conformance to specifications, standards, and good workmanship; (2) adherence to contract schedules; (3) history of reasonable and cooperative behavior; (4) commitment to customer satisfaction; and (5) the contractor's businesslike concern for the interest of the customer. In using this information during the evaluation process, the Policy Letter states:

Past performance information should be used to assess risk. Each performance evaluation and risk assessment should consider the number and severity of a contractor's problems, the effectiveness of corrective actions taken, and the contractor's overall work record. The assessment of performance risk should consider the relative merits of the contractor's prior experience and performance as compared to that of other competing offerors.

The OFPP's interim "A Guide to Best Practices for Past Performance"[30] recommends that past performance be weighted at least equally with any noncost evaluation factor and no less than 25% if a numeric score is used. The guide identifies six areas of contractor past performance that should be evaluated: product/service quality, timeliness of performance, cost control, business practices, customer satisfaction, and performance of key personnel.

Responsibility Determination

The CO must have sufficient information to establish that a prospective contractor currently meets the minimum standards of responsibility outlined in FAR 9.104.1. These standards require a prospective contractor to

- Have or be able to obtain adequate financial resources to perform the contract
- Be able to meet the required delivery schedule
- Have a satisfactory performance record
- Have a satisfactory record of integrity and business ethics
- Have or be able to obtain the necessary organization, experience, accounting and operations controls, and technical skills
- Have or be able to obtain the necessary equipment and facilities

The CO should make maximum practical use of currently valid information already on file or within the knowledge of agency personnel in making the responsibility determination. Additionally, information may be obtained from any of the following sources:

- Lists of debarred, suspended, or ineligible concerns or individuals
- The prospective contractor's representations and other information in, or attached to, bids and proposals, replies to questionnaires, and such financial data as balance sheets, profit or loss statements, and cash forecasts
- Other information existing in the agency, including records on file and knowledge of personnel within the purchasing office making the procurement
- Publications, including credit ratings, trade and financial journals, business directories, and registers
- Other sources, including suppliers, subcontractors, customers of the prospective contractor, banks, and financial institutions

A preaward survey is generally required when the information available to the CO is inadequate to determine the responsibility of a prospective contractor. This is normally the case when the agency has had no previous experience with the offeror or when the anticipated level of activity with the company is to be significantly increased. In a preaward survey, the procuring agency evaluates whether the prospective contractor is capable of performing the proposed contract. The survey may be made by using data already in the agency files, data obtained from other government or commercial sources, on-site inspection of plants and facilities, or any combination of the above.

When a CO determines that a preaward survey is desirable, his or her technical and financial advisors are directed to make the necessary reviews. The surveying activity completes the applicable parts of the multiform Preaward Survey of Prospective Contractor:

- SF 1403—General (Appendix 3.6)
- SF 1404—Technical (Appendix 3.7)
- SF 1405—Production (Appendix 3.8)
- SF 1406—Quality Assurance (Appendix 3.9)
- SF 1407—Financial Capability (Appendix 3.10)
- SF 1408—Accounting System (Appendix 3.11)

The objective of the financial capability survey is to determine whether the contractor's finances are adequate to perform the contract. In certain instances, a sound decision may be possible after a relatively simple review of a company's financial position and production commitments. In other circumstances, a more comprehensive review and analysis may be required. If private financing is needed to supplement any government financing that may be provided, the auditor normally verifies the availability of such financing.

A preaward accounting system survey is usually made to determine the adequacy and suitability of the contractor's accounting practices to accumulate costs under the type of contract to be awarded. Accordingly, the survey may emphasize the ability of the contractor's cost accounting system to provide specific information required for the anticipated contract. If the contemplated contract is a cost-type contract or a fixed-price contract with progress payment provisions, the auditor will normally review the accounting system to ensure that it has the capability to accumulate cost by contract.

Because the time available to complete the preaward survey is normally limited, the survey may not be extensive in scope or depth. Nevertheless, a major deficiency in a cost accounting system, such as the inability to satisfy government reporting requirements, could preclude the contract award. Consequently, companies undergoing such a survey should insist on immediately learning any defects the government reviewers have noted. In anticipation of such a government survey, it may be well for management to conduct its own review and correct any deficiencies.

Contract Negotiation

The contracting process is not complete until the parties reach a consensus on the contractual agreement to cover the work being done. In sealed bidding, that consensus is achieved when a prospective contractor accepts the terms and conditions stated by the government and submits a responsive bid. When an award is not based on sealed bidding, the final agreement is achieved through negotiation.

The actual bargaining that takes place depends primarily on whether the negotiation is competitive or other than competitive. In any case, the government begins by evaluating the proposals and the prospective contractors in accordance with the evaluation criteria specified in the RFP. In a formal source selection, the detailed procedures in the source selection plan are followed. Those performing the evaluation are prohibited from discussing the proposals with offerors until after the competitive range is determined. The result of this evaluation is the CO's judgment of the competitive range. The acquisition regulations offer some guidance by stating that the competitive range should be determined by price or cost and by technical and other salient factors and should include proposals that have a reasonable chance of being selected for award.

The solicitation must state whether proposals are intended to be evaluated and awarded (1) after discussions with offerors or (2) without discussions with offerors. If discussions with offerors are intended, the CO must conduct written or oral discussions with all responsible offerors that submit proposals within the competitive range. The government uses the discussions, which may be written or oral, to clarify ambiguities and to identify to the offerors any deficiencies in their proposals.

These discussions are not to result in what is referred to as leveling or auctioning. "Leveling" is defined as a condition in which the best features of each proposal are incorporated into all other competing proposals. The government is sensitive to this transfusion among proposals and has sought ways to prevent it. "Auctioning" occurs when the discussions take the form of a request to competing offerors to meet a certain price or when indications are given to an offeror that its proposed price is not low enough to obtain further consideration.

Discussions need not be held if it can be demonstrated that accepting an initial proposal would result in a fair and reasonable price and that the solicitation provided for award without discussions. If discussions are conducted, a competitive range comprised of all of the most higly rated proposals is established unless the range is further reduced for efficiency. FAR 15.306(c)(2), as revised October 10, 1997, permits the CO to limit the number of proposals in the competitive range to the greatest number that will permit an efficient competition among the most highly rated proposals. Written notice is provided to offerors whose proposals have been eliminated. At the conclusions of discussions, each offeror still in the competitive range is given the opportunity to submit a final proposal revision.

Reductions to the originally proposed price should be supported by identifiable changes in circumstances involving the work to be performed or the costs to be incurred. Arbitrary reductions may not be considered favorably by the government in its evaluation of the proposal. If, after reviewing the revised proposals, the government concludes that its requirements have changed, additioinal discussions must be held and a new request for revised proposals should be issued.

The DOD previously utilized a four-step source selection procedure for procurements that emphasize technical excellence. The proposed revision to DFARS, published on November 26, 1997[31] to conform with the FAR Part 15 rewrite, deleted the discussion of this alternate source selection procedure.

Discussions held with all the offerors that submitted proposals within the competitive range are distinguishable from those held with the selected source. The former discussions are directed primarily at obtaining information for source selection. The latter discussions are intended to lead to a contractually binding document.

Before the source selection, the CO needs assurance that the proposed price is fair and reasonable and that the source selection evaluation factors and subfactors have been met. The acquisition regulations governing negotiated procurements require the CO to use all appropriate organizational tools, such as the advice of specialists in the fields of contracting, finance, law, contract audit, engineering, and price analysis. As a result of this requirement, the offeror may be visited by a contract auditor, a technical representative, and a cost/price analyst—all to review and evaluate the proposal. The contract auditor reviews the offeror's books, records, and relevant cost data. If cost or pricing data have been submitted, to determine currency, completeness and accuracy of cost or pricing data, and whether the estimated costs appear reasonable and realistic. The technical evaluation covers such things as the overall approach the company is proposing to solve the government's problem and the need to include in the proposal various kinds and quantities of labor hours, material, and other purchased items.

Throughout this evaluation process, the CO is the government's exclusive agent with the authority to enter into contracts. All of the specialists assisting the CO are merely advisers.

After all the input has been received from the specialists, final price negotiations can take place. The government's objective is to establish a fair and reasonable price and a contract type that will sustain the price. The company's objective is to provide a reasonable return on investment and establish a contract type that reflects an acceptable assumption of risk, based on the degree of uncertainty involved in performing the contract. To accomplish the government's objective, the contracting officer formulates a negotiation plan, sets objectives, assembles a team, and develops a strategy. The offeror should do no less. The offeror should enter into the negotiation process fully armed with data relevant to the proposal. Every reasonable attempt should have been made to learn about the aspects of the proposal that the government will be questioning. Often, in response to the offeror's request, the government will provide a copy of the contract auditor's and technical specialist's reports. If such reports are not released, every effort should be made to elicit, during the proposal evaluation, information from the auditor and technical representatives regarding any unresolved technical or cost issues that may have arisen during their reviews. While the government auditor or technical specialist is not authorized to disclose the final recommendations, the factual bases for the judgment are appropriate matters for discussion.

Contractors should exercise care in forming the negotiation team. Personnel from manufacturing and from support departments may be needed to respond to specific issues during the negotiation, and each team member's role in the negotiation should be clearly defined. It is important that the company's official spokesperson be established "up front," and that the company speak with one voice.

Finally, negotiation objectives should be established. The contractor's lead negotiator must understand the statement of work, related specifications, products or services to be procured by the government, and performance schedules. The negotiator, of course, must understand the price level at which it would not be reasonable for the company to accept a contract. During negotiations, the government may change the scope of work from that used as the basis for the estimate. When this occurs, the company must decide whether the effect of the change in scope, quantities, or schedules can be reflected in the price without suspending the negotiation. It may be necessary to request a recess in order to develop a revised proposal. Depending on the extent of the change, it may be hazardous to estimate its impact while sitting around the negotiation table.

Perhaps the best way to summarize the negotiation process is to include a slightly paraphrased version of the "Don't But Do" list of ideas that the government provides its negotiators.

- Don't dictate; negotiate. Be a reasonable person.

- Don't expose anyone to ridicule or insult.

- Don't try to make anyone look bad.

- Don't be predictable in your approach.

- Do be discriminating. Accept a good offer.

- Do fight hard on the important points; win the war, not the battles. Don't start fights you have no chance of winning or which, even if you do win, would not be worth the fight.

- Do be courteous and considerate. Do what you say you will. Have integrity.

- Do know when to talk and when to listen. Do stop talking when you've made your point, won your case, or reached agreement.

- Do remember that negotiation is a two-way street and that prenegotiation preparation is the most important attribute of successful selling.

3-4. SUBCONTRACTORS

Often companies are involved in government business as subcontractors. The contractual relationship in this case is with another company, the prime contractor or a higher-tier subcontractor, rather than a government agency. Perhaps the most important consideration in this relationship is that the terms and conditions in the prime contractor's agreement with the government generally flow down to the subcontractor. In other words, the subcontractor is equally bound to comply with the applicable acquisition rules and regulations. Generally, all of our previous comments applicable to prime contractors are equally applicable to subcontractors.

While the prime contractor is contractually obligated to administer its subcontracts, the government reserves the right to interject itself into the process on the premise of "protecting the public interest." Therefore, subcontractors may find both the prime contractor and the government reviewers looking over their shoulders.

As mentioned above, the acquisition regulations assert that basic responsibility rests with the prime contractor for selecting the subcontractors, pricing the subcontracts, and ensuring satisfactory subcontractor performance. To ensure that the prime contractor has appropriately evaluated its subcontractors' proposals, the government may review the prime contractor's purchasing procedures or evaluate the actions taken by the prime contractor to validate the reasonableness of the specific subcontract price and the ability of the subcontractor to perform the statement of work. However, in some instances, the government conducts separate independent reviews, especially when the CO is not satisfied.

The prime contractor may request the government to review the subcontractor's proposal in lieu of making its own review. In fact, the subcontractor may object to giving the prime contractor access to its books and records because of their competitive relationship. While the prime contractor is not contractually relieved of its responsibility for its subcontractors, the government will conduct those reviews that require access to the subcontractor's formal books and records. The results of the reviews are provided to the prime contractor, which uses them to price or settle the subcontract.

3-5. SUMMARY

If a government agency is the potential customer, the process for making the sale is likely to be more complex, formal, and structured than that used in selling to private industry. The federal government has rather clearly defined steps to follow—from preparing and submitting the initial offer through contract execution. Companies pursuing this market must be well informed about how the government procurement process works and what is expected. It is important to know the government officials involved, their responsibilities and authority, the regulations that govern their actions, and how they go about making procurement decisions. These procedures generally apply also to subcontractors, even though their relationship is not directly with the government.

Management should not be lulled into thinking that the elaborate procedures described in this chapter eliminate the need for aggressive, imaginative marketing. In addition to obtaining all of the published information available, successful contractors establish effective working relationships with the procurement and technical officials in the buying offices to whom they sell. These contacts are usually helpful in obtaining timely marketing information on anticipated procurement actions. In dealing with the federal government, getting the opportunity to make an offer is only the critical first step. Whether the company succeeds in receiving the contract depends largely on how well the offeror copes with the (1) rules and regulations that govern the content and format of the proposal, (2) government reviews and discussions, and (3) formal contract negotiation. Only after all these bridges have been successfully crossed can one be assured that the government's business has been obtained.

3-6. NOTES

1. U.S. Government Purchasing and Sales Directory.
2. Office of Federal Procurement Policy Act Amendments of 1988, 41 U.S.C. §423, 97 Stat. 1325, enacted Nov. 17, 1988, Pub. L. 100-679, §27.
3. Fiscal Year 1990–1991 National Defense Authorization Act, enacted Nov. 29, 1989, Pub. L. 101-189, §814.
4. National Defense Authorization Act for Fiscal Year 1991, enacted Nov. 5, 1990, Pub. L. 101-510, §815.
5. Fiscal Year 1996 National Defense Authorization Act, 110 Stat. 186, enacted Feb. 10, 1996, Pub. L. 104-106.
6. Byrd Amendment, Department of the Interior and Related Agencies Appropriations Act, 103 Stat. 701, 41 U.S.C. §319 enacted Oct. 13, 1989, Pub. L. 101-121.
7. Federal Regulation of Lobbying Act, Ch 753, 60 Stat. 839 2 U.S.C. §261, 262–270, enacted Aug. 2, 1946.
8. Lobbying Disclosure Act, 2 U.S.C. §1601, enacted Dec. 19, 1995, Pub. L. 104-65.
9. National Defense Authorization Act for Fiscal Year 1998, 111 Stat. 1629, enacted Nov. 18, 1997, Pub. L. 105–85.
10. Federal Acquisition Streamlining Act of 1994, 41 U.S.C. §251, enacted Oct. 13, 1994, Pub. L. 103-355, Title IX.
11. Small Business Act, Ch 282, 67 Stat. 232 and 69 Stat., 15 U.S.C. §644, enacted July 30, 1953 and July 30, 1955.
12. 13 CFR Business Credit and Assistance, §121, Small Business Size Regulations.
13. National Defense Authorization Act for Fiscal Year 1993, enacted Oct. 23, 1992, Pub. L. 101-510.
14. Federal Acquisition Streamlining Act of 1984, supra, note 9, §7101(a).
15. Adarand Constructors Inc. v. Pena, U.S. S. Ct. No. 93-1841, June 12, 1995.
16. Small Business Act, Ch. 282, 67 Stat. 232 and 69 Stat. 15 U.S.C. §637, §8(a), enacted July 30, 1953 and July 30, 1955.

17. 13 CFR Business Credit and Assistance, §1245, Minority Small Business and Capital Ownership Development/Small Disadvantaged Business Status Protest and Appeal Procedures, §124.105, Social Disadvantage.

18. 13 CFR, Subpart 124.10.

19. Cortez III Service Corp. v. NASA, DCDC Civil Action No. 96-01 301 (SS), Nov. 27, 1996, 950 F.Supp. 357.

20. National Defense Authorization Act for Fiscal Year 1991, enacted Nov. 1990, Pub. L. No. 101-510, §831.

21. Department of Transportation, 49 CFR 23.

22. Defense Production Act Amendments of 1992, 50 U.S.C. §§Appx. 2062, 2074, 2077 enacted Oct. 28, 1992, Pub. L. No. 102-558, §108.

23. Small Business Research and Development Enhancement Act of 1992, 15 U.S.C. §631, enacted Oct. 28, 1992, Pub. L. No. 102-564, §103(f).

24. Stevenson–Wydler Technology Innovation Act of 1980, 15 U.S.C. §3701, enacted Oct. 21, 1980, Pub. L. No. 96-480.

25. Small Business Credit and Business Opportunity Enhancement Act of 1992, 15 U.S.C. §631 and 648 enacted Sept. 4, 1992, Pub. L. No. 102-366, and Aug. 13, 1993, Pub. L. 103-81.

26. Competition in Contracting Act, 41 U.S.C. 253, 10 U.S.C. 2304, enacted July 18, 1984, Pub. L. 98-369.

27. Armed Services Procurement Act of 1947, 10 U.S.C., 62 Stat. 21, enacted Feb. 19, 1948 and 70A Stat. L., enacted August 10, 1956, Pub. L. 84-1028.

28. Federal Property and Administrative Services Act of 1949, 41 U.S.C., 63 Stat. 378, enacted June 30, 1949, Pub. L. 81-152.

29. The Armed Services Procurement Act of 1947 authorized 16 specific negotiation exceptions to procurement by formal advertising. The Federal Property and Administrative Services Act of 1949 contained 14 exceptions for the civilian agencies, omitting those for duplication of investment or delay (Exception 14) and defense mobilization requirements (Exception 16). Cf. 10 U.S.C. 2304(a); 41 U.S.C. 252(c).

30. Office of Federal Procurement Policy, "A Guide to Best Practices for Past Performance, Interim Edition, May 1995." Copies can be obtained by calling the Executive Office of the President's Publication Office, (202) 395-7332, or by writing to Office of Publications, 725 17th Street, N.W., Room 2200, New Executive Office Building, Washington, DC 20503.

31. Federal Register, Vol. 62, No. 228, Nov. 26, 1997, pp. 63050–63062.

DISCLOSURE OF LOBBYING ACTIVITIES

Complete this form to disclose lobbying activities pursuant to 31 U.S.C. 1352

(See reverse for public burden disclosure.)

Approved by OMB

0348-0046

1. Type of Federal Action:	2. Status of Federal Action:	3. Report Type:
☐ a. contract b. grant c. cooperative agreement d. loan e. loan guarantee f. loan insurance	☐ a. bid/offer/application b. initial award c. post-award	☐ a. initial filing b. material change **For Material Change Only:** year _____ quarter _____ date of last report _____

4. Name and Address of Reporting Entity: ☐ Prime ☐ Subawardee Tier _____, *if known*: **Congressional District**, *if known*:	5. If Reporting Entity in No. 4 is a Subawardee, Enter Name and Address of Prime: **Congressional District**, *if known*:
6. Federal Department/Agency:	7. Federal Program Name/Description: CFDA Number, *if applicable*: _____
8. Federal Action Number, *if known*:	9. Award Amount, *if known*: $
10. a. Name and Address of Lobbying Entity (*if individual, last name, first name, MI*):	b. Individuals Performing Services (*including address if different from No. 10a*) (*last name, first name, MI*):

(attach Continuation Sheet(s) SF-LLLA, if necessary)

11. Amount of Payment (*check all that apply*): $ _____ ☐ actual ☐ planned 12. Form of Payment (*check all that apply*): ☐ a. cash ☐ b. in-kind; specify: nature _____ value _____	13. Type of Payment (*check all that apply*): ☐ a. retainer ☐ b. one-time fee ☐ c. commission ☐ d. contingent fee ☐ e. deferred ☐ f. other; specify: _____

14. Brief Description of Services Performed or to be Performed and Date(s) of Service, including officer(s), employee(s), or Member(s) contacted, for Payment Indicated in Item 11:

(attach Continuation Sheet(s) SF-LLLA, if necessary)

15. Continuation Sheet(s) SF-LLLA attached:	☐ Yes ☐ No

16. Information requested through this form is authorized by title 31 U.S.C. section 1352. This disclosure of lobbying activities is a material representation of fact upon which reliance was placed by the tier above when this transaction was made or entered into. This disclosure is required pursuant to 31 U.S.C. 1352. This information will be reported to the Congress semi-annually and will be available for public inspection. Any person who fails to file the required disclosure shall be subject to a civil penalty of not less that $10,000 and not more than $100,000 for each such failure.	Signature: _____ Print Name: _____ Title: _____ Telephone No.: _____ Date: _____

Federal Use Only:	Authorized for Local Reproduction Standard Form LLL (Rev. 7-97)

Appendix 3.1 OMB Standard Form LLL, Disclosure of Lobbying Activities

60

INSTRUCTIONS FOR COMPLETION OF SF-LLL, DISCLOSURE OF LOBBYING ACTIVITIES

This disclosure form shall be completed by the reporting entity, whether subawardee or prime Federal recipient, at the initiation or receipt of a covered Federal action, or a material change to a previous filing, pursuant to title 31 U.S.C. section 1352. The filing of a form is required for each payment or agreement to make payment to any lobbying entity for influencing or attempting to influence an officer or employee of any agency, a Member of Congress, an officer or employee of Congress, or an employee of a Member of Congress in connection with a covered Federal action. Use the SF-LLLA Continuation Sheet for additional information if the space on the form is inadequate. Complete all items that apply for both the initial filing and material change report. Refer to the implementing guidance published by the Office of Management and Budget for additional information.

1. Identify the type of covered Federal action for which lobbying activity is and/or has been secured to influence the outcome of a covered Federal action.

2. Identify the status of the covered Federal action.

3. Identify the appropriate classification of this report. If this is a followup report caused by a material change to the information previously reported, enter the year and quarter in which the change occurred. Enter the date of the last previously submitted report by this reporting entity for this covered Federal action.

4. Enter the full name, address, city, State and zip code of the reporting entity. Include Congressional District, if known. Check the appropriate classification of the reporting entity that designates if it is, or expects to be, a prime or subaward recipient. Identify the tier of the subawardee, e.g., the first subawardee of the prime is the 1st tier. Subawards include but are not limited to subcontracts, subgrants and contract awards under grants.

5. If the organization filing the report in item 4 checks "Subawardee," then enter the full name, address, city, State and zip code of the prime Federal recipient. Include Congressional District, if known.

6. Enter the name of the Federal agency making the award or loan commitment. Include at least one organizational level below agency name, if known. For example, Department of Transportation, United States Coast Guard.

7. Enter the Federal program name or description for the covered Federal action (item 1). If known, enter the full Catalog of Federal Domestic Assistance (CFDA) number for grants, cooperative agreements, loans, and loan commitments.

8. Enter the most appropriate Federal identifying number available for the Federal action identified in item 1 (e.g., Request for Proposal (RFP) number; Invitation for Bid (IFB) number; grant announcement number; the contract, grant, or loan award number; the application/proposal control number assigned by the Federal agency). Include prefixes, e.g., "RFP-DE-90-001."

9. For a covered Federal action where there has been an award or loan commitment by the Federal agency, enter the Federal amount of the award/loan commitment for the prime entity identified in item 4 or 5.

10. (a) Enter the full name, address, city, State and zip code of the lobbying entity engaged by the reporting entity identified in item 4 to influence the covered Federal action.

    (b) Enter the full names of the individual(s) performing services, and include full address if different from 10 (a). Enter Last Name, First Name, and Middle Initial (MI).

11. Enter the amount of compensation paid or reasonably expected to be paid by the reporting entity (item 4) to the lobbying entity (item 10). Indicate whether the payment has been made (actual) or will be made (planned). Check all boxes that apply. If this is a material change report, enter the cumulative amount of payment made or planned to be made.

12. Check the appropriate box(es). Check all boxes that apply. If payment is made through an in-kind contribution, specify the nature and value of the in-kind payment.

13. Check the appropriate box(es). Check all boxes that apply. If other, specify nature.

14. Provide a specific and detailed description of the services that the lobbyist has performed, or will be expected to perform, and the date(s) of any services rendered. Include all preparatory and related activity, not just time spent in actual contact with Federal officials. Identify the Federal official(s) or employee(s) contacted or the officer(s), employee(s), or Member(s) of Congress that were contacted.

15. Check whether or not a SF-LLLA Continuation Sheet(s) is attached.

16. The certifying official shall sign and date the form, print his/her name, title, and telephone number.

Appendix 3.1   (Continued)

SOLICITATION MAILING LIST APPLICATION	1. TYPE OF APPLICATION ☐ INITIAL ☐ REVISION	2. DATE	OMB No. 900-0002 Expires: 10/31/97

NOTE: Please complete all items on this form. Insert N/A in items not applicable. See page 2 for instructions.

Public reporting burden for this collection of information is estimated to average .58 hours per response, including the time for reviewing instructions, searching existing data sources, gathering and maintaining the data needed, and completing and reviewing the collection of information. Send comments regarding this burden estimate or any other aspect of this collection of information, including suggestions for reducing this burden, to the FAR Secretariat (MVR), Federal Acquisition Policy Division, GSA, Washington, DC 20405.

3. SUBMIT TO

a. FEDERAL AGENCY'S NAME

b. STREET ADDRESS

c. CITY | d. STATE | e. ZIP CODE

4. APPLICANT

a. NAME

b. STREET ADDRESS | c. COUNTY

d. CITY | e. STATE | f. ZIP CODE

5. TYPE OF ORGANIZATION (Check one)

☐ INDIVIDUAL   ☐ NON-PROFIT ORGANIZATION

☐ PARTNERSHIP   ☐ CORPORATION, INCORPORATED UNDER THE LAWS OF THE STATE OF:

6. ADDRESS TO WHICH SOLICITATIONS ARE TO BE MAILED (If different than Item 4)

a. STREET ADDRESS | b. COUNTY

c. CITY | d. STATE | e. ZIP CODE

7. NAMES OF OFFICERS, OWNERS, OR PARTNERS

a. PRESIDENT	b. VICE PRESIDENT	c. SECRETARY
d. TREASURER	e. OWNERS OR PARTNERS	

8. AFFILIATES OF APPLICANT

NAME	LOCATION	NATURE OF AFFILIATION

9. PERSONS AUTHORIZED TO SIGN OFFERS AND CONTRACTS IN YOUR NAME (Indicate if agent)

NAME	OFFICIAL CAPACITY	TELEPHONE NUMBER AREA CODE NUMBER

10. IDENTIFY EQUIPMENT, SUPPLIES, AND/OR SERVICES ON WHICH YOU DESIRE TO MAKE AN OFFER (See attached Federal Agency's supplemental listing and instructions, if any)

11a. SIZE OF BUSINESS (See definitions on page 2) ☐ SMALL BUSINESS (If checked, complete Items 11B and 11C) ☐ OTHER THAN SMALL BUSINESS	11b. AVERAGE NUMBER OF EMPLOYEES (Including affiliates) CALENDAR QUARTERS FOR FOUR PRECEDING	11c. AVERAGE ANNUAL SALES OR RECEIPTS FOR PRECEDING THREE FISCAL YEARS $

12. TYPE OF OWNERSHIP (See definitions on page 2) (Not applicable for other than small businesses) ☐ DISADVANTAGED BUSINESS ☐ WOMAN-OWNED BUSINESS	13. TYPE OF BUSINESS (See definitions on page 2) ☐ MANUFACTURER OR PRODUCER ☐ CONSTRUCTION CONCERN ☐ SURPLUS DEALER ☐ SERVICE ESTABLISHMENT ☐ RESEARCH AND DEVELOPMENT	

14. DUNS NO. (If available)	15. HOW LONG IN PRESENT BUSINESS?

16. FLOOR SPACE (Square Feet/M²)		17. NET WORTH	
a. MANUFACTURING	b. WAREHOUSE	a. DATE	b. AMOUNT $

18. SECURITY CLEARANCE (If applicable, check highest clearance authorized)

FOR	TOP SECRET	SECRET	CONFIDENTIAL	c. NAMES OF AGENCIES GRANTING SECURITY CLEARANCES	d. DATES GRANTED
a. KEY PERSONNEL					
b. PLANT ONLY					

The information supplied herein (including all pages attached) is correct and neither the applicant nor any person (or concern) in any connection with the applicant as a principal or officer, so far as is known, is now debarred or otherwise declared ineligible by any agency of the Federal Government from making offers for furnishing materials, supplies, or services to the Government or any agency thereof.

19a. NAME OF PERSON AUTHORIZED TO SIGN (Type or print)	20. SIGNATURE	21. DATE SIGNED
19b. TITLE OF PERSON AUTHORIZED TO SIGN (Type or print)		

AUTHORIZED FOR LOCAL REPRODUCTION
Previous edition not usable

J61298
04-24-97

STANDARD FORM 129 (REV. 12-96)
by GSA - FAR (48 CFR) 53.214(e)

Appendix 3.2   Standard Form 129, Solicitation Mailing List Application

INSTRUCTIONS

Persons or concerns wishing to be added to a particular agency's bidder's mailing list for supplies or services shall file this properly completed Solicitation Mailing List Application, together with such other lists as may be attached to this application form, with each procurement office of the Federal agency with which they desire to do business. If a Federal agency has attached a Supplemental Commodity list with instructions, complete the application as instructed. Otherwise, identify in Item 10 the equipment, supplies, and/or services on which you desire to bid. (Provide Federal Supply Class or Standard Industrial Classification codes, if available.) The application shall be submitted and signed by the principal as distinguished from an agent, however constituted.

After placement on the bidder's mailing list of an agency, your failure to respond (submission of bid, or notice in writing, that you are unable to bid on that particular transaction but wish to remain on the active bidder's mailing list for that particular item) to solicitations will be understood by the agency to indicate lack of interest and concurrence in the removal of your name from the purchasing activity's solicitation mailing for items concerned.

SIZE OF BUSINESS DEFINITIONS
(See Item 11A.)

a.   Small business concern - A small business concern for the purpose of Government procurement is a concern, including its affiliates, which is independently owned and operated, is not dominant in the field of operation in which it is competing for Government contracts, and can further qualify under the criteria concerning number of employees, average annual receipts, or the other criteria, as prescribed by the Small Business Administration. (See Code of Federal Regulations, Title 13, Part 121, as amended, which contains detailed industry definitions and related procedures.)

b.   Affiliates - Business concerns are affiliates of each other when either directly or indirectly (i) one concern controls or has the power to control the other, or (ii) a third party controls or has the power to control both. In determining whether concerns are independently owned and operated and whether or not affiliation exists, consideration is given to all appropriate factors including common ownership, common management, and contratual relationship. (See Items 8 and 11A.)

c.   Number of employees - (Item 11B) in connection with the determination of small business status, "number of employees" means the average employment of any concern, including the employees of its domestic and foreign affiliates, based on the number of persons employed on a full-time, part-time, temporary or other basis during each of the pay periods of the preceding 12 months. If a concern has not been in existence for 12 months, "number of employees" means the average employment of such concern and its affiliates during the period that such concern has been in existence based on the number of persons employed during each of the pay periods of the period that such concern has been in business.

TYPE OF OWNERSHIP DEFINITIONS
(See Item 12.)

a.   "Disadvantaged business concern" - means any business concern (1) which is at least 51 percent owned by one or more socially and economically disadvantaged individuals; or, in the case of any publicly owned business, at least 51 percent of the stock of which is owned by one or more socially and economically disadvantaged individuals; and (2) whose management and daily business operations are controlled by one or more of such individuals.

b.   "Women-owned business" - means a business that is at least 51 percent owned by a woman or women who are U.S. citizens and who also control and operate the business.

TYPE OF BUSINESS DEFINITIONS
(See Item 13.)

a.   "Manufacturer or producer" - means a person (or concern) owning, operating, or maintaining a store, warehouse, or other establishment that produces, on the premises, the materials, supplies, articles or equipment of the general character of those listed in Item 10, or in the Federal Agency's Supplemental Commodity List, if attached.

b.   "Service establishment" - means a concern (or person) which owns, operates, or maintains any type of business which is principally engaged in the furnishing of nonpersonal services, such as (but not limited to) repairing, cleaning, redecorating, or rental of personal property, including the furnishing of necessary repair parts or other supplies as a part of the services performed.

● COMMERCE BUSINESS DAILY - The Commerce Business Daily, published by the Department of Commerce, contains information concerning proposed procurements, sales, and contract awards. For further information concerning this publication, contact your local Commerce Field Office.

STANDARD FORM 129 (REV. 12-96) PAGE 2

SOLICITATION, OFFER AND AWARD	1. THIS CONTRACT IS A RATED ORDER UNDER DPAS (15 CFR 350)	▶ RATING	PAGE OF	PAGES

2. CONTRACT NO.	3. SOLICITATION NO.	4. TYPE OF SOLICITATION ☐ SEALED BID (IFB) ☐ NEGOTIATED (RFP)	5. DATE ISSUED	6. REQUISITION/PURCHASE NO.

7. ISSUED BY	CODE	8. ADDRESS OFFER TO (If other than Item 7)

NOTE: In sealed bid solicitations "offer" and "offeror" mean "bid" and "bidder".

SOLICITATION

9. Sealed offers in original and _____ copies for furnishing the supplies or services in the Schedule will be received at the place specified in Item 8, or if handcarried, in the depository located in _____ until _____ local time _____

(Hour)   (Date)

CAUTION - LATE Submissions, Modifications, and Withdrawals: See Section L, Provision No. 52.214-7 or 52.215-10. All offers are subject to all terms and conditions contained in this solicitation.

10. FOR INFORMATION CALL: ▶	A. NAME	B. TELEPHONE NO. (Include area code) (NO COLLECT CALLS)

11. TABLE OF CONTENTS

(√)	SEC.	DESCRIPTION	PAGE(S)	(√)	SEC.	DESCRIPTION	PAGE(S)
		PART I - THE SCHEDULE				PART II - CONTRACT CLAUSES	
	A	SOLICITATION/CONTRACT FORM			I	CONTRACT CLAUSES	
	B	SUPPLIES OR SERVICES AND PRICES/COSTS				PART III - LIST OF DOCUMENTS, EXHIBITS AND OTHER ATTACH.	
	C	DESCRIPTION/SPECS./WORK STATEMENT			J	LIST OF ATTACHMENTS	
	D	PACKAGING AND MARKING				PART IV - REPRESENTATIONS AND INSTRUCTIONS	
	E	INSPECTION AND ACCEPTANCE			K	REPRESENTATIONS, CERTIFICATIONS AND OTHER STATEMENTS OF OFFERORS	
	F	DELIVERIES OR PERFORMANCE					
	G	CONTRACT ADMINISTRATION DATA			L	INSTRS., CONDS., AND NOTICES TO OFFERORS	
	H	SPECIAL CONTRACT REQUIREMENTS			M	EVALUATION FACTORS FOR AWARD	

OFFER (Must be fully completed by offeror)

NOTE: Item 12 does not apply if the solicitation includes the provisions at 52.214-16, Minimum Bid Acceptance Period.

12. In compliance with the above, the undersigned agrees, if this offer is accepted within _____ calendar days (60 calendar days unless a different period is inserted by the offeror) from the date for receipt of offers specified above, to furnish any or all items upon which prices are offered at the price set opposite each item, delivered at the designated point(s), within the time specified in the schedule.

13. DISCOUNT FOR PROMPT PAYMENT (See Section I, Clause No. 52-232-8) ▶	10 CALENDAR DAYS %	20 CALENDAR DAYS %	30 CALENDAR DAYS %	CALENDAR DAYS %

14. ACKNOWLEDGMENT OF AMENDMENTS (The offeror acknowledges receipt of amendments to the SOLICITATION for offerors and related documents numbered and dated:	AMENDMENT NO.	DATE	AMENDMENT NO.	DATE

15A. NAME AND ADDRESS OF OFFEROR	CODE	FACILITY	16. NAME AND TITLE OF PERSON AUTHORIZED TO SIGN OFFER (Type or print)

15B. TELEPHONE NO. (Include area code)	15C. CHECK IF REMITTANCE ADDRESS IS DIFFERENT FROM ABOVE - ENTER SUCH ADDRESS IN SCHEDULE. ☐	17. SIGNATURE	18. OFFER DATE

AWARD (To be completed by Government)

19. ACCEPTED AS TO ITEMS NUMBERED	20. AMOUNT	21. ACCOUNTING AND APPROPRIATION

22. AUTHORITY FOR USING OTHER THAN FULL AND OPEN COMPETITION:
☐ 10 U.S.C. 2304(c)( )   ☐ 41 U.S.C. 253(c)( )

24. ADMINISTERED BY (If other than Item 7)   CODE

23. SUBMIT INVOICES TO ADDRESS SHOWN IN (4 copies unless otherwise specified) ▶	ITEM
25. PAYMENT WILL BE MADE BY	CODE

26. NAME OF CONTRACTING OFFICER (Type or print)	27. UNITED STATES OF AMERICA (Signature of Contracting Officer)	28. AWARD DATE

IMPORTANT - Award will be made on this Form, or on Standard Form 26, or by other authorized official written notice.

NSN 7540-01-152-8064
PREVIOUS EDITION NOT USABLE

33-134

STANDARD FORM 33 (REV. 4-85)
Prescribed by GSA
FAR (48 CFR) 53.214(c)

J61118
05-28-97

Appendix 3.3   Standard Form 33, Solicitation, Offer and Award

53.302-308 Optional Form 308, Solicitation
and Offer—Negotiated Acquisition.

	SOLICITATION AND OFFER - NEGOTIATED ACQUISITION	PAGE	OF	PAGES

I. SOLICITATION

1. SOLICITATION NUMBER	2. DATE ISSUED	3. OFFERS DUE BY	4. OFFERS VALID FOR 60 DAYS UNLESS A DIFFERENT PERIOD IS ENTERED HERE

5. ISSUED BY	6. ADDRESS OFFER TO (If other than Item 5)

7. FOR INFORMATION CALL (No collect calls)

A. NAME	B. TELEPHONE		C. E-MAIL ADDRESS
	AREA CODE	PHONE NUMBER	

8. BRIEF DESCRIPTION

9. TABLE OF CONTENTS

(X)	SEC.	DESCRIPTION	PAGE(S)	(X)	SEC.	DESCRIPTION	PAGE(S)
		PART I - THE SCHEDULE				PART II - CONTRACT CLAUSES	
	A	SOLICITATION/CONTRACT FORM			I	CONTRACT CLAUSES	
	B	SUPPLIES OR SERVCIES AND PRICES/COSTS				PART III - LIST OF DOCUMENTS, EXHIBITS AND OTHER ATTACH.	
	C	DESCRIPTION/SPECS./WORK STATEMENT			J	LIST OF ATTACHMENTS	
	D	PACKAGING AND MARKING				PART IV - REPRESENTATIONS AND INSTRUCTIONS	
	E	INSPECTION AND ACCEPTANCE				REPRESENTATIONS, CERTIFICATIONS AND OTHER	
	F	DELIVERIES OR PERFORMANCE			K	STATEMENTS OF OFFERORS	
	G	CONTRACT ADMINISTRATION DATA			L	INSTRS., CONDS., AND NOTICES TO OFFERORS	
	H	SPECIAL CONTRACT REQUIREMENTS			M	EVALUATION FACTORS FOR AWARD	

II. OFFER

The undersigned agrees to furnish and deliver the items or perform services to the extent stated in this document for the consideration stated. The rights and obligations of the parties to the resultant contract shall be subject to and governed by this document and any documents attached or incorporated by reference.

10A. PERSONS AUTHORIZED TO NEGTIATE	10B. TIITLE	10C. TELEPHONE	
		AREA CODE	NUMBER

11. NAME AND ADDRESS OF OFFEROR	12A. SIGNATURE OF PERSON AUTHORIZED TO SIGN
	12B. NAME OF SIGNER
	12C. TITLE OF SIGNER
	12D. DATE / 12E. TELEPHONE (AREA CODE / NUMBER)

OPTIONAL FORM 308 (9-97)
Prescribed by GSA - FAR (48 CFR) 53.215-1(f)

Appendix 3.4   Optional Form (OF) 308, Solicitation and Offer—Negotiated Aquisition

<u>Material and Services</u>

Provide a consolidated priced summary of individual material quantities included in the various tasks, orders, or contract line items being proposed and the basis for pricing (vendor quotes, invoice prices, etc.). Include raw materials, parts, components, assemblies, and services to be produced or performed by others. For all items proposed, identify the item and show the source, quantity, and price. Conduct price analyses of all subcontractor proposals. Conduct cost analyses of all subcontractor proposals. Conduct cost analyses for all subcontracts when cost or pricing data are submitted by the subcontractor. Include these analyses as part of your own cost or pricing data submissions for subcontracts expected to exceed the appropriate threshold in FAR 15.403-4. Submit the subcontractor cost or pricing data as part of your own cost or pricing data as required in paragraph IIA(2) of this table. These requirements also apply to all subcontractors if required to submit cost or pricing data.

Adequate Price Competition. Provide data showing the degree of competition and the basis for establishing the source and reasonableness of price for those acquisitions (such as subcontracts, purchase orders, material order, etc.) exceeding, or expected to exceed, the appropriate threshold set forth at FAR 15.403-4 priced on the basis of adequate price competition. For interorganizational transfers priced at other than the cost of comparable competitive commercial work of the division, subsidiary, or affiliate of the contractor, explain the pricing method (see FAR 31.205-26(e)).

All Other. Obtain cost or pricing data from prospective sources for those acquisitions (such as subcontracts, purchase orders, material order, etc.) exceeding the threshold set forth in FAR 15.403-4 and not otherwise exempt, in accordance with FAR 15.403-1(b) (i.e., adequate price competition, commercial items, prices set by law or regulation or waiver). Also provide data showing the basis for establishing source and reasonableness of price. In addition, provide a summary of your cost analysis and a copy of cost or pricing data submitted by the prospective source in support of each subcontract, or purchase order that is the lower of either $10,000,000 or more, or both more than the pertinent cost or pricing data threshold and more than 10 percent of the prime contractor's proposed price. The Contracting Officer may require you to submit cost or pricing data in support of proposals in lower amounts. Subcontractor cost or pricing data must be accurate, complete and current as of the date of final price agreement, or an earlier date agreed upon by the parties, given on the prime contractor's Certificate of Current Cost or Pricing Data. The prime contractor is responsible for updating a prospective subcontractor's data. For standard commercial items fabricated by the offeror that are generally stocked in inventory, provide a separate cost breakdown, if priced based on cost. For interorganizational transfers priced at cost, provide a separate breakdown of cost elements. Analyze the cost or pricing data and submit the results of your analysis of the prospective source's proposal. When submission of a prospective source's cost or pricing data is required as described in this paragraph, it must be included along with your own cost or pricing data submission, as part of your own cost or pricing data. You must also submit any other cost or pricing data obtained from a subcontractor, either actually or by specific identification, along with the results of any analysis performed on that data.

<u>Direct Labor</u>

Provide a time-phased (e.g., monthly, quarterly, etc.) breakdown of labor hours, rates, and cost by appropriate category, and furnish bases for estimates.

<u>Indirect Costs</u>

Indicate how you have computed and applied your indirect costs, including cost breakdowns. Show trends and budgetary data to provide a basis for evaluating the reasonableness of proposed rates. Indicate the rates used and provide an appropriate explanation.

<u>Other Costs</u>

List all other costs not otherwise included in the categories described above (e.g., special tooling, travel, computer and consultant services, preservation, packaging and packing, spoilage and rework, and Federal excise tax on finished articles) and provide bases for pricing.

<u>Royalties</u>

If royalties exceed $1,500, you must provide the following information on a separate page for each separate royalty or license fee:

1. Name and address of licensor.
2. Date of license agreement.
3. Patent numbers.
4. Patent application serial numbers, or other basis on which the royalty is payable.
5. Brief description (including any part or model numbers of each contract item or component on which the royalty is payable).
6. Percentage or dollar rate of royalty per unit.
7. Unit price of contract item.
8. Number of units.
9. Total dollar amount of royalties.
10. If specifically requested by the Contracting Officer, a copy of the current license agreement and identification of applicable claims of specific patents (see FAR 27.204 and 31.205-37).

<u>Facilities Capital Cost of Money</u>

When you elect to claim facilities capital cost of money as an allowable cost, you must submit Form CASB-CMF and show the calculation of the proposed amount (see FAR 31.205-10).

Appendix 3.5 Excerpts from FAR 15.408–Table 15-2 Instructions for Submitting Cost/Pricing Proposals When Cost or Pricing Data are Required

PREAWARD SURVEY OF PROSPECTIVE CONTRACTOR
(GENERAL)

	1. SERIAL NO. (For surveying activity use)	FORM APPROVED OMB NO. 9000-0011

Public reporting burden for this collection of information is estimated to average 24 hours per response, including the time for reviewing instructions, searching existing data sources, gathering and maintaining the data needed, and completing and reviewing the collection of information. Send comments regarding this burden estimate or any other aspect of this collection of information, including suggestions for reducing this burden, to the FAR Secretariat (VRS), Office of Federal Acquisition and Regulatory Policy, GSA, Washington, D.C. 20405; and to the Office of Management and Budget, Paperwork Reduction Project (9000-0011), Washington, D.C. 20503.

SECTION I - REQUEST (For Completion by Contracting Office)

2. NAME AND ADDRESS OF SURVEYING ACTIVITY	3. SOLICITATION NO.	4. TOTAL OFFERED PRICE $
	5. TYPE OF CONTRACT	

6A. NAME AND ADDRESS OF SECONDARY SURVEY ACTIVITY (For surveying activity use)	7A. NAME AND ADDRESS PROSPECTIVE CONTRACTOR

6B. TELEPHONE NO. (Include AUTOVON, WATS or FTS, if available)	7B. FIRM'S CONTACT	7C. TELEPHONE NO. (with area code)

8. WILL CONTRACTING OFFICE PARTICIPATE IN SURVEY?
☐ YES ☐ NO

13. NAME AND ADDRESS OF PARENT COMPANY (If applicable)

9. DATE OF THIS REQUEST	10. DATE REPORT REQUIRED

11. PROSPECTIVE CONTRACTOR REPRESENTS THAT IT ☐ IS, ☐ IS NOT A SMALL BUSINESS CONCERN.

12. WALSH-HEALEY CONTRACTS ACT (Check applicable box(es))
A. IS NOT APPLICABLE
B. IS APPLICABLE AND PROSPECTIVE CONTRACTOR REPRESENTS HIS CLASSIFICATION AS:
☐ MANUFACTURER   ☐ REGULAR DEALER
☐ OTHER (Specify)

14A. PLANT AND LOCATION (If different from Item 7, above)

15A. NAME OF REQUESTING ACTIVITY CONTRACTING OFFICER	14B. POINT OF CONTACT	14C. TELEPHONE NO. (with area code)

15B. SIGNATURE	16A. NAME OF CONTACT POINT AT REQUESTING ACTIVITY (If different from Item 15A)

15C. TELEPHONE NO. (Include AUTOVON, WATS or FTS, if available)

17. RETURN PREAWARD SURVEY TO THIS ADDRESS:	16B. TELEPHONE NO. (Include AUTOVON, WATS or FTS, if available)

ATTN:

SECTION II - DATA (For Completion by Contracting Office)

18A. ITEM NO.	18B. NATIONAL STOCK NUMBER (NEW) AND NOMENCLATURE		18C. TOTAL QUANTITY	18D. UNIT PRICE	18E. DELIVERY SCHEDULE				
					(a)	(b)	(c)	(d)	(e)
		SOLICITED							
		OFFERED		$					
		SOLICITED							
		OFFERED		$					
		SOLICITED							
		OFFERED		$					
		SOLICITED							
		OFFERED		$					
		SOLICITED							
		OFFERED		$					
		SOLICITED							
		OFFERED		$					
		SOLICITED							
		OFFERED		$					

AUTHORIZED FOR LOCAL REPRODUCTION
Previous edition is usable.
J61185
10-09-96

EXPIRATION DATE: 9-30-91

1403-103

STANDARD FORM 1403 (REV. 9-88)
Prescribed by GSA - FAR (48 CFR) 53.209 - 1(a)

Appendix 3.6 Standard Form 1403, Preaward Survey of Prospective Contractor

SECTION III - FACTORS TO BE INVESTIGATED

19. MAJOR FACTORS	CHK. (a)	SAT. (b)	UN-SAT. (c)	20. OTHER FACTORS (Provide specific requirements in Remarks)	CHK. (a)	SAT. (b)	UN-SAT. (c)
A. TECHNICAL CAPABILITY				A. GOVERNMENT PROPERTY CONTROL			
B. PRODUCTION CAPABILITY				B. TRANSPORTATION			
C. QUALITY ASSURANCE CAPABILITY				C. PACKAGING			
D. FINANCIAL CAPABILITY				D. SECURITY			
E. ACCOUNTING SYSTEM				E. SAFETY			

21. IS THIS A SHORT FORM PREAWARD REPORT? (For completion by surveying activity)

☐ YES ☐ NO

22. IS A FINANCIAL ASSISTANCE PAYMENT PROVISION IN THE SOLICITATION? (For completion by contracting activity)

☐ YES ☐ NO

F. ENVIRONMENTAL/ENERGY CONSIDERATIONS			
G. FLIGHT OPERATIONS/FLIGHT SAFETY			
H. OTHER (Specify)			

23. REMARKS (For Contracting Activity Use)

SECTION IV - SURVEYING ACTIVITY RECOMMENDATIONS

24. RECOMMEND	25A. NAME AND TITLE OF SURVEY APPROVING OFFICIAL	25B. TELEPHONE NO.
☐ A. COMPLETE AWARD		
☐ B. PARTIAL AWARD (Quantity _____)	25C. SIGNATURE	25D. DATE
☐ C. NO AWARD		

J61186
10-09-96

STANDARD FORM 1403 (REV. 9-88) PAGE 2

Appendix 3.6 (Continued)

**PREAWARD SURVEY OF PROSPECTIVE CONTRACTOR
TECHNICAL**

SERIAL NO. (For surveying activity use)	FORM APPROVED OMB NUMBER
	9000-0011
PROSPECTIVE CONTRACTOR	

1. RECOMMENDED

☐ a. COMPLETE AWARD ☐ b. PARTIAL AWARD (Quantity: _____) ☐ c. NO AWARD

2. NARRATIVE (Include the following information concerning key personnel who will be involved with the prospective contract: (1) Names, qualifications/experience and length of affiliation with prospective contractor; (2) Evaluate technical capabilities with respect to the requirements of the proposed contract or item classification; (3) Description of any technical capabilities which the prospective contractor lacks. Comment on the prospective contractor's efforts to obtain the needed technical capabilities.)

**IF CONTINUATION SHEETS
ATTACHED - MARK HERE** ☐

3. FIRM HAS AND/OR UNDERSTANDS (Give explanation for any items marked "NO" in 2. narrative)

a. SPECIFICATIONS	☐ YES ☐ NO	b. EXHIBITS	☐ YES ☐ NO
c. DRAWINGS	☐ YES ☐ NO	d. TECHNICAL DATA REQUIREMENTS	☐ YES ☐ NO

4. SURVEY MADE BY	a. SIGNATURE AND OFFICE (Include typed or printed name)	b. TELEPHONE NO. (Include area code)	c. DATE SIGNED
5. SURVEY REVIEWING OFFICIAL	a. SIGNATURE AND OFFICE (Include typed or printed name)	b. TELEPHONE NO. (Include area code)	c. DATE REVIEWED

AUTHORIZED FOR LOCAL REPRODUCTION   EXPIRATION DATE: 9-30-91   1404-103   **STANDARD FORM 1404**   (REV. 9-88)
Previous edition is usable.   Prescribed by GSA · FAR (48 CFR) 53.209-1(b)
J61187
10-09-96

Appendix 3.7   Standard Form 1404, Preaward Survey of Prospective Contractor Technical

PREAWARD SURVEY OF PROSPECTIVE CONTRACTOR

TECHNICAL

SERIAL NO. (For surveying activity use)	FORM APPROVED OMB NO.
	9000-0011
PROSPECTIVE CONTRACTOR	

Public reporting burden for this collection of information is estimated to average 24 hours per response, including the time for reviewing instructions, searching existing data sources, gathering and maintaining the data needed, and completing and reviewing the collection of information. Send comments regarding this burden estimate or any other aspect of this collection of information, including suggestions for reducing this burden, to the FAR Secretariat (VRS), Office of Federal Acquisition and Regulatory Policy, GSA, Washington, D.C. 20405; and to the Office of Management and Budget, Paperwork Reduction Project (9000-0011), Washington, D.C. 20503.

1. RECOMMENDED

☐ a. COMPLETE AWARD   ☐ b. PARTIAL AWARD (Quantity: _____)   ☐ c. NO AWARD

2. NARRATIVE (Include the following information concerning key personnel who will be involved with the prospective contract: (1) Names, qualifications/experience and length of affiliation with prospective contractor; (2) Evaluate technical capabilities with respect to the requirements of the proposed contract or item classification; (3) Description of any technical capabilities which the prospective contractor lacks. Comment on the prospective contractor's efforts to obtain the needed technical capabilities.)

IF CONTINUATION SHEETS
ATTACHED - MARK HERE ☐

3. FIRM HAS AND/OR UNDERSTANDS (Give explanation for any items marked "NO" in 2. narrative)

a. SPECIFICATIONS	☐ YES ☐ NO	b. EXHIBITS	☐ YES ☐ NO
c. DRAWINGS	☐ YES ☐ NO	d. TECHNICAL DATA REQUIREMENTS	☐ YES ☐ NO

4. SURVEY MADE BY	a. SIGNATURE AND OFFICE (Include typed or printed name)	b. TELEPHONE NO. (Include area code)	c. DATE SIGNED
5. SURVEY REVIEWING OFFICIAL	a. SIGNATURE AND OFFICE (Include typed or printed name)	b. TELEPHONE NO. (Include area code)	c. DATE REVIEWED

AUTHORIZED FOR LOCAL REPRODUCTION
Previous edition is usable.   EXPIRATION DATE: 9-30-91   1404-103   STANDARD FORM 1404   (REV. 9-88)
Prescribed by GSA - FAR (48 CFR) 53.209-1(b)

Appendix 3.7   (Continued)

70

PREAWARD SURVEY OF PROSPECTIVE CONTRACTOR PRODUCTION

SERIAL NO. (For surveying activity use)	FORM APPROVED OMB NO.
	9000-0011
PROSPECTIVE CONTRACTOR	

Public reporting burden for this collection of information is estimated to average 24 hours per response, including the time for reviewing instructions, searching existing data sources, gathering and maintaining the data needed, and completing and reviewing the collection of information. Send comments regarding this burden estimate or any other aspect of this collection of information, including suggestions for reducing this burden, to the FAR Secretariat (VRS), Office of Federal Acquisition and Regulatory Policy, GSA, Washington, DC 20405; and to the Office of Management and Budget, Paperwork Reduction Project (9000-0011), Washington, DC 20503.

SECTION I - RECOMMENDATION

1. RECOMMENDED

☐ a. COMPLETE AWARD   ☐ b. PARTIAL AWARD (Quantity: _____)   ☐ c. NO AWARD

2. NARRATIVE (Cite those sections of this report which substantiate the recommendations. List any other backup information in this space or on attached sheet if necessary. Identify any formal systems reviews and state results.)

IF CONTINUATION SHEETS ATTACHED - MARK HERE ☐

	a. SIGNATURE AND OFFICE (Include typed or printed name)	b. TELEPHONE NO. (Include area code)	c. DATE SIGNED
3. SURVEY MADE BY			
4. SURVEY REVIEWING OFFICIAL	a. SIGNATURE AND OFFICE (Include typed or printed name)	b. TELEPHONE NO. (Include area code)	c. DATE REVIEWED

AUTHORIZED FOR LOCAL REPRODUCTION   EXPIRATION DATE: 9-30-91   1405-103   **STANDARD FORM 1405**   (REV. 9-88)
Previous edition is usable.   Prescribed by GSA - FAR (48 CFR) 53.209-1(c)

J61188
10-09-96

Appendix 3.8   Standard Form 1405, Preaward of Prospective Contractor Production

SECTION II - PLANT FACILITIES

1. SIZE OF TRACT		4. DESCRIPTION AND TYPE OF BUILDING(S) ☐ OWNED
2. SQUARE FEET UNDER ROOF	3. NO. OF BUILDINGS	☐ LEASED (Give expiration date)

5. SPACE					6. MISCELLANEOUS PLANT OBSERVATIONS		
	TYPE	SQUARE FEET	ADE-QUATE	INADE-QUATE	(Explain any items marked "NO" on an attached sheet.)	YES	NO
MANUFAC-TURING	a. TOTAL MANUFACTURING SPACE				a. GOOD HOUSEKEEPING MAINTAINED		
	b. SPACE AVAILABLE FOR OFFERED ITEM				b. POWER AND FUEL SUPPLY ADEQUATE TO MEET PRODUCTION REQUIREMENTS		
STORAGE	c. TOTAL STORAGE SPACE				c. ALTERNATE POWER AND FUEL SOURCE AVAILABLE		
					d. ADEQUATE MATERIAL HANDLING EQUIPMENT AVAILABLE		
	d. FOR INSPECTION LOTS				e. TRANSPORTATION FACILITIES AVAILABLE FOR SHIPPING PRODUCT		
	e. FOR SHIPPING QUANTITIES						
	f. SPACE AVAILABLE FOR OFFERED ITEM				OTHER (Specify) f. _____		
	g. AMOUNT OF STORAGE THAT CAN BE CONVERTED FOR MANUFACTURING, IF REQUIRED				g. _____ h. _____		

SECTION III - PRODUCTION EQUIPMENT

LIST MAJOR EQUIPMENT REQUIRED (Include GFP and annotate it as such)	QUANTITY REQUIRED FOR PROPOSED CONTRACT	TOTAL QTY. REQD. DUR-ING LIFE OF PROPOSED CONTRACT	QUANTITY ON HAND	CONDI-TION (e)			QUANTITY SHORT* (Col. (c) minus (d))	SOURCE, IF NOT ON HAND	VERIFIED DELIVERY DATE
MANUFACTURING	(b)	(c)	(d)	G	F	P	(f)	(g)	(h)
1. MANUFACTURING									
2. SPECIAL TOOLING									
3. SPECIAL TEST									

* Coordinate shortage information for financial implications.

STANDARD FORM 1405 (REV. 9-88) PAGE 2

J61189
10-09-96

Appendix 3.8 (Continued)

SECTION IV - MATERIALS, PURCHASED PARTS AND SUBCONTRACTS

1. PARTS/MATERIALS/SUBCONTRACTS WITH LONGEST LEAD TIME OR CRUCIAL ITEMS

DESCRIPTION (a)	SOURCE (b)	VERIFIED DELIVERY DATE TO MEET PROD. (c)

2. DESCRIBE THE MATERIAL CONTROL SYSTEM, INDICATING WHETHER IT IS CURRENTLY OPERATIONAL, AND EVALUATE ITS ABILITY TO MEET THE NEEDS OF THE PROPOSED ACQUISITION.

SECTION V - PERSONNEL

1. NUMBER AND SOURCE OF EMPLOYEES						2. SHIFTS ON WHICH WORK IS TO BE PERFORMED
TYPE OF EMPLOYEES	NO. ON BOARD	ADD. NO. REQUIRED	AVAIL. YES	NO	SOURCE	☐ FIRST ☐ SECOND ☐ THIRD
a. Skilled Production						3. UNION AFFILIATION
b. Unskilled Production						AGREEMENT EXPIRATION DATE ▶
c. Engineering						4. RELATIONSHIP WITH LABOR INDICATES PROBLEMS AFFECTING TIMELY PERFORMANCE OF PROPOSED CONTRACT (If "Yes," explain on attached sheet)
d. Administrative						☐ YES ☐ NO
e. TOT. (Lines a thru d)						

SECTION VI - DELIVERY PERFORMANCE RECORD

J61190
10-09-96

Appendix 3.8 (Continued)

SECTION VII - RELATED PREVIOUS PRODUCTION (Government)

PAST YEAR PRODUCTION		GOVERNMENT CONTRACT NUMBER 1/	PERFORMANCE		QUANTITY	DOLLAR VALUE ($000)
ITEM NOMENCLATURE (a)	NATIONAL STOCK NO. (NSN) (b)	(c)	ON SCHED. (d)	DELIN-QUENT (e)	(f)	(g)

1/ Identify identical items by an asterisk (*) after the Government contract number.

SECTION VIII - CURRENT PRODUCTION
(Government and civilian concurrent production schedule using same equipment and/or personnel as offered item.)

ITEM(S) (Include Government Contract No., if applicable. Identify unsatisfactory performance with asterisk (*).)	MONTHLY SCHEDULE OF CONCURRENT DELIVERIES (Quantity)										
	1st	2nd	3rd	4th	5th	6th	7th	8th	9th	10th	BAL.
BEING PRODUCED — 1.											
PENDING AWARD — 2.											

SECTION IX - ORGANIZATION AND MANAGEMENT DATA

Provide the following information in SECTION I NARRATIVE:

1. Describe the relationship between management, production, and inspection. Attach an organizational chart, if available.

2. Describe the prospective contractor's production control system. State whether or not it is operational.

3. Evaluate the prospective contractor's production control system in terms of (a) historical effectiveness, (b) the proposed contract, and (c) total production during performance of the proposed contract.

4. Comment on or evaluate other areas unique to this survey (include all special requests by the contracting office and any other information pertinent to the proposed contract or item classification).

STANDARD FORM 1405 (REV. 9-88) PAGE 4

J61191
10-09-96

Appendix 3.8   (Continued)

PREAWARD SURVEY OF PROSPECTIVE CONTRACTOR
QUALITY ASSURANCE

SERIAL NO. (For surveying activity use)	FORM APPROVED OMB NO.
	9000-0011
PROSPECTIVE CONTRACTOR	

Public reporting burden for this collection of information is estimated to average 24 hours per response, including the time for reviewing instructions, searching existing data sources, gathering and maintaining the data needed, and completing and reviewing the collection of information. Send comments regarding this burden estimate or any other aspect of this collection of information, including suggestions for reducing this burden, to the FAR Secretariat (VRS), Office of Federal Acquisition and Regulatory Policy, GSA, Washington, D.C. 20405; and to the Office of Management and Budget, Paperwork Reduction Project (9000-0011), Washington, D.C. 20503.

SECTION I - RECOMMENDATION

1. RECOMMEND: ☐ AWARD ☐ NO AWARD (Provide full substantiation for recommendation in 4. NARRATIVE)

2. IF PROSPECTIVE CONTRACTOR RECEIVES AWARD, A POST AWARD CONFERENCE, IS RECOMMENDED. ☐ YES ☐ NO

3. AN ON-SITE SURVEY WAS PERFORMED. ☐ YES ☐ NO

4. NARRATIVE

IF CONTINUATION
SHEETS - MARK HERE ☐

5. SURVEY MADE BY	a. SIGNATURE AND OFFICE (Include typed or printed name)	b. TELEPHONE NO. (Include area code)	c. DATE SIGNED
6. SURVEY REVIEWING OFFICIAL	a. SIGNATURE AND OFFICE (Include typed or printed name)	b. TELEPHONE NO. (Include area code)	c. DATE REVIEWED

AUTHORIZED FOR LOCAL REPRODUCTION EXPIRATION DATE: 9-30-91 1406-103 **STANDARD FORM 1406** (REV. 9-88)
Previous edition is usable. Prescribed by GSA · FAR (48 CFR) 53.209-1(d)
J61192
10-09-96

Appendix 3.9 Standard Form 1406, Preaward of Prospective Contractor Quality Assurance

SECTION II - COMPANY AND SOLICITATION DATA

1. QUALITY ASSURANCE ORGANIZATION (Describe briefly and attach organization chart.)

2. QUALITY ASSURANCE OFFICIALS CONTACTED (Names, titles, and years of quality assurance experience)

3. QUALITY, RELIABILITY, MAINTAINABILITY REQUIRE- MENTS WHICH APPLY	MIL-I-45208	MIL-STD-45662	☐ OTHER (Specify)	
	MIL-I-45607	MIL-STD-785		
	MIL-Q-9858	MIL-STD-470	MIL-S-52779	

4. ☐ IDENTICAL OR ☐ SIMILAR ITEMS HAVE BEEN ☐ PRODUCED ☐ SERVICED BY PROSPECTIVE CONTRACTOR

(If similar items. identify:

SECTION III - EVALUATION CHECKLIST

STATEMENTS		YES	NO
1. AS PERTAINS TO THE CONTRACT, THESE ITEMS ARE UNDERSTOOD BY THE CONTRACTOR	a. Exhibits, technical data, drawings, specifications, and approval requirements.		
	b. Preservation, packaging, packing, and marking requirements.		
	c. OTHER (Specify)		
2. Records available indicate that the prospective contractor has a satisfactory quality performance record during the past twelve (12) months for similar items.			
3. Used or reconditioned material and former Government surplus material will be furnished by the prospective contractor. (If Yes, explain in Section I NARRATIVE)			
4. Prospective contractor will require unusual assistance from the Government.			
5. Did prospective contractor fulfill commitments to correct deficiencies, as proposed on previous surveys, when awarded that contract?			
6. Quality control, inspection, and test personnel.	NUMBER SKILLED / NUMBER SEMI-SKILLED		
7. Inspection to production personnel ratio.	RATIO		
The following are available and adequate. (If not applicable, show "N/A" in "Yes" column.)			
8. Inspection and test equipment, gauges, and instruments for first article and production (including solicitation specified equipment).			
9. Calibration/metrology program.			
10. Written procedures and instructions for inspections, tests, process controls, and other requirements; conformance thereto; in conjunction with other planning control functions.			
11. Control of specifications, drawings, changes and modifications, work/process instructions.			
12. Quality assurance/control organizational structure.			
13. System for determining inspection, test, and measurement requirements.			
14. Controls for selecting qualified suppliers and assuring the quality of purchased materials.			
15. Material control: identification, segregation, maintenance, preservation, and correction of defects.			
16. Government furnished property controls.			
17. In-process inspection controls.			
18. System for timely identification and correction of deficiencies to prevent recurrence.			
19. Preservation, packaging, packing, marking controls.			
20. Quality control records (such as: inspection, test, corrective actions, calibration, etc.)			
21. Controls for investigation of customer complaints and correction of deficiencies.			
22. Reliability and/or maintainability program.			
23. Computer software (deliverable and/or non-deliverable) quality assurance program.			

STANDARD FORM 1406 (REV. 9-88) PAGE 2

J61193
10-09-96

Appendix 3.9 (Continued)

PREAWARD SURVEY OF PROSPECTIVE CONTRACTOR FINANCIAL CAPABILITY

SERIAL NO. (For surveying activity use)	FORM APPROVED OMB NO.
	9000-0011
PROSPECTIVE CONTRACTOR	

Public reporting burden for this collection of information is estimated to average 24 hours per response, including the time for reviewing instructions, searching existing data sources, gathering and maintaining the data needed, and completing and reviewing the collection of information. Send comments regarding this burden estimate or any other aspect of this collection of information, including suggestions for reducing this burden, to the FAR Secretariat (VRS), Office of Federal Acquisition and Regulatory Policy, GSA, Washington, D.C. 20405; and to the Office of Management and Budget, Paperwork Reduction Project (9000-0011), Washington, D.C. 20503.

SECTION I - RECOMMENDATION

1. RECOMMENDED
   ☐ a. COMPLETE AWARD   ☐ b. PARTIAL AWARD (Quantity: _____)   ☐ c. NO AWARD

2. TOTAL OFFERED PRICE

3. NARRATIVE (Cite those sections of the report which substantiate the recommendations. Give any other backup information in this space or on an attached sheet, if necessary.)

IF CONTINUATION SHEETS
ATTACHED - MARK HERE ☐

4. SURVEY MADE BY	a. SIGNATURE AND OFFICE (Include typed or printed name)	b. TELEPHONE NO. (Include area code)	c. DATE SIGNED
5. SURVEY REVIEWING OFFICIAL	a. SIGNATURE AND OFFICE (Include typed or printed name)	b. TELEPHONE NO. (Include area code)	c. DATE REVIEWED

AUTHORIZED FOR LOCAL REPRODUCTION   EXPIRATION DATE: 9-30-91   1407-103   **STANDARD FORM 1407**   (REV. 9-88)
Previous edition is usable.   Prescribed by GSA · FAR (48 CFR) 53.209-1(e)

J61194
10-09-96

Appendix 3.10   Standard Form 1407, Preaward of Prospective Contractor Financial Capability

SECTION II - GENERAL

1. TYPE OF COMPANY	3. NAME AND ADDRESS OF:
☐ CORPORATION ☐ PARTNERSHIP	a. PARENT CO.
☐ SUBSIDIARY ☐ DIVISION	
☐ PROPRIETORSHIP ☐ OTHER (Specify)	b. SUBSIDIARIES
2. YEAR ESTABLISHED:	

SECTION III - BALANCE SHEET/PROFIT AND LOSS STATEMENT

PART A · LATEST BALANCE SHEET		PART B · LATEST PROFIT AND LOSS STATEMENT		
1. DATE	2. FILED WITH	1. CURRENT PERIOD		2. FILED WITH
		a. FROM	b. TO	

3. FINANCIAL POSITION				
a. Cash	$	3. NET SALES	a. CURRENT PERIOD	$
b. Accounts Receivable			b. First prior fiscal year	
c. Inventory			c. Second prior fiscal year	
d. Other Current Assets		4. NET PROFITS BEFORE TAXES	a. CURRENT PERIOD	$
e. Total Current Assets			b. First prior fiscal year	
f. Fixed Assets			c. Second prior fiscal year	
g. Current Liabilities		PART C · OTHER		
h. Long Term Liabilities		1. FISCAL YEAR ENDS (Date):		
i. Total Liabilities		2. BALANCE SHEETS AND PROFIT AND LOSS STATEMENTS HAVE BEEN CERTIFIED ►	a. THROUGH (Date)	b. BY (Signature)
j. Net Worth				

4. WORKING CAPITAL (Current Assets less Current Liabilities)

5. RATIOS			3. OTHER PERTINENT DATA
a. CURRENT ASSETS TO CURRENT LIABILITIES	b. ACID TEST (Cash, temporary investments held in lieu of cash and current receivables to current liabilities)	c. TOTAL LIABILITIES TO NET WORTH	

SECTION IV - PROSPECTIVE CONTRACTOR'S FINANCIAL ARRANGEMENTS

Mark "X" in appropriate column.	YES	NO	4. INDEPENDENT ANALYSIS OF FINANCIAL POSITION SUPPORTS THE STATEMENTS SHOWN IN ITEMS 1, 2, AND 3
1. USE OF OWN RESOURCES			☐ YES ☐ NO (If "NO", explain)
2. USE OF BANK CREDITS			
3. OTHER (Specify)			

SECTION V - GOVERNMENT FINANCIAL AID

1. TO BE REQUESTED IN CONNECTION WITH PERFORMANCE OF PROPOSED CONTRACT	2. EXPLAIN ANY "YES" ANSWERS TO ITEMS 1a, b, AND c

Mark "X" in appropriate column.	YES	NO
a. PROGRESS PAYMENT(S)		
b. GUARANTEED LOAN		
c. ADVANCE PAYMENTS		

3. FINANCIAL AID CURRENTLY OBTAINED FROM THE GOVERNMENT

a. PROSPECTIVE CONTRACTOR RECEIVES GOVERNMENT FINANCING AT PRESENT	Complete items below only if Item a., is marked "YES."			
	b. IS LIQUIDATION CURRENT?	c. AMOUNT OF UNLIQUIDATED PROGRESS PAYMENTS OUTSTANDING	DOLLAR AMOUNTS	(a) AUTHORIZED	(b) IN USE
☐ YES ☐ NO	☐ YES ☐ NO	$	a. Guaranteed loans	$	$
			b. Advance payments	$	$

4. LIST THE GOVERNMENT AGENCIES INVOLVED	5. SHOW THE APPLICABLE CONTRACT NOS.

STANDARD FORM 1407 (REV. 9-88) **PAGE 2**

J61195
10-09-96

Appendix 3.10   (Continued)

SECTION VI - BUSINESS AND FINANCIAL REPUTATION

1. COMMENTS OF PROSPECTIVE CONTRACTOR'S BANK

2. COMMENTS OF TRADE CREDITORS

3. COMMENTS AND REPORTS OF COMMERCIAL FINANCIAL SERVICES AND CREDIT ORGANIZATIONS (Such as, Dun & Bradstreet, Standard and Poor, etc.)

4. MOST RECENT CREDIT RATING ▶ a. DATE	b. BY

5. DOES PRICE APPEAR UNREALISTICALLY LOW? ☐ YES ☐ NO (If YES, explain in Section I NARRATIVE)

6. DESCRIBE ANY OUTSTANDING LIENS OR JUDGEMENTS

SECTION VII - SALES (000'S) FOR NEXT SIX QUARTERS							
CATEGORY	1	2	3	4	5	6	TOTAL
1. CURRENT CONTRACT SALES (Backlog)	$	$	$	$	$	$	$
A. GOVERNMENT (Prime & Subcontractor)							
B. COMMERCIAL							
2. ANTICIPATED ADDITIONAL SALES							
A. GOVERNMENT (Prime and Subcontractor)							
B. COMMERCIAL							
3. TOTALS							

STANDARD FORM 1407 (REV. 9-88) PAGE 3

J61196
10-09-96

Appendix 3.10   (Continued)

PREAWARD SURVEY OF PROSPECTIVE CONTRACTOR ACCOUNTING SYSTEM

SERIAL NO. (For surveying activity use)	FORM APPROVED OMB NO.
	9000-0011
PROSPECTIVE CONTRACTOR	

Public reporting burden for this collection of information is estimated to average 24 hours per response, including the time for reviewing instructions, searching existing data sources, gathering and maintaining the data needed, and completing and reviewing the collection of information. Send comments regarding this burden estimate or any other aspect of this collection of information, including suggestions for reducing this burden, to the FAR Secretariat (VRS), Office of Federal Acquisition and Regulatory Policy, GSA, Washington, D.C. 20405; and to the Office of Management and Budget, Paperwork Reduction Project (9000-0011), Washington, D.C. 20503.

SECTION I - RECOMMENDATION

1. PROSPECTIVE CONTRACTOR'S ACCOUNTING SYSTEM IS ACCEPTABLE FOR AWARD OF PROSPECTIVE CONTRACT.

☐ YES   ☐ NO (Explain in 2. NARRATIVE)

☐ YES, WITH A RECOMMENDATION THAT A FOLLOW ON ACCOUNTING SYSTEM REVIEW BE PERFORMED AFTER CONTRACT AWARD (Explain in 2. NARRATIVE)

2 NARRATIVE (Clarification of deficiencies, and other pertinent comments. If additional space is required, continue on plain sheets of paper.)

IF CONTINUATION SHEETS ATTACHED - MARK HERE ☐

3. SURVEY MADE BY	a. SIGNATURE AND OFFICE (Include typed or printed name)	b. TELEPHONE NO. (Include area code)	c. DATE SIGNED
4. SURVEY REVIEWING OFFICIAL	a. SIGNATURE AND OFFICE (Include typed or printed name)	b. TELEPHONE NO. (Include area code)	c. DATE REVIEWED

AUTHORIZED FOR LOCAL REPRODUCTION   EXPIRATION DATE: 9-30-91   1408-103
Previous edition is usable.

STANDARD FORM 1408   (REV. 9-88)
Prescribed by GSA - FAR (48 CFR) 53.209-1(f)

J61197
10-09-96

Appendix 3.11   Standard Form 1408, Preaward Survey of Prospective Contractor Accounting System

80

SECTION II - EVALUATION CHECKLIST

MARK "X" IN THE APPROPRIATE COLUMN (Explain any deficiencies in SECTION I NARRATIVE)	YES	NO	NOT APPLI-CABLE
1. EXCEPT AS STATED IN SECTION I NARRATIVE, IS THE ACCOUNTING SYSTEM IN ACCORD WITH GENERALLY ACCEPTED ACCOUNTING PRINCIPLES APPLICABLE IN THE CIRCUMSTANCES?			
2. ACCOUNTING SYSTEM PROVIDES FOR:			
a. Proper segregation of direct costs from indirect costs.			
b. Identification and accumulation of direct costs by contract.			
c. A logical and consistent method for the allocation of indirect costs to intermediate and final cost objectives. (A contract is a final cost objective.)			
d. Accumulation of costs under general ledger control.			
e. A timekeeping system that identifies employees' labor by intermediate or final cost objectives.			
f. A labor distribution system that charges direct and indirect labor to the appropriate cost objectives.			
g. Interim (at least monthly) determination of costs charged to a contract through routine posting of books of account.			
h. Exclusion from costs charged to government contracts of amounts which are not allowable in terms of FAR 31, Contract Cost Principles and Procedures, or other contract provisions.			
i. Identification of costs by contract line item and by units (as if each unit or line item were a separate contract) if required by the proposed contract.			
j. Segregation of preproduction costs from production costs.			
3. ACCOUNTING SYSTEM PROVIDES FINANCIAL INFORMATION:			
a. Required by contract clauses concerning limitation of cost (FAR 52.232-20 and 21) or limitation on payments (FAR 52.216-16).			
b. Required to support requests for progress payments.			
4. IS THE ACCOUNTING SYSTEM DESIGNED, AND ARE THE RECORDS MAINTAINED IN SUCH A MANNER THAT ADEQUATE, RELIABLE DATA ARE DEVELOPED FOR USE IN PRICING FOLLOW-ON ACQUISITIONS?			
5. IS THE ACCOUNTING SYSTEM CURRENTLY IN FULL OPERATION? (If not, describe in Section I Narrative which portions are (1) in operation, (2) set up, but not yet in operation, (3) anticipated, or (4) nonexistent.)			

STANDARD FORM 1408 (REV. 9-88) PAGE 2

J61198
10-09-96

Appendix 3.11 (Continued)

Chapter Four

Profit

4-1. BACKGROUND

Over the years, the government has struggled to achieve fairness, uniformity, and consistency in its profit policy and regulations. Different methods for establishing contract profit objectives have been used by different agencies, and the methods have changed in an unending attempt to make them more equitable and responsive to changing needs. As an important aspect of government contracting, the methods used by contracting officers (COs) in establishing contract profit objectives warrant serious attention by businesses involved in this market and by those planning to enter the market.

Following World War I, the Vinson–Trammel Act[1] of 1934 limited profits on military aircraft and naval vessels to 12% and 10%, respectively. In 1942, the profit limitation on military procurement was expanded when the first Renegotiation Act[2] was passed. In 1951, the Renegotiation Board was established to determine whether the overall profits earned on Department of Defense (DOD) contracts over a specified threshold were excessive. While the Renegotiation Act was effective, the Vinson–Trammell Act was held in abeyance.

Profit limitation activity under the Renegotiation Act ceased in 1979. The application of Vinson–Trammel was suspended indefinitely in 1982 but allowed the President to reinstate profit limitation regulations in the event of war or national emergency. Currently, there are no requirements for renegotiating federal contracts for the purpose of eliminating excess profits.

How to use the profit motive to provide an incentive to contractors to reduce costs while satisfactorily meeting contract requirements is a continuing challenge for the government. Prior to the mid-1970s, profit policies followed by government agencies rewarded companies that incurred higher costs in performing certain negotiated contracts. As a result of a study called Profit '76, the DOD revised the profit policy to give greater weight to contractor investment in cost-saving facilities and decreased the effect of the contractor's cost input. The DOD continued to review the profit policy, making changes to achieve the elusive objective of removing the disincentive for contractors to decrease the costs of performing negotiated contracts. A notable change was implemented in 1986 to assign even greater weight to contractor investment in productivity-enhancing equipment and less to costs incurred. Profit policies utilized on nondefense contracts still focus on contract cost as the primary factor in the negotiation of fee or profit.

4-2. GOVERNMENT PROFIT POLICY

Contracting officers are charged with ensuring that the prices the government pays for the goods and services it requires are fair and reasonable. When the government purchase is a result of sealed bidding or a negotiated contract in which cost or pricing data are not required, profit is not separately considered. The amount of profit is normally of no concern to the government. In such situations, fixed-price contracts are usually awarded to the lowest responsible offeror. The force of competition ensures fair and reasonable pricing and protects the government from paying too much. If the contractor earns a large profit, it is considered the normal reward of efficiency in a competitive environment.

In procurements that require cost or pricing data, profit becomes a separate element to be considered by COs. While methods for determining specific profit objectives have varied, the general government profit policy has been relatively consistent. This policy is set forth in Federal Acquisition Regulation (FAR) 15.404(a)(2) and (3):

> It is in the Government's interest to offer contractors opportunities for financial rewards sufficient to (1) stimulate efficient contract performance, (2) attract the best capabilities of qualified large and small business concerns to Government contracts, and (3) maintain a viable industrial base. Both the Government and contractors should be concerned with profit as a motivator of efficient and effective contract performance. Negotiations aimed merely at reducing prices by reducing profit, without proper recognition of the function of profit, are not in the Government's interest.

Few would argue with this statement of policy; it does appear to promote a fair, reasonable, and equitable approach to profit determination. Nevertheless, the application of this profit policy affects the ultimate profits of businesses engaged in government contracting. While contractors have pointed with alarm to the low profit rates experienced on government contracts, Congress has viewed with suspicion the alleged high return on investment shown by many defense firms.

The government's periodic studies of its profit policies frequently result in changes to the implementing regulations. These constantly changing guidelines confuse contractors, who are trying to respond to the government's interest while optimizing profits. The use of profit to promote the three sometimes contradictory objectives of rewarding (1) quality contract performance, (2) capital investment, and (3) support for national socioeconomic policies, as well as the constantly shifting emphasis among the three objectives, has contributed to the confusion.

Limitations on Cost-Reimbursement Contracts

Notwithstanding the various methods of determining prenegotiation profit objectives, cost-reimbursement contracts are limited to a maximum fee of 10% of the estimated contract cost, except that contracts for experimental, developmental, or research work are limited to a maximum fee of 15% of the estimated contract cost. In the case of cost-plus-fixed-fee contracts, these limits are statutory. The FAR extends these limits to cost-plus-award-fee contracts and cost-plus-incentive-fee contracts.

Prenegotiation Profit Objectives

The profit included in the price of any negotiated contract for which cost data have been submitted is subject to negotiation between the CO and the contractor, subject to the limits for cost-type contracts. FAR 15.406-1(b) requires the CO to establish a prenegotiation objective before negotiating any contract pricing action. The prenegotiation profit or fee objective is a distinct part of the required prenegotiation objectives.

FAR 15.404-4(B) directs COs to use a structured approach in determining the profit or fee objective in noncompetitive awards requiring cost analysis. This approach uses mechanical procedures that measure and assign weight values to such factors as contractor effort, contract cost risk, federal socioeconomic program support, capital investment, past performance, and independent research and development (IR&D). Unstructured methods, which also consider the above performance factors, do not quantify the individual risk elements. When establishing a structured method, agencies may adopt another agency's method and may prescribe specific exemptions where the mandatory use of a structured approach would be clearly inappropriate.

4-3. DOD WEIGHTED GUIDELINES

Within the DOD, whenever cost analysis is performed, COs are required to establish profit objectives for contract negotiations that:

- Reward contractors that undertake more difficult work requiring higher skills
- Allow contractors an opportunity to earn profits commensurate with the extent of the cost risk they are willing to assume
- Reward contractors that provide their own facilities and financing and establish their competence through development work undertaken at their own risk
- Reward contractors for productivity increases

The DOD's structured method for determining prenegotiation profit objectives is called weighted guidelines. This method includes fairly precise guidance on implementing and applying the weighted guidelines and on tailoring profits to the circumstances of each contract. This approach fosters long-range cost-reduction objectives and spreads profits commensurate with varying circumstances.

The DOD has revised its weighted guidelines several times as a result of internal studies. In 1985, the Defense Financing and Investment Review, concluded that the DOD profit structure was generally sound. Two of the findings, however, were to have a significant impact on defense contractors; the study found that overall profit had increased about 1% since the previous profit study and that the profit policy was not effectively motivating contractors to invest in capital facilities.

As a result of this study and a General Accounting Office (GAO) analysis of the study, Congress mandated that the DOD revise its profit policy to incorporate certain of the recommendations. To back up its demand, Congress removed about $700 million from the fiscal year 1987 budget—approximately the amount by which negotiated profits would be reduced under the new policy. Consequently, the DOD completely revised its profit approach and issued new weighted guidelines. The interim regulation was effective on all solicitations released after October 18, 1986, and the final regulation was effective August 1, 1987.

DOD FAR Supplement (DFARS) 215.404-70, requires contractors to provide to COs the distribution of capital assets into three separate categories: (1) land, (2) buildings, and (3) equipment. Different weight factors are assigned to asset values in each category, and COs use these data to calculate profit objectives.

The CO has the latitude to use another structured method if the weighted guidelines do not produce a reasonable profit objective. This action requires the written approval of the head of the contracting activity. Another structured method should also be used in the following situations:

- Architect–engineer contracts
- Construction contracts
- Contracts primarily requiring delivery of material supplied by subcontractors
- Termination settlements
- Cost-plus-award-fee contracts
- Contracts not expected to exceed $500,000

When the weighted guidelines method is not used, a similar structured approach must be used that still considers the three primary factors of (1) performance risk, (2) contract-type risk (with a working capital adjustment for fixed-price contracts), and (3) facilities capital investment.

Contractors are encouraged to use the weighted guidelines in setting profit objectives for their negotiated subcontracts and to voluntarily submit with their proposals an analysis of their proposed profit in the weighted guidelines format.

The form used to determine the prenegotiation profit objective is DD Form 1547. This form is used both as a worksheet for the CO and as a transmittal sheet for statistical purposes. In addition, the CO is required to prepare DD Form 1861 to report the facilities capital cost of money (FCCOM) negotiated and to partially develop the facilities capital employed portion of the prenegotiation profit objective.

Performance Risk

The portion of the prenegotiation profit objective based on performance risk is the product of the contracting officer's prenegotiation cost objective (excluding FCCOM, IR&D/B&P [bid and proposal], and general and administrative [G&A] expense) and an assigned weight and value. In assigning the weight and value, the CO considers the relative importance of three broad categories of contract performance: technical, management, and cost. A weight is assigned as a percentage to each category, with the total of the three to equal 100%. Then, a value between 2% and 6% (standard range) is assigned to each category. (Four percent is considered the normal value.) Each of the three categories is independently assessed. The regulation identifies an extensive number of factors to be considered in assigning the value to each category. The CO is not limited to these considerations but must explain any other factors considered. The values for all categories are based on the CO's judgment and are combined to arrive at the overall performance risk weight value shown in Table 4.1.

Contractor Risk Factors	Assigned Weight	Assigned Value	Computation (not shown on form)
Technical	40%	5.0	2.0
Management	30%	4.0	1.2
Cost control	30%	5.0	1.5
Performance risk (composite)		4.7	

Table 4.1   Performance Risk Factors

Since research and development (R&D) and service-type organizations often require minimum facilities capital for contract performance, the guidelines permit the CO to use an alternate range between 4% and 8%, with a normal value of 6% for performance risk, in lieu of the standard range previously described. If the alternate range is used, no profit is calculated for facilities capital employed.

Contract-Type Risk

The portion of the prenegotiation profit objective based on contract-type risk is the product of the CO's prenegotiation cost objective (excluding FCCOM, IR&D/B&P, and G&A) and an assigned value for contract-type risk. Contracting officers are directed to consider the extent to which costs have been incurred before contract definitization as a factor in reducing contract-type risk. The normal values and ranges are shown in Table 4.2.

Contract Type	Contracts with No (or Limited) Progress Payment Provisions		Contracts with Progress Payment Provisions	
	Range	Normal Value	Range	Normal Value
Firm-fixed-price	4%–6%	5%	2%–4%	3%
Fixed-price-incentive	2%–4%	3%	0%–2%	1%
Cost-plus-incentive-fee	0%–2%	1%		
Cost-plus-fixed-fee, time and material, labor hour, and fixed-price-level-of-effort	0%–1%	.5%		

Table 4.2   Contract Type Risk Factors

The working capital adjustment applies only to fixed-price contracts with provisions for progress payments. The CO's prenegotiation cost objective, this time including IR&D/B&P and G&A costs but not FCCOM, is multiplied by the percent of costs financed by the contractor (one minus the progress payment rate) and by a contract length factor taken from a table in DFARS 215.404-71-3(f). This product is then multiplied by the Treasury rate, which is published semiannually. There is an upward limit on the adjustment of 4% of the cost objective.

Facilities Capital Employed

The facilities capital employed portion of the prenegotiation profit objective is based on the contractor's investment in buildings and equipment. To compute this amount, it is necessary to obtain the percentage of the net book values related to land, buildings, and equipment for each business unit for each year of the contract and also the allocation base amounts used to calculate the indirect rates for each pool. These calculations are made on DD Form 1861.

The contract facilities capital cost of money is calculated for each pool and fiscal year by multiplying the FCCOM factor (from column 7 of the CASB-CMF form, discussed in Chapter 8) by the estimated allocation base in the prenegotiation objective for the pool. The pools and fiscal years are summed into a single value and divided by the current Treasury rate. The percentages of land, buildings, and equipment for each pool are used to redistribute the facilities capital employed to the three asset types. The results are the base for determining the facilities capital employed profit objective.

The CO then assesses the usefulness of the assets to present and future DOD contracts and, on DD Form 1547, assigns a value within the ranges shown in Table 4.3. The assigned value for each asset type is multiplied by the base for each asset type, and the sum of the products for buildings and equipment is the profit objective for facilities capital employed.

Asset Type	R&D and Service Contracts Awarded to Highly Facilitized Manufacturers		All Other Contracts	
	Range	Normal Value	Range	Normal Value
Land	0%	0%	0%	0%
Buildings	0%–10%	5%	10%–20%	15%
Equipment	15%–25%	20%	20%–50%	35%

Table 4.3   Facilities Capital Employed Factors

The CO's total prenegotiation profit objective is the sum of the performance risk, contract type (including the working capital adjustment, if applicable), and facilities capital employed profit objectives. The forms are straightforward and easy to prepare once the method is understood and the required data are available. Appendices 4.1 through 4.5 illustrate a completed set of forms applying the DOD weighted guidelines method.

4-4. NASA PROFIT APPROACH

In determining profit objectives, the National Aeronautics and Space Administration (NASA) uses a structured approach that is similar to the DOD policy in effect before October 18, 1986. Weight ranges are prescribed for each major type of cost of the contractor's effort and for each of several other factors. The ranges for contractor effort vary in proportion to the value added by the type of cost element being evaluated. NASA FAR Supplement 1815.404-70 directs NASA COs on the criteria for selecting specific values within the given ranges. For the other factors, the regulations direct COs to evaluate the contractor's relative cost risk;

investment in facilities, equipment, and processes; past performance; and support for the government's socioeconomic programs. There is also an adjustment factor for special situations not adequately covered by the other factors.

NASA FAR Supplement 1815.404-70 requires direct reduction of the profit objective by the allowable amount of the facilities capital cost of money included in the contractor's proposal. NASA's weighted guidelines are illustrated in Table 4.4.

Profit Factors	Weight Ranges
Contractor Effort	
Material acquisition	1%–4%
Direct labor	4%–12%
Overhead	3%–8%
Other costs	1%–3%
General management	4%–8%
Other Factors	
Cost risk	0%–7%
Investment	−2% to +2%
Performance	−1% to +1%
Socioeconomic programs	−5% to +5%
Special situations	

Table 4.4 NASA Weighted Guidelines

4-5. OTHER CIVILIAN AGENCY APPROACHES

Each of the major civilian agencies now uses a structured approach to determine prenegotiation profit objectives. Most other agency approaches resemble the NASA policy in that much of the profit is based on contractor effort, as reflected in the Department of Energy (DOE) and Environmental Protection Agency (EPA) policies illustrated in Tables 4.5 and 4.6, respectively. Individual

Profit Factors	Weight Ranges
Contractor effort	
Material acquisition	
Purchased parts and other materials	1%–3%
Subcontracted items	1%–4%
Direct Labor	
Technical and managerial	8%–20%
Manufacturing	4%–8%
Support services	4%–14%
Overhead	
Technical and managerial	5%–8%
Manufacturing	3%–6%
Support services	3%–7%
Other direct costs	3%–8%
G&A expenses	5%–7%
Cost risk	0%–8%
Investment	5%–20%
Independent research and development	0%–20%
Special program participation	−5% to +5%
Other considerations	−5% to +5%

Table 4.5 DOE Weighted Guidelines

Profit Factors	Weight Ranges
Contractor effort	
Purchases	1%–4%
Subcontracts	1%–5%
Equipment	1%–2%
Engineering labor	8%–15%
Engineering overhead	6%–9%
Manufacturing labor	5%–9%
Manufacturing overhead	4%–7%
Consultants	2%–5%
Other direct costs	1%–3%
G&A expenses	5%–8%
Other factors	0%–6%
Cost risk	0%–6%

Table 4.6 EPA Weighted Guidelines

agency regulations should be consulted to determine the specific weights and categories used by each agency.

4-6. SUMMARY

Profit is generally considered the reward or compensation for (1) efforts or services performed and resources provided (both human and facilities) and (2) the uncertainty or risk undertaken. The more resources provided and the higher the skills or risk involved, the higher the expected level of profit. Although government contracting differs from the commercial environment in ways that need to be understood, these same general principles apply. Contractors are willing to enter the government contracting market only if reasonable profit levels are provided in relation to the risks involved and the alternative opportunities for using resources.

When competition exists, profit is generally not analyzed by the government. However, when cost analysis of the contractor's proposal is required, detailed requirements for profit analysis come into play, and each agency is generally required to use a structured method to determine prenegotiation cost objectives.

The DOD's weighted guidelines are intended to produce different profit levels depending on the complexity and quality of expected contract performance and the amount of contractor investment in buildings and equipment. The current guidelines include profit factors for performance risk, contract-type risk (including a working capital adjustment for fixed-price contracts with progress payment provisions), and facilities investment. Their objective is to encourage greater contractor investment in productivity-enhancing capital facilities.

NASA and the other civilian agencies use other approaches to establishing prenegotiation profit objectives. These agencies use structured methods which base profit objectives on the type of contractor effort and selected other factors. The FAR supplement for each agency specifically identifies the factors and values used.

4-7. NOTES

1. Vinson–Trammel Act of 1934, 48 Stat. 503, 10 U.S.C. §§2382, 7300, 7342, 7343, 40 U.S.C. §474, March 27, 1934.
2. Renegotiation Act, Ch. 247, 56 Stat. 245, 50 U.S.C. Appx. 1191, enacted April 28, 1942.

Contract length (months)	24
Contract type	FFP
Progress payments	75%
Cost incurred before definitization	$0
Percent of business unit assets	
Land	2%
Building	24%
Equipment	74%
	Contract Costs
Subcontracts	$17,200
Parts and material	19,067
Material subtotal	36,267
Manufacturing direct labor	624,704
Off-site direct labor	83,769
Field engineering labor	13,235
Manufacturing overhead	877,668
Off-site engineering overhead	55,715
Field engineering overhead	5955
Other direct	34,321
Total cost input	1,731,634
G&A, R&D, and B&P	268,366
Total cost	**$2,000,000**

Appendix 4.1 Contract Cost Data for Use in Weighted Guidelines Example.

RECORD OF WEIGHTED GUIDELINES APPLICATION

REPORT CONTROL SYMBOL
DD-P&L(Q)1751

1. REPORT NO.	2. BASIC PROCUREMENT INSTRUMENT IDENTIFICATION NO.				3. SPIIN	4. DATE OF ACTION	
	a. PURCHASING OFFICE	b. FY	c. TYPE PROC INST CODE	d. PRISN		a. YEAR	b. MONTH

5. CONTRACTING OFFICE CODE

ITEM	COST CATEGORY	OBJECTIVE
13.	MATERIAL	19,067
14.	SUBCONTRACTS	17,200
15.	DIRECT LABOR	721,708
16.	INDIRECT EXPENSES	939,338
17.	OTHER DIRECT CHARGES	34,321
18.	SUBTOTAL COSTS (13 thru 17)	1,731,634
19.	GENERAL AND ADMINISTRATIVE	268,366
20.	TOTAL COSTS (18 + 19)	2,000,000

6. NAME OF CONTRACTOR

7. DUNS NUMBER

8. FEDERAL SUPPLY CODE

9. DOD CLAIMANT PROGRAM

10. CONTRACT TYPE CODE

11. TYPE EFFORT

12. USE CODE

WEIGHTED GUIDELINES PROFIT FACTORS

ITEM	CONTRACTOR RISK FACTORS	ASSIGNED WEIGHTING	ASSIGNED VALUE	BASE (ITEM 18)	PROFIT OBJECTIVE
21.	TECHNICAL	40.0 %	5.0		
22.	MANAGEMENT	30.0 %	4.0		
23.	COST CONTROL	30.0 %	4.0		
24.	PERFORMANCE RISK (COMPOSITE)		4.7	1,731,634	81,387
25.	CONTRACT TYPE RISK		3.5	1,731,634	60,607

		COSTS FINANCED	LENGTH FACTOR	INTEREST RATE	
26.	WORKING CAPITAL	500,000	.65	6.375 %	20,719

	CONTRACTOR FACILITIES CAPITAL EMPLOYED	ASSIGNED VALUE	AMOUNT EMPLOYED	
27.	LAND		5,629	
28.	BUILDINGS	11	111,062	12,217
29.	EQUIPMENT	37	370,599	137,122
30.	TOTAL PROFIT OBJECTIVE			312,052

NEGOTIATION SUMMARY

		PROPOSED	OBJECTIVE	NEGOTIATED
31.	TOTAL COSTS	2,000,000		
32.	FACILITIES CAPITAL COST OF MONEY (DD Form 1861)	27,867		
33.	PROFIT	312,052		
34.	TOTAL PRICE (Line 31 + 32 + 33)	2,339,919		
35.	MARKUP RATE (Line 32 + 33 divided by 31)	17.00 %	%	%

CONTRACTING OFFICER APPROVAL

36. TYPED / PRINTED NAME OF CONTRACTING OFFICER (Last, First, Middle Initial)	37. SIGNATURE OF CONTRACTING OFFICER	38. TELEPHONE NO.	39. DATE SUBMITTED (YYMMDD)

OPTIONAL USE

96.	97.	98.	99.

J61051
10-08-96 **DD Form 1547, AUG 87**   *Previous editions are obsolete.*   184/259

Appendix 4.2   DD Form 1547, Record of Weighted Guidelines Application

CONTRACT FACILITIES CAPITAL COST OF MONEY

Form Approved
OMB No. 0704-0267
Expires Feb 28, 1995

Public reporting burden for this collection of information is estimated to average 10 hours per response, including the time for reviewing instructions, searching existing data sources, gathering and maintaining the data needed, and completing and reviewing the collection of information. Send comments regarding this burden estimate or any other aspect of this collection of information, including suggestions for reducing this burden, to Washington Headquarters Services, Directorate for Information Operations and Reports, 1215 Jefferson Davis Highway, Suite 1204, Arlington, VA 22202-4302, and to the Office of Management and Budget, Paperwork Reduction Report (0704-0267), Washington, DC 20503.

PLEASE DO NOT RETURN YOUR COMPLETED FORM TO EITHER OF THESE ADDRESSES.
RETURN COMPLETED FORM TO YOUR CONTRACTING OFFICIAL.

1. CONTRACTOR NAME	2. CONTRACTOR ADDRESS
3. BUSINESS UNIT	
4. RFP / CONTRACT PIIN NUMBER	5. PERFORMANCE RECORD July 1, 1996 - June 30, 1998

6. DISTRIBUTION OF FACILITIES CAPITAL COST OF MONEY

POOL a.	ALLOCATION BASE b.	FACILITIES CAPITAL COST OF MONEY c.	
		FACTOR (1)	AMOUNT (2)
FY 1997 Manufacturing	316,502	.03764	11,913
Offsite	41,024	.00747	306
Field	5,632	.00033	2
G&A	869,565	.00271	2,357
FY 1988 Manufacturing	308,202	.03562	10,978
Offsite	42,745	.00800	342
Field	7,603	.00034	3
G&A	862,069	.00228	1,966
d. TOTAL			27,867
e. TREASURY RATE			6.375 %
f. FACILITIES CAPITAL EMPLOYED (TOTAL DIVIDED BY TREASURY RATE)			437,129

7. DISTRIBUTION OF FACILITIES CAPITAL EMPLOYED

	PERCENTAGE a.	AMOUNT b.
(1) LAND	1.25 %	5,464
(2) BUILDINGS	24.57 %	107,403
(3) EQUIPMENT	74.18 %	324,262
(4) FACILITIES CAPITAL EMPLOYED	100%	437,129

J61078
10-08-96 **DD Form 1861, MAR 93**   *PREVIOUS EDITION IS OBSOLETE*

Appendix 4.3 DD Form 1861, Contract Facilities Cost of Money

FORM CASB-CMF

FACILITIES CAPITAL
COST OF MONEY FACTORS COMPUTATION

Contractor:
Business Unit:

Address:

COST ACCOUNTING PERIOD: FY 1997		1. Applicable Cost of Money Rate 6.375 %	2. Accumulation & Direct Distribution of N.B.V.	3. Allocation of Undistributed	4. Total Net Book Value	5. Cost of Money for the Cost Accounting Period	6. Allocation Base for the Period	7. Facilities Capital Cost of Money Factors
				Basis of Allocation	Columns 2 + 3	Columns 1 x 4	In Unit(s) of Measure	Columns 5 ÷ 6
BUSINESS UNIT FACILITIES CAPITAL	Recorded		13,132,510					
	Leased Property		350,750					
	Corporate or Group		450,000					
	Total		13,933,260					
	Undistributed		194,150					
	Distributed		13,739,110					
OVERHEAD POOLS	Manufacturing		11,275,110	194,150	11,469,260	731,165	19,425,000	.03764
	Offsite		287,060		287,060	18,300	2,450,000	.00747
	Field		1,800		1,800	115	350,000	.00033
G&A EXPENSE POOLS	G&A Expense		2,175,140		2,175,140	138,665	51,216,500	.00271
TOTAL			13,739,110	194,150	13,933,260	888,245	///////	///////

Appendix 4.4 Facilities Capital Cost of Money Factors Computation, Form CASB-CMF.

94

FORM CASB-CMF

FACILITIES CAPITAL
COST OF MONEY FACTORS COMPUTATION

Contractor:
Business Unit:

Address:

COST ACCOUNTING PERIOD: FY 1998

		1. Applicable Cost of Money Rate 6.375 %	2. Accumulation & Direct Distribution of N.B.V.	3. Allocation of Undistributed — Basis of Allocation	4. Total Net Book Value — Columns 2 + 3	5. Cost of Money for the Cost Accounting Period — Columns 1 x 4	6. Allocation Base for the Period — In Unit(s) of Measure	7. Facilities Capital Cost of Money Factors — Columns 5 ÷ 6
BUSINESS UNIT FACILITIES CAPITAL	Recorded		13,484,660					
	Leased Property		350,750					
	Corporate or Group		450,000					
	Total		14,285,410					
	Undistributed		194,150	194,150				
	Distributed		14,091,260					
OVERHEAD POOLS	Manufacturing		11,720,920	194,150	11,915,070	759,586	21,325,000	.03562
	Offsite		327,650		327,650	20,888	2,610,000	.00800
	Field		1,880		1,880	120	350,000	.00034
G&A EXPENSE POOLS	G &A Expense		2,040,810		2,040,810	130,102	56,975,000	.00228
TOTAL			14,091,260	194,150	14,285,410	910,695	///////	///////

Appendix 4.5 Facilities Capital Cost of Money Factors Computation, Form CASB-CMF.

Chapter Five

Defective Pricing

5-1. REQUIREMENTS OF THE TRUTH IN NEGOTIATIONS ACT

Since 1948, defense contractors have been required to submit cost or pricing data for negotiating government contracts. The regulations were later strengthened to require certificates of current pricing for certain negotiated procurements and to give the government the right to reduce a contract price if cost or pricing data proved defective. Continued congressional concern led to the 1962 enactment of the Truth in Negotiations Act,[1] which included requirements for a new certificate and a defective pricing data clause. A new contract clause also provided a right of audit, after contract award, to determine the accuracy, completeness, and currency of the cost or pricing data that formed the basis of the contractor's proposal.[2] The Federal Procurement Regulation (FPR) was subsequently amended to make these requirements applicable to all government agencies, and the requirements were later incorporated into Federal Acquisition Regulation (FAR), Subpart 15.8. With the FAR Part 15 rewrite, effective October 10, 1997, these requirements were moved to FAR Subpart 15.4.

Although the Truth in Negotiations Act (TINA) has been amended on numerous occasions, the underlying requirement has remained unchanged. The act initially required submission of cost or pricing data used to support a proposal for any negotiated contract or subcontract over $100,000, with certain exceptions. The threshold for requiring cost or pricing data was raised from $100,000 to $500,000 in 1981,[3] but reverted back to $100,000 with the enactment of the Competition in Contracting Act,[4] effective April 1, 1985. The threshold was raised back again to $500,000, effective for all prime contract awards by the Department of Defense (DOD), the National Aeronautics and Space Administration (NASA), and the Coast Guard after December 5, 1990.[5] The $500,000 threshold was extended to subcontracts and modifications awarded after December 5, 1991, under DOD, NASA, or Coast Guard prime contracts, provided that the prime contractor requested modification of its contract to incorporate the higher threshold.[6] The threshold was re-established at $500,000 on a government-wide basis with the passage of the Federal Acquisition Streamlining Act (FASA) 1994.[7]

The contractor must certify that the submitted or disclosed data are accurate, current, and complete as of the date of the price agreement. A clause included in the negotiated contract or subcontract provides for a downward price adjustment if the negotiated price was increased because of submission of incomplete, inaccurate, or noncurrent cost or pricing data. An additional price reduction clause is included in both sealed-bid and negotiated contracts over $500,000 for contract modifications in excess of $500,000. Prime contractors who are required to submit certified cost or pricing data must also obtain certified cost or pricing data from prospective subcontractors in support of each subcontract estimate over $500,000 that is not otherwise exempt from the TINA.

The TINA also applies to modifications of negotiated and advertised contracts for other than the acquisition of commercial items, contract termination actions, and price adjustments under cost accounting standards where any of these actions exceed $500,000.

Forward pricing rate agreements do not require certification that the data are current, accurate, and complete when the rates are agreed upon. The certificate ultimately signed for the contract negotiation covers the data submitted in connection with the rates negotiation. Consequently, forward pricing rates may require updating prior to finalizing individual contract negotiations, even though formal forward pricing rate agreements are in place.

The $500,000 limitation applicable to a contract modification is not the net contract modification cost but is based on additive and deductive costs aggregating $500,000 or more. For example, the requirement applies to a $40,000 modification resulting from a reduction of $300,000 and an increase of $340,000. It could also apply to a no-cost modification, such as when the modification results from an increase of $600,000 offset by a decrease of $600,000.

Except where an exception applies, the contracting officer may request cost or pricing data for pricing actions over the streamlined acquisition threshold when it is considered necessary to establish a fair and reasonable price, despite the statutory $500,000 threshold for submitting cost or pricing data.

5-2. EXCEPTIONS FROM SUBMISSION OF COST OR PRICING DATA

Prior to October 1, 1995, based on the discretionary language in the statute and FAR 15.804-3(b)(2), 15.804-3(c)(8), and 15.804-6(e) contracting officers (COs) and prime contractors often asked for cost or pricing data when the criteria for adequate price competition or established catalog or market pricing were met, even though unnecessary requests for cost or pricing data were clearly discouraged. The Armed Services Board of Contract Appeals (ASBCA) concluded the following in *Sperry Flight Systems*:[8]

> ... [T]he determination as to whether to accept the catalog price or to undertake negotiations enlightened by cost data from appellant was within the discretion of the Administrative Contracting Officer (ACO), pursuant with his fundamental duty to secure a fair and reasonable price for the supplies ... The statute clearly states only that the contracting officer "need not" secure certified cost or pricing data where the price is based on established catalog prices, etc., not that he cannot or should not. The regulatory guidelines also fall short of unequivocally forbidding a contracting officer from demanding cost data for catalog-priced items. Rather, they stress the necessity for the contracting officer's judgment and analysis on a case-by-case basis (ASPR 3-807.1(b)(2)) ....

A May 29, 1992, memorandum issued by the Director of Defense Procurement discouraged requests for submission of cost or pricing when exemptions were available.

> Contracting officers shall not require the submission or certification of cost or pricing data when contract price is based on adequate price competition, based on established catalog or market prices of commercial items sold in substantial quantities to the general public, or set by law or regulation. This policy applies to subcontracts as well as prime contracts, and contracting officers should not require a prime contractor to obtain cost or pricing data from a subcontractor that qualifies for an exemption. This policy may also apply to a portion of a contract or subcontract when, for example, a contractor will provide both an item that qualifies for a catalog exemption and a service that does not qualify for an exemption. If the portion of the contract that does not qualify for the exemption exceeds the threshold for submission of cost or pricing data (currently $500,000), cost or pricing data should be obtained for that portion of the contract only.[9]

Issuance of this memorandum did little, however, to stem the tide of unnecessary requests for submission of cost or pricing data. Statutory revisions to the TINA, enacted with the FASA, would be required to accomplish that.

With the implementation of the FASA and the Clinger–Cohen Act of 1996[10] into FAR 15.403-1, the exceptions to the requirement for submission of cost or pricing data are as follows:

- Adequate price competition
- Prices set by law or regulation
- Acquisitions of commercial items
- Waivers granted by the head of the contracting activity in exceptional cases
- Modifications to contracts or subcontracts that do not change the commercial nature of the item acquired and that were awarded either on the basis of adequate price competition, prices set by law or regulation, or the acquisition of a commercial item

Former FAR 15.804-1 (now FAR 15.403-1) was revised on October 1, 1995, to prohibit the request for cost or pricing data when the CO determines that the criterion for an exception has been met. However, a new category of data called "information other than cost or pricing data" may be required to support a determination of price reasonableness or cost realism. Such data is not subject to certification.

Adequate Price Competition

Prior to enactment of the FASA, price competition was presumed to exist [FAR 15.805-3(a)] if at least two responsible offerors, competing independently, submitted priced offers responsive to the solicitation's express requirements, and a contract was to be awarded to the responsive and responsible offeror submitting the lowest evaluated price. Under such conditions, the CO was to determine that price competition was adequate and exempt the offerors from submission of cost or pricing data unless:

- The solicitation was made under conditions that unreasonably denied to one or more known and qualified offerors an opportunity to compete.
- The low competitor had such a determinative advantage over other competitors that it was essentially immune to the stimulus of competition in proposing a price.
- The CO made a written finding, supported by the facts, that the lowest price was not reasonable, and the finding was approved at a level above the CO.

A price was assumed to be based on adequate price competition if it resulted directly from such competition or if price analysis (not cost analysis) showed clearly that the price was reasonable in comparison with current or recent prices of the same or substantially the same items procured in comparable quantities under contracts awarded with adequate competition.

Under *Libby Welding Company, Inc.*,[11] the ASBCA concluded that if the submitted price was based on adequate price competition, the CO was prohibited from requesting cost or pricing data, let alone requiring certification of its accuracy, completeness, and currency. This situation also was addressed in *Sperry Flight Systems, Division of Sperry Rand Corp.*[12] in which the ASBCA, while addressing a separate point, stated, "That the ASPR authors know how unequivocally to forbid contracting officers from requesting cost or pricing data is shown by the admonition that: 'Where there is adequate price competition, cost or pricing data shall not be requested regardless of the dollar amount involved.'"

The DOD strengthened the regulatory exemption language in September 1989 with the following revision to Defense FAR Supplement (DFARS) 215.804-3(a)(1)(i):

> Where there is a reasonable expectation that adequate price competition will result in a particular procurement, the contracting officer should rarely have a need to require the submission or certification of cost or pricing data regardless of the type of contract. Unnecessarily requiring the submission of cost or pricing data is not in the best interest of the government because it leads to increased proposal preparation costs, extends procurement lead time and wastes both contractor and government resources.

However, neither prior case law nor the DFARS revision effectively reduced requests for submission of cost or pricing data. True reform came with the enactment of the FASA.

To implement the FASA, FAR 15.804-1(b)(1) was revised effective October 1, 1995, to expand the exception to the requirement to submit cost or pricing data by establishing a presumption of adequate price competition if

- at least two offerors compete for an award to be made to a responsible offeror whose proposal offers either (1) the greatest value to the government and price is a substantial factor in source selection, or (2) the lowest evaluated price; or

- only one offer was received but there was a reasonable expectation that two or more responsible offerors would compete for the award.

A 1987 Deputy Assistant Secretary of Defense for Procurement policy memorandum[13] emphasized that the "lowest evaluated price" does not mean "lowest price" and that adequate price competition can exist when an award is made to other than the lowest offeror, provided price was a significant factor in the evaluation criteria. The memorandum concluded that adequate price competition can exist even if price constitutes only 20% of the overall evaluation factor for the procurement. Comptroller General decisions have also concluded that price competition exists as long as "more than one offeror is within the competitive range and price is a substantial though not necessarily determinative factor in the prescribed evaluation criteria."[14]

Although awards based on adequate price competition are excepted from the requirement to submit cost or pricing data, additional information may be requested to determine price reasonableness or cost realism.

Commercial Items

Prior to enactment of the Clinger–Cohen Act of 1996, a proposal for the acquisition of commercial products or services could be excepted from the submission of cost or pricing data on the basis of either (1) established catalog or market prices of commercial items sold in substantial quantities to the general public or (2) acquisitions of commercial items. This second exception could be used only if the CO didn't have sufficient information to support an exception based on adequate price competition, established catalog or market prices of items sold in substantial quantities to the general public, or prices set by law or regulation. Not surprisingly, the existence of two separate and distinct exceptions relating to commercial items caused considerable confusion. These terms were defined as follows:

- An *established catalog price* was a price included in a catalog, price list, schedule, or other form that (1) was regularly maintained by the manufacturer or vendor, (2) was published or otherwise available for inspection by customers, and (3) stated current sales prices.

- An *established market price* was a current price established in the usual and ordinary course of trade between buyers and sellers free to bargain, which could be substantiated from sources independent of the manufacturer or vendor.

- A *commercial item* was an item that included both supplies and services of a class or kind that was (1) regularly used for other than government purposes and (2) sold or traded to the general public in normal business operations.

- *Substantial quantity* was not precisely defined. Prior to the enactment of FASA, FAR 15.804-3(f)(2), addressed three categories of sales: category A, sales to the U.S. government or to contractors for U.S. government use; category B, sales to the general public at catalog prices; and category C, sales to the general public at other than catalog prices. Sales to the public were considered substantial if: Categories B and C were not negligible in themselves and totaled 55% or more of the total category A, B, and C sales; and Category B sales totaled 75% or more of the total of category B and C sales. If category B and C sales totals were less than 35% of the total category A, B, and C sales, and if category B sales were less than 55% of the total of category B and C sales, the CO would rarely grant an exemption. When percentages fell between those stated, the CO was encouraged to perform an analysis before granting an exemption. The exemption was claimed on Standard Form 1412, Claim for Exemption from Submission of Certified Cost or Pricing Data. The FASA eliminated Standard Form 1412, as well as the requirement to identify the three categories of sales. Thus, a relational test is no longer applicable.

Clinger–Cohen eliminated the definitions relating to "established catalog or market price of commercial items sold in substantial quantities to the general public" and combined the two exceptions that relate to commercial items. A commercial item is now broadly defined to include the following:

- Any item, other than real property, that is of a type that is customarily used commercially and that has been sold, leased, or licensed, or offered for sale, lease, or license to the general public. Items being developed, but not yet available in the commercial marketplace, can be considered commercial items if they will be available in time to satisfy delivery requirements under a government contract

- An otherwise commercial item with modifications customarily available in the commercial marketplace, or with minor modifications made to meet federal government requirements
- A combination of items otherwise meeting the requirements or items that are customarily combined and sold in combinations to the general public
- Installation services, maintenance services, repair services, training services, and other services for commercial items, provided the following two criteria are met:
  - The services are offered to the general public and the government contemporaneously and under similar terms and conditions.
  - The same workforce provides the services to the general public and the government.
- Services offered and sold competitively in substantial quantities in the commercial marketplace based on established catalog or market prices for specific tasks performed and under standard commercial terms and conditions
- Any item, combination of items, or service, of a type referred to above, that is transferred between or among separate divisions, subsidiaries, or affiliates of a government contractor
- A nondevelopmental item that was developed exclusively at private expense and sold in substantial quantities on a competitive basis to multiple state and local governments. A nondevelopmental item includes the following:
  - Any item that is used by the federal government, a state or local government, or a foreign government with which the United States has a mutual defense cooperation agreement
  - Any item described above that requires minor modification or modification customarily available in the commercial marketplace to meet the requirements of the procuring agency
  - Any item being produced that does not otherwise meet the requirements solely because the item is not yet in use

The exception from the requirement to submit cost or pricing data extends to any modification of a commercial item that does not change the item from a commercial item to a noncommercial item.

Information relating to the prices at which the same or similar commercial items have previously been sold may be requested to enable the contracting office to determine the reasonableness of the proposed price.

The FASA and Clinger–Cohen provisions were implemented in FAR, effective October 1, 1995, and January 2, 1997, respectively.

Waivers by Agency Heads

FAR 15-403-1(b)(4) permits the agency head to grant a waiver to a company from the requirement to submit cost or pricing data in exceptional cases. While the regulation does not provide guidance on what circumstances qualify as exceptional, FAR 15.403-1(c)(3) now authorizes COs to consider a waiver if sufficient information is available to determine price reasonableness. Prior to enactment of the FASA, waivers were generally granted only to firms with unique products that the government required. Because such firms had no other government contracts requiring submission of cost or pricing data, they typically did not have accounting or estimating systems that met government requirements and were unwilling to establish them for such a minor portion of their total business volume. The waiver must be in writing and must include the reasons for granting it. Granting a waiver to a prime contractor or higher-tier subcontractor does not exempt lower-tier subcontractors from the requirement to submit cost or pricing data unless the waiver explicitly includes the subcontracts.

5-3. COST OR PRICING DATA

Definition

If one of the exceptions is not met, the critical question becomes: What are cost or pricing data that must be disclosed? FAR 15.401 defines cost or pricing data as follows:

> ... all facts that, as of the date of price agreement ... prudent buyers and sellers would reasonably expect to affect price negotiations significantly. Cost or pricing data are data requiring certification in accordance with 15.406-20. Cost or pricing data are factual, not judgmental, and are verifiable. While they do not indicate the accuracy of the prospective contractor's judgment about estimated future costs or projections, they do include the data forming the basis for that judgment. Cost or pricing data are more than historical accounting data; they are all the facts that can be reasonably expected to contribute to the soundness of estimates of future costs and to the validity of determinations of costs already incurred. They also include such factors as vendor quotations; nonrecurring costs; information on changes in production methods and in production or purchasing volume; data supporting projections of business prospects and objectives and related operations costs; unit-cost trends such as those associated with labor efficiency; make-or-buy decisions; estimated resources to attain business goals; and information on management decisions that could have a significant bearing on costs.

In *FMC Corp.*,[15] the ASBCA adopted the then substantially similar version of ASPR "as a reasonable definition of 'cost or pricing data' in the context of the clauses relating to price competition for defective pricing in the subject contracts."

Attempts to clarify the meaning of data and to distinguish fact from judgment have not been wholly successful, and disputes have continued to arise over these terms. The 1987 TINA amendments[16] attempted to clarify the definition of cost or pricing data by expressly acknowledging that cost or pricing data included the factual information from which a judgment was derived, but not the judgmental information itself. The Conference Report accompanying the 1987 TINA amendments also included the following comments:

> The conferees were very concerned with clarifying the definition of cost or pricing data that a contractor is not required to provide and certify to data relating to judgments, business strategies, plans for the future or estimates. A contractor is required, on the other hand, to disclose any information relating to execution or implementation of any such strategies or plans. For example, a corporate decision to attempt to negotiate a new labor rate structure with its employee union, although verifiable, is not cost or pricing data for purposes of this section. If the company has made an offer to the union, the fact than an offer has been made, and the details and status of the offer, on the other hand, is information that should be conveyed to the government.

Largely as a result of criticism from the government procurement community, the Conference Report accompanying the 1988 TINA amendments[17] effectively reversed the comments quoted above from the 1987 Conference Report by adding the following additional clarification:

The conferees acknowledge that such "cost or pricing data" must in some instances include information that would be considered judgmental. Although "cost or pricing data" do not indicate the accuracy of the contractor's judgment about estimated future costs or projections, they do include the data forming the basis for that judgment. The factual data underlying judgments have been and should remain subject to disclosure. Furthermore, "cost or pricing data" may include facts and data so intertwined with judgments that the judgments must be disclosed in order to make the facts or data meaningful. As such, the conferees believe that a contractor should disclose a decision to act on judgmental data, even though it has not been implemented. As currently provided in the regulations, when a contractor is required to disclose judgmental information, the certification should not be taken to mean that the judgment is correct, only that the contractor has accurately and completely disclosed its current estimate.

In April 1993, the DOD Inspector General issued *The Truth in Negotiations Act Handbook*[18] as a reference guide for government personnel. Included in the *Handbook* is the following list of 13 "Examples of Potential Defective Cost of Pricing Data":

1. Operating budget plan usually involving indirect costs which contain data that are different from the data in the proposal to the Government

2. Labor hour standards not current. Defective pricing can occur when new standards exist and are not disclosed or more current data from which the standards are computed are not disclosed

3. Labor hour estimates, other than estimates based on pure judgment, not complete, not current, or not accurate

4. Valuation of contractor inventory erroneously computed or latest valuation not reflected in contractor's proposal

5. Contractor pricing personnel or negotiator's failure to follow contractor internal pricing policy or estimating and/or purchasing manual instructions and updates.

6. Quantity errors in required material and parts caused by co-production buys or failure to read current specification drawings correctly or use of obsolete drawings

7. Contractor failure to reveal evaluation of vendor or subcontractor quotes and failure to reveal changes to the contractor evaluations

8. Contractor nondisclosure of production or program directives affecting current and future business volumes and changes which affect overhead and general and administration rates

9. Canceled purchase order not disclosed to the Government

10. Duplication of costs included in contractor's proposals

11. Change in make or buy decisions by prime contractor or subcontractor not disclosed (may be related to new or revised manufacturing processes not disclosed)

12. Contractor distortion of time periods, especially for labor hours, when computing averages for purpose of proposal to Government

13. Contractor failure to disclose vendor quotes, voluntarily reduced at request of prime

In *Texas Instruments, Inc.*[19] the ASBCA addressed the issue of disclosing factual information that had elements of judgment involved. Essentially, the Board concluded that judgments must be disclosed when they are critical to understanding the factual data. Thus, while the accuracy of judgments is not certified, disclosure of judgmental information may be required.

Numerous defective pricing disputes have arisen over the issue of undisclosed vendor quotes.

- The ASBCA concluded in *Cutler–Hammer, Inc.*[20] that failure to disclose an unsolicited vendor quote constituted defective pricing. Cutler–Hammer's proposed material costs included a vendor quote from a company that had produced the item in the past. After receiving the unsolicited proposal from another company for a much lower price, Cutler–Hammer requested technical data which were finally received just two days before Cutler–Hammer signed the certificate of current cost or pricing data. Although the company's technical people apparently were examining these technical data, the official signing the certificate had no knowledge of these developments and the bid was not disclosed to the government. After the prime contract was awarded, Cutler–Hammer continued negotiations and discussions with the new vendor; issued a purchase order for a limited quantity; and, as the product proved satisfactory, issued additional purchase orders. Although the ASBCA conceded that the lower vendor bid was far from representing data on which a firm price reduction could have been made by the government, it conjectured that, had this information been disclosed, the government might have excluded the item from the contract price, reserving it for further negotiation.

- The ASBCA later tempered this decision in *Sparton Corp., Sparton Electronics Division,*[21] when it stated the following:

  > In our opinion, unless specifically asked to do so under the contract clause in this case, a prospective contractor is not required to list each and every quote received from prospective vendors whose responsibility had not previously been evaluated and where the quote concerns a part deemed to be critical.... In our opinion, under the facts stated, the Government does not prove its case unless it shows that the contractor, at the time the data is submitted, did not intend to deal with the vendor listed, but did intend to do business with the lower cost vendor.

- Since that time, the ASBCA has issued decisions that reflect a middle ground between the above positions. The ASBCA ruled that Aerojet General Corp.[22] was liable for defective pricing because it did not submit or disclose a nonresponsive vendor quotation. The Board reasoned that

  > ... [A] non-responsive quotation may not always be so meaningless or unreliable that no prudent buyers and sellers would reasonably expect the quotation to have a significant effect on the price negotiations. Under certain conditions, the quotation can have a significant impact on the negotiation and thus would become cost or pricing data which must be disclosed to the government.

- The ASBCA ruled in *EDO Corp.*[23] that the government was entitled to a price reduction for defective pricing because EDO was unable to document that it disclosed to the government a reduced price quotation from its prospective second-tier subcontractor.

The issue of subcontract cost/price analyses has also been the subject of dispute.

- The ASBCA concluded in *Aerojet General Corp.*[24] that disclosure of subcontract cost analyses was required when such analyses contained underlying factual data that prudent buyers and sellers would reasonably expect to have a significant effect on price negotiation.

- In *Grumman Aerospace Corp.*,[25] the ASBCA ruled that disclosure of a subcontract cost analysis report was required because

    > ... [T]he narrative analysis adds meaning to the raw figures and cannot be said to lack factual content simply because it contains elements of judgment. We therefore conclude that the nature of a Cost Analysis Report, including both its narrative analysis and statistical data, is said as to constitute "fact" to be disclosed as cost and pricing data.

While defective pricing issues related to the pricing of direct labor occur less frequently than those related to the pricing of material costs, disputes also occur in this area.

- The ASBCA concluded in *Litton Systems, Inc., Amecom Division*,[26] that an estimated standard labor hours report was not cost or pricing data because it was merely "an accumulation of estimates and judgments of appellant's standard labor hours." The ASBCA noted that the report contained only judgments, not a mixture of facts and judgments.

- The government raised two defective pricing issues in *Aerojet Ordnance Tennessee* (AOT)[27] related to an alleged overstatement of manufacturing hours: nondisclosure of various reports generated under AOT's internal operating control (IOC) systems and failure to provide any allowance for improvement: the learning process even though it was apparent. With regard to learning curves, the Board noted: "Learning curves may be important estimating tools. Nevertheless, even if a learning curve indicates that a curve can be fitted to the data with some degree of confidence, the parties' conduct during the negotiation can rule out its use." Testimony at the hearing clearly showed that the CO did not like to use formal learning curves and that "prior to agreement on price no one from the Government suggested that the negotiation strategy should be built around the use of learning curves, although everyone on the government side recognized that learning was occurring." As a result, the Board concluded that measuring the extent of defective pricing through the use of learning curves was not justified. With regard to the IOC reports, the Board concluded that the IOC labor actuals could be traced to the accounting records but that the government would have looked to the accounting records to rationalize any differences between the IOC report actuals and accounting actuals. Thus, the government did not demonstrate that the parties would have relied on the IOC reports in negotiating manufacturing labor.

- In *Rosemont, Inc.*[28] the government asserted that the proposed labor hours were defectively priced because the contractor failed to project the hours on the basis of a learning curve. Rosemont's proposed labor hours were based on monthly closed job order reports. The Defense Contract Audit Agency (DCAA) preaward audit report concluded that the proposed hours were reasonable. The defective pricing audit was performed by auditors from the Department of Defense Office of the Inspector General (DODIG). The DODIG auditors, using the same data reviewed by the DCAA preaward auditors, plotted a learning curve and calculated an alleged overstatement. In concluding that Rosemont had not failed to disclose any underlying factual data, the Board noted: "[I]t is clear a contractor does not have to either use the cost information or analyze it for the Government, but rather must only submit it so the Government can make its own analysis." The Board further cautioned that "[c]are must be taken to tie the assessment to a consideration of the parties' actions at the time and to avoid imposing an after-the-fact perspective on how the negotiations could have been conducted to produce improved results from the Government's perspective."

Issues relating to the disclosure of indirect cost rate information have occasionally been the subject of dispute. The ASBCA addressed the currency, completeness, and accuracy of general and administrative (G&A) expense rate data disclosed by Motorola's subcontractor, Aydin Computer Systems Division.[29] Aydin exercised its right to disclose indirect cost rate information solely to DCAA, rather than to Motorola, one of its competitors. The ASBCA concluded that Aydin properly disclosed its current historical G&A expense rate to the DCAA auditor who provided a report to the government procurement office that handled the negotiation of Motorola's contract modification. Aydin failed to disclose, however, that its historical G&A expense rate reflected an unallowable imputed interest charge assess by the Aydin corporate office. That portion of the G&A expense rate represented by the unallowable imputed interest change was found to have been defectively priced.

Numerous decisions have focused on the disclosure of management decisions.

- A key issue arises as to when a decision has actually been made. The ASBCA denial of Grumman Aerospace Corporation's motion for summary judgment relating to disclosure of its subcontract cost analysis report indicates that a decision may have been made even though the formal decision-making process has not yet been completed. The decision stated the following:

  > The fact that Grumman management did not formally approve the [cost analysis report] approach until after the agreement on price is not necessarily determinative of when that decision might have been reached *informally* or should have been recognized as *sufficiently likely* to have required full disclosure to the Navy.[30]

- The *Grumman* decision is distinguishable from *Lockheed Corp.*,[31] in which the ASBCA denied the government's claim that goals established by Lockheed Corporation's human resources organizations to negotiate a new labor wage structure with its union constituted a management decision. The Board noted that a management decision should occur "at a level of management which has the authority actually to approve or disapprove actions affecting the cost element." The Board concluded that only Lockheed's senior management—not the human resources organizations—had such authority, and the government failed to prove that senior management had approved the plan.

- In *Aerojet Ordnance Tennessee*,[32] the Board ruled that the company had failed to disclose a key management decision as to how hazardous waste would be disposed of. For the instant contract, AOT proposed to transport its hazardous waste to Richland, Washington, rather than to Barnwell, North Carolina, because the contract would generate higher levels of waste than its monthly cubic feet allotment at Barnwell. However, AOT failed to disclose its intention to temporarily hold the waste in inventory at its own facility until the lower-cost storage space became available in Barnwell.

Another defective pricing decision addressed the requirement to disclose a pending cost accounting practice change. In definitizing the restructure modification on October 31, 1985, for full-scale engineering development of the C17 aircraft, Douglas Aircraft Company (DAC), subsidiary of McDonnell Douglas

Corporation,[33] utilized the accounting practices disclosed in its then-current Cost Accounting Standards (CAS) disclosure statement. On November 1, 1985, DAC notified its ACO, pursuant to the CAS administration clause, that it intended to make several significant cost accounting practice changes effective January 1, 1986. The ACO was not apprised that the C17 negotiation was completed the previous day. Douglas Aircraft executed its Certificate of Current Cost or Pricing Data on November 15, 1986. The government ultimately concluded that DAC's failure to disclose its decision to change its cost accounting practice constituted defective pricing and calculated an alleged overpricing in the amount of $9 million. Douglas Aircraft's motion for summary judgment argued that (1) the planned cost accounting practice change did not constitute cost or pricing because the changes had not occurred, and (2) DAC had no choice, pursuant to CAS 401, to estimate in accordance with its practices for accumulating costs. With regard to these arguments, the Board noted the following:

> Whether Douglas was required, or even permitted, to reprice its proposal for the restructure modification to reflect its planned cost accounting practice changes is not at issue. The only relevant question is whether, prior to reaching agreement on the price ... , verifiable facts about the planned accounting changes "reasonably could be expected to have a significant bearing on costs under" that contract and "to contribute to sound estimates of future costs." ... [T]he gravamen of the claim here is that Douglas submitted and certified (incomplete and inaccurate) cost or pricing data because it failed to disclose verifiable facts about its planned accounting changes, which prudent buyers and sellers would reasonably expect to have a significant effect on price negotiations and that such defective data caused the price of modification P00044 to be increased by significant sums.

The Board concluded that the facts going to the defectiveness of the data Douglas submitted were in dispute and remained to be proved. Consequently, DAC's motion for summary judgment was denied.

The meaning of the term "significant" in the phrase "which prudent buyers and sellers would reasonably expect to have a significant effect on the price negotiations" was addressed in an ASBCA decision involving Sylvania Electric Products, Inc., which was upheld by the Court of Claims.[34] Sylvania argued that, although it did not make specific disclosure that its proposed material costs were in error, documents that were furnished should have enabled the government to discover errors in the material cost breakdown. The ASBCA concluded that the contractor's disclosures were inadequate. In its decision, it noted the following:

> It does not suffice to make available or physically hand over for Government inspection files which, if examined, would disclose differences between proposal costs and lower historical costs. It is also necessary, in order to make a disclosure, to advise the Government representatives involved in the proposed procurement, of the kind and content of the cost or pricing data and their bearing on the prospective contractor's proposal which examination of the files would disclose.

The court noted that if the company's argument were to be adopted, the TINA could be easily circumvented; therefore, the term *significant* should relate to effect on negotiation and not to amount.

The ASBCA also addressed the term *significant* in *Kaiser Aerospace and Electronics Corp.*,[35] by ruling as follows:

> Although the amount of overpricing in this appeal which resulted from defective cost data ($5,527.82) might appear to be insignificant compared to the total prices negotiated for the three orders ($2,754,581), constituting only two-tenths of one percent, thereof, we nevertheless are bound by the decision in Conrac Corporation v. United States, supra, which declined to hold that the statutory provision requiring refund of "significant" sums vests in a contractor a right to

retain amounts earned through supplying defective price data to the government. Consequently, the government is entitled to a refund of $5,527.82.

From this decision, it appears that the government may impose a contract price reduction for virtually any amount attributable to noncompliance with the TINA.

Data Submission

A contractor is expected to disclose existing verifiable data, judgmental factors used to project from known data to the estimate, and contingencies included in the proposed price. In short, the contractor's estimating process itself must be disclosed. Any doubt about whether information should be submitted should be resolved in favor of submitting it. Merely making data available is not sufficient.

Numerous decisions have established a precedent that was incorporated in the Defense Acquisition Regulation (DAR) and later FAR 15.408, note 1 to Table 15-2.

> There is a clear distinction between submitting cost or pricing data and merely making available books, records and other documents without identification. The requirement for submission of cost or pricing data is met when all accurate cost or pricing data reasonably available to the offeror have been submitted either actually or by specific identification, to the Contracting Officer or an authorized representative.

In *M-R-S Manufacturing Co. v. United States*,[36] the Court of Claims ruled that a company must either physically deliver all accurate, complete, and current pricing information relevant to negotiations or make its significance known to the government. If a contractor does neither, it has not fulfilled its duty under the TINA. The contractor's primary argument before the court was that it actually met its duty to submit accurate, complete, and current cost or pricing data because the auditor who performed the initial price evaluation: (1) received a bill of materials, including all parts and parts numbers; (2) knew previous production runs had been completed; and (3) knew how to obtain all the information in the contractor's files. Because the files included all the data available to the contractor, the obligation to submit current, accurate, and complete data was fulfilled, according to the contractor. The court concluded, however, that if the contractor possesses information relevant to contract negotiations and neither physically delivers the data to the government nor makes the government aware of the information's significance to the negotiation process, "then he has not fulfilled his duty under the Act to furnish such information to the government."

In *The Singer Co., Librascope Division*,[37] the contractor was declared to have failed to "submit," even though it did submit the data in question for a purpose other than the pricing proposal involved. The ASBCA said that even physically handing over data to the government may not suffice because "it is also necessary to advise the Government representatives involved in the proposed procurement of the kind and content of the cost or pricing data and their bearing on the prospective contractor's proposal which examination of the files would disclose."

While these rulings would appear to place a substantial obligation on the contractor to specifically identify each significant item affecting price negotiations, the ASBCA has ruled that there are reasonable limits. *Hardie–Tynes Manufacturing Co.*[38] had submitted a proposal that reflected a quotation from vendor B, although the lowest quote was from vendor C. The latter was not used because of the contractor's substantial doubts about C's ability to make the parts. The government alleged that the lack of disclosure of C's quote represented defective pricing. The DCAA auditor who had initially reviewed the pricing proposal testified that he couldn't recall whether he had seen C's quotation but that he would have noted it if he had. The contractor testified that C's quote was in a separate folder that was furnished to the auditor and that the contractor "adequately submitted that quotation to the auditor." The ASBCA noted the following:

> The [C] quote was not "hidden in a mass of information" but was in a folder containing only two other quotes and three replies indicating "no quote." . . .

> The absence of a notation on the pre-award auditor's work sheets as to why the [C] quote was not being used could indicate a failure of the auditor to realize that the quote was low or a failure in this instance to follow the prescribed policy of making such notations. In any event, the absence of a notation is not conclusive evidence of a nondisclosure. . . .

> Under these particular circumstances, appellant was not obligated to "lead the auditor by the hand" by pointing out to him that [C] quote was low but was not being used for the reasons indicated.

In a postaward audit of a contract awarded to AOT, the DCAA identified numerous lower-priced vendor quotes, invoices, and purchase orders that were not disclosed prior to price agreement. AOT's negotiator advised the CO orally during price negotiations that it was experiencing a "ten percent decline in billet use and a five to ten percent drop in billet price." The ASBCA concluded that these statements were "not at all meaningful when viewed against numerous and detailed quotations. If anything, the generality of the comments is at odds with a meaningful disclosure."[39] The ASBCA ruled that The Boeing Company[40] had met its disclosure requirement when it provided newly negotiated rates to the negotiator with a statement that the rates were lower than those on the proposal being negotiated, even though it did not reprice the proposal. The fact that the government considered the lower rates in evaluating Boeing's best and final offer appeared key to the court's decision. The decision stated, "Thus, the Government negotiators were in possession of all facts necessary to place the Government in a position equal to appellant with respect to making judgments on pricing."

Although the defective pricing clause and the requirements of the law are such that current, accurate, and complete data must be submitted, there is no specific requirement that they be used to determine the negotiated price. In *Dworshak Dam Constructors*,[41] the Army Corps of Engineers Appeals Board stated the following:

> This approach erroneously assumes that the Truth in Negotiations Act dictates that contract prices must be based on the submitted cost or pricing data. The Act does not prescribe that the government adopt a contractor's actual cost in pricing situations. Further, the Act operates in the price area only after certification provisions have not been properly observed and the price to the government inflated thereby.

A dispute involving Hughes Aircraft[42] addressed the creation of pricing documents specifically for government use and proposal updates. The Board noted the following:

> It (appellant) does not have to change its accounting system to specifically develop documents for the Government's own convenience in estimating price. However, it cannot give the Government the second best of what it actually has if to do so would significantly put the Government at a disadvantage vis-a-vis the appellant in estimating price. . . .

> The appellant does not have to "update" its proposal, but it does have to make a meaningful disclosure to put the Government in an essentially equal position for purposes of pricing.

As previously discussed, cost or pricing data are defined as all facts "as of the time of price agreement." FAR 15.406-2(c) addresses the time when cost or pricing data are reasonably available to the contractor as follows:

Closing or cutoff dates should be included as part of the data submitted with the proposal and, before agreement on price, data should be updated by the contractor to the latest closing or cut-off dates for which the data are available. Use of cutoff dates coinciding with reports is acceptable, as certain data may not be reasonably available before normal periodic closing dates (*e.g.*, actual indirect costs). Data within the contractor's or a subcontractor's organization on matters significant to contractor management and to the Government will be treated as reasonably available. What is significant depends upon the circumstances of each acquisition.

The importance of the phrase *contractor's organization* cannot be overemphasized. The contractor's responsibility is not limited by the personal knowledge of the signer of the certificate if the contractor has information reasonably available at the time of agreement showing that the negotiated price is not based on accurate, complete, and current data. The government's interpretation of this requirement is that the signer of the certificate represents the entire company's belief and knowledge as to the accuracy and completeness of the data being certified. This requirement for absolute knowledge on the part of the certificate signer may be lessened somewhat by the provisions of FAR 15.406-2(c), concerning such items as actual indirect costs; however, significant matters are considered to be known to the contractor up to the time of agreement on price and "reasonably available as of that date."

In *American Bosch Arma Corp.*,[43] the cutoff date when cost or pricing data were reasonably available was related to the contractor's recordkeeping system. In determining when the data were "reasonably available," the ASBCA considered the time it took the contractor to properly process information into its records and the time it would have taken the contractor to extract the information from the records for negotiation purposes. However, the ASBCA later ruled in *Sylvania Electric Products*[44] that the contractor's obligations were not reduced by a lack of administrative effort or the subjective lack of knowledge on the part of the negotiating team. In its decision, the ASBCA stated the following:

> ... [T]he entire evidence shows that the gathering of current pricing data by the negotiation team at Mountain View was left to the initiative of its members, essentially its cost estimator, without any procedures within Sylvania other than the useless commitment run to help them assemble this information. Their duty to take the initiative and collect current pricing data on their own was clearly not fulfilled by deciding that none of the items here involved were important enough to require checking. As this Board said in Aerojet General Corporation, ASBCA No. 12264, 69-1 BCA Paragraph 7664, at p. 35,583: "Appellant's obligation to furnish accurate, complete, and current cost and pricing data to the extent that the data are significant and reasonably available cannot be reduced either by the lack of administrative effort to see that all significant data are gathered and furnished by the Government, or by the subjective lack of knowledge of such data on the part of appellant's negotiators or the person who signed the certificate."

Contractor Certification

The effect of a contractor's failure to certify that the data submitted are current, accurate, and complete has changed through case law. In *American Bosch Arma Corp.*,[45] the ASBCA ruled that "the applicability of the price reduction clause does not depend on the existence of a valid and meaningful certificate of current cost or pricing data." The ASBCA reiterated this position in *Lockheed Aircraft Corp.*,[46] when it stated that "the certificate and the clause are not interdependent but are independent and each stands on its own." The ASBCA reversed this position in *Libby Welding Co., Inc.*,[47] by concluding that in the absence of a certificate of current cost or pricing data, the contractor is not liable under the "price reduction for defective cost pricing data" clause in its contract. The board again reversed its position in *S.T. Research Corp.*[48] by ruling that failure to certify cost data did not preclude the government from asserting a defective pricing claim. The Board's conclusion was based on the facts that (1) the defective pricing clause required certification of cost or pricing data, and (2) the statute itself prohibited the submission of defective data.

The ambiguities raised by these conflicting decisions were resolved by the 1987 TINA amendments,[49] which stated that "it is not a defense to an adjustment of the price of a contract . . . that . . . the prime contractor or subcontractor did not submit a certification of cost or pricing data relating to the contract."

When a certificate of current cost or pricing data is required, the CO must obtain an executed certificate in the form specified below and include it in the contract file. (See Figure 5.1.) The contractor certifies that the cost data are accurate, complete, and current as of the date the contract price was agreed to. However, the certificate provides for a delay in the date of executing the certificate as distinguished from the date of agreement. The intervening period should be used to verify that the data submitted were in fact current, accurate, and complete. This process has become known as a "sweep." A delay of a week or two is normally considered reasonable for this purpose.

Companies should be aware that the government may seek to reduce the agreed-to price when additional data found during the sweep are disclosed.

5-4. CONTRACT PRICE ADJUSTMENT

When cost or pricing data are required, the resultant contract contains a Price Reduction for Defective Cost or Pricing Data clause, which is excerpted in Figure 5.2.

This clause gives the government a contractual right to price adjustment plus interest for inaccurate, incomplete, or noncurrent cost or pricing data from

---

This is to certify that, to the best of my knowledge and belief, the cost or pricing data (as defined in Section 15.401 of the Federal Acquisition Regulation [FAR] and required under FAR, Subsection 15.403-4) submitted, either actually or by specific identification in writing to the Contracting Officer or to the Contracting Officer's representative in support of ____[a] are accurate, complete, and current as of ____.[b] This certification includes the cost or pricing data supporting any advance agreements and forward pricing rate agreements between the offeror and the Government that are part of the proposal.

Firm   _____

Name _____

Title   _____

Date of Execution _____[c]

[a]Identify the proposal, quotation, request for price adjustment, or other submission involved, giving the appropriate identifying number (e.g., RFP No. ____).

[b]Insert the date, month, and year when price negotiations were concluded and price agreement was reached, or if applicable, an earlier date agreed upon between the parties that is as close as practicable to the date of agreement on price.

[c]Insert the date, month, and year of signing, which should be as close as practicable to the date when the price negotiations were concluded and the contract price was agreed to.

Figure 5.1 Certificate of Current Cost or Pricing Data.

(a) If any price, including profit or fee, negotiated in connection with this contract, of any cost reimbursable under this contract, was increased by any significant amount because (1) the Contractor or a subcontractor furnished cost or pricing data that were not complete, accurate, and current as certified in its Certificate of Current Cost or Pricing Data; (2) a subcontractor of prospective subcontractor furnished the Contractor cost or pricing data that were not complete, accurate, and current as certified in the Contractor's Certificate of Current Cost or Pricing Data; or (3) any of these parties furnished data of any description that were not accurate, the price or cost shall be reduced accordingly and the contract shall be modified to reflect the reduction.

(b) Any reduction in the contract price under paragraph (a) of this clause due to defective data from a prospective subcontractor that was not subsequently awarded the subcontract shall be limited to the amount, plus applicable overhead and profit markup, by which (1) the actual subcontract or (2) the actual cost to the Contractor, if there was no subcontract, was less than the prospective subcontract cost estimate submitted by the Contractor; *provided* that the actual subcontract price was not itself affected by defective cost or pricing data....

* * * * *

(d) If any reduction in the contract price under this clause reduces the price of items for which payment was made prior to the date of the modification reflecting the price reduction, the Contractor shall be liable to and shall pay the United States at the time such overpayment is repaid—(1) Simple interest on the amount of such overpayment to be computed from the date(s) of overpayment to the Contractor to the date the Government is repaid by the Contractor at the applicable underpayment rate effective for each quarter prescribed by the Secretary of the Treasury under 26 U.S.C. 6621(a)(2); and (2) A penalty equal to the amount of the overpayment, if the Contractor or subcontractor knowingly submitted cost or pricing data which were incomplete, inaccurate, or noncurrent.

Figure 5.2   Excerpt from "Price Reduction for Defective Cost or Pricing Data" Clause, FAR 52.215-10.

either the prime contractor or a prospective or actual subcontractor. An additional penalty equal to the overpayment is assessed against defense contracts if the submission of defective data was deemed to be deliberate.

Because the TINA pertains to the adequacy of data submitted for negotiations, profitability (or lack thereof) on a specific contract is not relevant in computing the downward price adjustment due to defective pricing. If a $1 million fixed-price contract that resulted in a $100,000 loss because of faulty judgments were, in fact, overpriced by $100,000 because of defective data, the government could reduce the contract by $100,000. The net result for the company would be a $200,000 loss.

Baseline of the Price Adjustment

Questions sometimes arise about what baseline should be used to compute the price adjustment. The DCAA's *Contract Audit Manual,*[50] Section 14-116.2a, concludes that the baseline should be the contractor's last proposal before price negotiations began, adjusted for any additional cost or pricing data up to the time of price agreement or disclosure of sweeps data ... for which the contractor addresses its significance on the proposal and submits it to the government." In reality, complete updated proposals are not always submitted, and the government's negotiation record may not always reflect updated data reviewed or concessions achieved on individual cost elements. However, this philosophy reflects conclusions drawn by various boards of contract appeals.[51] In *Sperry Corp. Computer Systems*,[52] the ASBCA departed from this traditional view of the contract baseline. The Board rejected the government's baseline position, which was to use the last DD Form 633 (predecessor to the SF 1411), because it did not reflect negotiated reductions and thus would duplicate concessions made during negotiations, which were completed in February 1981. The court also rejected Sperry's computation of the impact, which considered the difference between the undisclosed lot data and October 1980 lot data that were disclosed, because Sperry did not base its last proposal solely on the October 1980 data. As an alternative, the court compared the individual November 1980 data to amounts relied on by the government and used in its prenegotiation clearance. While the *Sperry* decision represented a more balanced approach under the circumstances, the case illustrates the difficulties the parties face in computing the cost impact of defective pricing. Companies should maintain accurate records of not only the data provided to the government but also concessions agreed to during negotiations—even if the final price is a "bottom line" agreement. Such documentation may prove helpful in computing a realistic cost impact when defective pricing has occurred.

Reliance on Defective Data

The doctrine of natural and probable consequences, previously contained in DAR 3-807.10, has been used as the basis for calculating downward price adjustments for defective pricing.

> In the absence of evidence to the contrary, the natural and probable consequence of defective data is an increase in the contract price in the amount of the defect plus related burden and profit or fee; therefore, unless there is a clear indication that the defective data were not used, or were not relied upon, the contract price should be reduced in that amount. In establishing that the defective data caused an increase in the contract price, the contracting officer is not expected to reconstruct the negotiation by speculating as to what would have been the mental attitudes of the negotiating parties if the correct data had been submitted at the time of agreement on price.

DFARS 215.407-1(b)(2) espouses a similar philosophy, by stating that unless there is clear evidence to the contrary, the contracting officer may presume the defective data were relied on and resulted in a contract price increase equal to the amount of the defect plus related overhead and profit or fee.

These provisions were based on *American Bosch Arma Corp.*,[53] in which the ASBCA stated that "in the absence of any more specific evidence tending to show what effect the nondisclosure of the pricing data had on the negotiated target cost, we are of the opinion that we should adopt the natural and probable consequence of the nondisclosure as representing its effect." However, in *Levison Steel Co.*,[54] the Board ruled that the government must show a cause–effect relationship between the defective data and any resulting increase in negotiated contract price before it can enforce a reduction in that price.

This was further addressed in *American Machine and Foundry Co.*,[55] when the ASBCA disagreed with the government estimate of the amount to be refunded by the contractor, noting that the government is not automatically entitled to a price reduction once an overstatement has been established.

> That it was not the intent of Congress in enacting the measure so severely to punish contractors, particularly in case of inadvertent withholding of pricing data pertaining to a component part which had little or no effect upon the final agreed price of the end item, is manifested by (1) the fact that the statute does not so expressly provide, as it readily could have; (2) by the failure

of the legislative history of the measure to so indicate; and (3) by the very wordage of the act itself.

> Rather, the remedy clearly envisioned by the statute where an overstatement in the cost of a component part has been established is an adjustment in the contract price of the end item "to exclude any significant sums by which it may be determined . . . that the price was increased because the contractor or any subcontractor . . . furnished cost or pricing data which . . . was inaccurate, incomplete, or noncurrent." In other words, the statute, rather than requiring an automatic price reduction in the end item equal to the amount of the dollar and cents overstatement of a component part, plus G&A and profit, as advocated by the Government, requires that first, as a sine qua non, there exists a causal connection between any inaccurate, incomplete, or noncurrent data with respect to a component part, on the one hand, and any increase of the contract price of the end item, on the other hand.

If the defective data were not relied on, the logical conclusion appears to be that the nondisclosed data did not affect the ultimate price negotiated. In *Universal Restoration, Inc.*,[56] the ASBCA stated that the burden of proof is upon the contractor to establish that the defective data were not relied upon. The Board said the following:

> . . . [O]nce disclosure has been established, it would be the natural and probable consequence that an overstated contract price resulted. The burden of persuasion is with the appellant to establish nonreliance on the part of the Government on the inaccurate data in order to rebut the natural and probable consequences of the nondisclosure. . . . The ultimate burden of showing the causal connection between the inaccurate data and an overstated contract price, however, remains with the Government.

The 1987 TINA amendments incorporated the concept of nonreliance as a defense against defective pricing allegations and specified circumstances when the government's nonreliance on defective data could not be asserted as a defense by companies. The language in the act is incorporated into FAR 52.215-10. Consequently, contractors may no longer raise the following matters as a defense against an assertion of defective pricing:

- The contract price would not have been modified even if defective cost or pricing data had been submitted by the contractor or subcontractor because the contractor or subcontractor was the sole source or in a superior bargaining position.

- The CO should have known that the cost or pricing data at issue were defective even though the contractor or subcontractor did not bring the data to the CO's attention.

- The contract price represented a bottom-line agreement between the contracting parties, with no agreement about the cost of each item procured under such contract.

- The prime contractor or subcontractor did not submit a certification of cost or pricing data.

The elimination of these defenses overrides previously established court precedence in such decisions as *Luzon Stevedoring Corp.*[57] and *Universal Restoration, Inc. v. United States*,[58] in which requiring companies to prove nonreliance by the government was the only criterion considered by the courts. In *Luzon Stevedoring Corp.*, the ASBCA ruled that the government was not entitled to a reduction in contract price, even though defective cost or pricing data may have been submitted, because the contractor's strong bargaining position effectively nullified the government's use of the data as a negotiation tool. The Federal Circuit Court came to a similar decision when it concluded that Universal Restoration, Inc.

would not have accepted an overhead rate lower than 115% since it was the only qualified company available to do the work.

Lack of reliance on contractor data was the basis for the ASBCA's decision that the Air Force was not entitled to a downward price adjustment of a contract modification negotiated with General Dynamics Corporation.[59] The Board noted that the Air Force Plant Representative Office negotiator had (1) concluded that the contractor's proposal was not acceptable as a basis for negotiating a factor value and (2) actually developed a negotiation objective based on material usage variance factors developed by DCAA and Air Force personnel.

FAR 15.407-1(d) requires the contracting officer to prepare a memorandum indicating (1) the contracting officer's determination as to whether or not the submitted data were accurate, complete, and current as of the certified date and whether or not the government relied on the data, and (2) the results of any corrective action taken. The absence of a statement in the price negotiation record that the data were not used in establishing the price generally is cited by the government as constituting evidence that the data were relied on. Any agreement to the contrary should be noted in the company's memorandum of negotiations.

Offsets of Other Defective Data

What if the defective data tended to reduce the cost to the government? Unfortunately, the company cannot obtain an increase in the contract price. However, the data may be used to offset other defective data that tended to increase the price to the government.

In *Cutler–Hammer, Inc. v. United States*,[60] the court held that the defective pricing clause allowed understatements to be set off against overstatements to the extent of the overstatements. In *Lockheed Aircraft Corp., Lockheed-Georgia Company Division v. United States*,[61] the court elaborated on its reasoning in *Cutler–Hammer* as follows:

> The reason we allowed offsets to the extent of overstatements in Cutler–Hammer, was that including both understatements and overstatements in a price proposal, negated any attempt on the part of the contractor at creating "artificial savings." This allows them to cancel each other out, at least to the extent of the overstatements, and means that only savings which were brought about through "demonstrated performance of the work" would be available as added profit.

> The allowance of offsets does not give the contractor a windfall, nor does it penalize the government. In both the Cutler–Hammer situation and the one which prevails here, allowing offsets according to our formula merely allows the setting of the negotiated price in an amount which reflects the true cost. If overstatements exceed understatements, the government is still allowed to reduce the contract price by the amount of the excess. No raising of the price is allowed, however.

The 1987 TINA amendments specifically addressed the question of offsets. For the first time, offsets were recognized and conditions were established for their recognition. Two conditions must be met.

1. The contractor must certify that to the best of its knowledge and belief, it is entitled to the offset.

2. The contractor must prove that the unsubmitted, understated cost or pricing data were available before the date of agreement on the price of the contract or modification.

The amendments also stated that offsets would not be permitted to reduce the amount of defective pricing in either of the following conditions:

- The certificate of current cost or pricing data was known to be false when signed.
- The government proves that submission of the understated cost or pricing data before the date of the price agreement would not have resulted in a price increase.

Insight into the reference to false certification can be found in the legislative history, as follows:

> The Senate recedes to the House with an amendment that would prohibit an offset, if the contractor intentionally withheld from the government information that would indicate a higher cost for an item or service and thus certified that the cost or pricing data is submitted was accurate, complete and current when, in fact, the contractor knew it to be false.[62]

Clearly, the intent was that companies must disclose all data related to the proposal under negotiation. This does not mean that a company may not judgmentally reduce its bid, but rather that the anticipated true cost must first be disclosed. At that point, the disclosure obligation is met and pricing decisions can be made.

Prior to the 1987 TINA amendments, Rogerson Aircraft[63] was permitted to use an intentional understatement of indirect costs as an offset against an overstatement of material costs due to submission of defective data. In a decision relating to a contract modification that was finalized on December 20, 1982, the ASBCA rules that Lockheed, unlike Rogerson Aircraft, did not intentionally understate its costs.[64] Price concessions that Lockheed offered at contract negotiations were not viewed by the Board as indicia that Lockheed expected its costs to be lower than those proposed. Thus, no cost understatements were available to offset statements of materials costs which had been stipulated by the parties.

5-5. SUBCONTRACTS: PRIME CONTRACTOR AND SUBCONTRACTOR RESPONSIBILITIES

The relationship between prime contractors and subcontractors relative to defective pricing is extremely complex, and subcontractors may face a higher risk than the prime contractor or upper-tier subcontractors. The latter two often limit their risk by including clauses in their purchase orders/subcontracts that obligate subcontractors to reimburse the prime contractor for all or part of the amount by which the government has reduced the contract price due to the subcontractor's defective pricing.

Many of the potential problems subcontractors face in submitting cost or pricing data to the contractor or higher-tier subcontractors are not addressed in the procurement regulations or court decisions.

Part of the problem emanates from the certificate itself. A subcontractor signs the certificate as of the date of the price agreement between the subcontractor and prime contractor. The prime contractor, however, certifies that its proposal, including subcontractor data, is current, accurate, and complete as of the date of price agreement with the government. While the subcontractor may not know when the contractor's date of price agreement occurred, it may be audited by the government to determine if its data were current, accurate, and complete on that date.

If a prime contractor finalizes negotiations with a subcontractor before agreeing on a price with the government, the issue of relevant dates is much clearer for defective pricing purposes. The subcontractor faces no risk of defective pricing, regardless of the type of contract negotiated between the prime contractor and the government, if the subcontractor's data were current, accurate, and complete when it agreed on price with the prime contractor. However, the government may be entitled to reduce the prime contract price if the prime contractor failed to disclose to the government its price agreement with the subcontractor.

When the prime contractor negotiates with a subcontractor after it has agreed on price with the government, however, the type of contract affects the remedies available to the parties in the event of subcontractor defective pricing.

- If the prime contract is firm-fixed-price, the government may be entitled to reduce the prime contract price only if the subcontractor's data were defective as of the date of price agreement between the prime contractor and the government.

- If the prime contract is other than firm-fixed-price, the date of price agreement between the prime contractor and the subcontractor is relevant. If the subcontractor's data are defective on the date of price agreement between the prime contractor and the government, the government may be entitled to reduce the prime contract price. If the subcontractor's data are not defective when the government and prime contractor agree on price but are defective when the prime contractor and subcontractor reach price agreement, the government will limit the prime contractor to costs that would have been paid if the subcontractor's data had not been defective. FAR 15.407-1(f)(2) states the following:

  > Under cost-reimbursement contracts and under all fixed-price contracts except (i) firm-fixed-price contracts and (ii) contracts with economic price adjustments, payments to subcontractors that are higher than they would be had there been no defective subcontractor cost or pricing data shall be the basis for disallowance or nonrecognition of costs under the clauses prescribed in 15.408(b) and (c). The Government has a continuing and direct financial interest in such payments that is unaffected by the initial agreement on prime contract price.

Because the subcontractor will not have certified its data as of the date of price agreement between the government and the prime contractor, the prime contractor might be able to recoup from the subcontractor only if the subcontract includes an indemnification clause.

According to FAR 15.407-1(f), the prime contract price adjustment due to defective subcontractor data is limited to the difference between the subcontract price included in the prime contractor's proposal and either the actual subcontract price or (if the work was not subcontracted) the actual cost to the contractor. This computation assumes that the actual subcontract price was not based on defective data. To the subcontractor's defective amount, the government will add the prime contractor's markups (indirect expenses and profit) to arrive at the prime contract price adjustment.

Both contractors and subcontractors should fashion a strategy to avoid defective pricing problems. First, a prime contractor should seek to award subcontracts using available exemptions from submission of cost or pricing data to the maximum extent possible. When cost or pricing data are required, prime contractors should request their major subcontractors to update their proposals before the prime contractor's final negotiations with the government. Subcontractors must be fully aware of their responsibilities under the TINA and must communicate with prime contractors, advising them of significant changes that may affect their proposals.

5-6. NOTES

1. Truth in Negotiations Act, Amendment to 10 U.S.C. 2306 by adding subsection (f), enacted Sept. 10, 1962, Pub. L. 87-653.
2. Pub. L. 90-512, Sept. 25, 1968, amended 10 U.S.C. 2305(f) by adding Paragraph (3), which states: "For the purpose of evaluating the accuracy, completeness, and currency of cost or pricing data required to be submitted by this subsection, any authorized representative of the head of the agency who is an employee of the United States Government shall have the right, until the expiration of three years after final payment under the contract or subcontract, to examine all books, records, documents, and other data of the contractor or subcontractor related to the negotiation, pricing, or performance of the contract or subcontract."
3. Department of Defense Authorization Act of 1981, 10 U.S.C. §2315, enacted Dec. 1, 1981, Pub. L. 97-86.
4. Competition in Contracting Act, 10 U.S.C. 2304, 41 U.S.C. 253, enacted July 18, 1984, Pub. L. 98-369.
5. The National Defense Authorization Act for Fiscal Year 1991, enacted Nov. 5, 1990, Pub. L. 101-510.
6. The National Defense Authorization Act For Fiscal Years 1992 and 1993, 105 Stat. 1290, enacted Dec. 5, 1991, Pub. L. 102-90.
7. Federal Acquisition Streamlining Act of 1994, 41 U.S.C. §251, enacted October 13, 1995, Pub. L. 103-355.
8. Sperry Flight Systems, Division of Sperry Rand Corp., ASBCA No. 17375, May 13, 1974, 74-1 BCA 10,648.
9. Director of Defense Procurement, Office of the Undersecretary of Defense, May 29, 1992, Memorandum to the Directors of Defense Agencies, Deputy Assistant Secretary of the Army for Procurement, ASA (RD&A), Deputy for Acquisition Policy, Integrity and Accountability, ASN (RD&A)/API&A, Deputy Assistant Secretary of the Air Force for Contracting, SAF/AQC, Executive Director Contracting, DLA-P, and Executive Director, Contract Management, DLA-A; subject: Certified Cost or Pricing Data.
10. Clinger–Cohen Act of 1996, formerly known as the Federal Acquisition Reform Act of 1996, enacted Feb. 10, 1996, Pub. L. 104-106.
11. Libby Welding Co., Inc. ASBCA No. 15084, Dec. 21, 1972, 73-1 BCA 9,859. See also Lockheed Shipbuilding and Construction Co., ASBCA No. 16494, June 29, 1973, 73-2 BCA 10,157.
12. Sperry Flight Systems, supra, note 8.
13. Deputy Assistant Secretary of Defense for Procurement, May 1, 1987. Memorandum for Assistant Secretary of Military Services and Directors of Defense Agencies. Subject: Adequate Price Competition.
14. Comp. Gen. No. B-194367, December 5, 1979, 27 CCF 80,001; see also Comp. Gen. No. B-189884, March 29, 1979, 26 CCF 83,224.
15. FMC Corp., ASBCA No. 10095 and 11113, March 31, 1966, 66-1 BCA 5,483.
16. 1987 Defense Authorization Act, TINA Amendments, enacted Dec. 4, 1987 Pub. L. 100-180.
17. 1988 TINA Amendments, Defense Authorization Act, §804, Pub L. 100–180.
18. Superintendent of Documents, Government Printing Office, The Truth in Negotiations Handbook, Attn.: Mail List Section, Washington, DC 20402.
19. Texas Instruments, Inc., ASBCA No. 23678, Sept. 28, 1987, 87-3 BCA 20,195.
20. Cutler–Hammer, Inc., ASBCA No. 10900, June 28, 1967, 67-2 BCA 6,432.
21. Sparton Corp., Sparton Electronics Division, ASBCA No. 11363, August 25, 1967, 67-2 BCA 6,539; aff'd. November 24, 1967, 68-1 BCA 6,730.
22. Aerojet-General Corp., ASBCA No. 12873, March 20, 1969, 69-1 BCA 7,585.
23. EDO Corp., ASBCA No. 41448, June 9, 1993, 93-3 BCA 26,135.
24. Aerojet-General Corp., ASBCA No. 12264, April 29, 1969, 69-1 BCA 7,664; aff'd in part Feb. 12, 1970, 70-1 BCA 8,140.
25. Grumman Aerospace Corp., ASBCA No. 27476, May 29, 1986, 86-3 BCA 19,091.
26. Litton Systems, Inc., Amecom Division, ASBCA No. 36509, Feb. 26, 1992, 92-2 BCA 24,842.
27. Aerojet Ordnance Tennessee, ASBCA No. 36089, Sept. 7, 1995, 95-2 BCA 27,922.

28. Rosemont, Inc., ASBCA No. 37520, June 19, 1995, 95-2 BCA 27,770.
29. Motorola, Inc., ASBCA No. 48841, July 25, 1996, 96-2 BCA 28,465.
30. Grumman Aerospace Corp., ASBCA No. 35185, April 27, 1992, 92-3 BCA 25,059.
31. Lockheed Corp., ASBCA Nos. 36420, 37495, 39195, May 23, 1995, 95-2 BCA 27,722.
32. Aerojet Ordnance Tennessee, supra, note 27.
33. McDonnell Douglas Corp., ASBCA No. 44637, July 31, 1995, 95-2 BCA 27,858.
34. Sylvania Electric Products, Inc., ASBCA No. 13622, July 14, 1970, 70-2 BCA 8,387; Ct. Cl. No. 378-70, 202 Ct. Cl. 16, June 20, 1973, 479 F.2d 1342.
35. Kaiser Aerospace and Electronics Corp., ASBCA No. 32098, Nov. 20, 1989, 90-2 BCA 22,695.
36. M-R-S Manufacturing Co. v. United States, ASBCA 14825, March 31, 1971, 71-1 BCA 8,821; 203 Ct. Cl. 551, Feb. 20, 1974, 492 F.2d 835.
37. The Singer Co., Librascope Division, ASBCA No. 17604, July 8, 1975, 75-2 BCA 11,401.
38. Hardie–Tynes Manufacturing Co., ASBCA No. 20717, Sept. 23, 1976, 76-2 BCA 12,121.
39. Aerojet Ordnance Tennessee, supra, note 27.
40. The Boeing Co., ASBCA No. 37579, April 21, 1989, 89-3 BCA 21,787.
41. Dworshak Dam Constructors, ENGBCA No. 3198, Dec. 16, 1971, 72-1 BCA 9,187.
42. Hughes Aircraft Co., ASBCA No. 30144, March 26, 1990, 90-2 BCA 22,847.
43. American Bosch Arma Corp., ASBCA No. 10305, Dec. 17, 1965, 65-2 BCA 5,280.
44. Sylvania Electric Products, Inc., supra, note 34.
45. American Bosch Arma Corp., supra, note 43.
46. Lockheed Aircraft Corp., Lockheed–Georgia Company Division, ASBCA No. 10453, Feb. 28, 1972, 72-1 BCA 9,370.
47. Libby Welding Co., supra, note 11.
48. S.T. Research Corp., ASBCA No. 29070, Aug. 1, 1984, 84-3 BCA 17,568.
49. 1987 Defense Authorization Act, §952, TINA Amendments supra, note 16, Paragraph (d)(3).
50. Superintendent of Documents, Government Printing Office, Defense Contract Audit Manual, Catalog No. D-1.461/2:7640.1/1283, P.O. Box 371954, Pittsburgh, PA 15250-7954.
51. Etowah Manufacturing Company, Inc., ASBCA No. 27267, July 25, 1988, 88-3 BCA 21,054. See also Aydin Monitor Systems, NASA BCA No. 381-1, April 3, 1984, 84-2 BCA 17,297.
52. Sperry Corp. Computer Systems, Defense Systems Division, ASBCA No. 29525, June 21, 1988, 88-3 BCA 20,975.
53. American Bosch Arma Corp., supra, note 43.
54. Levison Steel Co., ASBCA No. 16520, May 1, 1973, 73-2 BCA 10,116.
55. American Machine and Foundry Co., ASBCA No. 15037, Dec. 13, 1973, 74-1 BCA 10,409.
56. Universal Restoration, Inc., ASBCA No. 22833, April 9, 1982, 82-1 BCA 15,762; overturned on reconsideration, 83-1 BCA 16,265; Ct. Cl. No. 77-84C, July 19, 1985, 8 Cl. Ct. 510.
57. Luzon Stevedoring Corp., ASBCA No. 14851, Feb. 24, 1971, 71-1 BCA 8,745.
58. Universal Restoration, Inc. v. United States, CAFC No. 85-2662, Aug. 22, 1986, F.2d 1400.
59. General Dynamics Corp., ASBCA Nos. 32660, 32661, Aug. 24, 1992, 93-1 BCA 25,378.
60. Cutler–Hammer, Inc. v. United States, 189 Ct. Cl. 76, Oct. 17, 1969, F.2d 1306.
61. Lockheed Aircraft Corporation, Lockheed–Georgia Company Division, 193 Ct. Cl. 86, Oct. 16, 1970, 432 F.2d 801; (202 Ct. Cl. 787, Oct. 17, 1973, 485 F.2d 584.)
62. 1987 Defense Authorization Act, TINA Amendments, Paragraph (d)(4)(A), supra, note 19.
63. Rogerson Aircraft Controls, ASBCA No. 27954, Oct. 15, 1984, 85-1 BCA 17,725; CAFC No. 27954, March 6, 1986, 785 F.2d 296.
64. Lockheed Corp., supra, note 31.

Chapter Six

Federal Supply Schedule Contracting

6-1. BACKGROUND

Contracting with the federal government is generally thought of in terms of multimillion-dollar defense contracts for high-tech weapons systems, super-secret stealth aircraft, nuclear submarines, and a host of other military hardware. However, multimillion-dollar government contracts are also awarded for common, everyday, off-the-shelf items. Each year the federal government spends billions of dollars on contracts for such items as lighting fixtures, soaps, clothing, recreational equipment, personal computers, office furniture, and tools. Almost every government agency purchases these items through the Federal Supply Schedule program.

The Federal Supply Schedule program is a procurement process directed and managed by the General Services Administration (GSA). The program allows federal agencies to purchase off-the-shelf items at prices that are generally associated with large-volume buying. It was established to simplify the government's purchasing process for commonly needed supplies and services. The program allows individual agencies to place orders, receive shipments, and make payments directly to contractors without the need for consolidated government buying or handling through a government warehouse system.

Under the program, the GSA awards indefinite-quantity, fixed-price contracts to commercial firms for stated periods of time. The contracts are awarded under either the sealed-bid method or the negotiated method of procurement and are placed on "lists," or schedules, according to product type. These schedules identify the supplies and services available to authorized government agencies by contract and include the names, addresses, and phone numbers of the GSA schedule contractors. They also include contract numbers, contract periods, geographical areas of coverage, order limitations, agencies required to use the schedule, and information on how to place orders. The GSA lists these schedules in a publication entitled *Federal Supply Schedules*.

There are over 200 different schedules under the Federal Supply Schedule program. About half of them are multiple-award/negotiated commercial item schedules, resulting in negotiated contracts with several suppliers for similar goods and services. There are no government specifications for the items listed in this type of schedule; all the items are similar in nature but have varying degrees of quality and features. The other half of the schedules are single-award schedules with contracts awarded to only one supplier. The contracts on this type of schedule are awarded to the lowest bidder whose supplies or services meet the government's specifications, using the sealed-bid procurement method. The New Item Introductory Schedule is used for introducing new items into the Federal Supply Schedule program. The GSA negotiates contracts for these items and puts them on this schedule for a trial period of time. If demand for the items is substantial, the GSA transfers the items to one of its other schedules previously noted.

The International Federal Supply Schedule is used as a supply source for U.S. government activities located overseas. This schedule includes items awarded under both the sealed-bid and the negotiated procurement methods.

This chapter focuses on the requirements related to multiple-award schedule contracts.

6-2. THE GENERAL SERVICES ADMINISTRATION

As discussed in Chapter 2, the GSA was created by the Federal Property and Administrative Services Act of 1949 to consolidate dozens of agencies involved in the government's many housekeeping activities. Such activities included purchasing supplies and equipment; keeping records; and acting as the federal architect, builder, and landlord. Each of these functions is the responsibility of a particular group or service within the GSA. It is the Federal Supply Service that awards Federal Supply Schedule contracts.

The Federal Supply Service (FSS) is responsible for thousands of common-use items, such as office supplies, scientific instruments, furniture, fixtures, and tools. It is now also responsible for procuring automated data processing (ADP) and telecommunications equipment, software, and services. This function was previously handled by the GSA's Information Technology Service. The ADP schedule includes contracts for mainframe and minicomputers, peripherals, software, supplies, and recently services. The telecommunications schedule has contracts for communications-related products, such as audio and video recorders, telephones, radios, and navigational equipment.

6-3. DEPARTMENT OF VETERANS AFFAIRS

In 1981, the GSA authorized the Department of Veterans Affairs (DVA), formerly the Veterans Administration, to award supply schedule contracts for medical items, which had previously been contracted for by the FSS.

The DVA has contracting responsibility for medical, dental, and veterinary equipment and supplies, as well as certain subsistence items (foodstuffs). The DVA awards and administers supply schedule contracts for these products using GSA's policies, procedures, and forms. The DVA is kept abreast of any changes in GSA practices and procedures by pronouncements issued by the FSS.

6-4. PURCHASING FROM FEDERAL SUPPLY SCHEDULES

Priorities for Sources of Supply

Government regulations require that agencies purchase from federal supply schedules before buying goods and services on the open market. In this respect, supply schedule contractors have an advantage over their nonschedule competitors. However, federal supply schedules are not the government's first priority for purchasing supplies and services. As provided by Federal Acquisition Regulation (FAR) 8.001, the government's priorities for sources of supplies are as follows:

1. Agency inventories
2. Excess from other agencies, through GSA's Personal Property Services Branch
3. Federal Prison Industries, Inc.
4. Procurement list of products available from the Committee for Purchase from the Blind and Other Severely Handicapped
5. The GSA Stock Program and other wholesale suppliers, such as the Defense Logistics Agency, the DVA, and military inventory control points
6. Mandatory federal supply schedules
7. Optional-use federal supply schedules
8. Commercial sources

The government's priorities for sources of services are as follows:

1. Procurement list of services available from the Committee for Purchase from the Blind and Other Severely Handicapped
2. Mandatory federal supply schedules and mandatory GSA term contracts for personal property rehabilitation
3. Optional-use federal supply schedules and optional GSA term contracts for personal property rehabilitation
4. Federal Prison Industries, Inc., or other commercial sources

Mandatory Users of Schedules

Each federal supply schedule identifies government agencies that are required to use the schedule contracts as a primary source of supply. Agencies designated as "mandatory users" of a schedule must first seek to buy items from a single-award contractor before going to a multiple-award schedule. If a "mandatory use" agency cannot find the products it needs from a supply schedule contract, it may look to nonschedule supply sources after obtaining the GSA's approval.

Although the GSA designates certain government agencies as mandatory users of the supply schedule contracts, there are exceptions to the rules, as follows:

- *Urgent delivery requirements.* A mandatory use agency will not be required to use a schedule if it has a legitimate urgent requirement for goods that cannot be delivered within the time necessary to meet its needs. For example, an agency urgently needs a certain computer system within three working days of placing the order, but the best delivery time on the schedule is one week. In this case, the agency would not be required to use the schedule if (time permitting) the contractor confirms in writing that it cannot meet the three-day delivery requirement.

- *Minimum and maximum orders.* Almost all multiple-award schedule (MAS) contracts contain a clause that limits the minimum and maximum order sizes the contractor is liable to accept. A mandatory-use agency is not required to use the schedule if its purchase order is for less than the minimum or more than the maximum order limitations of the contract. The maximum order limitation will be discussed in further detail later.

- *Legislative and judicial agencies.* Except in certain circumstances, agencies in the legislative and judicial branches of the government are not mandatory users of federal supply schedules.

- *Geographic locations.* All MAS contracts identify specific geographic delivery limitations. If the ordering agency's delivery location is outside the geographic scope of the contract, the agency is not mandated to use the schedule contract.

- *Lower prices.* If a mandatory-use agency can find the same or similar item included in a multiple-award schedule contract at a price that is lower than the contract price offered by a nonschedule commercial source, the agency will not be required to use the schedule contract. However, in considering price, the agency must consider the overall price, including such things as warranties, delivery terms, and transportation costs.

- *Nonmandatory use of federal supply schedules.* Federal agencies not designated as mandatory users by the GSA are not required to use the supply schedules but may do so at their own option.

Ordering Agency Responsibilities

Although the GSA awards schedule contracts and administers the Federal Supply Schedule program, the individual government agencies are responsible for placing orders, receiving shipments, and making payments to the schedule contractors.

To place an order against a schedule contract, an ordering agency prepares and issues a purchase order to the contractor. Federal Acquisition Regulation 8.405-2 requires all purchase orders to contain the following information:

- Shipping and billing address
- Contract number and date
- Agency order number
- Freight-on-board (F.O.B.) order point
- Discount and delivery terms
- Special item number or national stock number
- Description of the items ordered
- Quantity, unit price, and total price
- Points of inspection and acceptance
- Level of preservation, packaging, and packing
- Other pertinent data

Inspection and Acceptance of Items Purchased from Federal Supply Schedules

Generally, it is the responsibility of the ordering agency to inspect, accept, reject, make price adjustments, seek replacement, and—in the case of default— terminate purchase orders under supply schedule contracts.

When delivered goods are defective in quality or do not comply with the con- tract requirements, the agency may accept them at a reduced price. On the other hand, the agency also has the right to demand corrections at the contractor's expense. If the company fails to make the corrections, the agency may terminate the purchase order and declare the company in default on the order. The goods and services may then be repurchased from another source, and the company may be held liable for any excess costs incurred by the government. However, the company does have the right to appeal to the GSA if it concludes that its failure to perform on the purchase order was excusable.

Government agencies placing orders under the contract are required to report all declarations of default to the GSA. Accordingly, the GSA also has the right to declare the company in default of its contractual obligations on an overall basis for any or all items covered by the contract.

6-5. MULTIPLE-AWARD SCHEDULE PROPOSALS

Specific data disclosure requirements must be met before the award of any MAS contract. These requirements pertain equally to the contracts awarded by both the DVA and the GSA.

Like other types of negotiated government contracts, MAS contracts are sub- ject to FAR provisions. Generally, prices offered under federal supply schedule contracts are for commercial items with catalog prices and are therefore exempt from the submission of certified cost or pricing data. However, the contracting officer (CO) still must determine that the prices offered are fair and reasonable before the award of any contract.

MAS Negotiation Policies

On October 25, 1982, the GSA issued policies and procedures to be followed when contracting for goods and services under the MAS program. The policy, developed in response to concerns expressed by Congress, federal agencies, and companies holding MAS contracts, applies to those contracts awarded by the GSA and the DVA.

The policy stated that the GSA's primary goal when awarding MAS contracts was "to obtain discounts equal to or greater than" the discounts offered to the firm's most favored customers. The GSA defined a "most-favored-customer dis- count" as "the best discount given by a contractor to any entity with whom the contractor does business other than dealers, distributors, or original equipment manufacturers." However, the GSA also considered the discounts offered to these classes of customers when establishing its negotiation objectives.

Under the 1982 policy, the offeror was required in its MAS pricing proposal to submit and certify to specific discount, sales, and marketing information relating to the same or similar products offered to the government. The format for dis- closing this information was the Discount Schedule and Marketing Data (DSMD) sheet, discussed later in this chapter and included for reference in Appendix 6.1.

The 1982 GSA MAS Policy Statement permitted the government to seek other than the most-favored-customer discount in certain circumstances. Section II under the Pricing Arrangement Section recognized that the government's terms and conditions might differ from those given a firm's most favored customer. Additionally, the Pricing Guide attached to Policy Statement at Paragraph 4D allowed the government to establish a negotiation objective other than the offeror's dealer/distributor discount when functions, such as warehousing, that are performed by dealers/distributors must be performed by the MAS contractor itself in selling to the GSA.

The General Accounting Office (GAO) report entitled "Multiple Award Schedule Contracting—Changes Needed in Negotiation Objectives and Data Requirements,"[1] issued in August 1993, also addressed this issue, as follows:

> GSA contracting staff must also consider legitimate differences in the terms and conditions of sales between the government's MAS purchases and vendor's other customers. If it is more expensive for a vendor to sell to the government than to the customer who receives the vendor's best discount or if the customer who receives the best discount performs certain value-added functions for the vendor that the government does not perform, then some reduction in the discount given to the government would be appropriate. To accomplish this, prospective vendors should identify and place a value on any differences in terms and conditions that prevent them from giving the government their best discounts.

Although the 1982 Policy Statement was canceled by GSA on February 16, 1996, GSAR 538.270 reiterates GSA's goal to obtain most-favored-customer pricing (best discount). However, the GSA recognizes that the terms and conditions of commercial sales vary, and there may be valid reasons why the best discount is not achieved.

The GSA rejected Best Power Technology's MAS proposal solely because it did not offer the most-favored-customer discount, even though the net prices offered to the GSA were lower than those of Best Power's competitors' products that were already on the schedule. Best Power subsequently filed a bid protest with the General Services Board of Contract Appeals (GSBCA).[2] The GSBCA focused only on the narrow issue of whether the CO was authorized to refuse to place an offeror on the schedule solely because the offeror declined to offer its most favored customer discount. The Board noted that the GAO had previously ruled, in *Baxter Healthcare Corp.*,[3] that the CO could take such action. Furthermore, the board concluded that in a multiple-award schedule, net price comparisons were not feasible because the products on the schedule were not identical. The Federal Circuit Court ruled that the GSBCA had no jurisdiction over the protest because the GSBCA's bid protest authority was limited to acquisitions of automatic data processing equipment (ADPE) and because the Best Power products that were the subject of the protest were not ADPE. The decision was vacated and the case remanded to the Board with an instruction to dismiss.[4] The Board dismissed the case for lack of jurisdiction on February 24, 1993.

Discount Schedule and Marketing Data Sheet

Prior to February 1992, all MAS solicitations contained the DSMD sheet. Multiple-award schedule contractors were required to disclose to the government the best discounts, regardless of quantity, terms, and conditions, that they offered to other than GSA/DVA contract users for the same or similar products offered to the government. Actual percentages for all classes of customers, such as distributors, dealers, and retailers, were required to be disclosed. Specifically, the government wanted to know about regular, quantity, aggregate, and prompt-payment discounts, as well as delivery terms, commissions, and related data on rebates, pricing agreements, and other concessions that can be expressed as a percentage of the product list price. For each product offered in the proposal, detailed sales information was also required.

The DSMD sheet, when properly prepared, allowed the government to (1) evaluate the pricing proposal, (2) determine if the products in the proposal met the government's "test of commerciality," and (3) determine if the prices were reasonable. Because the data provided form the basis for MAS contract negotiations, those data were required to be accurate, complete, and current.

The DSMD sheets were broken down into two parts. Part A was used to obtain general information about the offeror, while Part B required specific discount information. Under Part A, the government wanted to know the following:

- Marketing category (Is the offeror a manufacturer or a dealer of the products?)
- The price list used as the basis for the offer
- The warranty (Is it the same warranty offered to other commercial customers?)
- The value of any warranty or installation provisions of the proposal
- End-of-contract discounts
- The amount of government sales under similar supply schedule contracts over the last 12-month period
- Projected sales under the contract

Part B of the DSMD sheets required the offeror to disclose specific information about discounting practices as well as product sales information for each special item number (SIN) in the proposal. A SIN is a number assigned by the government to identify specific groups of products. With regard to discount information, the government asked the following:

- The number of catalog items in the proposal
- The discount(s) offered to the government, including prompt payment and quantity discounts, as well as other beneficial terms or concessions, such as renewal discounts, purchase options, or rebates of any kind
- The best discounts and concessions resulting in the lowest net price (regardless of quantity, terms, or conditions) offered to other than authorized schedule contract users from the price list for the same or similar products offered to the government, including actual percentages and delivery terms

The DSMD sheets listed the following classes of customers: (1) dealers/retailers; (2) distributors/wholesalers; (3) educational institutions; (4) state, county, city, and local governments; (5) original equipment manufacturers (OEMs); and (6) others (e.g., national accounts). The offeror was not limited to the customer classes specifically identified in the DSMD sheets; other classes of customers could be specifically identified in a supplemental data sheet appended to the proposal.

When necessary, supplemental data sheets could be prepared to explain customer classifications, discounts, or sales and marketing information. Companies could always explain any pricing agreements or discounts that resulted in lower net prices than those offered to the government and any allowances and/or reduced prices for trade-ins, returns, samples, demonstrators, or reconditioned or floor models that are not available to a schedule contract user.

On February 18, 1992, the GSA's Office of Acquisition Policy temporarily amended the General Services Administration Regulation (GSAR), Subparts 515 and 538, to test a revised format for the DSMD sheets. This format consisted of four parts rather than the current two.

- Part A—General Information and Discounts Offered the Government
- Part B—Commercial Discounting Practices
- Part C—Sales Information
- Part D—Certification

The test format deleted the requirement to list best discounts by class of customer. Instead, it required the offeror to identify discounts to all customers that exceeded the discount offered to the government. If the government was offered a discount equal to or greater than the offeror's best commercial discount, the offeror was required only to identify the best discount and the customers receiving that discount. The test format also expressly recognized that differences between discounts offered to commercial customers and those offered to the government may be warranted.

Commercial Sales Practices Format

The GSA amended GSAR, Subparts 515, 538, and 552, to implement provisions of the Federal Acquisition Streamlining Act's (FASA)[5] and the Clinger–Cohen Act of 1996[6] relating to the Truth in Negotiations Act (TINA)[7] and the acquisition of commercial items. The GSAR revisions, were initially issued as an interim rule on February 16, 1996 and applied to solicitations for commercial items and open season solicitations issued after March 4, 1996. The final rule was issued August 21, 1997 for mandatory application to solicitations issued on or after December 19, 1997.

The GSAR revisions replaced the DSMD with the Commercial Practices Format, included in Appendix 6.2. The level of discount data required to be furnished with the Commercial Practices Format depends on the offeror's response to the question of whether the discounts offered are equal to or greater than the offeror's best discount to any customer for the same offered items. If the best discount is offered in the MAS proposal (a "yes" response to the discount question), the only information required to be furnished with the Commercial Practices Format is the identity of the customer(s) that received the best discount. If an offeror does not offer its best discount in the MAS proposal (a "no" response to the discount question), the offeror must supply discount data for all customers that received a discount equal to or better than the discount offered in the MAS proposal for the same offered items.

The term *discount* is defined in GSAR 552.212-70 as "a reduction to catalog prices and includes rebates, quantity discounts, purchase option credits, and any other terms or conditions which reduce the amount of money a customer ultimately pays for goods or services ordered or received." The term *customer* is defined in the Commercial Practices Format as "any entity except the Federal Government including original equipment manufacturers, value-added resellers, state and local governments, dealers and distributors, educational institutions, national accounts, and other end users."

Price Analysis

While the price of an item offered on an MAS contract qualifies for an exemption from the requirement to submit certified cost or pricing data, the CO is required to perform some form of "price analysis" to determine the reasonableness of the proposed price(s).

The government's requirement for the submission of former DSMD sheets or the new Commercial Practices Format stems from FAR 15.404-1(b), which directs the CO to obtain information on the prices at which the same item or similar items been sold in order to evaluate the reasonableness of the proposed price through price analysis.

When establishing negotiation objectives and determining price reasonableness, COs will compare the terms and conditions of agreements with customers. The CO will consider the following factors to determine the government's price negotiation objectives:

1. Aggregate volume of anticipated purchases
2. The purchase of a minimum quantity or a pattern of historic purchases
3. Discounts/prices offered
4. Length of the contract period
5. Warranties, training, maintenance included in the purchase price or provided at additional cost to the product prices
6. Ordering and delivery practices
7. Any other relevant information, including differences between the MAS solicitation and commercial terms and conditions that may warrant differentials between the offer and the discounts offered to the best customers; in cases in which the best discount is not offered to the government, the offeror is responsible for identifying, substantiating, and valuing any asserted differences

The CO may not award a contract containing pricing that is less favorable than the best discount the offeror extends to any commercial customer purchasing under circumstances comparable to the government, unless the CO makes a written determination that (1) the prices offered to the government are fair and reasonable, even though comparable discounts were not negotiated; and (2) award of a contract is otherwise in the best interest of the government.

Certifications

Prior to the passage of the FASA and the Clinger–Cohen Act of 1996, the 1982 Policy Statement required the offeror to certify at the conclusion of negotiations that all the information provided to the government up to the date of negotiations was accurate, complete, and current. The FASA eliminated that requirement.

If the previously certified pricing data are subsequently found to have been inaccurate, incomplete, or noncurrent as of the effective date of the certificate, the government is entitled to an adjustment of the contract price. Such adjustment may include any significant sum by which the price was increased because of defective data, provided the data were relied on by the government. Prior to issuance of the GSAR revision, the Basis for Price Negotiation clause (M-FSS-330) stated the following:

If subsequent to the award of any contract resulting from this solicitation it is found that any price negotiated in connection with this contract was increased by any significant amount because the prices, data, and facts were not as stated in the offeror's *Certificate of Established Catalog or Market Price*, then the contract price(s) shall be reduced by such amount and the contract shall be modified in writing to reflect such adjustment. Failure to agree on such a reduction, subsequent to a "final decision" by the Contracting Officer in this matter, shall be a dispute concerning a question of fact within the meaning of the "disputes" clause of the contract.

The GSAR revision introduced a new clause (GSAR 552.215-72), Price Adjustment for Incomplete, Not Current, or Inaccurate Information Other Than Cost or Pricing Data. The clause provides for a price reduction if the submitted discount data and information are determined to be incomplete, inaccurate, or noncurrent.

Many in the contracting community believe that the revised GSAR requirements do not reflect the spirit of the TINA amendments, or the procedures for acquiring commercial products that were mandated by the FASA and Clinger–Cohen.

The GSA has successfully pursued a number of MAS contract defective pricing issues as violations of the False Claims Act. However, in *United States v. Data Translation, Inc.*,[8] a jury found Data Translation not guilty of any False Claims Act violations. Key to the decision was, undoubtedly, the judge's instruction to the jury that "the DSMD sheets were so confusing that . . . there could not have been a meeting of the minds on the meaning of these forms prior to award." In affirming the lower court decision, the Court of Appeals found "the language of the discount provisions virtually unintelligible if read literally . . . [but] one may give the language a practical interpretation which makes them intelligible."[9] The court concluded that an intelligible reading of the GSA's 78-page "Solicitation Offer and Award" required disclosure of "significantly relevant discounts that DTI normally provided to other customers making purchases roughly comparable to the agency purchases the Government contemplated would occur under the MAS program." In the court's view, Data Translation met that disclosure requirement.

6-6. MAS CONTRACT ADMINISTRATION

A number of contractual obligations must be fulfilled after award of an MAS contract. These obligations include reporting price reductions during the contract term and providing the CO with reports of sales made under the contract and the corresponding industrial funding fee calculation.

Price Reductions

All MAS contracts contain a Price Reductions clause (GSAR 552.238-76) to ensure that the government maintains its relative price/discount advantage in relation to the commercial price/discount on which the contract is predicated. This relationship is agreed to at the end of contract negotiations.

Any price reductions are effective for the contract at the same time that they are effective for the class of customer on which the contract is predicated. In the case of temporary, government-only price reductions, the effective date was the date of acceptance by the CO. The contractor must invoice its government customers at the reduced prices and must indicate on the invoice that the price reduction is pursuant to the Price Reductions clause until the contract is modified.

The Price Reductions clause was revised on October 19, 1994, to clarify its applicability, reduce contractor reporting requirements, and eliminate price reductions based on lower price to federal agencies.

Price Reductions to Customers Other Than Federal Agencies

The Price Reductions clause states that before the MAS contract award, the CO and the offeror should reach agreement on the price relationship between the government and the identified customer or category of customers on which the contract award is predicated (referred to as the award class of customer). This relationship is maintained throughout the contract period. If the contractor, after contract award, makes any change in the commercial pricing arrangements for the identified customer or category of customers that disturbs this relationship, it will be deemed a "price reduction" under the terms of the MAS contract. A price reduction is also triggered if, after contract negotiations have been completed, the price list upon which the contract award was predicated is reduced. Operation of the price reduction provision is illustrated in Figure 6.1.

The contractor must report to the CO all price reductions made during the contract period, along with an explanation of the conditions under which the reductions were made. Those reductions that do not disturb the government's price position relative to the identified customer or class of customers are not subject to the provisions of the clause. However, the information will more than likely be used during negotiations for the following contract period.

The Price Reductions clause is not invoked when a contractor receives a firm-fixed-price, definite-quantity order with specified delivery above the maximum order limitation specified in the contract. The CO also may waive the clause for any sale at a price below the contract price if caused by an error in quotation or billing, provided adequate documentation is furnished to the CO as soon as the error is discovered.

Price Reductions to Federal Agencies

Price reductions to any federal agency after the effective contract date, other than temporary "government-only" price reductions, previously triggered an equivalent price reduction on sales to federal agencies under MAS contracts awarded by the FSS. This price reduction requirement was eliminated on October 19, 1994.

Reporting Price Reductions

Prior to October 19, 1994, the contractor was required to notify the CO, in writing, of any price reductions as soon as possible, but not later than 10 calendar days after the effective date. If the contractor failed to do so, the price reductions (including temporary price reductions) applied to the contract for its duration or until the price was further reduced. Such failure could also constitute a basis for termination for default of the contract.

In addition, the contractor was required to furnish, within 10 calendar days after the end of the contract period, a statement certifying that either (1) there were no applicable reductions during the contract period, or (2) any price reductions were reported to the CO. For each reported price reduction, the contractor had to show the date when the CO was notified.

Effective October 19, 1994, price reduction notification requirements were

The category of customer upon which the contract is predicated is "dealers." On January 1, 19xx, the company negotiates MAS contract prices as follows:

		Dealer		GSA	
	Quantity				
List Price	Ordered	Discount	Dealer Price	Discount	GSA Price
$20.00	1-5	25%	$15.00	30%	$14.00
$15.00	6-10	35%	$ 9.75	40%	$ 9.00
$10.00	11-up	40%	$ 6.00	45%	$ 5.50

On May 1, 19xx, the company reduces the dealer quantity price of 6-10 units from $9.75 to $9.00, resulting in a 5% increase in the discount percentage to dealers. A price reduction of 7.7% per unit may apply to all subsequent GSA contract orders, as shown below:

	List Price	Discount Offered	Net Price
To the government	$15.00	44.6%	$8.31
To dealers	$15.00	40.0%	$9.00

Price reduction granted to dealers on May 1 = $.75

($9.75 - $9.00 = $.75)

Price reduction percentage granted to dealers = 7.7%

($.75/$9.75)

Comparable price reduction per unit to the government = $.69

($9.00 x 7.7%)

New government price = $8.31

(9.00 - $.69)

New government discount = 44.6%

($15.00 - $8.31 = $6.69/$15.00)

Figure 6.1 Example of a Price Reduction Computation

eased. Contractors must now report price reductions to the award class of customer within 15 calendar days after the effective date. The end-of-contract statement of reported price reductions was eliminated.

Contractor's Report of Sales

Under the terms of an MAS contract, the contractor is required to report to the CO the dollar value of all sales made, during the preceding two- or three-month contract period. A separate report is required for each special item number under the contract.

Unless otherwise stated in the contract, the contractor must use GSA Form 72A for these reports. This form is simply a data input card identifying each special item number. The contract will specify the due dates for each report; the company is required to submit reports even during periods of no sales activity. Prior to the introduction of the industrial funding fee, the requirement was to report orders received under the contract.

Industrial Funding Fee

In 1995, the GSA implemented an industrial funding fee to ordering activities to recoup the costs of operating the Federal Supply Schedule program. The DVA has also adopted the imposition of the fee. Contractors pay the fee as a percentage of sales reported on the GSA Form 72A.

Maximum Order Limitations

In March 1983, FSS Procurement Letter 359-4 required that a Maximum Order Limitation clause be included in all MAS solicitations to limit the maximum dollar value of each order placed under a contract. The limit varied, depending on the special item number ordered. If an ordering agency's need for any item on the schedule exceeded the maximum, the agency was to solicit bids from the open market for the higher volume it needed. The idea behind the maximum limitation was that an ordering agency should be able to get a better price in the open market than it would get through the MAS schedule contract. The specific limitation, established at the conclusion of negotiations, depended on the discount(s) offered to the government and the sales level at which lower prices were likely to be offered by other suppliers under other types of contracts.

The Maximum Order Limitation clause was replaced in August 1995 with the Requirements Exceeding the Maximum Order clause (IFSS-125). The clause states that when an agency has a need to place an order over the maximum order amount, it should contact the vendor for a reduced price. Vendors may (1) offer a new, lower price for this requirement (the Price Reduction clause is not applicable to orders placed over the maximum order in FAR 52.216-19); (2) offer the lowest price available under the contract; or (3) decline the order. Sales for orders that exceed the maximum order are reportable and includable in the Contractor's Report of Sales.

Requote Procedures

Instructional Letter FSS-IL-87-12, dated November 10, 1987, described requote or ordering procedures for orders exceeding the maximum order limitation on MAS contracts. The procedures allowed agencies to place over-the-limit orders against existing schedule contracts. These procedures were designed to encourage more price competition among schedule contractors and to reduce administrative costs. Schedule contractors having the required items on contract were advised of the over-the-limit order by either the ordering agency or the GSA and were given the exclusive opportunity to compete for the order with the other contractors on the current schedule.

In response to a bid protest filed by Komatsu Dresser Company, the GAO concluded that the Requote Arrangements clause violated the Competition in Contracting Act,[10] since orders over the maximum order limitation are restricted to contractors already on the current schedule. The GAO concluded that such awards should be subject to full and open competition.

6-7. SUMMARY

Selling standard commercial products to the U.S. government can provide a company an excellent opportunity to increase market share while taking on only some of the red tape that usually accompanies government sales. This business opportunity stems from the fact that federal agencies, in conducting their day-to-day operations, require many of the same products used by the general public. To meet its needs for off-the-shelf products, the federal government is willing to pay prevailing market prices.

However, before venturing into this market, a company should have a good understanding of the Federal Supply Schedule program and have the proper controls in place to ensure that its reporting system can produce timely the detailed data required.

As in any separate and distinct marketplace, the entrepreneur must understand the process as well as the factors that affect the environment in which the company operates. If a company understands the most-favored-customer discount requirements and other associated requirements, supply schedule contracting is probably no more nor less treacherous than any other marketplace. However, if the company lacks a basic knowledge of the rules and regulations, or if it ignores the rules and regulations, the risk of loss or the expense of litigation can be considerable.

6-8. NOTES

1. Multiple Award Schedule Contracting—Changes Needed in Negotiation Objectives and Data Requirements, August 1993, United States General Accounting Office, GAO/GGD-93-123.
2. Best Power Technology Sales Corp., GSBCA No. 11400-P, Nov. 13, 1991, 92-1 BCA 24,625.
3. Baxter Healthcare Corp., Comp. Gen. No. B-230580.5, April 26, 1990, 5 CGEN 104,333.
4. Best Power Technology Sales Corp. v. Austin, CAFC No. 92-1118, -1254, Jan. 21, 1993, 984 F.2d 1172.
5. Federal Acquisition Streamlining Act, enacted Oct. 13, 1995, Pub. L. No. 103-355.
6. Clinger–Cohen Act of 1996, formerly known as Federal Acquisition Reform Act, enacted Feb. 10, 1996, Pub. L. 104-106.
7. Truth in Negotiations Act, amendment to 10 U.S.C. 2306 by adding subsection (f), enacted Sept. 10, 1962, Pub. L. 87-653.
8. United States v. Data Translation, Inc., DC Mass., No. 89-2192, Feb. 10, 1992.
9. United States v. Data Translation, Inc., CA1, No. 92-1496, Dec. 31, 1992.
10. Competition in Contracting Act, 10 U.S.C. §2304 and 41 U.S.C. §253, enacted July 18, 1984, Pub. L. 98-369.

INSTRUCTIONS TO OFFERORS:

PART A. General Information, applies to each GSA Special Item Number (SIN) for which an offer is submitted. (If all information is the same, SINs may be combined.)

PART B. Separate discount and sales information, must be completed for each Special Item Number for which an offer is submitted. (If discount information is the same for all products under each SIN, SINs may be combined. However, separate sales information requested under Part B IV must be provided for each SIN.)

Information required by each space must be furnished. If not applicable, indicate by "N/A". Information furnished in Part B relating to discounts, allowances and sales information will be treated as "CONFIDENTIAL" by the Government except for final prices and discounts awarded by the Government. Failure to provide current, accurate and complete information under Part A and B may subject the offeror to liability for refunds pursuant to the price reductions or Defective Pricing Clauses.

Part A - General Information (applicable to all special item numbers)

I. Offeror's Marketing Category (check applicable item)

    (a) __ Manufacturer selling direct - has no dealers.
    (b) __ Manufacturer selling direct to the Government even though he has dealers.
    (c) __ Manufacturer selling to the Government through dealers.
    (d) __ Dealer selling direct to the Government. (Dealer must submit manufacturer's price list).
    (e) __ Other (specify) _____

II. Identification of a pricelist as the basis for this offer (check and attach __ copies of the pricelist)

    (a) __ Manufacturer's catalog/pricelist _____
          (indicate type)
    (b) __ Dealer's catalog/pricelist
    (c) __ Retailer's catalog/pricelist
    (d) __ Other (specify) _____

III. Warranty

    (a) Submit your commercial warranty or specify where it may be found in your catalog or pricelist included with this offer.
    (b) The warranty offered to GSA is more favorable __ less favorable __ or equal to _____ the commercial warranty? (check one). Describe and provide the value (expressed as a percentage of the catalog price) if more favorable or less favorable __%.

IV. Installation and Instruction

    (a)   Are installation and instruction included in this offer?
          Yes__, No__ (check one).
          If yes, give details or indicate where the information may be found in your catalog or pricelist.
    (b)   Are installation and instruction provisions offered herein to the Government more favorable than those in commercial customers?
          Yes__, No__ (check one). If yes, describe and provide the value (expressed as a percentage) __%.

V. Other Data: (Answer "Yes" or "No" for each question)

    (a) __ Do you maintain stock on hand of the items offered?
    (b) __ Do you display the Special Item Number(s) offered in showroom?
    (c) __ Do you provide any design and layout assistance related to this Special Item Number free of charge?
    (d) __ If you are a dealer, will you arrange to have other dealers participate in the schedule contract should you receive a contract?
    (e) __ Will you administer all incoming orders, including requests for expediting and follow-up?

Appendix 6.1   Discount Schedule and Marketing Data Sheet

Name of Offeror   GSA Special Item Number

I. Identification of Items Offered. How many Model/type of catalog items do you offer under this GSA Special Item Number ____ (enter number).

II. Discounts. The following concessions are offered to the Government for delivery FOB destination. In ADTS solicitations, list also concessions to the Government for delivery FOB origin.

(a)   Discount offered on the above GSA Special Item Number is ___% from pricelist dated _____, plus prompt payment discount, as stated on the first page of this solicitation (additional details may be entered below or attached). If discounts vary, show discounts on pricelist.

(b)   Aggregate or end of a contract additional discounts. An additional discount of ____ percent is offered to the Government which will be applied to the actual aggregate sales in excess of the following base figure under this contract:

       1. For current MAS contractors, aggregate sales (annualized) to the Government for most recent 12 month period under similar contract(s) is $___, based on sales during the period ____ to ____.

       2. For other offerors, projected aggregate sales under this contract is $_____.

(c)   Quantity Discounts. List below any quantity discounts included in this offer. Question (2) below applies only to FSS.

       1. Can models/products be combined within Special Item Number?
          Yes___ No____. If yes, provide details.

       2. Can Special Item Numbers be combined?
          Yes___ No____. If yes, provide details.

(d)   Other beneficial terms, discounts, or concessions included in this offer such as prompt renewal discounts, purchase option credits, etc. (List below and provide detail explanations.) (This section applies only to FSS solicitations).

Appendix 6.1   (*Continued*)

III. a. List below the best discount and/or concessions resulting in the lowest net price (regardless of quantity and terms and conditions) to other than authorized GSA contract users from pricelist for the same or similar products or services offered to the Government under this solicitation. (Show actual percentage and delivery terms)

	Regular Discounts %	Quantity Discounts %	Aggregate Discounts	Commissions to other than employees %	Prompt Payment	FOB Point	Other
(1) to dealers/ retailers							
(2) to distributors/ wholesalers							
(3) to educational institutions							
(4) to state, county, city and local governments							
(5) to original equipment manufacturers (OEM)							
(6) to others (specify); e.g., nat'l accts. sales agreements, etc.							
(7) If a dealer, indicate discount from mfg's pricelist							

Appendix 6.1   *(Continued)*

III. b.   Do you have in effect, for any customer of any class within the MOL or outside of the MOL, other discounts and/or concession including but not limited to the following, regardless of pricelist, which result in lower net prices than those offered to the Government in this offer?

Yes_ No_ rebates of any kind, including year-end or end of contract discounts?
Yes_ No_ multiple quantity unit pricing plan?
Yes_ No_ cumulative discounts of any type which cover items being offer?
Yes_ No_ products (models)/services that may be combined for maximum discounts?
Yes_ No_ others (specify).

If answer to any of the above is "Yes", provide detailed explanation including the value expressed as a percentage of the list price.

IV. (a)   Are any of the models/products offered herein sold by the offeror under a different trade name(s)? Yes__, No ___. If "Yes", explain and provide applicable pricelists.

   (b)   To your knowledge, are there identical products offered herein contained in any other GSA Federal Supply Schedule contract? Yes___, No ___. If "Yes", identify the product, schedule and contract.

   (c)   Summarize any significant changes in concessions offered herein as compared with those set forth in any current GSA contract.

V.   Allowances: (This section only applies to FSS solicitations). Do you offer any of the following allowances to any customer which are not available to a GSA contract user under this contract? (Enter "yes" or "no" for each. If yes, explain.)

   (a) _ Trade-in allowances?
   (b) _ Return/Exchange goods policy?
   (c) _ Reduced prices on samples, demonstrator models, reconditioned items or floor models?
   (d) _ Do you give any allowances not mentioned above?

VI. Sales Information (This section only applies to FSS solicitations).

   Estimate the percentage of your sales made to the U.S. Government under Federal Supply Schedule Blanket Purchase Arrangements (check one of the following):

   None ___   25% or less ___   25% to 49% ___

   50% to 75% ___   75% or more ___

   List agencies below:

   1. _____
   2. _____
   3. _____
   4. _____
   etc.

Appendix 6.1   (*Continued*)

138

Solicitation No. _____ Special Item No. _____ Offeror Name _____

VII.

A. This section requires (1) that sales information be provided to enable the contracting officer to determine that the items meet the test of commerciality in FAR 15.804-3 and ASPM Vol. 1, Chapter 9; and (2) that pricing data is furnished in sufficient detail to enable the contracting officer to perform a price analysis in accordance with FAR 15.804-3(h).

B. The offeror certifies that, except for the individual models/types or catalog numbers cited in paragraph C below, all other models/types or catalog numbers offered in response to this solicitation meet the tests of commerciality in FAR 15.804-3 and ASPM Vol. 1, Chapter 9. Of the individual models/types or catalog numbers so certified, sales information shall be provided in the table below for each of the __ models/types or catalog numbers with the largest dollar sales volume. The sales information provided is _ for the prior 12 months, from __ to __ for this special item number.

1. Total annual sales to the Government under this special item number $_____.
2. Total annual sales (to all entities) under this special item number $_____.

1	2	3	4	5	6		7		8
Model/Type or catalog no.	Total annual sales to Fed. Govt.	Total annual sales to nongovernment customers at catalog price (less published discounts).	Total annual sales to nongovernment customers at other than catalog price.	Total annual sales: Columns 2, 3, and 4	Provide information below for largest discount granted to any nongovernment customer		List the largest discount at which the item was sold for comparable sales/quantities shown in column 2 to any nongovernment customer during the past year		Is the discount in block number 6 greater than your current offer under this solicitation? Yes_ No_. If yes, provide complete documentation and rationale of the difference. Merely terms and conditions of commercial contracts, commercial warranties, etc. will not be adequate to justify the difference.
	$ / % of column 5		% of column 3 if more than 25% / $		Qty	Discount	Qty	Discount	

Appendix 6.1 (Continued)

139

VII. - contd.

C. Sales information in the table below shall be provided for each individual model/type or catalog number in the above special item number that is not certified commercial when experienced annual government sales are $100,000 or more.

1	2		3	4		5	6		7		8
Model/Type or catalog no.	Total annual sales to Fed. Govt.		Total annual sales to nongovernment customers at catalog price (less published discounts).	Total annual sales to nongovernment customers at other than catalog price.		Total annual sales: Columns 2, 3, and 4	Provide information below for largest discount granted to any nongovernment customer		List the largest discount at which the item was sold for comparable sales/quantities shown in column 2 to any nongovernment customer during the past year		Is the discount in block number 6 greater than your current offer under this solicitation? Yes_ No_. If yes, provide complete documentation and rationale of the difference. Merely terms and conditions of commercial contracts, commercial warranties, etc. will not be adequate to justify the difference.
		% of column 5			% of column 3 if more than 25%		Qty	Discount	Qty	Discount	
	$			$							

Note: 1. Federal Government sales include all sales to U.S. Government and its instrumentalities and for U.S. Government use, sales directly to U.S. Government prime contractors and to their subcontractors or suppliers at any time, for use as an end item or as part of an end item, by the U.S. Government.

2. Nongovernment customer is defined as other than Government or affiliates (include sales to distributors, dealers, OEM, national accounts, educational institutions, state, etc.).

3. Discounts are reductions to catalog or market prices (published or unpublished) applicable to any customer, including OEMs, dealers, distributors, national accounts, states, etc.; and any other form of price reduction such as concessions, rebates, quantity discounts, allowances, services, warranties, installation, free parts, etc., which are granted to any customer.

Appendix 6.1   (Continued)

COMMERCIAL SALES PRACTICES FORMAT

NAME OF OFFEROR:
SIN(S):

INSTRUCTIONS:

Please refer to clause 552.212-70, PREPARATION OF OFFER (MULTIPLE AWARD SCHEDULE), for additional information concerning your offer. Provide the following information for each SIN (or group of SINs or SubSIN) for which information is the same.

1. Provide the dollar value of sales to the general public at or based on an established catalog or market price during the previous 12 month period of the offeror's last fiscal year. $_____. State beginning and ending of the 12 month period. Beginning: _____. Ending: _____. In the event that a dollar value is not an appropriate measure of the sales, provide and describe your own measure of the sales of the item(s).

2. Show your total projected annual sales to the government under this contract for the contract term, excluding options, for each SIN offered. If you currently hold a Federal Supply Schedule contract for the SIN the total projected annual sales should be based on your most recent 12 months of sales under that contract. SIN: _____ $ _____; SIN: _____ $ _____; SIN: _____ $ _____.

3. Based on your written discounting policies (standard commercial sales practices in the event you do not have written discounting policies), are the discounts and any concessions which you offer the government equal to or better than your best price (discount and concessions in any combination) offered to any customer acquiring the same items regardless of quantity or terms and conditions? YES ___ NO ___. (See definition of "concession" and "discount" in 552.212-70.)

4. Information by SIN

   a) Based on your written discounting policies (standard commercial sales practices in the event you do not have written discounting policies), provide information as requested for each SIN (or group of SINs for which the information is the same) in accordance with the instructions at Table 515-1 which is provided in this solicitation for your convenience. The information should be provided in the chart below or in an equivalent format developed by the offeror. Rows should be added to accommodate as many customers as required. See definition of "concession" and "discount" in 552.212-70.

COLUMN 1 CUSTOMER	COLUMN 2 DISCOUNT	COLUMN 3 QUANTITY/VOLUME	COLUMN 4 FOB TERM	COLUMN 5 CONCESSIONS

   b) Do any deviations from your written policies or standard commercial sales practices disclosed in the above chart ever result in better discounts (lower prices) or concessions than indicated? YES ___ NO ___. If YES, explain deviations in accordance with the instructions at Table 515-1 which is provided in this solicitation for your convenience.

5. If you are a dealer/reseller without significant sales to the general public, you should provide manufacturers' information required by paragraphs (1) through (4) above for each item/SIN offered, if the manufacturer's sales under any resulting contract are expected to exceed $500,000. You must also obtain written authorization from the manufacturer(s) for government access, at any time before award or before agreeing to a modification, to the manufacturer's sales records for the purpose of verifying the information submitted by the manufacturer. The information is required in order to enable the government to make a determination that the offered price is fair and reasonable. To expedite the review and processing of offers, you should advise the manufacturer(s) of this requirement. The contracting officer may require the information be submitted on electronic media with commercially available spreadsheet(s). The information may be provided by the manufacturer directly to the government. If the manufacturer's item(s) is being offered by multiple dealers/resellers, only one copy of the requested information should be submitted to the government. In addition, you must submit the following information along with a listing of contact information regarding each of the manufacturers whose products and/or services are included in the offer (include the manufacturer's name, address, the manufacturer's contact point, telephone number, and FAX number) for each model offered by SIN:

   a) Manufacturer's Name
   b) Manufacturer's Part Number
   c) Dealer's/Reseller's Part Number
   d) Product Description
   e) Manufacturer's List Price
   f) Dealer's/Reseller's percentage discount from list price or net prices.

Appendix 6.2 Commercial Sales Practices Format

Chapter Seven

Government Contract Cost Principles

7-1. HISTORICAL PERSPECTIVE

Cost criteria for government contracts first surfaced during World War I but addressed only allowability, not allocability. Renewed interest in building up the nation's defenses led to the passage of the Vinson–Trammell Act[1] and the Merchant Marine Act,[2] which addressed limitations on profit, but not the broader issue of costs against which profits are measured. Treasury Decision 5000 was issued in August 1940 to provide criteria for determining costs under the Vinson–Trammel Act. This document, a joint effort of the Treasury, Navy, and War Departments, addressed not only cost allowability but also cost allocability. An April 1942 booklet, known as the "Green Book," contained the cost principles for determining costs under defense contracts, as established by Treasury Decision 5000, and remained in effect until the first Armed Services Procurement Regulation (ASPR), Section XV, was issued in 1949. That section consisted of a tersely written 12-page promulgation establishing cost principles for cost-type contracts.

In 1955, the Hoover Commission recommended the development of cost principles for cost-reimbursement-type contracts that reflected generally accepted accounting principles for commercial organization and audit guidelines for determining costs on fixed-price-type contracts. The Department of Defense (DOD) subsequently undertook an ambitious project to completely revise the cost principles. The revised ASPR cost principles, discussed extensively with industry associations before their final promulgation in 1959, were somewhat similar to the current principles, but their application was limited to cost-reimbursement-type contracts. In 1970, ASPR, Section XV, was made applicable to all defense contracts in which cost was a factor in arriving at the price. The ASPR was redesignated as the Defense Acquisition Regulation (DAR) in 1978. During this period, the Federal Procurement Regulations (FPR) for civilian agencies were established by the Administrator of the General Services Administration (GSA). The FPR tended to follow and largely adopt the cost principles in DAR, Section XV.

The Federal Acquisition Regulation (FAR) and departmental FAR supplements, applicable to contracts awarded on or after April 1, 1984, replaced all the cost principles previously in effect. The various departments and agencies that have issued procurement cost principles are listed in Appendix 7.1.

Because the FAR citations differ from those in the prior regulations, a cross-reference list is provided in Appendix 7.2.

The FAR and FAR supplements contain separate cost principles for contracts and/or grants awarded to the following types of organizations that have substantially differing characteristics:

- Commercial organizations (Although construction and architect–engineer contracts are subject to the cost principles for commercial organizations, separate cost principles are provided for owning, operating, and renting construction equipment.)
- Educational institutions
- State, local, and federally recognized Indian tribal governments
- Nonprofit organizations

The Department of Veterans Affairs (DVA) also has separate cost principles for vocational rehabilitation and education contracts.

7-2. ADVANCE AGREEMENTS ON PARTICULAR COST ITEMS (FAR 31.109)

It is difficult to apply allowability and allocability concepts to the many different kinds of industries and accounting systems. Because of differences by industry, by contract, and by other circumstances, and in an effort to avoid unnecessary disputes on cost allowability, the cost principles apply broadly to many accounting systems in varying contract situations. Thus, the reasonableness and allocability of certain cost items to a given contract may be difficult to determine, particularly when firms or organizational divisions within firms may not be subject to effective competitive restraints.

To avoid possible disallowance or dispute based on unreasonableness or non-allocability, contractors are encouraged to seek advance agreement with the government on the treatment to be accorded special or unusual costs. Such agreements may also be initiated by the government. Advance agreements may be negotiated either before or during contract performance but ideally should be negotiated before the cost covered by the agreement is incurred. Agreements must be in writing, executed by both contracting parties, and incorporated in the applicable contracts. Contracting officers (COs) are not authorized to enter into advance agreements for the treatment of cost inconsistent with the other provisions of the cost principles. For example, an advance agreement may not allow interest or entertainment cost, since these costs are expressly stated to be unallowable in the Selected Costs section of the cost principles.

Examples of costs for which advance agreements may be particularly important include the following:

- Compensation for personal services
- Use charges for fully depreciated assets
- Deferred maintenance costs
- Precontract costs

- Independent research and development (IR&D) and bid and proposal (B&P) costs
- Royalties and other costs for use of patents
- Selling and distribution costs
- Travel and relocation costs as related to special or mass personnel movements, contractor-owned, -leased, or -chartered aircraft, or maximum per diem rates
- Costs of idle facilities and idle capacity
- Severance pay to employees on support service contracts
- Plant reconversion
- Professional services
- General and administrative (G&A) expenses particularly related to: construction; job site; architect–engineer; facilities; and government-owned, contractor-operated plant contracts
- Costs of construction plant and equipment
- Costs of public relations and advertising
- Training and education costs

Given the potentially controversial nature of many of these costs, it is readily understandable why they are suggested as items for which advance agreements may be appropriate.

7-3. COMPOSITION OF TOTAL ALLOWABLE COSTS

The cost principles of commercial organizations define the "total cost of a contract" as the sum of the allowable direct and indirect costs allocable to the contract, less allocable credits, plus any allocable cost of money.

Direct versus Indirect

The distinction between direct and indirect costs is a significant concept in the cost principles. A direct cost is identifiable with a specific final cost objective (e.g., the contract), whereas indirect costs are incurred for more than one cost objective. However, direct costs of insignificant amounts may be treated as indirect costs for administrative convenience. Consistent application of criteria for identifying costs as either direct or indirect is emphasized. Once a cost is identified as a direct cost to a particular contract, the same type of cost, incurred in similar circumstances, may not be included in any indirect expense pool allocated to that contract or any other contract. The cost principles do not prescribe which costs should be charged as direct as opposed to indirect. The criteria for charging direct versus indirect should be based on an analysis of the nature of the particular contractor's business and contracts. The criteria should be codified into a written statement of accounting principles and practices for classifying costs and for allocating indirect costs to contracts.

Allocation of Indirect Costs

Indirect expenses should be accumulated into logical cost groupings to permit distribution of expenses in relation to benefits received by the cost objectives.

The techniques or methods used to measure the amount of pooled costs to be allocated to cost objectives should be based on the extent of benefit derived from activities included in each pool.

The indirect expense allocation criteria contained in the acquisition regulations do not mandate the use of any particular cost distribution base. Rather, they permit any distribution base that equitably distributes indirect costs to appropriate cost objectives. The flexibility reflected in the criteria is illustrated by the Department of Housing and Urban Development (HUD) Contract Appeals Board's decision, which overruled the government's demand that Abeles, Schwartz, Haeckel, and Silverblatt, Inc.,[3] a small business not covered by cost accounting standards, allocate its G&A expenses on a total cost input base.

Once an appropriate allocation base has been established, the base cannot be fragmented by removing unallowable costs.[4]

Factors Affecting Allowability

Costs are not allowable merely because they were determined by application of the company's established accounting system. Factors considered in determining the allowability of individual cost items include: (1) reasonableness; (2) allocability; (3) cost accounting standards, if applicable, or generally accepted accounting principles and practices appropriate in the particular circumstances; (4) terms of the contract; and (5) limitations specified in the cost principles. A company should succeed in obtaining reimbursement for incurred costs if the CO believes that all these criteria have been met.

7-4. REASONABLENESS (FAR 31.201-3)

Reasonableness has been one of the more difficult concepts in the regulations, and understandably so in view of the substantially subjective nature of the concept. The cost principles consider a cost to be reasonable if, in its nature and amount, it does not exceed that which would be incurred by a prudent person in the conduct of competitive business.

The cost principles recognize that reasonableness must often be determined on a case-by-case basis, considering the specific circumstances, nature, and amount of the cost in question.

Reasonableness determinations depend upon a variety of considerations and circumstances, including the following:

- Is the cost generally recognized as ordinary and necessary for conducting business or performing the contract?

- Does the cost reflect sound business practices, arm's length bargaining, and the requirements of federal and state laws and regulations?

- Would a prudent businessperson take similar action, considering his or her responsibilities to the business owners, employees, customers, the government, and the public?

- Are significant deviations from established contractor practices inordinately increasing contract costs?

Case Law

Before 1987, costs incurred by the contractor were presumed to be reasonable. As a result, the government had the burden of establishing, by a preponderance of evidence, that an incurred cost was unreasonable. As might be expected, the government frequently failed to meet that burden of proof.

- In *Bruce Construction Corp., et al. v. United States,*[5] the Court of Claims concluded that:

  > Where there is an alleged disparity between "historical" and "reasonable" costs, the historical costs are presumed reasonable. Since the presumption is that a contractor's claimed cost is reasonable, the Government must carry the very heavy burden of showing that the claimed cost was of such a nature that it should not have been expended, or that the contractor's costs were more than were justified in the particular circumstance.

- In *Western Electric Company, Inc.,*[6] the Armed Services Board of Contract Appeals (ASBCA) concluded that "if a cost is of a type that is generally recognized as ordinary and necessary for the conduct of a particular business or the performance of particular contracts, it bears the primary indication of reasonableness and allowability." While the Board recognized that reasonableness related to amount as well as to activities, it concluded that the government "failed to overcome appellant's prima facie showing of reasonableness as to the amount of its 1960 expenditures, or that appellant abused its discretion by incurring costs far in excess of what was necessary under the circumstances."

- In 1983, the ASBCA overruled the government's disallowance of Data-Design Laboratories'[7] reimbursements to employees for overtime hours spent in business travel outside the normal workday. In concluding that the government failed to support its assertion of unreasonableness, the Board observed the following:

  > ...[T]he Government cannot merely superimpose its opinion in contradiction to that of the contractor. It must show why the contractor's actions were not those which a prudent business person would have taken. A presumption of reasonableness attaches to costs which were actually incurred by a contractor and is measured by the situation which existed at the time of performance.

- In *Stanley Aviation Corp.,*[8] the government, without objecting to any specific overhead item, disallowed a portion of the allocable overhead on the premise that the overhead rates were unreasonably high. The ASBCA rejected the government's argument, concluding that "the appellant is entitled to be reimbursed at the actually-experienced overhead rates" and "that there is no provision of the contract or of the Section XV cost principles ... requiring that costs or rates be competitive in order to be reasonable."

- In *General Dynamics Corp., Convair Division,*[9] the ASBCA rejected the government's disallowance of direct material costs that were asserted to have been unreasonably incurred. The Board concluded that "a preponderance of evidence shows that these subcontracts incurred by the prime contractor were reasonable costs under the prime contracts and are allowable thereunder."

Before 1987, the government had little success in disallowing cost based on unreasonableness except when it established that the contractor had abused its discretion by incurring the cost in question. In one such case, the Court of Claims denied General Dynamics Corporation's[10] request for reimbursement of losses incurred in the construction of employee housing. The court concluded that the contractor acted unreasonably in undertaking a housing construction project when, in fact, the government had declined to approve the project and had warned that the cost would not be allowed in the contract.

Effective July 30, 1987, the presumption of reasonableness that was previously associated with the incurrence of costs was eliminated. FAR 31.201-3 was revised to shift the burden of proof, with respect to reasonableness, to the contractor once the CO initially challenged a specific cost. Although this change has not necessarily resulted in a significant decrease in cost recovery on issues related to cost reasonableness, contractors, of necessity, have expended considerably more effort justifying their costs than was required prior to implementation of this change.

Contractor Weighted Average Share in Cost Risk

In 1966, the DOD developed a technique called Contractor Weighted Average Share in Cost Risk (CWAS) to determine and to express numerically the degree of cost risk a contractor assumed based on the mix of contract types that it agreed to perform. For CWAS-qualified contractors, selected costs designated "CWAS" were presumed reasonable in nature and amount, even if the amounts exceeded stated ceilings. In July 1983, CWAS coverage was deleted from the DAR, Part 15, and was never incorporated into the FAR, Part 31. The decision to eliminate CWAS reflected an emerging government philosophy that a substantial volume of commercial and/or competitively awarded government firm-fixed-price contracts did not, in itself, sufficiently motivate a contractor to conserve resources. The elimination of CWAS significantly affected defense contractors whose corporate offices were CWAS-qualified because costs previously designated as CWAS qualified, which were incurred either at the corporate office or pursuant to corporate policy, were no longer shielded from government challenges of reasonableness.

7-5. ALLOCABILITY (FAR 31.201-4)

The second factor affecting allowability of cost is allocability. Although the concept is not complicated, its application can become extremely difficult and frequently controversial. The cost principles consider a cost to be allocable if it is assignable or chargeable to one or more cost objectives in accordance with the relative benefits received or other equitable relationship. Subject to the foregoing, a cost is allocable to a government contract if it:

- Is incurred specifically for the contract
- Benefits both the contract and other work, or both government work and other work, and can be distributed to them in reasonable proportion to the benefits received or
- Is necessary to the overall operation of the business, although a direct relationship to any particular cost objective cannot be shown

Disputes in this area usually do not address whether an expenditure is allocable, but rather how it is allocable. If it is direct, the entire cost is recoverable against a specific contract; if indirect, only an appropriate portion of the expense can be recovered on a given contract. Frequently, litigation in this area has focused on the extent of "benefit" to the government. In *General Dynamics/Astronautics*,[11] the ASBCA ruled that the contractor's payment to the state of California to partially underwrite the cost of constructing a highway overpass near its plant directly benefited the government program from the standpoint of efficiency in conserving employee working time. The Board concluded its decision by observing, "And this view is not altered by circumstances that the accrued benefit is perhaps not susceptible of precise mathematical measurement."

As discussed under Selected Costs, a number of disputes related to professional and consultant service fees have centered on the issue of allocability to government contracts.

7-6. COST ACCOUNTING STANDARDS AND THEIR PRIMACY OVER GENERALLY ACCEPTED ACCOUNTING PRINCIPLES

While cost accounting standards are discussed in depth in Chapter 8, a few comments on the relationship of the standards to the allowability of costs are appropriate at this point. Cost accounting standards relate to allocability, not allowability, of costs. In its "Statement of Objectives, Policies, and Concepts," dated May 1992, the Cost Accounting Standards Board (CASB) noted the following:

> While the Board has exclusive authority for establishing Standards governing the measurement, assignment and allocation of costs, it does not determine the allowability of categories or individual items of cost. Allowability is a procurement concept affecting contract price and in most cases is established in regulatory or contractual provisions. An agency's policies on allowability of costs may be derived from law and are generally embodied in its procurement regulations. A contracting agency may include in contract terms or in its procurement regulations a provision that will refuse to allow certain costs incurred by contractors that are unreasonable in amount or contrary to public policy. In accounting terms, those same costs may be allocable to the contract in question.[12]

When cost accounting standards have been specifically incorporated into the cost principles (Appendix 7.3), a practice inconsistent with these standards is subject to disallowance under the cost principles as well as a finding of noncompliance with the standards. Excess costs resulting from practices not consistent with established practices will also be disallowed. The ASBCA concluded in *The Boeing Co.*[13] that, if conflicting allocability criteria exist between Cost Accounting Standards (CAS) and the cost principles, CAS prevails. However, as discussed further in Chapter 8, the continued validity of that decision was cast in doubt in *Rice v. Martin Marietta Corp.*[14] In that decision, the Federal Circuit Court concluded that DAR 15-203(c) (now FAR 31.201-3) did not conflict with CAS 410 because CAS 410 addressed allocation, whereas the DAR provision simply disallowed the allocable cost.

If cost accounting standards are not applicable, generally accepted accounting principles (GAAP) may be an authoritative reference for determining appropriate accounting treatment.

Pursuant to Statement on Auditing Standards (SAS) No. 69,[15] issued by the American Institute of Certified Public Accountants (AICPA), the phrase *generally accepted accounting principles* is derived from four sources:

1. Category (a), officially established accounting principles, consists of Financial Accounting Standards Board (FASB) statements of financial

accounting standards and interpretations, Accounting Principles Board (APB) opinions, and AICPA accounting research bulletins.

2. Category (b) consists of FASB technical bulletins and, if cleared by the FASB, AICPA industry audit and accounting guides and AICPA statements of position.

3. Category (c) consists of AICPA Accounting Standards Executive Committee (AcSEC) practice bulletins that have been cleared by the FASB and consensus positions of the FASB Emerging Issues Task Force.

4. Category (d) includes AICPA accounting interpretations and implementation guides ("Qs and As") published by the FASB staff, and practices that are widely recognized and prevalent either generally or in the industry.

Considerable weight is generally given to GAAP when more definitive accounting treatment is not prescribed in the acquisition regulations, CAS, or the contract itself. In *Blue Cross Association and Blue Cross of Virginia*,[16] the ASBCA observed that normally the contractor's established allocation practices that are in accord with GAAP should be accepted unless they are required to be changed by a new contractual provision or unless re-examination of the practices is warranted as a result of unusual circumstances. However, the boards and courts have also cautioned against relying on GAAP to determine the allocability of costs to government contracts by noting that "such principles have been developed for asset valuation and income measurement and 'are not cost accounting principles' as such, although 'cost accounting concepts ... may evolve out of them."[17] When the cost accounting treatment permitted by GAAP is contrary to the criteria provided in the CAS, cost principles, or the contract, these latter criteria generally prevail. In *Grumman Aerospace Corp. v. United States*,[18] the court rejected the contractor's argument that, under GAAP, its 1968 state franchise tax refund resulting from the carryback of its 1971 net operating loss should be credited to 1971 costs, not 1968 costs. In its decision, the court concluded that "with regard to how GAAP and sound accounting logic might treat the refund for income tax accounting purposes, the contract language prevails here." The ASBCA reached a similar conclusion in *Physics International Co.*,[19] when it decided that "even if appellant's intercompany allocations are consistent with the generally accepted accounting principles, they cannot dictate reimbursability by the Government when the cost item in question does not meet the ASPR specific allowability criteria."

7-7. SELECTED COSTS

The acquisition regulations address specific limitations or exclusions for numerous cost items. Contracts awarded before April 1, 1984, remain subject to the prior regulations (e.g., DAR). To some extent, the FAR enhanced uniformity in determining acceptable costs under government contracts, but agency differences still exist, as indicated in Appendix 7.4.

The cost principles have changed over the years with disturbing regularity in response to unique aspects of government contracting, such as public policy considerations, administrative convenience, and congressional interest. The cost principles essentially establish three categories of costs.

1. Expressly allowable
2. Partially unallowable or require special consideration
3. Expressly unallowable

The acquisition regulations require that expressly unallowable costs, plus all directly associated costs, be identified and excluded from proposals, billings, and claims submitted to the government. *Directly associated costs* are defined as those that would not have been incurred if the other cost (e.g., the unallowable cost) had not been incurred. Salary costs of employees who engage in activities that result in unallowable costs, such as acquisitions and mergers, are generally unallowable only if the employees expend a substantial portion of their time on the unallowable activity; however, for certain proscribed activities (e.g., lobbying and certain legal proceedings), the salary costs are themselves unallowable, regardless of amount. In *General Dynamics Corp.*,[20] the ASBCA concluded that only variable costs should be considered directly associated costs of unallowable flights on corporate aircraft and therefore subject to disallowance.

A contractor must have a process for distinguishing unallowable costs from otherwise allowable costs. Without that capability, a company is vulnerable to a determination of noncompliance with CAS 405 or execution of a false indirect cost certificate for failure to delete expressly unallowable costs from claims and proposals submitted to the government.

The cost principles do not address each cost that may be incurred, and the absence of a cost principle for a particular cost item does not imply that it is either allowable or unallowable. The cost principles previously provided that determinations of allowability in these instances should be based on the principles and standards included in the subpart and, when appropriate, on the treatment of similar or related items. Federal Acquisition Regulation 31.204 was revised effective June 17, 1988, to provide the following:

> When more than one subsection in 31.205 is relevant to a contractor cost, the cost shall be apportioned among the applicable subsections, and the determination of allowability of each portion shall be based on the guidance contained in the applicable subsection. When a cost, to which more than one subsection in 31.205 is relevant, cannot be apportioned, the determination of allowability shall be based on the guidance contained in the subsection that most specifically deals with, or best captures the essential nature of, the cost at issue.

Cost items described in the cost principles as either expressly allowable (assuming reasonableness and allocability tests are met) or expressly unallowable are summarized in Appendix 7.5. Certain costs that warrant special consideration or that may be either allowable or unallowable, depending on the particular circumstances, are discussed in the remainder of this chapter.

Public Relations and Advertising Costs (FAR 31.205-1)

Effective April 7, 1986, this cost principle was retitled and revised to add coverage on public relations to the existing coverage on advertising. While the revision did not substantively change the advertising provisions, the coverage on public relations limited allowable public relations costs to a narrower range of activities. The cost principle also provides that costs that are unallowable under this principle are not allowable under other cost principles and vice versa. The cost principle discusses advertising in the context of media advertising (e.g., magazines, newspapers, radio and television, direct mail, trade papers, outdoor advertising, dealer cards and window displays, conventions, exhibits, and free goods and samples) and directly associated costs. It defines *public relations* as all functions and activities related to maintaining, protecting, and enhancing the image of a concern or its products and maintaining or promoting reciprocal understanding and favorable relations with the public at large or any segment of the public. This definition includes activities associated with such areas as advertising and customer relations.

Allowable advertising costs are limited to those that are solely for the following:

- Recruitment of personnel for performing government contracts, when considered in conjunction with all other recruitment costs
- Procurement of scarce items for performing government contracts
- Disposal of scrap or surplus materials acquired under government contracts

Costs of this nature, if incurred for more than one contract or for both contract work and other work of the contractor, are allowable to the extent that they are reasonably apportioned among the various benefiting objectives.

Other advertising costs, such as those related to sales promotion, are not allowable. The ASBCA characterized such costs in *Aerojet-General Corp.*[21] as

> ... the paid use of time or space to promote the sale of products either directly by stimulating interest in a product or product line, or indirectly by disseminating messages calling favorable attention to the advertiser for the purpose of enhancing its overall image to sell its products. In both instances the advertiser controls form and content of the message and selects the medium of presentation and its timing.

The government's disallowance of advertising related to sales promotions stems from two considerations.

1. Companies do not have to sell to the government in the same manner that they sell to the general public. Sales to the government are accomplished through direct contacts and submission of solicited and unsolicited proposals, and these costs are allowable as selling or bidding costs.
2. The annual Defense Appropriation Acts forbid the use of appropriated funds for any advertising other than that specified above.

Allowable public relations costs are limited to the following:

- Activities specifically required by contract
- Responses to inquiries on company policy and activities and communications with the public, press, stockholders, creditors, and customers
- Communicating with the public, press, stockholders, creditors, and customers
- General liaison with news media and government public relations officers, limited to activities that are necessary to keep the public informed on matters of public concern, such as contract awards, plant closings or openings, employee layoffs or rehires, and financial information
- Participation in community service activities
- Plant tours and open houses
- Keel laying, ship launching, and rollout ceremonies, to the extent specifically provided for by contract
- Activities to promote sales of products normally sold to the U.S. government which contain significant efforts to promote exports from the United States

Companies should properly distinguish between costs for advertising, image-enhancement public relations, B&P, information dissemination, and selling activities in their indirect expense accounts. B&P costs and costs associated with information-disseminating activities are allowable. In *Aerojet-General Corp.*[22] the Board concluded that the following items that had been challenged as unallowable advertising costs did not fall into the definition of advertising and were thus allowable.

- A monthly magazine, circulated outside the company, which contained semitechnical summaries of the company's developments in technologies, progress on government programs, and changes in personnel
- Salaried costs for the company's public communications department, which provided liaison with news media and government public information offices
- A company profile brochure which was prepared in response to business inquiries and replied to factual questions about the company (Copies were provided to interested parties.)
- A brochure describing the company's effort to increase employees' knowledge and participation in the political process (Copies were sent to interested companies and political parties.)
- A reprint of a speech made by the company president (Copies were sent to interested parties and the news media.)
- Photographs and fact sheets for news releases (The fact sheets were distributed to the news media.)

Even before the cost principle was revised, the ASBCA observed in *Blue Cross/Blue Shield,*[23] that "where the major purpose of the message was image enhancement or sales, we concluded no share of the cost be allocated [to the government contract]." The board went on to decide, however, that mass media messages relating to health education, health care cost containment, and subscriber services did not fall into the category of image enhancement or sales; therefore, the costs should not be considered unallowable.

Civil Defense Cost (FAR 31.205-5)

Reasonable costs of civil defense measures undertaken on the company's premises, pursuant to suggestions or requirements of civil defense authorities, are allowable. Contributions to local civil defense funds and projects are unallowable.

Compensation for Personal Services (FAR 31.205-6)

Compensation for personal services is essentially defined in the cost principles as all remuneration paid currently or accrued for services rendered by employees during contract performance.

Reasonableness

Allowable total compensation of individual employees must be reasonable for the services rendered. Certain types of compensation, such as bonuses, incentive compensation, and severance pay, must also be paid pursuant to an employer–

employee agreement or an established plan that has been consistently followed. Allowable compensation must reflect the terms and conditions of established compensation plans or practices. No presumption of allowability exists if the government did not receive advance notice of major changes in compensation plans.

The cost principles identify the following circumstances that the government will closely scrutinize in determining whether compensation paid is reasonable:

- Compensation to owners of closely held corporations, partners, sole proprietors, or persons who have a significant financial interest in the business entity
- Increases in the company's compensation policy that coincide with an increase in government business
- Absence of a competitive environment that would help to control the reasonableness of all costs, including employee compensation
- Provisions of labor–management agreements that appear unwarranted or discriminatory against the government

In *Lockheed Corp. v. United States*,[24] the Department of Justice declined to pursue the government's disallowance of compensation costs for secretarial and security personnel paid in accordance with a negotiated union agreement. The Defense Contract Audit Agency (DCAA) questioned the reasonableness of the costs, because they were out of line with wages paid for similar services by other companies in the same geographical area. The government stipulated in its confession of judgment that Lockheed was entitled to the full relief it was seeking.

As a result of this case, the DOD Director of Defense Procurement issued a March 14, 1991, memorandum to the Director of the DCAA,[25] stating that "arms length" negotiated labor–management agreements should be considered reasonable unless the provisions of the agreement were either unwarranted by the character and circumstance of the work or discriminatory against the government. In the absence of union agreements, factors to be considered in evaluating reasonableness of compensation would include, among other things, wages paid for similar services by other companies in the same geographical area.

The cost principle was revised in 1986 to provide more detailed guidelines for determining the reasonableness of compensation practices. The current language makes clear that compensation is reasonable if each element of the compensation package is reasonable and that the contractor has the burden of proof in demonstrating the reasonableness of each element that may be challenged by the government. The contractor may, however, within certain specified limits, introduce other offsetting compensation elements when the reasonableness of some part of the program is challenged. Such offsets are considered only between the following allowable elements of an employee's (or a class of employees) compensation costs:

- Wages and salaries
- Incentive bonuses
- Deferred compensation
- Pension and savings plan benefits
- Health insurance benefits
- Life insurance benefits
- Compensated personal absences

Since 1995, contractors have been subject to statutory caps on the allowability of compensation costs.

- The Fiscal Year 1995 Defense Appropriations Act[26] capped allowable individual compensation at $250,000 per year for applicability to defense contracts awarded after April 15, 1995, and funded by fiscal year 1995 appropriations. The ceiling, applicable to DOD awards to commercial contractors, educational institutions, state and local governments, and nonprofit organizations, was implemented in DFARS 231.205-6(a)(2)(i)(A), 231.202, 231.603, and 231.703, effective December 14, 1994. The ceiling was (1) applied to the broad definition of compensation contained in FAR 31.205-6 (which includes salaries and wages, bonuses, differential and overtime pay, deferred compensation, pensions, fringe benefits, etc.); and (2) computed on the basis of amounts incurred, not amounts allocated to DOD awards.

- The *Fiscal Year 1996 Defense Appropriations Act*[27] capped allowable individual compensation at $200,000 per year for applicability to new defense contracts awarded after July 1, 1996, and funded with fiscal year 1996 appropriations. The implementing regulation, found in DFARS 231.205-6(a)(2)(i)(B), was effective July 10, 1996.

- Congress passed separate compensation cost allowability limits in the Fiscal Year 1997 Defense Appropriations[28] and Defense Authorization[29] Acts. The Appropriations Act provision, which applies to defense contracts and subcontracts funded with fiscal year 1997 appropriations, was implemented in DFARS 231.205-6(a)(2)(ii). The Authorization Act, which applies to non-DOD contracts and subcontracts awarded during fiscal year 1997 was implemented in FAR 31.205-6(p), effective January 1, 1997. Both statutory provisions define compensation as the total amount of taxable wages paid to the employee plus any elective deferred compensation, [e.g., 401(k) contributions] earned for the year. The statutes did not, however, apply the ceilings to the same employees. The Appropriations Act ceiling applied to all defense contractor personnel, whereas the Authorization Act ceiling applied only to the five highest compensated personnel at a contractor's home office, each intermediate home office, and each segment.

- Congress included in the Fiscal Year 1997 Authorization Act the requirement for a comprehensive review of senior executive compensation. The study legislative proposal, entitled the "Contract Costs Act of 1997" was forwarded to Congress by the Director of the Office of Management and Budget (OMB) on February 28, 1997. The proposal defined compensation on a basis consistent with the Fiscal Year 1997 Defense Authorization Act and limited allowable compensation to an amount derived from the 50th percentile of a compensation survey or surveys that were commercial or otherwise independent and determined to be appropriate to the contractor by the cognizant administrative contracting officer (ACO). In lieu of the ceiling methodology proposed by the OMB, the Fiscal Year 1998 National Defense Authorization Act[30] adopted a provision for the Administrator for Procurement Policy to establish an annual ceiling at the median compensation paid to all senior executives of U.S. publicly owned corporations with annual sales over $50 million. For purposes of the cap, compensation is defined as wages, bonuses and deferred compensation that is recorded on the contractor's cost accounting records. The compensation limits apply to compensation incurred after January 1, 1998 and earned by the five highest compensated personnel at corporate headquarters and each segment and intermediate home office that reports directly to company's headquarters.

Over the years, government auditors have questioned the level of compensation paid to chief executive officers, particularly of smaller companies. In situations in which compensation is being questioned on a basis other than the statutory ceilings, several ASBCA cases may assist companies in establishing the reasonableness of executive compensation. Although the first three decisions cited below were issued when the burden of proof was squarely on the government, they still have relevance. Contractors must now simply justify the reasonableness of challenged compensation through such means as determining the compensation levels paid by comparable firms.

- In *Lulejean and Associates, Inc.*,[31] the ASBCA reinstated the government's disallowances of executive salaries that exceeded the midpoint of salaries for comparable positions within the industry. The Board noted that for the year in which the study was made, the salaries of the Lulejean executives were within the range recommended by the government analyst. In the Board's view:

  > There is no explanation in the record why the ACO selected the midpoint of each range as "acceptable" salary or why a salary which was above the midpoint, but still within the recommended range, was unreasonable. Since levels of reasonable compensation can be more meaningfully represented by ranges below and above a certain figure than by a precise figure, we perceive no reason why the actual salaries of these five persons were unreasonable.

- In *Space Services of Georgia, Inc.*,[32] the Board considered the annual chief executive's salary of $100,000 to be reasonable compensation in April 1980 for a company providing mess attendant services with sales between $5 and $10 million.

- In *Burt Associates, Inc.*,[33] the Board considered annual chief executive compensation of $63,000 ($53,000 salary and $10,000 bonus) to be reasonable compensation in 1977 for a research and consulting corporation with annual revenues of $409,000. Significantly, the Board acknowledged that executives who own their own companies tend to be compensated at higher levels than those who do not. In its decision, the Board concluded:

  > When measured against average compensation of the highest paid executives ... Dr. Burt's compensation appears to be on the high side. However, when measured against the total compensation of executives who are majority owners of their companies, Dr. Burt's compensation falls within the range of compensation received by such executives. ... [O]n the record before us we cannot discount Dr. Burt's overwhelming responsibility for the success of his company and the long hours devoted to achieving that success. We conclude that Dr. Burt's compensation in fiscal year 1977 was reasonable under the circumstances.

- Based on Techplan Corporation's sustained growth and profitability,[34] the ASBCA agreed that the 75th percentile of an appropriate survey was a more appropriate basis for comparison to the chief executive officer's compensation than either the median or the average. In addition, the Board rejected the government's argument that a 10% range of reasonableness could not be used at the 75th percentile.

Bonuses

The Fiscal Year 1996, 1997 and 1998 Defense Appropriation Acts, as implemented in DFARS 231.205-6, prohibit reimbursement with fiscal year 1996 or subsequent year funds of employee bonuses in excess of normal salary when paid pursuant to restructuring associated with a business combination.

Employee Severance

A DCAA guidance memorandum issued January 27, 1995,[35] concluded that costs associated with employee separation and general release agreements were unallowable. This position was reversed and superseded by a DCAA guidance memorandum issued November 24, 1995,[36] which indicated that the allowability of such agreements was subject to a case-by-case review.

Stock Options and Stock Appreciation Rights

Since 1987, the allowable costs of stock appreciation rights (SARs) have been limited to the difference between the SAR base price (i.e., the price from which stock appreciation will be measured) and the market price on the first date on which both the number of shares and the SAR base price are known. Accordingly, when the SAR base price is equal to or greater than the market price on that date (as is usually the case), no costs are allowed for contract costing purposes.

Before 1987, allowable costs of stock options and SARs were limited to the difference between the option or SAR price and the market price of the stock on the measurement date (i.e., the first date on which the number of shares and the options or SAR price are known). This provision had validity for a stock option plan because the measurement date is almost always the award date—the first date on which both the number of shares and the option price are known. However, the measurement date for SARs is the exercise date; by definition, appreciation can be ascertained only at a specific future date.

The language in the 1987 revision clarified that the government's intent was to virtually disallow all SAR costs. The revision also made moot the decision in *The Boeing Co.*,[37] when the ASBCA overruled the government disallowance of the SAR costs by concluding the following:

- The costs were allowable under existing cost principles.
- Stock Appreciation Rights "are far more readily described not as 'options' but as 'bonuses including stock bonuses.'"
- The "requirement that the agreement be entered into 'before the services are rendered' is satisfied," inasmuch as SAR participants were required to remain in the firm's employ for at least six months before exercising an SAR.

Employee Stock Ownership/Purchase Plans

Contributions to employee stock ownership plans (ESOPs) are generally allowable, except that they normally may not exceed 15% of gross payroll (25% when a money purchase plan is included). However, neither contributions arising under tax reduction act ownership plans nor contributions made under payroll-based tax credit stock ownership plans are allowable costs. A proposed revision to FAR

31.205-6, published on November 7, 1995,[38] would have disallowed interest costs on leveraged ESOPs, thus placing them on the basis as unleveraged ESOPs. The proposal was negatively received by industry based on concerns that it would discourage the establishment of new ESOPs and foster the cancellation of existing ESOPs. The proposed rule was withdrawn, pending further study.

- The ASBCA ruled that Ralph M. Parsons Company's ESOP contributions were allowable because they did not exceed 25% of gross payroll.[39] The Board concluded that the costs were reasonable even though they were triple prior-year contributions and were being used to finance the plan's leveraged buyout of the firm.

- A case involving *Singer Co.*[40] dealt with a stock purchase plan in which company stock was available to virtually all employees at a 20% discount from the market price. The company treated the discount as compensation costs on the books of its division; however, in the consolidated financial statements, the discounts were charged directly to an equity account.

  In its final decision, the Board concluded that the plan was not a stock option plan within the meaning of the cost principle. Accordingly, the cost would be considered allowable as compensation unless precluded by some other provision of DAR, Section XV. As to the government's argument that the company's accounting practice violated GAAP and thus precluded reimbursement of the costs, the Board concluded that the alleged inconsistency had no effect on the appeal's disposition. The Board did not consider that disallowing amounts that otherwise would be recoverable was the appropriate redress for failure to follow GAAP in the financial statements. The Board also concluded that the plan was, in fact, compensation in the year the stock restrictions were removed, since the company was entitled to an income tax deduction in that year. The Board also disagreed with the government's argument that the discount should be disallowed as a financing charge. Because the plan was voluntary, the Board concluded that the employee stock purchase plan was primarily an inducement and incentive for retaining employees, rather than a vehicle for raising capital.

- In *Honeywell, Inc.*[41] the ASBCA also overruled the government's challenge to the allowability of employee stock discount costs. The costs were similar to those incurred by Singer. The Honeywell Employee Stock Ownership Plan permitted employees to purchase company stock at 85% of the market price. The discount was taxable to the employees. Like Singer, Honeywell recorded the discount as an adjustment to equity rather than as a charge against earnings on its financial statements. However, it did allocate the discount costs to the appropriate division for inclusion in its indirect cost submissions. The government disallowed the costs on the basis that the contractor's treatment of these costs for third-party financial reporting and government costing purposes was inconsistent, and the plan was noncompensatory under APB Opinion 25.

  On the first point, the Board merely recited its earlier opinion in the *Singer* case; since the company treated the discount as a deductible compensation cost for tax purposes, it should be treated as a compensation cost for government contract costing purposes. On the second point, the Board found that the Honeywell plan did not meet one of the four characteristics essential for qualifying as a noncompensable plan under Section 423 of the

Internal Revenue Code. Therefore, the criteria in APB 25 did not support the government position.

- The ASBCA disallowed employee stock discount costs incurred by GTE Government Systems Corporation[42] in 1980. The GTE employee stock purchase plan (ESPP) permitted employees to purchase company stock at 85% of the market price. Unlike Singer or Honeywell, Inc., GTE did not deduct the stock discount costs on its federal income tax return. The cost principle in effect in 1981 [DAR 15-205.6(a)(1)], stated that costs must not exceed "those costs which are allowable by the Internal Revenue Code" as a criterion for government contract cost allowability purposes. The Federal Circuit[43] overruled the ASBCA, noting that the DAR provision used the broader term *allowable* rather than *deductible* or *deducted*; thus, the Internal Revenue Code language should not be given an overly restrictive reading. In its decision, the court opined that GTE's decision to voluntarily forego its tax deduction, in order to provide a more favorable tax treatment for the employee "... does not require that its case be distinguished from *Singer* and *Honeywell* ... Construing the term allowable to refer to costs of the nature and type generally deductible, ... we conclude that GTE's ESPP discount costs are properly reimbursable." The precedential value of this decision was short-lived since the reference to federal tax deductibility was deleted from the cost principle in March of 1983.

Pensions and Deferred Compensation

Cost accounting standards have had a significant effect on the compensation cost principle since it incorporated CAS 412, Composition and Measurement of Pension Cost; CAS 413, Adjustment and Allocation of Pension Cost; and CAS 415, Accounting for the Cost of Deferred Compensation. Thus, even contractors not otherwise subject to CAS must calculate pension and deferred compensation costs in accordance with these standards in order for the costs to be considered allowable.

The issuance of FAS 87 by the FASB changed in several respects the way pension costs are calculated for financial accounting purposes. Because the FAS 87 requirements for amortizing actuarial gains and losses and for valuing pension fund assets differ from the CAS 412 and 413 requirements, contractors have to prepare separate actuarial valuations for financial accounting and cost accounting purposes. The disposition of the excess of the value of plan assets over plan liabilities, generally referred to as a reversion, which often results from plan terminations, segment closures, and curtailments of benefits is addressed in FAR 31.205-6(j) and clause FAR 52.215-27 which is included in all contracts requiring certified cost or pricing data. The cost principle provision and clause provides that the government will receive its "equitable share" of any reversion. As discussed in Chapter 8, these issues were also addressed in the March 30, 1995, revisions to CAS 412 and 413.

The U.S. District Court for the Middle District of Florida ruled in *United States v. Bicoastal Corp.*[44] that the federal government was entitled to receive its equitable share of the surplus of certain overfunded pension plans attributable to segments of companies that were *closed* as defined in CAS 413. The court concluded that the company's various segments were closed by virtue of an ownership change and that the revised FAR 31.205-6(j)(4) provision became effective upon segment closure. This decision reversed and remanded an earlier bankruptcy court order permitting the merger of Bicoastal's overfunded and underfunded plans. The U.S. Bankruptcy Court for the Middle District of Florida[45] subsequently ruled that the FAR 31.205-6(j)(4) cost principle revision did not apply because it became effective after the change in ownership. The Bankruptcy Court further concluded that because neither FAR nor CAS established a trust interest between the government and the contractor, the government's claim to any portion of pension plan overfunding would be allowed only as an unsecured claim against the debtor.

The ASBCA allowed the costs of The Boeing Company's[46] Supplemental Executive Retirement Plan, which was funded only when the costs ultimately became deductible for IRS purposes. The requirements of the then-existing CAS 412, and the cost principle on compensation in FAR 31.205-6, applicable to the contract subject to the dispute, were in conflict. The then-existing CAS 412 required the actuarially computed pension costs to be assigned to a cost accounting period and allocated to cost objectives (e.g., contracts) of that period if the pension cost was funded or if payment of the benefits could be compelled. The FAR more restrictively limited cost allowability to the lesser of the actuarially computed pension costs or the amount deductible for federal income tax purposes for the year. The government disallowed the plan's costs since they were not funded in the year the costs were claimed. In its decision, the Board observed that "whether based on its own official standing or on the basis of its incorporation in the Defense Acquisition Regulation, CAS 412 has the force and effect of law. . . . We hold that CAS 412 is controlling with respect to the determination, measurement, assignment and allocation of [the retirement plan] costs." The precedence of this decision ended with the March 30, 1995, revision to CAS 412, which essentially requires funding as a condition of cost recognition, as discussed further in Chapter 8.

In a complex dispute stemming from *NI Industries'* termination of its defined-benefit plan, the ASBCA[47] ruled that the government's flexibly priced contracts had a right to share in the reversion. On active cost-type and fixed-price incentive contracts, that right stemmed from the credits provision in the cost principles. On closed cost-type contracts, that right stemmed from the Contractor's Assignment of Refunds, Rebates, Credits, and Other Amounts executed upon contract closure. The ASBCA[48] reached a similar conclusion with regard to pension plan reversions that resulted from *Gould, Inc.'s* sale of five divisions in 1987 and 1988. The *Gould, Inc.* decision is discussed in further detail in Chapter 8 in the section on CAS 413, Adjustment and Allocation of Pension Costs.

Other Postretirement Benefits

Other postretirement employee benefits (primarily medical and insurance benefits) have traditionally been accounted for on a pay-as-you-go basis. Financial Accounting Standards Board Statement (SFAS) 106, which required that the cost of these benefits be accrued over the working lives of the workforce was issued in 1989. The FAR was revised on June 25, 1991, to require that, to be allowable, the costs of the benefits must be paid to either (1) an insurer, provider, or other recipient as current-year costs or premiums; or (2) an insurer or trustee to establish or maintain a fund or reserve for the sole purpose of providing retirement benefits. If the latter option is selected, cost allowability is further limited to amounts permitted under GAAP and funded by the tax return time. Funded SFAS 106 costs are allowable to the extent that they do not exceed amounts assigned under the delayed methodology described in Paragraphs 112 and 113 of the SFAS. Accounting for these retirement costs under GAAP (accrual accounting) and the FAR (cost basis accounting) now differ widely.

Compensation Incidental to Business Acquisitions

In 1989, the compensation cost principles on business acquisitions were revised [FAR 31.205-6(1)]. The revisions specifically disallowed the costs of *golden parachutes*—special compensation in excess of severance pay in the event of termination—and *golden handcuffs*—special compensation, in addition to normal pay, to induce employees to remain with the company.

Cost of Money (FAR 31.205-10)

Facilities Capital Cost of Money

Facilities capital cost of money (FCCOM), as defined and computed in CAS 414, is allowable, except on Postal Service contracts, provided the cost is specifically identified or proposed in cost proposals. (The calculation of FCCOM is illustrated in Figure 8.4 in Chapter 8.) The cost principle was modified in October 1984 to disallow the cost of money associated with goodwill. It was revised again, effective July 23, 1990, to disallow the cost of money associated with the stepped-up value of assets acquired in business combinations that use the purchase method of accounting.

The instructions for calculating FCCOM, contained in Form CASB-CMF, state that the facilities capital values should be the same values that are used to generate depreciation and amortization for contract costing purposes. The instructions go on to state that land integral to the regular operations of the business should be included.

Numerous decisions on the recovery of cost of money are discussed in Chapter 8.

Cost of Money as an Element of the Cost of Capital Assets under Construction

This cost of money, as defined and computed in CAS 417, is allowable and is thus included in the depreciable base of the constructed asset. Unlike CAS 417, however, the cost principle does not allow any alternative methods for calculating the cost, such as the method prescribed for financial reporting in FAS 34. Under FAS 34, interest expense on certain capital assets is capitalized at a rate based on the company's outstanding borrowings.

Depreciation (FAR 31.205-11) and Asset Valuations Resulting from Business Combinations (FAR 31.205-52)

Contractors with contracts subject to CAS 409, Depreciation of Tangible Capital Assets, must follow its provisions on these contracts and may elect to follow the standard on their non–CAS-covered contracts. For contracts not subject to CAS, the acquisition regulations rely primarily on tests of reasonableness and the Internal Revenue Code. Depreciation is ordinarily considered reasonable if depreciation policies and procedures used for contract costing are (1) consistent with the policies and procedures followed by the company in its commercial business, (2) reflected in the company's books of account and financial statements, and (3) used and accepted for federal income tax purposes.

If different depreciation costs are computed for financial statement and tax purposes, allowable depreciation is limited to the amounts used for book and statement purposes, determined in a manner consistent with the depreciation policies used on other than government business.

The FAR, like the predecessor DAR and NASA Procurement Regulation, incorporated FAS 13, Accounting for Leases, except when sale and lease-back transactions are involved. Financial Accounting Standards 13 requires that a lease be classified as a capital lease for financial reporting purposes if it meets any one of the following four criteria; otherwise, it is classified as an operating lease.

1. Automatic transfer of title
2. Bargain purchase option
3. Lease term of at least 75% of the estimated economic life of the leased property
4. Present value of the minimum lease payments of at least 90% of the excess of the leased property's fair value over any related investment tax credit retained by the lessor

Items acquired through a capital lease, as defined by FAS 13, are subject to the depreciation cost principle and CAS 404, Capitalization of Tangible Assets. In a sale and lease-back situation, the allowable lease cost is limited to the amount the company would be allowed if it had retained title.

The FPR never referenced FAS 13; consequently, costs of capital leases allocated to federal contracts subject to those regulations were governed by the rental cost principle, not the cost principle for depreciation.

The allowability of depreciation resulting from the step-up in asset values arising from business combinations has been the subject of numerous disputes.

- In *Gould Defense Systems, Inc.*,[49] the additional depreciation resulting from the stepped-up asset base was allowed by the ASBCA. Clevite, a previously independent company, was acquired by and merged into Gould Defense Systems, Inc. Clevite ceased to exist as a result of the merger, and Clevite's contracts were novated to recognize Gould as the new contracting entity.
- In *The Marquardt Co.*,[50] the ASBCA disallowed depreciation costs resulting from the write-up of the value of Marquardt's assets following its acquisition by ISC Electronics, Inc. Marquardt had formerly been a wholly owned subsidiary of CCI Corporation. ISC recorded the acquisition in accordance with the requirements of APB 16. Under the purchase method, the acquiring company allocates the cost of the acquisition to the identifiable individual assets acquired and liabilities assumed on the basis of their fair values. On the basis of language in CAS 404.50(d), Marquardt claimed the depreciation expense attributable to the stepped-up basis of its capital assets as an allowable cost and included this cost in its provisional and forward-pricing indirect cost rates. The CO disallowed the increased depreciation expense on the basis that the sale of Marquardt merely represented a stock transfer from CCI to ISC. After the acquisition, Marquardt still maintained the same name, management, assets, and corporate status.

  The Board concurred with the CO's final decision by concluding as follows:

  > Marquardt's arguments lose sight of the fact that Marquardt and not its new parent [ISC] is the contracting party here. Paragraph 1 of APB 16 states that a business combination occurs

when one or more businesses are brought together in one accounting entity, and "The single entity carries on the activities of the previously separate, independent enterprises." Appellant's reliance on APB 16 is misplaced, since Marquardt remained an independent entity. … APB 16, under these circumstances, has nothing to do with how the acquired corporation is to value its assets when it is acquired by another company. APB 16 deals solely with how an acquiring corporation [ISC] is to value the assets it has acquired … As a result of the transaction, [ISC] incurred the cost, not Marquardt, and if [ISC] is to recover the purchase cost of acquiring Marquardt it can only do so under its own Government and commercial contracts. Marquardt remains a separate legal entity, obligated to perform its contracts and these contracts cannot be burdened with costs incurred by a third party.

Marquardt's situation was perceived by the Board as clearly different from *Gould*. No novation agreement was required as a result of the ISC Electronics acquisition because Marquardt's separate corporate status was not changed.

- The ASBCA allowed a $47 million step-up in asset values, resulting from Times Fiber Communications' spin-off from its former parent, Insilco.[51] The Board, distinguishing its decision from *Marquardt*, concluded that Times Fiber Communications became a "new and significantly different company" after the business combination, whereas Marquardt continued to exist as it had before the acquisition. The most significant aspect of this decision, however, is that $39 million of the total asset step-up consisted of engineering software (manufacturing instructions, calibration software, and assembly drawings), which had previously been expensed by Insilco. Times Fiber Communication continued to expense the costs of developing additional software after the business combination.

Effective July 23, 1990, the depreciation cost principle was revised and a new principle, 31.205-52, Asset Valuations Resulting from Business Combinations, was issued. The changes disallow the depreciation associated with the stepped-up value of assets acquired in business combinations using the purchase method of accounting. Under FAR 31.205-52, when the purchase method of accounting for a business combination is used, allowable amortization, cost of money, and depreciation are limited to the total of the amount that would have been allowed had the combination not taken place. The government believes that it should not be at risk of paying higher prices simply due to ownership changes. As discussed further in Chapter 8, CAS 404 was revised in 1995 to eliminate the reference to Accounting Principles Board Opinion 16 regarding business combinations. The cost principle revision, as well as the CAS 404 revisions, are contrary to GAAP and are inequitable. The novation agreement already protects the government from increased cost on contracts in progress when acquisition occurs. If the predecessor contractor is dissolved, future awards are made to a new contracting entity. The acquiring contractor is now denied the right to recover depreciation and cost of money on the same basis as a contractor that acquires its assets on the open market.

Financial Accounting Standards Board Statement (SFAS) 121 requires assets to be written down to fair value when events, such as environmental damage or declining business that results in idle facilities, indicate that carrying values may not be fully recoverable. SFAS 121 applies to fiscal years beginning after December 15, 1995. Federal Acquisition Regulations 31.205-11 and FAR 31.205-16 were revised on December 14, 1995, to clarify that depreciation and gains/losses on disposed assets must be accounted for in accordance with CAS, not GAAP. The cost principle revisions specifically state the following:

- Depreciation of impaired assets that have been written down to fair value will not exceed the amounts established on depreciation schedules used prior to the write-down.

- No loss will be recognized for a write-down resulting from asset impairment.

Employee Morale, Health, Welfare, Food Service, and Dormitory Costs and Credits (FAR 31.205-13)

Prior to October 1, 1995, costs incurred to enhance working conditions, labor relations, employee morale, and employee productivity were generally allowable, but special limitations applied to food and dormitory service losses. The FAR originally provided that when the company did not attempt to break even on its food and dormitory services, the loss was unallowable except in unusual circumstances (such as when commercial facilities were not reasonably available or when it was necessary to operate the facility at less than an economically practicable volume). The cost principle was amended in 1986 to broaden the criteria for allowability of losses on contractor-operated cafeteria and lodging operations and to establish more businesslike criteria for evaluating these operations. The negative impacts of reduced cafeteria volume or cessation of operations are now addressed. That is, when workers eat away from the contractor's property, the result may be longer lunch periods, and when cafeterias are closed, many of the fixed occupancy costs do not diminish but are absorbed into other indirect cost pools of the contractor operations.

Federal Acquisition Regulation 31.205-13 was revised effective October 1, 1995, and reduced the recovery of employee welfare costs by disallowing the costs of gifts, other than employee service awards, and the costs of employee recreation activities, except for employee sports teams or employee organizations designed to improve company loyalty, teamwork, or physical fitness. The revision does not address purely social activities such as holiday parties or picnics; however, the entertainment cost principle appears to disallow such costs.

The allowability of company parties and outings to enhance employee morale had previously been the subject of dispute between the government and contractors. In *Brown Engineering Co.*,[52] the ASBCA recognized the cost of a party for employees as allowable to improve employer–employee relations. As stated by the Board, "The costs of the patio party for the female employees we also believe are appropriate for inclusion. We do not believe the party to have been purely social or for entertainment. It was designed to improve employer–employee relations." In *Cotton & Co.*,[53] the Department of Energy (DOE) Board of Contract Appeals agreed that Friday afternoon get-togethers, to which all company personnel were invited, were held to improve employer–employee relations, employee morale, and employee performance, and that the costs were allowable under FAR 31.205-13. As the Board stated, "The affidavits establish that everyone in the firm was invited and that the purpose of these get-togethers was to boost employee morale." The significance of these decisions is seriously clouded by the October 1995 cost principle revision.

Entertainment (FAR 31.205-14)

Before April 1986, the FAR defined *unallowable entertainment* as the costs of amusement, diversion, social activities, and such directly associated costs as transportation and/or gratuities. In 1986, the FAR cost principle was revised to expand unallowable costs to include memberships in social, dining, and country clubs, regardless of whether the costs are considered taxable income to the recipient. Effective October 1, 1995, the FAR cost principle was again revised to expressly state that costs made unallowable under this provision are not allowable under any other cost principle. Prior to this change, costs associated with employee social or recreation activities and tickets to shows or sports events given to employees were considered allowable employee relations costs, provided the costs were reasonable in total.

Fines, Penalties, and Mischarging Costs (FAR 31.205.15)

This cost principle was expanded in 1989 to include not only fines and penalties but also mischarging costs. Previously, the cost principle dealt solely with the unallowable fine and penalty costs resulting from violations of, or failure to comply with, federal, state, local, or foreign laws and regulations. The revised provision initially disallowed costs "incurred to identify, measure, or otherwise determine the magnitude of improper charging and costs incurred to remedy or correct the mischarging, such as the costs to rescreen and reconstruct records." This language was so broad that it could literally result in a disallowance of a contractor's internal audit activity devoted to federal contract compliance. As a result of concerns voiced by industry, the rule was revised in 1991 to limit the disallowance of costs incurred in connection with the mischarging of costs to situations where the "costs are caused by, or result from, alteration or destruction of records, or other false or improper charging or recording of costs." The rule goes on to state that "such costs include those incurred to measure or otherwise determine the magnitude of the improper charging, such as the costs to rescreen and reconstruct records." The cost required to "identify" improper charging was deleted by the change to make clear that the costs of contract self-governance programs are allowable.

Idle Facilities and Idle Capacity Costs (FAR 31.205.17)

Ownership costs attributable to completely unused and excess facilities are generally unallowable unless the facilities must be maintained to accommodate workload fluctuations. However, if facilities become idle because of unforeseen events, such as a termination, the costs will be allowed for a reasonable period, generally not exceeding one year. In extenuating circumstances, the ASBCA has granted recovery of idle facilities costs for periods in excess of one year.[54]

Bid and Proposal and Independent Research and Development Costs (FAR 31.205-18 and FAR 31.205-48)

Bid and proposal (B&P) costs are incurred in preparing, submitting, and supporting bids and proposals on potential government or nongovernment contracts. Independent research and development (IR&D) costs are the costs for technical effort that is not sponsored by a contract, grant, or other arrangement and that falls in the areas of basic and applied research, development, and/or systems and other concept formulation studies.

For the purpose of allocating indirect expenses other than G&A expense, B&P and IR&D projects are accounted for as if they were contracts. Thus, B&P and IR&D costs consist of all direct labor, material, other direct costs, and all allocable indirect costs except G&A expense. IR&D and B&P costs are generally allocated to contracts on the same basis used to allocate G&A expenses.

Disputes occasionally arise over whether costs classified as IR&D are properly chargeable to an existing contract. The issue revolves around FAR 31.205-18, which defines IR&D as excluding "costs of effort sponsored by a grant or required in the performance of a contract." The U.S. District Court concluded that Martin Marietta[55] mischarged to IR&D the costs of six tasks that were explicitly required to perform a Navy contract to design and build a full-scale model of a Supersonic Law Altitude Target (SLAT). In concluding that the effort charged to IR&D should have been charged direct to the SLAT contract, the court rejected the argument that the six tasks potentially benefited future contracts. In its denial of Martin Marietta's motion to dismiss, the court opined as follows:

> When the Government hires a contractor to do research and development work, that work inevitably benefits other contemplated contracts. Certainly, scientific research is rarely so narrow that it fails to benefit other projects. [R]esearch and development inevitably benefits one very particular contract—the contract to build what it is that is being researched and developed....
>
> Martin Marietta's argument would make the very notion of a research and development fixed-price contract impossible. That cannot be. The Government is entitled to hire contractors to perform research and development services and to limit the amount paid to an agreed upon sum.

This decision does not resolve the controversy revolving around research and development effort that is implicitly required by a contract. The government sometimes takes the position that such effort is also a direct charge to the contract and not IR&D. Industry, on the other hand, generally disagrees. However, neither interpretation is expressly stated in the FAR cost principle.

Disputes over where research and development costs implicitly required by a contract are properly chargeable to IR&D or to a contract usually occur because (1) neither the contractor nor the government has clearly addressed the issue; and (2) the contract requirements do not specify how the contract may be affected by a particular contractor IR&D project.

The following are some of the circumstances that may lead to problems:

- Independent research and development projects that originate either before or after the receipt of a contract that implicitly requires the application of similar technology.

- Technology developed under an IR&D program addresses future business requirements of the contractor, but an awarded contract affords the contractor an opportunity to apply the new technology.

- An existing product is improved to meet the implicit requirements of a production contract.

Each of these circumstances raises an issue of equity—did the government procure product or IR&D effort?

Companies should act proactively to avoid allegations of labor mischarging. Policies and procedures should clearly distinguish between the IR&D and contract effort, and require complete disclosure of all information necessary to support the contractor's position. In light of the *Martin Marietta* decision, contractors must be certain that a contract does not explicitly require any effort proposed for an IR&D project.

Bid and Proposal/Independent Research and Development Ceilings for Periods Preceding Contractor Fiscal Year 1993—Companies Required to Negotiate an Advance Agreement

Prior to 1992, any company that received government payments over a specified threshold for both IR&D and B&P in its prior fiscal year had to negotiate an advance agreement on a ceiling for allowable IR&D and B&P expenses for the current year. A DOD tri-service CO was designated to negotiate the agreement. The specified threshold included only those recoverable IR&D and B&P costs allocated to government prime contracts and subcontracts for which submission and certification of cost or pricing data were required. The penalty for not obtaining a required advance agreement was severe. No IR&D or B&P costs were allowed if a company failed to initiate the negotiations of a required advance agreement before the start of the next fiscal year. If negotiations were held but agreement was not reached by the end of the fiscal year, payment for IR&D and B&P costs were reduced by at least 25% of the amount that, in the CO's opinion, the company or profit center would otherwise have been entitled to receive under an advance agreement. Required advance agreements could be negotiated at the corporate level and/or with those profit centers that contract directly with the government and that in the preceding year allocated more than a specified threshold in recoverable IR&D and B&P costs to DOD contracts and subcontracts for which certified cost or pricing data were required.

The total B&P and IR&D costs allocated to DOD contracts could not exceed the total expenditures for B&P and IR&D projects with a potential military relationship. The DOE also limited recovery of IR&D costs to the lesser of the amount calculated in accordance with the FAR provision or the amount having a potential benefit to DOE programs. The 1991 DOD Authorization Act[56] expanded the allowability of IR&D/B&P costs to those incurred on projects of "potential interest to the Department of Defense." Such projects include those that: (1) strengthen the U.S. defense industrial and technology base; (2) enhance industrial competitiveness; (3) promote the development of various critical technologies, including those useful to private, commercial, and public sectors; and (4) develop technologies achieving environmental benefits (e.g., environmental clean-up and restoration and environmentally safe facilities management).

Bid and Proposal/Independent Research and Development Ceilings for Periods Preceding Contractor Fiscal Year 1993—Companies Not Required to Negotiate an Advance Agreement

Total B&P and IR&D costs allocated to DOD contracts could not exceed the total expenditures for projects with a potential military relationship. The FAR, like the prior DAR and DOE Procurement Regulation, established cost ceilings for companies not required to negotiate an advance agreement by using a formula based on historical IR&D and B&P costs and sales data for the preceding three years. The formula could be applied on either a company-wide basis or by profit center. The mechanics of the formula are illustrated in Figure 7.1. (The FPR and NASA PR contained no ceiling.)

If the formula gave an inequitable result, the CO was authorized to negotiate an advance agreement establishing the IR&D/B&P ceiling. In *Dynatrend, Inc.*,[57] the ASBCA concluded that the company was entitled to higher recovery of B&P costs than resulted from the formula. The contracting officer's refusal to negotiate an advance agreement with the contractor was considered an abuse

	Sales ($000)	IR&D & B&P ($000)	Percentage
Period for application of ceiling			
Year 4	$4,500	$350	
Prior three periods			
Year 1	$5,000	$300	6.0
Year 2	$7,000	$350	5.0
Year 3	$4,000	$320	8.0
Calculation of ceiling			
Historical ratio[1]			7.0
Average annual cost[1]		$335	
Limits			
120% of average (upper limit)		$402	
80% of average (lower limit)		$268	
Product			
Current year sales X historical ratio ($4,500 X 7%)		$315	
Year 4 ceiling[2]		$315	
Cost disallowed		$35	

[1]Average of the two highest of the prior three years.
[2]The ceiling equals the product of the current-year sales and the historical ratio, provided that amount is not less than 80% of greater than 120% of the average.

Figure 7.1 Formula for Determining IR&D/B&P Ceiling for Companies Not Required to Negotiate an Advance Agreement (Applies to Periods Preceding Fiscal Year 1993)

of discretion. Of particular significance is the fact that the contractor's request for advance agreement, which covered both its prior and current fiscal year, was sustained by the board.

Elimination of Bid and Proposal/Independent Research and Development Ceilings

The National Defense Authorization Act for 1992 and 1993,[58] as implemented in FAR 31.205-18 for both defense and nondefense awards, eliminated the requirement for establishing cost ceilings by either an advance agreement or a formula. For nonmajor contractors, the ceilings were eliminated on September 24, 1992. For major contractors, the ceilings were eliminated over a three-year period commencing with fiscal years beginning on or after October 1, 1992. A *major contractor* is defined as a contractor that allocated more than $10 million in IR&D/B&P costs to flexibly priced awards over $100,000 in its prior fiscal year. In determining whether the $10 million threshold was met, only segments that allocated $1 million or more to flexibly priced awards over $100,000 were counted. During each of the three years in the transition period, allowable costs for major contractors were capped at a 5% increase over the allowable costs for the prior year, plus the lesser of (1) the percentage increase in actual IR&D/B&P costs over the prior year or (2) the percentage increase in the price escalation index for the Research Development Test and Evaluation account.

Major contractors must still submit certain financial and technical data to support their IR&D/B&P costs.

Insurance (FAR 31.205-19)

Insurance that is required or approved under the contract or that is maintained in the general conduct of business is allowable, except for the following restrictions:

- For purchased insurance, the cost of the normal deductibles is allowable if reasonable in amount
- Business interruption insurance must exclude any coverage of profit
- Life insurance on principals of the business is allowable only to the extent that it represents additional compensation (e.g., the principals, heirs, or estate are the beneficiaries)
- Property insurance premiums covering cost in excess of acquisition cost are allowable only if the contractor's written policy requires the basis of any new asset to reflect the book value of the replaced asset, adjusted for the difference between the insurance proceeds and actual replacement cost
- Contractors subject to CAS 416, Accounting for Insurance Costs, or desiring to establish a self-insurance program, must
  - comply with the self-insurance provisions of CAS 416
  - submit their self-insurance programs to the ACO if self-insurance costs allocated to negotiated federal contracts are at least $200,000 and 50% of the total self-insurance costs
  - provide to the ACO such information as statements, loss histories, and formulas for establishing reserves

Lobbying and Political Activity Costs (FAR 31.205-22)

The cost principles related to legislative and executive lobbying have changed significantly over the years. The separate cost principles for legislative lobbying and executive lobbying were combined under FAR 31.205-22, effective August 19, 1996. Currently, the following activities are unallowable:

- Attempts to influence legislation
- Participation in political activities, including political contributions
- Legislative liaison activities which support or are in knowing preparation for an effort to engage in unallowable activities
- Attempts to improperly influence, either directly or indirectly, executive branch employees or officers regarding a regulatory or contract matter

The following legislative activities, when adequately documented, are allowable under FAR 31.205-22(b)(1):

- Participation in legislative public hearings or meetings in response to a specific invitation from the legislative source
- State or local lobbying undertaken to directly reduce contract costs or avoid impairment of the contractor's authority to perform a contract
- Any activity specifically authorized by statute to be undertaken with contract funds

Adequate records must be maintained to demonstrate that lobbying costs have been excluded. Prior to June 20, 1996, specific language permitted the use of estimates of time spent on unallowable lobbying activity by indirect employees, provided less than 25% of the employee's time was spent on such activities and the company did not materially misstate any allowable or unallowable costs within the prior five years. This provision was eliminated because it conflicted with the recordkeeping requirements in 31.201-6(c) and was inconsistent with the requirement in FAR 52.203-12 to disclose lobbying activities.

Manufacturing and Production Engineering (FAR 31.205-25)

Effort related to developing and deploying new or improved materials, systems, processes, methods, equipment, tools, and techniques should be considered manufacturing and production engineering if the developed items are intended for use: in improving current production functions; in producing the current or anticipated products or services; on production lines; or in production suitability analysis and manufacturing optimization. These costs are allowable but must be carefully distinguished from efforts to develop or deploy items that are intended for sale. Such costs should be considered IR&D, as discussed previously in this chapter.

Material Costs (FAR 31.205-26)

Material costs are generally allowable provided the costing method reasonably measures actual costs. However, the purchase of items from affiliates is particularly sensitive. An item may be transferred at a price that includes profit rather than at cost only when it is a commercial item or when the price is the result of "adequate price competition."

Prior to October 1, 1995, the price also had to be reasonable and no higher than the transferor's current sale price to its most favored customer. The most-favored-customer pricing requirement was eliminated on October 1, 1995.

The terms *commercial item* and *adequate price competition* are discussed in Chapter 5.

In *Materials Science Corp.*,[59] the ASBCA ruled that the cost of ADPE services provided by a supplier under common ownership did not qualify for transfer at market-based prices because (1) the ADPE services were not provided to the general public, and (2) the award to the supplier was not made after obtaining quotations on an equal basis from the supplier and one or more outside services.

Patents and Royalties (FAR 31.205-30 and 31205-37)

The cost principle limits the allowability of patent costs to those applicable to the following:

- Specific patents that are required by contract or for which the government has royalty-free use
- General counseling services relating to patent matters

Contractors should ensure that their cost accounting systems are capable of separately identifying allowable and unallowable patent and royalty costs.

Royalty costs are allowable unless: the government has a royalty-free license; the patent has been deemed invalid; or the patent is expired. Royalties that have been established as a result of less-than-arm's length bargaining are particularly scrutinized to assure that amounts are reasonable.

In *Rocket Research Co.*,[60] the ASBCA held that costs incurred in making patent searches and preparing and prosecuting patent applications, which were claimed as indirect expenses on a cost-type contract, were unallowable. The Board reasoned that the costs were not required for contract performance. The contractor contended that the disputed provision did not apply to patent costs that were charged indirectly. The Board disagreed and ruled that the sole purpose of the 1971 revision to DAR 15-205.26(b) "was to disallow all patent costs not necessary to a particular contract's performance."

Plant Reconversion Costs (FAR 31.205-31)

Costs related to restoring or rehabilitating a contractor's facility to the condition that existed before undertaking contract work are unallowable except for costs of removing government property and repairing damage resulting from such removal.

Precontract Costs (FAR 31.205-32)

Precontract costs are incurred before the effective contract date directly pursuant to the negotiation and in anticipation of the contract award. Such costs are allowable to the extent they were necessary to comply with the proposed contract delivery schedule and would have been allowable if incurred after the contract date.

In *AT&T Technologies, Inc.*,[61] the Department of Transportation (DOT) Contract Appeals Board resoundingly overruled the CO's determination that "AT&T had not substantiated its entitlement of such costs and in any event, allowance was at the discretion of the contracting officer." In its decision, the DOT Board concluded the following:

> ... [I]n the instant case, (i) the precontract work performed by AT&T and the cost of such work were necessary to contract performance, (ii) the cost of such work had been included in the contract price, (iii) the work was directed only to the development of the Radio Controlled Equipment for this particular Federal Aviation Administration (FAA) need expressed in this Request for Proposals and defined during negotiations, and (iv) the FAA benefited from the work. In this posture, for the FAA to refuse to acknowledge and recognize those costs is an effort to obtain something for nothing. This Board has traditionally looked with disfavor upon such attempts; there is no such thing as a free lunch. ...

> With regard to the contracting officer's decision statement that recognition of the precontract costs is vested in the discretion of the contracting officer, the Board noted that Federal Acquisition Regulation 31.205-32 "Precontract Costs" does not state that the contracting officer "may" recognize such costs. Rather, it says that, if the conditions of the section are met, "Such costs are allowable ..." [emphasis added]. The selection of words removes any vestige of discretion from the provision if the conditions are met.

The recovery of precontract costs is often an issue in contract termination settlements and has been litigated in numerous occasions, as discussed in Chapter 12.

In 1991, a FAR change was proposed that would have required the contracting parties to establish a firm date for recognizing precontract costs and a maximum amount for such costs. The proposed rule also would also have required that the costs, to be allowable on a contract, be authorized in a contract clause. The proposed cost principle revision was formally withdrawn on July 23, 1992.

Professional and Consultant Services (FAR 31.205-33) and Costs Related to Legal and Other Proceedings (FAR 31.205-47)

In recent years, these cost principles have been revised significantly to broaden the scope of disallowed costs. The principles now provide that reasonable costs of in-house and outside professional and consultant services are allowable provided that:

- Outside fees are not contingent upon recovery of costs from the government
- Retainer fees are for necessary and customary services
- The costs do not pertain to
  - Company organizations and reorganizations
  - Defense of antitrust suits
  - Patent infringement litigation
  - Prosecution of claims against the government or defense of government claims or appeals
  - Protests of federal awards or defense against protests of contract awards unless such defense costs are incurred as a result of a written request from the CO
  - Litigation between contractors arising from a joint venture, a teaming arrangement, or a dual sourcing coproduction program
  - Defense of qui tam suits, unless the suits are deemed unmeritorious by the CO
  - Defense of any proceeding brought by a federal, state, local, or foreign government for noncompliance with laws or regulations
  - Services: to improperly obtain, distribute, or use information or data prohibited by law or regulation; to improperly influence the content of solicitations, the evaluation of proposals or quotations, or source selection; that violate any statute or regulation prohibiting improper business practices or conflicts of interest; or that are not consistent with the purpose and scope of the services contracted for or otherwise agreed to
- The nature and scope of services performed (on other than a retainer basis) are documented. Documentation supporting allowable consulting services shall include: details of agreements; invoices or billings submitted, including details on time expended and the nature of services provided; and consultant work products, trip reports, minutes of meetings, and collateral memoranda and reports.

Costs incurred in the defense of any proceeding brought by federal, state, local, or foreign governments for noncompliance with laws or regulations are totally unallowable if (1) the contractor is convicted in a criminal proceeding; (2) the contractor is found liable in a civil or administrative proceeding involving an allegation of fraud; (3) a monetary penalty is imposed against the contractor in a civil or administrative proceeding that does not involve an allegation of fraud; or (4) the agency debars or suspends the contractor, rescinds the contract, or terminates the contract for default for violating a law or regulation.

If the allegation is settled through consent or compromise, up to 80% of the costs incurred may be allowed. The cost principle also disallows the costs incurred in defending individuals (e.g., employees or officers) who are convicted of violating a law or regulation or who are held liable in a proceeding unless the company is legally bound to provide such defense. Industry representatives have severely criticized this principle as a violation of due process.

Federal Acquisition Regulations 31.205-47 resulted, to some extent, from the ASBCA's decision in *John Doe Co., Inc.*,[62] which addressed the allowability of legal costs included in provisional billing rates and incurred in connection with a criminal investigation. The government contended that the costs should be disallowed "because of their possible linkage with prior costs that might have been fraudulently charged." The contractor asserted that, regardless of the outcome of the fraud investigation, legal defense costs are ordinary and necessary expenses, reasonable in nature, and properly includable in a G&A pool. In concluding that both positions were flawed, the Board ruled the following:

> ... [P]ending completion of an investigation and possible prosecution, the Board has no assurance whether the retention of legal services and the expenditure of all costs related to alleged fraud are, in all respects, reasonable in nature. Accordingly, we may not conclude that the reasonableness in nature and allocability of such costs may not be made to depend in some cases on the ultimate outcome of an investigation and prosecution. But we may and do rule negatively; that such costs may not properly be disallowed simply because they are incurred in defense of such an investigation; nor may they be disallowed as not allocable, without regard to the circumstances, because some act of fraud might be established. ... Unless the Government has evidence of other grounds for disallowance, e.g., that the costs are otherwise unreasonable, they should be reimbursed provisionally.

The ASBCA established the allowability of costs of labor settlements arrived at before judgments in which there was insufficient evidence of wrongdoing on the part of the contractor. The ASBCA concluded in *Ravenna Arsenal, Inc.*[63] that conciliation agreements entered into with two applicants who had filed discrimination suits". . . did not result from what have been shown to be unlawful employment practices on the part of RAI. They were entered into on the basis of a reasonable business decision to settle the controversies at a minimum cost rather than incur the relatively expensive costs of litigation."

The DCAA uses similar guidance in the *Contract Audit Manual*, Section 7-802.2a,[64] which states the following:

> If the dispute arose from actions that would be taken by a prudent businessman (FAR 31.201-3), the costs will be allowable. However, if the dispute was occasioned by actions which appear unreasonable or were found by the agency or board ruling on the dispute to be caused by unlawful, negligent or other malicious conduct, the costs would be unallowable and should be questioned.

A number of allowability disputes have arisen over the allowability of legal fees and settlements to wrongful termination suits.

- In *Hirsch Tyler Co.*,[65] the ASBCA allowed the legal fees incurred in the defense an employment discrimination suit even though the court found in favor of the complainant. The Board noted the following:

  > ... [A]n ordinarily prudent person in the conduct of competitive business is often obliged to defend lawsuits brought by third parties, some of which are frivolous and others of which have merit. In either event, the restraints or requirements imposed by generally accepted sound business practices dictate that, except under the most extraordinary circumstances, a prudent businessman would incur legal expenses to defend a litigation and that such expenses are of the type generally recognized as ordinary and necessary for the conduct of a competitive business. Accordingly, legal expenses incurred in defending a civil litigation brought by a third party, regardless of the outcome thereof, are prima facie reasonable and are allowable, unless shown to have been incurred unreasonably or reimbursement is expressly prohibited by an extraordinary cost principle.

- In a 1995 decision involving *Northrop Worldwide Aircraft Services, Inc.*,[66] the

ASBCA caveated the *Hirsch Tyler* decision, in which costs incurred were considered presumptively reasonable under the then-existing cost principles and case law. Since 1986, the cost principles have not attached any presumption at reasonable to the incurrence of costs. Northrop Worldwide Aircraft Services' legal costs were incurred in defending a suit in which former employees alleged wrongful termination resulting from their refusal to falsify inspection reports on a government contract. In the civil state court proceedings, a jury awarded the former employees both compensatory and punitive damages. In denying both the government's and Northrop's motions for summary judgment, the Board observed that, because a substantially justified litigation position can fail to carry the day, evidence offered by the parties as to the reasonableness of incurring legal fees to defend the wrongful termination would have to be considered. The Board cautioned, however, that the jury verdict would require an inference in favor of the government.

A number of other disputes have also addressed allowability of legal fees.

- In *Bos'n Towing & Salvage Co.*,[67] the ASBCA concluded the following:

  "Protests," either to GAO or to the General Services Board of Contract Appeals, covered under FAR Subpart 33.1—Protests, do not fall within the definition of "claim" in section 33.201 nor within the meaning of the term "claims or appeals" in FAR 31.205-33(d). Similarly, proceedings before the Small Business Administration (SBA) involving the determination of status as a small business concern, as covered under FAR Subpart 19.3, are beyond the purview of the term "claims or appeals" as used in FAR 31.205-33(d). Accordingly, we hold that professional services costs incurred in connection with legal proceedings before either GAO or SBA involving either protests affecting contract awards or determinations of small business concern status are not made unallowable by FAR 31.205-33(d).

  However, this decision was made partially moot by a revision to FAR 31.205-47, which disallowed the costs associated with protests unless the costs were incurred by interested parties to defend against such protest (i.e., intervenors).

- In *P&M Industries, Inc.*,[68] the ASBCA denied recovery of the costs incurred for a consultant who had assisted the contractor in submitting claims for equitable adjustments, but the costs of a quality consultant who had provided administrative services rather than claim-related services were deemed allowable.

- The ASBCA allowed the recovery claim preparation costs incurred by Bill Strong Enterprises[69] in preparing a Request for Equitable Adjustment (REA) because the company's intent in incurring the costs was to negotiate a REA, not to prosecute a claim against the government. The convoluted history concerning Bill Strong Enterprises is discussed further in Chapter 13.

- The HUD Board of Contract Appeals concluded that legal and accounting fees incurred in an attempt to negotiate the close-out payment prior to submission of the second disputed invoice were allowable contract administration costs, not unallowable claim prosecution costs.[70]

The DCAA *Contract Audit Manual,* Section 7-2118.10, concludes that costs related to defending shareholder suits are unreasonable.

A number of disputes over professional and consulting fees have centered on the allocability of such costs to government contracts.

- In *Walter Motor Truck Co.*,[71] legal fees were not considered allocable as an indirect expense because they were incurred for a particular cost objective, a commercial joint venture.

- In a similar decision, *Dynalectron Corp.*,[72] the ASBCA held that legal defense fees for a suit arising from the guarantee of a commercial sales contract were direct costs, chargeable either to the contract or to commercial business generally. The Board was not persuaded by the contractor's argument that the legal fees should not be treated as direct costs since the contractor had no way of including in the original contract price the costs of litigation that would occur in a subsequent period. The Board observed that the definition of direct costs simply does not address the "condition of ready assimilability into an accounting system." On appeal, the Court of Claims sustained the ASBCA, concluding the following:

    ... [T]he alleged benefit to the Government is far too remote and speculative to be relevant.... The costs in dispute ... are not allocable to the Government contracts ... under subparagraph (iii) because they were not necessary to the overall operation of the business, but had a direct relationship to a particular cost objective, namely, the commercial guarantee venture.[73]

- In *Celesco Industries, Inc.*,[74] the contractor was not permitted to charge a consultant fee as an indirect cost because the consulting service applied to a specific government contract. The Board ruled that the amount should have been charged directly to the particular contract.

- The ASBCA decided in *FMC, Inc.*[75] that legal costs incurred in preparing and settling a dispute with a subcontractor must be allocated as a direct cost to the contract. Consistent with earlier decisions, the Board considered the costs to be direct, since they were incurred specifically for, and identified specifically to, the contract. The Board concluded that the financial benefit to other contracts from pursuit of the claim was too remote to justify allocation of the legal costs to all contracts as part of the G&A rate.

- In a dispute with a somewhat similar result, the court in *JANA, Inc.*[76] concluded that legal fees expended by a contract awardee whose award was being protested by a losing offeror must allocate such legal costs as a direct charge to the newly awarded contract.

The requirement to treat costs such as legal expenses as direct has the unfortunate consequence of generally precluding contractors operating in a firm-fixed-price environment from obtaining full cost recovery. Because the need for professional services of this nature cannot be predicted in advance of contract award, it is virtually impossible to include such costs in the proposal used as a basis for negotiating a contract price. Consequently, unless the contractor is able to recover the costs as part of an equitable price adjustment, the costs remain allocable to, but unrecoverable under a fixed-price contract.

Recruiting Costs and Relocation Costs (FAR 31.205-34 and 31.205-35)

Costs incident to recruiting employees and permanently relocating new or existing employees are generally allowable subject to certain ceilings based on time, percentages, and absolute dollar amounts (see Figure 7-2).

Time limitation for incurring transition costs (house-hunting, temporary residence, etc.)	60 days
Closing costs and continuing costs of ownership of residence being sold (as percentage of sales price)	
New employees	14%[1]
Existing employees	14%[1]
Costs incidental to acquiring a new home (as percentage of purchase price)	
New employees	5%[2]
Existing employees	5%[2]
Time limitation for incurring mortgage interest and rental differential payments	3 years
Loss on sale of home	Not allowable
Cancellation of unexpired lease	No ceiling
Employee income taxes incident to reimbursed relocation costs	Not allowable
Job counseling and placement assistance for non-employee spouses and dependents	Not allowable

[1]Continuing mortgage principal payments are unallowable.
[2]Commissions, litigation, insurance, property taxes, and operating/maintenance costs are unallowable.

Figure 7.2   Ceilings on Allowable Relocation Costs

The Defense Acquisition Regulatory (DAR) Council has established Case No. 97-032 to consider revising the relocation cost principle to remove the cost ceilings, allow the payment of lump-sum relocation allowances, allow tax gross-ups, and allow the cost of employment assistance for spouses. The recruiting cost principle restricts the content of "help wanted" advertising (e.g., use of color is prohibited) and the use of recruitment incentives intended to pirate personnel from other companies.

Rental Costs (FAR 31.205-36)

Under the FAR, as well as the predecessor DAR and NASA PR, rental costs of operating leases (as defined by FAS 13) are generally allowable to the extent that the rates are reasonable at the time of the decision to lease the property, except that:

- Rental costs under a sale and lease-back arrangement are limited to amounts that would have been allowed if title had been retained.

- Costs of rentals between entities under common control are generally limited to normal ownership costs.

"Build–lease" transactions are not sale and lease-back arrangements subject to the rental cost limitation. In *HRB-Singer, Inc.*,[77] the contractor sold land to an independent party who constructed buildings that were then leased back to the contractor. The government disallowed rent paid for the facilities to the extent that it exceeded the cost of ownership on the basis that the transaction was a sale and lease-back. In disagreeing with the government's position, the ASBCA concluded the following:

> The most that can be said is that it sold the land upon which the buildings were built and leased it back with the building. This land did not constitute a plant facility, specified in paragraph (c) [of ASPR 15-205.34], until the buildings were built. Even if it did, the relative value of the unimproved land ... was so small in comparison to the value of the buildings that it cannot be

considered a material factor in this question. We accordingly find that there was no sale and leaseback in this situation.

In *A.S. Thomas, Inc.*,[78] the ASBCA decision is enlightening on the issue of common control. In that case, the lessee was able to demonstrate that even though he was treasurer and owned 43% of his brother's company (lessor), there was no common control because neither brother took an active role in managing the other brother's company. Common officers coupled with substantial ownership would potentially give a contractor the ability to significantly influence the operations and financial policies of another business entity. Therefore, the management role assumed by a contractor's owners or officers in another business venture owning assets that are leased to the contractor is a critical factor in determining whether common control exists.

In *Data Design Laboratories*,[79] the ASBCA concluded that common control did not exist with respect to a building leased to the company by a partnership of several company officers and employees. The Board noted that this management group never owned more than 10% of the company's stock and that the company's board of directors consisted of different individuals, primarily representatives of the company's original financial backers.

When constructive ownership costs are allowed in lieu of actual rental payments, the cost of money on the capitalized value used in calculating the constructive ownership cost may be recovered. The calculation of the cost of money is covered in Chapter 8 in the discussion of CAS 414.

Under the FPR in effect before issuance of the FAR, allowability criteria were discussed in the context of short-term and long-term leases. Allowable long-term lease costs were generally limited to constructive ownership costs. Short-term lease costs (two years or less for personal property and five years or less for real property) were generally allowable if:

- The rates were reasonable at the time of the decision to lease.
- No material equity in the property accrued to the lessee other than that available to the public at large.

The allowability criteria for sale and lease-back transactions and rentals between entities under common control are the same as those previously discussed.

The separate cost principle on Automatic Data Processing Equipment (ADPE) Leasing Costs (FAR 31.205-2) was eliminated, effective December 31, 1996. The cost principle previously required an annual demonstration that ADPE leasing costs were reasonable, necessary for the conduct of business, and did not give rise to a material equity in the equipment other than that given to the industry at large. Contracting officer approval was also required if either total ADPE costs were allocated to flexibly priced contracts or ADPE costs for the plant, division, or cost center exceeded $500,000 per year and at least 50% of the cost is allocated to flexibly priced contracts.

Selling Costs (FAR 31.205-38)

Selling and marketing costs, as defined in the cost principle, are allowable to the extent that they are reasonable, direct selling expenses, consulting, and demonstration activities, as well as negotiation and customer liaison.

The principle on selling costs was revised in 1986 to clarify that elements of selling covered in other cost principles, such as advertising, B&P costs, corporate image enhancement, and entertainment are governed by other, more specific principles when determining allowability. Costs of activities correctly classified and disallowed under such cost principles may not be reconsidered under the selling cost principle. The revised language identifies which selling and marketing costs are allowable and requires separate identification of unallowable costs.

The FAR cost principle was also revised in 1986 to provide that foreign selling expenses were unallowable, not unallocable. This change led many contractors with foreign sales of military products to establish separate selling expense pools (domestic and foreign), since the clear implication was that foreign selling costs would be disallowed in total if they were included in a single-selling, G&A pool allocated to all contracts. The disallowance of foreign selling costs has been rescinded. DFARS 231.205-38 (effective December 1988) and FAR 31.205-38(c)(2) (effective May 1991) made allowable broadly targeted and direct-selling and short-term planning efforts incurred in connection with a significant effort to promote export sales of products generally sold to the U.S. government. Allowable foreign selling costs for those business segments that allocated $2.5 million or more of such costs to government contracts were limited to 110% of foreign selling costs incurred by the segment in the previous fiscal year until May 16, 1997, at which time the ceiling was also eliminated.

The allocation of selling costs has been subject to numerous disputes. Unfortunately, these cases have not been decided on a totally consistent basis, as noted below.

- In *Cubic Corp.*,[80] the ASBCA addressed the allowability of selling costs that were subject to two different selling cost principles: ASPR Section XV in effect before Revision 50, and ASPR Section XV as changed by Revision 50. Commercial sales commissions before Revision 50 were disallowed because the products sold to the government (sophisticated tracking systems) were distinct from the catalog items sold commercially and because the selling costs related to government and commercial products were clearly severable. The Board acknowledged, however, that even under the strict cost allowability criteria in effect prior to Revision 50, it could have held for the appellant if "the products upon which the commissions were paid are related in some affirmative way (such as being the same type or class of product) to the products or services being purchased by the Government."

  With regard to sales commissions that were subject to the Revision 50 cost principle, the ASBCA concluded that the sales expenses should be accumulated into at least two pools—one pool for selling costs which met the criteria to ASPR 15-205.37, and the other pool for selling costs that did not meet such criteria and that the costs accumulated in each pool should be distributed against the class of sales to which each applies. Having reached that conclusion, however, the Board then acknowledged that the company's recordkeeping system did not easily permit a literal application of the selling cost principle. In view of other provisions of the cost principles addressing advance agreements, allowability factors, and logical cost groupings for indirect expenses, the Board concluded that a pro rata allocation of total selling expenses to all contracts was acceptable in the circumstances. Because certain selling expenses (e.g., salaries of in-house sales personnel) supported government sales, while other selling expenses (e.g., outside sales commissions) supported commercial sales, the Board concluded that the total selling expense pool could be equitably allocated to all contracts, both government and commercial.

- In *General Dynamics Corp., Convair Division*,[81] the ASBCA concluded that selling expenses of the company's commercial division were allocable to the Air Force contracts performed by the military division.

- In *Lockheed–Georgia Co.* (commonly referred to as GELAC),[82] the Board overruled the government's disallowance of excess commercial sales expenses. In rejecting the government's argument that the company had failed to allocate selling costs in reasonable proportion to the benefits received, the Board quoted from the *General Dynamics* decision cited above by stating that for the government to prevail "it must show that due to the particular circumstances involved further use of a particular base would be inequitable." The Board further observed the following:

> Respondent ... does not contend that GELAC's accounting system for overhead and G&A costs failed to comply with GAAP. ... Respondent has also stipulated that GELAC's use of a direct labor allocation base is in accordance with GAAP (id.), and there is no evident inequity in the use of such a base here. ... GELAC's accounting practices were in accord with its own established policies which were consistently followed during the period at issue. ... We have found that GELAC's system met the ASPR requirements regarding proper classification of costs and logical cost groups. ... Given that conclusion, as well as the court's "sound method" test for judging allocation, we conclude on these facts that GELAC allocated its commercial costs in reasonable proportion to the benefit received.

This broad view of benefits received was not adopted by the Claims Court in *KMS Fusion, Inc.*,[83] which sustained DOE's disallowance of marketing costs related to multiplexer units that were allocated to contracts under the DOE's Inertial Confinement Fusion (ICF) program. The DOE concluded that the costs of marketing the multiplexer were costs that went directly to that product itself, and that any benefit to the government was too remote and insubstantial to make the cost allocable to the DOE contracts.

Several disputes focused on the allowability of foreign selling expenses before the 1986 change in the cost principle.

- The ASBCA denied *Emerson Electric Co.'s*[84] motion for summary judgment against the government's disallowance of foreign selling expenses incurred from 1979 to 1984. The Board focused on two key provisions of the then-existing cost principle that selling costs "are allowable to the extent they are allocable" to government contracts, and foreign military products selling costs "shall not be allocable to" domestic government contracts. In the Board's view:

> It should be unmistakable to any person possessing a rudimentary familiarity with the English language and principles of deductive reasoning that the foregoing two phrases represent the first two legs of a syllogism. The third and final leg of the syllogism clearly is: Therefore, foreign military products selling costs are not allowable under domestic Government contracts.

- In *General Electric Co.*,[85] the court also effectively prohibited inclusion of foreign selling costs as an expense chargeable to GE's government contracts. General Electric argued that (1) the inclusion of domestic and foreign selling costs in the G&A cost pool was permitted by CAS 410; (2) DAR 15-205.37(b) was inconsistent with CAS 410 because it purported to address allocability as opposed to allowability; and (3) since CAS exclusively governs allocability of costs, the conflicting DAR provision was invalid. To support its position, GE cited the Boeing supplemental executive retirement plan decision,[86] in which the ASBCA ruled that cost accounting standards take precedence over conflicting DAR provisions governing the allocability of unfunded pension costs. In ruling against GE, the court concluded that no conflict existed between CAS 410 and the DAR. The court held that CAS 410 permits, but does not mandate, the inclusion of selling costs in G&A and that even if the inclusion of selling costs in the G&A is consistent with CAS 410, it does not necessarily mean that costs are allowable. The court further concluded that costs can plainly be properly allocable yet not allowable and that even if costs are not allowable, they must be allocated. The court also referred to the previously discussed *Emerson Electric* case, in which ASBCA held that the intent of the DAR was to disallow foreign military product selling costs on domestic contracts.

- The ASBCA reached an entirely different conclusion in *Daedalus Enterprises, Inc.*[87] The government challenged Daedalus' selling expenses on two grounds: (1) Foreign sales commissions should be charged direct, and (2) foreign selling costs were not allocable to government contracts. The government lost on both issues. In its opinion, the ASBCA concluded the following:

  > In the contract before us in this appeal the Government benefited not potentially, but actually, from the reduced G&A rate as a result of the foreign business.
  >
  > Cases in which this Board has found the element of benefit insufficient for allocation are distinguishable on the facts. . . . None of these cases involved the potential of clear inequity in the different treatment of salaries and commissions found in Cubic and in the instant appeal. The Board has recognized a degree of business judgment, which properly belongs to the contractor, in deciding what is necessary to the overall operation or expansion of its business. . . .
  >
  > We conclude that neither the FAR nor the case law precludes the allocation of the foreign sales commissions under the factual circumstances here present.

- The ASBCA[88] concluded that Aydin Corporation's consistent practice of including sales commissions in its G&A expense pool resulted in an inequitable distribution of sales commissions to government contracts where one contract had a disproportionately large commission. The commission generated by Aydin's SOLAR II contract represented over 91% of the total sales commissions paid in 1989, whereas the SOLAR II contract costs represented only 19% of the 1989 G&A base. The ASBCA ruled that Aydin's only choices were to either: (1) charge the SOLAR II commission direct and charge all other commissions to G&A expense; or (2) calculate a special allocation of G&A expense to the SOLAR II contract to eliminate the inequitable distribution of G&A expense to other contracts. The Federal Circuit[89] disagreed. Because the SOLAR II sales commission did not differ in purpose or circumstances from other sales commissions, the court concluded that the SOLAR II sales commission had to remain in the G&A pool. This Aydin decision is discussed in further detail in Chapter 8 in the section on CAS 410—Allocation of Business Unit G&A to Final Cost Objectives.

Needless to say, this cost principle has generated considerable criticism from industry representatives who contend that selling costs are:

- Necessary to the overall operation of a business
- Only one of many indirect costs incurred by a company and should not be subject to a separate analysis of benefit to the government. Unfortunately, a number of board and court decisions have failed to recognize the govern-

ment's inconsistent accounting treatment of B&P costs and selling costs. Bid and proposal costs that relate primarily to government work are required to be allocated to all work, including commercial contracts. In contrast, selling expenses have, at times, been considered allocable on a class of customer basis (e.g., commercial sales). This potential inequity was recognized in *General Dynamics Corp., Convair Division*,[90] when the ASBCA observed the following:

> It is apparent that during these years commercial contracts benefited more from the allocation of selling and distribution costs to all contracts at the expense of military products. The opposite appears to be true with respect to proposal and bidding cost for civilian and military costs during the same period.

Taxes (FAR 31.205-41)

Taxes, which are accounted for in accordance with GAAP, are generally allowable, except for the following:

- Federal income and excess profits taxes
- Taxes for which an exemption is available
- Taxes related to financing, refinancing, and reorganization
- Special assessments on land
- Taxes on real or personal property or on the value, use, possession, or sale of property used solely for nongovernment work
- Taxes on funding deficiencies or prohibited transactions relating to employee deferred compensation plans
- Deferred income taxes (tax effects of differences between taxable income and pretax income reported on the financial statements)

The unallowability of deferred taxes has generated considerable controversy. Many believe that a tax should become a cost when the conditions giving rise to the tax (such as profitable contract performance) occur, rather than when the liability is identified on the tax return. Generally accepted accounting principles require that taxes be recorded based on pretax accounting income and not when paid (Accounting Principles Board Opinion 11, *Accounting for Income Taxes*). The acquisition regulations are, therefore, contrary to GAAP.

Over the years, major disputes have arisen on the allocation of state and local taxes to segments. These cases are discussed in Chapter 8 in the section on CAS 403, Allocation of Home Office Expenses to Segments.

The rationale for the government's disallowance of taxes on property used solely for nongovernment work is that real or personal property, which is charged directly to flexibly priced contracts (or to fixed-price contracts for which the contractor has received progress payments), is exempt from such taxes since title vests with the government.

In *United States v. State of New Mexico*,[91] the U.S. Court of Appeals concluded that the following items were subject to the New Mexico gross receipts tax:

- Sales of tangible personal property to the Energy Research and Development Administration (now DOE) through its management contractors
- Advanced funds used for government operations under those management contracts

The court held that the contractors were not agents of the government; consequently, they were not immune from state tax assessment.

A 1990 court decision raised some new issues for contractors with operations in California. The California Court of Appeals ruled in *The Aerospace Corp. v. State Board of Equalization*[92] that materials and supplies purchased for overhead accounts and allocated to federal contracts containing title provisions were exempt from sales and use taxes. The court concluded that title to indirect materials and supplies passes to the government under the Government Property clause [FAR 52.245-5(c)(3)(iii)] in cost-reimbursement contracts, the Progress Payments clause [FAR 52.232-16(d)] in fixed-price contracts, or equivalent DAR clauses. Contractors may be obligated to file claims for refunds and to either pay some of the refunds to the government or adjust some contract prices downward to reflect the refunds. In other cases, contractors may be eligible for refunds and not be obligated to pass them on. The effect of this ruling on the refund's disposition is complex since the impact is different for fixed-price contracts than for cost-reimbursement contracts.

A number of contractual issues must be addressed as a result of this decision. To whom do refunds belong? Are progress payments affected? How should contractors calculate the amount of refunds, credits, and price adjustments to which the government may be entitled? Are subcontractors entitled to refunds?

A significant impact of this decision is that these taxes may become unallowable in the future. Federal Acquisition Regulation 31.205-41(b)(3) states that "taxes from which exemptions are available to the contractor directly, or available to the contractor based on an exemption afforded the Government" are unallowable unless the CO determines that the administrative burden in obtaining the exemption outweighs the corresponding benefits to the government. Consequently, contractors may not be permitted to classify California sales and use taxes as allowable costs for contract pricing and subsequent costing for government contracts with a title clause unless the potential refund is so small that it is not significantly greater than the administrative costs the company would have to incur to calculate and obtain the exemption. Furthermore, the government will likely assert its rights to benefit from refunds of sales and use taxes incurred in prior periods for which the contractor may still file a refund claim.

In another decision dealing with sales and use tax, the U.S. District Court for the Western District of Missouri (*United States v. Benton*)[93] addressed sales and use tax assessed by the State of Missouri. The State of Missouri taxed Olin for sales and use tax on tangible personal property purchased for the plant. These taxes were subsequently reimbursed by the government. The Missouri sales and use tax statute exempts from taxation purchases made for resale in any form. Under Olin's Army contract, title passes to the government when the property is delivered to Olin. The government argued that this passage of title effects a resale. Missouri argued that Olin's transfer of title of the property under the contract was not a resale, because Olin retained an ownership interest on the property it managed and operated the tangible personal property after title passed.

In its decision, the court stated: "To the extent Olin has an interest in the property, its interest is subservient to that of the United States, which is contractually obligated to pay Olin for the property." The court did not view Olin's continuing interest as holding that a resale did not occur.

Superfund tax payments that were made from the inception of the tax in 1986 to January 22, 1991, are unallowable. Federal Acquisition Regulations 31.205-41 was amended, effective January 22, 1991, to allow the cost of such payments.

Trade, Business, Technical, and Professional Activity Costs (FAR 31.205-43)

Costs of memberships and subscriptions related to trade, business, technical, and professional organizations are allowable. Costs of meetings and conferences are allowable if their primary purpose is to disseminate information or enhance production. Documentation of claimed costs, including conference participants and the purpose of the meeting, is therefore critical. The DCAA *Contract Audit Manual* provides the following guidance to DCAA auditors on the expected level of documentation for business conference expenses:

I. Section 7-1103.3 Documentation
   A. The contractor should maintain adequate records supplying the following information on properly prepared travel vouchers or expense records, supported by copies of paid invoices, receipts, charge slips, etc.: (1) date and location of meeting, including the name of the establishment; (2) names of employees and guests in attendance; (3) purpose of the meeting; and (4) cost of the meeting, by item.
   B. The above guidelines closely parallel the current record-keeping requirements in Section 274 of the Internal Revenue Code for entertainment costs as a tax, deductible expense. Where satisfactory support assuring the claimed costs are allowable conference expenses is not furnished, the claimed conference/meal costs and directly associated costs . . . should be questioned.
   C. Meal expense: Expenses for meals of contractor personnel, not in travel status, who act as hosts as contractor-sponsored business luncheons or dinners are allowable if it is determined that the activity constitutes a business meeting or conference associated with the active conduct of the contractor's business and not a social function.
II. Section 7-1103.4 Standards of Conduct—Federal Employee

Guest expenses for meals or other incidentals applicable Federal employees should normally be questioned as unnecessary, and hence unreasonable, costs, except under limited circumstances, since they are prohibited from accepting gratuities by Executive Order 11222 of 1965, 5 CFR 735(c), and various departmental implementing directives (e.g., DOD 5500.7, Standards of Conduct).

Training and Educational Costs (FAR 31.205-44)

Costs of training at the noncollege level to increase employees' vocational effectiveness are allowable. Costs of education at the college level are allowable to the extent that the course or degree pursued relates to the field in which the employee is working or may be reasonably expected to work, except for the following:

- Allowable, straight-time compensation of employees attending classes part time during working hours is generally limited to 156 hours per year.
- Allowable costs of full-time education at the postgraduate level are generally limited to two school years per employee trained.

Also, costs of specialized programs for existing or potential executives or managers are allowable up to 16 weeks per employee per year. Grants to educational or training institutions are considered unallowable contributions.

Travel Costs (FAR 31.205-46)

In 1986, FAR coverage on travel costs went through some major changes, which have had an impact on firms doing business with the government. Before those revisions, travel costs incurred by employees in travel status while on company business were generally allowable with certain exceptions. The excess of first-class airfare over less than first-class accommodations generally was allowable only when less than first-class accommodations were not reasonably available. The cost of contractor-owned aircraft was allowable if: (1) it was reasonable; (2) the use of such aircraft was necessary for the conduct of business; and (3) any increase in cost, compared with alternative means of transportation, was commensurate with the advantages gained.

The first of the 1986 FAR changes dealt with corporate aircraft costs, company-furnished automobiles, and unallowable commercial airfare costs. The revised criteria limit allowable costs of contractor-owned, -leased, or -chartered aircraft to the lowest customary coach airfare unless travel by such aircraft is specifically required by the contract or a higher amount is approved by the CO. A higher amount may be agreed to under circumstances justifying higher-than-standard airfare as described in the cost principle. Manifest/logs for all flights on company aircraft must be maintained and made available as a condition of allowability. Costs of contractor-owned or -leased automobiles are allowed to the extent they are used for company business. Costs associated with the personal use of the automobiles (including travel to and from work) are now specifically cited as unallowable.

Airfare costs in excess of the lowest standard coach or equivalent airfare offered during normal business hours are unallowable, unless certain exceptions apply.

The most significant change, applicable to all contracts resulting from solicitations issued on or after July 31, 1986, concerned allowable reimbursement for lodgings, meals, and incidental expenses. The amendment limits reimbursement for such expenses to the maximum per diem rates applicable to government employees. If a contractor reimburses its employees per diem in lieu of actual costs, detailed receipts or other documentation are not required. However, if employee reimbursement is based on actual costs incurred, documentation, similar to the Internal Revenue Code requirements, must be maintained. In special circumstances, actual costs up to three times the maximum per diem rates may be allowed. The special circumstances are addressed in the Federal Travel Regulation.[94]

The cost principle was revised on September 23, 1991, to clarify that: (1) contractors are not subject to separate ceilings for lodging and meals/incidentals; and (2) maximum per diems rates do not constitute a reasonable daily charge for partial travel days or travel days without lodging. The revision not only affects the amount of reimbursable travel costs but may require administrative effort on the part of contractors to demonstrate that subsistence costs for partial travel days and travel days with no lodging are reasonable.

The DCAA Contract Audit Manual Section 7-1002.4 concludes that a statistical sampling approach to identifying the excess costs does not satisfy the requirements of CAS 405, Accounting for Unallowable Costs, and that contractors are required to specifically identify the unallowable travel costs except under circumstances addressed in CAS 405-50(c).[95] In lieu of specifically identifying unallowable costs, the Cost Accounting Standard permits the contracting parties to reach agreement on an alternate method based on materiality.

The Federal Acquisition Streamlining Act (FASA) of 1994[95] eliminated the statutory requirement that limited the recovery of contractor travel subsidence costs to the same per diem limitations applicable to federal employees. The intent of Congress was to streamline the acquisition process and minimize burdensome, government-unique requirements. This action was consistent with the Section 800 Panel Report, which recommended repeal on the basis that per diem limitations for contractors were unreasonable, because contractors generally could not obtain either the hotel rates or the state and city tax exemptions that were available to federal employees. Unfortunately, the proposed revision to FAR 31.205-46, Travel Costs,[96] did not eliminate the per diem ceilings as the basis for determining reasonable and allowable travel subsistence costs. Rather, the proposal merely added a new paragraph (a)(7), which provides as follows:

> Contractors may propose an alternative set of maximum per diem rates to replace the rates prescribed by subparagraph (a)(2) of this subsection. The contracting officer may approve alternative rates if the contractor demonstrates that the alternative rates are reasonable, are derived from the contractor's normal travel cost reimbursement system, and do not exceed amounts normally paid under that system. In order to be allowable, the alternative rates must be approved prior to the incurrence of the travel costs.

Industry criticism of the proposed FAR revision was vociferous, because the revision fell far short of the relief envisioned by the statute. The proposed rule has not been finalized.

Big Three Industries, Inc.[97] dealt with the allowability of the costs of company-owned aircraft. The ASBCA made a presumptive determination of reasonableness of such costs because the firm had obtained fixed-price contracts under competitive conditions and thus had a strong economic incentive to keep down its costs. The Board further relied on IRS acceptance of the company's aircraft as necessary to the conduct of its business. Finally, the Board concluded that the government had the burden to prove that the contractor's aircraft expense was more costly than alternative means of transportation. Since the government in this case had made no attempt to demonstrate that the use of the aircraft was more costly, the disputed cost was allowed in full. The applicability of this decision to future challenges to the allocability of corporate aircraft costs was effectively limited by the 1986 cost principle revision.

In *United Technologies Corp.*,[98] the ASBCA allowed the costs relating to five of the eight aircraft owned by the corporate office. The company demonstrated, through an internal cost-benefit analysis, that the full costs of operating the aircraft were less than the total of (1) commercial airfare, subsistence, freight, and relocation costs that would have been incurred if corporate aircraft had not been used; and (2) the productivity savings by corporate personnel that would have been lost had the corporate aircraft not been used. Productivity savings were computed by applying a 2.5 multiplier to the passengers' hourly rate, which was then multiplied by actual flight time. The 2.5 multiplier was based on typical contractual billing rates for individuals (e.g., technicians who were billed on an hourly, daily, or weekly basis).

In *General Dynamics Corp.*,[99] the ASBCA concluded that the benefits outweighed the costs for all of the aircraft owned by the corporate office. While both the contractor and the government made internal cost-benefit analyses that focused on both cost avoidances and productivity savings, the results of the two studies were dramatically different. The contractor's study concluded that benefits outweighed costs by $17 million for the six years at issue. In contrast, the government's study concluded that costs exceeded benefits by $19 million. Two of the principal differences in the methodologies used to calculate productivity saving in these studies were the multiplier and the passengers' hourly compensation rates. The General Dynamics study reflected (1) an hourly compensation rate that included both base salary and incentive compensation and (2) multipliers of 5, 10, or 15, depending on the executive positions of the passengers. The multiplier of 15 was restricted to the chief executive officer (CEO). The government study reflected only the base salary and used the 2.5 multiplier that had been accepted by ASBCA in *United Technologies.*

In deciding for the contractor, the Board concluded the following:

> Weighing the evidence before us, we find General Dynamics' unchallenged analysis to be more persuasive. We reach this conclusion because General Dynamics' analysis was supported by the testimony of experts and because its analysis was based on proven facts peculiar to General Dynamics. In contrast, the Government's analysis was based on an attempt to fit General Dynamics' situation into a cost-benefit formula designed for another company. It was an awkward fit at best. While we do not necessarily subscribe to all the theories and conclusions of General Dynamics' experts, we conclude that General Dynamics has demonstrated that the advantages gained in using corporate aircraft outweighed the costs of the aircraft.

Goodwill (FAR 31.205-49)

In 1984, the Defense Acquisition Regulatory Council issued a new cost principle disallowing any cost for expensing, writing off, or writing down goodwill. *Goodwill* is defined in FAR 31.205-49 as an unidentifiable, intangible asset that "originates under the purchase method of accounting for a business combination when the price paid by the acquiring company exceeds the sum of the identifiable individual assets acquired less liabilities assumed, based on their fair values."

This action was not entirely unexpected in light of the ASBCA decision in *Gould Defense Systems.*[100] As further discussed in Chapter 8, the central issue in this appeal was whether goodwill was properly includable as an element of facilities capital under CAS 414. The Board concluded the following:

> [Goodwill] amortization expense generally is an allowable cost under the Defense Acquisition Regulation. There are no specific references in the Defense Acquisition Regulation cost principles to the recoverability of goodwill amortization costs nor does the Defense Acquisition Regulation preclude recovery of such costs. Amortization of goodwill not only is recognized as a cost under generally accepted accounting principles, it currently is required for financial reporting purposes. Thus, when properly incurred, goodwill amortization cost meets the general requirements of DAR 15-201.1 ... that costs be determined in accordance with a "generally accepted" method.

When the cost principle was ultimately promulgated in FAR 31.205-49 in 1984, the dispute over goodwill was, from a contractor's perspective, unfortunately just another case of winning the battle and losing the war.

Cost of Alcoholic Beverages (FAR 31.205-50)

This cost principle, added on April 7, 1986, specifically disallows the cost of alcoholic beverages.

Environmental Clean-up Costs

Although there has been considerable discussion related to this issue, no cost principle exists regarding the allowability of environmental clean-up costs. In 1990, the issuance of an environmental cost principle was proposed. The draft generated considerable controversy because it categorized environmental remediation costs as unallowable unless a contractor could prove that it:

- Created the damage while performing a government contract
- Acted prudently, at the time the damage occurred, to comply with the then-existing industry practices and environmental laws and regulations
- Acted promptly to minimize the damage and to mitigate the cost of remediation
- Exhausted all insurance and indemnifiable sources to defray the costs

The draft cost principle was never promulgated.

The DCAA Contract Audit Manual Section 7-2120.1 concludes that environmental clean-up costs are generally allowable if the contractor can demonstrate that the contamination was not caused by contractor wrongdoing or actions that should have been avoided. A guidance memorandum[101] jointly issued by the Defense Contract Management Command (DCMC) and DCAA on April 13, 1994, addresses specific questions that have arisen as to the treatment of environmental costs. The guidance concludes the following:

- Costs to clean up property that was not contaminated when acquired should be expensed; whereas costs to clean up property that was already contaminated when acquired should be capitalized as an improvement to the land in accordance with CAS 404, Capitalization of Tangible Capital Assets.

- If contamination occurred both before and after acquisition, clean-up costs should be apportioned to the responsible parties using a reasonable allocation base.

- If a contractor is legally required to pay another potentially responsible party's (PRP) share of the clean-up costs and cannot collect from the other PRP who is out of business with no successor having assumed its liabilities, the costs should not be characterized as a bad debt. However, if a contractor cannot collect from another PRP but either the other PRP is still in business or a successor company assumed the other PRP's liabilities, the uncollected amounts are considered bad debts, and thus unallowable costs.

External Restructuring Costs (DFARS 231.205-70)

A memorandum issued by the Undersecretary of Defense (Acquisition) on July 21, 1993,[102] permitted the amortization of allowable restructuring costs resulting from either an acquisition or merger, if such costs were expected to result in cost savings to the DOD. A joint DCMC/DCAA guidance,[103] issued in January 1994, provided detailed guidance on the process to be followed in the submission and evaluation of restructuring costs and savings proposals and negotiation of advance agreements. Prior to enactment of the Fiscal Year 1995 National Defense Authorization Act, Congress hotly debated whether external restructuring costs (restructuring costs resulting from an acquisition or merger) should be reimbursed to contractors. The act[104] ultimately permitted reimbursement of external restructuring costs with certain restrictions. Restructuring costs were also addressed in the National Defense Appropriation Act for 1997[105] and the National Defense Authorization Act for 1998.[106] The statutory provisions are implemented in DFARS 231.205-70. External restructuring activities are those restructures activities occurring after a business combination that affect the operations of companies not previously under common control. As a direct outgrowth of the business combination, they are generally initiated within three years of the business combination. Allowability of otherwise allowable external restructuring costs is conditioned on the following:

- Performance of an audit of the contractor's proposed restructuring costs and restructuring savings
- An ACO determination that the proposed restructuring efforts are expected to result in savings to the DOD
- Certification by the Undersecretary of Defense (Acquisition Technology) or a senior designee that projected future restructuring savings are based on audited cost data and should result in overall reduced costs to the DOD (Certification is not required for any business combination for which other restructuring costs were reimbursed or an advance agreement was negotiated prior to August 15, 1994.)
- Execution of an advance agreement by the contractor and the ACO which establishes cost ceilings for restructuring costs
- For business combinations occurring after September 30, 1996, no fiscal year 1997 or subsequent year appropriated funds can be used for reimbursement of restructuring costs unless: (1) the audited savings exceed the costs allowed by a factor of two to one; or (2) the savings exceed allowed costs and the Secretary of Defense determines that the business combination will preserve a critical capability that might otherwise be lost to DOD.

External restructuring costs must be separately identified and excluded from billings, contract settlements, and final indirect cost rate settlements until the DOD certification has been obtained.

A proposed addition to DFARS 231.205-70, issued for comment on January 12, 1995,[107] would have conditioned the allowability of otherwise allowable internal restructuring costs on the following:

- The performance of an audit of the contractor's restructuring proposal
- An ACO determination that proposed restructuring efforts are expected to result in DOD savings
- Execution of an ACO/contractor advance agreement as to restructuring cost ceilings

Industry vigorously opposed the promulgation of this proposed rule because it was not statutorily mandated, would be costly to implement, and could result in a significant disallowance of previously allowable costs. The proposal was withdrawn October 13, 1995.[108]

The DCAA guidance on restructuring costs is contained in the *Contract Audit Manual* Section 7-190C.

Defense Capability Preservation Agreements

The 1996 Defense Authorization Act[109] included a provision authorizing the Secretary of Defense to enter into agreements to permit a contractor to allocate to commercial contracts only the direct costs of performance plus variable indirect expenses. All remaining indirect costs (e.g., fixed costs) would be allocated solely to government business. The purpose of the statutory provision was to facilitate the entry of defense contractors into commercial markets. Implementing regulations were incorporated into DFARS 231.205-71.

7-8. RETROACTIVE DISALLOWANCES

Boards of contract appeals and the courts have consistently applied the doctrine of estoppel in preventing the government from retroactively disallowing a cost or allocation method that had previously been accepted. Cases in which this doctrine figured in the decision included *Litton Systems,*[110] *H&M Moving, Inc.,*[111] *Falcon Research & Development Co.,*[112] *Data Design Laboratories, Inc.,*[113] and *Gould Defense Systems, Inc.*[114] The following elements must be present to establish the defense of estoppel:

- The party to be estopped must know the facts.
- The party to be estopped must intend that his or her conduct will be acted upon or must so act that the party asserting estoppel has a right to believe it is so intended.
- The party asserting estoppel must be ignorant of the true facts.
- The party asserting estoppel must rely on the other party's conduct to his or her injury.

In an interesting sequel to the *Data Design Laboratories'* case,[115] the Board later barred the government from retroactively disallowing the costs before issuing the CO's final decision. The Board concluded the following:

> The DCAA Form 1 was a recommendation to the contracting officer on treatment of costs but was not, itself, a final decision disallowing such costs. Therefore, issuance of the DCAA Form 1 was not in and of itself conclusive that these costs would be disallowed. In this case, especially, the record indicates that some modification of this position by the contracting officer might have been achieved. Therefore, we conclude that under the facts here present the issuance of the DCAA Form 1 did not, in and of itself, constitute a disallowance or such likelihood of disallowance that continuing to make the expenditure became the risk of the contractor. . . .
>
> Here, the contractor did appeal to the administrative contracting officer and was successful in negotiating approval of three of four costs for which the auditor had recommended disallowance. . . .
>
> We, therefore, conclude that it was reasonable under the facts here present for appellant to believe it would again be successful in establishing the reasonableness of the first class air fare costs with the contracting officer and to continue to incur such costs prior to the receipt of the contracting officer's final decision so that disallowance of such costs would be a retroactive disallowance. . . .

The precedent of previous estoppel decisions became somewhat uncertain as a result of a 1991 Court of Appeals for the Federal Circuit decision involving *JANA, Inc.*[116] The court observed the following:

> It is also not entirely clear whether the defense of estoppel is still available against the government in light of the Supreme Court's decision in *OPM v. Richmond*, 110 S. Ct. 2465 (1990), which held that, absent fraud by the government, estoppel could never be asserted against it in suits to compel the payment of money from the public treasury in contravention of eligibility requirements contained in an Act of Congress.

In 1992, the ASBCA appeared to reaffirm the validity of the estoppel doctrine in a decision involving *General Dynamics Corp.*[117] but concluded that it did not bar the government from disallowing certain corporate aircraft costs, because the government had never accepted the costs. As the Board observed:

> The facts do not support application of the doctrine of the bar against retroactive disallowance in this case. Although the Government had knowledge of General Dynamics' corporate aircraft, the evidence provided no support that the Government approved of or acquiesced in the aircraft. . . .

there was no doubt that General Dynamics clearly understood and had "reasonably adequate" notice since the time it acquired its first corporate aircraft that the Government was "taking great exception to [its] corporate aircraft costs."

A 1993 ASBCA decision reaffirmed the validity of the estoppel doctrine in a limitation of funds issue involving *Dynamic Concepts, Inc.*[118] The Board ruled that the government's conduct estopped it from citing the contractor's failure to provide proper notification of a contract overrun, because the four-element estoppel test had been met.

Establishing that the four elements of estoppel have been met, however, will not necessarily protect a company against an asserted violation of the False Claims Act. The Federal Circuit[119] rejected Martin Marietta's assertion that the government was estopped from claiming fraudulent mischarging of labor costs because the contracting officer was informed of the contractor's intent to charge to IR&D six tasks required on performance of research and development contract. The court opined as follows:

> Even assuming that Martin Marietta did inform the Government of its precise actions, a government officer cannot authorize a contractor to violate federal regulations. . . .

> Martin Marietta's notice to the Government might also negate any contention that the company intended to deceive the Government. However, intent to deceive is not an element of the False Claims Act. . . . [A] contractor who tells a government contracting officer that a claim is false still violates the statute when the false claim is submitted.

7-9. CREDITS

Credits are defined as the applicable portion of income, rebates, allowances, and other credits that relate to allowable costs. Credits can be given to the government as either cost reductions or cash refunds.

The issue of the government's entitlement to credits has been litigated on numerous occasions. In *Celesco Industries, Inc.*,[120] the government was precluded from sharing in a gain on a sale of land acquired through the exercise of an option under a rental agreement. In its decision, the ASBCA concluded that the regulatory provision was only intended to:

> . . . [A] apply to situations where the Government has reimbursed the contractor for costs incurred and the contractor has simultaneously recovered a portion of the *same costs from another source*. . . . The Government did not participate with the contractor in the payment of any additional rental costs attributable to the option price or other factors. The gain realized was not income, rebate, allowance, or other credits related to an allowable cost within the meaning of ASPR 15-201.5. [Emphasis added.]

In a somewhat similar decision, *RMK–BRJ, A Joint Venture*,[121] the government was precluded from sharing in the portion of an insurance refund that corresponded to the percentage of premiums contributed by the company's employees. In sustaining the contractor's appeal, the Board observed the following:

> It is not every refund which a contractor may receive to which the Government is entitled. Before any entitlement arises, the Government must have paid the costs to which the refund is applicable. . . . The Government's rights in the refund are tied to and dependent upon the amount of costs which it has reimbursed to appellant. Not one dime of the portion of the premiums paid by the employees ever became a cost of this contract or was ever reimbursed by the Government. . . .

> All the refund which related to the costs which respondent had paid was credited to the Government. The ASPR cost principles do not require any more than that.

In a Court of Claims decision, *Northrop Aircraft, Inc., v. United States*,[122] the contractor was required to offset interest income against contract costs because the interest income was derived from a tax refund and because the government had been allocated its share of the original tax payment. The court construed the interest on the refund as a reduction in the taxes previously charged to government contracts.

In *Colorado Dental Service (Delta Dental Plan of Colorado)*,[123] the Board ruled that the government was entitled to interest income on monies placed in an interest-bearing account that the contractor received in advance for paying dental claims under government contracts. Consistent with the *Northrop* decision, the Board concluded that the interest income related to allowable contract costs since it was attributable solely to the government's advance reimbursement to the contractor of insurance payments that had not yet been received by claimants and deducted from the contractor's bank account.

In *KMS Fusion, Inc.*,[124] the Court of Claims overruled the DOE's attempt to credit the profit realized on the sale of an option to purchase real property against the costs of an operating lease for the same property. Although the lease and the option to purchase were executed concurrently, they were separate transactions; there was no evidence that the price of the option had any bearing on the rental rate negotiated with the property owner.

The ASBCA ruled in *NI Industries*[125] that the credits provision entitled the government's flexibly priced contracts to an appropriate share of the reversion resulting from the termination of a defined benefit pension plan.

7-10. INDIRECT COST RATES

The Allowable Cost and Payment clause (FAR 52.216-7) provides for reimbursing costs incurred in contract performance that are deemed "allowable" by the CO, in accordance with procurement regulation cost principles and contract terms. In establishing the allowable indirect costs under a contract, indirect cost rates are applied to allowable contract base costs.

Billing Rates

Because indirect cost rates can be definitively determined only at the completion of a contractor's fiscal year, estimated rates are required to reimburse contractors on an interim basis. These rates, referred to as billing rates, are based on the anticipated final annual rates. To prevent substantial overpayment or underpayment, the billing rates should be adjusted as needed during the year. The contractor must determine the continued appropriateness of previously established billing rates given the passage of time and experience. The ACO or auditor responsible for determining the final indirect cost rates is usually responsible for establishing the billing rates to be used.

Final Indirect Cost Rates

Final indirect cost rates, which are determined after the contractor's fiscal period ends, are used to determine indirect expenses applicable to cost-reimbursement-type contracts, as well as fixed-price redeterminable and incentive-type contracts. Under the Allowable Cost and Payment clause, the contractor is required to submit the final indirect cost rate proposal to the ACO and auditor within six months after expiration of the fiscal year.[126] The proposal must include cost data supporting the indirect cost rate computations (i.e., indirect costs and base costs incurred for the year, as well as an identification of the flexibly priced contracts to which the rates apply).

Before October 1985, final rates were established either by procurement determination (negotiation) or audit determination.

- The procedure for establishing final rates by negotiation was initiated by submitting the contractor's overhead proposal to the ACO. The auditor made a review and issued an advisory report to the ACO. Negotiations ensued and culminated in an agreement on rates. If the parties failed to agree, the ACO made a unilateral final decision on behalf of the government, which could be appealed in accordance with the Disputes clause of the contract.

- The procedure for establishing rates by audit determination was also initiated by the contractor's submission of an overhead rate proposal. However, in this case, the proposal was submitted to the auditor, who made the review and discussed the audit findings with the contractor. The auditor prepared a written overhead rate agreement to be jointly signed by the contractor and the auditor. In the event an agreement could not be reached, the auditor issued a formal notice of costs suspended and/or disapproved (DCAA Form 1) (see Appendix 9.3), detailing the exceptions, which the contractor could appeal to the ACO. The ACO's decision was appealed through the normal disputes procedure.

- Overhead rates were "negotiated" at major contractor locations where a corporate administrative contracting officer was assigned or where an ACO was in residence. Audit-determined rates were applicable for other business concerns.

On October 17, 1985, the Deputy Secretary of Defense officially transferred to the DCAA the responsibility for final indirect cost rate determinations for all commercial contractor locations. This action extended the same procedures used by the DCAA in determining the rates at smaller contractors to the larger commercial contractor locations, in which final rates had been settled by procurement negotiation. Indirect cost settlement procedures remained unchanged for educational and similar institutions. To permit as orderly a transition as possible, ACOs retained settlement responsibility for open years in which an audit report had been issued and negotiations had begun. The DCAA settlement authority began with the following year. In June 1988, responsibility for determining final indirect cost rates of major contractor locations was returned to the ACOs. As a result, the final indirect cost rate settlement procedures that were in effect before October 1985 are again applicable.

Certification

A certification requirement was created on March 12, 1985, amid a series of congressional hearings delving into assertions that defense contractors were improperly charging the government with unallowable costs.

The initial certificate required corporate officials to declare, under penalty of perjury, that no unallowable costs were included in the billing and final indirect cost rate proposals and that all costs that were included "benefited the Department of Defense and were demonstrably related to or necessary for the performance of the Department of Defense contracts covered by the claim."

Industry was understandably concerned about the ramifications of this requirement, since the language in the certificate could lead one to believe that the DOD would seek criminal prosecution if costs, claimed and certified in good faith to be allowable, were later disallowed. In addition, the definition of "overhead" costs in the initial certificate was inconsistent with acquisition regulations and cost accounting standards, since it appeared to preclude the reimbursement of costs necessary for the overall operation of the business, even though a direct relationship to a particular contract could not be shown.

A letter from the DOD General Counsel[127] later advised the following:

- The certificate did not require the signer to ensure that the costs will be finally allowed; the signer was certifying in good faith that the costs were believed allowable and that he or she had reviewed the claim.

- The purpose of the perjury declaration was to remind the signer of the importance of the certification and the need to ensure that it accurately states his/her actual knowledge and belief.

- The certificate was not intended to change the FAR that defines the standards for allocating indirect costs to government contracts. The purpose of the certificate was to ensure that the signer, in good faith, actually applied those established principles in determining which costs he/she claimed to be chargeable to the contract.

The certificate was revised in April 1986 to recognize that "the certification is a good faith assertion, not an absolute guarantee. Costs are properly allocable to defense contracts if they are allocated in accordance with applicable acquisition regulations." The FASA extended to all civilian agencies the same indirect cost certification provisions that previously applied to defense contracts. Implementing regulations FAR 42.703-2 and 52.242-4 were effective October 1, 1995. The certification requirement relative to billing rate proposals and the requirement to execute the certificate under penalty of perjury were eliminated, effective January 1, 1997.

The certificate must be signed by a senior management official at a level no lower than vice president or chief financial officer. A contract clause entitled Certificate of Indirect Costs (see Appendix 7.6) is included in all contracts that provide for establishment of final indirect cost rates.

Including unallowable costs in proposals for settlement of indirect costs awarded since 1987 subjects the contractor to penalties as discussed further in Chapter 15.

The certification requirements should not be taken lightly. To adequately protect itself, a defense contractor should ensure that effective internal controls exist to properly screen unallowable costs from indirect expense proposals. The development of forward pricing, provisional, and final indirect cost also should be addressed in written policies and procedures. The suggested content for a policy and procedure covering the year-end indirect cost rate proposal is outlined below. First, the written policy should provide a mechanism for the following:

- Documenting how the indirect cost proposal is prepared
- Identifying the roles and responsibilities of personnel involved in the process

- Providing management with the tools necessary to prudently evaluate proposals before certification

Based on the above policy, the written procedure should address the following:

- Accounts and/or departments for which costs are to be voluntarily withdrawn as unallowable
- Costs requiring special analyses (e.g., cost issues raised by the DCAA in prior indirect cost proposal audit report) to ascertain amounts to be withdrawn, if any
- Disclosure of costs whose allowability is the subject of a formal dispute
- Methods used to develop indirect expense rates
- Documentation required to provide clear audit trails between the proposal and the general books of account and to permit a prudent management review of the proposal's adherence to federal regulations and company policies
- Independent management review and approval of indirect expense proposals, including:
  - Responsibility for review by an individual knowledgeable of federal acquisition regulations and independent of the proposal preparation process
  - Evaluation criteria to ensure that the review process is sufficiently detailed to document the proper exclusion of unallowable costs, the disposition of costs requiring special analysis, and the disposition of cost issues previously raised by the DCAA
  - Designation of the individual responsible for executing the certificate of indirect cost

7-11. SUMMARY

Costs are not allowable simply because they are incurred and properly recorded in the accounting records. Rather, cost allowability is determined based on such factors as reasonableness, allocability, CAS, GAAP, contractual terms, and limitations specified in the cost principles.

The regulatory environment affecting cost allowability is indeed dynamic. A company must keep abreast of the changes in allowability criteria to obtain optimal cost recovery and must take appropriate measures to exclude expressly unallowable costs from proposals, billings, and claims submitted to the government.

7-12. NOTES

1. Vinson–Trammel Act, 48 Stat. 503,10 U.S.C. §§2382, 7300, 7342, 7343, 40 U.S.C. §474, enacted March 27, 1934.
2. Merchant Marine Act of 1970, 84 Stat. 1018, §5 U.S.C. §5315, enacted Oct. 21, 1970, Pub L. 91-469.
3. Abeles, Schwartz, Haeckel, and Silverblatt, Inc., HUDBCA No. 81-625-C31, Sept. 4, 1984, 84-3 BCA 17,605.
4. Donald B. Rice, Secretary of the Air Force v. Martin Marietta Corp., CAFC No. 93-1025, Dec. 29, 1993, 13 F.3d 1563.
5. Bruce Construction Corporation, et al. v. United States, 163 Ct. Cl. 197, Nov. 15, 1963, 324 F.2d 516.

6. Western Electric Company, Inc., ASBCA No. 11056, April 18, 1969, 69-1 BCA 7,660.

7. Data-Design Laboratories, ASBCA No. 24534, June 16, 1983, 83-2 BCA 16,665.

8. Stanley Aviation Corp., ASBCA No. 12292, June 12, 1968, 68-2 BCA 7,081.

9. General Dynamics Corp. (Convair Division), ASBCA Nos. 8759, 9264, 9265, and 9266, Jan. 31, 1965, 66-1 BCA 5,368.

10. General Dynamics Corp. v. United States, 187 Ct. Cl. 597, May 16, 1969, 410 F.2d 404.

11. General Dynamics/Astronautics, ASBCA No. 6899, May 17, 1962, 1962 BCA 3,391.

12. Federal Register, Vol. 57, No. 134, July 13, 1992, pp. 31036–31040.

13. The Boeing Co., ASBCA No. 28342, Sept. 17, 1985, 85-3 BCA 18,435, aff'd. CAFC No. 86-927, Oct. 1, 1986, 802 F.2d 1390.

14. Donald B. Rice, Secretary of the Air Force v. Martin Marietta Corp., supra, note 4.

15. American Institute of Certified Public Accountants, AICPA Professional Standards as of Feb. 15, 1997, Statements on Auditing Standards, No. 69, AU §411, Paragraph 10.

16. Blue Cross Association and Blue Cross of Virginia, ASBCA No. 25776, Sept. 17, 1981, 81-2 BCA 15,359.

17. Celesco Industries, Inc., ASBCA No. 22402, Jan. 31, 1980, 80-1 BCA 14,271.

18. Grumman Aerospace Corp. v. United States, Ct. Cl. 1978, Nov. 15, 1978, 587 F.2d 498.

19. Physics International Co., ASBCA No. 17700, June 16, 1977, 77-2 BCA 12,612.

20. General Dynamics Corp., ASBCA No. 31359, Jan. 6, 1992, 92-1 BCA 24,698.

21. Aerojet-General Corp., ASBCA No. 13372, June 25, 1973, 73-2 BCA 10, 164; aff'd. Oct. 10, 1973, 73-2 BCA 10,307.

22. Ibid.

23. Blue Cross Association and Blue Shield Association (in the matter of Group Hospitalization, Inc., and Medical Services of the District of Columbia), ASBCA No. 25944, April 28, 1983, 83-1 BCA 16,524.

24. Lockheed Corp. v. United States, Ct. Cl. Nos. 261-88C, 90-168C, Nov. 7, 1990; CAFC No. 91-5061, settled May 1, 1991.

25. DOD Director of Defense Procurement Memorandum, reference DP/CPF, dated March 14, 1991, Subject: Impact of the Lockheed Case on the Determination of Unreasonable Compensation.

26. Fiscal Year 1995 Defense Appropriations Act, enacted Oct. 5, 1994, §8117, Pub. L. 103-337.

27. Fiscal Year 1996 Defense Appropriations Act, Pub. L. 104-61.

28. Fiscal Year 1997 Defense Appropriations Act, 110 Stat. 3009, enacted Sept. 30, 1996, Pub. L. 104-208.

29. Fiscal Year 1997 Defense Authorizations Act, 110 Stat. 2422, enacted Sept. 23, 1996, Pub. L. 104-201.

30. Fiscal Year 1998 Defense Authorization Act 111 Stat. 1629, enacted Nov. 18, 1997, Pub. L. 105-85.

31. Lulejean and Associates, Inc., ASBCA No. 20094, April 27, 1976, 76-1 BCA 11,880.

32. Space Services of Georgia, Inc., ASBCA No. 26021, July 19, 1982, 82-2 BCA 15,952.

33. Burt Associates, Inc., ASBCA No. 25884, April 20, 1982, 82-1 BCA 15,764.

34. Techplan Corp., ASBCA Nos. 41470, 45387, 45388, July 2, 1996, 96-2 BCA 28,426.

35. Memorandum for Regional Directors, DCAA and Director Field Detachment DCAA, Jan. 27, 1995, PAD 730.32/95-8, 95-PAD-021(R); subject: Allowability of Costs Associated with Employee Separation and General Release Agreements.

36. Memorandum for Regional Directors, DCAA and Director Field Detachment DCAA, Nov. 24, 1995; subject: Allowability of Costs Associated with Employee Separation and General Release Agreements.

37. The Boeing Co., ASBCA No. 24089, Dec. 15, 1980, 81-1 BCA 14,864; aff'd. April 30, 1981, 81-1 BCA 15,121.

38. Federal Register, Vol. 60, No. 215, Nov. 7, 1995, pp. 56216–56217.

39. Ralph M. Parsons Co., ASBCA Nos. 37931, 37946, 37947, Dec. 20, 1990, 91-1 BCA 23,648.

40. Singer Co., Kearfott Division, ASBCA No. 18857, March 17, 1975, 75-1 BCA 11,185; rev'd. and rem'd. Ct. Cl. No. 381-79C, Oct. 3, 1980, 225 Ct. Cl. 637; on remand May 4, 1981, 81-2 BCA 15,167; rem'd. Ct. Cl. Order, Nov. 13, 1981, 229 Ct. Cl. 589; on remand March 4, 1982, 82-2 BCA 15,684.

41. Honeywell Inc., ASBCA Nos. 28814, 29140, Sept. 28, 1984, 84-3 BCA No. 17,690.

42. GTE Government Systems Corp., ASBCA No. 37176, April 22, 1991, 91-2 BCA 23,987.

43. GTE Government Systems Corp. v. Perry, CAFC No. 91-1424, July 18, 1995, 61 F.3d 920.

44. United States v. Bicoastal Corp., DCM Fla. No. 90-573-CIV-T-17-3, March 29, 1991.

45. Bicoastal Corp., fka Singer Co., Bank. Ct. MD Fla. No. 89-8191, 8 Pl, Jan. 15, 1992.

46. The Boeing Co., supra, note 13.

47. NI Industries, Inc., ASBCA No. 34943, Nov. 29, 1991, 92-1 BCA 24,631; aff'd. April 6, 1992, 92-2 BCA 24,980.
48. Gould, Inc., ASBCA No. 46759, Sept. 19, 1997, 97-2 BCA 29,254.
49. Gould Defense Systems, Inc., ASBCA No. 24881, June 10, 1983, 83-2 BCA 16,676.
50. The Marquardt Co., ASBCA No. 29888, July 19, 1985, 85-3 BCA 18,245.
51. Times Fiber Communications, Inc. and Times Fiber Microwave Systems, Inc., ASBCA No. 37301, Jan. 23, 1991, 91-2 BCA 24,013.
52. Brown Engineering Co., ASBCA Nos. 6830 and 6831, Nov. 24, 1961, 61-2 BCA 3,225.
53. Cotton & Co., EBCA No. 426-6-89, Jan. 23, 1990, 90-2 BCA 22,828.
54. Aerojet-General Corp., ASBCA No. 15703, 15704, Jan. 31, 1973, 73-1 BCA 9932; see also General Dynamics, ASBCA No. 19607, May 3, 1978, 78-1 BCA 13,203.
55. United States ex rel Jerry J. Mayman v. Martin Marietta Corp., DCDM, Civil Action No. MJG-91-1853, April 27, 1995.
56. Fiscal Year 1991 Defense Authorization Act, 104 Stat. 1485, 10 U.S.C. §§372, 942, 2431, enacted Nov. 5, 1990, Pub. L. 101-510.
57. Dynatrend, Inc., ASBCA No. 23463, July 15, 1980, 80-2 BCA 14,617.
58. National Defense Authorization Act for 1992 and 1993, 106 Stat. 2315, 10 U.S.C. §§2687, 12001, enacted Oct. 23, 1992, Pub. L. 102-484.
59. Materials Science Corp., ASBCA No. 47067, May 7, 1996, 96-2 BCA 28,329.
60. Rocket Research Co., ASBCA No. 24972, Aug. 10, 1981, 81-2 BCA 15,307.
61. AT&T Technologies, Inc., DOTCAB No. 2007, July 14, 1989, 89-3 BCA 22,104.
62. John Doe Co., Inc., ASBCA No. 24576, July 28, 1980, 80-2 BCA 14,620.
63. Ravenna Arsenal, Inc., ASBCA No. 17802, Oct. 31, 1974, 74-2 BCA 10,937.
64. Superintendent of Documents, U.S. Government Printing Office, Defense Contract Audit Manual, P.O. Box 371954, Pittsburgh, PA 15250-7954.
65. Hirsch Tyler Co., ASBCA No. 20962, Aug. 23, 1976, 76-2 BCA 12,075.
66. Northrop Worldwide Aircraft Services, Inc., ASBCA No. 45877, Feb. 15, 1995, 95-1 BCA 27,503; Sept. 19, 1996, 96-2 BCA 28,574.
67. Bos'n Towing & Salvage Co., ASBCA No. 41357, Feb. 27, 1992, 92-2 BCA 24,864.
68. P&M Industries, Inc., ASBCA No. 38759, Sept. 29, 1997, 93-1 BCA 25,471.
69. Bill Strong Enterprises, Inc., ASBCA Nos. 42946, 43896, 43946, July 16, 1996, 96-2 BCA 26,428.
70. Pearl Properties, HUDBCA No. 95-C-118-C4, March 4, 1996, 96-1 BCA 28,219.
71. Walter Motor Truck Co., ASBCA No. 8054, Feb. 10, 1966, 66-1 BCA 5,365.
72. Dynalectron Corp., ASBCA No. 16895, Feb. 7, 1973, 73-1 BCA 9,909.
73. Ibid.
74. Celesco Industries, Inc., ASBCA No. 20569, March 11, 1977, 77-1 BCA 12,445.
75. FMC Corp., Northern Ordnance Division, ASBCA No. 30130, April 30, 1987, 87-2 BCA 19,791.
76. JANA, Inc., ASBCA No. 32447, March 11, 1988, 88-2 BCA 20,651.
77. HRB Singer, Inc., ASBCA No. 10799, Oct. 17, 1966, 66-2 BCA 5,903.
78. A.S. Thomas, Inc., ASBCA No. 10745, March 7, 1966, 66-1 BCA 5,438.
79. Data Design Laboratories, ASBCA No. 26753, Dec. 27, 1984, 85-1 BCA 17,825.
80. Cubic Corp., ASBCA No. 8125, June 17, 1963, 1963 BCA 3,775.
81. General Dynamics Corp., Convair Division, ASBCA No. 7963, March 5, 1964, 1964 BCA 4,133.
82. Lockheed Corp., Lockheed–Georgia Co., ASBCA No. 27660, April 26, 1990, 90-3 BCA 22,957.
83. KMS Fusion, Inc. v. United States, Ct.Cl. No. 649-87C, Dec. 4, 1991, 24 Cl. Ct. 582.
84. Emerson Electric Corp., ASBCA No. 30090, Nov. 19, 1986, 87-1 BCA 19,478.
85. General Electric Co., Aerospace Group, Ct. Cl. No. 25-89C, July 19, 1990, 21 Ct.Cl. 72; aff'd. CAFC No. 90-5157, March 29, 1991, 929 F.2d 679.
86. The Boeing Co., supra, note 37.
87. Daedalus Enterprises, Inc., ASBCA No. 43602, May 18, 1992, 93-1 BCA 25,499.
88. Aydin Corp. (West), ASBCA No. 42760, April 18, 1994, 94-2 BCA 26,899; on remand Dec. 12, 1995, 96-1 BCA 28,134.
89. Aydin Corp. (West) v. Sheila E. Widnall, Secretary of the Air Force, CAFC No. 94-1441, Aug. 10, 1995, 61 F.3d 1571; CAFC No. 96-1267, July 24, 1997, 1997 U.S. App. LEXIS 18959.
90. General Dynamics Corp., Convair Division, supra, note 81.
91. United States v. State of New Mexico; Bureau of Revenue of the State of New Mexico; and Fred L. O'Cheskey, as Commissioner of Revenue of the State of New Mexico, and his successors in office, CA-10 1980, No. 78-1755, June 2, 1980, 624 F.2d 111; aff'd. March 24, 1982, 102 S. Ct. 1373, 455 U.S. 720.
92. The Aerospace Corp. v. State Board of Equalization, No. B036583, Sup. Ct. Nos. C-41,6134 and C-578611, July 7, 1988; CA C of A, 2d, Div. 7, March 20, 1990.

93. United States v. Benton, DC WDMO, No. 89-0608-CV-W-3, March 25, 1991, 1991 U.S. Dist. Lexis 4707.

94. Available, on a subscription basis, from the Superintendent of Documents, U.S. Government Printing Office, Federal Travel Regulation, Washington, D.C. 20402, Stock No. 022-001-81003-7.

95. Federal Acquisition Streamlining Act of 1994, 41 U.S.C. §251, enacted Oct. 13, 1995, Pub. L. 103-355, Section 2191.

96. Federal Register, Vol. 59, No. 239, Dec. 14, 1994, pp. 64542–64543.

97. Big Three Industries, Inc., ASBCA Nos. 16949 and 17331, Jan. 31, 1974, 74-1 BCA 10,483.

98. United Technologies Corp., ASBCA No. 25501, Aug. 25, 1987, 87-3 BCA 20,193.

99. General Dynamics Corp., supra, note 20.

100. Gould Defense Systems, Inc., supra, note 49.

101. The DCMC and DCAA Memorandum for Environmental Pilot Project Teams, dated April 13, 1994 (PAD 730.47/94-9); subject: Guidance Addressing Questions Raised Related to the 14 Oct. 1992 Guidance Paper on Environmental Costs.

102. Undersecretary of Defense Memorandum for Commander, DCMC, dated July 21, 1993; subject: Allowability of Restructuring Costs on Novated Contracts.

103. DCMC and DCAA Memorandum for District Commanders, DCAA, Regional Directors, DCAA and Director, Field Detachment, DCAA, dated Jan. 14, 1994 (AQCOH/PAD 730.45/94-2); subject: Guidance Paper on Restructuring Costs.

104. Fiscal Year 1995 Defense Authorization Act, 108 Stat. 2821, 10 U.S.C. §§555, 2208, 12001, enacted Oct. 5, 1994, Pub. L. 103-337, §818.

105. National Defense Appropriations Act for Fiscal Year 1997, supra note 28. §8115.

106. National Defense Authorization Act for Fiscal Year 1998, supra note 30, §804.

107. Federal Register, Vol. 60, No. 8, Jan. 12, 1995, p. 2924.

108. Federal Register, Vol. 60, Oct. 13, 1995, p. 53321.

109. The National Defense Authorization Act for Fiscal Year 1996, 110 Stat. 186, enacted Feb. 10, 1996, Pub. L. 104-106.

110. Litton Systems, Inc., 196 Ct. Cl. 133, Oct. 15, 1971, 449 F.2d 392.

111. H&M Moving, Inc., Ct. Cl. No. 37-73, June 19, 1974, 499 F.2d 660.

112. Falcon Research & Development Co., ASBCA No. 19784, Jan. 6, 1977, 77-1 BCA 12,312; aff'd. Oct. 4, 1977, 77-2 BCA 12,795.

113. Data Design Laboratories, Inc., ASBCA No. 21029, May 29, 1981, 81-2 BCA 15,190; aff'd. July 8, 1982, 82-2 BCA 15,932.

114. Gould Defense Systems, Inc., supra, note 49.

115. Data Design Laboratories, Inc., supra, note 79.

116. JANA, Inc., CAFC No. 91-5012, June 13, 1991, 936 F.2d 1265.

117. General Dynamics Corp., supra, note 20.

118. Dynamic Concepts, Inc., ASBCA No. 44738, Dec. 21, 1992, 93-2 BCA 25,689.

119. United States ex rel Jerry J. Mayman v. Martin Marietta Corp., supra, note 55.

120. Celesco Industries, Inc., supra, note 74.

121. RMK–BRJ, A Joint Venture, ASBCA No. 16031, March 18, 1974, 74-1 BCA 10,535.

122. Northrop Aircraft, Inc. v. United States (1955), 130 Ct. Cl. 626.

123. Colorado Dental Service (Delta Dental Plan of Colorado), ASBCA No. 24,666, May 28, 1982, 82-2 BCA 15,836.

124. KMS Fusion, Inc., supra, note 83.

125. NI Industries, Inc., supra, note 47.

126. Prior to Feb. 9, 1998, final indirect cost rate proposals were due no later than three months after the expiration of the fiscal year. The time frame for submission of the proposal was extended from three months to six months via Federal Acquisition Circular 97-03.

127. Letter dated April 4, 1984, from Chapman B. Cox, General Counsel of the Department of Defense to the Council of Defense and Space Industry Associations and Machinery and Allied Products Institute.

Code of Federal Regulations Title	Organization	Procurement Acquisition Regulation	FPR/FAR System Chapter No.
Before issuance of FAR			
32	DOD	DAR	--
41	Civilian agencies	FPR	1
41	AID	AID PR	7
41	VA	VA PR	8
41	DOE	DOE PR	9
41	EPA	EPA PR	15
41	NASA	NASA PR	18
41	ICA	ICA PR	19
After issuance of FAR			
48	Federal agencies	FAR	1
48	DOD	DFARS	2
48	GSA	GSAR	5
48	Dept. of State	State FAR Suppl.	6
48	USAID	AID FAR Suppl.	7
48	DVA	DVA FAR Suppl.	8
48	DOE	DEAR	9
48	DOT	DOT FAR Suppl.	12
48	OPM, FEHB Prog.	FEHBAR	16
48	NASA	NASA FAR Suppl.	18
48	NRC	NRC FAR Suppl.	20
48	OPM, FEGLI Prog	FEGLIFAR	21
48	DOJ	DOJ FAR Suppl.	28
48	DOL	DOL FAR Suppl.	29
48	Panama Canal Commission	Panama Canal FAR Suppl.	35

Appendix 7.1   Cost Principles Contained in the Acquisition Regulations.

	FAR 31.205	Regulations in Effect Prior to FAR		
		DAR 15-205	NASA PR 15.205	FPR 1-15.205
Public relations & advertising costs	-1	.1	-1	-1
Bad debts	-3	.2	-2	-2
Bonding costs	-4	.4	-4	-4
Civil defense costs	-5	.5	-5	-5
Compensation for personal services	-6	.6	-6	-6
Contingencies	-7	.7	-7	-7
Contributions and donations	-8	.8	-8	-8
Cost of money	-10	.50	-50	-51
Depreciation	-11	.9	-9	-9
Economic planning costs	-12	.47	-47	-47
Employee morale, health, welfare, food service, and dormitory costs and credits	-13	.10	-10	-10
Entertainment costs	-14	.11	-11	-11
Fines, penalties and mischarging costs	-15	.13	-13	-13
Gains and losses on disposition or impairment of depreciable property or capital assets	-16	.32	-32	-32
Idle facilities and idle capacity costs	-17	.12	-12	-12
Independent research and development and bid and proposal costs	-18	.3 and .35	-3 and -35	-3 and -35
Insurance and indemnification	-19	.16	-16	-16
Interest and other financial costs	-20	.17	-17	-17
Labor relations costs	-21	.18	-18	-18
Lobbying and political activity costs	-22	.51	-51	-52
Losses on other contracts	-23	.19	-19	-19
Maintenance and repair costs	-24	.20	-20	-20
Manufacturing and production engineering costs	-25	.21	-21	-21
Material costs	-26	.22	-22	-22
Organization costs	-27	.23	-23	-23
Other business expenses	-28	.24	-24	-24

Appendix 7.2   Selected Costs—Reference Citations.

	FAR 31.205	Regulations in Effect Prior to FAR		
		DAR 15-205	NASA PR 15.205	FPR 1-15.205
Plant protection costs	-29	.28	-28	-28
Patent costs	-30	.26	.26	-26
Plant reconversion costs	-31	.29	-29	-29
Precontract costs	-32	.30	-30	-30
Professional and consultant service costs	-33	.31	-31	-31
Recruitment costs	-34	.33	-33	-33
Relocation costs	-35	.25	-25	-25
Rental costs	-36	.34	-34	-34
Royalties and other costs for use of patents	-37	.36	-36	-36
Selling costs	-38	.37	-37	-37
Service and warranty costs	-39	.38	-38	-38
Special tooling and special test equipment costs	-40	.40	-40	-40
Taxes	-41	.41	-41	-41
Termination costs	-42	.42	-42	-42
Trade, business, technical, and professional activity costs	-43	.43	-43	-43
Training and educational costs	-44	.44	-44	-44
Transportation costs	-45	.45	-45	-45
Travel costs	-46	.46	-46	-46
Costs related to legal and other proceedings	-47	.52	-52	-53
Deferred research and development costs	-48	.49		
Goodwill	-49			
Cost of alcoholic beverages	-51			
Asset valuations resulting from business combinations	-52			

Appendix 7.2 (*Continued*)

Cost Accounting Standards	Extent of Incorporation Into FAR
402- Consistency in Allocating Cost Incurred for the Same Purpose	FAR 31.202(a) and 31.203(a) require compliance with the standard on all contracts.
403- Allocation of Home Office Expenses to Segments	FAR 31.203(d) requires allocation methods to comply with CAS on CAS-covered contracts.*Otherwise, the method should be in accordance with GAAP.
404- Capitalization of Tangible Assets	FAR 31.205-11(m) provides that items acquired by means of a capital lease, as defined by FAS 13, are subject to the standard.
405- Accounting for Unallowable Costs	FAR 31.201-6 requires compliance with the standard on all contracts.
406- Cost Accounting Period	FAR 31.203(e) requires compliance with the standard on all CAS-covered contracts.* For contacts not subject to CAS, a period shorter than a fiscal year may be appropriate in certain circumstances.
409- Depreciation of Tangible Capital Assets	FAR 31.205-11(b) requires compliance with the standard for all CAS-covered contracts* and permits contractors to elect adoption of the standard for all non-CAS-covered contracts.
410- Allocation of Business Unit General and Administrative Expenses to Final Cost Objectives	Same coverage as for CAS 403.
412- Composition and Measurement of Pension Cost	FAR 31.205-6(j)(2) requires compliance with the standard on all contracts.
413- Adjustment and Allocation of Pension Cost	Same coverage as for CAS 412.
414- Cost of Money as an Element of the Cost of Facilities Capital	FAR 31.205-10 provides that cost of money computed in accordance with the standard is an allowable cost on all contracts.
415- Accounting for the Cost of Deferred Compensation	FAR 31.205-6(k)(2) requires compliance with the standard on all contracts.
416- Accounting for Insurance Costs	FAR 31.205-19(a) requires compliance with the self-insurance provisions of the standard for all CAS-covered contracts* and for all non-CAS-covered contracts where the contractor wishes to establish a self-insurance program.
417- Cost of Money as an Element of the Cost of Capital Assets under Construction	FAR 31.205-10 provides that cost of money, computed in accordance with the standard, is includible in the capitalized acquisition cost of the asset, except that actual interest in lieu of the calculated imputed cost of money is unallowable.
418- Allocation of Direct and Indirect Costs	Same coverage as for CAS 403.
420- Accounting for Independent Research and Development Cost and Bid and Proposal Cost	FAR 31.205-18(b) requires contracts subject to full CAS coverage to account for IR&D and B&P costs in accordance with the provisions of CAS 420. Contracts that are exempt from CAS or subject to only modified CAS coverage, but awarded while contracts subject to full CAS coverage are being performed, must also account for IR&D and B&P costs in accordance with the provisions of CAS 420. Other contracts must comply with all CAS 420 provisions except those pertaining to allocability. When IR&D and B&P costs cannot be allocated equitably to these contracts through the G&A base, the contracting officer may approve another base.
* Contracts subject to full CAS coverage.	

Appendix 7.3   Cost Accounting Standards Incorporated into the FAR.

	DOD	AID	DOE	DOT	OPM, FEHB	NASA	NRC	OPM, FEGI	DOJ	Panama Canal
Compensation	X	X			X	X		X		
COM	X					X				
IR&D/B&P	X		X			X				
Lobbying	X									
Restructuring	X									
Travel		X								X
Overseas recruiting incentives		X								
Precontract costs			X	X		X	X	X	X	
OPMFEBAR										
Taxes					X			X		
PR & advertising					X			X		
Bad debts					X			X		
Interest exp.					X					
Losses on other contracts					X					
Selling costs					X			X		
Startup and other nonrecurring					X					
Printed material costs					X					
Mandatory statutory reserves					X					
Major subcontractor service charges					X			X		
Trade, business, techn & prof. activity costs								X		
Reinsurer administrative exp. costs								X		

Appendix 7.4   Unique Cost Allowability Criteria in Agency FAR Supplements.

Expressly Allowable Costs	Expressly Unallowable Costs
Bonding costs FAR 31.205-4	Bad debts FAR 31.205-3,
Cost of Money FAR 31.205-10	Contingencies FAR 31.205-7
Depreciation FAR 31.205-11	Contributions and donations FAR 31.205-8.
Economic planning costs FAR 31.205-12	Entertainment FAR 31.205-14.
Labor relations costs FAR 31.205-21	Fines and penalties FAR 31.205-15.
Service and warranty costs FAR 31.205-39	Gains or losses on disposition of capital assets other than depreciable property FAR 31.205-16
Maintenance and repair costs FAR 31.205-24	Interest and other financial costs FAR 31.205-20.
Manufacturing and production engineering costs FAR 31.205-25	Lobbying and political activity costs FAR 31.205-22 .
Other business expenses (e.g., recurring costs for stock registry and transfer, shareholder meetings and reports, reports for taxing and regulatory bodies, etc.) FAR 31.205-28	Losses on other contracts FAR 31.205-23
Plant protection costs FAR 31.205-29	Organization costs FAR 31.205-27
Precontract costs (but an advance agreement is recommended) FAR 31.205-32	Goodwill FAR 31.205-49
Special tooling and special test equipment FAR 31.205-40	Alcoholic beverages FAR 31.205-51
Transportation costs FAR 31.205-45	Asset valuations resulting from business combinations FAR 31.205-52

Appendix 7.5 Cost Principles-Selected Costs.

CERTIFICATE OF INDIRECT COSTS

This is to certify that I have reviewed this proposal to establish final indirect cost rates and to the best of my knowledge and belief:

1. All costs included in this proposal (identify, proposal and date) to establish final indirect cost rates for (identify period covered by rate) are allowable in accordance with the cost principles of the Federal Acquisition Regulations and its supplements applicable to the contracts to which the final indirect cost rates will apply.

2. This proposal does not include any costs which are expressly unallowable under applicable cost principles of the FAR or its supplements.

Firm: _____

Signature: _____

Name of Corporate Official: _____

Title: _____

Date of Execution: _____

(End of clause)

Appendix 7.6 Certificate of Final Indirect Costs Clause, FAR 52.242-4.

Chapter Eight

Cost Accounting Standards

8-1. STATUTORY AND REGULATORY PERSPECTIVE

Public Law 90-370

When the Defense Production Act came up for renewal in 1968, Admiral Hyman G. Rickover testified that, because generally accepted accounting principles (GAAP) allowed contractors to use such a wide variety of accounting practices, it was nearly impossible to analyze contract costs and compare prices proposed by competing contractors. In challenging Congress to develop uniform accounting standards and to require contractors to comply with them, Rickover predicted that $2 billion in savings could be achieved through such action. As a result, the Defense Production Act Amendments of 1968[1] directed the Comptroller General to study the feasibility of applying uniform cost accounting standards (CAS) to negotiated defense contracts and subcontracts.

The Comptroller General's study,[2] submitted to Congress in January 1970, concluded the following:

- It was feasible to establish and apply CAS to provide more uniformity and consistency in cost accounting as a basis for negotiating and administering contracts.

- Cost accounting standards should not require the application of precisely prescribed methods of computing each different type of cost.

- Cost accounting standards should not be limited to defense cost-reimbursement-type contracts but should apply to all types of negotiated government contracts and subcontracts.

- Cumulative benefits from establishing CAS should outweigh the cost of implementation.

- Cost accounting standards for contract costing should evolve from sound commercial cost accounting practices and should not be incompatible with GAAP.

- New mechanisms should be established to develop CAS and to perform the continuing research and updating that will be required for effective administration.

- Contractors should be required to maintain records of contract performance in conformity with the CAS and with the approved practices set forth in disclosure agreements.

Public Law 91-379

After vigorous debate, Congress included a provision in the Defense Production Act Amendments of 1970,[3] which established the Cost Accounting Standards Board (CASB).

The law established a five-member CASB as an agent of Congress and independent of the executive departments. The Board consisted of the Comptroller General, as chairman, and four members appointed by him for four-year terms. Two of the appointees were from the accounting profession (one knowledgeable in the cost accounting problems of small business), one an industry representative, and one from the federal government.

The Board was directed by statute to promulgate standards designed to achieve uniformity and consistency in the cost accounting principles followed by defense prime contractors and subcontractors in estimating, accumulating, and reporting costs in connection with the pricing, administration, and settlement of negotiated procurements.

Period of Transition

The CASB ceased to exist on September 30, 1980, after Congress declined to further fund the Board. During its turbulent ten-year life, the CASB promulgated accounting practice disclosure requirements and 19 cost accounting standards which considered to have the full force and effect of law. Executive departments continued to enforce and monitor the standards' provisions, and the General Accounting Office (GAO) maintained a program for executive agency implementation of the standards.

Following a Department of Justice opinion that the Department of Defense (DOD) was legally free to adopt, reject, or grant exemptions to the CAS, the DOD incorporated the standards into Part 30 of the Federal Acquisition Regulation (FAR) in September 1987. Federal Acquisition Regulation, Part 30, was revised to raise the minimum capitalization threshold in CAS 404 from $1,000 to $1,500, and to substitute the Treasury rate for state rates in discounting certain self-insured losses to present value in CAS 416.

Public Law 100-679

In November 1988, the Office of Federal Procurement Policy (OFPP) Act Amendments of 1988[4] reestablished a new CASB, placing it in the executive branch partly to eliminate assertions by The Boeing Company[5] that the original CASB, established in the legislative branch, was unconstitutional.

This CASB also has five members but is chaired by the OFPP Administrator. The other four members consist of a DOD member (appointed by the Secretary of Defense), a General Services Administration (GSA) member (appointed by the Administrator of General Services), an industry member, and a private-sector member knowledgeable in cost accounting matters. The latter two are appointed by the OFPP Administrator. The DOD and GSA members are the Director of the Defense Contract Audit Agency (DCAA) and the GSA Assistant Inspector General for Auditing, respectively. This Board has essentially the same authority as the original CASB.

The Board got off to a relatively slow start, and appointments were not completed until May 1991. The standards, which were previously codified in both Title 4 of the Code of Federal Regulations and in FAR 30, were rescinded and repromulgated in Chapter 99 of the FAR System, on April 17, 1992.

Relationship to the Federal Acquisition Regulation

Cost Accounting Standards administration requirements are contained in the FAR, Part 30; they deal with the concepts of cost measurement, assignment to cost accounting periods, and allocability to cost objectives. They do not specifically address the question of cost allowability. The acceptability of a specific cost for reimbursement by the government is under the purview of other laws or procurement regulations issued by the various government agencies. In *The Boeing Co.*,[6] the Armed Services Board of Contract Appeals (ASBCA) held that when contradictory cost accounting requirements are imposed by the Defense Acquisition Regulation (DAR)/FAR cost principles and CAS, CAS is controlling with respect to the determination, measurement, assignment, and allocation of costs. However in *Rice v. Martin Marietta Corp.*[7] the Federal Circuit came to a somewhat different decision. The court concluded that DAR 15-203(c) (now FAR 31.201-3) did not conflict with CAS 410, because the DAR provision, despite its express discussion of allocability, really only disallowed an otherwise allocable cost.

Cost Accounting Standards Steering Committee

In 1976, the DOD established a Cost Accounting Standards Steering Committee to develop policy guidelines on integrating the CASB regulations into the DOD's procurement practices and to provide liaison with the CASB. Twenty-five CAS Steering Committee interim guidance papers (see Appendix 8.1) were published on a variety of matters relating to the standards, contract coverage, disclosure statements, and determination of price adjustments. Although the papers do not constitute either regulatory or contractual requirements, they reflect the DOD's interpretation of what CAS requires. The National Aeronautics and Space Administration (NASA) and GSA also refer to the CAS Steering Committee papers for guidance.

8-2. POLICIES, RULES, AND REGULATIONS OF THE BOARD

Objectives, Policies, and Concepts

A Statement of Objectives, Policies, and Concepts was issued by the Board in July 1992[8] to present the framework within which it formulates cost accounting standards and related rules and regulations. The document includes the CASB's general objectives among which uniformity, consistency, allowability, allocability, fairness, and verifiability assume primary importance; its cost allocation concepts;

and a statement of operating policies. The document also explains the promulgation process by which the CASB develops standards.

Promulgation Process

Original Cost Accounting Standards Board

The CASB circulated questionnaires and/or statements of issues to selected contractors, government agencies, and business and professional groups to obtain information on current practices as well as views and comments. A preliminary draft standard subsequently was prepared and distributed for comment. After considering comments on the draft standard, the proposed standard was published in the *Federal Register* for comments. After review and analysis of the public comments, the final version of the standard was published in the *Federal Register* and submitted simultaneously to Congress. Both houses of Congress had 60 days of continuous session in which to pass a concurrent resolution on any proposed final standard that they did not favor. Absent such a resolution, the standard, carrying the force of law, became effective at the beginning of the second fiscal quarter following 30 days after final publication unless CASB provided a later effective date.

Current Cost Accounting Standards Board

The Board adopted the standards issued by the original CASB, adjusted for the 1987 revisions to CAS 404 and 416 that had been incorporated into FAR Part 30. Before promulgating new standards, amendments, or interpretations, the Board is required to publish an advance notice of proposed rulemaking in the *Federal Register*. Interested parties have at least 60 days to submit comments. After the Board considers those comments, a notice of proposed rulemaking is published in the *Federal Register*. Interested parties again have at least 60 days to respond. The Board is supposed to consult with the Comptroller General, contractors, professional accounting and industry associations, and other interested parties before finalizing new or revised standards or interpretations. Once the procedure, standard, rule, or regulation is published in final form in the *Federal Register*, it becomes effective within 120 days unless a longer period is authorized by the Board. Applicability dates for contractors and subcontractors are no later than the start of the contractor's second fiscal year after the standard's effective date. This process has not necessarily been followed, however, with regard to interpretations.

Contract Coverage

Cost Accounting Standards coverage is determined at the segment or business unit level of a company. A *segment* is defined as a subdivision of an organization, such as a division, product department, or plant, which usually has profit responsibility and/or produces a product or service. A *business unit* can be either an individual segment or an entire business organization that is not divided into segments.

The threshold for CAS coverage through December 31, 1974, was $100,000. On January 1, 1975, the CASB amended its regulations to provide that CAS coverage at a business unit was triggered by the award of a negotiated defense prime contract or subcontract in excess of $500,000. After receiving such an award, a business unit was required to comply with all applicable standards for subsequently awarded negotiated prime contracts and subcontracts in excess of $100,000, unless otherwise exempt.

Effective March 10, 1978, two levels of coverage were provided. Modified coverage subjected a business to only CAS 401 and 402, whereas full coverage subjected it to all CASB standards. The following were conditions that determined the extent of CAS applicability:

- Business units that had not received a negotiated defense prime contract or subcontract in excess of $500,000, which required submission of a cost proposal, were exempt from complying with CAS.
- Once a business unit received a negotiated CAS covered contract/subcontract in excess of $500,000, that contract and future negotiated contracts/subcontracts in excess of $100,000, which required submission of cost data and were awarded before completion of the $500,000 contract, were subject to either the full CAS clause or the modified CAS clause.
  - Negotiated national defense and nondefense contracts/subcontracts over $100,000 were eligible for modified coverage if the business unit's total defense CAS-covered awards in the preceding cost accounting period were less than $10 million and less than 10% of the business unit's total sales.
  - Negotiated defense and nondefense contracts/subcontracts over $100,000 were subject to full coverage if the business unit's total defense CAS-covered awards in the preceding cost accounting period were more than 10% of the business unit's total sales or $10 million or more.
  - Business units receiving a single defense award of $10 million or more were subject to full coverage.

Between April 17, 1992, and November 4, 1993, negotiated contracts/subcontracts in excess of $500,000, which required submission of cost data, were subject to either the "full" CAS clause or the "modified" CAS clause, based on the following criteria:

- Negotiated contracts/subcontracts over $500,000 were eligible for modified coverage if the business unit's total CAS-covered awards in the preceding cost accounting period were less than $10 million and less than 10% of the business unit's total sales.
- Negotiated contracts/subcontracts over $500,000 were subject to full coverage if the business unit's CAS-covered awards in the preceding cost accounting period were more than 10% of the business unit's total sales or $10 million or more.
- Business units receiving a single negotiated award of $10 million or more, which required submission of cost data, became subject to full coverage.

On November 4, 1993, the CASB revised the CAS coverage criteria (in 48 CFR 9903.201) as follows:

- Negotiated contracts/subcontracts over $500,000 but less than $25 million, which require submission of cost data, are eligible for modified coverage if the business unit's net covered awards in the prior cost accounting period were either (1) less than $25 million or (2) greater than $25 million but did not include a single covered net award exceeding $1 million. Modified coverage was expanded to require compliance with:

- CAS 401—Consistency in Estimating Accumulating and Reporting Costs
- CAS 402—Consistency in Allocating Costs Incurred for the Same Purpose
- CAS 405—Accounting for Unallowable Costs
- CAS 406—Cost Accounting Period

    An eligible contractor must elect modified coverage; otherwise, full coverage will apply.

- Negotiated contracts/subcontracts over $500,000 but less than $25 million, which require submission of cost data, are subject to full coverage if the business unit's CAS-covered awards in the prior cost accounting period exceeded $25 million, provided at least one covered award exceeded $1 million.

- An individual negotiated contract/subcontract with a net award value of $25 million or more, which requires submission of cost data, is subject to full CAS coverage.

The CASB eliminated the CAS exemption in 9903.201-1 for educational institutions, effective January 9, 1995. CAS coverage now applies to any educational institution that receives a negotiated award over $500,000 unless the award is eligible for one of the established CAS exemptions. The new coverage for educational institutions in 48 CFR 9903.201-2(c) consists of four standards that are similar to modified coverage for commercial companies:

- CAS 501—Consistency in Estimating, Accumulating, and Reporting Costs by Educational Institutions
- CAS 502—Consistency in Allocating Costs Incurred for the Same Purpose by Educational Institutions
- CAS 505—Accounting for Unallowable Costs
- CAS 506—Cost Accounting Period

Criteria for Determining Cost Accounting Standards Applicability

The criteria for determining CAS applicability are illustrated in Appendix 8.2.

Basic agreements and basic ordering agreements are, by definition, not contracts but written understandings about future procurements. The individual orders issued under these agreements are contracts, and they establish the basis for determining the applicability of CAS.

Modifications to covered contracts are subject to CAS. If the original contract is exempt, modifications are generally awarded on the same basis. The CASB concluded in the preamble to its 1972 publication that its regulations:

> ... should not cover negotiated modifications to contracts exempt at their inception. ... however, the Board intends that the annual extension of existing negotiated contracts and similar contract modifications would not be exempt from the Board's rules, regulations and Cost Accounting Standards.[9]

Cost Accounting Standards apply to letter contracts if it is expected that the definitized contract will be covered. Whether CAS applies should be determined when the letter contract is awarded. The definitized letter contract is viewed as a modification rather than an original award.

On November 4, 1993, the CASB redefined "Net Awards" to mean the total value of negotiated covered prime contract and subcontract awards, *including the potential value of contract options* received during the reporting period. This definition is a complete reversal from the prior definition included in 9903.301, which stated: "Net awards, used in the chapter, means the *total obligated value* of negotiated prime contract and subcontract awards received during the reporting period." The definition as revised in the November 4, 1993, final rule seems inappropriate, because the government has no obligation to buy option items until the option is exercised. Furthermore, the definition, as revised, contradicts FAR 17.201, which states that an option provision in a contract merely gives the government a unilateral right to purchase additional supplies or services.

Exemptions and Waivers

Statutory exemptions from CAS apply to the following:

1. Awards based on sealed bidding
2. Negotiated awards under $500,000
3. Negotiated awards in which the price is set by law or regulation
4. Acquisitions of commercial items[10]

In 1976, the Comptroller General ruled that statutory exemptions are mandatory and "do not allow for agency discretion as to whether to grant the exemption."[11]

In addition to the statutory exemptions, the CASB has also exercised its authority to exempt from its rules, regulations, and standards the following:

- Any contract or subcontract awarded to a small business concern, as defined by Small Business Administration regulations
- Any contract or subcontract awarded to a foreign government or its agencies or instrumentalities
- Any contract or subcontract awarded to a foreign concern, except for CAS 401 and 402
- Any contract or subcontract made with a U.K. contractor for performance substantially in the United Kingdom, provided that the contractor has filed with the U.K. Ministry of Defence a completed CASB Disclosure Statement; if the contractor is already required to follow U.K. government accounting conventions, the disclosed practices must be in accordance with the requirements of those conventions
- Any firm-fixed-price contract or subcontract awarded without submission of cost data
- Contracts executed and performed entirely outside the United States or its territories and possessions

The CASB is also authorized to waive, at the request of designated executive agency officials, all or part of its standards or rules for particular contracts or subcontracts. Such waivers are granted on the basis of whether the procurement agency establishes, to the CASB's satisfaction, that the contract involved is essentially a sole-source procurement with such urgency that finding an alternative supplier is not feasible.

Aydin Corporation (West) argued that the CAS clauses included in its contract were voidable and that the contract was thus exempt from CAS coverage pursuant to 4 CFR 331.30 [now 48 CFR 9903.201-1(b)(15)], because the contract was awarded without the submission of certified cost or pricing data. However, informal costs were submitted to permit the contracting officer (CO) to check for mistakes or major omissions in offers, not to negotiate price. Both ASBCA and the Federal Circuit rejected Aydin's argument, noting that with regard to the phrase *any cost data* under Section 331.30(b)(9), "The modifier 'any' sweeps all types of cost data within the coverage of the regulation including informal cost data."[12]

Contract Clauses

An agency implements CAS by first including a notice in the solicitation to offerors, and then inserting a CAS clause in the negotiated contract. Contracts subject to CASB regulations include either the full-coverage clause or the modified-coverage clause, a distinction which, in fact, determines the number of standards to be applied. Both clauses also contain provisions for handling disputes, examining contractor's records, and including an applicable CAS clause in all covered subcontracts.

Full Cost Accounting Standards Coverage

The clause applicable to full coverage (Cost Accounting Standards, FAR 52.230-3 requires a contractor to:

- Describe in writing its cost accounting practices when a business unit is part of a company that is required to submit a Disclosure Statement.
- Follow its cost accounting practices consistently.
- Comply with all cost accounting standards in effect either on the contract award date or on the date of the signed certificate of current cost or pricing.
- Comply prospectively with all cost accounting standards that become applicable during contract performance.
- Agree to an adjustment of contract price, or cost allowance (as described below) when it fails to comply with existing standards or to follow its cost accounting practices and when making changes to its existing practices.

Modified Coverage

The clause applicable to modified coverage (Disclosure and Consistency of Cost Accounting Practices, FAR 52.230-5) requires a contractor not otherwise exempt to:

- Comply with CAS 401, 402, 405, and 406.
- Describe in writing its cost accounting practices when a business unit is part of a company that is required to submit a disclosure statement.
- Consistently follow its cost accounting practices.
- Agree to an adjustment of contract price, or cost allowance (as described below) when it fails to comply with applicable standards or to follow its cost accounting practices.

Cost Accounting Standards Administration Clause

The clause for full or modified CAS coverage is accompanied by an Administration of Cost Accounting Standards (FAR 52.230-4) clause, which outlines the procedures and time requirements for the contractor to notify the CO about anticipated changes in any cost accounting practice. The notification must include a written description of any change to be made, together with a general dollar cost impact showing the shift of costs between CAS-covered contracts by contract type and other work. For required changes, the description must be provided no later than the date of submission of the proposal which uses the change to estimate costs. For desirable or voluntary changes, the description is generally required no later than 60 days before the applicability date of the change or the date of submission of the proposal which uses the change to estimate costs.

The Administration clause requires a contractor to agree to appropriate contract or subcontract amendments to reflect price adjustments or cost allowances resulting from changes in cost accounting practices or noncompliance. It also provides for the flow of CAS requirements down to lower-tier subcontractors that are not otherwise exempt from CAS. Further, the contractor must advise the CO within 30 days, or any other mutually agreed-upon date, of an award of a CAS-covered subcontract.

Proper administration of this clause requires a system for identifying contracts and subcontracts containing the CAS clauses. A contractor is responsible for maintaining such a system. The administrative contracting officer (ACO) is responsible for ensuring that the system functions effectively.

Price Adjustments

Contract price adjustments to CAS-covered contracts can arise, as outlined below:

- A contract is eligible for equitable adjustment when the contractor (1) is initially required to apply a standard (required change) or (2) implements an accounting change that the CO has found to be desirable and not detrimental to the government's interests (desirable change). The price adjustment is the net increase or decrease in costs resulting from the application of the new standard(s) or desirable changes to all covered contracts. Equitable adjustments may cause the government to pay increased costs to the contractor or may reduce the contract price. These adjustments are applied prospectively from the change date to covered prime contracts and subcontracts awarded before the accounting change occurred. All uncompleted contracts subject to CAS must be recosted and repriced from the date the change is implemented to completion of the contract to determine the amount of the equitable adjustment. Criteria to be used in determining whether an accounting change is desirable encompass the tests of being appropriate, warranted, equitable, fair, or reasonable.

- Price adjustments for the effect of voluntary changes in practice that the CO has not found to be in the government's interest (voluntary changes) are limited to no net increased costs to the government resulting from the prospective application of the revised practice to all covered contracts. Adjustments are made only in favor of the government.

- Adjustments arising from failure to comply with applicable standards and disclosed practices, are made only in favor of the government. Public Law

91-379 required repayment of the net increased cost resulting from the non-compliance, plus an annual interest rate not to exceed 7%. Public Law 100-679 requires payment of the net resulting increased cost plus interest at the annual rate established by the Internal Revenue Service. Adjustments are made retroactively back to the date of the noncompliance.

Increased cost is defined as (1) cost paid by the government that, as a result of a changed practice or a CAS noncompliance, is higher than the cost that would have been paid had the change or noncompliance not occurred; and (2) the excess of the negotiated price on a fixed-price contract over the price that would have been negotiated if the proposal had been priced in accordance with the practices actually used during contract performance. Increased costs exist when costs allocated to firm-fixed-price contracts as a result of a changed practice are less than would have been allocated if the change had not occurred.

Cost Accounting Standards legislation established the contract price adjustment as the only remedy for failure to comply with CASB rules, regulations, and standards. What happens when the cost impact of contractor noncompliance cannot be determined? The ASBCA concluded in *AiResearch Manufacturing Co.*,[13] that even the possibility that no cost impact could be computed would not deny it jurisdiction over the question of whether the contractor's practices complied with the standards.

Cost Accounting Practices and Cost Accounting Practice Changes

The primary purpose of the contract adjustment procedures is to hold contractors accountable for the practices used to cost government contracts. To accomplish this important objective, the CASB defined a cost accounting practice and a cost accounting practice change in 48 CFR 9903.302.

The term *cost accounting practice* is defined as any accounting method or technique used to measure cost, assign cost to cost accounting periods, or allocate cost to cost objectives. Cost measurement encompasses accounting methods and techniques to define cost components, determine bases for cost measurement, and establish criteria for alternative cost measurement techniques. Cost assignment encompasses the criteria used to determine the timing of the cost occurrence [e.g., the cost accounting period(s) to which the cost should be charged]. Examples of assignment methods or techniques include the accrual versus cash basis of accounting. Cost allocations encompass methods or techniques to accumulate cost, to determine whether a cost is to be directly or indirectly allocated, to determine the selection and composition of cost pools, and to determine selection and composition of appropriate allocation bases.

A *cost accounting practice change* is defined as an alteration in a cost accounting practice, including pool combinations, pool split-outs, and functional transfers, except that:

- The initial adoption of a cost accounting practice for the first time a cost is incurred, or a function is created, is not a change in cost accounting practice.
- The partial or total elimination of a cost or the cost of a function is not a change in cost accounting practice.
- The revision of a cost accounting practice for a cost that previously had been immaterial is not a change in cost accounting practice.

To clarify the definition, the CASB regulations (9903.302-3 and 9903.302-4) provide practical examples of circumstances that are, and are not, changes in cost accounting practice.

In significant decisions involving Martin Marietta,[14] both the ASBCA and the Federal Circuit ruled that realignments of cost pools that do not change the composition of the pools or the allocation bases are not cost accounting practice changes. The decisions relied on an illustration in the then-existing CASB regulations in which one segment that previously allocated overhead by direct labor hours and a second segment that allocated overhead by direct labor dollars merged into a single new segment. The successor entity adopted the direct labor dollar method. The only change in cost accounting practice identified in the illustration was the change in the first segment's overhead allocation base from hours to dollars. Significantly, the illustration did not identify either the expanded overhead pool or the expanded overhead base of the merged entity as a cost accounting practice change.

On July 14, 1997,[15] the CASB issued a Supplemental Notice of Proposed Rulemaking (NPRM) on Changes in Cost Accounting Practices, which proposes to:

- Revise the current definitions and illustrations governing changes in cost accounting practices.
- Add a new subpart to address the process for determining cost impacts on costs and/or prices of CAS-covered contracts resulting from cost accounting practice changes, failure to follow an applicable standard, or failure to follow established cost accounting practices.

Most contractors and accountants in the private sector continue to strenuously disagree with the Board's premise that the concept of a change to a cost accounting practice must be expanded to include indirect cost pool combinations or split-outs that undergo no change in either the composition of the pool(s) or the allocation base(s). The proposal does not treat the transfer of an existing function from "make" to "buy" or vice versa as a change in cost accounting practice, but does consider the transfer of an existing function from one pool to a different pool to constitute a change in cost accounting practice. Both types of transfers are made at the discretion of the company; both transfers can result in the same kind of cost shifts between contracts. Yet, inexplicably, the two types of transfers will have dramatically different consequences from the perspective of cost recovery under the Board's proposed rule.

Unfortunately, this proposal represents the government's typical reaction to losing a case before a board of contract appeals or court—the regulation gets changed. The prefatory comments characterize the proposed rule change as a clarification of what constitutes a change in cost accounting practice. However, the proposed rule is not a clarification; it is a major expansion of the definition of a cost accounting practice change.

The proposal expands the discussion of desirable change by concluding that a change will be deemed to be desirable and not detrimental when

- It is necessary for a contractor to remain in compliance
- Aggregated cost savings will occur under existing and/or future CAS covered awards
- The contractor's written justification clearly demonstrates that the change is desirable and not detrimental to the interests of the government

Cost Shift by Contract Type		Actions to Be Taken
Flexibly Priced	Firm-Fixed-Price	
Higher	Higher	No upward price adjustments. Disallow the higher level of costs on flexibly priced.
Lower	Higher	Limit FFP upward price adjustments to amount of flexibly priced downward price adjustments.
Lower	Lower	Adjust FFP and flexibly priced contract prices downward by the amount of the net downward price adjustment.
Higher	Lower	Limit upward adjustments on flexibly priced contract prices to amount of downward adjustments on FFP contracts. Disallow any excess increased costs on flexibly priced contract prices.

Figure 8.1   Actions to Preclude Payment of Increased Costs—Voluntary Change

The CO's finding should not be based solely on the financial impact of the change. A change may be deemed to be desirable even though costs of existing contracts increase, if benefits are expected on future government awards. For voluntary changes that are not deemed to be desirable, the proposal provides for the CO to take the actions summarized in Figure 8.1 to preclude payment of the excess costs by the government.

To preclude payment of excess costs by the government as a result of the correction of noncompliant estimating practices, the proposal provides for the CO to take the actions outlined in Figure 8.2.

The processes outlined above in Figures 8.1 and 8.2, while certainly controversial, are not new concepts. The government has for years utilized such techniques in teaching auditors and COs how to adjust contract prices. Formal inclusion of these adjustment processes in the CAS regulation will at least bring greater uniformity and consistency to the process.

The efforts of the Board to deal meaningfully with the concept of materiality in 9903.407-1 and 9903.407-2 are encouraging. The use of examples that use materiality criteria such as "contracts having an impact in excess of $500,000" and "contracts that have an impact that exceeds both $500,000 and 0.5% of the contract value" will significantly streamline the cost impact process.

Change in Cost Est. by K Type		Actions to be taken
Flexibly Priced	FFP	
Higher	Higher	No contract price adjustment required.
Lower	Higher	Limit FFP upward price adjustment to flexibly-priced contract downward adjustments.
Lower	Lower	Adjustment contract prices downward.
Higher	Lower	Limit upward price adjustments on flexibly-priced contracts to downward price adjustments on FFP contracts.

Figure 8.2   Actions to Preclude Payment of Increased Costs—Estimating Noncompliance

8-3. DISCLOSURE STATEMENTS

Purposes and Uses

When CAS-covered awards exceed specified thresholds, contractors must disclose in writing their cost accounting principles, including methods of distinguishing direct costs from indirect costs and the basis used for allocating indirect costs.

Cost Accounting Standards Board-DS-1, promulgated for entities other than educational institutions, was first issued in 1972. The CASB-DS-1 included in the Recodification of Cost Accounting Standards Board Rules and Regulations dated April 17, 1992, was updated to revise certain regulatory and statutory references. A revised statement, promulgated on February 28, 1996, is reproduced in Appendix 8-3.

On November 8, 1994, the CASB promulgated a separate disclosure statement, CASB-DS-2, for colleges and universities. It is reproduced in Appendix 8-4.

The ACO is designated to review the adequacy of the statements and to notify the contractor of any reporting deficiencies. The ACO delegates this review to the DCAA.

Disclosure statements are not made public when, as a condition of filing the statement, a contractor requests confidentiality. An action challenging the validity of that regulation was brought under the Freedom of Information Act (FOIA) by the Corporate Accountability Research Group.[16] The case was dismissed following an agreement by the CASB to provide aggregate data on disclosure statement responses. The CASB also agreed to comply with all disclosure statement FOIA requests when the information sought was submitted by a respondent who did not request that it be kept confidential.

Filing Thresholds

Entities Other Than Educational Institutions

Initially, the CASB required only those companies, including all divisions and subsidiaries, whose negotiated national defense prime contracts totaled less than $30 million during federal fiscal year 1971 to file disclosure statements. From 1974 to 1977, the filing thresholds were lowered to $10 million of CAS-covered negotiated defense prime contracts and subcontracts awarded in the prior fiscal year or the single award of a $10 million CAS-covered negotiated defense prime contract or subcontract. The April 17, 1992, recodification of the CASB Rules and Regulations, revised the filing thresholds to exempt companies whose negotiated CAS-covered prime contracts and subcontracts, at all divisions and subsidiaries, totaled less than $10 million during the company's prior fiscal year. On November 4, 1993, the CASB liberalized the threshold for disclosure statement filing but instituted a more complicated two-part test. A company meets the disclosure statement filing threshold if net covered awards for all segments in the prior cost accounting period exceeded $25 million *and* at least one of the covered awards exceeded $1 million. Once a company, as a whole, has met that disclosure statement filing threshold, segments must file disclosure statements only if, in the prior cost accounting period, the covered awards were at least 30% of segment sales or $10 million. A $25 million covered award triggers disclosure statement filing prior to award for the segment receiving the award and for related group office/home offices.

When the cost accounting practices under contracts are identical for more than one business unit, only one statement need be submitted, but each unit must be identified. Disclosure statements are due within 90 days after the close of the contractor's fiscal year, following the fiscal year in which the threshold was exceeded. Amendments to disclosure statements are processed by submitting the changed pages, together with a new cover sheet, to the administrative contracting officer and the auditor.

Educational Institutions

An educational institution meets the disclosure statement filing threshold if net covered awards for all segments exceeded $25 million in the preceding cost accounting period and at least one award exceeded $1 million, or if a currently covered award exceeds $25 million.

To avoid the requirement for universities to file disclosure statements at the same time, the CASB devised a method for phasing in disclosure statement filings applicable to contracts awarded on or before December 31, 1995 to a business unit of an educational institution that is listed on Exhibit A of the Office of Management and Budget (OMB) Circular A-21.

For a business unit of an educational institution that is not listed in Exhibit A of OMB Circular A-21, a disclosure statement was required to be submitted within six months after award of a covered contract. Awarding agencies were authorized to waive preaward disclosure statement submission for awards between January 1, 1996, and June 30, 1997, if a due date for submission has previously been established under the transition periods enumerated here.

Subcontractors

The flow-down provisions of the CAS clause require subcontractors to submit disclosure statements if they have met the filing requirements. Generally, the CAS regulations provide for submission of the subcontractor's disclosure statement to the prime contractor for review.

However, 48 CFR 9903.202-8(c)(1) permits subcontractors to submit disclosure statements to the government instead of to the prime contractor if the subcontractor does not want to divulge competitive information to the prime contractor. If the disclosure statement is submitted to the government, the prime contractor is not relieved of its responsibility for ascertaining subcontractor compliance with the requirements of the CAS clause. Because of this, the CASB noted in its regulations that a prime contractor might wish to include an indemnification clause in its subcontracts.

Determinations of Adequacy and Compliance

When the threshold for filing has been met, a contract may not be awarded until the ACO has determined that the disclosure statement is adequate. However, FAR 30.202-6(b) permits the CO to waive the requirement for an adequacy determination before award when necessary to protect the government's interest. Federal Acquisition Regulation 30.202-7 defines an adequate disclosure statement as one that is current, accurate, and complete. The ACO must specifically determine whether a statement is adequate and notify the contractor of that determination in writing. Submission of a disclosure statement does not, in itself, establish that the practices disclosed are correct. A disclosed practice is not, merely by virtue of such disclosure, approved practice for pricing proposals or accumulating and reporting contract performance costs data. Submission of a disclosure statement is a serious matter. Not only does it provide a written, measurable baseline from which to measure compliance and the consistent application of accounting practices, but it also can have a serious effect on the award of contracts.

Neither the CAS regulations nor the acquisition regulations require the ACO to determine, before contract award, that the disclosure statement complies with applicable standards. However, after the adequacy determination, the auditor must review the disclosed practices for compliance with applicable standards and report the audit findings to the ACO. The ACO is required to obtain a revised disclosure statement and negotiate any required price adjustments if the disclosed practices are determined to be in noncompliance with applicable standards. Some of the items in the disclosure statement pertain to cost accounting practices addressed in specific standards.

Changes to disclosure statements are reviewed by the government concurrently for adequacy and compliance.

Contents and Problem Areas

The key to avoiding a deficient disclosure statement is complete disclosure. Auditors are admonished to be alert for vague, incomplete, or ambiguous answers which could lead to alternative accounting interpretations. Materiality is a major factor in determining the level of detail required to be disclosed. A description of the disclosure statement follows.

- *Cover Sheet and Certification:* Identifies the company or reporting unit, its address, and the company official to be contacted regarding the statement. A certification of the statement's completeness and accuracy must be executed by an authorized signatory of the reporting unit.

- *General Information (Part I):* Includes industry classification, sales volume, proportion of government business to total, type of cost system, and extent of integration of the cost system with the general accounts.

- *Direct Costs (Part II):* Contractors are asked to define direct material, direct labor, and other direct costs and to disclose the bases for making direct charges. Accounting for variances under standard costs is explored in depth. In describing classes of labor, sufficient information is required to distinguish the principal labor rate categories.

- *Direct vs. Indirect Costs (Part III):* Contractors must designate how various functions, cost elements, and transactions are treated and, if indirect, what aggregate pools are used. Disagreements have involved the extent of detail required to describe the criteria for determining whether costs are charged directly or indirectly.

- *Indirect Costs (Part IV):* Allocation bases must be identified and described for all overhead, service center, and general and administrative pools used by the contractor.

- *Depreciation and Capitalization (Part V):* The criteria for capitalization, the methods of depreciation used, the bases for determining useful lives, and the treatment of gains and losses from disposition are to be specified.

- *Other Costs and Credits (Part VI):* This part covers the methods used for charging or crediting vacation, holiday, sick pay, and other compensation for personal absence.

- *Deferred Compensation and Insurance Costs (Part VII):* This part addresses the accounting for pension plans, deferred compensation plans, postretirement benefits other than pension plans, employee stock ownership plans, and insurance costs.

- *Corporate or Group Expenses (Part VIII):* Pooling patterns and allocation bases for distributing corporate group expenses (home-office expenses) to organizational segments must be specified and described.

Parts I through VII must be submitted for each covered segment (e.g., profit center, division, or other organizational unit). Part I and Part VIII must be submitted for each group or home office with costs allocated to one or more CAS-covered segment. Where a home office either establishes practices related to the costs described in Parts V through VII, or incurs and allocates such costs, the home office may complete Parts V through VII for inclusion in the segment disclosure statement. The Cover Sheet and Certificate must be submitted with each filing.

The current CASB-DS-1 is more complex than the prior version and will likely require considerably more effort to prepare than the 40 hours estimated by the CASB. Significant changes to the prior and current disclosure statements are summarized in Figure 8.3.

Item No.	Change
1.5.0	Differences between contract cost accounting and financial accounting records must be identified.
1.6.0	The treatment of unallowable costs must be described.
3.2.2, 3.2.3	Additional items of cost were added.
4.1.0–4.3.0	The disclosure of a segment's indirect cost methodology has been reformatted.
4.7.0	A separate disclosure requirement related to facilities capital cost of money has been added.
7.1.0–7.1.3	Substantially more information must be disclosed about a segment's pension plans.
7.2.0–7.2.2	A new section has been added to address the disclosure of a segment's postretirement benefit plans.
7.3.0–7.3.1	More information must be disclosed about a segment's employee group insurance plans.
7.4.0–7.4.2	More information must be disclosed about a segment's deferred compensation plans.
7.5.0–7.5.1	A new section has been added to address the disclosure of a segment's employee stock ownership plans.
7.6.0–7.6.1	More information must be disclosed about a segment's worker compensation, liability, and property insurance plans. The reporting of information has been reformatted.
8.1.0	The following information must be disclosed: • Segments and other intermediate home offices reporting to the home office • Each reporting unit having CAS-covered sales • CAS-covered sales as a percent of total sales for each segment with CAS-covered sales
8.3.0–8.3.3	The disclosure of the home office cost methodology has been reformatted.

Figure 8.3 Significant Changes in CASB-DS-1

8-4. THE COST ACCOUNTING STANDARDS

The General Concept of the Standards

As defined in the CASB's Statement of Objectives, Policies, and Concepts, a cost accounting standard is a statement that enunciates a principle or principles to be followed, establishes practices to be followed, or specifies criteria to be used in selecting from alternative principles and practices for estimating, accumulating, and reporting costs. It may be stated in general or specific terms. The Comptroller General's feasibility report stated that cost accounting standards should:

> ... [R]elate to assertions which guide or which point toward accounting procedures or applicable governing rules. Cost accounting standards are not the same as standardized or uniform cost accounting which suggests prescribed procedures from which there is limited freedom to depart.[17]

Notwithstanding that conceptual framework, the 19 standards and four interpretations promulgated to date have run the gamut from generalized statements providing for little more than consistency in certain circumstances to highly detailed dissertations on the treatment of specific costs. Which category a specific standard falls into should be readily evident from a review of the standard.

Each standard has an effective date and an applicability date. In some standards, these dates are the same. The effective date designates the point in time when pricing of future covered contracts must reflect the requirements of the standard. The applicability date marks the time by which the contractor's accounting and reporting systems must actually conform to the standard.

As stated in its "Statement of Objectives, Policies, and Concepts," the CASB's primary objective in promulgating standards has been to achieve greater uniformity in accounting practices among government contractors and consistency in accounting treatment of specific costs by individual contractors. The concept of uniformity relates to a comparison of two or more contractors, and the Board's objective is to achieve comparable accounting treatment among contractors operating under similar circumstances. Consistency, on the other hand, pertains to the practices used by a single contractor over periods of time. When the criteria used to measure costs, assign costs to cost accounting periods, and allocate costs to cost objectives remain unchanged, the results of operations under similar circumstances can be compared over different time periods.

Summaries of the Standards

Provided below are brief summaries of the 19 CASB standards. To fully understand each standard, the entire standard, including prefatory comments (preambles), should be read. (The complete standards appear in 48 CFR, Chapter 99.)

Consistency in Estimating, Accumulating, and Reporting Costs (Standard 401—48 CFR 9904.401)

The purpose of CAS 401 is to ensure consistency in each of the contractor's cost accounting practices used to estimate, accumulate, and report costs on government contracts. The objective is to enhance the likelihood that a contractor will treat comparable transactions alike. The standard requires that consistency be applied as follows:

- The practices used in estimating costs for a proposal must be consistent with the cost accounting practices followed by the contractor in accumulating and reporting actual contract costs. The standard permits grouping of like costs when it is not practicable to estimate contract costs by individual cost element or function. However, costs estimated for proposal purposes must be presented in such a manner and in sufficient detail so that any significant cost can be compared with the actual cost accumulated and reported.

- The standard specifically requires consistency in: (1) classification of elements or functions of cost as direct or indirect; (2) indirect cost pools to which each element or function of cost is charged or proposed to be charged; and (3) methods used in allocating indirect costs to the contract.

The standard does not specify the level of detail required to support particular proposed costs when compared with the actual costs accumulated and reported on contracts. The standard does not require that costs, as presented in proposals, reflect exactly the same detail as the actual costs that are accumulated and reported; it requires only that the practices be consistent and in sufficient detail to permit a valid comparison. The important consideration is to produce reasonable "trails" from the cost included in the proposal to those accumulated in the accounting records and subsequently reported to the government.

Compliance with this standard may require changes to cost accounting and estimating systems; however, it may not be necessary for the contractor to change its formal accounting system, since informal records are acceptable. Preamble A to CAS 401 addresses the use of memorandum records as follows:

> Commentators stated that the purpose of the standards would require each contractor to revise his formal system of accounts in order to maintain them on a basis used for estimating Government contracts. The Board did not intend that requirement. The standard does not contain any requirement that a contractor must revise his formal system of accounts. Cost accounting records are supplemental to, and generally subsidiary to a contractor's financial records. However, it is necessary that the cost accounting records be reconcilable to the contractor's general financial records.

In late 1976, the CASB issued Interpretation No. 1 to CAS 401 in response to questions concerning consistency in estimating and recording scrap or other losses of direct materials. The interpretation does not prescribe the level of detail required to be maintained. However, it requires, when a significant part of material cost is estimated by means of percentage factors, that the practice be supported by appropriate accounting, statistical, or other relevant records that document the actual scrap or other losses.

In *Texas Instruments, Inc.*,[18] the ASBCA ruled that CAS 401 does not require costs to be estimated, accumulated, and reported by contract when job order costing is not consistent with the nature of the contractor's operations. The contractor used a production-line cost system to manufacture homogeneous units for the covered contract as well as for other orders. The costs assigned to the contract were the average cost of units produced on a production run.

In *Dayton T. Brown, Inc.*,[19] estimated bid and proposal (B&P) costs on the basis of amounts allocated from the corporate office but reported its B&P costs at the divisional level in computing the cost ceiling under the formula in the procurement regulations. The ASBCA initially ruled that the contractor's practice was consistent, since the application of the formula was a procedure for determining allowability and therefore outside the purview of CAS. On a motion for reconsideration, however, the ASBCA reversed its earlier decision and found that the contractor's practices were in violation of CAS 401.

The standard became effective July 1, 1972.

Consistency in Allocating Costs Incurred for the Same Purpose (Standard 402—48 CFR 9904.402)

The standard requires that each type of cost be allocated only once and on only one basis. Its intent is to preclude the "double counting" of costs. Double counting occurs when cost items are allocated directly to cost objectives without eliminating like items from indirect cost if pools. An example of double counting is charging the cost of inspecting units produced directly to a contract and, at the same time, including similar inspection costs incurred in substantially the same circumstances in an overhead pool that is allocated to all cost objectives, including that contract. Thus, CAS 402 prohibits a contract from being charged more than once for the same type of cost by requiring that a cost incurred for the same purpose, in like circumstances, be classified as either direct cost only or indirect cost only. The standard relates to the system as a whole and not necessarily to the treatment on individual contracts. Thus, a CAS noncompliance occurs if a cost is charged to a specific contract as a direct cost, and the same cost incurred in like circumstances is also included in an overhead pool but not allocated to that contract.

The key element, however, is whether the cost is incurred for the same purpose and in like circumstances. If either the purpose or the circumstances differ, the accounting practices related to the two separate transactions need not be consistent and would not be covered by this standard.

Disagreements between contractors and government auditors over the standard's requirements usually involve identifying and classifying costs incurred for the same purpose, in like circumstances. To avoid challenge, contractors must support their classification of costs and demonstrate that the accounting treatment of all costs of a similar type and nature, incurred in like circumstances, is the same. If a contractor has submitted a disclosure statement, it should provide sufficient criteria for determining whether a particular cost in a given circumstance is treated as a direct or indirect cost.

The CAS Steering Committee Interim Guidance Paper W.G. 77-15 addressed the interrelationship between the procurement cost principle for termination cost practices and CAS 401, 402, and 406. The paper recognized that direct charging to the terminated contract of certain costs that would have been charged indirectly if the contract had been completed is not a violation of CAS 402. Since a contract termination is a significant change in circumstances, it is unreasonable to extend the requirement of consistency to an event that was never anticipated in the estimate.

Interpretation No. 1 to CAS 402 dealt with the question of whether B&P costs are always incurred for the same purpose and in like circumstances. The interpretation makes clear they are not. B&P costs specifically required by contractual terms and conditions can, on a consistent basis, be properly treated as direct costs, while other contractor B&P costs may be recorded as indirect costs. The condition of being "specifically required" under a contract exists, for example, when a contract option is repriced and when proposals result from contract provisions, such as the Changes clause.

The Federal Circuit[20] reversed an earlier ASBCA decision (No. 29793) that The Boeing Company's practice constituted noncompliance with the provisions of CAS 402. Boeing charged the cost of contractually required proposals as direct cost. Submission of a proposal for a Phase 2 contract was required as a specific line item in the Phase 1 contract subject to this dispute. The contractor identified as a direct cost only the B&P costs incurred between receipt of the Phase 2 request for proposal and submission of the Phase 2 proposal. Before receiving the request, the contractor performed a number of technical B&P activities to enhance its probability of obtaining the Phase 2 contract. The contractor also incurred B&P costs in preparing a best and final offer after submission of the Phase 2 proposal. The contractor concluded that these costs were charged indirectly as part of the total independent research and development (IR&D) and B&P pool. The ASBCA concluded that all B&P costs relating to the Phase 2 proposal should have been treated consistently as directly chargeable to the contract. In reversing the ASBCA decision, the Federal Circuit ruled that only the Phase 2 proposal costs incurred between receipt of the Phase 2 request for proposal and the Phase 2 proposal submission were specifically required by the Phase 1 contract and, therefore, directly chargeable to the contract. Since no Phase 1 contractual requirement differentiated the remainder of the Phase 2 proposal costs from other B&P costs, it was proper to allocate the remaining Phase 2 proposal costs as indirect B&P costs.

The Comptroller General ruled, in a bid protest filed by CACI Inc.,[21] that the government's addition of certain hours to direct cost on the protester's proposal for evaluation purposes was improper, because the protester consistently accounted for those hours as an indirect cost. The GAO concluded that CAS 402 required the contractor and the government to treat the function consistently with the contractor's past practice.

In a somewhat contradictory decision, the Comptroller General ruled in *Syscon Corp.*[22] that a request for proposals for a time-and-materials contract did not violate CAS 402, because the materials estimate was not to include relocation cost. The Navy advised that it would reimburse the successful contractor for relocation costs only to the extent that such costs were included in the proposed fixed-labor rates. The protester asserted that since it was precluded by its established cost accounting practice from factoring relocation costs into its labor rates, the RFP violated CAS 402. The Comptroller General concluded that the RFP requirement was not inconsistent with the CAS because it only informed offerors that costs other than materials and travel expenses would be recoverable only if included in the labor rates; it did not define how such costs were to be classified for the purpose of the firms' accounting systems. This decision clearly ignored the basic premises of CAS 401 and 402 that (1) cost estimating and cost accumulation practices must be consistent; and (2) a cost may not be proposed for indirect cost recovery on one contract if the same cost is proposed as a direct cost on other contracts.

In *Aydin Corp.*,[23] the Federal Circuit overruled an ASBCA decision that a large commission on a foreign contract (Solar II) could be charged direct while other commissions remained in the contractor's general and administrative expense pool. The court observed that CAS 402 requires similar treatment for similar costs unless "different circumstances justify different accounting treatment" and that the disproportionate size of a cost does not justify a different treatment. Aydin's sales commission for the Solar II contract represented 91% of total sales commission for the year, while costs incurred to perform the contract represented only 19% of Aydin's general and administrative (G&A) base. The Federal Circuit remanded the issue to ASBCA on November 20, 1995, to explain how the Solar II foreign sales commissions differed in purpose or circumstances, if at all, from other sales commissions. On remand,[24] the ASBCA found no difference, other than size, in the purpose or circumstance, between the Solar II sales commission and other sales commission; thus, direct assignment of the Solar II commission to the contract was not possible.

The standard became effective July 1, 1972.

Allocation of Home Office Expenses to Segments (Standard 403—48 CFR 9904.403)

This standard governs the allocation of the home-office expenses to the segments (business units) under its control. Allocation from segments to final cost objectives is covered by CAS 410. CAS 403 divides home office expenses into three categories.

- Expenses incurred for specific segments. Such costs should be allocated directly to those segments to the maximum extent practical.
- Expenses incurred for various segments, such as centralized services, certain line and staff management, and centralized payments and accruals, whose relationship to those segments can be measured on some objective basis. Such expenses should be grouped in logical and homogeneous expense pools and allocated on the most objective basis available. The standard sets forth the following hierarchy of allocation techniques for centralized services:
  - *Preferred:* A measure of the activity of the organization performing the function for supporting functions that are labor-oriented, machine-oriented, or space-oriented
  - *First alternative:* A measure of the output of the supporting function, measured in terms of the units of end products produced
  - *Second alternative:* A measure of the activity of the segments receiving the service

  The standard also suggests several types of allocation bases for these categories of home office expenses. The methods suggested support the standard's requirement that home office expenses be allocated on the basis of the beneficial or causal relationship between supporting and receiving activities.
  - Expenses incurred to manage the organization as a whole that have no identifiable relationship to any specific segment or segments. The aggregate of such residual expenses must be allocated to segments either (1) on the basis of a three-factor formula (payroll dollars, operating revenue, and net book value of tangible capital assets plus inventories); or (2) on any basis representative of the segments' total activity. The three-factor formula is required when total residual expenses exceed stated proportions of the aggregate operating revenues of all segments for the previous fiscal year as follows:
  - 3.35% of the first $100 million
  - 0.95% of the next $200 million
  - 0.30% of the next $2.7 billion
  - 0.20% of the amounts over $3 billion
- A special allocation of home office expenses to particular segments is permitted when it can be shown that the benefits from the expense pool to

the segment(s) are significantly different from the benefits accruing to the segments.

The first CAS 403 issue to progress through the formal disputes process related to The Boeing Company's allocation of state and local taxes.[25] Property, sales, use, and fuel and vehicle taxes were accumulated at the home office and were allocated to segments on the basis of head count. The ASBCA agreed with the government that using the basis on which the taxes were assessed met the standard's requirements, whereas the contractor's method of using head count did not comply. Boeing appealed the decision to the Court of Claims, asserting that: (1) The ASBCA inappropriately rejected the "broad benefit test"; and (2) the CASB was unconstitutional, and all of its standards were therefore void. The court affirmed the ASBCA decision,[26] noting that "by literal terms of the standard, the assessment base is permissible and the head-count approach seems improper." The court effectively avoided the issue of whether the CASB was constitutional by ruling that the DOD's adoption of CAS 403 in the Defense Acquisition Regulation negated the contractor's entitlement to monetary relief. Boeing appealed to the U.S. Supreme Court,[27] but the Supreme Court declined to accept the case.

Numerous CAS 403 noncompliance issues have related to the allocation of state and local taxes that are calculated based on income. The standard provides an illustration pertaining specifically to the allocation of such taxes. The illustration suggests that the allocation should be made using a base or by a method that results in an amount that equals or approximates a segment's proportionate share of the tax imposed by the jurisdiction in which the segment does business. In most states, the measures for determining taxable income are combinations of the following factors: sales, payroll dollars, and tangible property.

Citing the illustrative allocation base included in the standard as support, the government concluded that only the factors determining the taxable income for a state can be used in allocating the expense. However, in *Lockheed Corp. and Lockheed Missiles and Space Co., Inc.*,[28] the ASBCA ruled that state and local taxes computed on the basis of income must include segment income as one of the factors of the allocation base under CAS 403. The CASB disagreed with the ASBCA ruling and subsequently issued CAS 403 Interpretation No. 1, which permits use of segment book income as a factor in allocating income tax expense to segments only when segment book income is expressly used by the taxing jurisdiction in computing the income tax. The ASBCA rejected the legal authority of that interpretation, since the CASB had neither published the interpretation for comment nor submitted it to Congress for review before promulgation. The issue was revisited by the ASBCA in 1985 in another Lockheed dispute in which the parties agreed to retain the same issues as in the previous dispute. The ASBCA again concluded that segment net income should be included as a factor in allocating state and local taxes.[29] The significance of the second dispute is that the contract was subject to the Contract Disputes Act and could be appealed by the government. The Court of Appeals for the Federal Circuit sustained the prior ASBCA decision.[30]

In another state income tax allocation case, *McDonnell Douglas Corp.*[31] allocated its multistate income and franchise taxes from the home office to its segments on the basis of gross payroll. The ASBCA concluded that neither the contractor's method nor the government's method (an approach similar to the government's position in the *Lockheed* case) complied with CAS 403. Failure to consider segment income in either method resulted in tax allocations that were not considered comparable to the various segments' proportionate shares of the taxes.

In a third state income tax allocation case, *Grumman Corp.*,[32] the ASBCA held that it was acceptable to include net operating losses in the allocation base used to distribute state franchise taxes and thereby assign credits to loss divisions. The government contended that CAS 403 limits the components of the allocation base to those factors used to apportion a company's total taxable income among the states—namely property, payroll, and sales. The company stressed the principle expressed in the standard that the allocation base should reflect the causal relationship between the tax cost and the receiving segment. Regression and correlation analyses showed virtually no correlation between the apportionment factors and the tax. The Board, in its opinion, clearly agreed by stating the following:

> [W]e conclude that income is both the primary cause of the Grumman tax and a factor which must be considered in the home office allocation of the NYFT [New York Franchise Tax] to attain compliance with the requirements in CAS 403.40(b)(4) that an allocation base 'representative of the factors' be used.

Interpretation No. 1 to CAS 403 that was rejected by the ASBCA was reaffirmed by the second CASB when it included the interpretation in the recodification of the standards incorporated into 4 CFR, Chapter 99. Consequently, the issues previously resolved by the *Lockheed*, *McDonnel*, *McDonnell Douglas*, and *Grumman* decisions may again be revisited.

In *R&D Associates*,[33] the Board rejected an attempt to allocate imputed state tax expenses to a subsidiary when the actual taxes paid were considerably less due to tax credits which the company allocated to a commercial subsidiary. The company relied on CAS 403, stating that the credits were the result of economic events at the commercial segment. The Board held that it was unnecessary to address the CAS allocation issues and relied on the acquisition regulation's definition of total cost. The Board disallowed the imputed costs since they represented amounts that would never be paid or incurred.

In *Hercules, Inc.*,[34] the government asserted that state income taxes resulting from a capital gain on the sale of the company's interest in a commercial joint venture were not allocable to Hercules' ammunition plant. The court disagreed; Hercules' proration of total corporate net income to the state and to the segments within the state based on the state's income tax assessment factors (payroll, property, and sales) was deemed to comply with CAS 403.

In *General Dynamics Corp.*,[35] the ASBCA ruled that the contractor's practice of allocating data-processing site office costs to user segments on the basis of an average site office cost was at variance with CAS 403. Since the site offices responded solely to ADP requests of specific facilities and divisions, the Board concluded that CAS 403 required allocation of the site costs to segments on the basis of services provided.

In another decision involving *General Dynamics Corp.*,[36] the ASBCA overruled the government's conclusion that CAS 403.40(a)(1) and CAS 418.60(h) required flights on corporate aircraft to be charged to the division traveled to, rather than the home office. After concluding that the CAS 418 requirements applied only to business units or segments and were not pertinent to the allocation of home office aircraft costs, the Board also noted the following:

> General Dynamics accumulated its headquarters flight costs in a residual pool. The Government appeared to suggest that General Dynamics had not allocated the flight costs to the division "to the maximum extent practical" as required by CAS 403(a)(1). The Government seemed to have taken the position that all flights to a division, ought to be, *ipso facto*, charged to that division. ... CAS 403(c) provides in part that "Typical residual expenses are those for the chief executive, the

chief financial officer, and any staff who are not identifiable with specific activities of segments." Flights out of St. Louis were taken principally by headquarters executives in connection with the management of the divisions by the home office. Thus, the flights were taken for home office purposes and not strictly for divisional purposes. In the absence of evidence to the contrary, we cannot conclude that General Dynamics' method of allocating home office aircraft expenses was in violation of CAS 403.

This standard originally became effective on July 1, 1973, and must now be followed by contractors as of the beginning of the next fiscal year after receipt of a contract subject to the standard. Contractors subject to Federal Management Circular 74-4 (Principles for Determining Costs Applicable to Grants and Contracts with State and Local Governments) are exempt from CAS 403.

Capitalization of Tangible Assets (Standard 404—48 CFR 9904.404)

The purpose of CAS 404 was to provide uniform capitalization criteria that could be used as a basis for determining the cost of capital assets applicable to government contracts. The CASB concluded that provisions of the Internal Revenue Code and GAAP addressed alternatives that were inappropriate for contract costing. The following are the more significant requirements of the standard:

- Contractors must establish and adhere to a written policy on tangible asset capitalization. The policy must designate the economic and physical characteristics on which the policy is based and identify, to the maximum extent practicable, the components of plant and equipment that are capitalized when asset units are initially acquired or replaced. Additionally, the contractor's policy must designate minimum service life and minimum acquisition cost criteria for capitalization, which may not exceed two years and $5,000, respectively. The dollar threshold was raised from $1,500 to $5,000 in February, 1996.[37]

- Tangible capital assets constructed for a contractor's own use must be capitalized at amounts that include all allocable indirect costs, including any G&A expenses that are identifiable with the constructed assets and material in amount. When the constructed assets are identical or similar to the contractor's regular product, such assets must be capitalized at amounts that include a full share of indirect costs.

- Donated assets that meet the contractor's criteria for capitalization must be capitalized at their fair value.

- A group of individual low-cost items acquired for the initial outfitting of a tangible capital asset, such as furnishings for a new facility, which in the aggregate represent a material investment, must be capitalized consistent with the contractor's written policy. The contractor may, however, designate a minimum acquisition cost criterion higher in the aggregate than the criterion for such original complements, provided it is reasonable in the contractor's circumstances.

- Costs incurred that extend the life or increase the productivity of an asset (betterments and improvements) must be capitalized when they exceed the contractor's specified minimum acquisition cost criterion for betterments and when the asset has a remaining life in excess of two years.

This standard does not require the use of any practices that depart from generally accepted accounting principles with regard to the basis for determining cost and the accounting for assets acquired at other than arm's length, for assets acquired through a business combination, for repair and maintenance costs, and for asset dispositions.

The original standard subjected capital assets acquired in a business combination under the purchase method of accounting to a step-up in basis when the fair value of the assets exceeded the purchase price. This position was reversed when the CASB revised CAS 404 in February 1996. The standard now provides the following:

- If the acquired company's assets generated depreciation or cost of money that was allocated, during the fiscal year prior to the business combination, to federal awards negotiated on the basis of cost, no "step-up" or "step-down" in asset value is permitted.

- Assets values can be adjusted if the assets did not generate depreciation or cost of money that was allocated, during the fiscal year prior to the business combination, to federal awards negotiated on the basis of cost. The assets can be adjusted to their fair market value if the acquisition price is equal to or greater than their book value. If the acquisition price is less than book value of the assets, the value of the assets acquired will be reduced by a proportional share of the excess.

The revision essentially formalizes the "no step-up/step-down" provision already contained in FAR cost principle 31.205-52, Asset Valuations Resulting from Business Combinations; consequently, the revision has little impact on asset valuations of acquired companies that perform cost-based awards. Where no depreciation or cost of money was allocated to cost-based awards in the acquired company's fiscal year prior to the business combination, step-ups or step-downs are permitted under CAS 404 but not under FAR 31.205-52. Unless the cost principle is changed to conform to the language in CAS 404, the cost principle presumably will prevail, based on the Federal Circuit's ruling that a cost principle provision limiting cost reimbursement is not an allocability provision in conflict with a cost accounting standard.[38]

In *Marquardt Co.*,[39] the increased asset values resulting from a business acquisition were disallowed, even though the write-up of assets was deemed to be in accordance with generally accepted accounting principles and CAS 404. The decision, which predated the revision to the standard, held that the business combination was merely the result of a stock ownership change; consequently, assets were to be revalued at the acquiring corporation and not at the acquired corporation which was responsible for performing government contracts.

This standard became effective on July 1, 1973, and was applicable to tangible capital assets acquired during a contractor's fiscal year, beginning on or after October 1, 1973. The standard's revision relating to gains or losses related to business combinations and the increase in the capitalization threshold was effective February 13, 1996, and became applicable at the start of a contractor's fiscal year following receipt of a contract subject to full CAS coverage.

Accounting for Unallowable Costs (Standard 405—48 CFR 9904.405)

This standard, effective on April 1, 1974, sets forth guidelines for identifying in the contractor's accounting records specific costs that are unallowable and the cost accounting treatment of such costs. The standard resulted from the general lack of uniformity and consistency in the accounting treatment accorded unallowable costs and the lack of any regulatory requirement for contractor identification of unallowable costs. Cost Accounting Standard 405 does not provide criteria for determining the allowability of costs; this is a function of the appropriate procurement or reviewing authority. It merely establishes the accounting treatment and reporting requirements after the costs are determined to be unallowable. The following are the fundamental requirements of the standard:

- Contractors must identify in their accounting records, and exclude from any proposal, billing, or claim, costs specifically described as unallowable either by the express wording of laws or regulations or by mutual agreement of the contracting parties. The CAS Steering Committee (W.G. 77-13) concluded that contractors must identify disputed allocable costs as unallowable in any billing, claim, or proposal, and that refusal to identify these unallowables represents noncompliance with this standard.

- Contractors must identify: (1) costs designated as unallowable as a result of a written decision by a CO pursuant to contract disputes procedures; (2) any costs incurred for the same purpose and in like circumstances as those specifically identified as unallowable; and (3) the costs of any work project not contractually authorized.

- Costs that are mutually agreed to be directly associated with unallowable costs must be identified and excluded from proposals, billings, or claims. Costs that are designated as directly associated with unallowable costs pursuant to contract dispute procedures must be identified in the accounting records. A directly associated cost is any cost that is generated solely as a result of the incurrence of another cost, and would not have been incurred had the other cost not been incurred.

- Costs specifically described as unallowable, as well as directly associated costs, must be included in any indirect allocation base or bases in which they would normally be included.

Industry's principal concern with the standard relates to the requirement that unallowable costs remain in any base for the allocation of indirect costs and bear their pro rata share of such indirect costs. The government has used this provision to treat otherwise allowable costs as unallowable, which to many is an inequitable result.

In *General Dynamics Corp.*,[40] the ASBCA overruled the government's finding that CAS 405.40(e) required the contractor to exclude the full costs of any flights on corporate aircraft that were deemed unallowable. In its decision, the ASBCA stated the following:

> We believe it is confusing and even misleading to characterize "variable" costs as "aircraft" costs. The concept of "directly associated costs," as articulated in CAS 405, is useful in drawing a distinction between "aircraft" costs and "flight-related" costs.

> "Variable" costs are costs directly associated with a flight. In other words, if the flight had not taken place, the "variable" costs would not have been incurred. It follows that if a flight is unallowable, its directly associated "variable" costs should also be unallowable. That, simply, is what CAS 405 required. . . .

> Accordingly, we hold that once General Dynamics has demonstrated that it is entitled to the "fixed" costs of an aircraft under DAR 15-205.46(g), none of the "fixed" costs need be conceded along with the "variable" costs of the conceded flights.

In *Martin Marietta Corp.*,[41] the ASBCA ruled that unallowable costs must be included in the G&A base to calculate the allowable G&A rate. The Board concluded that Martin Marietta's exclusion of a significant unallowable expense from the total cost input base used to allocate G&A expenses violated CAS 405 on the basis that once an allocation base is established, all costs should be included, irrespective of their allowability.

Cost Accounting Period (Standard 406—48 CFR 9904.406)

Except in the following specific circumstances, CAS 406 requires a contractor to use its normal fiscal year as its cost accounting period.

- When costs of an indirect function exist for only part of a cost accounting period, they may be allocated to cost objectives of that same part of the period.

- Another fixed annual period other than a fiscal year may be used upon mutual agreement with the government if it is an established practice and is consistently used.

- Transitional periods may be used in connection with a change in fiscal year. If the transition period between the end of the previous fiscal year and the beginning of the next fiscal year is three months or less, it may be (1) treated as a stand-alone cost accounting period, (2) combined with the previous fiscal year, or (3) combined with the next regular fiscal year. If the transition period is more than three months, it must be treated as a stand-alone period.

- Where an expense, such as pension cost, is identified with a fixed, recurring annual period that is different from the contractor's cost accounting period, and is consistently employed, its use may be continued.

In all cases, however, the cost accounting period used for accumulating costs in an indirect cost pool must be the same as the period used for establishing related allocation bases. Indirect expense rates used for estimating, accumulating, and reporting costs, including progress payments and public vouchers, should be based on the established annual cost accounting period.

Interpretation 1 to CAS 406 was issued as a final rule on June 6, 1997, effective August 15, 1997. The CASB had previously issued this guidance as an interim rule on March 8, 1995, entitled Interpretation 95-01, Allocation of Contractor Restructuring Costs under Defense Contracts. Although the CASB did not follow the promulgation process established in 9901.305 with regard to the interim rule, government and industry generally agree with the promulgated guidance which:

- Recognizes that restructuring costs may be either expensed or deferred and amortized over a period not to exceed five years.

- Permits treatment of restructuring costs incurred for the first time as an initial adoption of a cost accounting practice if the contractor does not have an established or disclosed practice covering such costs.

- Deems the resultant change in cost accounting practice to be desirable and not detrimental to the interests of the government if a contractor has previously expensed restructuring costs and now wishes to defer and amortize such costs, thus enabling the contractor to obtain equitable adjustment for the impact of such costs on CAS-covered awards.

In *Aerojet General Corp.*,[42] the ASBCA ruled that the contractor's allocation of mass severance pay to in-house contracts in the year in which the severance was paid complied with the provisions of CAS 406. The government had concluded that this method was inequitable and had allocated the costs over all contracts to be completed after management decided to close the plant. The Board concluded that the government had not demonstrated how its reallocation of the severance costs would not be inconsistent with CAS 406.

The CAS Steering Committee Interim Guidance Paper W.G. 77-15 addressed the interrelationship between the procurement cost principle for termination cost practices and CAS 401, 402, and 406. The paper specifically precluded the application of shorter accounting periods to contracts terminated early in the accounting year.

The standard became effective on July 1, 1974, and was applicable at the start of the next fiscal year, following the receipt of a contract subject to the standard.

Use of Standard Costs for Direct Material and Direct Labor (Standard 407—48 CFR 9904.407)

Cost Accounting Standards 407 provides criteria for establishing and revising standard costs, as well as disposing of variances from standard costs, for those contractors who elect to use such costs in estimating, accumulating, and reporting costs of direct material and direct labor. The standard was promulgated because practices concerning the use of standard costs had not been well defined in government procurement regulations. This standard requires the following:

- Standard costs must be entered into the books of account.

- Standard costs and related variances must be accounted for at the production unit level. The standard defines a *production unit* as a group of activities that either uses homogeneous input (e.g., direct labor and material) or yields homogeneous outputs.

- Practices relating to setting and revising standards, using standard costs, and disposing of variances must be stated in writing and consistently followed.

- Variances must be allocated to cost objectives at least annually on the basis of material or labor cost at standard, labor hours at standard, or units of output, whichever is most appropriate in the circumstances. If variances are immaterial, they may be included in appropriate indirect cost pools for allocation to applicable cost objectives.

Because of the requirement to accumulate variances at the production unit level, some users of standard cost accounting systems must revise those systems to comply with the standard. A labor-rate standard may be used for a category of direct labor only if functions performed within that category are not materially different and employees involved perform interchangeable functions. A labor-rate standard can be set for a group of direct labor workers who perform different functions only when the group works in a single production unit yielding homogeneous outputs or when the group forms an integral team. As a result, utilization of standard costs by organizational structure (e.g., departments) may not be acceptable under the standard.

This standard became effective on October 1, 1974, and was applicable at the start of the next fiscal year, following the receipt of a contract subject to the standard.

Accounting for Costs of Compensated Personal Absence (Standard 408—48 CFR 9904.408)

Cost Accounting Standards 408 provides criteria for measuring, for a cost accounting period, costs of vacation, sick leave, holiday, and other compensated personal absences, such as jury duty, military training, mourning, and personal time off. The standard requires that the costs of compensated personal absences be assigned to the cost accounting period or periods in which the entitlement was earned (accrual basis) and that such costs for an entire cost accounting period be allocated pro rata on an annual basis among that period's final cost objectives. The following are the more significant principles that govern the allocation of these costs:

- Entitlement is determined when the employer becomes liable to compensate the employee for such absence if the employee was terminated. Probationary periods may be included as a part of the service time creating entitlement.

- Each plan or custom for compensated personal absence must be considered separately in determining when the entitlement is earned.

- In the absence of a determinable liability, compensated personal absence will be considered to be earned only in the cost accounting period in which paid.

- In determining the liability for compensated personal absence, current or anticipated wage rates may be used; however, the estimated liability must be reduced to allow for anticipated nonuse when such amounts are material.

- An adjustment occasioned by the initial adoption of the standard, the adoption of a new plan, or a change of an existing plan must be carried in a "suspense account" and recognized as a contract cost only to the extent that the suspense account balance at the beginning of the cost accounting period exceeds the ending liability for such compensated absence in a future fiscal year. Since the suspense account balance comprises the compensated absence liabilities of individual employees, it can be reduced as the liability for specific employees is reduced to zero (e.g., upon retirement or severance), even though the ending liability for such compensated absence for all employees exceeds the aggregate balance in the suspense account.

The standard became effective on July 1, 1975, and was applicable at the start of the next fiscal year, following the receipt of a contract subject to the standard. Contractors subject to Federal Management Circular 74-4 are exempt from this standard.

Depreciation of Tangible Capital Assets (Standard 409—48 CFR 9904.409)

This standard sets forth criteria for assigning costs of tangible capital assets to cost accounting periods and for allocating such costs to cost objectives within such periods. The purpose of the standard is to match depreciation costs with the accounting period and cost objectives that benefit from the use of the fixed assets. The following are the more important provisions of CAS 409:

- Estimated service lives for contracting purposes must be reasonable approximations of expected actual periods of usefulness, supported by records of past retirements, disposals, or withdrawals from service. Periods for which assets are retained for stand-by or incidental use can be excluded from estimated service lives. However, stand-by or incidental use must be supported by sufficiently detailed records. A two-year period, measured from the beginning of the fiscal year in which a contractor must first comply with the standard, was provided for the contractors to develop and maintain such records. Lives based on past experience may be modified to reflect expected changes in physical or economic usefulness, but the contractor bears the burden of justifying estimated service lives that are shorter than those experienced.

Estimated service lives used for financial accounting purposes also must be used for government contract costing purposes until adequate records supporting the periods of usefulness are available, if the estimated lives are not unreasonable under the standard's criteria. Assets acquired for which the contractor has no available data or prior experience must be assigned service lives based on a projection of expected usefulness; however, these service lives may not be less than the asset guideline period (midrange) published by the Internal Revenue Service. Use of any such alternative lives must cease as soon as a contractor can develop service lives supported by its own experience.

Sampling techniques may be used to support estimated service lives. The prefatory comments accompanying the standard state that procurement agencies are expected to be reasonable in enforcing the supporting record requirements.

- The depreciation method used for financial accounting purposes must be used for contract costing unless it: (1) does not reasonably reflect the expected consumption of services as measured by the expected activity or physical output of the assets, or (2) is unacceptable for federal income tax purposes. If the method used for financial accounting purposes does not meet these tests, the contractor must adopt a method that best measures the expected consumption of services. When a contractor selects a depreciation method for new assets that is different from the method used for like assets in similar circumstances, that new method must be supported by a projection of the expected consumption of services. In its prefatory comments, the CASB stated "it is not the intent of the Board to introduce uncertainty into contract negotiation and settlement by encouraging challenge of contractor's depreciation methods. If the method selected is also used for external financial reporting and is acceptable for income tax purposes, the Board's expectation is that it will be accepted."

- Gain or loss on the disposition of assets recognized for contract costing purposes must be limited to the difference between the original acquisition cost and the undepreciated balance. The gain or loss, if material in amount, must be allocated in the same manner as depreciation cost; however, if such amounts are immaterial, they may be included in an appropriate indirect cost pool. The standard was modified in 1996 to clarify that the provisions relating to gains and losses on disposition of tangible capital assets do not apply to business combinations. The carrying value of tangible capital assets acquired subsequent to a business combination are established in accordance with the provisions of CAS 404.

This standard received a lot of attention and criticism from industry, primarily because of the requirement that service lives be based on actual periods of usefulness. Industry argued that such a requirement inappropriately extended the period over which the cost of the asset was recovered, ignored the economic realities of inflation, provided little incentive for companies to contract with the government because of the standard's impact on earnings and cash flow, and eroded the productivity of government contractors. Because of the mitigating effect of CAS 414, however, the primary long-range impact of the standard has been limited to additional administrative costs stemming from the necessity to maintain separate capital asset records for contracting purposes.

As the standard allows a two-year grace period within which to develop records to supporting asset lives, equitable adjustment procedures should be applied to CAS-covered contracts existing at the end of the grace period (i.e., not just those contracts existing at the more usual "effective date").

The standard became effective on July 1, 1975. Contractors must apply the standard to assets acquired after the beginning of the next fiscal year, following receipt of a covered contract, and are required to support asset lives used in computing depreciation within two years of becoming subject to the standard. This standard does not apply when compensation for the use of tangible capital assets is based on use allowances in lieu of depreciation. The revision relating to gains and losses relating to business combinations became effective April 15, 1996, and applicable at the start of a contractor's next full cost accounting period after receipt of a contract or subcontract subject to full CAS coverage.

Allocation of Business Unit General and Administrative Expenses to Final Cost Objectives (Standard 410—48 CFR 9904.410)

The purpose of CAS 410 is to provide criteria for allocating business unit G&A expenses to final cost objectives. To accomplish its purpose, the standard narrowly defines "G&A expenses" to include only expenses that are incurred for the general management and administration of the business unit as a whole and that do not have a directly measurable relationship to particular cost objectives. Such expenses are thus only the "residual expenses" that exclude management and administrative expenses having measurable beneficial or causal relationships to cost objectives. Home office expenses that meet the definition of segment G&A expense are includable in the receiving segment's G&A expense pool. Insignificant expenses that do not qualify by definition as G&A expenses may be included in G&A expense pools. Other significant requirements of the standard are as follows:

- The G&A expense pool must be allocated to final cost objectives (i.e., contracts) by means of one of three cost input bases: (1) total cost input (total production costs), (2) value-added cost input (total production costs excluding material and subcontract costs), or (3) single-element cost input (direct labor dollars or hours), whichever is most appropriate in the circumstances.

- Special allocation is permitted when the benefits from G&A expense to a particular final cost objective significantly differ from the benefits accruing to other final cost objectives. When a special allocation is used, the expense allocated must be excluded from the residual G&A pool, and the cost input of the cost objective must be removed from the cost input base used.

- Contractors that include selling costs in a cost pool separate and apart from the G&A expense pool may continue to do so, or they may opt to include selling costs in their G&A pool. However, CAS Steering Committee Interim Guidance Paper W.G. 78-21 requires a separate allocation of selling expenses when a significant disparity exists in marketing activity (e.g., between domestic and foreign). On September 19, 1996, the CASB issued a Staff Discussion Paper on Allocation of Selling and Marketing Costs.[43] The paper raises questions about the causal/beneficial relationship between selling costs and final cost objectives, the appropriate indirect cost pool to accumulate selling and marketing costs, and the selection of an appropriate allocation base. Because this is the first step of a four-part CAS promulgation process, no final action by the Board is imminent.

- Items produced for stock or inventory must be included in the input base in the year the item is produced. When the standard first becomes applicable to a contractor, stock items in inventory must be included in the G&A input base in the cost accounting period in which they are assigned to final cost objectives.

- To reduce the impact of deferred G&A costs that could have occurred when the standard was first adopted by a contractor, a transitional procedure was provided for contractors that were using an output base (e.g., sales or cost of sales) to allocate G&A when the standard became effective. The transition method was elective, not mandatory.

The CAS Steering Committee issued three guidance papers on CAS 410. Interim Guidance Paper W.G. 77-11 deals largely with problems initially encountered by contractors that elected the transition method. Interim Guidance Paper W.G. 78-21, as revised by Amendment No. 1, dated April 14, 1981, covers a number of issues in a question-and-answer format. The following are the more significant of these:

- *Types of items includable in the residual G&A pool and the cost input base.* For example, significant functional costs should not be included in the residual G&A pool, and interdivisional transfers should be included in the total cost input base.

- *Criteria for using the value-added and single-element cost input base.* The value-added base is mandated when significant distortions are reflected in a total cost input base; the existence of a wide range of material and subcontract content among contracts may signal the precondition for potential significant distortion. The single-element base is acceptable if labor dollars are significant and if other input costs are a less significant measure of a segment's activities.

- *Separate allocations of home office expenses under CAS 403.* They should be identified by the receiving segment; residual home office expenses are includable in the segment's residual G&A pool.

Interim Guidance Paper W.G. 79-24 covers circumstances in which significant facilities contracts dictate the use of a special allocation base to avoid excessive allocation of G&A expenses by using a total cost input allocation.

Government and contractor representatives have frequently disagreed about what circumstances justify the use of a special allocation. Disagreements have also related to the appropriate cost input base, particularly the conditions under which including material and subcontract costs in the base distort the allocation of G&A expenses to final cost objectives. Disproportionate levels of material and subcontract costs among a contractor's cost objectives were a major consideration in a significant ASBCA decision[44] involving CAS 410. The government argued that the standard mandated the use of total cost input to allocate segment G&A unless it could be shown that using such a base distorted the allocation. The appellant, *Ford Aerospace and Communications Corp., Aeronutronic Division*, contended that a value-added base (total cost input less materials and subcontracts) was required because including materials and subcontracts in the base destroyed the base's ability to distribute G&A expenses to final cost objectives based on benefits received. In its decision, the ASBCA dealt meaningfully with the critical issue of how one determines whether an allocation of G&A expenses is, in fact, distorted. The Board concluded that (1) the material and subcontract content of the contracts was disproportionate, and (2) the contractor's general management expenses provided substantially more benefit to its labor-intensive development contracts than to its material-intensive production contracts.

Two disputes involving *Emerson Electric Co.*[45] and *General Electric Co.*[46] resulted in decisions that the allocability criteria in the selling cost principle (FAR 31.205-38 and its predecessor DAR 15-205.37) do not conflict with the language in CAS 410, which permits allocation of selling expenses as part of the G&A expense pool. General Electric (GE) argued that CAS 410 permitted the inclusion of domestic and foreign selling costs in the G&A cost pool; that DAR 15-205.37(b) was inconsistent with CAS 410 because it stated that foreign military selling costs were not allocable to U.S. government contracts for U.S. requirements, and that, since CAS exclusively governs cost allocability, the conflicting DAR provision was invalid. In ruling against GE, the court stated that DAR 15-205.37(b) did not conflict with CAS 410 because CAS 410 permits, but does not mandate, the inclusion of selling costs in G&A.

After the promulgation of CAS 410, the Progress Payment clause was revised for contractors electing the CAS 410 transition method. Such contractors were prohibited from including G&A expenses in the costs eligible for progress payments until the work-in-process inventories of the post-CAS 410 contracts exceeded the amount in the suspense account. Once the work-in-process inventory exceeded the suspense account balance, the contractor's progress billings were limited to a pro rata share of the G&A allocable to the excess. *Westinghouse Electric Corp.'s*[47] assertion that the Progress Payment clause was unconstitutional was rejected by the ASBCA and by the Court of Appeals for the Federal Circuit.

In 1992, the ASBCA ruled in *Martin Marietta Corp.*[48] that unallowable costs included in the G&A base should not be burdened with a pro rata share of G&A expenses. Martin Marietta had excluded certain unallowable costs from the cost input base to allocate G&A expenses. While the Board agreed that CAS 410 required the unallowable cost to be included in the total cost input base, it also ruled that CAS 410 did not mandate that a pro rata share of allowable G&A be allocated to unallowable costs. Thus, the DAR requirement that "all items properly includable in an indirect cost base should bear a pro rata share of indirect costs irrespective of their acceptance as Government contract costs" conflicted with CAS 410. Consistent with prior decisions, the Board ruled that CAS 410 prevailed. However, the ASBCA decision was reversed by the Federal Circuit,[49] which concluded that the cost principle provision did not conflict with CAS 410. In its decision, the court concluded the following:

Because DAR 15-203(c) operates to disallow a share of G&A expense proportionate to unallowable costs after the G&A has been allocated to a final cost objective, we conclude that DAR 15-203(c) is not an allocability provision in conflict with CAS 410. Accordingly DAR 15-203(c) is valid and can be applied by a government agency to limit reimbursement to a government contractor for G&A expense.

Although the inability to recoup all allowable G&A expenses may be inequitable, there is little a company can do to argue for recoupment.

The ASBCA concluded that Aydin Corporation's inclusion in the G&A pool of a large sales commission related to a foreign contract (SOLAR II) violated CAS 410, because it resulted in an inequitable distribution of the commission to U.S. government contracts. On remand, the ASBCA directed Aydin to account for the foreign sales commissions by means of a special allocation of G&A expenses under CAS 410.50(j) [now 48 CFR 9904.410-50(j)].[50] The Federal Circuit reversed,[51] concluding that the SOLAR II sales commission must remain in the G&A pool "... because it does not differ in purpose or circumstances from other sales commissions."

CAS 410 became effective on October 1, 1976, and was applicable after the start of a contractor's next fiscal year, beginning after January 1, 1977. Contractors subject to Federal Management Circular 74-4 are exempt from this standard.

Accounting for Acquisition Costs of Material (Standard 411—48 CFR 9904.411)

Cost Accounting Standard 411 sets forth criteria for accumulating and allocating material costs and contains provisions on the use of certain inventory-costing methods. This standard resulted from what the CASB viewed as an absence in existing procurement regulations of a requirement that the same costing method be used for similar categories of material within the same business unit. The following are the more important requirements of this standard:

- First-in, first-out; last-in, first-out; weighted or moving average; and standard cost are all acceptable methods of inventory costing. The method(s) selected must be used consistently for similar categories of material within the same business unit and must be applied "in a manner which results in systematic and rational costing of issues of materials to cost objectives." Although this standard permits the use of the last-in, first-out method, the provision that the method used should result in systematic and rational costing has been interpreted by the CASB to require costing on a reasonably current basis.

- The standard provides for the direct allocation of the cost of units of a category of material, as long as the cost objective is identified at the time of purchase or production.

- The cost of material used for indirect functions may be allocated to cost objectives through an indirect cost pool when it is not a significant element of production cost. When the cost of such inventories remaining at the end of any cost accounting period significantly exceeds the cost at the beginning of the period, the difference must be capitalized as inventory and the indirect cost pool reduced correspondingly.

- Contractors are required to maintain in writing, and consistently apply, their accounting policies and practices for accumulating and allocating costs of materials.

The standard became effective on January 1, 1976, and must be observed for materials purchased or produced after the start of the next fiscal year, following the receipt of a contract subject to the standard.

Composition and Measurement of Pension Cost (Standard 412—48 CFR 9904.412)

Cost Accounting Standards 412 establishes the components of pension cost, the bases for measuring such cost, and the criteria for assigning pension cost to cost accounting periods. Two types of pension plans are recognized: a defined-contribution plan in which benefits are determined by the amount of the contributions established in advance, and a defined-benefit plan in which the benefits are stated in advance and the amount to be paid is actuarially calculated to provide for the future stated benefits. Multiemployer collective-bargaining plans and state university plans are considered to be defined-contribution plans. Cost Accounting Standards 412 originally became effective in 1976 and became woefully out of date because it was promulgated:

- Prior to FAS-87, which significantly changed the financial accounting requirements for the costs of pensions
- Prior to the Omnibus Budget Reconciliation Act of 1987, which introduced a more restrictive full funding limitation and a stiff excise tax for funding pension costs in excess of the maximum tax deductible amount
- During an era in which pension plans were more likely to be underfunded than overfunded

The standard was significantly revised in 1995. The following are the more important provisions of the current standard:

- For defined-contribution plans, the components of pension cost for a cost accounting period are the payments made, less dividends and other credits. For defined-benefit plans, the components are the normal cost, a part of the unfunded liability, plus interest equivalent and adjustment of actuarial gains and losses.
- Pension costs may not include prior unallowable costs under government regulations, excise taxes assessed for delayed funding, or interest attributable to pension costs computed for the cost accounting period that are not funded in that period.
- Unfunded actuarial liabilities must be consistently amortized in equal annual installments, and such liabilities must be determined by using the same actuarial assumptions as are used for the other pension cost components. No change in amortization period for unfunded liabilities is required when the amortization began before this standard; however, unfunded liabilities for new plans and improvements in existing plans must be amortized within 10 to 30 years.
- The costs of defined-benefit pension plans, other than those accounted for under the pay-as-you-go method, must be measured using an immediate gain actuarial method (one that separately identifies actuarial gains and losses from normal costs). The standard originally permitted the use of a spread-gain actuarial cost method if such a method was used for financial accounting purposes. Because FAS 87 requires the use of an immediate-gain method for financial accounting purposes, companies that were using a spread-gain method had to change to an immediate-gain method for

government cost accounting purposes. Such a change is a cost accounting change.

- Actuarial assumptions must be separately identified and validated. Assumptions used should reflect long-term rather than short-term trends.

- Pension costs must be measured (1) by a payroll percentage or as an annual accrual based on the service attribution of the benefit formula if the benefit is based on salaries and may include salary projections, or (2) by employee service if the benefit is not based on salaries.

- Funding is a condition for assignment and allocation.

  - For qualified plans, computed pension costs are assigned to a cost accounting period and allocable to cost objectives only to the extent funded. However, if the computed cost exceeds the maximum tax deductible amount, the excess (referred to as an assignable cost deficit) is assigned to future periods and amortized over 10 years. Any unfunded actuarial liability that occurs in the first cost accounting period after the assignable pension cost has been so limited will be treated like an actuarial gain or loss and amortized over 15 years. If the computed cost is less than zero (e.g., the plan is fully funded and net actuarial gains exceed normal cost), the computed negative pension cost (referred to as an assignable cost credit) is also assigned to future periods and amortized over 10 years.

  - For nonqualified plans that provide nonforfeitable benefits (and the right to the nonforfeitable benefit is communicated to the participant), the computed cost is assignable and allocable to the extent that it is funded through a funding agency at a level at least equal to the percentage of the complement of the highest corporate tax rate in effect on the first day of the accounting period. Because this contribution is not deductible for federal income tax purposes, the required funding level is equal to the after-tax effect of the amount funded for qualified plans. Funding at a lower level than the complement of the highest tax rate will result in a proportional reduction in assigned cost. For example, if the computed pension cost is $100 and the highest tax rate is 35%, pension cost funding of $65 is required; if only $50 is funded, 77% ($50/$65) of the $100 computed cost or $77 is assignable and allocable to the current period.

  - For nonqualified defined-benefit plans that do not meet the communication, nonforfeiture, or funding criteria or are accounted for under the pay-as-you-go cost method, the amount assignable and allocable is the net benefit paid for the period, plus a level 15-year annual installment required to amortize any amount paid to irrevocably settle an obligation for current of future benefits.

- With regard to prior unfunded accruals and unallocated credits:

  - Prior accruals that were not assigned to prior years and which were unfunded because they exceeded full funding/maximum deductible limits can be assigned to future periods.

  - Prior year unfunded accruals that were previously assigned to prior years because the payment of benefits could be compelled must be treated as assets and applied against the actuarial accrued liability or the benefits paid under the pay-as-you-go method.

The 1995 revision to CAS 412 effectively made moot prior ASBCA and Federal Circuit decisions that allowed the costs of the Boeing Company's[52] Supplemental

Executive Retirement Plan. The plan was funded only when the costs ultimately became deductible for IRS purposes. Since the payment of benefits could be compelled, the then-existing CAS 412 required the actuarially computed pension costs to be assigned to a cost accounting period and allocated to that period's cost objectives (e.g., contracts). The FAR cost principle at the time limited cost allowability to the lesser of the actuarially computed pension costs or the amount deductible for federal income tax purposes for the year. In its decision, the Board observed that "whether based on its own official standing or on the basis of its incorporation in the Defense Acquisition Regulation, CAS 412 has the force and effect of law. . . . We hold that CAS 412 is controlling with respect to the determination, measurement, assignment and allocation of [the retirement plan] costs."

The original standard became effective on January 1, 1976, and was applicable on the start of the next cost accounting period, following receipt of a covered contract. The standard was revised on March 30, 1995, and must be followed on or after the start of the next fiscal year after receipt of a covered contract.

Adjustment and Allocation of Pension Cost (Standard 413—48 CFR 9904.413)

Cost Accounting Standards 413 provides guidelines for (1) measuring actuarial gains and losses and assigning them to cost accounting periods, (2) valuing pension fund assets, and (3) allocating pension costs to segments. Cost Accounting Standards 413 was also significantly revised in 1995. The following are the more important provisions of the current standard:

- Actuarial gains and losses must be calculated annually and amortized over a 15-year period. Gains and losses that are not material may be included as a component of the current or following year's pension cost. The amount included in the current year must include the amortized amount of the gain or loss for the year plus interest for the unamortized balance as of the beginning of the period.

- Any recognized pension fund valuation method may be used. However, if the method results in a value that is outside a corridor of 80% to 120% of the assets' market value, the value must be adjusted to the nearest boundary of the corridor.

- Pension costs for segments generally may be calculated either on a composite basis or by separate computation. However, pension costs must be separately calculated for a segment when the costs at the segment are materially affected by any of the following conditions:

  - The segment experiences material termination gains or losses.

  - The level of benefits, eligibility for benefits, or age distribution is materially different for the segment than for the company as a whole.

  - The aggregate of actuarial assumptions for termination, retirement age, or salary scale is materially different for the segment than for the company as a whole.

  - The ratios of pension fund assets to actuarial liabilities for merged segments are different after applying the benefits in effect after the merger.

- Contractors that separately calculate pension costs for one or more segments have the option of establishing a separate segment for inactive participants, such as retirees.

- When either a pension plan is terminated, a segment is closed, or benefits are curtailed, the contractor must determine the difference between the market value of the pension fund assets allocated to the segment and the segment's actuarial accrued liability (measured by either the payment to the Pension Benefit Guarantee Corporation or the payment to settle all benefit obligations). The difference, calculated as of the date of the event, is treated as an adjustment of previously determined pension costs. The adjustment amount is reduced by any excise tax imposed on the assets withdrawn from the fund. The government's share of any pension plan reversion or unfunded liability is determined by the ratio of (1) the pension costs allocated to fully CAS-covered contracts for a period representative of the government's participation in the pension plan to (2) total pension costs assigned during the same period. The government's share may be recognized by modifying one or more contracts or by some other suitable technique.

  – A segment closing occurs when a segment (1) has been sold or its ownership transferred, (2) has discontinued operations, or (3) has discontinued doing or actively seeking government business under contracts subject to the standard.

  – A plan termination occurs when either the pension plan ceases to exist and all benefits are settled by purchase of annuities or other means, or the trusteeship of the plan is assumed by the Pension Benefit Guarantee Corporation or other conservator. The plan may or may not be replaced by another plan.

  – Benefits are curtailed when the pension plan is frozen and no further material benefits accrue. Further service may be the basis for vesting of nonvested benefits existing at the time of the curtailment. The plan may hold assets, pay benefits already accrued, and receive additional contributions for unfunded benefits. The employees may or may not continue working for the contractor.

In *Teledyne Continental Motors, General Products Division*,[53] the Board ruled that use of an active employee head-count base to allocate past service costs, supplemental benefits costs, and retirement bonus costs did not comply with CAS 413.50(c)(1), which requires that the base be representative of the factors on which the pension benefits are based.

In a decision addressing the standard's original provisions,[54] the ASBCA concluded as follows in *NI Industries, Inc.*:

- Terminating a defined-benefit plan and replacing it with a defined-contribution plan is not a change in cost accounting practice. Rather, "[t]he establishment for the first time of a defined contribution pension plan for salaried employees at the Vernon Division amounts to the 'initial adoption of an accounting practice for the first time incurrence of a cost [which] is not a change in cost accounting practice.'"

- Because the then-existing CAS 413 did not address the situation in which a pension plan is terminated but no segment is closed, the Board had "no authority to overcome such omission by creating a new standard to cover a 'situation' somewhat 'similar to' that described in CAS 413.50(c)(12). Any attempt to do so would usurp powers expressly granted to the CASB."

- A reversion resulting from the termination of a defined-benefit pension plan is not an actuarial gain; therefore, the reversion is not required to be amortized over current and future cost accounting periods.

- An appropriate share of the reversion relating to allowable pension costs that were allocated to cost-type and fixed-price incentive awards should be credited to the government. The government's share is payable on active cost-type and fixed-price incentive contracts pursuant to the "credits" provision in the cost principles. The government's share is payable on closed cost-type contracts pursuant to the Contractor's Assignment of Refunds, Rebates, Credits, and Other Amounts, executed at contract closing.

The second and fourth points effectively became moot as a result of the March 30, 1995 revision to CAS 413.

In a complex decision addressing the treatment of pension revision resulting from Gould, Inc.'s sale of five divisions in 1987 and 1988,[55] the ASBCA again interpreted the requirements outlined in the original CAS 413-50(c)(12). This provision required a final accounting of the difference between the actuarial liability and the market value of the pension fund assets if a segment was closed. Gould's pensions plans were not terminated as a result of the sales. Highlights of the Board's decision are as follows:

- The sales of the Gould divisions constituted segment closings within the meaning of CAS 413-50(c)(12).

- Actuarial assumptions used in the final accounting can only be revised from those used in the measurement of annual pension costs to the extent that such assumptions are impacted by the changed circumstances, that is, the closure of the segment. The Board rejected Gould's change in assumptions related to interest rates and mortality because the amount of interest the fund would earn and the rate at which participants would die was not affected by the sales of the divisions. The Board accepted Gould's change in the assumption relating to retirement age, however, because the divisions' sales could impact the decisions by Gould's former employees as to whether to continue working or retire earlier and immediately draw a Gould pension.

- The government was not entitled to recover that portion of the reversion allocable to firm-fixed-price contracts. (This point is effectively made moot by the March 30, 1995 revision to CAS 413).

The original standard became effective on March 10, 1978, and was applicable at the start of the next cost accounting period, following receipt of a covered contract. The standard was revised on March 30, 1995. The revised standard must be followed on or after the start of the next fiscal year after receipt of a covered contract.

Cost of Money as an Element of the Cost of Facilities Capital (Standard 414—48 CFR 9904.414)

Cost Accounting Standards 414 recognizes facilities capital cost of money (FCCOM) as an allocable contract cost. The standard provides criteria for measuring and allocating the cost of capital committed to facilities. The following are the more important provisions of the standard:

- Facilities capital cost of money is an imputed cost which is identified with the facilities capital associated with each indirect expense pool. Facilities capital cost of money is allocated to contracts over the same base used to allocate the other expenses in the cost pool in which it is included. For example, manufacturing cost of money is allocated to contracts using the same manufacturing direct labor base that is used to allocate manufacturing overhead.

- The FCCOM rate is based on rates published semiannually by the Secretary of the Treasury.

- Form CASB-CMF is used for calculating FCCOM factors. (See Appendix 8.5.)

- The following are procedures for calculating FCCOM:

  - The average net book value of facilities for each indirect expense pool is identified from accounting data used for contract costing. Unless there is a major fluctuation, the beginning and ending asset balances for the year may be averaged to arrive at the average net book value. The facilities capital values should be the same values used to generate depreciation or amortization that is allowed for federal contract costing purposes plus the value of land that is integral to the regular operation of the business unit. Since the standard provides that the facilities should be used in the regular business activity, the following should be eliminated from the cost of money computation: facilities or facility capacity that have been determined to be excess or idle and assets that are under construction or have not yet been put into service.

  - The FCCOM devoted to facilities capital for each indirect pool is the product of these net book values and the cost of money rates published by the Secretary of the Treasury.

  - FCCOM factors are computed by dividing the cost of money for each pool by the appropriate allocation base.

  - FCCOM is separately estimated, accumulated, and reported for each contract.

Once FCCOM indirect expense rates are calculated, they must be applied to the base costs incurred or estimated for each contract. Worksheet memorandum records may be used to allocate FCCOM to the incurred base costs of flexibly priced contracts. A worksheet distributing FCCOM to contracts is illustrated in Figure 8.4.

The net book value of assets and the resultant cost of money must be segregated between land, buildings, and equipment to calculate FCCOM applicable to a particular proposal. The calculations are made on DD Form 1861 and are included on the cost proposal as separate cost elements. The use of this form in calculating the preaward negotiation profit objective is discussed in greater detail in Chapter 4.

Two CAS Steering Committee interim guidance papers were issued in connection with CAS 414. Interim Guidance Paper W.G. 77-18 covers a number of issues, including: (1) types of facilities not subject to cost of money; (2) allocation of FCCOM to IR&D and B&P projects; (3) revisions to disclosure statements to include procedures related to CAS 414; and (4) application of CAS 414 to price proposals. Interim Guidance Paper W.G. 77-18 concluded that the cost of facilities capital allocable to IR&D and B&P costs is unallowable if it exceeded

Cost Element	FCCOM Factor	Contract A	Contract B	Contract C
Direct material costs		$1,100,000	$200,000	$1,000,000
Material COM	15.00%	$ 1,650	$ 300	$ 150,000
Engineering direct Labor $		$ 330,000	$ 50,000	$ 200,000
Engineering COM	4.2019%	$ 13,866	$ 2,101	$ 8,404
Manufacturing Direct labor $		$1,210,000	$125,000	$ 800,000
Manufacturing COM	18.9844%	$ 229,711	$ 23,730	$ 151,875
Technical computer hours		280	100	200
Technical computer COM	16.4311/hr	$ 4,601	$ 1,643	$ 3,286
Total cost input base		$5,369,000	$705,000	$3,250,000
G&A COM	.1035%	$ 5,557	$ 730	$ 3,364

Figure 8.4 Allocation of Facilities Capital Cost of Money to Government Contracts

negotiated IR&D and B&P ceiling. While contractors voiced strong and persistent disagreement with the DOD's position, the issue has become moot since ceilings are no longer applied to IR&D and B&P costs. Interim Guidance Paper W.G. 77-19 discusses the treatment of leased property under CAS 414 and concludes that cost of money should be included as an ownership cost in determining whether allowable cost will be based on cost of ownership or leasing costs.

In *Gould Defense Systems Inc.*,[56] the ASBCA addressed the inclusion of goodwill in the net book value of the assets used to calculate FCCOM on Form CASB-CMF. The Board concluded that, under the then-existing cost principles, goodwill, if properly amortized and allocated, would generate allowable amortization cost and could be used in computing the cost of FCCOM. The precedence established by the decision was short lived, because the FAR cost principles were soon revised to disallow goodwill amortization costs and cost of money resulting from including goodwill in the asset base. Because of Gould's historical failure to amortize goodwill and claim it as an allowable cost, the disallowance of cost of facilities capital attributable to goodwill was sustained from October 1979 until amortization and allocation commenced. However, because of the government's prior approval of Gould's practice, the government was estopped from excluding goodwill in the CAS 414 calculations before October 1979.

In *Fiesta Leasing and Sales, Inc.*[57] the ASBCA focused on the reclassification of depreciation and FCCOM costs from indirect to direct as the result of contract termination. The Board allowed the continuing cost of depreciation on buses used in contract performance and the FCCOM associated with the facilities capital invested in the buses on Fiesta's terminated bus leasing contract.

In *Williams International Inc.*,[58] the ASBCA concluded that the contractor could not include the net book value of corporate aircraft in the asset base used to calculate FCCOM if an advance agreement precluded recovery of the corporate aircraft costs.

In *Engineering, Inc.,*[59] the issue was whether FCCOM should be included as an element of constructive ownership costs in determining allowable operating lease costs in a related-party lease, if FCCOM was waived as an allowable cost under the contract. Engineering, Inc. did not propose facilities capital cost of money in its NASA cost-type contract. It did, however, propose the full operating lease costs of two buildings leased from a trust whose beneficiary was the company president. The cost principle on rental costs limited those costs between related parties to the normal costs of ownership, such as depreciation, taxes, insurance, facilities capital cost of money, and maintenance. The government contended that since cost of money was waived under the subject contract, it should be excluded from ownership cost in determining the amount to be allowed. The Board disagreed. In concluding that Interim Guidance Paper W.G. 77-19 did not support the government's interpretation, the Board noted that the guidance paper

> ... does not dictate exclusion of FCCOM from the cost of ownership comparison when it is otherwise an unallowable cost under a particular contract. It states, without qualification, that FCCOM should be included as an ownership cost in determining whether allowable cost is to be based on constructive ownership costs or rental costs.

In *Raytheon Co.,*[60] the Board addressed the treatment of land held for expansion. Following the guidance in CAS Steering Committee Interim Guidance Paper W.G. 77-18, the government concluded that land held for expansion should be eliminated from the asset base used to calculate FCCOM. Raytheon's land had been purchased to expand the facilities of one of its divisions, but the planned expansion was prevented because of zoning restrictions imposed by the local government. Noting that a business must expand to stay competitive and meet growing demands for its products, the Board concluded the following:

> ... [S]uch expansion is therefore integral to the regular operation of the business unit for purposes of the Form CASB-CMF instructions, and it meets the benefit test of necessary to the overall operation of the business.

Accounting for the Cost of Deferred Compensation (Standard 415—48 CFR 9904.415)

Cost Accounting Standards 415 provides criteria for measuring deferred compensation costs and assigning such costs to cost accounting periods. The standard covers deferred compensation awards made in cash, stock, stock options, or other assets. The following are the more important provisions of the standard:

- Deferred compensation costs must be assigned to current cost accounting periods whenever a valid obligation has been incurred (accrual basis) and future funding is assured. The following criteria are provided for determining whether a valid obligation for deferred compensation costs has been incurred.
  - A future payment is required.
  - The payment is to be made in money, other assets, or shares of stock of the contractor.
  - The amount due can be measured with reasonable accuracy.
  - The recipient is known.
  - There is a reasonable probability that any conditions required for the payment will occur.
  - There is a reasonable probability that any stock options will be exercised.

If no obligation is incurred before payment, the cost should be assigned to the period(s) of payment.

- The cost of deferred compensation (i.e., amounts to be paid in the future) must be measured by the present value of the future benefits to be paid. A commercial borrowing rate published semiannually by the Secretary of the Treasury is prescribed for discounting the future payments.

- For awards that require future service, costs should be assigned to cost accounting periods as the future services are performed.

- The cost of deferred compensation must be reduced by forfeitures in the cost accounting periods in which the forfeitures occur. A recipient's voluntary failure to exercise stock options is not considered a forfeiture.

- For deferred compensation to be paid in money, various methods are described to recognize interest, if provided for in the award.

- The cost assignable for stock awards is the market value of the stock on the date the shares are awarded.

- The cost assignable for stock options is the excess of the market value of the stock over the option price on the date the options for the specific number of shares are awarded. Consequently, no cost is assigned to options awarded at market value.

The standard became effective on July 10, 1977, and was applicable at the start of the next cost accounting period, following award of a covered contract.

Accounting for Insurance Costs (Standard 416—48 CFR 9904.416)

Cost Accounting Standards 416 provides criteria for measuring, assigning, and allocating insurance costs. The principle requirement of the standard is that the insurance cost assigned to a cost accounting period is the projected average loss for that period plus insurance administration expenses. Other important provisions are as follows:

- Insurance premiums or payments to a trusteed fund, properly prorated and adjusted for applicable refunds, dividends, or additional assessments, should represent the projected average loss.

- For exposure to risk of loss not covered by insurance premiums or payments to a trusteed fund, a program of self-insurance accounting must be developed. If insurance can be purchased against the self-insured risk, the cost of such insurance may be used to estimate the projected average loss. If purchased insurance is not available, the projected average loss should be based on the contractor's experience, relevant industry experience, and anticipated conditions using appropriate actuarial principles. Actual losses can only be charged to insurance expense when they are expected to approximate the projected average loss or are paid to retirees under a self-insurance program.

- Actual loss experience must be evaluated regularly for comparison with the self-insurance cost used to estimate the projected average loss. Actual losses should be measured by the actual cash value of property destroyed, amounts paid or accrued to repair damages, amounts paid or accrued to estates and beneficiaries, and amounts paid or accrued to compensate claimants.

- Insurance costs should generally be allocated on the basis of the factors used to determine the premium or assessment.
- Necessary records must be maintained to substantiate amounts of premiums, refunds, dividends, losses, and self-insurance charges and the measurements and allocation of insurance costs.

The standard became effective on July 10, 1979, and was applicable at the start of the next fiscal year, following receipt of a contract subject to the standard.

Cost of Money as an Element of the Cost of Capital Assets Under Construction (Standard 417—48 CFR 9904.417)

Cost Accounting Standards 417 provides for including an imputed cost of money in the capitalized cost of assets constructed for a contractor's own use. The concept is the same as that in CAS 414, which provides criteria for measuring and allocating cost of money as part of the cost of facilities capital. Pertinent provisions are as follows:

- The cost of money to be capitalized must reflect the application of the commercial borrowing rates published semiannually by the Secretary of the Treasury to a representative investment amount for the period that considers the rate at which construction costs are incurred.
- Other methods for calculating cost of money, such as the method used for financial reporting, may be used, provided the result is not substantially different from the amount calculated as described above.

The standard became effective on December 15, 1980, and was applicable at the start of the next cost accounting period, following receipt of a covered contract.

A calculation of COM for a capital asset under construction is illustrated in Figure 8.5.

Allocation of Direct and Indirect Cost (Standard 418—48 CFR 9904.418)

Cost Accounting Standards 418 requires that a contractor have a written policy for distinguishing between direct and indirect costs and that such costs be consistently classified. A *direct cost* is defined as a cost that is identified specifically with a particular final cost objective. An *indirect cost* is defined as a cost that is identified with two or more final cost objectives or with at least one intermediate cost objective. Pertinent provisions of the standard are as follows:

- Indirect costs must be accumulated in homogeneous cost pools. A cost pool is considered homogeneous if: (1) the major activities in the pool have similar beneficial/causal relationships to cost objectives, or (2) separate allocations of costs of dissimilar activities would not result in substantially different amounts.
- Materiality is a key consideration in whether heterogeneous cost pools must be separately allocated. No changes in the existing indirect cost pool structure are required if the allocations resulting from the existing base(s) are not materially different from the allocations that would result from using discrete homogeneous cost pools.

	Fiscal Year 1	Fiscal Year 2	Total Period of Construction in Progress
Months project under construction	10	3	
Average investment for months under construction (A)	$245,000[1]	$1,234,000[2]	
Time-weighted cost of money (COM) rate based on rates in effect during the construction period (B)	8.75%[3]	8.5%[3]	
Portion of year to which COM rate should be applied (C)	10/12	3/12	
Amount of COM to be capitalized (A) (B) (C)	$ 17,865	$ 26,223	$ 44,088
Total construction cost			$1,500,000
COM capitalized			$ 44,088
Depreciable base for completed asset			$1,544,088

[1]If costs are incurred at a fairly uniform rate, a simple average of the beginning and ending balances may be used to find the representative amount. If costs are not incurred at a uniform rate, each of the month-end balances should be totaled to compute the average investment.

[2]The average investment includes the COM capitalized in the prior fiscal year.

[3]The COM rates are weighted by the number of months each rate is in effect during the construction period.

Figure 8.5   Calculation of Cost of Money for an Asset under Construction

- A cost pool that includes a significant amount of direct labor or direct material management activities should be allocated on a base representative of the activity being managed. A machine-hour base may be used if the costs in the pool are predominantly facility-related. A unit of production base is appropriate if there is common production of comparable units. A material costs base is appropriate if the activity being managed or supervised is a material-related activity. If none of these bases are appropriate, a direct labor hour or direct labor cost base will be used, whichever is more likely to vary in proportion to the cost included in the pool. A cost pool that does not include a significant amount of labor or material management activities should be allocated in accordance with the following hierarchy of preferred bases: (1) a resource consumption measure, (2) an output measure, and (3) a surrogate representative of resources consumed.

- A special allocation of indirect costs is permitted where a particular cost objective receives significantly more or less benefit from an indirect cost pool than would result from a normal allocation of such costs.

Problems have occasionally surfaced regarding the extent and frequency of analyses required to demonstrate that separate allocations of dissimilar activities would not result in materially different allocations from amounts allocated under existing cost pools.

The standard became effective on September 20, 1980, and was applicable on the start of the second fiscal year after receipt of a covered contract.

In *Litton Systems, Inc.*,[61] the ASBCA overruled the ACO's determination that CAS 418 unequivocally prohibits the use of multifacility, division-wide average direct labor rates and overhead rates. In its decision, the Board observed:

[T]he indirect cost pools are not considered homogeneous for the purpose of CAS 418 unless (1) all significant activities in the pool has [*sic*] the same or a similar beneficial or causal relationship to cost objectives; or (2) the costs, if allocated separately, would not result in [a] materially different allocation than the allocation from the common pool. There is no proof that a "materially different" allocation would have resulted if separate indirect cost pools were established. The Government did not carry its burden to prove CAS 418 noncompliance of the indirect costs.

Accounting for Independent Research and Development Costs and Bid and Proposal Costs (Standard 420—48 CFR 9904.420)

Cost Accounting Standards 420 provides criteria for accumulating IR&D and B&P costs and for allocating those costs to final cost objectives. Independent research and development expenses are identified as technical effort that is neither sponsored by a grant nor required for performance of a contract, and that falls into the area of basic and applied research, development, or systems and other concept formulation studies. Bid and proposal costs are those incurred in preparing, submitting, or supporting any bid or proposal that is neither sponsored by a grant nor required for contractor performance. The standard covers such costs incurred at both the home office and the business unit levels. The major provisions are as follows:

- Independent research and development and B&P costs are to be identified and accumulated by project, except when the costs of individual projects are not material.

- Independent research and development and B&P project costs include all allocable costs except business unit G&A. In essence, IR&D and B&P projects are treated like final cost objectives except for the allocation of G&A expenses.

- Independent research and development costs generally may not be deferred, and B&P costs may not be deferred.

- Independent research and development and B&P projects performed by one segment for another segment are considered final cost objectives of the performing segment, rather than IR&D and B&P projects, unless the work is part of an IR&D or B&P project of the performing segment. In that case, the IR&D or B&P project will be transferred to the home office for reallocation to the benefiting segments.

- Independent research and development and B&P costs accumulated at the home office level are allocated to specific segments where projects are identified with such segments; otherwise, the costs are allocated to all segments using the CAS 403 residual expense allocation base. Segment IR&D and B&P costs are allocated to contracts using the G&A base.

- The standard provides for a special allocation of IR&D and B&P costs at either the home office or the segment level if a particular segment (for home office costs) or a particular final cost objective (for segment costs) receives significantly more or less benefit from IR&D and B&P costs than would result from the normal allocation of such costs.

The DOD's Indirect Cost Monitoring Office[62] concluded in 1981 that a segment using a total cost input base to allocate G&A expense may, under CAS 420, use a "modified" total cost input base to allocate IR&D/B&P expense. The guidance considered the modified base appropriate when certain contracts receive significantly more or less benefit from IR&D/B&P than would be allocated under the normal G&A base. This situation could occur, for example, if particular contracts contain subcontracts for work that is outside the contractor's normal product line.

The ASBCA denied QuesTech, Inc.'s attempt to retroactively allocate IR&D costs to two domestic segments that performed government work after it learned about a military application for the research.[63] QuesTech Ventures, Inc. (QVI), a subsidiary of QuesTech, Inc., was established to perform the R&D. QuesTech, Inc. argued that QVI was not a segment and, therefore, the R&D costs incurred by QVI were properly accumulated as home office R&D and allocated to the two domestic segments. However, QuesTech's annual report identified QVI as one of three domestic segments that were formed to focus on distinct markets and specific customer bases. The ASBCA ruled that QVI was a segment within the meaning of CAS 420 and that the R&D costs were properly accumulated as QVI's costs, not home office costs. In the Board's view, even though QVI's only activity was a single IR&D project, its efforts were typical of those of a new business venture.

Educational Institutions

Consistency in Estimating, Accumulating, and Reporting Costs by Educational Institutions (Standard 501—48 CFR 9905.501)

This standard requires that consistency be applied as follows:

- The practices used in estimating costs for a proposal must be consistent with the cost accounting practices followed by the institution in accumulating and reporting actual contract costs. The standard permits grouping of like costs when it is not practicable to estimate contract costs by individual cost element or function. However, costs estimated for proposal purposes must be presented in such a manner and in sufficient detail so that any significant cost can be compared with the actual cost accumulated and reported.

- The standard specifically requires consistency in: (1) classification of elements or functions of cost as direct or indirect; (2) indirect cost pools to which each element or function of cost is charged or proposed to be charged; and (3) methods used in allocating indirect costs to the contract.

Unlike CAS 401, which applies to commercial companies, CAS 501 does not contain any illustrations of practices that are deemed to be either "consistent" or "nonconsistent."

The standard became effective January 9, 1995.

Consistency in Allocating Costs Incurred for the Same Purpose by Educational Institution (Standard 502—48 CFR 9905.502)

The standard requires that each type of cost be allocated only once and on only one basis. Its intent is to preclude the "double counting" of costs that occurs when cost items are allocated directly to cost objectives without eliminating like items from indirect cost pools. An example of double counting is charging the cost of travel directly to a contract and, at the same time, including similar costs incurred in substantially the same circumstances in an overhead pool that is allocated to all cost objectives, including that contract. The standard relates to the system as a whole and not necessarily to the treatment of individual contracts.

Cost Accounting Standards 501 does not permit a specific contract to receive a cost charged to it as a direct cost if the same cost incurred in like circumstances is also included in an overhead pool, but not allocated to that contract.

The key is determining whether the cost is incurred for the same purpose and in like circumstances. If either the purpose or the circumstances differ, the accounting practices related to the two separate transactions need not be consistent and would not be covered by this standard. If an institution has submitted a disclosure statement, it should provide sufficient criteria for determining whether a particular cost in a given circumstance is treated as a direct or indirect cost.

Interpretation No. 1 to CAS 502 addresses the question of B&P costs. The interpretation makes clear that B&P costs are not always incurred for the same purpose and in like circumstances. Bid and proposal costs specifically required by contractual terms and conditions, on a consistent basis, can be properly treated as direct costs, whereas other B&P costs may be recorded as indirect costs.

The standard became effective January 9, 1995.

Accounting for Unallowable Costs (Standard 505—48 CFR 9905.505)

The standard sets forth guidelines for identifying in the institution's accounting records specific costs that are unallowable and the cost accounting treatment of such costs. Cost Accounting Standards 505 does not provide criteria for determining the allowability of costs; this is a function of the appropriate procurement or reviewing authority. Rather, the standard establishes the accounting treatment and reporting requirements after the costs are determined to be unallowable. The following are the fundamental requirements of the standard:

- Institutions must identify in their accounting records, and exclude from proposals, billings, or claims, costs specifically described as expressly unallowable or unallowable by mutual agreement of the contracting parties, including directly associated costs that are mutually agreed to be unallowable.
- Institutions must identify (1) costs designated as unallowable as a result of a written decision by a CO pursuant to contract dispute procedures; and (2) the costs of any work project not contractually authorized.
- Costs specifically described as unallowable, as well as directly associated costs, must be included in any indirect allocation base or bases in which they would normally be included.

The standard became effective January 9, 1995.

Cost Accounting Period (Standard 506—48 CFR 9905.506)

Except in the following specific circumstances, CAS 506 requires an institution to use its normal fiscal year as its cost accounting period.

- When costs of an indirect function exist for only part of a cost accounting period, they may be allocated to cost objectives of that same part of the period.
- Another fixed annual period other than a fiscal year (e.g., the school year), may be used upon mutual agreement with the government if it is an established practice and is consistently used.

- Transitional periods may be used in connection with a change in fiscal year. If the transition period between the end of the previous fiscal year and the beginning of the next fiscal year is three months or less, it may be (1) treated as a stand-alone cost accounting period, (2) combined with the previous fiscal year, or (3) combined with the next regular fiscal year. If the transition period is more than three months, it must be treated as a stand-alone period.

- When an expense, such as pension cost, is identified with a fixed, recurring annual period that is different from the contractor's cost accounting period, and is consistently employed, its use may be continued.

The cost accounting period used for accumulating costs in an indirect cost pool must be the same as the period used for establishing related allocation bases. Indirect expense rates used for estimating, accumulating, and reporting costs—including progress payments and public vouchers—should be based on the established annual cost accounting period.

The standard became effective on January 9, 1995.

8-5. SUMMARY

The cost accounting standards affect many organizations doing business with the federal government and have significantly affected many accounting systems. In addition to the records needed for financial reporting and tax return preparation, some contractors must maintain a third set of records to comply with the standards. These problems are a particular concern to contractors whose government business is immaterial in relation to their total business.

The impact of CAS on accounting systems varies with the amount of government business performed by the contractor, the contractor's size, and the sophistication of its recordkeeping function. The contractor whose principal business is with the government may change its cost accounting practices used for financial reporting purposes to conform with cost accounting standards, unless management finds that such costing techniques are not responsive to its operational requirements. Medium-sized and smaller contractors may find it necessary, upon becoming subject to cost accounting standards, to make significant changes in their formal cost accounting practices if separate memorandum recordkeeping is not economically or practically feasible.

As a result of CASB disclosure statement requirements, contractors have found it necessary to formalize and reduce to writing their cost accounting practices. These practices serve management in the detailed operational analysis and control of their businesses. Changing business conditions and management philosophy, as well as improvements in accounting and operational techniques, often require contractors to alter their practices. Contractors find the procedures cumbersome for effecting such changes in cost accounting practices.

The impact of cost accounting standards goes beyond the need to develop and maintain new accounting systems. Standards can affect companies' profits and resulting capital accumulation and, if such effect is adverse, can discourage companies from pursuing government work and thus weaken the base of suppliers available to satisfy the government's needs. The more significant issues raised by industry are: (1) CASB standards are too detailed and rigid, favor the government, and give little attention to alternatives; and (2) the costs of adoption have not been sufficiently weighed against the benefits to be derived.

However, there have been some positive effects from cost accounting standards. By requiring more objective allocation techniques and by limiting alternative accounting procedures through more specified criteria, contract costing has become more comparable and consistent. Cost Accounting Standards regulations have also provided a more structured framework for effecting changes in cost accounting practices. Finally, the disclosure statement has proven to be a useful document for gaining a mutual understanding of the practices to be used in costing government contracts.

Compliance with cost accounting standards should not be taken lightly. Since failure to comply can result in adverse adjustments of costs and profits, companies subject to CAS, as well as those potentially subject and their lawyers and accountants, must become knowledgeable in this significant area.

8-6. NOTES

1. Defense Production Act Amendments, 82 Stat. 279, 50 U.S.C.S. Appx. 2162, 2166, 2167, enacted July 1, 1968, Pub. L 90-370.
2. Elmer B. Staats, Report on Feasibility of Applying Uniform Cost Accounting Standards to Negotiated Defense Contracts B-39995. Washington, DC: Government Printing Office, 1970.
3. Defense Production Act Amendments, 84 Stat. 796, 50 U.S.C.S. Appx. 2091, 2152, 2166, 2168, enacted Aug. 15, 1970, Pub. L. 91-379.
4. Office of Federal Procurement Policy Act Amendments of 1988, 41 U.S.C. §422, 97 Stat. 1325, enacted Nov. 17, 1988, Pub. L. 100-679.
5. The Boeing Co., Ct. Cl. 1982, No. 268-79C, June 2, 1982, 680 F.2d 132.
6. The Boeing Co., ASBCA No. 28342, Sept. 17, 1985, 85-3 BCA 18,435.
7. Donald B. Rice, Secretary of the Air Force v. Martin Marietta Corp., CAFC No. 93-1025, Dec. 29, 1993, 13 F.3d 1563.
8. Federal Register, Vol. 57, No. 134, July 13, 1992, pp. 31036–31040.
9. Cost Accounting Standards Preamble A, Item 6, Feb. 29, 1972.
10. Clinger–Cohen Act of 1996, formerly known as Federal Acquisition Reform Act of 1996, enacted Feb. 10, 1996, Pub. L. 104–106.
11. Gulf Oil Trading Co., Comp. Gen. No. B-184333, March 11, 1976, 55 Comp. Gen. 881.
12. Aydin Corp. (West), ASBCA No. 42760, April 18, 1994, 94-2 BCA 26,899; aff'd. in part, CAFC No. 94-1441, Aug. 10, 1995, 61 F.3d 1571.
13. AiResearch Manufacturing Co., ASBCA No. 20998, Nov. 29, 1976, 76-2 BCA 12,150; aff'd. May 13, 1977, 77-1 BCA 12,546.
14. Martin Marietta Corp., ASBCA Nos. 38920, 41565, Sept. 4, 1992, 92-3 BCA 25,175; CAFC No. 93-1164, Feb. 10, 1995, 47 F.3d 1134.
15. Federal Register, Vol. 62, No. 134, July 14, 1997, pp. 37654–37692.
16. Peter J. Petkas vs. Elmer B. Staats, Civil Action No. 2238-72, DC D of C, Aug. 23, 1973; No. 73-2153, CA DC, July 25, 1974.
17. Elmer B. Staats, supra, note 2.
18. Texas Instruments, Inc., ASBCA No. 18621, March 30, 1979, 79-1 BCA 13,800; aff'd. Nov. 20, 1979, 79-2 BCA 14,184.
19. Dayton T. Brown, Inc., ASBCA No. 22810, Sept. 29, 1978, 78-2 BCA 13,484; rev'd June 11, 1980, 80-2 BCA 14,543.
20. The Boeing Co., Boeing Military Airplane Division, ASBCA No. 29793, Dec. 3, 1987, 88-1 BCA 20,380; rev'd CAFC No. 88-1298, Nov. 30, 1988, 862 F.2d 290.
21. CACI, Inc., Comp. Gen. No. B-216516, Nov. 19, 984, 32 CCF 73,159.
22. Syscon Corp., Comp. Gen. No. B-233478, March 7, 1989, 3 Comp. Gen. 102974.
23. Aydin Corp. (West), supra, note 12.
24. Aydin Corp. (West), ASBCA No. 42760, Dec. 12, 1995, 96-1 BCA 28,134.
25. The Boeing Co., ASBCA No. 19224, Feb. 4, 1977, 77-1 BCA 12,371; aff'd. Jan. 31, 1979, 79-1 BCA 13,708.
26. The Boeing Co., supra, note 5.

27. The Boeing Co., Petition for a Writ of Certiorari, No. 82-1024; cert. denied April 18, 1983.

28. Lockheed Corp. and Lockheed Missiles and Space Co., Inc., ASBCA No. 22451, Dec. 26, 1979, 80-1 BCA 14,222; aff'd. June 5, 1980, 80-2 BCA 14,509.

29. Lockheed Corp. and Lockheed Missiles and Space Co., Inc., ASBCA No. 27921, Dec. 11, 1985, 86-1 BCA 18,612.

30. Lockheed Corp. and Lockheed Missiles and Space Co., Inc., CAFC No. 86-1177, April 15, 1987, 817 F.2d 1565.

31. McDonnell Douglas Corp., ASBCA No. 19842, Dec. 26, 1979, 80-2 BCA 14,223; aff'd. June 9, 1980, 80-2 BCA 14,508.

32. Grumman Aerospace Corp. and Grumman Corp., ASBCA No. 23219, Feb. 16, 1982, 82-1 BCA 15,661; aff'd. July 8, 1982, 82-2 BCA 15,933.

33. R&D Associates, ASBCA No. 30750, May 7, 1986, 86-2 BCA 19,062.

34. Hercules, Inc., Ct. Cl. No. 49-89C, Jan. 14, 1991. 22 Cl. Ct. 301.

35. General Dynamics Corp., ASBCA No. 25919, April 18, 1985, 85-2 BCA 18,074.

36. General Dynamics Corp., ASBCA No. 31359, Jan. 6, 1992, 92-1 BCA 24,698.

37. The threshold has been increased periodically since the original promulgation. The $5,000 threshold was established on Feb. 13, 1996.

38. Martin Marietta Corp., supra, note 7.

39. The Marquardt Co., ASBCA No. 29888, July 18, 85-3 BCA 18245; aff'd. June 1, 1986, 86-3 BCA 19,100, CAFC No. 86-1546, 822 F.2d 1573.

40. General Dynamics Corp., supra, note 36.

41. Martin Marietta Corp., ASBCA No. 35895, June 5, 1992, 92-3 BCA 25,094.

42. Aerojet-General Corp., ASBCA No. 34202, Nov. 27, 1989, 90-1 BCA 22,634.

43. Federal Register, Vol. 61, No. 183, Sept. 19, 1996, pp. 49351–49356.

44. Ford Aerospace and Communications Corp., ASBCA No. 23833, Aug. 31, 1983, 83-2 BCA 16,813.

45. Emerson Electric Co., ASBCA No. 30090, Nov. 19, 1986, 87-1 BCA 19,478.

46. General Electric Co., Ct. Cl. No. 25-89C, July 19, 1990, 21 Cl. Ct. 72; aff'd. CAFC No. 90-5157, March 29, 1991, 21 Cl. Ct. 72.

47. Westinghouse Electric Corp., ASBCA No. 25787, Jan. 30, 1985 and Feb. 13, 1985, 85-1 BCA 17,910; aff'd. CAFC No. 85-2200, Feb. 3, 1986, 782 F.2d 1017.

48. Martin Marietta Corp., supra, note 41.

49. Donald B. Rice, Secretary of the Air Force v. Martin Marietta Corp., supra, note 7.

50. Aydin Corp. (West), ASBCA No. 42760, April 18, 1994, 94-2 BCA 26,899; on remand Dec. 12, 1995.

51. Aydin Corp. (West) v. Sheila E. Widnall, Secretary of the Air Force, July 24, 1997, CAFC No. 96-1267, 1997 U.S. App. LEXIS 18959.

52. The Boeing Co., ASBCA No. 28342, Sept. 17, 1985, 85-3 BCA No. 18435; aff'd. CAFC No. 86-927, Oct. 1, 1986, 802 F. 2d 1390.

53. Teledyne Continental Motors, General Products Division, ASBCA No. 24,758, March 22, 1989, 89-2 BCA 21,780.

54. NI Industries, Inc., ASBCA No. 34943, Nov. 29, 1991, 92-1 BCA 24,631; aff'd. April 6, 1992, 92-2 BCA 24,980.

55. Gould, Inc., ASBCA No. 46759, Sept. 22, 1997, 97-2 BCA 29,254.

56. Gould Defense Systems, Inc., ASBCA No. 24881, June 10, 1983, 83-2 BCA 16,676.

57. Fiesta Leasing and Sales, Inc., ASBCA No. 29311, Jan. 30, 1987, 87-1 BCA No. 19,622; aff'd. Jan. 13, 1988, 88-1 BCA 20,499.

58. Williams International Corp., ASBCA No. 28389, Jan. 4, 1988, 88-1 BCA 20,480.

59. Engineering, Inc., NASABCA No. 187-2, May 26, 1988, 88-2 BCA 20,792; aff'd. Nov. 14, 1988, 89-1 BCA No. 21,435.

60. Raytheon Co., ASBCA No. 32419, June 14, 1988, 88-3 BCA 20,899.

61. Litton Systems, Inc., ASBCA No. 37131, Feb. 23, 1994, 94-2 BCA 26,731.

62. Indirect Cost Monitoring Office Memorandum, dated May 11, 1981, reference NAVMAT 08CD/RWL; subject: Application of Cost Accounting Standard 420.50 (f)(2), Special Allocation—IR&D/B&P.

63. QuesTech, Inc., ASBCA No. 45127, June 7, 1995, 95-2 BCA 27,743.

W.G. No.	Subject	Date
76- 1	Implementing CAS 412	Feb. 24, 1976
76- 2	Application of CAS to Contract Modifications and to Orders Placed Under Basic Agreements	Feb. 24, 1976
76- 3	Application of CAS to Subcontracts	Mar. 18, 1976
76- 4	Determining Increased Costs to the Government for CAS Covered FFP Contracts	Oct. 1, 1976
76- 5	Treatment of Implementation Costs Related to Changes in Cost Accounting Practices	Oct. 1, 1976
76- 6	Application of CAS Clauses to Changes in Contractor's Established Practices When a Disclosure Statement Has Been Submitted	Oct. 1, 1976
76- 7	Significance of "Effective" and "Applicability" Dates Included in Cost Accounting Standards	Oct. 1, 1976
76- 8	Use of the Offset Principle in Contract Price Adjustments Resulting From Accounting Changes	Dec. 17, 1976
76- 9	Measurement of Cost Impact of FFP Contracts	Dec. 17, 1976
77-10	Retroactive Implementation of Cost Accounting Standards When Timely Compliance Is Not Feasible	Feb. 2, 1977
77-11	Implementation of CAS 410	Feb. 2, 1977
77-12	Deliberate Noncompliance and Inadvertent Noncompliance	Mar. 29, 1977
77-13	Applicability of CAS 405 to Costs Determined Unallowable on the Basis of Allocability	Mar. 29, 1977
77-14	Early Implementation of New Cost Accounting Standards Issued by the CAS Board	Mar. 29, 1977
77-15	Influence of CAS Regulations on Contract Terminations	Mar. 29, 1977
77-16	Applicability of CAS to Letter Contracts	June 14, 1977
77-17	Identification of CAS Contract Universe at a Contractor's Plant	June 14, 1977
77-18	Implementation of CAS 414 and DPC 76-3	June 14, 1977
77-19	Administration of Leased Facilities Under CAS 414	Aug. 18, 1977
77-20	Policy for Withdrawing Determination of Adequacy of Disclosure Statement	June 14, 1977
78-21	Implementation of CAS 410	Jan. 16, 1978
Amend. 1 to 78-21	Implementation of CAS 410	Apr. 10, 1981
78-22	CAS 409 and the Development of Asset Service Lives	Feb. 6, 1978
79-23	Administration of Equitable Adjustments for Accounting Changes Not Required by New Cost Accounting Standards	Jan. 2, 1979
79-24	Allocation of Business Unit General and Administrative (G&A) Expense to Facilities Contracts	Jan. 26, 1979
81-25	Change in Cost Accounting Practice for State Income and Franchise Taxes as a Result of Change in Method of Reporting Income From Long-Term Contracts	Feb. 10, 1981

Appendix 8.1 Index of CAS Steering Committee Interim Guidance Papers

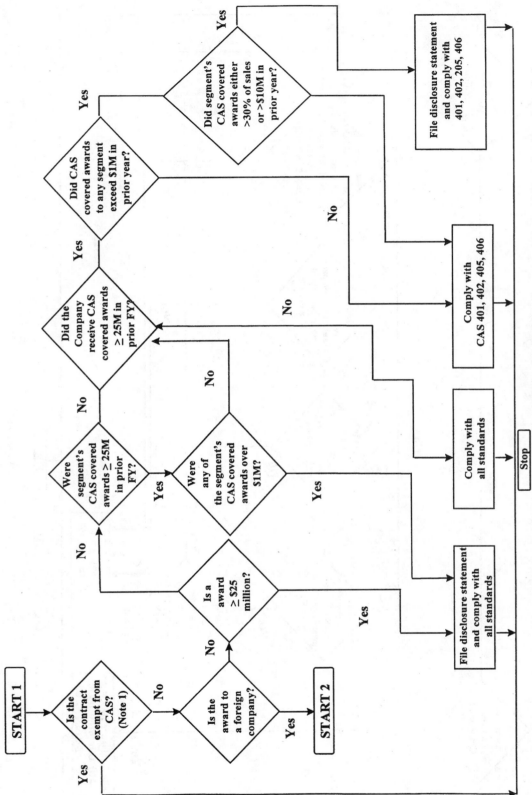

Note 1. Exemptions include all sealed bid contracts and any negotiated awards: (a) that are under $500,000; (b) that are for commercial items; (c) that are based on prices set by law or regulation; (d) to small business concerns; (e) to foreign governments; or (f) for which no cost data was submitted.

Appendix 8.2   CAS Applicability

257

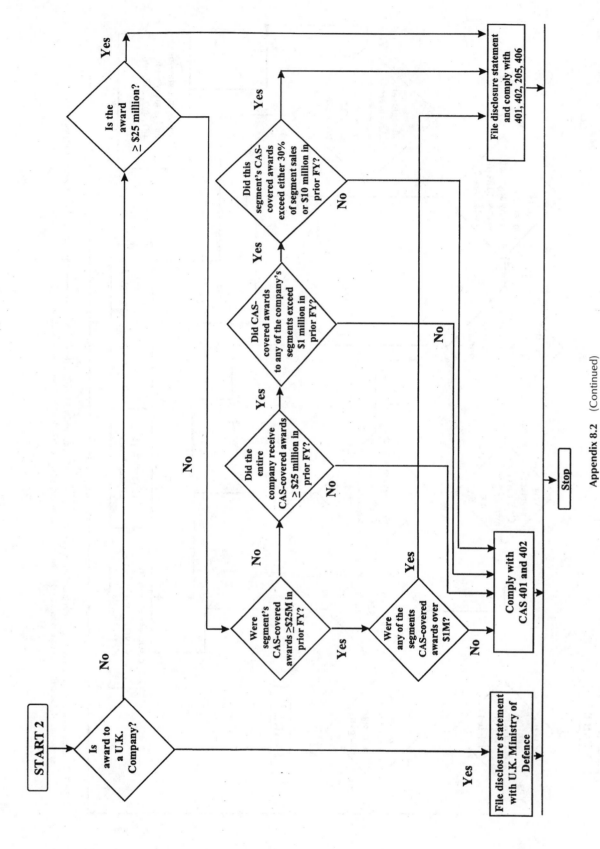

258

Appendix 8.2 (Continued)

FORM APPROVED OMB NUMBER
0348-0051

Appendix 8.3   Form CASB DS-1, Cost Accounting Standards Board Disclosure Statement Required by Public Law 100-679

259

1. This Disclosure Statement has been designed to meet the requirements of Public Law 100-679, and persons completing it are to describe the contractor and its contract cost accounting practices. For complete regulations, instructions and timing requirements concerning submission of the Disclosure Statement, refer to Section 9903.202 of Chapter 99 Of Title 48 CFR (48 CFR 9903.202).

2. Part I of the Statement provides general information concerning each reporting unit (e.g., segment, Corporate or other intermediate level home office, or a business unit). Parts II through VII pertain to the types of costs generally incurred by the segment or business unit directly performing Federal contracts or similar cost objectives. Part VIII pertains to the types of costs that are generally incurred by a Home office and are allocated to one or more segments performing Federal contracts. For a definition of the term "home office", see 48 CFR 9904.403.

3. Each segment or business unit required to disclose its cost accounting practices should complete the Cover Sheet, the Certification, and Parts I through VII.

4. Each home office required to disclose its cost accounting practices for measuring, assigning and allocating its costs to segments performing Federal contracts or similar cost objectives shall complete the Cover Sheet, the Certification, Part I and Part VIII of the Disclosure Statement. Where a home office either establishes practices or procedures for the types of costs covered by Parts V, VI and VII, or incurs and then allocates these types of cost to its segments, the home office may complete Parts V, VI and VII to be included in the Disclosure Statement submitted by its segments. While a home office may have more than one segment submitting Disclosure Statements, only one Statement needs to be submitted to cover the home office operations.

5. The Statement must be signed by an authorized signatory of the reporting unit.

6. The Disclosure Statement should be answered by marking the appropriate line or inserting the applicable letter code which describes the segment's (reporting unit's) cost accounting practices.

7. A number of questions in this Statement may need narrative answers requiring more space than is provided. In such instances, the reporting unit should use the attached continuation sheet provided. The continuation sheet may be reproduced locally as needed. The number of the question involved should be indicated and the same coding required to answer the questions in the Statement should be used in presenting the answer on the continuation sheet. Continuation sheets should be inserted at the end of the pertinent Part of the Statement. On each continuation sheet, the reporting unit should enter the next sequential page number for that Part and, on the last continuation sheet used, the words "End of Part" should be inserted after the last entry.

8. Where the cost accounting practice being disclosed is clearly set forth in the contractor's existing written accounting policies and procedures, such documents may be cited on a continuation sheet and incorporated by reference at the option of the contractor. In such cases, the contractor should provide the date of issuance and effective date for each accounting policy and/or procedures document cited. Alternatively, copies of the relevant parts of such documents may be attached as appendices to the pertinent Disclosure Statement Part. Such continuation sheets and appendices should be labeled and cross-referenced with the applicable Disclosure Statement number and follow the page number specified in paragraph 7. Any supplementary comments needed to adequately describe the cost accounting practice being disclosed should also be provided.

9. Disclosure Statements must be amended when cost accounting practices are changed to comply with a new CAS or when practices are changed with or without knowledge of the Government (Also see 48 CFR 9903.202-3).

FORM CASB DS-1 (REV 2/96)   (i)

Appendix 8.3   (Continued)

10. Amendments shall be submitted to the same offices to which submission would have been made were an original Disclosure Statement filed.

11. Each amendment, or set of amendments should be accompanied by an amended cover sheet (indicating revision number and effective date of the change) and a signed certification. For all resubmissions, on each page, insert "Revision Number ____" and "Effective Date _____" in the Item Description block; and, insert a revision mark (e.g., "R") in the right hand margin of any line that is revised. Completely resubmitted Disclosure Statements must be accompanied by similar notations identifying the items which have been changed.

12. Use of this Disclosure Statement, amended February 1996, shall be phased in as follows:

A) <u>New Contractors</u>. This form shall be used by new contractors when they are initially required to disclose their cost accounting practices pursuant to 9903.202-1.

B) <u>Existing Contractors</u>. If a contractor has disclosed its cost accounting practices on a prior edition of the Disclosure Statement (CASB DS-1), such disclosure shall remain in effect until the contractor amends or revises a significant portion of the Disclosure Statement in accordance with CAS 9903.202-3. Minor amendments to an existing DS-1 may continue to be made using the prior form. However, when a substantive change is made, a complete Disclosure Statement must be filed using this form. In any event, all contractors and subcontractors must submit a new Disclosure Statement (this version of the CASB DS-1) not later than the beginning of the contractor's next full fiscal year after December 31, 1998.

ATTACHMENT -   Blank Continuation Sheet

FORM CASB DS-1 (REV 2/96)   (ii)

Appendix 8.3   (Continued)

COST ACCOUNTING STANDARDS BOARD DISCLOSURE STATEMENT REQUIRED BY PUBLIC LAW 100-679	COVER SHEET AND CERTIFICATION

0.1 **Company or Reporting Unit.**

    Name

    Street Address

    City, State, & Zip Code

    Division or Subsidiary of (if applicable)

0.2 **Reporting Unit:** (Mark one.)

    A. _____ **Business Unit comprising an entire business organization which is not divided into segments.**
    B.1. _____ **Corporate Home Office**
    2. _____ **Intermediate Level Home Office**
    3. _____ **Segment or business unit reporting directly to a home office.**

0.3 **Official to Contact Concerning this Statement.**

    Name and Title

    Phone number (including area code and extension)

0.4 **Statement Type and Effective Date:**

    A. (Mark type of submission. If a revision, enter number)
    (a) _____ **Original Statement**
    (b) _____ **Revised Statement; Revision No.** _____

    B. Effective Date of this Statement/Revision: _____

0.5 **Statement Submitted To** (Provide office name, location and telephone number, include area code and extension):

    (a) **Cognizant Federal Agency:** _____
    (b) **Cognizant Federal Auditor:** _____

CERTIFICATION

I certify that to the best of my knowledge and belief this Statement, as amended in the case of a revision, is the complete and accurate disclosure as of the above date by the above-named organization of its cost accounting practices, as required by the Disclosure Regulation (48 CFR 9903.202) of the Cost Accounting Standards Board under P.L. 100-679.

_____
(Name)

_____
(Title)

THE PENALTY FOR MAKING A FALSE STATEMENT IN THIS DISCLOSURE IS PRESCRIBED IN 18 U.S.C. § 1001

FORM CASB DS-1 (REV 2/96)   C - 1

Appendix 8.3 (Continued)

COST ACCOUNTING STANDARDS BOARD DISCLOSURE STATEMENT REQUIRED BY PUBLIC LAW 100-679	PART I - GENERAL INFORMATION
	NAME OF REPORTING UNIT

Item No.	Item description

Part I Instructions

Sales data for this part should cover the most recently completed fiscal year of the reporting unit. "Government CAS Covered Sales" includes sales under both prime contracts and subcontracts. "Annual CAS Covered Sales" includes intracorporate transactions.

1.1.0 Type of Business Entity of Which the Reporting Unit is a Part. (Mark one.)

    A. _____ Corporation
    B. _____ Partnership
    C. _____ Proprietorship
    D. _____ Not-for-profit organization
    E. _____ Joint Venture
    F. _____ Federally Funded Research and Development Center (FFRDC)
    Y. _____ Other (Specify) _____

1.2.0 Predominant Type of Government Sales. (Mark one.) 1/

    A. _____ Manufacturing
    B. _____ Research and Development
    C. _____ Construction
    D. _____ Services
    Y. _____ Other (Specify)_____

1.3.0 Annual CAS Covered Government Sales as Percentage of Total Sales (Government and Commercial). (Mark one. An estimate is permitted for this section.) 1/

    A. _____ Less than 10%
    B. _____ 10%-50%
    C. _____ 51%-80%
    D. _____ 81% - 95%
    E. _____ Over 95%

1.4.0 Description of Your Cost Accounting System for Government Contracts and Subcontracts. (Mark the appropriate line(s) and if more than one is marked, explain on a continuation sheet.) 1/

    A. _____ Standard costs - Job order
    B. _____ Standard costs - Process
    C. _____ Actual costs - Job order
    D. _____ Actual costs - Process
    Y. _____ Other(s) 2/

1/ Do not complete when Part I is filed in conjunction with Part VIII.
2/ Describe on a Continuation Sheet.

COST ACCOUNTING STANDARDS BOARD DISCLOSURE STATEMENT REQUIRED BY PUBLIC LAW 100-679	PART I - GENERAL INFORMATION
	NAME OF REPORTING UNIT

Item No.	Item description
1.5.0	<u>Identification of Differences Between Contract Cost Accounting and Financial Accounting Records.</u> List on a continuation sheet, the types of costs charged to Federal contracts that are supported by memorandum records and identify the method used to reconcile with the entity's financial accounting records.
1.6.0	<u>Unallowable Costs.</u> Costs that are not reimbursable as allowable costs under the terms and conditions of Federal awards are identified as follows: (Mark all that apply and if more than one is marked, describe on a continuation sheet the major cost groupings, organizations, or other criteria for using each marked technique.)
1.6.1	Incurred costs. A. _____ Specifically identified and recorded separately in the formal financial accounting records. B. _____ Identified in separately maintained accounting records or workpapers. C. _____ Identifiable through use of less formal accounting techniques that permit audit verification. D. _____ Determinable by other means. <u>1/</u>
1.6.2	Estimated costs. A. _____ By designation and description (in backup data, workpapers, etc) which have specifically been identified and recognized in making estimates. B. _____ By description of any other estimating technique employed to provide appropriate recognition of any unallowable amounts pertinent to the estimates. C. _____ Other. <u>1/</u>
1.7.0	<u>Fiscal Year:</u> _____ (Specify twelve month period used for financial accounting and reporting purposes, e.g., 1/1 to 12/31.)
1.7.1	<u>Cost Accounting Period:</u> _____ (Specify period. If the cost accounting period used for the accumulation and reporting of costs under Federal contracts is other than the fiscal year identified in Item 1.7.0, explain circumstances on a continuation sheet.) _1/_ Describe on a Continuation Sheet.

Appendix 8.3 (Continued)

Item No.	Item description

COST ACCOUNTING STANDARDS BOARD   **PART II - DIRECT COSTS**
DISCLOSURE STATEMENT
REQUIRED BY PUBLIC LAW 100-679

NAME OF REPORTING UNIT

COST ACCOUNTING STANDARDS BOARD **DISCLOSURE STATEMENT** **REQUIRED BY PUBLIC LAW 100-679**	**PART II - DIRECT COSTS**
	NAME OF REPORTING UNIT

Part II Instructions

This part covers the three major categories of direct costs, i.e., Direct Material, Direct Labor, and Other Direct Costs.

It is not the intent here to spell out or define the three elements of direct costs. Rather, each contractor should disclose practices based on its own definitions of what costs are, or will be, charged directly to Federal contracts or similar cost objectives as Direct Material, Direct Labor, or Other Direct Costs. For example, a contractor may charge or classify purchased labor of a direct nature as "Direct Material" for purposes of pricing proposals, requests for progress payments, claims for cost reimbursement, etc.; some other contractor may classify the same cost as "Direct Labor," and still another as "Other Direct Costs." In these circumstances, it is expected that each contractor will disclose practices consistent with its own classifications of Direct Material, Direct Labor, and Other Direct Costs.

2.1.0   <u>Description of Direct Material.</u> Direct material as used here is <u>not</u> limited to those items of material actually incorporated into the end product; they also include material, consumable supplies, and other costs when charged to Federal contracts or similar cost objectives as Direct Material. (Describe on a continuation sheet the principal classes or types of material and services which are charged as direct material; group the material and service costs by those which are incorporated in an end product and those which are not.)

2.2.0   <u>Method of Charging Direct Material.</u>

2.2.1   <u>Direct Charge Not Through an Inventory Account at</u>: (Mark the appropriate line(s) and if more than one is marked, explain on a continuation sheet.)

     A. _____ Standard costs (Describe the type of standards used.) 1/
     B. _____ Actual Costs
     Y. _____ Other(s) 1/
     Z. _____ Not applicable

2.2.2   <u>Charged Direct from a Contractor-owned Inventory Account at</u>: (Mark the appropriate line(s) and if more than one is marked, explain on a continuation sheet.)

     A. _____ Standard costs 1/
     B. _____ Average Costs 1/
     C. _____ First in, first out
     D. _____ Last in, first out
     Y. _____ Other(s) 1/
     Z. _____ Not applicable

1/ Describe on a Continuation Sheet.

Item No.	Item description

2.3.0   <u>Timing of Charging Direct Material.</u> (Mark the appropriate line(s) to indicate the point in time at which direct material are charged to Federal contracts or similar cost objectives, and if more than one line is marked, explain on a continuation sheet.)

       A. _____ When orders are placed
       B. _____ When both the material and invoice are received
       C. _____ When material is issued or released to a process, batch, or similar intermediate cost objective
       D. _____ When material is issued or released to a final cost objective
       E. _____ When invoices are paid
       Y. _____ Other(s) 1/
       Z. _____ Not applicable

2.4.0   <u>Variances from Standard Costs for Direct Material.</u> (Do not complete this item unless you use a standard cost method, i.e., you have marked Line A of Item 2.2.1, or 2.2.2. Mark the appropriate line(s) in Items 2.4.1, 2.4.2, and 2.4.4, and if more than one line is marked, explain on a continuation sheet.)

2.4.1   <u>Type of Variance.</u>

       A. _____ Price
       B. _____ Usage
       C. _____ Combined (A and B)
       Y. _____ Other(s) 1/

2.4.2   <u>Level of Production Unit used to Accumulate Variance.</u> Indicate which level of production unit is used as a basis for accumulating material variances.

       A. _____ Plant-wide Basis
       B. _____ By Department
       C. _____ By Product or Product Line
       Y. _____ Other(s) 1/

2.4.3   <u>Method of Disposing of Variance.</u> Describe on a continuation sheet the basis for, and the frequency of, the disposition of the variance.

2.4.4   <u>Revisions.</u> Standard costs for direct materials are revised:

       A. _____ Semiannually
       B. _____ Annually
       C. _____ Revised as needed, but at least once annually
       Y. _____ Other(s) 1/

1/ Describe on a Continuation Sheet.

Item No.	Item description
2.5.0	**Method of Charging Direct Labor:** (Mark the appropriate line(s) for each Direct Labor Category to show how such labor is charged to Federal contracts or similar cost objectives, and if more than one line is marked, explain on a continuation sheet. Also describe on a continuation sheet the principal classes of labor rates that are, or will be applied to Manufacturing Labor, Engineering Labor, and Other Direct Labor, in order to develop direct labor costs.

Direct Labor Category

	Manufacturing	Engineering	Other Direct
A. Individual/actual rates	___	___	___
B. Average rates -- uncompensated overtime hours included in computation 1/	___	___	___
C. Average rates -- uncompensated overtime hours excluded from computation	___	___	___
D. Standard costs/rates 1/			
Y. Other(s) 1/	___	___	___
Z. Labor category is not applicable	___	___	___

Item No.	Item description
2.6.0	**Variances from Standard Costs for Direct Labor.** (Do not complete this item unless you use a standard costs/rate method, i.e., you have marked Line D of Item 2.5.0 for any direct labor category. Mark the appropriate line(s) in each column of Items 2.6.1, 2.6.2, and 2.6.4. If more than one is marked, explain on a continuation sheet.)
2.6.1	**Type of Variance.**

Direct Labor Category

	Manufacturing	Engineering	Other Direct
A. Rate	___	___	___
B. Efficiency	___	___	___
C. Combined (A and B)	___	___	___
Y. Other(s) 1/	___	___	___
Z. Labor category is not applicable	___	___	___

1/ Describe on a Continuation Sheet.

COST ACCOUNTING STANDARDS BOARD DISCLOSURE STATEMENT REQUIRED BY PUBLIC LAW 100-679	**PART II - DIRECT COSTS** **NAME OF REPORTING UNIT**

Item No.	Item description
2.6.2	**Level of Production Unit used to Accumulate Variance.** Indicate which level of production unit is used as a basis for accumulating the labor variances.

<table>
<tr><td></td><td colspan="3" align="center">Direct Labor Category</td></tr>
<tr><td></td><td>Manufacturing</td><td>Engineering</td><td>Other Direct</td></tr>
<tr><td>A. Plant-wide basis</td><td>____</td><td>____</td><td>____</td></tr>
<tr><td>B. By department</td><td>____</td><td>____</td><td>____</td></tr>
<tr><td>C. By product or product line</td><td>____</td><td>____</td><td>____</td></tr>
<tr><td>Y. Other(s) 1/</td><td>____</td><td>____</td><td>____</td></tr>
<tr><td>Z. Labor category is not applicable</td><td>____</td><td>____</td><td>____</td></tr>
</table>

2.6.3	**Method of Disposing of Variance.** Describe on a continuation sheet the basis for, and the frequency of, the disposition of the variance.
2.6.4	**Revisions.** Standard costs for direct labor are revised:

    A. _____ Semiannually
    B. _____ Annually
    C. _____ Revised as needed, but at least once annually
    Y. _____ Other(s) 1/

2.7.0	**Description of Other Direct Costs.** Other significant items of cost directly identified with Federal contracts or other final cost objectives. Describe on a continuation sheet the principal classes of other costs that are always charged directly, that is, identified specifically with final cost objectives, e.g., fringe benefits, travel costs, services, subcontracts, etc.
2.7.1	When Employee Travel Expenses for lodging and subsistence are charged direct to Federal contracts or similar cost objectives the charge is based on:

    A. _____ Actual Costs
    B. _____ Per Diem Rates
    C. _____ Lodging at actual costs and subsistence at per diem
    Y. _____ Other Method 1/
    Z. _____ Not Applicable

2.8.0	**Credits to Contract Costs.** When Federal contracts or similar cost objectives are credited for the following circumstances, are the rates of direct labor, direct materials, other direct costs and applicable indirect costs always the same as those for the original charges? (Mark one line for each circumstance, and for each "No" answer, explain on a continuation sheet how the credit differs from the original charge.)

Circumstance	A. Yes	B. No	Z. Not Applicable
(a) Transfers to other jobs/contracts	____	____	____
(b) Unused or excess materials remaining upon completion of contract	____	____	____

1/ Describe on a Continuation Sheet.

COST ACCOUNTING STANDARDS BOARD DISCLOSURE STATEMENT REQUIRED BY PUBLIC LAW 100-679	PART III - DIRECT VS. INDIRECT COSTS
	NAME OF REPORTING UNIT

Item No.	Item description
3.1.0	<u>Criteria for Determining How Costs are Charged to Federal Contracts Or Similar Cost Objectives.</u> Describe on a continuation sheet your criteria for determining when costs incurred for the same purpose, in like circumstances, are treated either as direct costs only or as indirect costs only with respect to final cost objectives.
3.2.0	<u>Treatment of Costs of Specified Functions, Elements of Cost, or Transactions.</u> (For each of the functions, elements of cost or transactions listed in Items 3.2.1, 3.2.2, and 3.2.3, enter one of the Codes A through F, or Y, to indicate how the item is treated. Enter Code Z in those lines that are not applicable to you. Also, specify the name(s) of the indirect pool(s) (as listed in 4.1.0, 4.2.0 and 4.3.0) for each function, element of cost, or transaction coded E or F. If Code E, Sometimes direct/Sometimes indirect, is used, explain on a continuation sheet the circumstances under which both direct and indirect allocations are made.)

Treatment Code

A. Direct material
B. Direct labor
C. Direct material and labor
D. Other direct costs

E. Sometimes direct/Sometimes indirect
F. Indirect only
Y. Other(s) <u>1/</u>
Z. Not applicable

3.2.1	<u>Functions, Elements of Cost, or Transactions Related to Direct Material</u>		Treatment Code	Name of Pool(s)
	(a)	Cash Discounts on Purchases	____	_____
	(b)	Freight in	____	_____
	(c)	Income from Sale of Scrap	____	_____
	(d)	Income from Sale of Salvage	____	_____
	(e)	Incoming Material Inspection (receiving)	____	_____
	(f)	Inventory adjustment	____	_____
	(g)	Purchasing	____	_____
	(h)	Trade Discounts, Refunds, Rebates, and Allowances on Purchases	____	_____

<u>1/</u> Describe on a Continuation Sheet.

FORM CASB DS-1 (REV 2/96) III - 1

Appendix 8.3 (Continued)

COST ACCOUNTING STANDARDS BOARD DISCLOSURE STATEMENT REQUIRED BY PUBLIC LAW 100-679	PART III - DIRECT VS. INDIRECT COSTS
	NAME OF REPORTING UNIT

Item No.	Item description		
3.2.2	**Functions, Elements of Cost, or Transactions Related to Direct Labor**	**Treatment Code**	**Name of Pool(s)**
	(a) **Incentive Compensation**	____	_____
	(b) **Holiday Differential (Premium Pay)**	____	_____
	(c) **Vacation Pay**	____	_____
	(d) **Overtime Premium Pay**	____	_____
	(e) **Shift Premium Pay**	____	_____
	(f) **Pension Costs**	____	_____
	(g) **Post Retirement Benefits Other Than Pensions**	____	_____
	(h) **Health Insurance**	____	_____
	(i) **Life Insurance**	____	_____
	(j) **Other Deferred Compensation** 1/	____	_____
	(k) **Training**	____	_____
	(l) **Sick Leave**	____	_____
	1/ **Describe on a Continuation Sheet.**		

COST ACCOUNTING STANDARDS BOARD **DISCLOSURE STATEMENT** **REQUIRED BY PUBLIC LAW 100-679**	**PART III - DIRECT VS. INDIRECT COSTS**
	NAME OF REPORTING UNIT

Item No.	Item description

3.2.3   <u>Functions, Elements of Cost,</u>
      <u>or Transactions - Miscellaneous</u>

			Treatment Code	Name of Pool(s)
(a)	Design Engineering (in-house)		____	_____
(b)	Drafting (in-house)		____	_____
(c)	Computer Operations (in-house)		____	_____
(d)	Contract Administration		____	_____
(e)	Subcontract Administration Costs		____	_____
(f)	Freight Out (finished product)		____	_____
(g)	Line (or production) Inspection		____	_____
(h)	Packaging and Preservation		____	_____
(i)	Preproduction Costs and Start-up Costs		____	_____
(j)	Departmental Supervision		____	_____
(k)	Professional Services (consultant fees)		____	_____
(l)	Purchased Labor of Direct Nature (on premises)		____	_____
(m)	Purchased Labor of Direct Nature (off premises)		____	_____
(n)	Rearrangement Costs		____	_____
(o)	Rework Costs		____	_____
(p)	Royalties		____	_____
(q)	Scrap Work		____	_____
(r)	Special Test Equipment		____	_____
(s)	Special Tooling		____	_____
(t)	Warranty Costs		____	_____
(u)	Rental Costs		____	_____
(v)	Travel and Subsistence		____	_____
(w)	Employee Severance Pay		____	_____
(x)	Security Guards		____	_____

FORM CASB DS-1 (REV 2/96)   III - 3

Appendix 8.3 (Continued)

	COST ACCOUNTING STANDARDS BOARD DISCLOSURE STATEMENT REQUIRED BY PUBLIC LAW 100-679	PART IV - INDIRECT COSTS
		NAME OF REPORTING UNIT

Item No.	Item description

<u>Part IV Instructions</u>

For the purpose of this part, indirect costs have been divided into three categories: (i) manufacturing, engineering, and comparable indirect costs, (ii) general and administrative (G&A) expenses, and (iii) service center and expense pool costs, as defined in Item 4.3.0. The term "overhead," as used in this part, refers only to the first category of indirect costs.

The following Allocation Base Codes are provided for use in connection with Items 4.1.0, 4.2.0 and 4.3.0.

A.	Sales	H.	Direct labor dollars
B.	Cost of sales	I.	Direct labor hours
C.	Total Cost input (direct material, direct labor, other direct costs and applicable overhead)	J.	Machine hours
		K.	Usage
		L.	Unit of production
D.	Value-added cost input (total cost input less direct material and subcontract costs)	M.	Direct material cost
		N.	Total payroll dollars (direct and indirect employees)
E.	Total cost incurred (total cost input plus G&A expenses)	O.	Headcount or number of employees (direct and indirect employees)
F.	Prime cost (direct material, direct labor and other direct cost)	P.	Square feet
		Y.	Other(s), or more than one basis (Describe on a cont. sheet.)
G.	Processing or conversion cost (direct labor and applicable overhead)	Z.	Pool not applicable

4.1.0   <u>Overhead Pools.</u> List all the overhead pools, i.e., pools of indirect costs, other than general and administrative (G&A) expenses, that are allocated to final cost objectives without any intermediate allocations. A segment or business unit may have only a single pool encompassing all of its overhead costs or alternatively it may have several pools such as manufacturing overhead, engineering overhead, material handling overhead, etc. For each pool listed indicate the base used for allocating such pooled expenses to Federal contracts or similar cost objectives. Also, for each of the pools indicate (a) the major functions, activities, and elements of cost included, and (b) the make up of the allocation base. Use a continuation sheet if additional space is required.

Allocation
<u>Base Code</u>

1.   _____   _____

     (a)   Major functions, activities, and elements of cost included:

              _____

              _____

     (b)   Description/Make up of the allocation base:

              _____

              _____

FORM CASB DS-1 (REV 2/96)   IV - 1

Appendix 8.3 (Continued)

	COST ACCOUNTING STANDARDS BOARD DISCLOSURE STATEMENT REQUIRED BY PUBLIC LAW 100-679	PART IV - INDIRECT COSTS
		NAME OF REPORTING UNIT

Item No.	Item description

4.1.0	**Continued.** **Allocation**
	Base Code
	
	    2. _____ _____
	
	      (a) Major functions, activities, and
	             elements of cost included:
	
	             _____
	
	             _____
	
	      (b) Description/Make up of the
	             allocation base:
	
	             _____
	
	             _____

4.2.0	<u>General and Administrative (G&A) Expense Pool(s).</u> Select among the three categories of pools below that describe(s) the manner in which G&A expenses are allocated. For each category of pool(s) selected indicate the base(s) used for allocating such pooled expenses to Federal contracts or similar cost objectives. Also, for each category of pool(s) selected, indicate (a) the major functions, activities, and elements of cost included, and (b) the make up of the allocation base(s). For example, if direct labor dollars are used, are fringe benefits included? If a total cost input base is used, is the imputed cost of capital included? Use a continuation sheet if additional space is required.
	
	                                           Allocation
	                                         Base Code
	
	    <u>Single Pool Containing G&A Expenses Only</u>
	
	    _____ _____
	
	      (a) Major functions, activities, and
	             elements of cost included:
	
	             _____
	
	             _____
	
	      (b) Description/Make up of the allocation base:
	
	             _____
	
	             _____

FORM CASB DS-1 (REV 2/96)   IV - 2

Appendix 8.3   (Continued)

Item No.	Item description

4.2.0 Continued.

<u>Single Pool Containing Both G&A and Non-G&A Expenses</u>

Allocation Base Code

_____   _____

   (a)   Major functions, activities, and elements of cost included:

      _____

      _____

   (b)   Description/Make up of the allocation base:

      _____

      _____

<u>Special Allocations</u>

Allocation Base Code

  1. _____   _____

      (a)   Major functions, activities, and elements of cost included:

         _____

         _____

      (b)   Description/Make up of the allocation base:

         _____

         _____

  2. _____   _____

      (a)   Major functions, activities, and elements of cost included:

         _____

         _____

      (b)   Description/Make up of the allocation base:

         _____

         _____

COST ACCOUNTING STANDARDS BOARD DISCLOSURE STATEMENT REQUIRED BY PUBLIC LAW 100-679	PART IV - INDIRECT COSTS
	NAME OF REPORTING UNIT

Item No.	Item description
4.3.0	**Service Center and Expense Pool Allocation Bases.**

Service centers are departments or other functional units which perform specific technical and/or administrative services primarily for the benefit of other units within a reporting unit. Expense pools are pools of indirect costs that are allocated primarily to other units within a reporting unit. Examples of service centers are data processing centers, reproduction services and communications services. Examples of expense pools are use and occupancy pools and fringe benefit pools.

Category Code

Generally, costs incurred by such centers or pools are, or can be, charged or allocated (i) partially to specific final cost objectives as direct costs and partially to other indirect cost pools (such as a manufacturing overhead pool) for subsequent reallocation to several final cost objectives, referred to herein as Category "A", and (ii) only to several other indirect cost pools (such as a manufacturing overhead pool, engineering overhead pool and G&A expense pool) for subsequent reallocation to several final cost objectives, referred to herein as Category "B".

Rate Code

Some service centers or expense pools may use predetermined billing or costing rates to charge or allocate the costs (Rate Code A) while others may charge or allocate on an actual basis (Rate Code B).

List all the service centers and expense pools and enter in column (1) Code A or B to indicate the category of pool. Enter in Column (2) one of the Allocation Base Codes A through P, or Y, listed on Page ___, to indicate the base used for charging or allocating service center or expense pool costs. Enter in Column (3) Rate Code A or B to describe the costing method used. Also, for each of the centers and pools indicate (a) the major functions, activities, and elements of cost included, and (b) the make up of the allocation base. Use a continuation sheet if additional space is required.

			Allocation		
	Service Center or Expense Pool		Category Code (1)	Base Code (2)	Rate Code (3)
1.	_____		___	___	___
	(a)	Major functions, activities, and elements of cost included: _____ _____			
	(b)	Description/Make up of the allocation base: _____ _____			
2.	_____		___	___	___
	(a)	Major functions, activities, and elements of cost included: _____ _____			
	(b)	Description/Make up of the allocation base: _____			

FORM CASB DS-1 (REV 2/96) IV - 4

Appendix 8.3 (Continued)

	COST ACCOUNTING STANDARDS BOARD DISCLOSURE STATEMENT REQUIRED BY PUBLIC LAW 100-679	PART IV - INDIRECT COSTS
		NAME OF REPORTING UNIT

Item No.	Item description

4.4.0	<u>Treatment of Variances from Actual Cost (Underabsorption or Overabsorption).</u> **Where predetermined billing or costing rates are used to charge costs of service centers and expense pools to Federal contracts or other indirect cost pools (Rate Code A in Column (3) of Item 4.3.0), variances from actual costs are: (Mark the appropriate line(s) and if more than one is marked, explain on a continuation sheet.)**
	
	    A. ____ Prorated to users on the basis of charges made, at least once annually
	    B. ____ All charged or credited to indirect cost pool(s) at least once annually
	    Y. ____ Other(s) <u>1/</u>
	    Z. ____ Service center is not applicable to reporting unit

4.5.0	<u>Application of Overhead and G&A Rates to Specified Transactions or Costs.</u>
	
	This item is directed to ascertaining your practice in special situations where, in lieu of establishing a separate indirect cost pool, allocation is made from an established overhead or G&A pool at a rate other than the normal full rate for that pool. In the case of such a special allocation, the terms "less than full rate" or "more than full rate" should be used to describe the practice. The terms do <u>not</u> apply to situations where, as in some cases of off-site activities, etc., a separate indirect cost pool and base are used and the rate for such activities is lower than the "in-house" rate.
	
	For each of the transactions or costs listed below, enter one of the following codes to indicate your indirect cost allocation practice with respect to that transaction or cost. If Code A, full rate, is entered, identify on a continuation sheet the pool(s) reported under items 4.1.0, 4.2.0, and 4.3.0, which are applicable. If Codes B or C, less than or more than the full rate, is entered, describe on a continuation sheet the major types of expenses that are covered by such a rate.
	
	    <u>Rate Code</u>
	    A. Full rate C. Special allocation at more than full rate
	    B. Special allocation at less than full rate D. No overhead or G&A is applied
	            Z. Transaction or cost is not applicable to reporting unit

Transaction or Cost to Which <u>Indirect Costs May be Allocated</u>	Rate <u>Code</u>
(a) Subcontract costs	____
(b) Purchased Labor	____
(c) Government-furnished materials	____
(d) Self-constructed depreciable assets	____
(e) Labor on installation of assets	____
(f) Off-site work	____
(g) Interorganizational transfers out	____
(h) Interorganizational transfers in (Also indicate on a continuation sheet the basis used by you as transferee to charge the cost or price of interogranizational transfers to Federal contracts or similar cost objectives. If the charge is based on cost, indicate whether the transferor's G&A expenses are included.)	____
(i) Other transactions or costs (Enter Code B or C on this line if there are other transactions or costs to which either less than full rate or more than full rate is applied. List such transactions or costs on a continuation sheet, and for each describe the major types of expenses covered by such a rate. If there are no other such transactions or costs, enter code Z.)	____

<u>1/</u> Describe on a Continuation Sheet.

Appendix 8.3 (Continued)

Item No.	Item description
4.6.0	**Independent Research and Development (IR&D) and Bid and Proposal (B&P) Costs.** Definitions of and requirements for the allocation of IR&D and B&P costs are contained in 48 CFR 9904.420. The full rate of all allocable manufacturing, engineering, and/or other overhead is applied to IR&D and B&P costs as if IR&D and B&P projects were under contract, and the "burdened" IR&D and B&P costs are: (Mark appropriate line(s).)

    A. _____ Allocated to Federal contracts or similar cost objectives by means of a composite pool with G&A expenses.

    B. _____ Allocated to Federal contracts or similar cost objectives by means of a separate pool.

    C. _____ Transferred to the corporate or home office level for reallocation to the benefiting segments.

    Y. _____ Other 1/

    Z. _____ Not applicable

| 4.7.0 | **Cost of Capital Committed to Facilities.** In accordance with instructions for Form CASB-CMF, undistributed facilities capital items are allocated to overhead and G&A expense pools: (Mark one.) |

    A. ____ On a basis identical to that used to absorb the actual depreciation or amortization from these facilities; land is assigned in the same manner as the facilities to which it relates.

    B. ____ On a basis not identical to that used to absorb the actual depreciation or amortization from these facilities. (Describe on a continuation sheet the difference for each step of the allocation process.)

    C. ____ By the "alternative allocation process" described in instructions for Form CASB-CMF.

    Z. ____ Not applicable.

1/ **Describe on a Continuation Sheet.**

FORM CASB DS-1 (REV 2/96)   IV - 6

Appendix 8.3 (Continued)

Item No.	Item description
	<div align="center">**COST ACCOUNTING STANDARDS BOARD** **DISCLOSURE STATEMENT** **REQUIRED BY PUBLIC LAW 100-679**</div> **PART V - DEPRECIATION AND** **CAPITALIZATION PRACTICES** **NAME OF REPORTING UNIT**

Part V Instructions

Where a home office either establishes practices or procedures for the types of costs covered in this Part or incurs and then allocates these costs to its segments, the home office may complete this Part to be included in the submission by the segment as indicated on page (i) 4., General Instructions.

5.1.0   <u>Depreciating Tangible Assets for Government Contract Costing.</u> (For each of the asset categories listed on Page ___, enter a code from A through H in Column (1) describing the method of depreciation (Code F for assets that are expensed); a code from A through C in Column (2) describing the basis for determining useful life; a code from A through C in Column (3) describing how depreciation methods or use charges are applied to property units; and a Code A, B or C in Column (4) indicating whether or not residual value is deducted from the total cost of depreciable assets. Enter Code Y in each column of an asset category where another or more than one method applies. Enter Code Z in Column (1) only, if an asset category is not applicable.)

Column (1)--Depreciation Method Code

A. Straight Line
B. Declining balance
C. Sum-of-the years digits
D. Machine hours
E. Unit of production
F. Expensed at acquisition
G. Use charge
H. Method of depreciation used under the applicable Internal Revenue Procedures
Y. Other or more than one method 1/
Z. Asset category is not applicable

Column (2)--Useful Life Code

A. Replacement experience adjusted by expected changes in periods of usefulness
B. Term of Lease
C. Estimated on the basis of Asset Guidelines under Internal Revenue Procedures
Y. Other, or more than one method 1/

Column (3)--Property Units Code

A. Individual units are accounted for separately
B. Applied to groups of assets with similar service lives
C. Applied to groups of assets with varying service lives
Y. Other or more than one method 1/

Column (4)--Residual Value Code

A. Residual value is estimated and deducted
B. Residual value is covered by the depreciation method (e.g., declining balance)
C. Residual value is estimated but not deducted in accordance with the provisions of 48 CFR 9904.409 1/
Y. Other or more than one method 1/

1/ **Describe on a Continuation Sheet.**

Item No.	Item description

5.1.0 Continued.

Asset Category	Depreciation Method Code (1)	Useful Life Code (2)	Property Units Code (3)	Residual Value Code (4)
(a) Land improvements	____	____	____	____
(b) Building	____	____	____	____
(c) Building improvements	____	____	____	____
(d) Leasehold improvements	____	____	____	____
(e) Machinery and equipment	____	____	____	____
(f) Furniture and fixtures	____	____	____	____
(g) Automobiles and trucks	____	____	____	____
(h) Data processing equipment	____	____	____	____
(i) Programming/reprogramming costs	____	____	____	____
(j) Patterns and dies	____	____	____	____
(k) Tools	____	____	____	____
(l) Other depreciable asset categories	____	____	____	____

(l) (Enter Code Y on this line if other asset categories are used and enumerate on a continuation sheet each such asset category and the applicable codes. Otherwise enter Code Z.)

5.2.0 Depreciation Practices for Costing, Financial Accounting, and Income Tax. Are depreciation practices the same for costing Federal contracts as for financial accounting and income tax? (Mark either (A) or (B) on each line under Financial Accounting and Income Tax. Not-for-profit organizations need not complete this item.)

Financial Accounting	A. Yes	B. No
(a) Methods	____	____
(b) Useful lives	____	____
(c) Property units	____	____
(d) Residual values	____	____

Income Tax	A. Yes	B. No
(e) Methods	____	____
(f) Useful lives	____	____
(g) Property units	____	____
(h) Residual values	____	____

FORM CASB DS-1 (REV 2/96) V - 2

Appendix 8.3 (Continued)

Item No.	Item description

5.3.0   <u>Fully Depreciated Assets.</u>   Is a usage charge for fully depreciated assets charged to Federal contracts?   (Mark one.)

          A.   _____   Yes <u>1</u>/
          B.   _____   No
          Z.   _____   Not applicable

5.4.0   <u>Treatment of Gains and Losses on Disposition of Depreciable Property.</u>   Gains and losses are: (Mark the appropriate line(s) and if more than one is marked, explain on a continuation sheet.)

          A.   _____   Credited or charged currently to the same overhead or G&A pools to which the depreciation of the assets was charged

          B.   _____   Taken into consideration in the depreciation cost basis of the new items, where trade-in is involved

          C.   _____   Not accounted for separately, but reflected in the depreciation reserve account

          Y.   _____   Other(s) <u>1</u>/

          Z.   _____   Not applicable

5.5.0   <u>Capitalization or Expensing of Specified Costs.</u>   (Mark one line on each item to indicate your practices regarding capitalization or expensing of specified costs incurred in connection with capital assets.   If the same specified cost is sometimes expensed and sometimes capitalized, mark both lines and describe on a continuation sheet the circumstances when each method is used.)

	<u>Cost</u>	A. <u>Expensed</u>	B. <u>Capitalized</u>
(a)	Freight-in	_____	_____
(b)	Sales taxes	_____	_____
(c)	Excise taxes	_____	_____
(d)	Architect-engineer fees	_____	_____
(e)	Overhauls (extraordinary repairs)	_____	_____

<u>1</u>/   Describe on a Continuation Sheet.

COST ACCOUNTING STANDARDS BOARD DISCLOSURE STATEMENT REQUIRED BY PUBLIC LAW 100-679	PART V - DEPRECIATION AND CAPITALIZATION PRACTICES
	NAME OF REPORTING UNIT

Item No.	Item description

5.6.0	<u>Criteria for Capitalization.</u> Enter (a) the minimum dollar amount of acquisition cost or expenditures for addition, alteration and improvement of depreciable assets capitalized, and (b) the minimum number of expected life years of capitalized assets.
	
	If more than one dollar amount or number applies, show the information for the majority of your depreciable assets, and enumerate on a continuation sheet the dollar amounts and/or number of years for each category or subcategory of assets involved which differ from those for the majority of assets.
	
	    (a) Minimum dollar amount capitalized _____
	
	    (b) Minimum service life years _____

5.7.0	<u>Group or Mass Purchase.</u> Are group or mass purchases (original complement) of low cost equipment, which individually are less than the capitalization amount indicated above, capitalized? (Mark one. If <u>Yes</u> is marked, provide the minimum aggregate dollar amount capitalized.)
	
	    A. ____ Yes
	
	    _____ Minimum aggregate dollar amount capitalized
	
	    B. ____ No

COST ACCOUNTING STANDARDS BOARD DISCLOSURE STATEMENT REQUIRED BY PUBLIC LAW 100-679	PART VI - OTHER COSTS AND CREDITS
	NAME OF REPORTING UNIT

Item No.	Item description

Part VI Instructions

Where a home office either establishes practices or procedures for the types of costs covered in this Part or incurs and then allocates these costs to its segments, the home office may complete this Part to be included in the submission by the segment as indicated on page (ii) 4., **General Instructions**.

6.1.0 — <u>Method of Charging and Crediting Vacation, Holiday, and Sick Pay.</u> (Mark the appropriate line(s) in each column of Items 6.1.1, 6.1.2, 6.1.3 and 6.1.4 to indicate the method used to charge, or credit any unused or unpaid vacation, holiday, or sick pay. If more than one method is marked, explain on a continuation sheet.)

			Salaried	
		Hourly (1)	Non-exempt 1/ (2)	Exempt 1/ (3)
6.1.1	**Charges for Vacation Pay**			
	A. When Accrued (earned)	____	____	____
	B. When Taken	____	____	____
	Y. Other(s) 2/	____	____	____
6.1.2	**Charges for Holiday Pay**			
	A. When Accrued (earned)	____	____	____
	B. When Taken	____	____	____
	Y. Other(s) 2/	____	____	____
6.1.3	**Charges for Sick Pay**			
	A. When Accrued (earned)	____	____	____
	B. When Taken	____	____	____
	Y. Other(s) 2/	____	____	____
6.1.4	**Credits for Unused or Unpaid Vacation, Holiday, or Sick Pay**			
	A. Credited to Accounts Originally charged at Least Once Annually	____	____	____
	B. Credited to Indirect Cost Pools at Least Once Annually	____	____	____
	C. Carried Over to Future Cost Accounting Periods 2/	____	____	____
	Y. Other(s) 2/	____	____	____
	Z. Not Applicable	____	____	____

1/   For the definition of Non-exempt and Exempt salaries, see the Fair Labor Standards Act, 29 U.S.C. 206.
2/   Describe on a Continuation Sheet.

FORM CASB DS-1 (REV 2/96)   VI - 1

Appendix 8.3   (Continued)

Item No.	Item description
6.2.0	**Supplemental Unemployment (Extended Layoff) Benefit Plans.** Costs of such plans are charged to Federal contracts: (Mark the appropriate line(s) and if more than one is marked, explain on a continuation sheet.)
	A. ____ When actual payments are made directly to employees
	B. ____ When accrued (book accrual or funds set aside but no trust fund involved)
	C. ____ When contributions are made to a nonforfeitable trust fund
	D. ____ Not charged
	Y. ____ Other(s) 1/
	Z. ____ Not applicable
6.3.0	**Severance Pay and Early Retirement.** Costs of normal turnover severance pay and early retirement incentive plans, as defined in FAR 31.2 or other pertinent procurement regulations, which are charged directly or indirectly to Federal contracts, are based on: (Mark the appropriate line(s) and if more than one is marked, explain on a continuation sheet.)
	A. ____ Actual payments made
	B. ____ Accrued amounts on the basis of past experience
	C. ____ Not charged
	Y. ____ Other(s) 1/
	Z. ____ Not applicable
6.4.0	**Incidental Receipts.** (Mark the appropriate line(s) to indicate the method used to account for incidental or miscellaneous receipts, such as revenues from renting real and personal property or selling services, when related costs have been allocated to Federal contracts. If more than one is marked, explain on a continuation sheet.)
	A. ____ The entire amount of the receipt is credited to the same indirect cost pools to which related costs have been charged
	B. ____ Where the amount of the receipt includes an allowance for profit, the cost-related part of the receipt is credited to the same indirect cost pools to which related costs have been charged; the profits are credited to Other (Miscellaneous) Income
	C. ____ The entire amount of the receipt is credited directly to Other (Miscellaneous) Income
	Y. ____ Other(s) 1/
	Z. ____ Not applicable
	1/ Describe on a Continuation Sheet.

FORM CASB DS-1 (REV 2/96)

VI - 2

Appendix 8.3 (Continued)

	COST ACCOUNTING STANDARDS BOARD DISCLOSURE STATEMENT REQUIRED BY PUBLIC LAW 100-679	PART VI - OTHER COSTS AND CREDITS
		NAME OF REPORTING UNIT

Item No.	Item description
6.5.0	<u>Proceeds from Employee Welfare Activities.</u> Employee welfare activities include all of those activities set forth in FAR 31.2 . (Mark the appropriate line(s) to indicate the practice followed in accounting for the proceeds from such activities. If more than one is marked, explain on a continuation sheet.)

A. ____   Proceeds are turned over to an employee-welfare organization or fund; such proceeds are reduced by all applicable costs such as depreciation, heat, light and power

B. ____   Same as above, except the proceeds are not reduced by all applicable costs

C. ____   Proceeds are credited at least once annually to the appropriate cost pools to which costs have been charged

D. ____   Proceeds are credited to Other (Miscellaneous) Income

Y. ____   Other(s) <u>1</u>/

Z. ____   Not applicable

<u>1</u>/ Describe on a Continuation Sheet.

FORM CASB DS-1 (REV 2/96)   VI - 3

Appendix 8.3   (Continued)

	PART VII - DEFERRED COMPENSATION AND INSURANCE COST
COST ACCOUNTING STANDARDS BOARD DISCLOSURE STATEMENT REQUIRED BY PUBLIC LAW 100-679	
	NAME OF REPORTING UNIT

Item No.	Item description
	### Part VII Instructions This part covers the measurement and assignment of costs for employee pensions, post retirement benefits other than pensions (including post retirement health benefits), certain other types of deferred compensation, and insurance. Some organizations may incur all of these costs at the corporate or home office level, while others may incur them at subordinate organizational levels. Still others may incur a portion of these costs at the corporate level and the balance at subordinate organizational levels. Where the segment (reporting unit) does not directly incur such costs, the segment should, on a continuation sheet, identify the organizational entity that incurs and records such costs, and should require that entity to complete the applicable portions of this Part VII. Each such entity is to fully disclose the methods and techniques used to measure, assign, and allocate such costs to the segment(s) performing Federal contracts or similar cost objectives. Necessary explanations required to achieve that objective should be provided by the entity on a continuation sheet. Where a home office either establishes practices or procedures for the types of costs covered in this Part VII or incurs and then allocates those costs to its segments, the home office may complete this Part to be included in the submission by the segment as indicated on page (i) 4., <u>General Instructions</u>.
7.1.0	<u>Pension Plans with Costs Charged to Federal Contracts.</u> Identify the types and number of pension plans whose costs are charged to Federal contracts or similar cost objectives: (Mark applicable line(s) and enter number of plans.)

	Type of Pension Plan	Number of Plans
A.	Defined-Contribution Plan (Other than ESOPs (see 7.5.0))	
	1. Non-Qualified	____
	2. Qualified	____
B.	Defined-Benefit Plan	
	1. Non-Qualified	
	a. Costs are measured and assigned on accrual basis	____
	b. Costs are measured and assigned on cash (pay-as-you-go) basis	____
	2. Qualified	
	a. Trusteed (Subject to ERISA's minimum funding requirements)	____
	b. Fully-insured plan (Exempt from ERISA's minimum funding requirements) treated as a defined-contribution plan	____
	c. Collectively bargained plan treated as a defined-contribution plan	____
Y.	____ Other 1/	____
Z.	____ Not Applicable (Proceed to Item 7.2.0)	

1/ Describe on a Continuation Sheet.

FORM CASB DS-1 (REV 2/96)   VII - 1

Appendix 8.3   (Continued)

Item No.	Item description
7.1.1	**General Plan Information.** On a continuation sheet for each plan identified in item 7.1.0, provide the following information:
	A. The plan name
	B. The Employer Identification Number (EIN) of the plan sponsor as reported on IRS Form 5500, if any
	C. The plan number as reported on IRS Form 5500, if any
	D. Is there a funding agency established for the plan?

	E. Indicate where costs are accumulated:
	     (1) Home Office
	     (2) Segment

	F. If the plan provides supplemental benefits to any other plan, identify the other plan(s).
7.1.2	**Defined-Contribution Plan(s) and Certain Defined-Benefit Plans treated as Defined-Contribution Plans.** Where numerous plans are listed under 7.1.0.A., 7.1.0.B.2.b., or 7.1.0.B.2.c., for those plans which represent the largest dollar amounts of costs charged to Federal contracts, or similar cost objectives, describe on a continuation sheet the basis for the contribution (including treatment of dividends, credits, and forfeitures) required for each fiscal year. (If there are not more than three plans, provide information for all the plans. If there are more than three plans, information should be provided for those plans that in the aggregate account for at least 80 percent of those defined-contribution plan costs allocable to this segment or business unit.)
	Z. _____ Not applicable. (Proceed to Item 7.1.3)
7.1.3	**Defined-Benefit Plan(s).** Where numerous plans are listed under 7.1.0.B. (excluding certain defined-benefit plans treated as defined-contribution plans reported under 7.1.0.B.2.b. and 7.1.0.B.2.c.), for those plans which represent the largest dollar amounts of costs charged to Federal contracts, provide the information requested below on a continuation sheet. (If there are not more than three plans, provide information for all the plans. If there are more than three plans, information should be provided for those plans that in the aggregate account for at least 80 percent of those defined-benefit plan costs allocable to this segment or business unit.):
	A. <u>Actuarial Cost Method.</u> Identify the actuarial cost method used, including the cost method(s) used to value ancillary benefits, for each plan. Include the method used to determine the actuarial value of assets. Also, if applicable, include whether normal cost is developed as a level dollar amount or as a level percent of salary. For plans listed under 7.1.0.B.1.b., enter "pay-as-you-go".
	B. <u>Actuarial Assumptions.</u> Describe the events or conditions for which significant actuarial assumptions are made for each plan. Do not include the current numeric values of the assumptions, but provide a description of the basis used for determining these numeric values. Also, describe the criteria used to evaluate the validity of an actuarial assumption. For plans listed under 7.1.0.B.1.b., enter "not applicable".
	C. <u>Market Value of Funding Agency Assets.</u> Indicate if all assets of the funding agency are valued on the basis of a readily determinable market price. If yes, indicate the basis for the market value. If no, describe how the market values are determined for those assets that do not have a readily determinable market price. For plans listed under 7.1.0.B.1.b., enter "not applicable".
	D. <u>Basis for Cost Computation.</u> Indicate whether the cost for the segment is determined as:
	1. An allocated portion of the total pension plan cost.
	2. A separately computed pension cost for one or more segments. If so, identify those segments.
	Z. _____ Not applicable, proceed to Item 7.2.0.

FORM CASB DS-1 (REV 2/96)   **VII - 2**

Appendix 8.3   (Continued)

COST ACCOUNTING STANDARDS BOARD DISCLOSURE STATEMENT REQUIRED BY PUBLIC LAW 100-679	PART VII - DEFERRED COMPENSATION AND INSURANCE COST
	NAME OF REPORTING UNIT

Item No.	Item description
7.2.0	**Post-retirement Benefits (PRBs) Other than Pensions (including post-retirement health care benefits) Charged to Federal Contracts.** Identify the accounting method used to determine the costs and the number of PRB plans whose costs are charged to Federal contracts or similar cost objectives. Where retiree benefits are provided as an integral part of an employee group insurance plan that covers active employees, report that plan under 7.3.0. (Mark applicable line(s) and enter number of plans.)

Method Used to Determine Costs   **Number of Plans**

A.   Accrual Accounting
B.   Cash (pay-as-you-go) Accounting   _____
C.   Purchased Insurance from unrelated Insurer   _____
D.   Purchased Insurance from Captive Insurer   _____
E.   Self-Insurance (including insurance
       obtained through Captive Insurer)
F.   Terminal Funding   _____
Y.   Other 1/
Z.   _____ Not Applicable (Proceed to Item 7.3.0)   _____

Item No.	Item description
7.2.1	**General PRB Plan Information.** On a continuation sheet for each plan identified in item 7.2.0, provide the following information grouped by method used to determine costs:

A.   The plan name

B.   The Employer Identification Number (EIN) of the plan sponsor as reported on IRS Form 5500, if any

C.   The plan number as reported on IRS Form 5500, if any

D.   Is there a funding agency or funded reserve established for the plan?

E.   Indicate where costs are accumulated:
     (1) Home Office
     (2) Segment

F.   Are benefits provided pursuant to a written plan or an established practice? If established practice, briefly describe.

G.   If this PRB plan is listed under 7.2.0.C., 7.2.0.D., or 7.2.0.E., indicate whether the plan is operated as an employee group insurance program. If this PRB plan is listed under 7.2.0.Y., indicate whether the plan is operated as a group insurance program. If the plan is operated as an employee group insurance program, report this plan under 7.3.0. and 7.3.1., as appropriate. If no, report the plan under 7.2.2.

1/ Describe on a Continuation Sheet.

Item No.	Item description
7.2.2	PRB Plan(s). Where numerous plans are listed under 7.2.0, for those plans which represent the largest dollar amounts of costs charged to Federal contracts, or other similar cost objectives, provide the information below on a continuation sheet. (If there are not more than three plans, provide information for all the plans. If there are more than three plans, information should be provided for those plans that in the aggregate account for at least 80 percent of those PRB costs allocable to this segment or business unit.)

A.   **Actuarial Cost Method.** Identify the actuarial cost method used for each plan or each benefit, as appropriate. Include the method used to determine the actuarial value of assets. Identify the amortization methods and periods used, if any. For plans listed under 7.2.0.B., enter "cash accounting". For plans listed under 7.2.0.F., enter "terminal funding" and identify the amortization methods and periods used, if any.

B.   **Actuarial Assumptions.** Describe the events or conditions for which significant actuarial assumptions are made for each plan. Do not include the current numeric values of the assumptions, but provide a description of the basis used for determining these numeric values. Also, describe the criteria used to evaluate the validity of an actuarial assumption. For plans under 7.2.0.B. or 7.2.0.F., enter "not applicable".

C.   **Funding.** Provide the following information on the funding practice for the costs of the plan: (For plans under 7.2.0.B. or 7.2.0.F., enter "not applicable".)

      1.   Describe the criteria for or practice of funding the measured and assigned cost; e.g., full funding of the accrual, funding is made pursuant to VEBA or 401(h) rules.
      2.   Briefly describe the funding arrangement.
      3.   Are all assets valued on the basis of a readily determinable market price? If yes, indicate the basis used for the market value. If no, describe how the market value is determined for those assets that are not valued on the basis of a readily determinable market price.

D.   **Basis for Cost Computation.** Indicate whether the cost for the segment is determined as:

      1.   An allocated portion of the total PRB plan cost
      2.   A separately computed PRB cost for one or more segments. If so, identify those segments.

E.   **Forfeitability.** Does each participant have a non-forfeitable contractual right to their benefit or account balance? If no, explain.

Z.   _____ Not applicable, proceed to item 7.3.0.

COST ACCOUNTING STANDARDS BOARD DISCLOSURE STATEMENT REQUIRED BY PUBLIC LAW 100-679	PART VII - DEFERRED COMPENSATION AND INSURANCE COST
	NAME OF REPORTING UNIT

Item No.	Item description
7.3.0	<u>Employee Group Insurance Charged to Federal Contracts or Similar Cost Objectives.</u> Does your organization provide group insurance coverage to its employees? (Includes coverage for life, hospital, surgical, medical, disability, accident, and similar plans for both active and retired employees, even if the coverage was previously described in 7.2.0.) A. _____ Yes (Complete Item 7.3.1) B. _____ No (Proceed to Item 7.4.0)
7.3.1	Employee Group Insurance Programs. For each program that covers a category of insured risk (e.g., life, hospital, surgical, medical, disability, accident, and similar programs for both active and retired employees), provide the information below on a continuation sheet, using the codes described below: (If there are not more than three policies or self-insurance plans that comprise the program, provide information for all the policies and self-insurance plans. If there are more that three policies or self-insurance plans, information should be provided for those policies and self-insurance plans that in the aggregate account for at least 80 percent of the costs allocable to this segment or business unit for the program that covers each category of insured risk identified.)

Description of Employee Group Insurance Program: _____

Policy or Self-Insurance Plan	Cost Accumulation (1)	Cost Basis (2)	Includes Retirees (3)	Purchased Insurance Rating Basis (4)	Self-Insurance	
					Projected Average Loss (5)	Insurance Admin. Expenses (6)

Column (1) -- <u>Cost Accumulation</u>

Enter Code A, B, or Y, as appropriate.

A. Costs are accumulated at the Home Office.
B. Costs are accumulated at Segment
Y. Other 1/

Column (2) -- <u>Cost Basis</u>

Enter code A, B, C, or Y, as appropriate.

A. Purchased Insurance from unrelated third party
B. Self-insurance
C. Purchased Insurance from a captive insurer
Y. Other 1/

1/ Describe on a Continuation Sheet.

Appendix 8.3   (Continued)

COST ACCOUNTING STANDARDS BOARD **DISCLOSURE STATEMENT** **REQUIRED BY PUBLIC LAW 100-679**	**PART VII - DEFERRED COMPENSATION** **AND INSURANCE COST**
	NAME OF REPORTING UNIT

Item No.	Item description
7.3.1	Continued. Column (3) – <u>Includes Retirees</u> Enter code A, B, C, or Y, as appropriate. A. No, does not include benefits for retirees. B. Yes, PRB benefits for retirees that are a part of a policy or coverage for both active employees and retirees are reported here instead of 7.2.0. C. Yes, PRB benefits for retirees are a part of a PRB plan previously reported under 7.2.0. Y. Other <u>1</u>/ Column (4) -- <u>Purchased Insurance Rating Basis</u> For each plan listed enter code A, B, C, Y, or Z, as appropriate. A. Retrospective Rating (also called experience rating plan or retention plan). B. Manually Rated C. Community Rated Y. Other, or more than one type <u>1</u>/ Z. Not applicable Column (5) – <u>Projected Average Loss</u> For each self-insured group plan, or the self-insured portion of purchased insurance, enter code A, B, C, Y, or Z, as appropriate. A. Self-insurance costs represent the projected average loss for the period estimated on the basis of the cost of comparable purchased insurance. B. Self-insurance costs are based on the contractor's experience, relevant industry experience, and anticipated conditions in accordance with accepted actuarial principles. C. Actual payments are considered to represent the projected average loss for the period. Y. Other, or more than one method <u>1</u>/ Z. Not applicable Column (6) -- <u>Insurance Administration Expenses</u> For each self-insured group plan, or the self-insured portion of purchased insurance, enter code A, B, C, D, Y, or Z, as appropriate, to indicate how administrative costs are treated. A. Separately identified and accumulated in indirect cost pool(s). B. Separately identified, accumulated, and allocated to cost objectives either at the segment and/or home office level (Describe allocation method on a Continuation Sheet). C. Not separately identified, but included in indirect cost pool(s). (Describe pool(s) on a Continuation Sheet) D. Incurred by an insurance carrier or third party (Describe accumulation and allocation process on a Continuation Sheet). Y. Other <u>1</u>/ Z. Not applicable <u>1</u>/ Describe on a Continuation Sheet.

	COST ACCOUNTING STANDARDS BOARD DISCLOSURE STATEMENT REQUIRED BY PUBLIC LAW 100-679	PART VII - DEFERRED COMPENSATION AND INSURANCE COST
		NAME OF REPORTING UNIT

Item No.	Item description
7.4.0	<u>Deferred Compensation, as defined in CAS 9904.415.</u> Does your organization award deferred compensation, other than ESOPs, which is charged to Federal contracts or similar cost objectives? (Mark one.) A. ____ Yes (Complete Item 7.4.1.) B. ____ No (Proceed to Item 7.5.0.)
7.4.1	General Plan Information. On a continuation sheet for all deferred compensation plans, as defined by CAS 9904.415, provide the following information: A. The plan name B. The Employer Identification Number (EIN) of the plan sponsor as reported on IRS Form 5500, if any C. The plan number as reported on IRS Form 5500, if any D. Indicate where costs are accumulated: (1) Home office (2) Segment E. Are benefits provided pursuant to a written plan or an established practice? If established practice, briefly describe.
7.4.2	Deferred Compensation Plans. Where numerous plans are listed under 7.4.1, for those plans which represent the largest dollar amounts of costs charged to Federal contracts, or other similar cost objectives, provide the information below on a continuation sheet. (If there are not more than three plans, provide information for all the plans. If there are more than three plans, information should be provided for those plans that in the aggregate account for at least 80% of these deferred compensation costs allocable to this segment or business unit): A. Description of Plan. 1. Stock Options 2. Stock Appreciation Rights 3. Cash Incentive 4. Other (explain) B. Method of Charging Costs to Federal Contracts or Similar Cost Objectives. 1. Costs charged when accrued and the accrual is fully funded 2. Costs charged when accrued and the accrual is partially funded or not funded 3. Costs charged when paid to employee (pay-as-you-go) 4. Other (explain)

FORM CASB DS-1 (REV 2/96) VII - 7

Appendix 8.3 (Continued)

291

Item No.	Item description
7.5.0	<u>Employee Stock Ownership Plans (ESOPs).</u> **Does your organization make contributions to fund ESOPs that are charged directly or indirectly to Federal contracts or similar cost objectives? (Mark one)** A. _____ Yes (Proceed to Item 7.5.1) B. _____ No (Proceed to Item 7.6.0)
7.5.1	**General Plan Information.** On a continuation sheet, for all ESOPs provide the following information: A. The plan name B. The Employer Identification Number (EIN) of the plan sponsor as reported on IRS Form 5500, if any C. The plan number as reported on IRS Form 5500, if any D. Indicate where costs are accumulated: (1) Home office (2) Segment E. Are benefits provided pursuant to a written plan or an established practice? If established practice, briefly describe. F. Indicate whether the ESOP plan is a defined-contribution plan subject to CAS 9904.412. (Answer Yes or No). G. Indicate whether the ESOP is leveraged or nonleveraged. H. <u>Valuation of Stock or Non-Cash Assets.</u> Are the plan assets valued on the basis of a readily determinable market price? If yes, indicate the basis for the market value. If no, indicate how the market value is determined for those assets that do not have a readily determinable market price. I. <u>Forfeitures and Dividends.</u> Describe the accounting treatment for forfeitures and dividends, on both allocated and unallocated shares, in the measurement of ESOP costs charged directly or indirectly to Federal contracts or similar cost objectives for each plan identified. J. <u>Administrative Costs.</u> Describe how the costs of administration of each plan listed are identified, grouped, and accumulated.

COST ACCOUNTING STANDARDS BOARD DISCLOSURE STATEMENT REQUIRED BY PUBLIC LAW 100-679	PART VII - DEFERRED COMPENSATION AND INSURANCE COST
	NAME OF REPORTING UNIT

Item No.	Item description
7.6.0	**Worker's Compensation, Liability, and Property Insurance.** Does your organization have insurance coverage regarding worker's compensation, liability and property insurance? A. _____ Yes (Complete Item 7.6.1.) B. _____ No (Proceed to Part VIII)
7.6.1	Worker's Compensation, Liability and Property Insurance Coverage. For each line of insurance that covers a category of insured risk (e.g., worker's compensation, fire and similar perils, automobile liability and property damage, general liability), provide the information below on a continuation sheet using the codes described below: (If there are not more than three policies or self-insurance plans that are applicable to the line of insurance, provide information for all the policies and self-insurance plans. If there are more than three policies or insurance plans, information should be provided for those policies and self-insurance plans that in the aggregate account for at least 80 percent of the costs allocable to this segment or business unit for each line of insurance identified.) Description of Line of Insurance Coverage: _____

			Crediting of Dividends	Self-Insurance	
Policy or Self-Insurance Plan	Cost Accumulation	Cost Basis	and Earned Refunds	Projected Average Loss	Insurance Administrative Expenses
	(1)	(2)	(3)	(4)	(5)

Column (1) -- Cost Accumulation

Enter code A, B, or Y, as appropriate.

A. Costs are accumulated at the Home Office.
B. Costs are accumulated at Segment
Y. Other 1/

Column (2) -- Cost Basis

Enter code A, B, C, or Y, as appropriate.

A. Purchased Insurance from unrelated third party
B. Self-insurance
C. Purchased Insurance from a captive insurer
Y. Other 1/

1/ Describe on a Continuation Sheet.

FORM CASB DS-1 (REV 2/96)   VII - 9

Appendix 8.3   (Continued)

293

Item No.	Item description
7.6.1	Continued.

Column (3) -- Crediting of Dividends and Earned Refunds

For each line of coverage listed, enter code A, B, C, D, E, Y, or Z, as appropriate.

A. Credited directly or indirectly to Federal contracts or similar cost objectives in the year earned

B. Credited directly or indirectly to Federal contracts or similar cost objectives in the year received, not necessarily in the year earned

C. Accrued each year, as applicable, to currently reflect the net annual cost of the insurance

D. Not credited or refunded to the contractor but retained by the carriers as reserves in accordance with 48 CFR 9904.416-50(a)(1)(iv)

E. Manually Rated - not applicable

Y. Other, or more than one 1/

Z. Not applicable

Column (4) -- Projected Average Loss

For each self-insured group plan, or the self-insured portion of purchased insurance, enter code A, B, C, Y, or Z, as appropriate.

A. Costs that represent the projected average loss for the period estimated on the basis of the cost of comparable purchased insurance.

B. Costs that are based on the contractor's experience, relevant industry experience, and anticipated conditions in accordance with generally accepted actuarial principles and practices.

C. The actual amount of losses are considered to represent the projected average loss for the period.

Y. Other, or more than one method. 1/

Z. Not applicable

Column (5) -- Insurance Administration Expenses

For each self-insured group plan, or the self-insured portion of purchased insurance, enter code A, B, C, D, Y, or Z, as appropriate, to indicate how administrative costs are treated.

A. Separately identified and accumulated in indirect cost pool(s).

B. Separately identified, accumulated, and allocated to cost objectives either at the segment and/or home office level (Describe allocation method on a Continuation Sheet).

C. Not separately identified, but included in indirect cost pool(s). (Describe pool(s) on a Continuation Sheet).

D. Incurred by an insurance carrier or third party. (Describe accumulation and allocation process on a Continuation Sheet).

Y. Other 1/

Z. Not applicable

1/ Describe on a Continuation Sheet.

FORM CASB DS-1 (REV 2/96)   VII - 10

Appendix 8.3   (Continued)

COST ACCOUNTING STANDARDS BOARD DISCLOSURE STATEMENT REQUIRED BY PUBLIC LAW 100-679	PART VIII - HOME OFFICE EXPENSES
	NAME OF REPORTING UNIT

Item No.	Item description
	Part VIII Instructions

FOR HOME OFFICE, AS APPLICABLE
(Includes home office type operations of subsidiaries, joint ventures, partnerships, etc.). 1/

This part should be completed only by the office of a corporation or other business entity where such an office is responsible for administering two or more segments, where it allocates its costs to such segments and where at least one of the segments is required to file Parts I through VII of the Disclosure Statement.

Data for this part should cover the reporting unit's (corporate or other intermediate level home office's) most recently completed fiscal year. For a corporate (home) office, such data should cover the entire corporation. For a intermediate level home office, they should cover the subordinate organizations administered by that group office.

8.1.0   Organizational Structure.

On a continuation sheet, provide the following information:

1. In column (1) list segments and other intermediate level home offices reporting to this home office,
2. In column (2) insert "yes" or "no" to indicate if reporting units have recorded any CAS-covered Government Sales, and
3. In column (3) provide the percentage of annual CAS-covered Government Sales as a Percentage of Total Sales (Government and Commercial), if applicable, as follows:

A. Less than 10%
B. 10%-50%
C. 51%-80%
D. 81%-95%
E. Over 95%

Segment or Other Intermediary Home Office (1)	CAS Covered Government Sales (2)	Government Sales as a Percentage of Total Sales (3)

8.2.0   Other Applicable Disclosure Statement Parts. (Refer to page (i) 4., General Instructions, and Parts V, VI and VII of the Disclosure Statement. Indicate below the parts that the reporting unit has completed concurrently with Parts I and VIII.)

A. _____ Part V - Depreciation and Capitalization Practices
B. _____ Part VI - Other Costs and Credits
C. _____ Part VII - Deferred Compensation and Insurance Costs
Z. _____ Not Applicable

1/ For definition of home office see 48 CFR 9904.403.

FORM CASB DS-1 (REV 2/96)   VIII - 1

Appendix 8.3   (Continued)

295

Item No.	Item description
8.3.0	**Expenses or Pools of Expenses and Methods of Allocation.**

For classification purposes, three methods of allocation, defined as follows, are to be used:

(i) Directly Allocated--those expenses that are charged to specific corporate segments or other intermediate level home offices based on a specific identification of costs incurred, as described in 9904.403;

(ii) Homogeneous Expense Pools--those individual or groups of expenses which are allocated using a base which reflects beneficial or causal relationships, as described in 9904.403; and

(iii) Residual Expense--the remaining expenses which are allocated to all segments by means of a base representative of the total activity of such segments.

Allocation Base Codes

A. Sales
B. Cost of Sales
C. Total Cost Input (Direct Material, Direct Labor, Other Direct Costs, and Applicable Overhead)
D. Total Cost Incurred (Total Cost Input Plus G&A Expenses)
E. Prime Cost (Direct Material, Direct Labor, and Other Direct Costs
F. Three factor formula (CAS 9904.403-50(c))
G. Processing or Conversion Cost (Direct Labor and Applicable Overhead)

H. Direct Labor Dollars
I. Direct Labor Hours
J. Machine Hours
K. Usage
L. Unit of Production
M. Direct Material Cost
N. Total Payroll Dollars (Direct and Indirect Employees)
O. Headcount or Number of employees (Direct and Indirect Employees)
P. Square Feet
Q. Value Added
Y. Other, or More than One Basis 1/

(On a continuation sheet, under each of the headings 8.3.1, 8.3.2, and 8.3.3 enter the type of expenses or the name of the expense pool(s). For each of the types of expense or expense pools listed, also indicate as item (a) the major functions, activities, and elements of cost included. In addition, for items listed under 8.3.2 and 8.3.3 enter one of the Allocation Base Codes A through Q, or Y, to indicate the basis of allocation and describe as item (b) the make up of the base(s). For example, if direct labor dollars are used, are ovetime premiums, fringe benefits, etc. included? For items listed under 8.3.2 and 8.3.3, if a pool is not allocated to all reporting units listed under 8.1.0, then list those reporting units either receiving or not receiving an allocation. Also identify special allocations of residual expenses and/or fixed mangement charges (see 9904.403-40(c)(3)).

1/ Describe on a Continuation Sheet.

COST ACCOUNTING STANDARDS BOARD DISCLOSURE STATEMENT REQUIRED BY PUBLIC LAW 100-679	PART VIII - HOME OFFICE EXPENSES
	NAME OF REPORTING UNIT

Item No.	Item description

Type of Expenses or Name of Pool of Expenses

8.3.1   **Directly Allocated**

    1.   _____

    (a)   **Major functions, activities, and elements of cost include:**

        _____
        _____

    2.   _____

    (a)   **Major functions, activities, and elements of cost include:**

        _____
        _____

8.3.2   **Homogeneous Expense Pools**   **Allocation Base Code**

    1.   _____   ____

    (a)   **Major functions, activities, and elements of cost include:**

        _____
        _____

    (b)   **Description/Make up of the allocation base:**

        _____
        _____

    2.   _____   ____

    (a)   **Major functions, activities, and elements of cost include:**

        _____
        _____

    (b)   **Description/Make up of the allocation base:**

        _____
        _____

Appendix 8.3   (Continued)

	COST ACCOUNTING STANDARDS BOARD DISCLOSURE STATEMENT REQUIRED BY PUBLIC LAW 100-679	PART VIII - HOME OFFICE EXPENSES
		NAME OF REPORTING UNIT

Item No.	Item description

8.3.3	**Residual Expenses** **Allocation Base Code**
	
	 _____ ____
	
	   (a) Major functions, activities, and elements of cost include:
	
	              _____
	              _____
	
	   (b) Description/Make up of the allocation base:
	
	              _____
	              _____

8.4.0	**Transfer of Expenses.** If there are normally transfers of expenses from reporting units to this home office, identify on a continuation sheet the classification of the expense and the name of the reporting unit incurring the expense.

FORM APPROVED OMB NUMBER
0348-0055

COST ACCOUNTING STANDARDS BOARD DISCLOSURE STATEMENT REQUIRED BY PUBLIC LAW 100-679 EDUCATIONAL INSTITUTIONS	INDEX

FORM CASB DS-2 (REV 10/94)

Appendix 8.4   Form CASB DS-2, Cost Accounting Standards Board
Disclosure Statement Required by Public Law 100-679 Educational Institutions

1.   This Disclosure Statement has been designed to meet the requirements of Public Law 100-679, and persons completing it are to describe the educational institution and its cost accounting practices. For complete regulations, instructions and timing requirements concerning submission of the Disclosure Statement, refer to Section 9903.202 of Chapter 99 of Title 48 CFR (48 CFR 9903).

2.   Part I of the Statement provides general information concerning each reporting unit (e.g., segments, business units, and central system or group (intermediate administration) offices). Parts II through VI pertain to the types of costs generally incurred by the segment or business unit directly performing under Federally sponsored agreements (e.g., contracts, grants and cooperative agreements). Part VII pertains to the types of costs that are generally incurred by a central or group office and are allocated to one or more segments performing under Federally sponsored agreements.

3.   Each segment or business unit required to disclose its cost accounting practices should complete the Cover Sheet, the Certification, and Parts I through VI.

4.   Each central or group office required to disclose its cost accounting practices for measuring, assigning and allocating its costs to segments performing under Federally sponsored agreements should complete the Cover Sheet, the Certification, Part I and Part VII of the Disclosure Statement. Where a central or group office incurs the types of cost covered by Parts IV, V and VI, and the cost amounts allocated to segments performing under Federally sponsored agreements are material, such office(s) should complete Parts IV, V, or VI for such material elements of cost. While a central or group office may have more than one reporting unit submitting Disclosure Statements, only one Statement needs to be submitted to cover the central or group office operations.

5.   The Statement must be signed by an authorized signatory of the reporting unit.

6.   The Disclosure Statement should be answered by marking the appropriate line or inserting the applicable letter code which describes the segment's (reporting unit's) cost accounting practices.

7.   A number of questions in this Statement may need narrative answers requiring more space than is provided. In such instances, the reporting unit should use the attached continuation sheet provided. The continuation sheet may be reproduced locally as needed. The number of the question involved should be indicated and the same coding required to answer the questions in the Statement should be used in presenting the answer on the continuation sheet. Continuation sheets should be inserted at the end of the pertinent Part of the Statement. On each continuation sheet, the reporting unit should enter the next sequential page number for that Part and, on the last continuation sheet used, the words "End of Part" should be inserted after the last entry.

FORM CASB DS-2 (REV 10/94)   (i)

Appendix 8.4 (Continued)

8.   Where the cost accounting practice being disclosed is clearly set forth in the institution's existing written accounting policies and procedures, such documents may be cited on a continuation sheet and incorporated by reference. In such cases, the reporting unit should provide the date of issuance and effective date for each accounting policy and/or procedures document cited. Alternatively, copies of the relevant parts of such documents may be attached as appendices to the pertinent Disclosure Statement Part. Such continuation sheets and appendices should be labeled and cross-referenced with the applicable Disclosure Statement item number. Any supplementary comments needed to fully describe the cost accounting practice being disclosed should also be provided.

9.   Disclosure Statements must be amended when disclosed practices are changed to comply with a new CAS or when practices are changed with or without agreement of the Government (Also see 48 CFR 9903.202-3).

10.   Amendments shall be submitted to the same offices to which submission would have to be made were an original Disclosure Statement being filed.

11.   Each amendment should be accompanied by an amended cover sheet (indicating revision number and effective date of the change) and a signed certification. For all resubmissions, on each page, insert "Revision Number ____" and "Effective Date _____" in the Item Description block; and, insert "Revised" under each Item Number amended. Resubmitted Disclosure Statements must be accompanied by similar notations identifying the items which have been changed.

ATTACHMENT - Blank Continuation Sheet

FORM CASB DS-2 (REV 10/94)   (ii)

Appendix 8.4   (Continued)

| COST ACCOUNTING STANDARDS BOARD DISCLOSURE STATEMENT REQUIRED BY PUBLIC LAW 100-679 EDUCATIONAL INSTITUTIONS | CONTINUATION SHEET |
| | NAME OF REPORTING UNIT |

Item No.	Item description

FORM CASB DS-2 (REV 10/94)

_ - _

Appendix 8.4   (Continued)

0.1 **Educational Institution**

    (a)   **Name**

    (b)   **Street Address**

    (c)   **City, State and ZIP Code**

    (d)   **Division or Campus of**
           (if applicable)

0.2 **Reporting Unit is: (Mark one.)**

    A.   ____   **Independently Administered Public Institution**
    B.   ____   **Independently Administered Nonprofit Institution**
    C.   ____   **Administered as Part of a Public System**
    D.   ____   **Administered as Part of a Nonprofit System**
    E.   ____   **Other (Specify)** _____

0.3 **Official to Contact Concerning this Statement:**

    (a)   **Name and Title**

    (b)   **Phone Number (include area code and extension)**

0.4 **Statement Type and Effective Date:**

    A.   **(Mark type of submission. If a revision, enter number)**

        (a)   ____   **Original Statement**
        (b)   ____   **Amended Statement; Revision No.** _____

    B.   **Effective Date of this Statement: (Specify)** _____

0.5 **Statement Submitted To (Provide office name, location and telephone number, include area code and extension):**

    A.   **Cognizant Federal Agency:** _____
                              _____

    B.   **Cognizant Federal Auditor:** _____
                              _____

FORM CASB DS-2 (REV 10/94)   **C - 1**

CERTIFICATION

I certify that to the best of my knowledge and belief this Statement, as amended in the case of a Revision, is the complete and accurate disclosure as of the date of certification shown below by the above-named organization of its cost accounting practices, as required by the Disclosure Regulations (48 CFR 9903.202) of the Cost Accounting Standards Board under 41 U.S.C. § 422.

Date of Certification: _____

_____
(Signature)

_____
(Print or Type Name)

_____
(Title)

THE PENALTY FOR MAKING A FALSE STATEMENT IN THIS DISCLOSURE IS PRESCRIBED IN 18 U.S.C. § 1001

FORM CASB DS-2 (REV 10/94)   C - 2

Appendix 8.4   (Continued)

COST ACCOUNTING STANDARDS BOARD DISCLOSURE STATEMENT REQUIRED BY PUBLIC LAW 100-679 EDUCATIONAL INSTITUTIONS	PART I - GENERAL INFORMATION
	NAME OF REPORTING UNIT

Item No.	Item description

Part I

1.1.0   <u>Description of Your Cost Accounting System</u> for recording expenses charged to Federally sponsored agreements (e.g., contracts, grants and cooperative agreements). (Mark the appropriate line(s) and if more than one is marked, explain on a continuation sheet.)

     A.   _____   **Accrual**

     B.   _____   **Modified Accrual Basis <u>1</u>/**

     C.   _____   **Cash Basis**

     Y.   _____   **Other <u>1</u>/**

1.2.0   <u>Integration of Cost Accounting with Financial Accounting</u>. The cost accounting system is: (Mark one. If B or C is marked, describe on a continuation sheet the costs which are accumulated on memorandum records.)

     A.   _____   **Integrated with financial accounting records (Subsidiary cost accounts are all controlled by general ledger control accounts.)**

     B.   _____   **Not integrated with financial accounting records (Cost data are accumulated on memorandum records.)**

     C.   _____   **Combination of A and B**

1.3.0   <u>Unallowable Costs</u>. Costs that are not reimbursable as allowable costs under the terms and conditions of Federally sponsored agreements are: (Mark one)

     A.   _____   **Specifically identified and recorded separately in the formal financial accounting records. <u>1</u>/**

     B.   _____   **Identified in separately maintained accounting records or workpapers. <u>1</u>/**

     C.   _____   **Identifiable through use of less formal accounting techniques that permit audit verification. <u>1</u>/**

     D.   _____   **Combination of A, B or C <u>1</u>/**

     E.   _____   **Determinable by other means. <u>1</u>/**

<u>1</u>/ **Describe on a Continuation Sheet.**

Appendix 8.4   (Continued)

COST ACCOUNTING STANDARDS BOARD DISCLOSURE STATEMENT REQUIRED BY PUBLIC LAW 100-679 EDUCATIONAL INSTITUTIONS	PART I - GENERAL INFORMATION
	NAME OF REPORTING UNIT

Item No.	Item description
1.3.1	Treatment of Unallowable Costs. (Explain on a continuation sheet how unallowable costs and directly associated costs are treated in each allocation base and indirect expense pool, e.g., when allocating costs to a major function or activity; when determining indirect cost rates; or, when a central office or group office allocates costs to a segment.)
1.4.0	Cost Accounting Period: _____ (Specify the twelve month period used for the accumulation and reporting of costs under Federally sponsored agreements, e.g., 7/1 to 6/30. If the cost accounting period is other than the institution's fiscal year used for financial accounting and reporting purposes, explain circumstances on a continuation sheet.)
1.5.0	State Laws or Regulations. Identify on a continuation sheet any State laws or regulations which influence the institution's cost accounting practices, e.g., State administered pension plans, and any applicable statutory limitations or special agreements on allowance of costs.
	1/ Describe on a Continuation Sheet.

FORM CASB DS-2 (REV 10/94)   I - 2

Appendix 8.4   (Continued)

306

COST ACCOUNTING STANDARDS BOARD DISCLOSURE STATEMENT REQUIRED BY PUBLIC LAW 100-679 EDUCATIONAL INSTITUTIONS	PART II - DIRECT COSTS
	NAME OF REPORTING UNIT

Item No.	Item description
	Instructions for Part II
	Institutions should disclose what costs are, or will be, charged directly to Federally sponsored agreements or similar cost objectives as Direct Costs. It is expected that the disclosed cost accounting practices (as defined at 48 CFR 9903.302-1) for classifying costs either as direct costs or indirect costs will be consistently applied to all costs incurred by the reporting unit.
2.1.0	<u>Criteria for Determining How Costs are Charged to Federally Sponsored Agreements or Similar Cost Objectives</u>. (For all major categories of cost under each major function or activity such, as instruction, organized research, other sponsored activities and other institutional activities, describe on a continuation sheet, your criteria for determining when costs incurred for the same purpose, in like circumstances, are treated either as direct costs only or as indirect costs only with respect to final cost objectives. Particular emphasis should be placed on items of cost that may be treated as either direct or indirect costs (e.g., Supplies, Materials, Salaries and Wages, Fringe Benefits, etc.) depending upon the purpose of the activity involved. Separate explanations on the criteria governing each direct cost category identified in this Part II are required. Also, list and explain if there are any deviations from the specified criteria.)
2.2.0	<u>Description of Direct Materials</u>. All materials and supplies directly identified with Federally sponsored agreements or similar cost objectives. (Describe on a continuation sheet the principal classes of materials which are charged as direct materials and supplies.)
2.3.0	<u>Method of Charging Direct Materials and Supplies</u>. (Mark the appropriate line(s) and if more than one is marked, explain on a continuation sheet.)
2.3.1	Direct Purchases for Projects are Charged to Projects at: A. _____ Actual Invoiced Costs B. _____ Actual Invoiced Costs Net of Discounts Taken Y. _____ Other(s) <u>1/</u> Z. _____ Not Applicable
2.3.2	Inventory Requisitions from Central or Common, Institution-owned Inventory. (Identify the inventory valuation method used to charge projects): A. _____ First In, First Out B. _____ Last In, First Out C. _____ Average Costs <u>1/</u> D. _____ Predetermined Costs <u>1/</u> Y. _____ Other(s) <u>1/</u> Z. _____ Not Applicable
	<u>1/</u> Describe on a Continuation Sheet.

FORM CASB DS-2 (REV 10/94)   II - 1

Appendix 8.4 (Continued)

COST ACCOUNTING STANDARDS BOARD DISCLOSURE STATEMENT REQUIRED BY PUBLIC LAW 100-679 EDUCATIONAL INSTITUTIONS	PART II - DIRECT COSTS
	NAME OF REPORTING UNIT

Item No.	Item description
2.4.0	**Description of Direct Personal Services.** All personal services directly identified with Federally sponsored agreements or similar cost objectives. (Describe on a continuation sheet the personal services compensation costs, including applicable fringe benefits costs, if any, within each major institutional function or activity that are charged as direct personal services.)
2.5.0	**Method of Charging Direct Salaries and Wages.** (Mark the appropriate line(s) for each Direct Personal Services Category to identify the method(s) used to charge direct salary and wage costs to Federally sponsored agreements or similar cost objectives. If more than one line is marked in a column, fully describe on a continuation sheet, the applicable methods used.)

<table>
<tr><td></td><td colspan="4">Direct Personal Services Category</td></tr>
<tr><td></td><td>Faculty
(1)</td><td>Staff
(2)</td><td>Students
(3)</td><td>Other 1/
(4)</td></tr>
<tr><td>A. Payroll Distribution Method (Individual time card/actual hours and rates)</td><td>____</td><td>____</td><td>____</td><td>____</td></tr>
<tr><td>B. Plan - Confirmation (Budgeted, planned or assigned work activity, updated to reflect significant changes)</td><td>____</td><td>____</td><td>____</td><td>____</td></tr>
<tr><td>C. After-the-fact Activity Records (Percentage Distribution of employee activity)</td><td>____</td><td>____</td><td>____</td><td>____</td></tr>
<tr><td>D. Multiple Confirmation Records (Employee Reports prepared each academic term, to account for employee's activities, direct and indirect charges are certified separately.)</td><td>____</td><td>____</td><td>____</td><td>____</td></tr>
<tr><td>Y. Other(s) 1/</td><td>____</td><td>____</td><td>____</td><td>____</td></tr>
</table>

1/ Describe on a Continuation Sheet.

FORM CASB DS-2 (REV 10/94) II - 2

Appendix 8.4 (Continued)

	COST ACCOUNTING STANDARDS BOARD DISCLOSURE STATEMENT REQUIRED BY PUBLIC LAW 100-679 EDUCATIONAL INSTITUTIONS	PART II - DIRECT COSTS
		NAME OF REPORTING UNIT

Item No.	Item description
2.5.1	**Salary and Wage Cost Distribution Systems.** Within each major function or activity, are the methods marked in Item 2.5.0 used by all employees compensated by the reporting unit? (If "NO", describe on a continuation sheet, the types of employees not included and describe the methods used to identify and distribute their salary and wage costs to direct and indirect cost objectives.) _____ Yes _____ No
2.5.2	**Salary and Wage Cost Accumulation System.** (Within each major function or activity, describe, on a continuation sheet, the specific accounting records or memorandum records used to accumulate and record the share of the total salary and wage costs attributable to each employee's direct (Federally sponsored projects, non-sponsored projects or similar cost objectives) and indirect activities. Indicate how the salary and wage cost distributions are reconciled with the payroll data recorded in the institution's financial accounting records.)
2.6.0	<u>Description of Direct Fringe Benefits Costs</u>. All fringe benefits that are attributable to direct salaries and wages and are charged directly to Federally sponsored agreements or similar cost objectives. (Describe on a continuation sheet <u>all</u> of the different types of fringe benefits which are classified and charged as direct costs, e.g., actual or accrued costs of vacation, holidays, sick leave, sabbatical leave, premium pay, social security, pension plans, post-retirement benefits other than pensions, health insurance, training, tuition, tuition remission, etc.)
2.6.1	**Method of Charging Direct Fringe Benefits.** (Describe on a continuation sheet, how each type of fringe benefit cost identified in item 2.6.0. is measured, assigned and allocated (for definitions, See 9903.302-1); first, to the major functions (e.g., instruction, research); and, then to individual projects or direct cost objectives within each function.)
2.7.0	<u>Description of Other Direct Costs</u>. All other items of cost directly identified with Federally sponsored agreements or similar cost objectives. (List on a continuation sheet the principal classes of other costs which are charged directly, e.g., travel, consultants, services, subgrants, subcontracts, malpractice insurance, etc.)

FORM CASB DS-2 (REV 10/94)   II - 3

Appendix 8.4   (Continued)

309

COST ACCOUNTING STANDARDS BOARD DISCLOSURE STATEMENT REQUIRED BY PUBLIC LAW 100-679 EDUCATIONAL INSTITUTIONS	PART II - DIRECT COSTS
	NAME OF REPORTING UNIT

Item No.	Item description
2.8.0	<u>Cost Transfers</u>. When Federally sponsored agreements or similar cost objectives are credited for cost transfers to other projects, grants or contracts, is the credit amount for direct personal services, materials, other direct charges and applicable indirect costs always based on the same amount(s) or rate(s) (e.g., direct labor rate, indirect costs) originally used to charge or allocate costs to the project (Consider transactions where the original charge and the credit occur in different cost accounting periods). (Mark one , if "No" , explain on a continuation sheet how the credit differs from original charge.) _____ Yes _____ No
2.9.0	<u>Interorganizational Transfers</u>. This item is directed only to those materials, supplies, and services which are, or will be transferred to you from other segments of the educational institution. (Mark the appropriate line(s) in each column to indicate the basis used by you as transferee to charge the cost or price of interorganizational transfers or materials, supplies, and services to Federally sponsored agreements or similar cost objectives. If more than one line is marked in a column, explain on a continuation sheet.)

	Materials (1)	Supplies (2)	Services (3)
A. At full cost <u>excluding</u> indirect costs attributable to group or central office expenses.	____	____	____
B. At full cost <u>including</u> indirect costs attributable to group or central office expenses.	____	____	____
C. At established catalog or market price or prices based on adequate competition.	____	____	____
Y. Other(s) <u>1/</u>	____	____	____
Z. Interorganizational transfers are not applicable	____	____	____

<u>1/</u> Describe on a Continuation Sheet.

FORM CASB DS-2 (REV 10/94)   II - 4

Appendix 8.4   (Continued)

Item No.	Item description
	Instructions for Part III

Institutions should disclose how the segment's total indirect costs are identified and accumulated in specific indirect cost categories and allocated to applicable indirect cost pools and service centers within each major function or activity, how service center costs are accumulated and "billed" to users, and the specific indirect cost pools and allocation bases used to calculate the indirect cost rates that are used to allocate accumulated indirect costs to Federally sponsored agreements or similar final cost objectives. A continuation sheet should be used wherever additional space is required or when a response requires further explanation to ensure clarity and understanding.

The following Allocation Base Codes are provided for use in connection with Items 3.1.0 and 3.3.0.

A.	Direct Charge or Allocation
B.	Total Expenditures
C.	Modified Total Cost Basis
D.	Modified Total Direct Cost Basis
E.	Salaries and Wages
F.	Salaries, Wages and Fringe Benefits
G.	Number of Employees (head count)
H.	Number of Employees (full-time equivalent basis)
I.	Number of Students (head count)
J.	Number of Students (full-time equivalent basis)
K.	Student Hours -- classroom and work performed
L.	Square Footage
M.	Usage
N.	Unit of Product
O.	Total Production
P.	More than one base (Separate Cost Groupings) 1/
Y.	Other(s) 1/
Z.	Category or Pool not applicable

1/   List on a continuation sheet, the category and subgrouping(s) of expense involved and the allocation base(s) used.

FORM CASB DS-2 (REV 10/94)   III - 1

Appendix 8.4   (Continued)

COST ACCOUNTING STANDARDS BOARD DISCLOSURE STATEMENT REQUIRED BY PUBLIC LAW 100-679 EDUCATIONAL INSTITUTIONS	PART III - INDIRECT COSTS
	NAME OF REPORTING UNIT

Item No.	Item description
3.1.0	**Indirect Cost Categories - Accumulation and Allocation.** This item is directed at the identification, accumulation and allocation of all indirect costs of the institution. (Under the column heading, "Accumulation Method," insert "Yes" or "No" to indicate if the cost elements included in each indirect cost category are identified, recorded and accumulated in the institution's formal accounting system. If "No," describe on a continuation sheet, how the cost elements included in the indirect cost category are identified and accumulated. Under the column heading "Allocation Base," enter one of the allocation base codes A through P, Y, or Z, to indicate the basis used for allocating the accumulated costs of each indirect cost category to other applicable indirect cost categories, indirect cost pools, other institutional activities, specialized service facilities and other service centers. Under the column heading "Allocation Sequence," insert 1, 2, or 3 next to each of the first three indirect cost categories to indicate the sequence of the allocation process. If cross-allocation techniques are used, insert "CA." If an indirect cost category listed in this section is not used, insert "NA.")

Indirect Cost Category	Accumulation Method	Allocation Base Code	Allocation Sequence
(a) Depreciation/Use Allowances/Interest			___
Building	___	___	
Equipment	___	___	
Capital Improvements to Land 1/	___	___	
Interest 1/	___	___	
(b) Operation and Maintenance	___	___	___
(c) General Administration and General Expense	___	___	___
(d) Departmental Administration	___	___	
(e) Sponsored Projects Administration	___	___	
(f) Library	___	___	
(g) Student Administration and Services	___	___	
(h) Other 1/	___	___	

1/ Describe on a Continuation Sheet.

FORM CASB DS-2 (REV 10/94)   III - 2

Appendix 8.4   (Continued)

312

Item No.	Item description
3.2.0	**Service Centers.** Service centers are departments or functional units which perform specific technical or administrative services primarily for the benefit of other units within a reporting unit. Service Centers include "recharge centers" and the "specialized service facilities" defined in Section J of Circular A-21. (The codes identified below should be inserted on the appropriate line for each service center listed. The column numbers correspond to the paragraphs listed below that provide the codes. Explain on a Continuation Sheet if any of the services are charged to users on a basis other than usage of the services. Enter "Z" in Column 1, if not applicable.)

(1) (2) (3) (4) (5) (6)

(a) **Scientific Computer Operations** __ __ __ __ __ __

(b) **Business Data Processing** __ __ __ __ __ __

(c) **Animal Care Facilities** __ __ __ __ __ __

(d) **Other Service Centers with Annual Operating Budgets exceeding $1,000,000 or that generate significant charges to Federally sponsored agreements either as a direct or indirect cost. (Specify below; use a Continuation Sheet, if necessary)**

_____ __ __ __ __ __ __

_____ __ __ __ __ __ __

(1) **Category Code:** Use code "A" if the service center costs are billed only as direct costs of final cost objectives; code "B" if billed only to indirect cost categories or indirect cost pools; code "C" if billed to both direct and indirect cost objectives.

(2) **Burden Code:** Code "A" -- center receives an allocation of all applicable indirect costs; Code "B" -- partial allocation of indirect costs; Code "C" -- no allocation of indirect costs.

(3) **Billing Rate Code:** Code "A" -- billing rates are based on historical costs; Code "B" -- rates are based on projected costs; Code "C" -- rates are based on a combination of historical and projected costs; Code "D" -- billings are based on the actual costs of the billing period; Code "Y" -- other (explain on a Continuation Sheet).

(4) **User Charges Code:** Code "A" -- all users are charged at the same billing rates; Code "B" -- some users are charged at different rates than other users (explain on a Continuation Sheet).

(5) **Actual Costs vs. Revenues Code:** Code "A" -- billings (revenues) are compared to actual costs (expenditures) at least annually; Code "B" -- billings are compared to actual costs less frequently than annually.

(6) **Variance Code:** Code "A" -- Annual variances between billed and actual costs are prorated to users (as credits or charges); Code "B" -- variances are carried forward as adjustments to billing rate of future periods; Code "C" -- annual variances are charged or credited to indirect costs; Code "Y" -- other (explain on a Continuation Sheet).

FORM CASB DS-2 (REV 10/94)

III - 3

Appendix 8.4   (Continued)

COST ACCOUNTING STANDARDS BOARD
DISCLOSURE STATEMENT
REQUIRED BY PUBLIC LAW 100-679
EDUCATIONAL INSTITUTIONS

PART III - INDIRECT COSTS

NAME OF REPORTING UNIT

Item No.	Item description
3.3.0	**Indirect Cost Pools and Allocation Bases** (Identify all of the indirect cost pools established for the accumulation of indirect costs, excluding service centers, and the allocation bases used to distribute accumulated indirect costs to Federally sponsored agreements or similar cost objectives within each major function or activity. For all applicable indirect cost pools, enter the applicable Allocation Base Code A through P, Y, or Z, to indicate the basis used for allocating accumulated pool costs to Federally sponsored agreements or similar cost objectives.)

<table>
<tr><td><u>Indirect Cost Pools</u></td><td>Allocation
Base Code</td></tr>
<tr><td>A. Instruction</td><td></td></tr>
<tr><td>_____ On-Campus
_____ Off-Campus
_____ Other 1/</td><td>_____
_____
_____</td></tr>
<tr><td>B. Organized Research</td><td></td></tr>
<tr><td>_____ On-Campus
_____ Off-Campus
_____ Other 1/</td><td>_____
_____
_____</td></tr>
<tr><td>C. Other Sponsored Activities</td><td></td></tr>
<tr><td>_____ On-Campus
_____ Off-Campus
_____ Other 1/</td><td>_____
_____
_____</td></tr>
<tr><td>D. Other Institutional Activities 1/</td><td>_____</td></tr>
</table>

Item No.	Item description
3.4.0	**Composition of Indirect Cost Pools**. (For each pool identified under Items 3.1.0 and 3.2.0, describe on a continuation sheet the major organizational components, subgoupings of expenses, and elements of cost included.)

1/ Describe on a Continuation Sheet.

Item No.	Item description
3.5.0	**Composition of Allocation Bases.** (For each allocation base code used in Items 3.1.0 and 3.3.0, describe on a continuation sheet the makeup of the base. For example, if a modified total direct cost base is used, specify which of the elements of direct cost identified in Part II, Direct Costs, that are included, e.g., materials, salaries and wages, fringe benefits, travel costs, and excluded, e.g., subcontract costs over first $25,000. Where applicable, explain if service centers are included or excluded. Specify the benefitting functions and activities included. If any cost objectives are excluded from the allocation base, such cost objectives and the alternate allocation method used should be identified. If an indirect cost allocation is based on Cost Analysis Studies, identify the study, and fully describe the study methods and techniques applied, the composition of the specific allocation base used, and the frequency of each recurring study .
3.6.0	**Allocation of Indirect Costs to Programs That Pay Less Than Full Indirect Costs.** Are appropriate direct costs of all programs and activites included in the indirect cost allocation bases, regardless of whether allocable indirect costs are fully reimbursed by the sponsoring organizations? A. ____ Yes B. ____ No 1/
	1/ Describe on a Continuation Sheet.

FORM CASB DS-2 (REV 10/94)   III - 5

Appendix 8.4   (Continued)

COST ACCOUNTING STANDARDS BOARD DISCLOSURE STATEMENT REQUIRED BY PUBLIC LAW 100-679 EDUCATIONAL INSTITUTIONS	PART IV - DEPRECIATION AND USE ALLOWANCES
	NAME OF REPORTING UNIT

Item No.	Item description
	Part IV
4.1.0	<u>Depreciation Charged to Federally Sponsored Agreements or Similar Cost Objectives</u>. (For each asset category listed below, enter a code from A through C in Column (1) describing the method of depreciation; a code from A through D in Column (2) describing the basis for determining useful life; a code from A through C in Column (3) describing how depreciation methods or use allowances are applied to property units; and Code A or B in Column (4) indicating whether or not the estimated residual value is deducted from the total cost of depreciable assets. Enter Code Y in each column of an asset category where another or more than one method applies. Enter Code Z in Column (1) only, if an asset category is not applicable.)

Asset Category	Depreciation Method (1)	Useful Life (2)	Property Unit (3)	Residual Value (4)
(a) Land Improvements	_____	_____	_____	_____
(b) Buildings	_____	_____	_____	_____
(c) Building Improvements	_____	_____	_____	_____
(d) Leasehold Improvements	_____	_____	_____	_____
(e) Equipment	_____	_____	_____	_____
(f) Furniture and Fixtures	_____	_____	_____	_____
(g) Automobiles and Trucks	_____	_____	_____	_____
(h) Tools	_____	_____	_____	_____
(i) Enter Code Y on this line if other asset categories are used and enumerate on a continuation sheet each such asset category and the applicable codes. (Otherwise enter Code Z.)	_____	_____	_____	_____

Column (1)--Depreciation Method Code

A. Straight Line
B. Expensed at Acquisition
C. Use Allowance
Y. Other or more than one method 1/

Column (2)--Useful Life Code

A. Replacement Experience
B. Term of Lease
C. Estimated service life
D. As prescribed for use allowance by Office of Management and Budget Circular No. A-21
Y. Other or more than one method 1/

Column (3)--Property Unit Code

A. Individual units are accounted for separately
B. Applied to groups of assets with similar service lives
C. Applied to groups of assets with varying service lives
Y. Other or more than one method 1/

Column (4)--Residual Value Code

A. Residual value is deducted
B. Residual value is not deducted
Y. Other or more than one method 1/

1/ Describe on a Continuation Sheet.

FORM CASB DS-2 (REV 10/94)   IV - 1

Appendix 8.4   (Continued)

COST ACCOUNTING STANDARDS BOARD DISCLOSURE STATEMENT REQUIRED BY PUBLIC LAW 100-679 EDUCATIONAL INSTITUTIONS	PART IV - DEPRECIATION AND USE ALLOWANCES
	NAME OF REPORTING UNIT

Item No.	Item description
4.1.1	**Asset Valuations and Useful Lives.** Are the asset valuations and useful lives used in your indirect cost proposal consistent with those used in the institution's financial statements? (Mark one.) A. _____ Yes B. _____ No 1/
4.2.0	<u>Fully Depreciated Assets</u>. Is a usage charge for fully depreciated assets charged to Federally sponsored agreements or similar cost objectives? (Mark one. If yes, describe the basis for the charge on a continuation sheet.) A. _____ Yes B. _____ No
4.3.0	<u>Treatment of Gains and Losses on Disposition of Depreciable Property</u>. Gains and losses are: (Mark the appropriate line(s) and if more than one is marked, explain on a continuation sheet.) A. _____ Excluded from determination of sponsored agreement costs B. _____ Credited or charged currently to the same pools to which the depreciation of the assets was originally charged C. _____ Taken into consideration in the depreciation cost basis of the new items, where trade-in is involved D. _____ Not accounted for separately, but reflected in the depreciation reserve account Y. _____ Other(s) 1/ Z. _____ Not applicable
4.4.0	<u>Criteria for Capitalization</u>. (Enter (a) the minimum dollar amount of expenditures which are capitalized for acquisition, addition, alteration, donation and improvement of capital assets, and (b) the minimum number of expected life years of assets which are capitalized. If more than one dollar amount or number applies, show the information for the majority of your capitalized assets, and enumerate on a continuation sheet the dollar amounts and/or number of years for each category or subcategory of assets involved which differs from those for the majority of assets.) A. Minimum Dollar Amount _____ B. Minimum Life Years _____
4.5.0	<u>Group or Mass Purchase</u>. Are group or mass purchases (initial complement) of similar items, which individually are less than the capitalization amount indicated above, capitalized? (Mark one.) A. _____ Yes 1/ B. _____ No
	1/ Describe on a Continuation Sheet.

FORM CASB DS-2 (REV 10/94)   **IV - 2**

Appendix 8.4   (Continued)

COST ACCOUNTING STANDARDS BOARD DISCLOSURE STATEMENT REQUIRED BY PUBLIC LAW 100-679 EDUCATIONAL INSTITUTIONS	PART V - OTHER COSTS AND CREDITS
	NAME OF REPORTING UNIT

Item No.	Item description
	Part V
5.1.0	<u>Method of Charging Leave Costs</u>. Do you charge vacation, sick, holiday and sabbatical leave costs to sponsored agreements on the cash basis of accounting (i.e., when the leave is taken or paid), or on the accrual basis of accounting (when the leave is earned)? (Mark applicable line(s))
	A. _____ Cash
	B. _____ Accrual <u>1/</u>
5.2.0	<u>Applicable Credits</u>. This item is directed at the treatment of "applicable credits" as defined in Section C of OMB Circular A-21 and other incidental receipts (e.g., purchase discounts, insurance refunds, library fees and fines, parking fees, etc.). (Indicate how the principal types of credits and incidental receipts the institution receives are usually handled.)
	A. _____ The credits/receipts are offset against the specific direct or indirect costs to which they relate.
	B. _____ The credits/receipts are handled as a general adjustment to the indirect pool.
	C. _____ The credits/receipts are treated as income and are not offset against costs.
	D. _____ Combination of methods <u>1/</u>
	Y. _____ Other <u>1/</u>
	<u>1/</u> Describe on a Continuation Sheet.

FORM CASB DS-2 (REV 10/94) V - 1

Appendix 8.4 (Continued)

Item No.	Item description
	Instructions for Part VI
	This part covers the measurement and assignment of costs for employee pensions, post retirement benefits other than pensions (including post retirement health benefits) and insurance. Some organizations may incur all of these costs at the main campus level or for public institutions at the governmental unit level, while others may incur them at subordinate organization levels. Still others may incur a portion of these costs at the main campus level and the balance at subordinate organization levels. Where the segment (reporting unit) does not directly incur such costs, the segment should, on a continuation sheet, identify the organizational entity that incurs and records such costs. When the costs allocated to Federally sponsored agreements are material, and the reporting unit does not have access to the information needed to complete an item, the reporting unit should require that entity to complete the applicable portions of this Part VI. (See item 4, page (i), General Instructions)
6.1.0	**Pension Plans.**
6.1.1	Defined-Contribution Pension Plans. Identify the types and number of pension plans whose costs are charged to Federally sponsored agreements. (Mark applicable line(s) and enter number of plans.)
	<u>Type of Plan</u> <u>Number of Plans</u>
	A. ____ Institution employees participate in ____ State/Local Government Retirement Plan(s)

	B. ____ Institution uses TIAA/CREF plan or ____
	          other defined contribution plan that
	          is managed by an organization not
	          affiliated with the institution

	C. ____ Institution has its own Defined- ____ Contribution Plan(s) <u>1/</u>
6.1.2	Defined-Benefit Pension Plan. (For each defined-benefit plan (other than plans that are part of a State or Local government pension plan) describe on a continuation sheet the actuarial cost method, the asset valuation method, the criteria for changing actuarial assumptions and computations, the amortization periods for prior service costs, the amortization periods for actuarial gains and losses, and the funding policy.)
	<u>1/</u> Describe on a Continuation Sheet.

	COST ACCOUNTING STANDARDS BOARD DISCLOSURE STATEMENT REQUIRED BY PUBLIC LAW 100-679 EDUCATIONAL INSTITUTIONS	PART VI - DEFERRED COMPENSATION AND INSURANCE COSTS
		NAME OF REPORTING UNIT

Item No.	Item description
6.2.0	Post Retirement Benefits Other Than Pensions (including post retirement health care benefits) (PRBs). (Identify on a continuation sheet all PRB plans whose costs are charged to Federally sponsored agreements. For each plan listed, state the plan name and indicate the approximate number and type of employees covered by each plan.) Z. [ ] Not Applicable
6.2.1	Determination of Annual PRB Costs. (On a continuation sheet, indicate whether PRB costs charged to Federally sponsored agreements are determined on the cash or accrual basis of accounting. If costs are accrued, describe the accounting practices used, including actuarial cost method, the asset valuation method, the criteria for changing actuarial assumptions and computations, the amortization periods for prior service costs, the amortization periods for actuarial gains and losses, and the funding policy.)
6.3.0	Self-Insurance Programs (Employee Group Insurance). Costs of the self-insurance programs are charged to Federally sponsored agreements or similar cost objectives: (Mark one.) A. _____ When accrued (book accrual only) B. _____ When contributions are made to a nonforfeitable fund C. _____ When contributions are made to a forfeitable fund D. _____ When the benefits are paid to an employee E. _____ When amounts are paid to an employee welfare plan Y. _____ Other or more than one method 1/ Z. _____ Not Applicable
6.4.0	Self-Insurance Programs (Worker's Compensation, Liability and Casualty Insurance.)
6.4.1	Worker's Compensation and Liability. Costs of such self-insurance programs are charged to Federally sponsored agreements or similar cost objectives: (Mark one.) A. _____ When claims are paid or losses are incurred (no provision for reserves) B. _____ When provisions for reserves are recorded based on the present value of the liability C. _____ When provisions for reserves are recorded based on the full or undiscounted value, as contrasted with present value, of the liability D. _____ When funds are set aside or contributions are made to a fund Y. _____ Other or more than one method 1/ Z. _____ Not Applicable
	1/ Describe on a Continuation Sheet.

FORM CASB DS-2 (REV 10/94)   VI - 2

Appendix 8.4   (Continued)

COST ACCOUNTING STANDARDS BOARD **DISCLOSURE STATEMENT** **REQUIRED BY PUBLIC LAW 100-679** **EDUCATIONAL INSTITUTIONS**	**PART VI - DEFERRED COMPENSATION AND** **INSURANCE COSTS**
	NAME OF REPORTING UNIT

Item No.	Item description
6.4.2	**Casualty Insurance.** Costs of such self-insurance programs are charged to Federally sponsored agreements or similar cost objectives: (Mark one.) A. _____ When losses are incurred (no provision for reserves) B. _____ When provisions for reserves are recorded based on replacement costs C. _____ When provisions for reserves are recorded based on reproduction costs new less observed depreciation (market value) excluding the value of land and other indestructibles. D. _____ Losses are charged to fund balance with no charge to contracts and grants (no provision for reserves) Y. _____ Other or more than one method 1/ Z. _____ Not Applicable 1/ **Describe on a Continuation Sheet.**

Item No.	Item description
	DISCLOSURE BY CENTRAL SYSTEM OFFICE, OR GROUP (INTERMEDIATE ADMINISTRATION) OFFICE, AS APPLICABLE. **Instructions for Part VII** This part should be completed <u>only</u> by the central system office or a group office of an educational system when that office is responsible for administering two or more segments, where it allocates its costs to such segments and where at least one of the segments is required to file Parts I through VI of the Disclosure Statement. The reporting unit (central system or group office) should disclose how costs of services provided by the reporting unit are, or will be, accumulated and allocated to applicable segments of the institution. For a central system office, disclosure should cover the entire institution. For a group office, disclosure should cover all of the subordinate organizations administered by that group office.
7.1.0	<u>Organizational Structure</u>. On a continuation sheet, list all segments of the university or university system, including hospitals, Federally Funded Research and Development Centers (FFRDC's), Government-owned Contractor-operated (GOCO) facilities, and lower-tier group offices serviced by the reporting unit.
7.2.0	<u>Cost Accumulation and Allocation</u>. On a continuation sheet, provide a description of: A. The services provided to segments of the university or university system (including hospitals, FFRDC's, GOCO facilities, etc.), in brief. B. How the costs of the services are identified and accumulated. C. The basis used to allocate the accumulated costs to the benefitting segments. D. Any costs that are transferred from a segment <u>to</u> the central system office or the intermediate administrative office, and which are reallocated to another segment(s). If none, so state. E. Any fixed management fees that are charged to a segment(s) in lieu of a prorata or allocation basis and the basis of such charges. If none, so state.

FORM CASB-CMF

FACILITIES CAPITAL
COST OF MONEY FACTORS COMPUTATION

CONTRACTOR:

BUSINESS UNIT:

ADDRESS:

COST ACCOUNTING PERIOD: C/Y 1997

		1. APPLICABLE COST OF MONEY RATE 6.375% (A)	2. ACCUMULATION & DIRECT DISTRIBUTION OF N.B.V.	3. ALLOCATION OF UNDISTRIBUTED — BASIS OF ALLOCATION	4. TOTAL NET BOOK VALUE — COLUMNS 2 + 3	5. COST OF MONEY FOR THE COST ACCOUNTING PERIOD — COLUMNS 1 x 4	6. ALLOCATION BASE FOR THE PERIOD — IN UNIT(S) OF MEASURE	7. FACILITIES CAPITAL COST OF MONEY FACTORS — COLUMNS 5 ÷ 6
BUSINESS UNIT FACILITIES CAPITAL	RECORDED	(B)	8,070,000					
	LEASED PROPERTY	(C)	200,000					
	CORPORATE OR GROUP	(D)	450,000					
	TOTAL		8,720,000					
	UNDISTRIBUTED	(F)	3,450,000					
	DISTRIBUTED	(E)	5,270,000					
OVERHEAD POOLS	Material		50,000	30,000	80,000	5,100	4,500,000	.1247%
	Engineering		270,000	726,000	996,000	63,495	2,000,000	3.1748%
	Manufacturing		4,750,000	2,800,000	6,750,000	430,312	3,000,000	14.3437%
	Technical Computer			444,000	444,000	28,305	2,280/hr.	12.4145/hr.
G&A EXPENSE POOLS	G &A Expense		200,000	250,000	450,000	28,688	36,700,000	.07822%
TOTAL			5,270,000	3,450,000	8,720,000	555,900	////////	////////

Appendix 8.5 Facilities Capital Cost of Money Factors Computation, Form CASB-CMF.

(A) When the facilities capital cost of money (FCCOM) is being calculated on a prospective basis for forward pricing proposals, the rate used should be the rate most recently published by the Secretary of Treasury. In calculating final fiscal year rates for application to flexibly priced contracts, the average rates incurred for the year should be used. For example, the FCCOM rate for fiscal year ended June 30, 1997 would be calculated as follows:

$$\frac{(7.0\% \times 6 \text{ mo.}) + (6.375\% \times 6 \text{ mo.})}{12 \text{ mo.}} = 6.6875\%$$

(B) Recorded capital assets are those that are owned and recorded on the books of the business unit.

(C) Leased property consists of the capitalized value of leases for which constructive ownership costs are allowed in lieu of rental costs under the procurement regulations (discussed in Chapter 7) under depreciation and rental costs). This category also includes the capitalized value of leases that are accounted for as capital leases under FAS 13 (discussed in Chapter 7 under depreciation costs).

(D) Corporate or group capital assets consist of the business unit's allocated share of corporate owned and leased (if meeting the criteria in the paragraph above) facilities.

(E) Distributed capital assets are those that are identified to specific primary indirect expense pools (e.g., manufacturing overhead and general and administrative expense).

(F) Undistributed capital assets are those that are identified to intermediate indirect expense pools (e.g., service centers) as well as any other capital assets not categorized as "distributed" e.g., land. Undistributed assets are allocated to the primary indirect expense FCCOM pools on (1) the same bases used to allocate the cost of the service centers to which the assets are identified, or (2) any other reasonable basis that approximates the absorption of depreciation/amortization of the facilities.

(G) The average net book value of distributed capital assets and allocated undistributed capital assets are added together.

(H) The FCCOM pools are calculated by applying the FCCOM rate to the total average net book values of the capital assets assigned to the various FCCOM indirect expense pools.

(I) The allocation bases are the same allocation bases used to allocate expenses in the primary indirect expense pools and any service centers that also allocate costs directly to contracts. For example, if manufacturing direct labor dollars are used to calculate a manufacturing overhead rate, those same manufacturing labor dollars would be used to calculate the manufacturing FCCOM rate.

Appendix 8.5 (Continued)

Chapter Nine

Payment and Contract Financing

9-1. BACKGROUND

In commercial contracting, the seller delivers and the buyer pays. With some exception, the government works the same way. Contractors deliver the supplies or services specified in the contract and submit an invoice, and the government eventually sends a check. Sometimes, the contract requires that the contractor's invoice include proof of delivery or proof of acceptance by the receiving agent specified in the contract. In any event, when the contractor completes the required performance, the government pays the amount specified in the contract.

9-2. COST-REIMBURSEMENT CONTRACTS

Allowable Cost and Payment

The Allowable Cost and Payment contract clause (Federal Acquisition Regulation [FAR] 52.216-7) provides for reimbursing costs incurred in contract performance that are deemed "allowable" by the contracting officer (CO), in accordance with government cost principles and contract terms. Notwithstanding the specific provisions of the cost principles (discussed in Chapter 7), the clause defines eligible costs to include only the following:

- Recorded costs for items or services purchased directly for the contract that, at the time of request for reimbursement, have been paid (not applicable to small business).
- Costs incurred, but not necessarily paid, for materials issued from the contractor's stored inventory, direct labor, direct travel, other direct in-house costs, and properly allocable and allowable indirect costs.
- Pension, deferred profit-sharing, and employee stock-ownership plan contributions that are, as a minimum, funded on a quarterly basis.
- Progress payments that have been paid to subcontractors.

Thus, for items purchased directly for a contract, the cash basis of accounting must be used unless the contractor is a small business. Furthermore, when pension, deferred profit-sharing, and employee stock-ownership plan contributions are funded less frequently than quarterly, the accrued cost must not be included in claimed indirect expenses until actually paid. The clause relies heavily on the contractor's accounting system to determine properly allocable costs. As discussed in Chapter 8, the allocation of costs to a government contract may be subject to some or all of the provisions of the CASB's rules, regulations, and standards.

The clause also (1) provides that, for other than small businesses, payment should not be made more frequently than biweekly; (2) gives the government the right to audit the invoices or vouchers and cost statements any time before final payment; and (3) describes the process for establishing billing rates and final indirect cost rates, which are discussed in Chapter 7.

Cost Reimbursement

A contractor is responsible for preparing and submitting reimbursement claims in accordance with the contract terms. Standard Forms 1034 (original) and 1034A (copy), Public Voucher for Purchases and Services Other Than Personal, are used to show the amount claimed for reimbursement. Standard Forms 1035 (original) and 1035A (copy), Public Voucher for Purchases and Services Other Than Personal—Continuation Sheet, are used for additional information required by the CO and/or the auditor. The public voucher forms may be reproduced from the FAR, obtained from an appropriate administrative contracting officer (ACO), or obtained at a nominal cost from the Government Printing Office. Unless the contractor is otherwise notified, public vouchers should be submitted to the auditor. The forms, together with instructions for their preparation, are illustrated in Appendices 9.1 and 9.2.

The Defense Contract Audit Agency's (DCAA) "Information for Contractors"[1] contains detailed information on preparing and processing public vouchers. The publication, which is available to the public, can be obtained from the Records Administrator, DCAA, Ft. Belvoir, VA 22060.

If a question on the allowability of direct or indirect cost is raised, the auditor, after coordinating with the ACO, may issue DCAA Form 1, Notice of Contract Costs Suspended and/or Disapproved (see Appendix 9.3), to deduct the cost from current payments. Defense Contract Audit Agency's Form 1 is distributed simultaneously to the contractor, the ACO, and the disbursing officer. The process for resolving disagreements with the deductions from current payments is described in FAR 42.803(b)(3).

Within one year (or longer when authorized by the CO) after completion of work under the contract, the contractor is required to submit to the government a completion invoice or completion voucher. The government is responsible for promptly paying to the contractor any allowable costs and fees that remain unpaid. Before final payment under the contract, the contractor and the assignee (if monies payable under the contract were assigned to a financial institution pursuant to the Assignment of Claims clause) must assign to the government any refunds, rebates, credits, or other amounts (including interest) properly allocable to costs for which the contractor has been reimbursed by the government under the contract. The assignment presumably extends indefinitely, so that any subsequent receipt of refunds or credits associated with amounts previously paid must be forwarded to the government. In addition, the contractor and assignee, if applicable, must provide a release discharging the government and its officials, agents, and employees from all liabilities, obligations, and claims arising out of or under the contract, subject to specified exceptions. Appendices 9.4 through 9.7 illustrate the Contractor's Release; Contractor's Assignment of Refunds, Rebates, Credits, and Other Amounts; Assignees's Release; and Assignees's Assignment of Refunds, Rebates, Credits, and Other Amounts.

Cost Reimbursement to Subcontractors

Costs incurred to reimburse a subcontractor under a cost-reimbursement-type subcontract, at any tier above the first fixed-price subcontract, are allowable to the extent that they are consistent with the cost principles. The subcontract may provide for the allowability determination to be made by either the prime contractor or the government CO, or the subcontract may not state who is to determine allowability. If the subcontractor also performs under prime contracts of its own and has a resident government auditor and CO, the subcontract may provide for the allowability determination by those government representatives. Under the contract's disputes procedures, a prime contractor has recourse to the government in the event of a disagreement concerning cost allowability; however, a subcontractor generally does not. As a result, subcontractors should avoid entering into any agreements that authorize government auditors or COs to make final cost decisions without preserving some means for review of their decisions.

Limitation of Cost or Funds

The Limitation of Cost clause (FAR 52.232-20) is used in fully funded cost-reimbursement contracts, whereas the Limitation of Funds clause (FAR 52.232-22) is inserted in incrementally funded cost-reimbursement contracts. These clauses generally obligate the contractor to notify the government when the contractor has reason to believe that within the next 60 days the cumulative cost incurred to date in performing the contract will exceed 75% of the estimated cost of, or funds allotted to, the contract. The contractor must also notify the government anytime the total contract cost is expected to be substantially more or less than the estimated cost or allotted funds.

The government is not obligated to reimburse the contractor for any cost in excess of the contract estimated cost or funds allotted to the contract, nor is the contractor obligated to continue performance or incur any costs in excess of the contract estimated costs or funds allotted. The Limitation of Cost or Funds clauses are designed to give the government an opportunity to decide whether it can and will provide additional funds necessary to complete the work.

Because of the reporting requirements of these clauses, companies contracting with the government must have adequate management-information systems to allow for timely notification of potential cost overruns. Boards and courts have ruled in numerous instances that an inadequate accounting or management-information system is not a valid excuse for not providing the notice required by the clauses.

- In *Research Applications, Inc.*,[2] the Armed Services Board of Contract Appeals (ASBCA) opined that "... the conclusion is inescapable that it was not the circumstances but appellant's own choice that produced the cost overrun as well as the lack of information on which a proper notice could have been based. Thus appellant cannot rely on the alleged unforeseeability of the overrun as an excuse."

- In *Datex Inc.*,[3] the ASBCA rejected the contractor's assertion that it was unaware when contract costs exceeded 75% of total estimated costs because actual overhead rates could not be determined until after contract completion and government audit. No notice was given to the government until settlement of final overhead rates (10 months after contract completion), at which time the contractor requested a contract modification to fund the contract overrun. In concluding that the contractor should have been able to foresee that its costs would exceed the estimated cost identified in the contract, the ASBCA cited a prior decision that a contractor is obligated to maintain an accounting and financial reporting system adequate to apprise the contractor of a possible overrun before the overrun occurs. The Board noted that the Limitation of Cost clause does not require an exact projection of the overrun but merely requires timely notice when the contractor believes total contract cost will exceed the estimated cost. The contractor was denied recovery of the overrun on the basis that it was not authorized to exceed the contractual estimated cost and that the CO was authorized to deny funding of the overrun.

- In an appeal heard by the Department of Transportation (DOT) Contract Appeals Board, *SAI Comsystems Corp.*[4] also lost its bid for government funding of its cost-plus-fixed-fee contract cost overrun. SAI claimed that the government's failure to make a timely audit excused the contractor's lack of notice and thus obligated the government to provide the requested funding. SAI also argued that, since the government knew that its indirect expense rates were higher than projected, the government should also have assumed that the contract cost would be overrun. The Board disagreed, noting that a contractor has a responsibility to maintain reasonable records and to expend reasonable effort in monitoring direct and indirect cost incurrence, in order to be able to ascertain when costs will approach the contract ceiling and to be able to cease performance in an orderly manner prior to reaching that level. The Board also rejected the notion that the government's knowledge of higher actual indirect expense rates automatically created either knowledge of the overrun or an obligation to provide funding. The Board emphasized that the Limitation of Cost clause limits the government's liability to reimburse costs incurred to the estimated cost. Consequently, unless the government obligates additional funds, mere notice of a probable overrun will not create a funding liability.

- The ASBCA denial of an appeal by *Varigas Research, Inc.*[5] for cost overrun funding emphasizes the critical nature of these control systems. Varigas was aware of the notification requirement and, upon reaching 75% of the estimated cost, notified the CO that it did not expect to overrun the contract. Yet, shortly before contract completion, Varigas suddenly realized that an overrun would occur, due primarily to an overrun subcontract. The CO denied the belated request for funding on the basis that the contractor's failure to comply with the notification requirement of the Limitation of Cost clause resulted from the contractor's poor management techniques and lack of control over the subcontractor. The ASBCA sustained the CO's decision and noted that "the subcontractor's failure to maintain adequate accounting records for its incurred costs and to notify the prime contractor of expected increases in the estimated cost does not excuse the prime contractor from the obligation to give notice to the government pursuant to the Limitation of Cost clause."

- The ASBCA denied Defense Systems Concepts, Inc.'s[6] request for funding its contract cost overrun. The Board concluded that the contractor should have provided timely notice of its pending overrun because it knew that (1) its actual indirect cost rates substantially exceeded provisional rates throughout contract performance, and (2) it was experiencing substantial schedule slippage in completing its final technical report.

The importance of monitoring costs incurred on cost-reimbursement-type contracts and of complying with the notification requirement is obvious; failure to comply can result in nonrecovery of cost. To ensure compliance and avoid the risk of financial loss, a contractor needs a cost accounting system that monitors costs incurred and a commitment system that monitors contractor obligations to suppliers and subcontractors.

Although the clauses explicitly relieve the government from any obligation to reimburse cost incurred in excess of the estimated cost, that does not mean that such overruns are never paid. The CO may recognize and fund an overrun when the contractor failed to give timely notice in strict compliance with the clause. This discretionary authority was emphasized in *ITT Defense Communications*,[7] when the ASBCA discussed the relationship between the notice requirement (paragraph [a] of the Limitation of Cost clause) and the government's action to fund an overrun (paragraph [b] of the clause):

> Paragraph [b] of the clause is in no way contingent upon the notice provision of paragraph [a]. The notice provides a means whereby the government receives advance notice of an anticipated shortage of funds to complete the contract, so as to give the government an opportunity to add funds in sufficient time to prevent the interruption of the work where additional funds are unavailable or unjustified. However, the government's exercise of its election under paragraph [b] is not conditioned on the contractor's compliance with the notice requirement of paragraph [a]. Even though there has been a flagrant violation of the notice requirement, the government may still, and frequently does, provide additional funds and continue the work under the contract. On the other hand, even though the contractor has complied fully and completely with the notice requirement, the government may still exercise its election not to provide additional funds and continue to work under the contract.

Since the decision to fund the overrun is discretionary, under what circumstances would the government most likely grant after-the-fact funding? A company would appear to have the strongest argument for funding when it can demonstrate that the overrun was unforeseeable and due to no fault of the contractor or when the government really needs the work.

- In *Metametrics, Inc.*,[8] the contract overrun was caused by an unforeseeable downturn in the contractor's business in the months following to contract completion. The dramatic drop-off in direct costs caused a substantial increase in the indirect expense rates allocable to the contract. In sustaining the contractor's appeal, the Department of Interior Board of Contract Appeals concluded the following:

> It is obvious that the reliability of overhead rate projections is dependent upon the timely acquisition of expected new business. An adequate accounting system is necessary to accurately project the effect that future business will have on the overhead rates. ... The more difficult problem involved in these cases is the lack of any standards by which to measure the adequacy of the contractor's new business projections. ... After the expected business has been lost with the resultant increase in overhead rates and a post-performance overrun, the conclusion is easily reached that the contractor should have known business would

be lost many months before, when it was time to give notice of an overrun. Procurement and award procedures do not support this conclusion. These procedures often stretch over many months or years. Lengthy interfaces between the government and contractors often precede the actual bidding or proposal effort. Evaluation and award after receipt of bids or proposals may involve extended periods. In actual practice, contractors rarely discontinue marketing efforts and expenditures until the expected business is awarded to another or a decision not to procure is announced. Under such circumstances, the placement of an unreasonable burden on the contractor to foresee the failure to secure expected business many months before the opportunity is actually lost results in reestablishing the total risk on the contractor to foresee and give notice of post-performance overhead induced overruns.

The post-performance overhead induced overrun should be funded where the contractor, through no fault or inadequacy in its accounting or business acquisition procedures, has no reason to foresee that a cost overrun will occur and the sole reason for refusal to pay the overrun is the contractor's failure to give proper notice. In the case before us, the parties agree on the adequacy of appellant's accounting system. The record discloses no basis on which appellant should have known, at the time that a notice of overrun should have been provided, that he would be markedly unsuccessful in acquiring new business.

- In *American Standard, Inc.* (also known as Melpar),[9] the ASBCA concluded that the CO erred in denying funding of costs that had been inadvertently omitted from an earlier funding request. In its decision, the Board reiterated the general requirements of an adequate accounting system:

  > With respect to the Melpar computer costs, incurred in December, 1967, Melpar admits that the omission of these cost entries from its books of account occurred through an internal error. A contractor has the responsibility of conducting an accounting system which gives up correct and timely data, sufficient to inform the contractor what his fiscal position might be vis-a-vis a cost ceiling or a cost limitation. We do not perceive this to be an unfair or an onerous burden, and certainly not an unconscionable responsibility, as argued by appellant. Generally where a contractor has put himself in an overrun position through his own error leading to unawareness of an overrun, contracting officers' denials of requests for funding have been sustained.

  However, the Board went on to note the mitigating circumstances of this particular appeal.

  > The error occurred before Melpar notified the contracting officer in March 1968, that an overrun was imminent. While the Limitation of Cost clause requires such a notice, as well as a notice when 75% of the estimated cost will be exceeded, the clause does not require that the specific amount of the overrun be given. It does require that the contractor provide a revised estimate of the cost to complete. The notice was given, but the estimate was obviously erroneous.

  > With respect to the omitted computer costs, it would be appropriate for the contracting officer to consider whether the $16,800 overrun would have been funded in the larger amount had the additional $5,215 also been presented as a cost; whether the government received the benefit of the work; whether the government did not specifically agree that verification of the existing data should be performed. ... Also for consideration is the fact that in the absence of an overrun, Melpar would not have been denied reimbursement for allowable costs at any time up to final payment under similar circumstances. In the Board's opinion, the contracting officer was not bound to deny the request for lack of notice. There was no bar to his exercising his discretion to allow this particular request. Accordingly, the Board will sustain the appeal with respect to the omitted computer costs only to the extent of remanding the matter to the contracting officer to permit exercise of his discretionary authority on the merits of appellant's request for additional funding for omitted computer costs.

- In *Clevite Ordinance*,[10] the ASBCA sustained the contractor's appeal for funding of the overrun on the basis that the government had constructively authorized the contractor to proceed. In its opinion, which was sharply critical of the procuring activity's actions, the Board concluded the following:

> The limitations on money and man-hours were reduced to meaningless ciphers by the conduct of the parties; performance by Appellant was prosecuted in obedience to explicit instructions of authorized and cognizant government personnel who were alert to the fiscal status of the contract on current and projected bases; and the government has reaped and enjoyed the benefits of Appellant's good faith performance in reliance upon assurance of reimbursement by an official bureau who we find to have been constituted in fact as the authorized representative of the contracting officer concerning the matters here in dispute.

- In *Dames & Moore*,[11] the Interior Board of Contract Appeals ruled that a contractor could recover its cost overrun on a cost-type contract despite failing to notify the government of the overrun as required by the Limitation of Costs clause. The Board's decision was consistent with previous decisions concerning contractors who maintained adequate accounting systems but could not reasonably foresee an overrun in time to notify the government. The increased overhead costs were attributable to (1) a lower level of business than previously projected and (2) the resolution of cost allowability issues between Dames & Moore and the DCAA. The Board concluded that the overrun resulted from cost issues that occurred near the end of the contract and were not resolved by the DCAA and the Environmental Protection Agency (EPA) until after the contract work had been completed. By that time, the contract had been fully funded. The Board ruled that the contractor was unable to avoid the incurrence of costs in excess of allocated funds and could not reasonably elect to cease work, therefore, the Limitation of Costs notice requirement was unenforceable.

- The ASBCA ruled that Dynamic Concepts, Inc.[12] was entitled to recover an amount in excess of the estimated cost stipulated for Option Year 1 of a time and material contract. Although the contractor gave no formal notice of overrun, it invoiced amounts for Option Year 1 that exceeded the Option Year 1 funded estimated cost. The CO knowingly paid such Option Year 1 invoices out of funds obligated for a two-month extension period designated as Option Year 2. The contractor's invoices for effort performed in (and funded for) Option Year 2 exceeded the funds remaining under the contract. The CO refused to pay the excess on the basis that the contractor had failed to provide timely notice of the overrun. The Board overruled the CO, concluding that the government had waived the notification requirement when it paid Option Year 1 invoices that exceeded the Option Year 1 estimated costs and funding obligation. In concluding that the four-element estoppel test had been met and that the government was thus estopped from relying on the notification requirement, the Board observed the following:

> There is no doubt that respondent knew of the overrun, element one, and appellant had the right to believe respondent's payment of overrun invoices was intended to induce continued performance, element two. Element three, the contractor must not be aware of the true facts that no implied funding of the overrun was intended, is not disproven by appellant's knowledge gained in litigation that respondent paid the latter Option Year 1 invoices out of funds allocated to the two-month extension period, since there is no proof that appellant knew so in September–October 1990. Appellant incurred continued performance costs in detrimental reliance on the respondent's conduct, element four.

Even with prompt reporting of possible overruns and requests for additional funds, a company may still be faced with the government's delay in providing written authority to continue. Whether to continue performance and risk not being paid is a management decision. Theoretically, perhaps the best approach is to maintain a timely record of expenditures, notify the government promptly, and then stop work when the ceiling is reached. However, while theoretically correct, this action is not altogether without risk. By stopping work, cost may be incurred that may be difficult or impossible to recover if and when work resumes. Also to be considered are the size of the contract in relation to the potential overrun, the government's funding situation, the possibility of follow-on work after the current contract, and the attitude of government representatives if the company does not complete the current contract.

Another area of risk is the performance, at the request of government employees, of additional tasks or functions that are not incorporated in the contract. The only person authorized to obligate the government to reimburse a contractor for effort performed is the CO. While the CO may rely on the advice of technical and financial experts, these other representatives may not obligate the government. Therefore, the company should obtain written approval from the CO for all changes in work and obtain overrun funding.

In *DBA Systems, Inc.,*[13] the contractor contended it was unable to give timely notice of its contract overrun because the overrun resulted from increased indirect expense rates recommended by the DCAA after contract completion. The CO was advised of the overrun in a letter dated one month after contract completion. The CO forwarded the letter to the contract specialist, who concluded that the contractor's position had merit; prepared a proposed contract modification to fund the overrun; and sent it to the CO, with a copy to the contractor. Before making his decision, the CO requested the ACO's opinion on the adequacy of the contractor's accounting methods and procedures. At the ACO's request, the DCAA concluded that the accounting system had, in fact, revealed the existence of the overrun on a timely basis. The CO rejected the contract modification because of the lack of timely notice of the overrun as required under the Limitation of Cost clause. The major issue in the appeal to the National Aeronautics and Space Administration (NASA) Board of Contract Appeals was whether the transmittal of the proposed contract modification to the contractor constituted notice, under the clause, of government approval to fund the overrun. The Board concluded it did not, since it was the CO, not the contract specialist, who was authorized to execute a contract on behalf of the government. Citing *Federal Crop Insurance Corporation v. Merrill,*[14] the Board concluded that "whatever the form in which the government functions, anyone entering into an arrangement with the government takes the risk of having accurately ascertained that he who purports to act for the government stays within the bounds of his authority."

9-3. FIXED-PRICE CONTRACTS

Invoicing

Contract Line Item Numbers

In structuring a contract, each unique product, part, item, or service is usually priced as a separate line item. Under the uniform contract format provided for in FAR 15.204-1, these contract line item numbers, known as CLINs, are listed in Section B of the contract. Typically, Section B also lists the part or service description, quantity, unit, unit price, and extended price.

For payment purposes, each line item is treated as a separate contract. Thus, a contractor may be paid the price of CLIN 1 of a contract even if work is still continuing on CLIN 2. To optimize cash flow on a contract, separate line item numbers should be established for severable portions of the work. Then, as each portion is completed and accepted by the government, the contractor can invoice for the price, including profit or fee, of that line item.

Fast Payment Procedure

The fast payment procedure allows payment, under limited conditions, to a contractor before government verification that supplies have been received and accepted. The conditions for using the procedure are as follows:

- Individual orders may not exceed $25,000.
- Supplies are delivered to locations that are geographically separate from, and lack adequate communications with, government receiving and disbursing activities, so it is impractical to make timely payment based on evidence of government acceptance.
- The purchasing instrument is a firm-fixed-price contract, purchase order, or delivery order.
- A system exists to ensure (1) documentation of performance, (2) timely feedback to the CO in case of contractor deficiencies, and (3) identification of suppliers that have a current history of abusing the fast payment procedure.

Fast payment orders are generally issued on DD Form 1155 (Appendix 9.8).

Prompt Payment Act

The Prompt Payment Act,[15] as amended on October 17, 1988, generally requires the federal government to pay business concerns from which goods and services are acquired within 30 days after receipt of a proper invoice unless the contract provides otherwise. Requests for interim financing, such as requests for progress payments and for interim billings on cost-type contracts, are not considered invoices for purposes of the act except in construction contracting. If the payment is not made within 15 days after the prescribed payment due date time, the government must pay interest to the contractor commencing the 30th day after receipt of the invoice. Interest is paid at the same rate applied to claims adjudicated under the Contract Disputes Act of 1978. The 30th day is calculated from the later of the date of receipt of a proper invoice or the seventh day after acceptance of the supplies or services as specified in the contract unless the contract specifies otherwise. In addition, if payment does not include interest when it is made, and if the agency does not remit interest owed within 10 days, contractors may request an interest penalty within 40 days of the incomplete payments. This penalty is a minimum of $25 and a maximum of $5,000.

A *business concern* is defined in the act as "any person engaged in trade or business and nonprofit entities operating as contractors." Thus, the law would appear to fully apply to foreign business concerns as well as U.S. firms.

A *proper invoice* is defined as an invoice that includes the following information:

- Date
- Name of contractor
- Address of contractor
- Address for sending payment

- Contract or order number
- Description of supplies or services provided
- Shipping information
- Quantity, unit price, and extended price
- Payment terms, if any
- Point of contact for additional information

A federal agency must notify a contractor within seven days of receipt of an invoice whenever an error or defect in the invoice would prevent the clock from running on the 30-day time period. If an error or defect is discovered in an invoice after the seventh day, the clock, for interest purposes, picks up where it was when the error or defect was discovered upon correction and resubmission by the contractor, except that the government once again has seven days to review and reject the invoice without further penalty.

The Office of Management and Budget (OMB) published OMB Circular No. A-125, Prompt Payment, which prescribes policies and procedures for implementing the act and requires each federal agency to report annually to the OMB the amount of interest penalties paid. The circular also requires agencies to take full advantage of the 30-day period before making payments. Therefore, for certain agencies that normally paid in considerably less than 30 days (such as the Department of Defense [DOD]), the Prompt Payment Act has actually slowed payments. On the other hand, for agencies that consistently took more than 30 days to pay their bills, the act has generally improved a contractor's cash flow.

The regulations implementing the Prompt Payment Act point up the importance of effective accounting and billing systems to ensure the timely submission of properly prepared invoices. In far too many instances, payment delay can be attributed to the contractor's failure to submit an acceptable invoice on a timely basis. Contractors should review their accounting and billing procedures to make certain that the systems are capable of taking full advantage of this act.

Contract Financing

The FAR, Part 32, defines government contract financing in terms of partial payments, progress payments, guaranteed loans, and advance payments for contracts other than cost-reimbursement contracts. Technically, partial payments are a form of payment, not contract financing, but they do reduce a contractor's need for contract financing by providing payments for partial deliveries.

If contract financing were not available, fewer contractors would be financially able to handle long-term contracts. It clearly is in the government's interest to have as many contractors as possible compete for government business. A broad base of suppliers enhances competition, opportunities for alternative selections, and expansion capability in times of national emergency. The government's financing policy is also an essential element in implementing its small business policy. While government financing is designed to broaden the supplier base, it is generally available to provide working capital only, not facilities expansion. An exception would be when the government procures facilities under contract.

To be considered eligible for government financing, a contractor must meet certain minimum standards for "responsibility," as prescribed in FAR 9.104-1. The contractor must:

- Have or be able to obtain (1) adequate financial resources (including government financing), (2) the necessary organization, and (3) the necessary facilities to perform the contract
- Be able to meet necessary performance and delivery schedules, considering existing commercial and government commitments
- Have a satisfactory performance record
- Have a satisfactory record of integrity and business ethics
- Have or be able to obtain the necessary organization, experience, accounting and operational controls, and technical skills
- Have or be able to obtain the necessary equipment and facilities
- Be qualified and eligible to receive a contract under applicable laws and regulations

Government financing may be necessary for successful contract performance. A competent and capable contractor that is considered responsible but requires some form of government financing will be treated no differently than a contractor that has no need for financial assistance. Federal Acquisition Regulation 32.107(a) states: "If the contractor or offeror meets the standards prescribed for responsible prospective contractors at 9.104, the contracting officer shall not treat the contractor's need for contract financing as a handicap for a contract award; e.g., as a responsibility factor or evaluation criterion."

A company that did not initially request government financing may request it after award. A determination that government financing is required will be made if financing is essential to successful contract performance. To this end, FAR 32.107(b) provides that "the contractor should not be disqualified from contract financing solely because the contractor failed to indicate a need for contract financing before the contract was awarded."

Several forms of financing are available to government contractors, ranging from those in which the government assumes no risk at all to those in which the government assumes total risk. Although the type of financing available depends on the specific situation and conditions, the nature of the contract, the contractor's needs, and regulatory or statutory restrictions, FAR 32.106 establishes the following order of preference:

1. Private financing (without governmental guarantee)
2. Customary progress payments (progress payments that conform to certain requirements for preproduction period, contract size, and percentage of payments) or progress payments based on a percentage or stage of completion (confined to contracts for construction; shipbuilding; and ship conversion, alteration, or repair)
3. Guaranteed loans (with appropriate participation of financial institutions)
4. Unusual progress payments, such as payments made more often than monthly or at a rate other than the customary progress payment rate
5. Advance payments

Private Financing and Assignment of Claims

For obvious reasons, the government prefers that contractors secure financing from the private sector. This may be accomplished in numerous ways, such as issuing stocks or bonds, using idle funds, or obtaining bank loans. The use of incentive-type contracts may enhance a company's ability to obtain financing from private sources through their potential to increase the percentage of profit.

Although federal law generally prohibits the assignment of claims against the government, contractors may use government contracts as collateral on loans under the provisions of the Assignment of Claims Act of 1940.[16] The standard Assignment of Claims clause (FAR 52.232-23), which is included in all government contracts, provides the contractual basis, pursuant to the act, for a government contractor to assign monies payable under the contract to a bank or other approved financial institution. The assignee is required to file written notice of the assignment and a copy of the assignment instrument with the CO, the disbursing officer, and the surety on any contract. Timely notice is important. An assignee's claim for funds paid to the contractor after execution of an assignment may be denied if the government disbursing officer has not received the required written notification from the assignee at the time of payment.[17]

The Assignment of Claims clause protects a bank that lends money on the basis of the assignment of payments under the government contract. Under the assignment, the government pays the bank or other approved financial institution directly. Once paid, the money is not subject to later recovery by the government. In addition, the clause provides, that in time of war or national emergency, amounts payable under the contract are generally not subject to setoff for any liability arising independently of the contract or for any liability arising from renegotiation, fines, penalties or taxes, or Social Security contributions, whether or not independent of the contract. This provision, however, does not exempt from setoffs any penalties withheld or collected in accordance with the contract terms. Thus, withholding that is required under the contract, such as for failure to comply with the federal labor laws, is not exempt from setoff.[18]

Since the Assignment of Claims Act no longer requires a loan to be tied to a particular security, the use of a revolving-credit financing device is considered acceptable. However, an assignment of a claim against the government should identify the particular contract(s) involved. Banks are entitled to payments due under government contracts by virtue of a blanket security agreement in which the existence of a valid assignment applicable to contract payments is adequately documented and the loan note that assigns all accounts receivable to the bank contains a schedule of the contractor's accounts receivable, including the contract account.[19] However, it has been determined that a bank is not entitled to monies owed the contractor when the blanket assignment does not comply with the Assignment of Claims Act, such as when the government has not been notified of the assignment or when the bank's security agreement has not been amended to make the agreement part of the blanket assignment.[20]

Private financing through assignment of claims keeps the government out of the financing business. It also benefits the contractor in that time is not consumed by government reviews prior to loan approval. The substantial disadvantage is that the interest expense incurred on commercial loans is not recoverable under government contracts.

Customary Progress Payments

Under the provisions of the Progress Payments clause (FAR 52.232-16), fixed-price contracts requiring the use of significant contractor working capital for extended periods generally provide for progress payments if the contractor is reliable, is in satisfactory financial condition, and has an adequate accounting and control system. Payments are made as work progresses, as measured by eligible costs incurred, percentage of completion, or other measure of the specific stages of physical completion. As previously stated, progress payments based on percentages or stages of physical completion are normally restricted to construction-type contracts or shipbuilding, conversion, alteration, or repair contracts. Consequently, most progress payments are based on incurred costs.

Customary progress payments are generally considered reasonably necessary when a contract or a grouping of contracts exceeds $1 million ($100,000 for small business concerns) and when lead time between the initial incurrence of cost and the first delivery or completion of service extends six months (four months for small business concerns). Progress payments are not permitted for quick-turnover items for which progress payments are not a customary commercial practice. Examples include clothing, medical supplies, and standard items not requiring the contractor's substantial accumulation of predelivery expenditures.

Payments are based on specified percentages applied to eligible costs incurred by the contractor in performing the contract. These customary progress payment rates, as set forth in FAR 32.501-1, are 80% for large business concerns and 85% for small business concerns.

As economic conditions change, the customary progress payment rates may be changed as well to reflect the changing availability of private financing. Once a contract is awarded, the progress payment rate in effect at the time of award stays in effect for that contract unless changed by a specific contract modification.

The DOD developed different customary rates for contracts awarded on or after July 1, 1991. Rates established at that time were 85% for large business concerns, 90% for small business concerns, and 95% for small disadvantaged business concerns. The DOD reduced the customary progress payment rate for large business concerns from 85% to 75% for contracts issued on or after November 11, 1993. This action was taken to implement Section 8155 of the DOD Appropriations Act for Fiscal Year 1994.[21] When the statutory requirement for the progress payment rate reduction expired September 30, 1994, the DOD was free to raise progress payment rates for large business concerns, but it declined to do so.

Department of Defense contractors used to be able to request flexible progress payments in lieu of the standard progress payments, on negotiated contracts over $1 million, provided that they were performed at least partially in the United States and that certified cost or pricing data were submitted before award. The Flexible Progress Payments clause was contained in Defense FAR Supplement (DFARS) 252.232-7004. The underlying DOD policy behind flexible progress payments was that contractors should maintain a minimum investment in contract work-in-process inventory over the contract performance period. By considering the contractor's cash flow on the specific contract, the flexible progress payment formula calculated the highest possible progress payment rate that still achieved the required contractor investment in the contract work-in-process inventory. Historically, this required investment in work in process was consistent with the progress payment rate; the sum of the required flexible investment rate and the customary progress payment rate equaled 100%. Flexible progress payments are not available for contracts awarded as a result of solicitations issued on or after November 11, 1993.

Eligible Costs. Eligible costs include all expenses of contract performance that are allowable, reasonable, allocable to the contract, consistent with sound and generally accepted accounting principles and practices, and not otherwise excluded by the contract. However, costs eligible for reimbursement under monthly progress payments are limited to the following:

- Recorded allowable costs that, at the time of request for reimbursement, have been paid for items or services purchased directly for the contract (For small businesses, these costs need not be paid.)
- Allowable costs incurred, but not necessarily paid, for materials issued from the contractor's stored inventory, direct labor, direct travel, other direct in-house costs, and properly allocable and allowable indirect costs
- Allowable pension, deferred profit-sharing, and employee stock-ownership plan contributions that are funded on a quarterly basis
- Unliquidated progress payments to subcontractors (However, these costs are fully allowed and not subject to reduction by applying progress payment rates.)

Thus, for items purchased directly for a contract, the cash basis of accounting must be used unless the contractor is a small business. Furthermore, when pension, deferred profit-sharing, and employee stock-ownership plan contributions are funded less frequently than quarterly, the accrued cost must be deleted from claimed indirect expenses until actually paid.

Title. The standard progress payment clauses provide that, upon signing the contract, title to all parts, materials, inventories, work in process, special tooling and test equipment, nondurable tools, jigs, dies, fixtures, molds, patterns, taps, gauges, other similar manufacturing aids, drawings, and technical data acquired or produced for and allocable to the contract vests immediately in the government. Title to all like property later acquired or produced and charged to the contract also vests in the government. Such property, however, is not considered government-furnished property. Vesting is intended to accomplish two things:

1. The government's interests are protected in that the assets are essentially used as collateral against progress payments made.
2. The vesting of title in the U.S. government makes it more difficult for local jurisdictions to impose property taxes on those items.

Although title transfers to the government, the risk of loss to the property remains with the contractor before delivery to the government. If the property is lost, stolen, damaged, or destroyed, the contractor must refund any progress payments attributable to those items. The property must also be handled and disposed of in accordance with contract provisions, such as the Default, Termination, and Special Tooling clauses, as well as the special default provisions included in the Progress Payments clause. Production scrap may be sold by the contractor without prior government approval, but the proceeds must be credited against the cost of performance. However, for the disposal of other property, prior government approval must be obtained and the cost allocable to the disposed property must be credited to the cost of contract performance, and the company must repay any prior progress payments allocable to the disposed property. Also, title to the government must be free of all encumbrances. The contractor's certification that title is free and clear is generally relied upon unless other available information indicates that the property may be subject to an encumbrance. If any encumbrances against the property arise to prevent the contractor from transferring clear title to the government, the government will act to protect its interest in such title. When the contract terms and conditions have been completely fulfilled and all progress payments have been liquidated, the title of any property remaining in the contractor's possession that is not deliverable to the government under the contract terms reverts to the contractor.

In *Marine Midland Bank v. United States,*[22] the Court of Claims took issue with the government's assertion that upon making progress payments, title for materials, work in progress, and so on actually passed to the government. The court concluded that progress payments were, in effect, loans and that the Progress Payments clause merely granted the government a lien against the items. The court noted that in the clause:

> "Title" is meant to carry no risks for the government and is shifted back to the contractor when it would be unneeded or undesired. In short, the government takes an interest in the contractor's inventory but does not want, and does not take, any of the responsibilities that go with ownership.
>
> The question raised, then, is what title vesting means for the purposes of the government's financing program, when it is evident that "title" is not used literally in the title vesting clause or the regulations. Indeed it would do violence to the system that the clause and regulations set up to say that the government "owns" covered property when it is apparent that the government specifically exempts itself from most of the incidents of ownership. Reading the clause and all of the regulations together, it is plain that ownership is not taken, but rather the government takes a security interest in the contractor's inventory, to secure the funds loaned to the contractor through progress payments. Such an interest is readily identifiable in common parlance as a lien, as plaintiff argues, despite the use of the term title.

However, even in light of this court decision, the government's interest still appears to be adequately protected, for the court concluded that "the rule of decision we choose for this case is to make the government's security interest under its title vesting procedures paramount to the liens of general creditors."

In *United States v. American Pouch Foods, Inc.,*[23] a U.S. District Court disagreed with the earlier *Marine Midland* decision and ruled that the Progress Payments clause granted to the government "full, absolute title in the property covered by the vesting clause." Because of these conflicting court decisions, this issue is likely to be further litigated.

The Progress Payments clause contains a specific reservation of government rights that protects the rights and remedies available to the government under other clauses.

Liquidation. As contract items are delivered, the progress payments previously made on the items delivered must be liquidated. The regulations prescribe what percentages of payments due under the contract for delivered items are to be liquidated against outstanding progress payments.

Under the ordinary method for liquidating progress payments, the same percentage used for billing progress payments is used for liquidating progress payments. The ordinary method is used when the original cost estimates are accurate and the resulting profit experienced under the contract is comparable to the profit estimated. Under certain conditions, contracts may be amended to reduce the progress payment liquidation rate so that the contractor retains the earned profit on items delivered and accepted.

The government may reduce or suspend progress payments or increase the liquidation rate if a contractor:

- Fails to comply with a material provision of the contract
- Endangers contract performance because of lack of progress or insecure financial condition
- Allocates excessive inventory to the contract
- Is delinquent in paying costs incurred under the contract

- Fails to make progress to the extent that unliquidated progress payments exceed the value of the work done on the undelivered portions

- Realizes less profit than that estimated and used in computing the liquidation rate

Action to reduce or suspend progress payments is not taken precipitantly. It requires notice to the contractor and an examination of the contractor's financial position, including the effect of a reduction in the progress payments. Although withholding financing is generally not in the government's interest, government representatives are obligated to protect the government's interest.

Federal Acquisition Regulation 32.503-6(g) prescribes a formula the government is to apply to individual progress payments for contracts considered to be in a loss position.

Preparing Progress Payment Requests.   Contracts that provide for progress payments require that the contractor maintain an adequate accounting system to accumulate contract costs. The contractor must also promptly furnish all reasonably requested reports, certificates, and financial statements. Another contract clause gives the government the right to review the contractor's books and records related to contract performance. However, the FAR specifically provides that unless the reliability or adequacy of the contractor's cost accounting system and controls is in question, progress payments may be made before completion of the review. Furthermore, FAR 32.503-4 states that when there is doubt about the amount of a progress payment request, only the amount in doubt should be withheld subject to later adjustment after the review. The DCAA has developed a time-share computer program known as PROPAY to assist in reviews of individual progress payment requests.

Requests for progress payments are submitted on a monthly or longer basis on Standard Form 1443, Contractor's Request for Progress Payment. The form and preparation instructions are presented in Appendix 9.9. The instructions are generally self-explanatory, but the estimate to complete (line 12b) is often given little attention by a contractor. However, from the government's viewpoint, it is one of the most critical items on the form, since a comparison of the estimate at completion with the contract price indicates whether the contract is in a loss position or is earning a substantially higher profit rate than was negotiated. In either event, the government may find it appropriate to change the liquidation rate. The relationship of the estimate at completion to contract price should be the same as the relationship of the cost of delivered/invoiced items to the price of delivered/invoiced items. Consequently, the government is concerned about an understatement of the estimate at completion, since it results in an overstatement of the costs eligible for progress payments applicable to undelivered/invoiced items. The instructions on the form require that the contractor update the estimate to complete at least every six months.

The Federal Circuit ruled in *Aydin Corp. v. Widnall*[24] that the Progress Payments clause included in defense contracts [DFARS 252.232-7007(a)] requires only accumulation of total contract costs, not costs by individual delivery orders within a contract. In its decision, the court noted:

> Nothing in the [progress payment] clauses directs Aydin to segregate its costs by delivery order. To the contrary, the clause focuses on "cumulative total costs" from delivery order to delivery order under this contract. ... The MUTES contract also does not incorporate regulations requiring Aydin to revamp its standard accounting practice of billing costs based on the overall contract.

On June 5, 1997, the DOD proposed to implement a requirement, effective October 1, 1997, for matching progress payments with contract accounting and appropriation classifications. Because contractor cost accounting systems do not generally accumulate costs by CLIN and accounting/appropriation classification, implementation of the proposal was projected to be quite costly. The proposal was put on hold in October 1997, pending further study. However, a second proposed rule was published on November 26, 1997,[25] that would require the CO to provide instructions for distributing contract financing payments on contracts with multiple accounting classification reference numbers (ACRNs) and progress payment provisions. The objective would be to distribute progress payments to ACRNs in reasonable proportion to the work performed. The distribution instructions would be developed from available information, including contract funds status reports, contract delivery schedules, profiles of anticipated contractor expenditures, from data furnished by the contractor.

Commercial Item Purchase Financing

The Federal Acquisition Streamlining Act of 1994[26] authorizes contract financing of commercial purchases; contract financing based on measures of contract performance are also authorized.

The FAR, Subpart 32.2, permits contract financing of commercial purchases when:

- The contract price exceeds the simplified acquisition threshold.
- The terms and conditions are customary and appropriate in the commercial marketplace.
- It is in the best interests of the government.
- Adequate security is obtained.
- The financing does not exceed 15% until some contract performance is accomplished.
- The contract is either awarded on the basis of competitive procedures, or when only one offer is solicited, adequate consideration is obtained if the financing is substantially more advantageous than normal commercial financing.
- The disbursing officer concurs with any liquidation provisions.

The clause entitled Installment Payments for Commercial Items (FAR 52.232-30) may be used in lieu of a clause that is tailored for a specific contract.

Performance-Based Payments

Under Defense Acquisition Regulation (DAR) Appendix E, in effect before FAR, fixed-price contracts with particularly long lead times between cost incurrence and first delivery could convert from customary progress payments to a type of partial payment known as a milestone billing after six months (four months for small businesses) of contract performance. To be eligible for milestone billings, contracts had to meet certain size and long-lead-time criteria.

The 1985 Defense Financial and Investment Review recommended that coverage of milestone billings be incorporated into the FAR, but such action was never taken. However, since no rules specifically prohibited milestone billings, they may still be requested and negotiated on a contract-by-contract basis.

In January 1993, NASA revised the NASA FAR Supplement, Parts 1832 and 1852, to allow milestone billings on fixed-price contracts over $10 million if lead times between the initial incurrence of cost and the delivery of the first end item extend at least 12 months. The revision limits milestone billing amounts to the government's best estimate of the cost to perform the milestone event.

NASA's view of how milestone billings relate to other forms of contract financing is illustrated in the following excerpt from NASA FAR Supplement 1832.7001:

> As authorized at FAR 32.102(e), milestone billing arrangements may be used for contract financing. Milestone billing arrangements fall between progress payments based on costs with unusual terms and advance payments in the order of preference specified in FAR 32.106. Milestone billing arrangements are contractual provisions which provide for payments to a contractor upon successful completion of specific performance events not involving physical deliveries to the Government. As milestone arrangements are interim payments with respect to total contract performance, they are fully recoverable, in the same manner as progress payments, in the event of default. Milestone payments shall not be considered as payments for contract items delivered and accepted, incentive price revisions, or inspection and acceptance provisions of the contract.

Effective October 1, 1995, FAR Subpart 32.10 was issued to address performance-based financing for sole-source, fixed-price, noncommercial purchases. Performance-based payments may be based on quantifiable performance measures, accomplishment of milestones or other quantifiable measures of results. Total performance-based payments cannot exceed 90% of the contract price.

Guaranteed Loans

Guaranteed loans are basically commercial loans by private lending institutions to a contractor that obligate the government, on demand of the lender, to purchase a stated percentage of the loan and/or share in any losses. Guaranteed loans are normally based on the undelivered portion of all defense contracts, subcontracts, or purchase orders, as opposed to contract-by-contract financing. Unless the contractor defaults in whole or in part on the primary loan, there is no cost to the government, since government funds are involved only when a percentage of the loan must actually be purchased. If government funds are expended to purchase a defaulted loan, the government recovers the amount through payments made by the contractor.

Requests for guaranteed loans are initiated by the lending institution. A contractor requiring financing applies to a private financial institution for a loan or revolving fund. If the lending institution considers a government guarantee to be necessary, it applies to its Federal Reserve Bank for the guarantee. The Federal Reserve Bank investigates the application and makes a recommendation to the Federal Reserve Board, which forwards a copy of the application to the appropriate guaranteeing agency to determine whether a contractor is eligible to receive a loan guarantee. The Departments of the Army, Navy, Air Force, Energy, Commerce, Interior, and Agriculture, as well as the General Services Administration (GSA), are designated as guaranteeing agencies under the Defense Production Act of 1950,[27] as amended, and under Executive Order 10480. If a company has undelivered contracts with more than one agency, the guaranteeing agency will generally be the one with the largest dollar volume of uncompleted work.

The application will be approved only if the guaranteeing agency can certify the following:

- The supplies or services are essential to the national defense.

- Other alternative sources are not available.
- The contractor is technically qualified and has adequate facilities to perform the contract.

If the guaranteeing agency approves the guarantee, the appropriate Federal Reserve Bank issues the guarantee agreement to the financial institution. The agreement generally requires that monies payable under the contracts be assigned to the bank unless the borrower's financial condition is particularly strong or unless the administration of contract assignments would be unduly onerous because of the many small contracts involved.

Loans are generally not guaranteed for more than 90% of the borrower's investment in defense production contracts. The Defense Production Act further limits a guaranteeing agency's maximum obligation to $20 million.

Unusual Progress Payments

Progress payments based on cost at higher rates than those specified in the Customary Progress Payments clause or payments made more frequently than monthly are considered unusual progress payments. The contractor must show an actual need for unusual progress payments. DFARS 232.501-2(a) prohibits DOD COs from modifying contracts to authorize unusual progress payments without the prior written consent of the Undersecretary of Defense (Acquisition and Technology).

Advance Payments

Advance payments, provided under the Advance Payment clause (FAR 52.232-12), are essentially loans that may be authorized for either subcontracts or prime contracts and for either cost-reimbursement-type or fixed-price contracts, including awards under formal advertising procedures. Advance payments may be paid up to the full amount of the unpaid contract price.

In contrast to progress payments, advance payments are loans made before, and in anticipation of, contract performance. They are authorized for defense contracts under the provisions of 10 U.S.C. 2307, as amended;[28] the National Defense Contract Authorization Act of August 28, 1958;[29] Public Law 85-804;[30] and Executive Order 10789. Advance payments for civilian procurements are authorized under Section 305 of the Federal Property and Administrative Services Act.

Except for certain specialized procurements, advance payments are authorized only when:

- No other means of adequate financing is available to the contractor except at excessive interest rates or charges.
- The amount of the advance payment reflects use of the contractor's own working capital to the extent possible.
- The contractor provides adequate security.
- It is in the public interest and furthers the national defense.

Once these conditions have been met, a contractor's request for advance payments is generally granted when:

- The payments are necessary to supplement other funds or credit.
- The contractor is otherwise considered responsible.
- The government will benefit from contract performance.
- Contract circumstances fit those specifically enumerated in the regulations as suitable for advance payments.

Letters of Credit. Treasury Department Circular 1075 governs the use of letters of credit for advance payments. Letters of credit enable a contractor to withdraw government funds in amounts necessary to cover its own disbursement of cash for contract performance. The Department of the Treasury favors this method of advance payments; it generates a lower cash flow impact on the government than other financing methods because the contractor is prohibited from withdrawing funds until checks have been forwarded to payees (float delay) or presented to the contractor's bank for payment. This type of advance funding arrangement may be terminated if the contractor is unwilling or unable to minimize the time between receipt of the advance and disbursement of the funds. In such cases, if reversion to normal payment methods is not feasible, a working capital method of advance payment may be used, which limits advances to the estimated disbursements for a given initial period and to actual cash disbursements for subsequent periods.

Interest on Advance Payments. All advance payments provide for the payment of interest, although interest may be waived in certain specialized circumstances. Interest on advance payments is charged at: (1) the greater of the published prime rate of the bank in which the special bank account is established; or (2) the rate established by the Secretary of the Treasury pursuant to Public Law 92-41.[31] It is a floating interest rate, subject to revision based on fluctuations in the prime rate and the semiannual determination by the Secretary of the Treasury.

Restrictions. Advance payments and all other payments to the contractor under the contract are deposited in a special bank account. None of the funds in the account may be commingled with other contractor funds before withdrawal by the contractor. Except in certain circumstances, funds are withdrawn by the contractor only by check signed by both an authorized company official and the CO or another designated government representative. Use of advance payments is restricted to payments of direct contract costs plus allocable indirect expenses. To protect the government's interest before repayment of the advance payments, the government has a lien, which is paramount to all other liens, on the balance in the special account, as well as on the materials, supplies, and property allocated to the contract.

Most contracts that provide for advance payments contain covenants prohibiting the contractor from doing the following, without prior government approval, while advance payments are outstanding:

- Mortgaging or pledging any assets
- Selling, assigning, or pledging any claims due
- Paying dividends
- Selling, conveying, or leasing all or a substantial part of the assets
- Acquiring for consideration any stock or security other than direct obligations of the United States

- Making loans or becoming liable on commercial paper
- Permitting an attachment to remain without remedial action
- Paying excessive salaries, commissions, bonuses, or other remuneration in any form or manner to the directors, officers, or key employees
- Changing the management, ownership, or control of the corporation
- Merging or consolidating with any firm or any other corporation
- Depositing funds in any bank or trust company not insured by the Federal Deposit Insurance Corporation
- Creating or incurring indebtedness for borrowed money or advances other than the advance payments themselves
- Making or agreeing to make capital expenditures exceeding a sum specified in the contract
- Permitting current assets, calculated in accordance with generally accepted accounting principles, to fall below a specified amount
- Paying, on account, obligations listed in the contract except in the manner and to the extent provided by the contract

While advance payments are usually provided for a single contract, they may be used to finance the performance of more than one contract under a single agreement. It may be advantageous to both the government and the contractor, when several contracts are to be financed by advance payments simultaneously, to agree to pool all such contracts and their advance payments. The arrangement can cover a broad area of the contractor's financial needs rather than piecemeal segments related to particular contracts. Arrangements of this type are generally used for financing nonprofit contracts with nonprofit educational or research institutions.

When an advance payment pool agreement is made, one of the contracts included in the pool will be the designated pool contract. This contract is the one to which all advance payments are charged; advances are not made on the other contracts in the pool. However, the monetary requirements of all the contracts are considered in determining the maximum amount of advance payments to be authorized.

9-4. SUMMARY

Many sources of financing are available to help companies successfully perform government contracts. Potential contractors should be aware that, under most circumstances, the need for financial assistance is not considered a hindrance to the receipt of government contracts.

9-5. NOTES

1. Information for Contractors, DCAA Pamphlet No. 7641.90, Aug. 1996.
2. Research Applications, Inc., ASBCA No. 23834, Oct. 4, 1979, 79-2 BCA 14,120.
3. Datex, Inc., ASBCA No. 24794, March 20, 1983, 81-1 BCA 15,060.
4. SAI Comsystems Corp., DOTCAB No. 1406, March 27, 1984, 84-2 BCA 17,234.
5. Varigas Research, Inc., ASBCA No. 28610, Jan. 25, 1984, 84-1 BCA 17,154.
6. Defense Systems Concepts, Inc., ASBCA No. 44540, Nov. 13, 1992, 93-2 BCA 25,568.

7. ITT Defense Communications, ITT Federal Laboratories, ASBCA No. 14270, June 25, 1970, 70-2 BCA 8,370.

8. Metametrics, Inc., IBCA No. 1552-2-82, Oct. 27, 1982, 82-2 BCA 16,095.

9. American Standard, Inc., ASBCA No. 15660, Sept. 24, 1971, 71-2 BCA 9,109.

10. Clevite Ordinance, ASBCA No. 5859, Navy Appeals Panel, March 26, 1962, 1962 BCA 3,330.

11. Dames & Moore, IBCA No. 2553, Oct. 7, 1992, 93-1 BCA 25,487.

12. Dynamic Concepts, Inc., ASBCA No. 44738, Dec. 21, 1992, 93-2 BCA 25,689.

13. DBA Systems, Inc., NASABCA No. 481-5, Nov. 20, 1981, 82-1 BCA 15,468.

14. Federal Crop Insurance Corp. v. Merrill, et al., Nov. 10, 1947, 332, US 380, 68 S. Ct. 1.

15. Prompt Payment Act, 31 U.S.C. §3901–3907, enacted Jan. 12, 1983, 96 Stat. 2474, Pub. L. 97-452; amended Oct. 17, 1988, 102 Stat. 2455.

16. Assignment of Claims Act of 1940, Ch. 779, 54 Stat. 1029, 31 U.S.C. §203, enacted Oct. 9, 1940.

17. Comptroller General Decision B-159494, Sept. 2, 1966.

18. Comptroller General Decision B-150528, Feb. 1, 1963.

19. Comptroller General Decision B-194945, June 16, 1979.

20. Comptroller General Decision B-195629, Sept. 7, 1979.

21. DOD Appropriations Act for Fiscal Year 1994, enacted Nov. 11, 1993, Pub. L. 103-139, §8155.

22. Marine Midland Bank v. United States, Ct. Cl. 1982, No. 308-81C, Aug. 25, 1982, 687 F.2d 395, S. Cl. No. 82-1026, March 21, 1983, 460 U.S. 1037; 103 S. Ct. 1427.

23. American Pouch Foods, Inc., Debtor, United States v. American Pouch Foods, Inc., DC NIII, Nos. VIII 81 C 1616, 80 B 14821, 80 A 2374; June 20, 1983.

24. Aydin Corp. (West) v. Widnall, CAFC No. 94-1441, Aug. 10, 1995, 61 F.3d 1571.

25. Federal Register, Vol. 62, No. 228, Nov. 26, 1997, pp. 63047–63050.

26. Federal Acquisition Streamlining Act of 1994, enacted Oct. 13, 1995, Pub. L. 103-355, §§2001 and 2051.

27. Defense Production Act of 1950, as amended, 64 Stat. 798, 50 U.S.C. App. 2061, enacted Sept. 8, 1950.

28. Armed Services Procurement Act, 62 Stat. 21, 10 U.S.C. 2307, enacted Feb. 19, 1948.

29. National Defense Contract Authorization Act of Aug. 28, 1958, also known as the Extraordinary Contractual Relief Act of 1958, 50 U.S.C. 1431.

30. Extraordinary Contractual Relief, Act of Aug. 28, 1958, 72 Stat. 972, Pub. L. 85-804.

31. Renegotiation Act, Ch. 247, 56 Stat. 245, 50 U.S.C. §Appx 1191, enacted April 28, 1942, Pub. L. 92-41.

Standard Form 1034 Revised January 1980 Department of the Treasury I TFRM 4-2000 1034-118	**PUBLIC VOUCHER FOR PURCHASES AND** **SERVICES OTHER THAN PERSONAL**	VOUCHER NO. (e)

U.S. DEPARTMENT, BUREAU, OR ESTABLISHMENT AND LOCATION (a)	DATE VOUCHER PREPARED (b)	SCHEDULE NO.
	CONTRACT NUMBER AND DATE (c)	**PAID BY**
	REQUISITION NUMBER AND DATE (d)	(f)

PAYEE'S NAME AND ADDRESS (h)

DATE INVOICE RECEIVED (f)
DISCOUNT TERMS (f)
PAYEE'S ACCOUNT NUMBER (q)

SHIPPED FROM (i)	TO (i)	WEIGHT (i)	GOVERNMENT B/L NUMBER (i)

NUMBER AND DATE OF ORDER	DATE OF DELIVERY OR SERVICE	ARTICLES OR SERVICES *(Enter description, item number of contract of Federal supply schedule, and other information deemed necessary)*	QUAN-TITY	UNIT PRICE		AMOUNT
				COST	PER	
(j)	(k)	(l)	(m)	(n)	(n)	(n)

(Use continuation sheet(s) if necessary)   (Payee must NOT use the space below)   **TOTAL**

PAYMENT: (o)	APPROVED FOR	EXCHANGE RATE	DIFFERENCES
☐ PROVISIONAL	(p) = $	(q) = $1.00	
☐ COMPLETE	BY [2]		
☐ PARTIAL			
☐ FINAL	(r)		Amount verified; correct for
☐ PROGRESS	TITLE		*(Signature of initials)*
☐ ADVANCE	(s)		

Pursuant to authority vested in me, I certify that this voucher is correct and proper for payment.

_____   _____   _____
(Date)   (Authorized Certifying Officer) [2]   (Title)

ACCOUNTING CLASSIFICATION

PAID BY	CHECK NUMBER	ON ACCOUNT OF U.S. TREASURY	CHECK NUMBER	ON *(Name of bank)*
	CASH $	DATE	PAYEE [3]	

1 When stated in foreign currency, insert name of currency.
2 If the ability to certify and authority to approve are combined in one person, one signature only is necessary; otherwise the approving officer will sign in the space provided, over his official title.
3 When a voucher is receipted in the name of a company or corporation, the name of the person writing the company or corporate name, as well as the capacity in which he signs, must appear. For example: "John Doe Company, per John Smith, Secretary", or "Treasurer", as the case may be.

PER

TITLE

Previous edition usable

NSN 7540-00-634-4206

J61174
10-08-96

Appendix 9.1 Standard Form 1034, Public Voucher for Purchases and Services other than Personal

Standard Form 1034 A Revised January 1980 Department of the Treasury I TFRM 4-2000	**PUBLIC VOUCHER FOR PURCHASES AND SERVICES OTHER THAN PERSONAL**	VOUCHER NO. (e)

U.S. DEPARTMENT, BUREAU, OR ESTABLISHMENT AND LOCATION	DATE VOUCHER PREPARED (b)	SCHEDULE NO.
	CONTRACT NUMBER AND DATE (c)	**PAID BY** (f)
	REQUISITION NUMBER AND DATE (d)	

PAYEE'S NAME AND ADDRESS   (h)

DATE INVOICE RECEIVED
(f)

DISCOUNT TERMS
(f)

PAYEE'S ACCOUNT NUMBER
(g)

SHIPPED FROM (i)	TO (i)	WEIGHT (i)	GOVERNMENT B/L NUMBER (i)

NUMBER AND DATE OF ORDER	DATE OF DELIVERY OR SERVICE	ARTICLES OR SERVICES *(Enter description, item number of contract of Federal supply schedule, and other information deemed necessary)*	QUAN-TITY	UNIT PRICE COST	PER	AMOUNT
(j)	(k)	(l)	(m)	(n)	(n)	(n)

(Use continuation sheet(s) if necessary)   (Payee must NOT use the space below)   **TOTAL**

PAYMENT: (o)		DIFFERENCES	
☐ PROVISIONAL			
☐ COMPLETE			
☐ PARTIAL		Amount verified; correct for	
☐ FINAL		*(Signature of initials)*	
☐ PROGRESS			
☐ ADVANCE			

MEMORANDUM

ACCOUNTING CLASSIFICATION

PAID BY	CHECK NUMBER	ON ACCOUNT OF U.S. TREASURY	CHECK NUMBER	ON *(Name of bank)*
	CASH $	DATE		

1034-213

NSN: 7540-00-634-4207

J81175
10-15-96

Appendix 9.1   (Continued)

Instructions for Preparing SF 1034/SF 1034A

(a) Insert the name and address of the military department or agency that negotiated the contract.

(b) Insert the date on which the public voucher is submitted to the auditor.

(c) Insert the number and date of the contract and task order (if applicable) under which reimbursement is claimed.

(d) Insert the requisition number and date if available; otherwise leave blank.

(e) Insert the appropriate serial number of the voucher. A separate series of consecutive numbers beginning with 1 should be sued for each new contract or task order (when applicable). Insert the word FINAL after the serial number on the completion voucher.

(f) Leave blank. The payer will complete this space.

(g) Leave blank unless such information is available.

(h) Insert the company name and correct address, except when an assignment has been made or the right to receive payment has been restricted. When the contractor has made an assignment, insert:

Name of Financial Institution
Assignee for X Company
Location (city and state) of Financial Institution

When the right to receive payment has been restricted, insert:

Name of Company
Location (city and state) of X Company
for deposit in the Y Financial Institution
Location (city and state) of Y Financial Institution
Name of Special Account

(i)-(j) Leave blank.

(k) Insert the month and year or beginning and ending dates with incurred costs claimed for reimbursement.

(l) Insert:

For detail, see SF 1035 – total amount of claim transferred from page ___ of ___ SF 1035.

On interim voucher, new COST REIMBURSABLE - PROVISIONAL PAYMENT

On final voucher , insert COST REIMBURSABLE – COMPLETION VOUCHER

(m) Leave blank.

(n) Insert the total amount claimed for the time indicated in (k). This should agree with the amount shown on SF 1035 – Continuation Sheet.

(o)-(s) Leave blank.

Appendix 9.1 (Continued)

Standard Form 1035 September 1973 4 Treasury FRM 2000 1035-110		PUBLIC VOUCHER FOR PURCHASES AND SERVICES OTHER THAN PERSONAL *CONTINUATION SHEET*			VOUCHER NO. (b)
					SCHEDULE NO. (c)
					SHEET NO. (d)

U.S. DEPARTMENT, BUREAU, OR ESTABLISHMENT
(a)

NUMBER AND DATE OF ORDER	DATE OF DELIVERY OR SERVICE	ARTICLES OR SERVICES *(Enter description, item number of contract or Federal supply schedule, and other information deemed necessary)*	QUAN- TITY	UNIT PRICE		AMOUNT
				COST	PER	
(e)		(f)	(g)			
		(h)	(j)			(k)
(i)						
(l)				xx		xx
(m)				xx		xx
(n)				xx		xx
(o)						
(p)						
(q)						
(r)						
(s)						

J61176
10-08-96

Appendix 9.2 Standard Form 1035, Public Voucher for Purchases and Services other than Personal—Continuation Sheet

350

Standard Form No. 1035-A September 1973 4 Treasury FRM 2000 1035-209-01	**PUBLIC VOUCHER FOR PURCHASES AND SERVICES OTHER THAN PERSONAL MEMORANDUM** *CONTINUATION SHEET*		VOUCHER NO. (b)
			SCHEDULE NO. (c)
			SHEET NO. (d)

U.S. DEPARTMENT, BUREAU, OR ESTABLISHMENT
(a)

NUMBER AND DATE OF ORDER	DATE OF DELIVERY OR SERVICE	ARTICLES OR SERVICES *(Enter description, item number of contract or Federal supply schedule, and other information deemed necessary)*	QUAN- TITY	UNIT PRICE		AMOUNT
				COST	PER	
(e)		(f)	(g)			
		(h)	(j)			(k)
(i)						
(l)			xx			xx
(m)			xx			xx
(n)			xx			xx
(o)						
(p)						
(q)						
(r)						
(s)						

J61177
10-15-96

Appendix 9.2 (Continued)

Instructions for Preparing SF 1035/SF 1035A

(a) Insert the name of the military department or agency that negotiated the contract.

(b) Insert the voucher number, as shown on SF 1034.

(c) Leave blank.

(d) Insert the sheet number in numerical sequence if more than one sheet is used. Use as many sheets as necessary to show the information required by the contracting officer or the auditor.

(e) Insert payee's name and address as shown on SF 1034.

(f) Insert the contract number and the task order number (when applicable).

(g) Insert the target or estimated costs, target or fixed-fee, total contract value, and amount of fee payable.

(h) Insert: Analysis of Claimed Current and Cumulative Costs and Fee Earned.

(i) Insert the major cost elements. Use additional SF 1035s if necessary to show computations of overhead adjustments from provisional rates to negotiated rates or allowable actual rates, or the computation of fee claimed.

(j) Insert the amount billed by the major cost elements, contract reserves and adjustments, and adjusted amounts claimed for the current period.

(k) Insert the cumulative amounts billed by the major cost elements, contract reserves, and adjusted amounts claimed to date of this billing.

(l) Insert the total costs for current and cumulative periods.

(m) Insert the target or fixed-fee earned and due for the current and cumulative periods and the formula for the computation (percentage of costs, percentage of completion, etc.).

(n) Insert the total costs claimed and the target or fixed-fee due for the current an cumulative periods.

(o) Insert the details of the contract reserves withheld in the current and cumulative periods. The contractor is responsible for reducing its claims for contract reserves.

(p) Show the status of all outstanding DCAA Form 1's, "Notice of Contract Costs Suspended and/or Disapproved." When amounts on an outstanding DCAA Form 1 are resubmitted, they should be shown in the current period column, and the corresponding cumulative total of outstanding suspensions or disapprovals should be reduced to cover the resubmission so that the cumulative amounts are "net".

(q) Insert the net reserves and adjustments.

(r) Show the costs and fee subject to reimbursement for the current and cumulative periods.

(s) Amount to be carried forward to SF 1034.

Appendix 9.2 (Continued)

	DEFENSE CONTRACT AUDIT AGENCY NOTICE OF CONTRACT COSTS SUSPENDED AND/OR DISAPPROVED		PAGE _____ OF _____ PAGE(S)	
TO: (Name and Address of Contractor)		Contract Number	Notice Number	
		Disbursing Office	Contract Administration Office	

1. This notice is issued pursuant to the authority of DoD Directive 5105.36, as implemented by the Federal Acquisition Regulation and DoD FAR Supplement. It constitutes notice of costs suspended and/or disapproved incident to the audit of contractor costs incurred under referenced contract(s). Description of items and reasons for the action are stated below.

2. SUSPENDED COSTS, as referred to herein, are costs which, for the reasons stated below, have been determined by the undersigned to be inadequately supported or otherwise questionable, and not appropriate for reimbursement under the contract terms at this time. Such costs may be determined reimbursable after the contractor provides the auditor additional documentation or explanation as specified below.

3. DISAPPROVED COSTS, as referred to herein, are costs which, for the reasons stated below, have been determined by the undersigned to be unallowable, that is not reimbursable under the contract terms.

4. If the contractor disagrees with this these determinations, the contractor may (1) request in writing the cognizant contracting officer to consider whether the unreimbursed costs should be paid and to discuss his of her findings with the contractor and/or (2) file a claim under the "Disputes" clause of the contract(s).

5. The auditor will submit copies of the acknowledged notice to the cognizant disbursing officer for appropriate action and to the cognizant

DCAA AUDITOR	Date of Notice	Address		Signature

CONTRACTOR'S ACKNOWLEDGMENT OF RECEIPT
The contractor or its authorized representative shall acknowledge receipt of this notice to the DCAA auditor.

Date of Receipt	Name and Title of Authorized Official	Signature

ITEM NO.	Description of Items and Reasons for Action	Amount of Costs	
		Suspended	Disapproved

DCAA Form 1 (EF)
February 1988

Supersedes August 1987 Edition of DCAA Form 1

Appendix 9.3 DCAA form 1, Defense Contract Audit Agency Notice of Contract Costs Suspended and/or Disapproved

CONTRACTOR'S RELEASE OF CLAIMS

CONTRACT NO. _____

Pursuant to the terms of Contract No. _____ and in consideration of the sum of
_____ Dollars ($_____) which has been or is to be paid under the said contract to
_____ (hereinafter called the Contractor) or its assignees, if any, the
Contractor, upon payment of the said sum by the UNITED STATES OF AMERICA (hereinafter called the
Government), does remise, release, and discharge the Government, its officers, agents, and employees, of and from all
liabilities, obligations, claims, and demands whatsoever arising out of or under this contract, subject only to the
following exceptions;

1. Specified claims in stated amounts, or in estimated amounts where the amounts are not susceptible of exact
   statement by the Contractor, as follows: _____;

2. Claims, together with reasonable expenses incidental thereto, based upon the liabilities of the Contractor to third
   parties arising out of the performance of this contract, which are not known to the Contractor on the date of the
   execution of this release, and of which the Contractor gives notice in writing to the Contracting Officer not more
   than six (6) years after the date of the release or the date of any notice to the Contractor that the Government is
   prepared to make final payment, whichever is earlier; and

3. Claims for reimbursement of costs (other than expenses of the Contractor by reason of his indemnification of the
   Government against patent liability), including reasonable expenses incidental thereto, incurred by the Contractor
   under the provisions of this contract relating to patents.

The Contractor agrees, in connection with patent matters and with claims which are not released as set forth above, to
comply with all of the provisions of the said contract, including without limitation those provisions relating to
notification to the Contracting Officer and relating to the defense or prosecution of litigation.

IN WITNESS WHEREOF, this release of claims has been executed this _____ day of _____ 19__.

_____ (Contractor)

BY _____

TITLE _____

Witnesses: (1) _____

               (2) _____

NOTE: In the case of a corporation, witnesses are not required, but the certificate below must be completed.

CERTIFICATE

I, _____, certify that I am the _____(official
title) of the corporation named as Contractor in the foregoing release; that _____,
who signed said release on behalf of the Contractor was the _____(official title) of said
corporation; that said release was duly signed for and in behalf of said corporation by authority of its governing body
and is within the scope of its corporate powers.

Signed: _____

CORPORATE SEAL

Appendix 9.4   Contractor's Release of Claims

CONTRACTOR'S ASSIGNMENT OF REFUNDS, REBATES OR CREDITS

CONTRACT NO. _____

Pursuant to the terms of Contract No. _____ and in consideration of the reimbursement of costs and payment of fee, as provided in the said contract and any assignment thereunder, the _____ (hereinafter called the Contractor) does hereby:

1. Assign, transfer, set over and release to the UNITED STATES OF AMERICA (hereinafter called the Government) all right, title and interest to all refunds, rebates, or credits (including any related interest), arising out of the materials portion of the said contract, together with all the rights of action accrued or which may hereafter accrue thereunder.

2. Agree to take whatever action may be necessary to effect prompt collection of all refunds, rebates, or credits, (including any related interest) due or which may become due, and to promptly forward to the Contracting Officer checks (made payable to the office designated for contract administration) for any proceeds so collected. The reasonable costs of any such action to effect collection shall constitute allowable costs when approved by the Contracting Officer as stated in the said contract and may be applied to reduce any amounts otherwise payable to the Government under the terms hereof.

3. Agree to cooperate fully with the Government as to any claim or suit in connection with refunds, rebates, or credits (including any related interest); to execute any protest, pleading, application, power of attorney, or other papers in connection therewith; and to permit the government to represent him at any hearing, trial, or other proceeding arising out of such claim or suit.

IN WITNESS WHEREOF, this assignment of refunds, rebates, or credits has been executed this _____ day of _____ 19__.

_____ (Contractor)

BY _____

TITLE _____

Witnesses: (1) _____

            (2) _____

NOTE: In the case of a corporation, witnesses are not required, but the certificate below must be completed.

CERTIFICATE

I, _____, certify that I am the _____ (official title) of the corporation named as Contractor in the foregoing assignment; that _____, who signed said assignment on behalf of the Contractor was the _____(official title) of said corporation; that said assignment was duly signed for and in behalf of said corporation by authority of its governing body and is within the scope of its corporate powers.

Signed: _____

CORPORATE SEAL

Appendix 9.5   Contractor's Assignment of Refunds, Rebates or Credits

ASSIGNEE'S RELEASE OF CLAIMS

CONTRACT NO. _____

Pursuant to the terms of Contract No. _____ and in consideration of the sum of
_____ Dollars ($_____) (total of amounts paid and payable) which has been or is to
be paid under the said contract upon payment of the said sum by the UNITED STATES OF AMERICA (hereinafter
called the Government), to the Contractor or its assignees, the _____
(Assignee's name and address),

      (i) a corporation organized and existing under the laws of the State of _____,

      (ii) a partnership consisting of _____,

      (iii) an individual trading as _____,

(hereinafter called the Assignee), upon receipt of that part of the said sum due under its assignment does
hereby remise, release, and discharge the Government, its officers, agents, and employees, of and from all
liabilities, obligations, claims, and demands whatsoever arising out of or under said contract and assignment,
subject only to the following exceptions;

1. Specified claims in stated amounts, or in estimated amounts where the amounts are not susceptible of exact
statement by the Contractor, as follows: _____;

2. Claims, together with reasonable expenses incidental thereto, based upon the liabilities of the Contractor to third
parties arising out of the performance of this contract, which are not known to the Contractor or Assignee on the
date of the execution of this release, and of which the Contractor or Assignee gives notice in writing to the
Contracting Officer within the time period specified in the said contract.

3. Claims for reimbursement of costs (other than expenses of the Contractor by reason of his indemnification of the
Government against patent liability), including reasonable expenses incidental thereto, incurred by the Contractor
under the provisions of this contract relating to patents.

4. When the contract includes an article entitled "Data Requirements," claims pursuant to such article when, within
the one-year period after final payment under the contract, the Contracting Officer requests in writing that the
Contractor furnish such data.

The Assignee further agrees that payments on amount of claims not released as set forth above shall be subject to
adjustment in accordance with paragraph (i) of the clause of the contract entitled "Incentive Fee," if such clause is a
provision of the contract.

IN WITNESS WHEREOF, this release of claims has been executed this _____ day of _____ 19__.

_____ (Assignee)

                  BY _____

                  TITLE _____

Witnesses: (1) _____

          (2) _____

NOTE: In the case of a corporation, witnesses are not required, but the certificate below must be completed.

CERTIFICATE

I, _____, certify that I am the _____ (official
title) of the corporation named as Assignee in the foregoing release; that _____,
who signed said release on behalf of the Assignee was the _____ (official title) of said
corporation; that said release was duly signed for and in behalf of said corporation by authority of its governing body
and is within the scope of its corporate powers.

                Signed: _____

CORPORATE SEAL

Appendix 9.6   Assignee's Release of Claims

ASSIGNEE'S ASSIGNMENT OF REFUNDS, REBATES, CREDITS, AND OTHER AMOUNTS

CONTRACT NO. _____

Pursuant to the terms of Contract No. _____ and in consideration of the reimbursement of costs and payment of fee, as provided in the said contract and assignment thereunder, the _____ (Assignee's name and address),

    (i)   a corporation organized and existing under the laws of the State of _____,

    (ii) a partnership consisting of _____,

    (iii) an individual trading as _____,

(hereinafter called the Assignee), does hereby assign, transfer, set over, and release to the UNITED STATES OF AMERICA, all right, title, and interest to all refunds, rebates, credits, and other amounts (including any interest thereon) arising out of the performance of the said contract, together with all the rights of action accrued or which may hereafter accrue thereunder.

IN WITNESS WHEREOF, this release of claims has been executed this _____ day of _____ 19__.

                                        _____ (Assignee)

                              BY _____

                            TITLE _____

Witnesses: (1) _____

            (2) _____

NOTE: In the case of a corporation, witnesses are not required, but the certificate below must be completed.

CERTIFICATE

I, _____, certify that I am the _____ (official title) of the corporation named as Assignee in the foregoing assignment; that _____, who signed said assignment on behalf of the Assignee was the _____ (official title) of said corporation; that said assignment was duly signed for and in behalf of said corporation by authority of its governing body and is within the scope of its corporate powers.

                              Signed: _____

CORPORATE SEAL

Appendix 9.7   Assignee's Assignment of Refunds, Rebates, Credits, and Other Amounts

ORDER FOR SUPPLIES OR SERVICES

(Contractor must submit four copies of invoice.)

Form Approved OMB No. 0704-0187 Expires Dec 31, 1993	PAGE 1 OF

Public reporting burden for this collection of information is estimated to average 1 hour per response, including the time for reviewing instructions, searching existing data sources, gathering and maintaining the data needed, and completing and reviewing the collection of information. Send comments regarding this burden estimate or any other aspect of this collection of information, including suggestions for reducing this burden, to Department of Defense, Washington Headquarters Services, Directorate for Information Operations and Reports, 1215 Jefferson Davis Highway, Suite 1204, Arlington, VA 22202-4302, and to the Office of Management and Budget, Paperwork Reduction Project (0704-0187), Washington, DC 20503.

PLEASE <u>DO NOT</u> RETURN YOUR FORM TO EITHER OF THESE ADDRESSES.
SEND YOUR COMPLETED FORM TO THE PROCUREMENT OFFICIAL IDENTIFIED IN ITEM 6.

1. CONTRACT / PURCH ORDER NO.	2. DELIVERY ORDER NO.	3. DATE OF ORDER (YYMMDD)	4. REQUISITION / PURCH REQUEST NO.	5. PRIORITY

6. ISSUED BY	CODE	7. ADMINISTERED BY (If other than 6)	CODE	

8. DELIVERY FOB
☐ DEST
☐ OTHER
(See Schedule if other)

9. CONTRACTOR	CODE	FACILITY CODE	10. DELIVER TO FOB POINT BY (Date) (YYMMDD)	11. MARK IF BUSINESS IS

NAME AND ADDRESS

☐ SMALL
☐ SMALL DISAD-VANTAGED
☐ WOMEN-OWNED

12. DISCOUNT TERMS

13. MAIL INVOICES TO

14. SHIP TO	CODE	15. PAYMENT WILL BE MADE BY	CODE	

MARK ALL PACKAGES AND PAPERS WITH CONTRACT OR ORDER NUMBER

16. TYPE OF ORDER		
DELIVERY	This delivery order is issued on another Government agency or in accordance with and subject to terms and conditions of above numbered contract.	
PURCHASE	Reference your	furnish the following on terms specified herein

ACCEPTANCE. THE CONTRACTOR HEREBY ACCEPTS THE OFFER REPRESENTED BY THE NUMBERED PURCHASE ORDER AS IT MAY PREVIOUSLY HAVE BEEN OR IS NOW MODIFIED, SUBJECT TO ALL OF THE TERMS AND CONDITIONS SET FORTH, AND AGREES TO PERFORM THE SAME.

NAME OF CONTRACTOR	SIGNATURE	TYPED NAME AND TITLE	DATE SIGNED (YYMMDD)

☐ If this box is marked, supplier must sign Acceptance and return the following number of copies:

17. ACCOUNTING AND APPROPRIATION DATA / LOCAL USE

18. ITEM NO.	19. SCHEDULE OF SUPPLIES / SERVICE	20. QUANTITY ORDERED / ACCEPTED *	21. UNIT	22. UNIT PRICE	23. AMOUNT

* If quantity accepted by the Government is same as quantity ordered, indicate by x. If different, enter actual quantity accepted below quantity ordered and encircle.	24. UNITED STATES OF AMERICA	25. TOTAL	
	BY:	29. DIFFERENCES	
	CONTRACTING / ORDERING OFFICER		

26. QUANTITY IN COLUMN 20 HAS BEEN	27. SHIP NO	28. D.O. VOUCHER NO.	30.
☐ INSPECTED ☐ RECEIVED ☐ ACCEPTED, AND CONFORMS TO THE CONTRACT EXCEPT AS NOTED	☐ PARTIAL ☐ FINAL	32. PAID BY	INITIALS

		31. PAYMENT	
DATE SIGNATURE OF AUTHORIZED GOVERNMENT REPRESENTATIVE	☐ COMPLETE	33. AMOUNT VERIFIED CORRECT FOR	
36. I certify this account is correct and proper for payment.	☐ PARTIAL	34. CHECK NUMBER	
DATE SIGNATURE AND TITLE OF CERTIFYING OFFICER	☐ FINAL	35. BILL OF LADING NO.	

37. RECEIVED AT	38. RECEIVED BY (Print)	39. DATE RECEIVED (YYMMDD)	40. TOTAL CONTAINERS	41. SR ACCOUNT NUMBER	42. SR VOUCHER NO.

DD Form 1155, APR 93
J61024
10-08-96

PREVIOUS EDITION MAY BE USED

460/

Appendix 9.8   DD form 1155, Order for Supplies or Services

ORDER FOR SUPPLIES OR SERVICES
(Commissary Continuation Sheet)

Form Approved
OMB No. 0704-0187
Expires Dec. 31, 1993

1. CONTRACTOR

2. PURCHASE OR DELIVERY ORDER NUMBER

3. DATE OF ORDER

4. PAGE NO.

5. NO. OF PAGES

6. ISSUED BY

7. CONTRACT NUMBER

8. VENDOR INVOICE NUMBER

9. RECEIVING REPORT NUMBER

10. ITEM NO.	11. SCHEDULE OF SUPPLIES / SERVICES	12. QUANTITY ORDERED*	13. QUANTITY ACCEPTED*	14. UNIT	15. UNIT PRICE	16. AMOUNT	17. RETAIL	
							a. UNIT PRICE	b. EXTENSION

* The supplies or services listed in the "Quantity Ordered" column were inspected and accepted, and quantities shown therein were received, unless otherwise noted in the "Quantity Accepted" column.

18. DATE

19. AUTHORIZED GOVERNMENT REPRESENTATIVE

J61025
10-08-96   DD Form 1155C-1, APR 93   PREVIOUS EDITION MAY BE USED

186/248

Appendix 9.8   (Continued)

CONTRACTOR'S REQUEST FOR PROGRESS PAYMENT

Form Approved
OMB No. 3090-0105

IMPORTANT: This form is to be completed in accordance with Instructions.

SECTION I - IDENTIFICATION INFORMATION

1. TO: NAME AND ADDRESS OF CONTRACTING OFFICE *(Include ZIP Code)*	2. FROM: NAME AND ADDRESS OF CONTRACTOR *(Include ZIP Code)*		
PAYING OFFICE			
	3. SMALL BUSINESS ☐ YES ☐ NO	4. CONTRACT NO.	5. CONTRACT PRICE $

6. RATES		7. DATE OF INITIAL AWARD		8A. PROGRESS PAYMENT REQUEST NO.	8B. DATE OF THIS REQUEST
A. PROG.PYMTS. %	B. LIQUIDATION %	A. YEAR	B. MONTH		

SECTION II - STATEMENT OF COSTS UNDER THIS CONTRACT THROUGH　　　(Date)

9. PAID COSTS ELIGIBLE UNDER PROGRESS PAYMENT CLAUSE		$
10. INCURRED COSTS ELIGIBLE UNDER PROGRESS PAYMENT CLAUSE		
11. TOTAL COSTS ELIGIBLE FOR PROGRESS PAYMENTS *(Item 9 plus 10)*		
12. a. TOTAL COSTS INCURRED TO DATE	$	
b. ESTIMATED ADDITIONAL COST TO COMPLETE		
13. ITEM 11 MULTIPLIED BY ITEM 6a		
14. a. PROGRESS PAYMENTS PAID TO SUBCONTRACTORS		
b. LIQUIDATED PROGRESS PAYMENTS TO SUBCONTRACTORS		
c. UNLIQUIDATED PROGRESS PAYMENTS TO SUBCONTRACTORS *(Item 14a less 14b)*		
d. SUBCONTRACTOR PROGRESS BILLINGS APPROVED FOR CURRENT PAYMENT		
e. ELIGIBLE SUBCONTRACTOR PROGRESS PAYMENTS *(Item 14c plus 14d)*		
15. TOTAL DOLLAR AMOUNT *(Item 13 plus 14e)*		
16. ITEM 5 MULTIPLIED BY ITEM 6b		
17. LESSER OF ITEM 15 OR ITEM 16		
18. TOTAL AMOUNT OF PREVIOUS PROGRESS PAYMENTS REQUESTED		
19. MAXIMUM BALANCE ELIGIBLE FOR PROGRESS PAYMENTS *(Item 17 less 18)*		

SECTION III - COMPUTATION OF LIMITS FOR OUTSTANDING PROGRESS PAYMENTS
* SEE SPECIAL INSTRUCTIONS ON BACK FOR USE UNDER THE FEDERAL ACQUISITION REGULATION.

20. COMPUTATION OF PROGRESS PAYMENT CLAUSE *(a(3)(i) or a(4)(i))* LIMITATION*	$	
a. COSTS INCLUDED IN ITEM 11, APPLICABLE TO ITEMS DELIVERED, INVOICED, AND ACCEPTED TO A DATE IN HEADING OF SECTION II.		
b. COSTS ELIGIBLE FOR PROGRESS PAYMENTS, APPLICABLE TO UNDELIVERED ITEMS AND TO DELIVERED ITEMS NOT INVOICED AND ACCEPTED *(Item 11 less 20a)*		
c. ITEM 20b MULTIPLIED BY ITEM 6a		$
d. ELIGIBLE SUBCONTRACTOR PROGRESS PAYMENTS *(Item 14e)*		
e. LIMITATION a(3)(i) or a (4)(i) *(Item 20c plus 20d)* *		
21. COMPUTATION OF PROGRESS PAYMENT CLAUSE *(a(3)(ii) or a(4)(ii))* LIMITATION *		
a. CONTRACT PRICE OF ITEMS DELIVERED, ACCEPTED AND INVOICED TO DATE IN HEADING OF SECTION II.		
b. CONTRACT PRICE OF ITEMS NOT DELIVERED, ACCEPTED AND INVOICED *(Item 5 less 21a)*		
c. ITEM 21b MULTIPLIED BY ITEM 6b		
d. UNLIQUIDATED ADVANCE PAYMENTS PLUS ACCRUED INTEREST		
e. LIMITATION *(a(3)(ii) or a(4)(ii)) (Item 21c less 21d)**		
22. MAXIMUM UNLIQUIDATED PROGRESS PAYMENTS *(Lesser of Item 20e or 21e)*		
23. TOTAL AMOUNT APPLIED AND TO BE APPLIED TO REDUCE PROGRESS PAYMENT		
24. UNLIQUIDATED PROGRESS PAYMENTS *(Item 18 less 23)*		
25. MAXIMUM PERMISSIBLE PROGRESS PAYMENTS *(Item 22 less 24)*		
26. AMOUNT OF CURRENT INVOICE FOR PROGRESS PAYMENT *(Lesser of Item 25 or 19)*		
27. AMOUNT APPROVED BY CONTRACTING OFFICER		

CERTIFICATION

I certify that the above statement (with attachments) has been prepared from the books and records of the above-named contractor in accordance with the contract and the instructions hereon, and to the best of my knowledge and belief, that it is correct, that all the costs of contract performance (except as herewith reported in writing) have been paid to the extent shown herein, or where not shown as paid have been paid or will be paid currently, by the contractor, when due, in the ordinary course of business, that the work reflected above has been performed, that the quantities and amounts involved are consistent with the requirements of the contact. That there are no encumbrances (except as reported in writing herewith, or on previous progress payment request No.

_____) against the property acquired or produced form, allocated or properly chargeable to the contract which would affect or impair the Government's title, that there has been no materially adverse change in the financial condition

of the contractor since the submission of the most recent written information dated _____ by the contractor to the Government in connection with the contract, that to the extent of any contract provision limiting progress payments pending

first article approval, such provision has been complied with, and that after the making of the requested progress payment the unliquidated progress payments will not exceed the maximum unliquidated progress apyments permitted by the contract.

NAME AND TITLE OF CONTRACTOR REPRESENTATIVE SIGNING THIS FORM	SIGNATURE
NAME AND TITLE OF CONTRACTING OFFICER	SIGNATURE

NSN 7540-01-140-5523
J61244
04-21-97

1443-101

STANDARD FORM 1443 (10-82)
Prescribed by GSA (FPR 1-16.808)
FAR (48 CFR) 53.232)

Appendix 9.9　Standard Form 1443, Contractor's Request for Progress Payment

INSTRUCTIONS

GENERAL - All entries on this form must be typewritten - all dollar amounts must be shown in whole dollars, rounded up to the next whole dollar. All line item numbers not included in the instructions below are self-explanatory.

SECTION I - IDENTIFICATION INFORMATION. Complete Items 1 through 8c in accordance with the following instructions:

Item 1. TO - Enter the name and address of the cognizant Contract Administration Office. PAYING OFFICE - Enter the designation of the paying office, as indicated in the contract.

Item 2. FROM - CONTRACTOR'S NAME AND ADDRESS/ZIP CODE - Enter the name and mailing address of the contractor. If applicable, the division of the company performing the contract should be entered immediately following the contractor's name.

Item 3. Enter an "X" in the appropriate block to indicate whether or not the contractor is a small business concern.

Item 5. Enter the total contract price, as amended. If the contract provides for escalation or price redetermination, enter the initial price until changed and not the ceiling price; if the contract is of the incentive type, enter the target or billing price, as amended until final pricing. For letter contracts, enter the maximum expenditure authorized by the contract, as amended.

Item 6A. PROGRESS PAYMENT RATES - Enter the 2-digit progress payment percentage rate shown in paragraph (a)(1) of the progress payment clause.

Item 6B. LIQUIDATION RATE - Enter the progress payment liquidation rate shown in paragraph (b) of the progress payment clause, using three digits - Example: show 80% as 800 - show 72.3% as 723.

Item 7. DATE OF INITIAL AWARD - Enter the last two digits of the calendar year. Use two digits to indicate the month. Example: show January 1982 as 82/01.

Item 8A. PROGRESS PAYMENT REQUEST NO. - Enter the number assigned to this request. All requests under a single contract must be numbered consecutively, beginning with 1. Each subsequent request under the same contract must continue in sequence, using the same series of numbers without omission.

Item 8B. Enter the date of the request.

SECTION II - GENERAL INSTRUCTIONS. DATE. In the space provided in the heading enter the date through which costs have been accumulated from inception for inclusion in this request. This date is applicable to item entries in Sections II and III.

Cost Basis. For all contracts with Small Business concerns, the base for progress payments is total costs incurred. For contracts with concerns other than Small Business, the progress payment base will be the total recorded paid costs, together with the incurred costs per the Computation of Amounts paragraph of the progress payment clause in FPR 1-30.510-1(a) or FAR 52.232-16, as appropriate. Total costs include all expenses paid and incurred, including applicable manufacturing and production expense, general and administrative expense for performance of contract, which are reasonable, allocable to the contract, consistent with sound and generally accepted accounting principles and practices, and which are not otherwise excluded by the contract.

Manufacturing and Production Expense, General and Administrative Expense. In connection with the first progress payment request on a contract, attach an explanation of the method, bases and period used in determining the amount of each of these two types of expenses. If the method, bases or periods used for computing these expenses differ in subsequent requests for progress payments under this contract, attach an explanation of such changes to the progress payment request involved.

Incurred Costs Involving Subcontractors for Contracts with Small Business Concerns. If the incurred costs eligible for progress payments under the contract include costs shown in invoices of subcontractors, suppliers and others, that portion of the costs computed on such invoices can only include costs for: (1) completed work to which the prime contractor has acquired title; (2) materials delivered to which the prime contractor has acquired title; (3) services rendered; and (4) costs billed under cost reimbursement or time and material subcontracts for work to which the prime contractor has acquired title.

SECTION II - SPECIFIC INSTRUCTIONS

Item 9. PAID COSTS ELIGIBLE UNDER PROGRESS PAYMENT CLAUSE - Line 9 will not be used for Small Business Contracts.

For large business contracts, costs to be shown in Item 9 shall include only those recorded costs which have resulted at time of request in payment made by cash, check, or other form of actual payment for items or services purchased directly for the contract. This includes items delivered, accepted and paid for, resulting in liquidation of subcontractor progress payments.

Costs to be shown in Item 9 are not to include advance payments, downpayments, or deposits, all of which are not eligible for reimbursement; or progress payments made to subcontractors, suppliers or others, which are to be included in Item 14. See "Cost Basis" above.

Item 10. INCURRED COSTS ELIGIBLE UNDER PROGRESS PAYMENT CLAUSE - For all Small Business Contracts, Item 10 will show total costs incurred for the contract.

Costs to be shown in Item 10 are not to include advance payments, downpayments, deposits, or progress payments made to subcontractors, suppliers or others.

For large business contracts, costs to be shown in Item 10 shall include all costs incurred (see "Cost Basis" above) for: materials which have been issued from the stores inventory and placed into production process for use on the contract; for direct labor; for other direct in-house costs; and for properly allocated and allowable indirect costs as set forth under "Cost Basis" above.

Item 12a. Enter the total contract costs incurred to date; if the actual amount is not known, enter the best possible estimate. If an estimate is used, enter (E) after the amount.

Item 12b. Enter the estimated cost to complete the contract. The estimate may be the last estimate made, adjusted for costs incurred since the last estimate; however, estimates shall be made not less frequently than every six months.

Items 14a through 14e. Include only progress payments on subcontracts which conform to progress payment provisions of the prime contract.

Item 14a. Enter only progress payments actually paid.

Item 14b. Enter total progress payments recouped from subcontractors.

Item 14d. For Small Business prime contracts, include the amount of unpaid subcontract progress payment billings which have been approved by the contractor for the current payment in the ordinary course of business. For other contracts, enter "0" amount.

SECTION III - SPECIFIC INSTRUCTIONS. This Section must be completed only if the contractor has received advance payments against this contract, or if items have been delivered, invoiced and accepted as of the date indicated in the heading of Section II above. EXCEPTION: Item 27 must be filled in by the Contracting Officer.

Item 20a. Of the costs reported in Item 11, compute and enter only costs which are properly allocable to items delivered, invoiced and accepted to the applicable date. In order of preference, these costs are to be computed on the basis of one of the following: (a) The actual unit cost of items delivered, giving proper consideration to the deferment of the starting load costs or, (b) projected unit costs (based on experienced costs plus the estimated cost to complete the contract), where the contractor maintains cost data which will clearly establish the reliability of such estimates.

Item 20d. Enter amount from 14e.

Item 21a. Enter the total billing price, as adjusted, of items delivered, accepted and invoiced to the applicable date.

Item 23. Enter total progress payments liquidated and those to be liquidated from billings submitted but not yet paid.

Item 25. Self-explanatory. (NOTE: If the entry in this item is a negative amount, there has been an overpayment which requires adjustment.)

Item 26. Self-explanatory, but if a lesser amount is requested, enter the lesser amount.

SPECIAL INSTRUCTIONS FOR USE UNDER FEDERAL ACQUISITION REGULATION (FAR).

Items 20 and 20e. Delete the references to a(3)(i) of the progress payment clause.

Items 21 and 21e. Delete the references to a(3)(ii) of the progress payment clause.

STANDARD FORM 1443 PAGE 2 (10-82)

Appendix 9.9   (Continued)

Chapter Ten

Other Contract Clauses

10-1. BACKGROUND

The procurement regulations require that government contracts include numerous clauses, many of which either directly or indirectly affect the renumeration the contractor ultimately will receive for contract performance. Other clauses impose requirements that are totally unrelated to contract remuneration. Because the clauses are often incorporated merely by reference into the contract's general provisions, a simple perusal of the contract terms provides little insight for assessing the impact of these clauses on the contract's potential profitability. Consequently, a more detailed review of these clauses is needed to enable a contractor to make informed judgments on the risks and requirements of government contracting.

Because of the sheer volume of contract clauses that can be incorporated into a given contract, it is not practical to discuss each of them in this chapter. The clauses discussed below pertain to record-retention requirements, price redetermination under redeterminable and incentive-type contracts, technical data, value engineering, government property, warranties, socioeconomic and environmental goals, and labor standards. Each of these clauses imposes significant contractual requirements for maintaining records or for specific actions. However, keep in mind that the clauses discussed in this and other chapters are still only a portion of the clauses that may be incorporated into government contracts and subcontracts.

10-2. RECORD-RETENTION REQUIREMENTS

The audit-negotiation clause (Federal Acquisition Regulation [FAR] 52.215-2) is required in contracts awarded under the procedures of FAR Part 15, Contracting by Negotiation, which exceed the simplified acquisition threshold. The audit-sealed bidding clause (FAR 52.214-26) is required in contracts awarded under the procedures of FAR Part 14, Sealed Bidding, expected to exceed $500,000. These

Retention Requirements	
2-Year Data	4-Year Data

Labor cost distribution cards
Petty cash records
Time and attendance cards
Payroll checks
Material and supply
  requisitions
	Accounts receivable invoice and supporting
	  data
	Material, work order, or service order files
	Cash advance recapitulations
	Paid, canceled, and voided checks
	Accounting payment records and supporting
	  data
	Payroll registers
	Maintenance work orders
	Equipment records
	Expendable property records
	Receiving inspection reports
	Purchase orders and supporting data
	Production records of quality records,
	  reliability, and inspection

Figure 10.1 Summary of Record Retention Requirements in FAR 4.705

two clauses form the basis of the government's access to contractor records, and require that contractors provide the contracting officer (CO), or a representative of the CO who is a government employee, with access to certain records whenever:

- Cost or pricing data is required
- A cost reimbursement or flexibly priced contract is used
- Cost, funding, or performance reports are required by the contract

In these situations, contractors must make available, in their original form, relevant books, records, documents and other data or evidence, and accounting procedures and practices. The data must be maintained for three years after final payment, except where shorter retention periods are prescribed in FAR 4.705 for certain specified types of data. Figure 10.1 summarizes these exceptions.

10-3. CONTRACT CLAUSES PROVIDING FOR SPECIFIC REPRICING ACTIONS

Several types of contract repricing actions simply respond to specific contract clauses that provide for anticipated repricing at contract inception. These repricing actions may be either positive or negative, and usually relate to uncertainties about the future that exist when the contract is awarded. The repricing action may also represent a vehicle for making an award or for making adjustments for less-than-anticipated levels of performance. Some of the types of contract clauses involved are discussed below.

Incentive Price Revision

Under fixed-price-incentive contracts, cost or performance targets are established, and adjustments to profit are based on performance as it relates to the

Example	Targets per Contract Terms	Assumption: Cost Underrun— $100,000	Assumption: Cost Overrun— $100,000
Sharing formula	75/25		
Cost	$1,000,000	$ 900,000	$1,100,000
Profit	$ 150,000	$ 175,000	$ 125,000
Price	$1,150,000	$1,075,000	$1,225,000
Price ceiling	$1,125,000	$1,250,000	$1,250,000

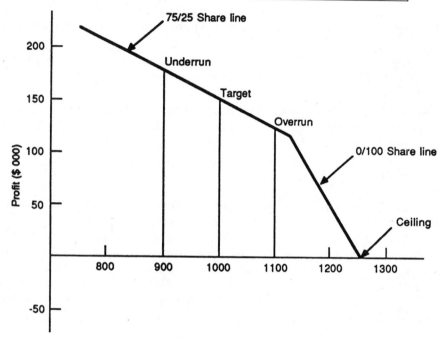

Figure 10.2 Application of Fixed-Price-Incentive Contract Formula for Final Price Determination

target. A target cost, target profit, total price ceiling, and formula for establishing the final profit and price are negotiated at the contract's outset. After the contract is completed, the final cost is negotiated and the final price determined through application of the formula. As illustrated in Figure 10.2, the formula provides greater profits when costs are less than the target cost; conversely, profits are reduced when the costs exceed the target cost. Fixed-price-incentive contracts may provide for either firm targets (FAR 52.216-16) or successive targets (FAR 52.216-17). Under the latter form, new targets are established at specified points in the contract's period of performance.

Cost-plus-incentive-fee contracts are similar to fixed-price-incentive contracts in that the amount of the ultimate fee earned depends on the level of cost incurred compared with the previously established target cost.

Economic Price Adjustment

These clauses are used to protect the contractor and the government against significant economic fluctuations in labor or material costs or to provide for contract price adjustments in the event of changes in the contract's established price. Upward or downward price adjustments are tied to the occurrence of certain contingencies that are specifically defined in the contract and are beyond the contractor's control. These clauses represent an excellent method of equitably distributing between the government and the contractor cost risks related to future economic events.

There are basically three types of economic price-adjustment provisions:

1. Adjustments based on established prices resulting from increases/decreases in the published or established prices of standard or semi-standard supplies (FAR 52.216-2 and FAR 52.216-3)

2. Adjustments based on labor or material costs (actual cost method) resulting from cost increases/decreases experienced by the contractor (FAR 52.216-4)

3. Adjustments based on labor or material costs (cost index method) resulting from increases/decreases in specified cost standards or indices

The standard contract clauses limit increases to 10% of the original unit price or labor rate. However, the clauses may be modified, upon approval by the chief of the contracting office, by raising the limit on aggregate increases.

Price Redetermination

There are two types of fixed-price redetermination clauses. The first provides for redetermination at stated intervals and is normally used when it is possible to negotiate a firm-fixed-price contract for a stated period but not beyond (FAR 52.216-5). The contract provides a fixed price for the stated period. Before the end of this period, the contractor submits a formal pricing proposal for the supplies to be delivered in the next period. The government and the contractor then negotiate prices for this period. The process continues for each succeeding period identified in the contract. This type of contract is used only when:

*   Given the conditions surrounding the procurement, it is clear that a firm-fixed-price or fixed-price-incentive arrangement does not meet the requirements of the contracting parties.

*   The contractor's accounting system is adequate for price redetermination purposes.

*   The prospective pricing period is compatible with the contractor's accounting system.

*   Timely price redetermination action is expected to be taken.

The second type of clause provides for a retroactive price redetermination after contract completion (FAR 52.216-6). Because the entire price is redetermined retroactively, the contract itself does not provide a quantifiable incentive for effective cost control. Accordingly, a contract ceiling, negotiated at the time of award, is designed to provide for a reasonable assumption of risk by the contractor.

When the contract is completed, the contractor submits a statement of total incurred costs. The contractor and the government then negotiate a contract price. The government's objective is to negotiate a price that recognizes the degree of management effectiveness and ingenuity exhibited during contract performance. Any amounts paid during contract performance that exceed the retroactively determined contract value must be repaid to the government immediately.

Retroactive price redetermination is used only for short-duration research and development (R&D) contracts when the estimated costs are $100,000 or less and:

- Establishing a fair and reasonable firm price at the time of contract award is not practical.
- A ceiling price will be negotiated for the contract at a level reflecting a reasonable sharing of risk by the contractor.
- A billing price was previously negotiated.
- The contractor's management effectiveness and ingenuity will be considered in retroactively redetermining the price.

10-4. VALUE ENGINEERING

Value engineering is a process to identify opportunities to achieve cost savings by changing an item's function or characteristics. Contractors whose profit is otherwise based on cost would not normally be incentivized to propose changes that might reduce cost and profit. Part 48 of the FAR describes the government's program to provide contractors with an incentive to identify and propose product or service changes which reduce cost and enhance value.

There are two value-engineering techniques: mandatory and voluntary. Under the voluntary approach, contractors use their own resources to develop and submit value-engineering change proposals (VECPs). The contract provides for sharing of savings and payment of allowable costs development and implementation costs only when the VECP is accepted. Under the voluntary program, contractors receive up to 50% of the net savings under fixed-price contracts and 25% of the net savings under cost-reimbursement contracts. The percentages are paid for savings on the "instant" contract, other affected contracts in effect, and future contracts for a specific period of time. The voluntary approach is used when detailed specifications exist and the likelihood of significant VECPs is not great. The mandatory approach provides lesser sharing of savings, but the cost of a program to seek out VECP opportunities is part of the cost or price of the contract. The contractor receives up to 25% of the net savings on fixed-price contracts and 15% of the net savings on cost-reimbursement contracts. This approach is used when significant opportunities to identify VECPs are anticipated, such as when specifications are less specific.

The Value Engineering clause (52.248-1) is required for contracts over $100,000, unless the contract:

- Provides for R&D other than full-scale development
- Provides for engineering services from a nonprofit or not-for-profit organization
- Provides for personal services
- Provides for product improvement
- Provides for commercial products, except for unique requirements
- Is exempted by agency head
- Provides for architect–engineer services

A separate Value Engineering clause (52.248-2) is included in architect–engineer contracts which require and fund specified value engineering effort. The clause must be flowed down to subcontractors meeting the requirements above.

Whether contractor costs incurred on unaccepted value engineering change proposals are allowable or unallowable has been the subject of controversy. The Civilian Agency Acquisition Council and the Defense Acquisition Regulation (DAR) Council published a proposed revision to FAR 48.101(b) in January 1990, which stated that the allowability of proposal development and implementation costs would be determined in accordance with the FAR Part 31 cost principles. A draft final rule, planned for inclusion in Federal Acquisition Circular No. 90-5, would have permitted direct charging of costs of accepted proposals and indirect charging of costs of unaccepted proposals. The draft final rule was withdrawn from the circular shortly before publication because of Defense Contract Audit Agency (DCAA) concerns that such accounting treatment violated the consistency requirements of Cost Accounting Standard (CAS) 402. A compromise position to require indirect costing of development costs for both accepted and unaccepted value engineering change proposals was published for comment in December 1992, but withdrawn on January 14, 1994. Consequently, FAR 48.101(b) has remained unchanged.

10-5. RIGHTS IN TECHNICAL DATA

Requirements for conveying technical data rights to the government have been especially confusing, particularly due to the many statutes, regulations, proposed statutes, and proposed regulations that have appeared in recent years. Much of the confusion started in 1984, when Congress enacted the Defense Procurement Reform Act[1] and the Small Business and Federal Procurement Enhancement Act,[2] which required defense contracts to include provisions that clearly delineated the contractor's responsibility for delivering technical data. However, because no government-wide regulations were promulgated, the military services tended to act independently in protecting the government's interest in data rights. The Fiscal Year 1987 Defense Authorization Act[3] amendments established a more reasoned approach for reviewing and challenging the propriety of data rights restrictions by emphasizing that when technology has been developed partly with federal sponsorship and partly at private expense, it is appropriate for the contracting parties to negotiate the data rights issues. The amendments also provided that contractors generally may not be forced, as a condition of responding to a solicitation's requirements, to relinquish legitimate data rights. To guide the DAR Council in defining the term *developed at private expense*, the conference report contained the following language:

> The conferees agree that, for purposes of determining whether an item or process has been developed at private expense, an item should generally be considered "developed" if the item or process exists and reasonable persons skilled in the applicable art would conclude that a high probability exists that the item or process will work as intended. ... In addition, the conferees agree that as a matter of general policy "at private expense" development was accomplished without direct government payment. Payments by the government to reimburse a contractor for its indirect costs would not be considered in determining whether the government had funded the development of an item. Thus reimbursement for independent research & development (IR&D) expenses and other indirect costs (capital funds and profits) although such payments are in indirect support of a development effort, are treated for the purposes of this Act as contractor funds.[4]

The revision to the Defense FAR Supplement (DFARS), Part 227, implementing the Fiscal Year 1987 Defense Authorization Act amendments, established a third category of data rights, in addition to "limited rights" and "unlimited rights," called "government purpose license rights." These rights apply when the contract has contributed more than 50% of the development cost. The DFARS revision also defines *developed at private expense* along the lines suggested in the 1987 Authorization Act conference report.

The 1992 Defense Authorization Act[5] required the Secretary of Defense to establish a joint Department of Defense (DOD)–industry committee to recommend proposed technical data rights regulations. The committee had difficulty reaching a consensus on the content of new regulations, particularly relating to the treatment of indirect manufacturing and production engineering costs. Original equipment manufacturers argued that data developed with costs charged to indirect cost pools should be treated as data developed at private expense, whereas spare parts replicators opposed this position on the basis that it would allow original manufacturers to restrict data that had not been restricted in the past. The committee ultimately concluded that data developed with the use of indirect cost funding met the criteria for development at private expense. The committee report was submitted to Congress by the Deputy Secretary of Defense in April 1994.

The DFARS, Subpart 227.4, Rights in Technical Data, and the related contract clause, 252.227-7013, Rights in Technical Data, were revised on June 28, 1995. With regard to commercial items or processes, the government is given specific license rights to use, modify, reproduce, release, perform, display, or disclose the data within the government. Except for emergency repair or overhaul, such data may not be released or disclosed to third parties without the contractor's written permission. Noncommercial items or processes are subject to standard license rights (unlimited, government purpose, or limited), based on the source of development funds. All indirect development costs are considered private expenses. The DFARS is designed to replicate commercial practice for commercial computer software and computer software documentation. Software and software documentation will be acquired under licenses customarily available to the public. Government rights in noncommercial computer software and computer software documentation are license rights. Standard license rights are (1) unlimited rights if the development was at government expense; (2) restricted rights if the development was at private expense; and (3) government purpose rights in the case of mixed development.

To assure that technical data rights are not inadvertently jeopardized, contractors need to be exceedingly careful in how they record costs incurred in developing technical data. Development costs not incurred for contract performance should be segregated and specifically identified to specific processes or products.

The technical rights requirements in FAR and DFARS are not identical, as demonstrated by the myriad of technical data rights clauses summarized in Figure 10.3. Consequently, contractors should carefully read data rights clauses included in each solicitation, prior to signing the contract. Contractors should also be diligent in placing proprietary markings on all technical data provided to the government that were developed, to any extent, with company-controlled funds.

10-6. CONTRACT WARRANTIES

The Fiscal Year 1985 Defense Authorization Act[6] revised the warranty requirements imposed on prime contractors that produce weapon systems. Defense FAR

Clause Description	FAR	DFARS
Rights in Data—General	52.227-14	
Rights in Technical Data—Noncommercial Items		252.227-7013
Rights in Noncommercial Computer Software and Noncommercial Computer Software Documentation		252.227-7014
Technical Data—Commercial Items		252.227-7015
Rights to Proposal Data	52.227-23	252.227-7016
Rights in Data—SBIR Program	52.227-20	252.227-7018
Rights in Data—Existing Works	52.227-18	252.227-7021
Rights in Data—Special Works	52.227-17	
Commercial Software—Restricted Rights	52.227-19	

Figure 10.3 Technical Data Rights Clauses

Supplement 246.7 requires the contracting officer to obtain cost-effective warranties on large, mature, full-scale production contracts for weapon systems. If a warranty provision is not considered cost-effective, a waiver may be obtained from a senior defense official.

In recognition of the need to tailor the warranty clause to unique contract requirements, no standard clause has been established. Defense FAR Supplement 246.777-3 provides the following guidance on appropriate content for warranty clauses:

> Since as the objectives and circumstances vary considerably among weapon system acquisition programs, contracting officers must tailor the required warranties on a case-by-case basis. The purpose of tailoring is to get a cost-effective warranty in light of the technical risk, or other program uncertainties, while ensuring that the Government still acquires the basic warranties described in 246.770-2. Tailoring shall not be used as a substitute for acquiring a warranty waiver.
>
> 1. Tailoring may affect remedies, exclusion, limitations, and duration provided such are consistent with the specific requirements of this section (see also FAR 46.706).
>
> 2. Clearly relate the duration of any warranty to the contract requirements and allow sufficient time to demonstrate achievement of the requirements after acceptance.
>
> 3. Tailor the terms of the warranty, if appropriate, to exclude certain defects for specified supplies (exclusions) or to limit the contractor's liability under the terms of the warranty (limitations).
>
> 4. Structure broader and more comprehensive warranties when advantageous or narrow the scope when appropriate. For example, it may be inappropriate to require warranty of all essential performance requirements for a contractor that did not design the system.
>
> Department of Defense policy is to exclude any terms that cover contracts liability for loss, damage or injury to third parties from warranty clauses.

10-7. GOVERNMENT PROPERTY

There are two classes of government property: government-furnished and contractor-acquired property. Government-furnished property is provided by the government under the contract terms for the contractor's use in the performing of the contract. Any other use must be approved by the CO. Contractor-acquired property is acquired or created by the contractor as part of the contract performance. Property may consist of materials, facilities, equipment, tooling, or military property.

Government regulations provide that possession or use of government property should not give one competing contractor an advantage over another. Consequently, government proposal evaluators must adjust the proposed prices of contractors that include the use of government property in their proposals to eliminate any advantage gained by such proposed use.

The FAR, Part 45, contains the regulations on government policies and procedures concerning government property. These regulations require the inclusion of a Government Property clause in nearly all government contracts. These clauses place extensive requirements on contractors for the responsibility and accountability for all government property in their possession. The standard clauses for fixed-price contracts (FAR 52.245-2) and cost-reimbursement, time-and-material, or labor hour contracts (FAR 52.245-5) require the contractor to comply with FAR 45.5, thereby effectively incorporating the subpart into the contract. In addition, the clauses provide that equitable adjustment is the contractor's exclusive remedy for disputes arising under the clause.

Title for contractor-acquired property passes to the government upon use or payment, whichever occurs first. This provision played a part in the decision in California that exempted contractors from sales and use tax on some purchases charged to indirect pools. The California court ruled that if title passes upon payment, it is, in effect, being sold to the government.[7] The federal government is exempt from state taxes.

The regulations in FAR 45.5 require contractors to maintain a property control system to control, protect, preserve, and maintain all government property in their possession or under their control. The contractor's property records are official government records. They must track all government property and include the following:

- Name, description, and national stock number
- Quantity
- Unit price
- Contract number
- Location
- Disposition
- Posting record and transaction data

10-8. CONTRACT CLAUSES RELATING TO SOCIOECONOMIC AND ENVIRONMENTAL PROTECTION GOALS

The federal government, primarily through legislative initiatives, has instituted a broad range of nonprocurement policies deemed to be in the public interest. While the pursuit of these socioeconomic objectives may increase the costs of the procurement process, the laws and regulations implementing these policies are an important and permanent part of contracting with the federal government.

Small, Small Disadvantaged, and Women-Owned Small Business Programs

The Utilization of Small, Small Disadvantaged, and Women-Owned Small Business Concerns clause (FAR 52.219-8) is included in contracts expected to exceed the simplified acquisition thresholds, except those performed entirely outside the United States or for personal services. The clause underscores the government's policy to maximize procurement opportunities for small, small disadvantaged, and women-owned small business concerns and requires contractors to implement that policy in awarding subcontracts.

The Small, Small Disadvantaged, and Women-Owned Small Business Subcontracting Plan clause (FAR 52.219-9) is included in all solicitations for negotiated or formally advertised contracts or modifications that (1) offer subcontracting possibilities; (2) are expected to exceed $500,000 ($1 million for public facility construction); and (3) are required to include the Utilization of Small, Small Disadvantaged, and Women-Owned Small Business Concerns clause. The clause is not included in solicitations that have been set aside for small businesses or that are to be procured through the Small Business Administration (SBA) Section 8(a) program. The clause requires the successful offeror/bidder to submit to the procurement CO a comprehensive subcontracting plan for incorporation into the contract. Failure to submit a subcontracting plan makes the offeror ineligible for contract award, and failure to comply in good faith with the plan is considered a material breach of contract. The plan must include the following:

- Percentage goals for using small and small disadvantaged subcontractors and dollars planned for subcontracting, in total, to small businesses and to small disadvantaged businesses

- The principal types of supplies and services to be subcontracted to all businesses, and in particular, to small, small disadvantaged, and women-owned small business concerns

- A description of the method used to develop the subcontracting goals

- A description of the method used to identify potential sources for solicitation purposes

- The name of the company representative who administers the plan

- A statement as to whether indirect costs were included in establishing subcontracting goals and a description of the method used to determine the proportionate share of indirect costs to be incurred with small, small disadvantaged, and women-owned small business concerns

- A description of the efforts that will be made to assure that small, small disadvantaged, and women-owned small business concerns have an equal opportunity to compete for subcontracts

- Assurance that the Utilization of Small, Small Disadvantaged, and Women-Owned Small Business Concerns clause will be inserted in all subcontracts that offer further subcontracting possibilities

- Assurance that any reports required to demonstrate compliance with the plan will be furnished. Standard Form 294, Subcontracting Report for Individual Contracts (see Appendix 10.1), and Standard Form 295, Summary Subcontract Report (see Appendix 10.2), must be submitted semiannually. Both forms were substantively revised, effective October 1, 1995

- Identification of records that will be maintained to document subcontracting actions, contacts with small and small disadvantaged businesses, and internal activities to provide guidance to buyers

Contractors may establish master subcontracting plans, on plant- or division-wide bases, that contain all of the plan elements described above, except for goals. Master plans are effective for one year after approval by the CO.

When a contractor fails to make a good faith effort to comply with its subcontracting plan, liquidated damages, equal to the dollar amount by which the contractor failed to meet its specified subcontracting goals, may be assessed pursuant to the Liquidated Damages—Small Business Subcontracting Plan clause (FAR 52.219-16).

Other Socioeconomic Clauses

The Utilization of Labor Surplus Area Concerns clause (formerly FAR 52.220-3), and Labor Surplus Area Subcontracting Program clause (formerly FAR 52.220-4) were eliminated on October 1, 1995.

The Equal Opportunity clause (FAR 52.222-26) is included in all contracts, except for transactions of $10,000 or less, work outside the United States, contracts with state or local governments, work on or near Indian reservations, and contracts exempted by Department of Labor Office of Federal Contractor Compliance Programs. This clause prohibits discrimination against qualified employees or applicants because of race, color, religion, sex, or national origin and requires submission of periodic reports of employment statistics as required by Executive Order 11246. Standard Form 100 (EEO-1) (see Appendix 10.3) must be filed 30 days following the contract award, unless the form was already filed within the preceding 12 months. Contractors determined to be in noncompliance with the Equal Opportunity clause or rules, regulations, and orders may be declared ineligible to receive further government contracts.

The Affirmative Action for Special Disabled Veterans and Vietnam Era Veterans clause (FAR 52.222-35) is included in all contracts for $10,000 or more, except for work performed outside the United States by employees who were not recruited within the United States. The clause prohibits discrimination against qualified employees or applicants on the basis that they are disabled veterans or veterans of the Vietnam era and requires reporting of employment openings and hirings.

A similar clause, Affirmative Action for Handicapped Workers (FAR 52.222-36), is included in all contracts for $2,500 or more, except for work performed outside the United States by employees who were not recruited within the United States. The clause prohibits discrimination against qualified employees or applicants on the basis of mental or physical handicap.

The Buy American Act—Trade Agreements—Balance of Payments Program clause (FAR 52.225-9) implements the Buy American Act, Trade Act Agreements, and the DOD Balance of Payments Program by providing a preference to domestic end products over certain foreign end products. The clause is inserted in all contracts subject to the Trade Agreements Act. The Buy American Act—North American Free Trade Agreement (NAFTA) Implementation Act—Balance of Payments Program clause (FAR 52.225-21) is inserted in contracts that are subject to NAFTA rather than the Trade Agreements Act.

The Clean Air and Water clause (FAR 52.223-2) is inserted in all contracts expected to exceed $100,000, or for which the contractor's facility has been the subject of a conviction of Air Act or Water Act violations and is listed by the Environmental Protection Agency (EPA) as a violating facility. The clause requires compliance with sections of the Air and Water Acts relating to inspection, monitoring, entry, reports, and information, and prohibits performance of contract work in facilities on the EPA List of Violating Facilities.

10-9. CONTRACT CLAUSES RELATING TO LABOR STANDARDS

The Walsh–Healy Public Contracts Act clause (FAR 52.222-20) is generally required in contracts over $10,000 performed in the United States, Puerto Rico, or the Virgin Islands for the manufacture or furnishing of noncommercial[8] materials, supplies, articles, or equipment. The act prohibits the following:

- The payment of employees of less than the prevailing minimum wages for persons employed on similar work within the geographic area
- Work by employees in excess of 40 hours in any one week except when an employer–employee agreement pursuant to Title 29, Section 207, of the United States Code provides otherwise
- The employment of children (males under 16 and females under 18) or convicts
- Contract performance under working conditions that are unsanitary, hazardous, or dangerous to the health and safety of employees

The Davis Bacon Act clause (FAR 52.222-6), included in construction contracts over $2,000, prohibits the payment to mechanics and laborers of less than the prevailing minimum wages for comparable classes or laborers and mechanics employed on similar construction projects in the same geographical area.

Construction contracts, as well as supply and R&D contracts, over the simplified acquisition threshold include the Contract Work Hours and Safety Standards Act—Overtime Compensation clause (FAR 52.222-4). This clause prohibits work by laborers or mechanics in excess of 40 hours in any one week without payment of overtime compensation at least at time and a half the basic pay rate.

The Service Contract Act of 1965 as Amended, clause (FAR 52.222-41), inserted in fixed-price service contracts over $2,500, prohibits the payment to employees of less than the prevailing minimum monetary wage and fringe benefits.

Either the Fair Labor Standards Act and Service Contract Act—Price Adjustment [Multiple Year and Option Contracts] clause (FAR 52.222-43) or the Fair Labor Standards Act and Service Contract Act—Price Adjustment clause (FAR 52.222-44) is required in contracts that are subject to the Service Contract Act and are over $2,500. The Fair Labor Standards Act specifies certain minimum wages and addresses overtime payments to nonsalaried employees for hours worked in excess of 40 hours a week.

A significant case involving Malcolm Pirnie, Inc., addressed the issue of whether certain engineers and other professional employees are exempt from the Fair Labor Standards Act overtime pay requirements. After discovering that it had inadvertently docked certain salaried employees for partial days not worked, Malcolm Pirnie immediately revised its employee handbook to prevent further docking practices. It also refunded the salary costs previously withheld, pursuant to the act's implementing regulations, which permit contractors to correct inadvertent deductions without losing the overtime exemption. The Department of Labor ruled that Malcolm Pirnie's employees were not exempt from the overtime requirements. While the District Court[9] upheld Malcolm Pirnie's position that its employees were salaried and that its inadvertent error had been corrected in accordance with the regulations, the Court of Appeals[10] reversed. Malcolm Pirnie appealed to the Supreme Court, but the Supreme Court declined to accept the case.[11] The implication of this decision is that any employer with partial-day docking procedures may be required to pay overtime to its salaried employees. The Department of Labor has been urged to modify its regulations.

10-10. RECOVERY OF NONRECURRING COSTS AND ROYALTY FEES ON COMMERCIAL SALES

Department of Defense 2140.2, Recoupment of Nonrecurring Costs on Sales of U.S. Products and Technology, as implemented in 32 CFR, Part 165, required contractors to pay recoupment whenever products or technologies developed under defense contracts were sold to nongovernment users or resulted in commercial spinoffs.

Fundamental to the DOD policy is language in the Arms Export Control Act, which requires recoupment on sales, under the Foreign Military Sales (FMS) program, of major defense equipment (MDE) that was previously developed under government contracts. The DOD policy, however, went beyond the act's requirements. The complex DOD rules, originally established in the 1960s, gradually expanded the Department's recoupment rights to

- Cover both domestic and international sales to which the U.S. government was not a party

- Cover major defense items and derivative items as well as MDE

- Assess fees that exceeded the Department's original contribution to the product or technology

Industry long pursued rescission of the policy on the grounds that it was unduly burdensome and severely inhibited the commercialization of government-funded technology. Recent developments have led to DOD actions to substantially liberalize the recoupment policy.

- On November 1, 1991, General Motors Corporation (GM), Allison Gas Turbine Division, reached a no-cost settlement with the U.S. government, bringing to a close a dispute in the Claims Court where GM was appealing the DOD's $35 million recoupment charge on non-U.S. government sales of aircraft engines.[12]

- On January 16, 1992, the Office of Information and Regulatory Affairs of the Office of Management and Budget (OMB) disapproved the information collection request in the DOD's revision to its recoupment rules. The OMB further noted that the recordkeeping and reporting requirements in the existing DOD recoupment rules had never been approved, in violation of the Paperwork Reduction Act.

- 32 CFR, Part 165, Recoupment of Nonrecurring Costs on Sales or Licensing of U.S. Items, was revised on July 2, 1992, to eliminate the requirement for recoupment on new DOD contracts other than those for FMS or commercial sales of MDE. On October 9, 1992,[13] an interim rule directed COs to modify existing contracts to delete the recoupment requirement except for FMS sales of MDE. The DOD finalized this rule on March 29, 1993, eliminating recoupment of nonrecurring costs on commercial sales of MDE on or after January 13, 1993.[14]

10-11. CONTRACT NOVATION

A third party may be recognized as a successor in interest to a government contract when the contractor's assets are sold or the assets involved in contract performance are sold. If the government agrees to recognize a successor in interest, a novation agreement must be executed. However, the CO must first determine that the successor in interest can fulfill all contractual responsibilities. The government is not obligated to novate contracts if the government does not deem the successor in interest to be responsible. Federal Acquisition Regulation 42.1204(b) specifically provides the following:

> When it is in the Government's interest not to concur in the transfer of a contract from one company to another company, the original contractor remains under obligation to the Government, and the contract may be terminated for default, should the original contractor not perform.

Prior to agreeing to novate any contracts, the COs will require the following:

- Evidence of the transferee's capability to perform the contracts
- Balance sheets of the transferor and transferee as of the dates immediately before and after the transfer of assets, certified for accuracy by independent accountants

The purpose of the certified balance sheets is to permit the government to compare the financial strength of the potential successor in interest to that of the current contractor.

Federal Acquisition Regulation 42.1204(e) provides a standard format for the novation agreement, including a provision that the government is not obligated to pay any cost increases directly or indirectly arising from the transfer or the novation agreement. This provision was invoked to bar recovery of home office costs on contracts novated by ITT Gilfillan, Inc.[15] The home office costs were assessed by ITT Gilfillan's new parent corporation (ITT). This provision was also cited by the NASA Board of Contract Appeals[16] to bar recovery of increased wind tunnel costs on novated contracts resulting from a cost accounting practice change. The accounting change was implemented to achieve consistent accounting treatment among the divisions of McDonnell Douglas Corporation, which resulted from the merger of the McDonnell Company and Douglas Aircraft Corporation.

The Undersecretary of Defense issued policy guidance on July 21, 1993,[17] regarding modification of the standard novation agreement to permit recovery of certain restructuring costs related to plant closure, employee severance, and plant/personnel relocation, etc., if an acquisition/merger is expected to result in overall reduced costs for the DOD or would preserve a critical defense capability. Recovery of external restructuring costs has been addressed in recent Defense Authorization Acts.[18] The statutory provisions are implemented in DFARS 231.205-70, as discussed in Chapter 7.

10-12. SUMMARY

The various contract clauses emphasize the fact that doing business with the federal government is far different from doing business with a typical commercial customer.

Because many clauses are incorporated into the contract only by reference, a contractor must become knowledgeable about their requirements. Before accepting any contract, a potential contractor should carefully read the complete text of each clause being incorporated into the contract to ensure that its requirements are understood and that reasonable compliance with its provisions during contract performance is achievable.

10-13. NOTES

1. Defense Procurement Reform Act, 10 U.S.C. §2301, enacted Oct. 19, 1984, Pub. L. 98-525.
2. Small Business and Federal Procurement Enhancement Act, 10 U.S.C. §2320, 2320a, 41 U.S.C. §416, enacted Oct. 30, 1984, Pub. L. 98-577.
3. Fiscal Year 1987 Defense Authorization Act, 100 Stat 3816, enacted Nov. 14, 1986, Pub. L. 100-26.
4. Fiscal Year 1987 Defense Authorization Act conference report, enacted Dec. 4, 1987, Pub. L. 100-80.
5. 1992 Defense Authorization Act, Pub. L., §807.
6. Fiscal Year 1985 Defense Authorization Act, 10 U.S.C. §2304, enacted Nov. 8, 1985, Pub. L. 99-145.
7. The Aerospace Corp. v. State Board of Equalization, CA Superior Ct., LA County, Nos. C-416134 and C-578611, June 13, 1988; aff'd. CA CMA, 2nd District, Division Seven, No. B-36583, March 22, 1990.
8. Federal Acquisition Circular No. 90-32, Item III, Sept. 18, 1995, exempted the acquisition of commercial items from the Walsh–Healy Act.
9. Martin v. Malcolm Pirnie, Inc., 758 F. Supp. 899, April 1, 1991.
10. Martin v. Malcolm Pirnie, Inc., CA 2 No. 91-6138, Nov. 20, 1991, 949 F. 2d 611.
11. Malcolm Pirnie, Inc. v. Martin, U.S. S. Ct., No. 91-1748, petition filed May 5, 1992, cert. denied.
12. Bureau of National Affairs, Federal Contracts Report, Vol. 56, Dec. 9, 1991, p. 784.
13. Undersecretary of Defense memorandum, dated Oct. 9, 1992, to the Assistant Secretary of the Army (Research, Development and Acquisition), Assistant Secretary of the Navy (Research, Development and Acquisition), Assistant Secretary of the Air Force (Acquisition), and Directors of Defense Agencies; subject: Recoupment of Nonrecurring Costs.
14. Federal Register, Vol. 58, No. 58, March 29, 1993, p. 16497.
15. ITT Gilfillan, Inc., ASBCA No. 11804, June 19, 1968, 68-2 BCA 7,086; Ct. Cl. No. 356-68, Jan. 18, 1973, 471 F.2d 1382.
16. McDonnell Douglas Corp., NASBCA No. 873-10, May 10, 1975, 75-1 BCA 11,337.
17. Undersecretary of Defense memorandum, dated July 21, 1993, to the Commander, Defense Contract Management Command; subject: Allowability of Restructuring Costs on Novated Contracts.
18. Fiscal Year 1995 Defense Authorization Act, §818, 108 Stat. 2821, enacted Oct. 5, 1994, Pub. L. 103-337, Fiscal Year 1997 Defense Authorization, §8115, 110 Stat. 3009, enacted Sept. 30, 1996, Pub. L. 104-208, Fiscal Year 1998 Defense Authorization Act.

SUBCONTRACTING REPORT FOR INDIVIDUAL CONTRACTS
(See instructions on page 2)

OMB No.: 9000-0006
Expires: 03/31/98

Public reporting burden for this collection of information is estimated to average 3 hours per response, including the time for reviewing instructions, searching existing data sources, gathering and maintaining the data needed, and completing and reviewing the collection of information. Send comments regarding this burden estimate or any other aspect of this collection of information, including suggestions for reducing this burden, to the FAR Secretariat (MVR), Federal Acquisition Policy Division, GSA, Washington, DC 20405.

1. CORPORATION, COMPANY OR SUBDIVISION COVERED

a. COMPANY NAME

b. STREET ADDRESS

c. CITY   d. STATE   e. ZIP CODE

2. CONTRACTOR IDENTIFICATION NUMBER

3. DATE SUBMITTED

4. REPORTING PERIOD FROM INCEPTION OF CONTRACT THRU:

☐ MAR 31   ☐ SEPT 30   YEAR

5. TYPE OF REPORT

☐ REGULAR   ☐ FINAL   ☐ REVISED

6. ADMINISTERING ACTIVITY *(Please check applicable box)*

☐ ARMY   ☐ GSA   ☐ NASA
☐ NAVY   ☐ DOE   ☐ OTHER FEDERAL AGENCY (Specify)
☐ AIR FORCE   ☐ DEFENSE LOGISTICS AGENCY

7. REPORT SUBMITTED AS *(Check one and provide appropriate number)*

☐ PRIME CONTRACTOR

☐ SUBCONTRACTOR

PRIME CONTRACT NUMBER

SUBCONTRACT NUMBER

8. AGENCY OR CONTRACTOR AWARDING CONTRACT

a. AGENCY'S OR CONTRACTOR'S NAME

b. STREET ADDRESS

c. CITY   d. STATE   e. ZIP CODE

9. DOLLARS AND PERCENTAGES IN THE FOLLOWING BLOCKS:

☐ DO INCLUDE INDIRECT COSTS   ☐ DO NOT INCLUDE INDIRECT COSTS

SUBCONTRACT AWARDS

TYPE	CURRENT GOAL		ACTUAL CUMULATIVE	
	WHOLE DOLLARS	PERCENT	WHOLE DOLLARS	PERCENT
10a. SMALL BUSINESS CONCERNS *(Include SDB, WOSB, HBCU/MI) (Dollar Amount and Percent of 10c.)*				
10b. LARGE BUSINESS CONCERNS *(Dollar Amount and Percent of 10c.)*				
10c. TOTAL *(Sum of 10a and 10b.)*				
11. SMALL DISADVANTAGED (SDB) CONCERNS *(Include HBCU/MI) (Dollar Amount and Percent of 10c.)*				
12. WOMEN-OWNED SMALL BUSINESS (WOSB) CONCERNS *(Dollar Amount and Percent of 10c.)*				

13. REMARKS

14a. NAME OF INDIVIDUAL ADMINISTERING SUBCONTRACTING PLAN

14b. TELEPHONE NUMBER

AREA CODE   NUMBER

AUTHORIZED FOR LOCAL REPRODUCTION
Previous edition is not usable

STANDARD FORM 294 (REV. 10-96)

Prescribed by GSA-FAR (48 CFR) 53.219(a)

J61306
05-07-97

Appendix 10.1   Standard Form 294, Subcontracting Report for Individual Contracts

378

GENERAL INSTRUCTIONS

1. This report is not required from small businesses.

2. This report is not required for commercial products for which a company-wide annual plan (i.e., a Commercial Products Plan) has been approved, nor from large businesses in the Department of Defense (DOD) Test Program for Negotiation of Comprehensive Subcontracting Plans. The Summary Subcontract Report (SF 295) is required for contractors operating under one of these two conditions and should be submitted to the Government in accordance with the instructions on that form.

3. This form collects subcontract award data from prime contractors/subcontractors that: (a) hold one or more contracts over $500,000 (over $1,000,000 for construction of a public facility); and (b) are required to report subcontracts awarded to Small Business (SB), Small Disadvantaged Business (SDB), and Women-Owned Small Business (WOSB) concerns under a subcontracting plan. For the Department of Defense (DOD), the National Aeronautics and Space Administration (NASA), and the Coast Guard, this form also collects subcontract award data for Historically Black Colleges and Universities (HBCUs) and Minority Institutions (MIs).

4. This report is required for each contract containing a subcontracting plan and must be submitted to the administrative contracting officer (ACO) or contracting officer if no ACO is assigned, semi-annually during contract performance for the periods ended March 31st and September 30th. A separate report is required for each contract at contract completion. Reports are due 30 days after the close of each reporting period unless otherwise directed by the contracting officer. Reports are required when due, regardless of whether there has been any subcontracting activity since the inception of the contract or since the previous report.

5. Only subcontracts involving performance with the U.S., its possessions, Puerto Rico, and the Trust Territory of the Pacific Islands should be included in this report.

6. Purchases from a corporation, company, or subdivision that is an affiliate of the prime/subcontractor are not included in this report.

7. Subcontract award data reported on this form by prime contractors/subcontractors shall be limited to awards made to their immediate subcontractors. Credit cannot be taken for awards made to lower tier subcontractors.

SPECIFIC INSTRUCTIONS

BLOCK 2: For the Contractor Identification Number, enter the nine-digit Data Universal Numbering System (DUNS) number that identifies the specific contractor establishment. If there is no DUNS number available that identifies the exact name and address entered in Block 1, contact Dun and Bradstreet Information Services at 1-800-333-0505 to get one free of charge over the telephone. Be prepared to provide the following information: (1) Company name; (2) Company address; (3) Company telephone number; (4) Line of business: (5) Chief executive officer/key manager; (6) Date the company was started; (7) Number of people employed by the company; and; (8) Company affiliation.

BLOCK 4: Check only one. Note that all subcontract award data reported on this form represents activity since the inception of the contract through the date indicated in this block.

BLOCK 5: Check whether this report is a "Regular," "Final," and/or "Revised" report. A "Final" report should be checked only if the contractor has completed the contract or subcontract reported in Block 7. A "Revised" report is a change to a report previously submitted for the same period.

BLOCK 6: Identify the department or agency administering the majority of subcontracting plans.

BLOCK 7: Indicate whether the reporting contractor is submitting this report as a prime contractor or subcontractor and the prime contract or subcontract number.

BLOCK 8: Enter the name and address of the Federal department or agency awarding the contract or the prime contractor awarding the subcontract.

BLOCK 9: Check the appropriate block to indicate whether indirect costs are included in the dollar amounts in blocks 10a through 12. To ensure comparability between the goal and actual columns, the contractor may include indirect costs in the actual column only if the subcontracting plan included indirect costs in the goal.

BLOCKS 10a through 12: Under "Current Goal," enter the dollar and percent goals in each category (SB, SDB, and, WOSB) from the subcontracting plan approved for this contract. (If the original goals agreed upon at contract award have been revised as a result of contract modifications, enter the original goals in Block 13. The amounts entered in Blocks 10a through 12 should reflect the revised goals.) Under "Actual Cumulative," enter actual subcontract achievements (dollar and percent) from the inception of the contract through the date of the report shown in Block 4. In cases where indirect costs are included, the amounts should include both direct awards and an appropriate prorated portion of indirect awards.

BLOCK 10a: Report all subcontracts awarded to SBs including subcontracts to SDBs and WOSBs. For DOD, NASA, and Coast Guard contracts, include subcontracting awards to HBCUs and MIs.

BLOCK 10b: Report all subcontracts awarded to large businesses (LBs).

BLOCK 10c: Report on this line the total of all subcontracts awarded under this contract (the sum of lines 10a and 10b).

BLOCKS 11 and 12: Each of these items is a subcategory of Block 10a. Note that in some cases the same dollars may be reported in both Block 11 and Block 12 (i.e., SDBs owned by women).

BLOCK 11: Report all subcontracts awarded to SDBs (including women-owned SDBs). For DOD, NASA, and Coast Guard contracts, include subcontract awards to HBCUs and MIs.

BLOCK 12: Report all subcontracts awarded to Women-Owned firms (including SDBs owned by women).

BLOCK 13: Enter a short narrative explanation if (a) SB, SDB, or WOSB accomplishments fall below that which would be expected using a straight-line projection of goals through the period of contract performance; or (b) if this is a final report, any one of the three goals was not met.

SPECIAL INSTRUCTIONS FOR COMMERCIAL PRODUCTS PLANS

DEFINITIONS

1. Commercial products means products sold in substantial quantities to the general public and/or industry at established catalog or market prices.

2. Subcontract means a contract, purchase order, amendment, or other legal obligation executed by the prime contractor/subcontractor calling for supplies or services required for the performance of the original contract or subcontract.

3. Direct Subcontract Awards are those that are identified with the performance of one or more specific Government contract(s).

4. Indirect costs are those which, because of incurrence for common or joint purposes, are not identified with specific Government contracts; these awards are related to Government contract performance but remain for allocation after direct awards have been determined and identified to specific Government contracts.

DISTRIBUTION OF THIS REPORT

For the Awarding Agency or Contractor:

The original copy of this report should be provided to the contracting officer at the agency or contractor identified in Block 8. For contracts with DOD, a copy should also be provided to the Defense Logistics Agency (DLA) at the cognizant Defense Contract Management Area Operations (DCMAO) office.

For the Small Business Administration (SBA):

A copy of this report must be provided to the cognizant Commercial Market Representative (CMR) at the time of a compliance review. It is NOT necessary to mail the SF 294 to SBA unless specifically requested by the CMR.

STANDARD FORM 294 (REV. 10-96) PAGE 2

J61307
05-06-97

Appendix 10.1 (Continued)

SUMMARY SUBCONTRACT REPORT
(See instructions on page 2)

1. CORPORATION, COMPANY OR SUBDIVISION COVERED

a. COMPANY NAME

b. STREET ADDRESS

c. CITY   d. STATE   e. ZIP CODE

2. CONTRACTOR IDENTIFICATION NUMBER

3. DATE SUBMITTED

4. REPORTING PERIOD:

☐ OCT 1- MAR 31   ☐ OCT 1- SEPT 30   YEAR

5. TYPE OF REPORT

☐ REGULAR   ☐ FINAL   ☐ REVISED

6. ADMINISTERING ACTIVITY *(Please check applicable box)*

☐ ARMY   ☐ DEFENSE LOGISTICS AGENCY   ☐ DOE

☐ NAVY   ☐ NASA   ☐ OTHER FEDERAL AGENCY *(Specify)*

☐ AIR FORCE   ☐ GSA

7. REPORT SUBMITTED AS *(Check one)*

☐ PRIME CONTRACTOR   ☐ BOTH

☐ SUBCONTRACTOR

8. TYPE OF PLAN

☐ INDIVIDUAL   ☐ COMMERCIAL PRODUCTS

IF PLAN IS A COMMERCIAL PRODUCT PLAN, SPECIFY THE PERCENTAGE OF THE DOLLARS ON THIS REPORT ATTRIBUTABLE TO THIS AGENCY. ▶

9. CONTRACTOR'S MAJOR PRODUCTS OR SERVICE LINES

a   c

b   d

CUMULATIVE FISCAL YEAR SUBCONTRACT AWARDS
(Report cumulative figures for reporting period in Block 4)

TYPE	WHOLE DOLLARS	PERCENT (To nearest tenth of a %)
10a. SMALL BUSINESS CONCERNS *(Include SDB, WOSB, HBCU/MI)* *(Dollar Amount and Percent of 10c.)*		
10b. LARGE BUSINESS CONCERNS *(Dollar Amount and Percent of 10c.)*		
10c. TOTAL *(Sum of 10a and 10b.)*		
11. SMALL DISADVANTAGED (SDB) CONCERNS *(Dollar Amount and Percent of 10c.)*		
12. WOMEN-OWNED SMALL BUSINESS (WOSB) CONCERNS *(Dollar Amount and Percent of 10c.)*		
13. HISTORICALLY BLACK COLLEGES AND UNIVERSITIES (HBCU) AND MINORITY INSTITUTIONS (MI) *(If applicable) (Dollar Amount and Percent of 10c.)*		

14. REMARKS

15. CONTRACTOR'S OFFICIAL WHO ADMINISTERS SUBCONTRACTING PROGRAM

a. NAME   b. TITLE   c. TELEPHONE NUMBER

AREA CODE   NUMBER

16. CHIEF EXECUTIVE OFFICER

a. NAME   c. SIGNATURE

b. TITLE   d. DATE

STANDARD FORM 295 (REV. 10-96)
Prescribed by GSA - FAR (48 CFR) 53.219(a)

J61308
05-07-97

Appendix 10.2   Standard Form 295, Summary Subcontract Report

GENERAL INSTRUCTIONS

1. This report is not required from small businesses.

2. This form collects subcontract award data from prime contractors/subcontractors that: (a) hold one or more contracts over $500,000 (over $1,000,000 for construction of a public facility); and (b) are required to report subcontracts awarded to Small Business (SB), Small Disadvantaged Business (SDB), and Women-Owned Small Business (WOSB) concerns under a subcontracting plan. For the Department of Defense (DOD), the National Aeronautics and Space Administration (NASA), and the Coast Guard, this form also collects subcontract award data for Historically Black Colleges and Universities (HBCUs) and Minority Institutions (Mis).

3. This report must be submitted semi-annually (for the six months ended March 31st and the twelve months ended September 30th) for contracts with the Department of Defense (DOD) and annually (for the twelve months ended September 30th) for contracts with civilian agencies, except for contracts covered by an approved Commercial Products Plan (see special instructions in right-hand column). Reports are due 30 days after the close of each reporting period.

4. This report may be submitted on a corporate, company, or subdivision (e.g., plant or division operating on a separate profit center) basis, unless otherwise directed by the agency awarding the contract.

5. If a prime contractor/subcontractor is performing work for more than one Federal agency, a separate report shall be submitted to each agency covering only that agency's contracts, provided at least one of that agency's contracts is over $500,000 (over $1,000,000 for construction of a public facility) and contains a subcontracting plan. (Note that DOD is considered to be a single agency; see next instruction.)

6. For DOD, a consolidated report should be submitted for all contracts awarded by military departments/agencies and/or subcontracts awarded by DOD prime contractors. However, DOD contractors involved in construction and related maintenance and repair must submit a separate report for each DOD component.

7. Only subcontracts involving performance within the U.S., its possessions, Puerto Rico, and the Trust Territory of the Pacific Islands should be included in this report.

8. Purchases from a corporation, company, or subdivision that is an affiliate of the prime/subcontractor are not included in this report.

9. Subcontract award data reported on this form by prime contractors/subcontractors shall be limited to awards made to their immediate subcontractors. Credit cannot be taken for awards made to lower tier subcontractors.

10. See special instructions in right-hand column for Commercial Products Plans.

SPECIFIC INSTRUCTIONS

BLOCK 2: For the Contractor Identification Number, enter the nine-digit Data Universal Numbering System (DUNS) number that identifies the specific contractor establishment. If there is no DUNS number avaible that identifies the exact name and address entered in Block 1, contact Dun and Bradstreet Information Services at 1-800-333-0505 to get one free of charge over the telephone. Be prepared to provide the following information; (1) Company name; (2) Company address; (3) Company telephone number; (4) Line of business; (5) Chief executive officer/key manager; (6) Date the company was started; (7) Number of people employed by the company; and; (8) Company affiliation.

BLOCK 4: Check only one. Note that March 31 represents the six months from October 1st and that September 30th represents the twelve months from October 1st. Enter the year of the reporting period, (i.e., Mar

BLOCK 5: Check whether this report is a "Regular," "Final," and/or "Revised" report. A "Final" report should be checked only if the contractor has completed all the contracts containing subcontracting plans awarded by the agency to which it is reporting. A "Revised" report is a change to a report previously submitted for the same period.

BLOCK 6: Identify the department or agency administering the majority of subcontracting plans.

BLOCK 7: This report encompasses all contracts with the Federal Government for the agency to which it is submitted, including subcontracts received from other large businesses that have contracts with the same agency. Indicate in this block whether the contractor is a prime contractor, subcontractor, or both (check only one).

BLOCK 8: Check only one. Check "Commercial Products Plan" only if this report is under an approved Commercial Products Plan. For a Commercial Products Plan, the contractor must specify the percentage of dollars in Blocks 10a through 13 attributable to the agency to which this report is being submitted.

BLOCK 9: Identify the major product or service lines of the reporting organization.

BLOCK 10a through 13: These entries should include all subcontract awards resulting from contracts or subcontracts, regardless of dollar amount, received from the agency to which this report is submitted. If reporting as a subcontractor, report all subcontracts awarded under prime contracts. Amounts should include both direct awards and an appropriate prorated portion of indirect awards. (The indirect portion is based on the percentage of work being performed for the organization to which the report is being submitted in relation to other work being performed by the prime contractor/subcontractor.) Do not include awards made in support in commercial business unless "Commercial Products" is checked in Block 8 (see Special Instructions for Commercial products Plans in right hand column).

Report only those dollars subcontracted this fiscal year for the period indicated in Block 4.

BLOCK 10a: Report all subcontracts awarded to SBs including subcontracts to SDBs and WOSBs. For DOD, NASA, and Coast Guard contracts, include subcontracting awards to HBCUs and Mis.

BLOCK 10b: Report all subcontracts awarded to large businesses (LBs).

BLOCK 10c: Report on this line the grand total of all subcontracts (the sum of lines 10a and 10b).

BLOCKS 11 and 13: Each of these items is a subcategory of Block 10a. Note that in some cases the same dollars may be reported on both Block 11 and Block 12 (i.e., SDBs owned by women); likewise subcontracts to HBCUs or Mis should be reported on both Block 11 and 13.

BLOCK 11: Report all subcontracts awarded to SDBs (including women-owned SDBs). For DOD, NASA, and Coast Guard contracts, include subcontract awards to HBCUs and Mis.

BLOCK 12: Report all subcontracts awarded to Women-Owned Small Business firms (including SDBs owned by women).

BLOCK 13: (For contracts with DOD, NASA, and Coast Guard): Enter the dollar value of all subcontracts with HBCUs/Mis.

SPECIAL INSTRUCTIONS FOR COMMERCIAL PRODUCTS PLANS

1. This report is due on October 30th each year for the previous fiscal year ended September 30th.

2. The annual report submitted by reporting organizations that have an approved company-wide annual subcontracting plan for commercial products shall include all subcontracting activity under commercial products plans in effect during the year and shall be submitted in addition to the required reports for other-than-commercial products, if any.

3. Enter in Blocks 10a through 13 the total of all subcontract awards under the contractor's Commercial Products Plan. Show in Block 8 the percentage of this total that is attributable to the agency to which this report is being submitted. This report must be submitted to each agency from which contracts for commercial products covered by an approved Commercial Products Plan were received.

DEFINITIONS

1. Commercial products means products sold in substantial quantities to the general public and/or industry at established catalog or market prices.

2. Subcontract means a contract, purchase order, amendment, or other legal obligation executed by the prime contractor/subcontractor calling for supplies or services required for the performance of the original contract or subcontract.

3. Direct Subcontract Awards are those that are identified with the performance of one or more specific Government contract(s).

4. Indirect Subcontract Awards are those which, because of incurrence for common or joint purposes, are not identified with specific Government contracts; these awards are related to Government contract performance but remain for allocation after direct awards have been determined and identified to specific Government contracts.

SUBMITTAL ADDRESSES FOR ORIGINAL REPORT

For DOD Contractors, send reports to the cognizant contract administration office as stated in the contract.

For Civilian Agency Contractors, send reports to awarding agency:

1. NASA: Forward reports to NASA, Office of Procurement (HC), Washington, DC 20546

2. OTHER FEDERAL DEPARTMENTS OR AGENCIES: Forward report to the OSDBU Director unless otherwise provided for in instructions by the Department or Agency.

FOR ALL CONTRACTORS:

SMALL BUSINESS ADMINISTRATION (SBA): Send "info copy" to the cognizant Commercial Market Representative (CMR) at the address provided by SBA. Call SBA Headquarters in Washington, DC at (202) 205-6475 for correct address if unknown.

STANDARD FORM 295 (REV. 10-96) **PAGE 2**

J61309
05-05-97

Appendix 10.2 (Continued)

EQUAL EMPLOYMENT OPPORTUNITY

- Equal Employment
  Opportunity Com-
  mission

EMPLOYER INFORMATION REPORT EEO—1

O.M.B. No. 3046-0007
EXPIRES 10/31/99
100-214

1997

- Office of Federal
  Contract Compli-
  ance Programs (Labor)

1   OF 1

```
S    A    M    P    L    E
S    A    M    P    L    E
S    A    M    P    L    E
S    A    M    P    L    E
S    A    M    P    L    E
S    A    M    P    L    E
S    A    M    P    L    E
S    A    M    P    L    E
S    A    M    P    L    E
```

RETURN COMPLETED REPORT TO:
THE JOINT REPORTING COMMITTEE
P.O. BOX 779
NORFOLK, VA 23501

PHONE: (757) 461-1213

Section A—TYPE OF REPORT
Refer to instructions for number and types of reports to be filed.

1. Indicate by marking in the appropriate box the type of reporting unit for which this copy of the form is submitted (MARK ONLY ONE BOX).

(1) ☐ Single-establishment Employer Report

Multi-establishment Employer:
(2) ☐ Consolidated Report (Required)
(3) ☐ Headquarters Unit Report (Required)
(4) ☐ Individual Establishment Report (submit one for each establishment with 50 or more employees)
(5) ☐ Special Report

2. Total number of reports being filed by this Company (Answer on Consolidated Report only) _____

Section B—COMPANY IDENTIFICATION (To be answered by all employers)

OFFICE
USE
ONLY

1. Parent Company

   a. Name of parent company (owns or controls establishment in item 2) omit if same as label

   a.

Address (Number and street)

b.

City or town	State	ZIP code

c.

2. Establishment for which this report is filed. (Omit if same as label)

   a. Name of establishment

   d.

Address (Number and street)	City or Town	County	State	ZIP code

e.

   b. Employer Identification No. (IRS 9-DIGIT TAX NUMBER)

f.

   c. Was an EEO–1 report filed for this establishment last year? ☐ Yes ☐ No

Section C—EMPLOYERS WHO ARE REQUIRED TO FILE (To be answered by all employers)

☐ Yes ☐ No 1. Does the entire company have at least 100 employees in the payroll period for which you are reporting?

☐ Yes ☐ No 2. Is your company affiliated through common ownership and/or centralized management with other entities in an enterprise with a total employment of 100 or more?

☐ Yes ☐ No 3. Does the company or any of its establishments (a) have 50 or more employees AND (b) is not exempt as provided by 41 CFR 60–1.5, AND either (1) is a prime government contractor or first-tier subcontractor, and has a contract, subcontract, or purchase order amounting to $50,000 or more, or (2) serves as a depository of Government funds in any amount or is a financial institution which is an issuing and paying agent for U.S. Savings Bonds and Savings Notes?

If the response to question C–3 is yes, please enter your Dun and Bradstreet identification number (if you have one): ☐☐☐☐☐☐☐☐☐

NOTE: If the answer is yes to questions 1, 2, or 3, complete the entire form, otherwise skip to Section G.

Appendix 10.3   Standard Form 100, Equal Employment Opportunity (Employer Information Report EEO–1)

☆ U.S. GOVERNMENT PRINTING OFFICE: 1997 425-479

Section D—EMPLOYMENT DATA

Employment at this establishment—Report all permanent full-time and part-time employees including apprentices and on-the-job trainees unless specifically excluded as set forth in the instructions. Enter the appropriate figures on all lines and in all columns. Blank spaces will be considered as zeros.

JOB CATEGORIES		OVERALL TOTALS (SUM OF COL. B THRU K)	MALE					FEMALE				
			WHITE (NOT OF HISPANIC ORIGIN)	BLACK (NOT OF HISPANIC ORIGIN)	HISPANIC	ASIAN OR PACIFIC ISLANDER	AMERICAN INDIAN OR ALASKAN NATIVE	WHITE (NOT OF HISPANIC ORIGIN)	BLACK (NOT OF HISPANIC ORIGIN)	HISPANIC	ASIAN OR PACIFIC ISLANDER	AMERICAN INDIAN OR ALASKAN NATIVE
		A	B	C	D	E	F	G	H	I	J	K
Officials and Managers	1	S	A	M	P	L	E					
Professionals	2	S	A	M	P	L	E					
Technicians	3	S	A	M	P	L	E					
Sales Workers	4	S	A	M	P	L	E					
Office and Clerical	5	S	A	M	P	L	E					
Craft Workers (Skilled)	6	S	A	M	P	L	E					
Operatives (Semi-Skilled)	7	S	A	M	P	L	E					
Laborers (Unskilled)	8	S	A	M	P	L	E					
Service Workers	9	S	A	M	P	L	E					
TOTAL	10	S	A	M	P	L	E					
Total employment reported in previous EEO-1 report	11	S	A	M	P	L	E					

NOTE: Omit questions 1 and 2 on the Consolidated Report.

1. Date(s) of payroll period used:

2. Does this establishment employ apprentices?
   1 ☐ Yes   2 ☐ No

Section E—ESTABLISHMENT INFORMATION (Omit on the Consolidated Report)

1. What is the major activity of this establishment? (Be specific, i.e., manufacturing steel castings, retail grocer, wholesale plumbing supplies, title insurance, etc. Include the specific type of product or type of service provided, as well as the principal business or industrial activity.)

OFFICE USE ONLY

g.

Section F—REMARKS

Use this item to give any identification data appearing on last report which differs from that given above, explain major changes in composition of reporting units and other pertinent information.

Section G—CERTIFICATION (See Instructions G)

Check one
1 ☐ All reports are accurate and were prepared in accordance with the instructions (check on consolidated only)
2 ☐ This report is accurate and was prepared in accordance with the instructions.

Name of Certifying Official	Title	Signature	Date
Name of person to contact regarding this report (Type or print)	Address (Number and Street)		
Title	City and State	ZIP Code	Telephone Number (Including Area Code)	Extension

All reports and information obtained from individual reports will be kept confidential as required by Section 709(e) of Title VII. WILLFULLY FALSE STATEMENTS ON THIS REPORT ARE PUNISHABLE BY LAW, U.S. CODE, TITLE 18, SECTION 1001.

Appendix 10.3   (Continued)

Chapter Eleven

Equitable Adjustments

11-1. BACKGROUND

Throughout the negotiation and administration of a government contract lurks the knowledge that the government has the right to change its mind, to revise what it wants or how it wants the job accomplished, or to just "stop and think about it." The government's right to change the terms and conditions of an existing contract originates in its need to be able to respond to new and different requirements for the products or services it buys. Such changes can relate to product design, government-furnished material or property, inspection, differing site conditions, cost accounting changes required or agreed to by the government, and so on. The government accepts the risk for potential future price increases or decreases resulting from such changes. This assumption of risk by the government manifests itself in various contract clauses, all of which provide for an equitable adjustment in the contract price for various government actions or inactions. Accordingly, changes required in a contract, and the need for a resulting adjustment in the contract price, are a normal part of contracting with the federal government. For these reasons, a contractor's need to submit a request for an equitable adjustment should not be looked upon as an undesirable or adversarial event.

11-2. CONTRACT CHANGES

The contract clauses providing for changes may vary from agency to agency and by type of contract, but all versions share some common concepts and contain words similar to those found in the Changes—Fixed Price clause (Federal Acquisition Regulation [FAR] 52.243-1):

> The Contracting Officer may at any time, by written order, and without notice to the sureties, if any, make changes within the general scope of this contract. ... If any such change causes an increase or decrease in the cost of, or the time required for, performance of any part of the work under this contract, whether or not changed by the order, the Contracting Officer shall make

an equitable adjustment in the contract price, the delivery schedule, or both, and shall modify the contract.

A change directed by the government under the provisions of these clauses is referred to as a formal or directed change. A change that occurs when government action or inaction, other than a formally directed change, causes a contractor to perform in a manner different from that required by the contract is referred to as a "constructive" change.

The government must fairly compensate the contractor for any increased costs attributable to a directed or constructive change in the contract. Because changes can occur for many and varied reasons, the techniques used to determine the necessary price adjustment are many and varied as well. This chapter discusses the circumstances under which either formal or constructive changes may take place and addresses some of the key accounting concepts related to pricing the resultant equitable adjustment. While the distinction between accounting and legal issues may not always be clear, it is not our intent to address the questions and concepts more appropriately covered in a legal forum. Accordingly, this chapter generally discusses the amount of the equitable adjustment when it has been determined that an adjustment is appropriate, rather than proof of entitlement or which party has the burden of proof and how that burden must be met.

11-3. DEFINITION OF EQUITABLE ADJUSTMENT

Certain clauses require that an equitable adjustment be made to the contract for any change made pursuant to the particular clause. The adjustment necessary to create equity may be highly dependent on the perspective of the parties to the action. A dictionary would probably define *equity* using terms such as fairness, impartiality, and justice. This type of definition has generally proved to be too broad for use in contract pricing actions. The Court of Claims recognized that the term had developed specific meaning in a federal government contracting environment. In *General Builders Supply Co., Inc. v. United States*,[1] the court stated the following:

> [T]he meaning of "equitable adjustment" 'has become so to speak, a "trade usage'" for those engaged in contracting with the Federal Government. The knowledgeable federal contractor would understand it, and plaintiff if it were not so knowledgeable, was charged with making itself aware of that usage. ... Since it was dealing with the government, as to which a whole body of special contract provisions has developed, plaintiff could hardly take the naive stance that it had the right to read its contract as an unsophisticated layman might, without bothering to inquire into the established meaning and coverage of phrases and provisions which appear to be unusual or special to federal procurement.

In a key case, *Bruce Construction Corp. et al. v. United States*,[2] the Court of Claims defined *equitable adjustment* as "simply corrective measures utilized to keep a contractor whole when the government modifies a contract." While this may sound simple enough, the long history of disputes and litigation would indicate that there is no clear-cut answer in many situations. In *Pacific Architects and Engineers, Inc. v. United States*,[3] the court addressed what is meant by "keeping a contractor whole."

> It is well established that the equitable adjustment may not properly be used as an occasion for reducing or increasing the contractor's profit or loss or for converting a loss to a profit or vice versa, for reasons unrelated to a change. A contractor who has understated his bid or encoun-

tered unanticipated expense or inefficiencies may not properly use a change order as an excuse to reform the contract or to shift its own risk or losses to the government.

In other words, the profit or loss that would be experienced on the portion of the contract not affected by the change should not be disturbed.

The calculation of the equitable adjustment was looked upon in much simpler terms in *Celesco Industries, Inc.*[4] where the Armed Services Board of Contract Appeals (ASBCA) stated that "the measure of the equitable price adjustment is the difference between the reasonable cost of performing without the change or deletion and the reasonable cost of performing with the change or deletion."

In summary, an equitable adjustment is designed to reimburse the contractor or the government, as the case may be, for the reasonable cost or savings resulting from the difference in cost of performance with and without the change, while not disturbing the profit or loss that will be experienced on the unchanged portion of the contract. As put succinctly in *Montag–Halvorson–Cascade–Austin*,[5] "the true objective of an equitable adjustment ... is to leave the parties in the same position costwise and profitwise as they would have occupied had there been no change, preserving to each as nearly as possible the advantages and disadvantages of their bargain. ..."

11-4. DEDUCTIVE CHANGES

Savings to the government may result from changes that reduce contractual requirements; if a deletion occurs before work associated with the deleted item is performed, costs will not be incurred. In this case, it will be necessary to estimate the amount of the equitable adjustment required to reflect the reduced contract requirements.

Because the equitable adjustment may not be used to increase profit or decrease a loss for reasons not related to the change, the boards of contract appeals and the courts have taken the position that the proper measure of a deductive change is the reasonable cost that would have been incurred for the deleted item, plus a profit on that cost. Thus, if the estimated cost of performance is less than the amount included in the contract for the item deleted, the contractor will retain the benefit of the difference.[6] Conversely, if the estimated cost of performance is greater than the contract price for the item, the contractor will suffer that loss. The estimated cost of performance for these calculations should be based on the information available when the change was directed or negotiated.

The government bears the burden of proof for a price reduction. In *Nager Electric Company, Inc.*,[7] the Court of Claims stated the following:

Another principle which is intricately involved in this case is that the government has the burden of proving how much of a downward equitable adjustment in price should be made on account of the deletion of the original [items]. Just as the contractor has that task when an upward adjustment is sought under the changes clause so the [government] has the laboring oar, and bears the risk of failure of proof, when a decrease is at issue.

If the costs have not been incurred, the burden of proof ascribed to the government may be difficult. However, if a portion of the costs was incurred before a change deleted the requirement for an item, the actual costs incurred, together with the estimate to complete, will be used to determine the amount of the adjustment.

11-5. ADDITIVE CHANGES

Just as changes can delete contract items, so can they add items or services or simply increase the cost of performance. Indeed, changes more often increase overall contractual obligations than reduce them. The accounting issues related to additive changes are generally the same as those for deductive changes, and the key task is determining the "reasonable costs" to perform the additional work. One of the critical issues concerning the reasonableness of costs is the timing of the pricing action. Such timing will determine the approach and information to be used in calculating the specific amounts involved. The timing of the action will also influence the determination of which party will bear the cost risk.

11-6. ESTIMATED QUANTITIES IN REQUIREMENTS CONTRACTS

Under a requirements contract, all actual requirements for supplies or services during a specified period are ordered under the contract, with deliveries or performance scheduled by placing orders with the contractor. The standard requirements clause (FAR 52.216-21) provides that quantities of supplies or services specified in the Schedule are estimates only. The clause specifically notes that "[e]xcept as this contract may otherwise provide, if the Government's requirements do not result in orders in the quantities described as 'estimated' or 'maximum' in the schedule, that fact shall not constitute the basis for an equitable adjustment." However, FAR 16.503 requires the solicitation and resultant contracts to provide a realistic estimated total quantity.

The ASBCA ruled that Contract Management, Inc.[8] was entitled to an equitable adjustment under the "changes" clause, because the government's estimates were not based on current information and did not reflect anticipated funding difficulties. In its decision, the Board opened: "We conclude that as of time of award the [government's] estimates were not prepared with due care and that CMI did not assume the risk that custodial services would be reduced because of budget constraints."

The U.S. Army Corps of Engineers Board of Contract Appeals (ENGBCA) reached a similar conclusion in *Pruitt Energy Sources, Inc.*[9] Because of faulty estimating techniques which significantly overstated the estimated quantity provided in the solicitation, the Corps' actual requirements were less than 20% of the estimate. In ruling that the contractor was entitled to an equitable adjustment, the Board concluded: "In assuming the risks entailed in this requirements contract, Pruitt was entitled to rely on the Corps' estimate as representing reasonably informed conclusions that were not misleading. The Corps could not carelessly or negligently use a faulty estimating method that resulted in an unreasonably inadequate estimate."

11-7. PROSPECTIVE VERSUS RETROACTIVE PRICING

Whether an equitable adjustment should be negotiated on a prospective or retroactive basis depends on the particular circumstances of each change. Because of the complexities normally encountered in actually implementing contract changes and the resulting need for contract repricing actions, many derivations of prospective changes may be used. Indeed, it is entirely likely that a combination of methods will prove to be the most desirable approach for a specific change.

In any case, the actual costs incurred, estimated costs to be incurred, or costs that would have been incurred are the starting point for determining the amount of an equitable adjustment resulting from a contract change. In fact, the pricing of equitable adjustments may not be significantly different from the activities associated with pricing an initial contract. A change may be related to the addition of one contract obligation for another or a combination of all of these. The pricing action may take place before the change has occurred, while the change is occurring, or after the change has occurred. Specific accounting records may measure the precise impact, or it may be necessary to resort to subjective approximations or estimates.

Prospective Pricing

For budgetary and funding purposes, the government generally prefers prospective pricing over retroactive pricing, particularly when the contractor can estimate the cost of performance with a high degree of confidence. It is not at all unusual for the government to request that the contractor submit an estimate or proposal for a change that is under consideration. It should be readily apparent in this situation that, to the extent the actual cost may be somewhat different than the estimated cost, the risk is placed primarily on the contractor. The importance of this assignment of risk depends on the type of contract adjustment to be negotiated (firm-fixed-price or cost-type) and how much confidence the contractor has in its ability to forecast the cost to be incurred.

Although the government's policy is to negotiate the equitable adjustment associated with the contract changes before performance of the changed activity, it will do so only if this will not adversely affect the government's interests. Federal Acquisition Regulation 43.102 notes that if a significant cost increase could result from a modification, and if time does not permit price negotiation, a maximum price will be negotiated before the work is performed, unless doing so would be impractical.

Because the prospective pricing of contract changes is substantially similar to the pricing activity associated with the initial award of a contract, the same rules of conduct generally apply. As discussed in Chapter 5, the Truth in Negotiations Act applies to any change orders for which estimated costs exceed the statutory limits. Whether or not the submission of cost or pricing data is required, the determination of the reasonable cost to perform the changed work should be based on the best information available when the contractor prepares the pricing proposal. To the extent that additional information becomes available after that time, but before the negotiation of the equitable adjustment for the change, this additional information should also be presented.

Retroactive Pricing

While the government prefers to negotiate the equitable adjustment before the changed work is performed, doing so is often not practical or desirable. If the contractor cannot estimate the cost of anticipated performance with a sufficient degree of confidence, it may be in the contractor's best interest to wait until after the costs have been incurred to negotiate the equitable adjustment. As discussed earlier, this tends to shift the cost risk to the government.

However, the use of retroactive pricing does place some additional burdens on the contractor, especially concerning the degree to which the contractor must "prove" the incurred cost. Even if incurred costs are presumed to be reasonable, they must be shown to have been incurred specifically for performance of, or allocable to, the changed effort. If incurred costs are the preferred basis for the retroactive pricing of a contract change, records showing incurred costs are generally needed for the contractor to successfully negotiate the adjustment.

The importance of incurred cost information was demonstrated in *Cen-Vi-Ro*,[10] in which the Court of Claims stated that the plaintiff "should have the opportunity to justify its equitable adjustment by a showing of actual costs. If . . . plaintiff is unable to come forward with acceptable records of its actual costs for particular claims, further adjustment as to those items should be denied." The court noted that the contractor was a subsidiary of a sophisticated, multidivision organization with an elaborate recordkeeping system. Thus, the detailed recordkeeping requirements implied in the decision may be limited to a contractor in the same circumstances. While it is possible to overcome a lack of adequate accounting records to support the amount of an equitable adjustment being priced on a retroactive basis, the contractor's request for an equitable adjustment is more vulnerable to a government challenge on reasonableness to the extent that actual cost data are not available.

Producing records showing the actual cost of performance for the changed effort is not only desired by the courts but is also in the contractor's best interest. Therefore, a contractor may want to evaluate the adequacy of its accounting system in terms of the system's ability to segregate the costs of changed work.

The government's recognition of the importance of incurred cost data in negotiating contract changes on a retroactive basis is evidenced in FAR 43.203, which states, in part:

> Contractors' accounting systems are seldom designed to segregate the costs of performing changed work. Therefore, before prospective contractors submit offers, the contracting officer should advise them of the possible need to revise their accounting procedures to comply with the cost segregation requirements of the Change Order Accounting clause . . . (FAR 52.243-6)

Under this clause, contractors may be directed to segregate change-order costs in their accounting records. Federal Acquisition Regulations 43.203 indicates that the following costs are normally segregable and accountable under the terms of the clause:

- Nonrecurring costs (e.g., engineering costs and costs of obsolete work or reperformed work)
- Costs of added distinct work caused by the change order (e.g., new subcontract work, new prototypes, or new retrofit or backfit kits)
- Costs of recurring work (e.g., labor and material costs)

11-8. COSTS OF CONTRACT CHANGES

Reasonable Costs

"Reasonable" costs are defined in FAR 31.201-3 as costs that do not exceed those that would be incurred by a prudent person in the conduct of competitive business. In discussing the reasonable cost of performance as the basis for equitable adjustments, the Court of Claims in *Nager Electric Company, Inc. and Keystone Engineering Corp. v. United States*[11] stated that "the objective focus is on the cost that would have been incurred by a prudent businessman placed in a similar overall competitive situation. . . . However, unless it also takes into account the subjective situation of the contractor a test of 'reasonable cost' is incomplete."

The result is that while the cost of having another contractor or the government perform a task that had been added or deleted may be used to evaluate the reasonableness of the adjustment, this test alone is not sufficient. If the anticipated or actual cost of performance by the contractor is not unreasonable, these outside estimates may not be appropriate measures of the equitable adjustment. In *Bruce Construction Corp, et al. v. United States*,[12] the Court of Claims, in quoting from a *Law Review* article, stated: "But the standard of reasonable cost must be viewed in the light of a particular contractor's cost . . . and not the universal objective determination of what the cost would have been to other contractors at large." The court also documented the presumption that incurred (historical) costs are considered to be reasonable by stating the following:

> To say that "reasonable cost" rather than "historical cost" should be the measure does not depart from the test applied in the past for the two terms are often synonymous. And where there is an alleged disparity between "historical" and "reasonable" costs, the historical costs are presumed reasonable.

> Since the presumption is that a contractor's claimed cost is reasonable, the Government must carry the very heavy burden of showing that the claimed cost was of such a nature that it should not have been expended, or that the contractor's costs were more than were justified in the particular circumstance.[13]

While *Bruce Construction* established the presumption of reasonableness, in 1987 the burden of proving reasonableness was shifted to the contractor in certain circumstances. Federal Acquisition Regulations 31.201-3 now attaches no presumption of reasonableness to the incurrence of costs by a contractor. If an initial review of the facts results in a challenge of a specific cost by the contracting officer (CO) or the CO's representative, the burden of proof falls on the contractor to establish that such cost is reasonable.

This FAR revision represented a dramatic change in the treatment of reasonable costs. Even if the presumption of reasonableness is sustained, the incurred costs must also meet the other tests of allowability provided for in the contract and in applicable procurement regulations

Direct Costs

In determining the amount of the equitable adjustment necessary as a result of a change, the cost calculation for direct costs is relatively easy. In general, direct costs are those that are incurred exclusively for performing a particular activity and are measurable with a reasonable degree of precision. As a result, once the changed activity is identified, determining the amount of direct cost may be a simple matter of applying the normal estimating and accounting processes to that activity. Therefore, adjustments related to the pricing of changes for direct labor, direct material purchases, subcontracts, and so on may be a straightforward exercise. However, difficulties in this area often relate to distinguishing between the costs incurred on changed work and the costs incurred on unchanged work.

Overhead

Determining the proper amount of overhead to be applied to the changed effort may not be so clear-cut. Some government agencies include, as a contract provision, a specific overhead percentage to be applied for changes, or provide for certain other costs and profit at a prescribed amount or rate. When a contract has such a provision, the equitable adjustment will normally be made using the stated percentage applied to the appropriate base (the normal base applied through the accounting system application or the base specified in the contract).

If the rate is not specified in the contract, a subjective evaluation of the circumstances is usually necessary. This may present some difficulties. In *Kemmons–Wilson, Inc.,*[14] the ASBCA stated that "it is always more desirable to reimburse a contracting party for its actual expended or incurred indirect costs, exactly in the same manner as direct costs if it is practicable or feasible."

The issues involved in determining the proper amount of contract overhead costs are substantially the same as those for other contract change costs. That is, the costs must be reasonable in amount, allowable under the contract cost principles, not prohibited by the contract, and properly allocable. It is this latter point that usually presents the most difficulty.

When the amount of change requiring the equitable adjustment is not so significant as to have a measurable impact on the allocation base, problems are not normally encountered. In this case, the normal overhead rate applied to all the contracts (either incurred or projected) would be applied to the component of the change that represents the normal allocation base for those indirect expenses. However, when the change is of such a magnitude that it affects the overhead rates for all jobs, the proper portion of the overhead expenses that should be applied to the equitable adjustment must be determined. Normally, an attempt is made to isolate the components of the indirect expenses that are affected by the change. This may be accomplished by account analysis of the indirect expenses pool or by a determination of the proportionate impact on the total pool. Determining the proper adjustment must, of necessity, be handled on a case-by-case basis. The ultimate objective is to isolate the impact of the change on the indirect expense pool much in the same manner as the impact on direct costs.

Costs of Accounting Changes

Cost accounting practices changes under CAS-covered contracts are addressed in Chapter 8. The Federal Circuit concluded in *Aydin Corp.*[15] that a CO's requirement to compute progress payments separately for each delivery order rather than for the contract as a whole constituted a constructive change. In awarding Aydin an equitable adjustment for the increased costs it incurred to segregate costs by delivery order, the court noted the following:

> [N]othing in the (progress payment) clauses directs Aydin to segregate its costs by delivery order. To the contrary, the clause focuses on "cumulative total costs" from delivery order to delivery order under this contract. . . . The MUTES contract also does not incorporate regulations requiring Aydin to revamp its standard accounting practice of billing costs based on the overall contract.

Delay-Related Costs

The concept of delay can be extremely complicated; however, it is important to distinguish between government-caused delays and other excusable delays. "Excusable delays" are generally defined in contract clauses as delays resulting from "causes beyond the control and without the fault or negligence of the contractor." Examples of such causes are acts of God, fires, floods, unusually severe weather, and labor strikes. The general criterion above takes precedence over the specific examples cited. For example, while strikes are listed as a cause for excusable delay, a contractor that was found to be engaged in an unfair labor practice would not be entitled to an excusable delay. In that case, the strike would not be "beyond the control and without the fault or negligence of the contractor." In the case of unusually severe weather, the basic issue is whether the weather was unusually severe—not necessarily the severity of the weather. If the weather was extremely severe, even to the point of making any work impossible, the delay would not be excusable if such weather conditions were not unusual for the location. If the effect of the weather could not have been foreseen in making the original cost estimate, the resulting delay should be excusable. However, the contractor must be able to prove that the delay was a direct result of unusual weather.

Excusable delays entitle a contractor to an increased period of performance. However, only excusable delays that are caused by the government entitle the company to an equitable adjustment for increased cost due to the delay. Because the government acts in the capacity of a sovereign, any delays caused by government action or inaction are considered to be excusable delays.

Various methods are used to calculate the impact of government-caused delays. However, the principal elements usually included in these methods are: (1) unabsorbed overhead and/or burden fluctuation; (2) idle labor and equipment; (3) loss of efficiency; and (4) performance in a later, higher-cost period.

Unabsorbed Overhead and/or Burden Fluctuation

When a government-caused delay requires that the contractor stop performance, certain expenses will continue to be incurred. Among these are fixed indirect (overhead) expenses. Such expenses should be considered to also include those variable expenses that cannot, as a practical matter, be prevented through good management procedures. Because the normal method of absorbing indirect expenses is to allocate them over direct activity, there is no way to recover these costs if direct activity ceases. Therefore, if performance of a contract is delayed, the indirect expenses that would have been absorbed by that contract will be absorbed by other contracts unless an adjustment is made. This is particularly true when the delay can be specifically identified with a reduction in the anticipated indirect expense allocation base. In recent years, the boards and courts have required contractors to demonstrate that they were actually damaged as a result of the government-caused delay.

Case law has established several formulas for computing unabsorbed overhead. The most widely used formula, particularly in construction contracts, is referred to as the Eichleay method. In *Eichleay Corp.*,[16] a daily overhead rate was calculated on the basis that there had been no delay. This daily rate was then applied to each day of delay. It is expressed in the following formula:

$$\frac{\text{Total billings for}}{\text{actual contract period}} \times \frac{\text{Total overhead incurred}}{\text{during contact period}} = \frac{\text{Overhead allocable}}{\text{to contract}}$$

$$\frac{\text{Contract billing}}{\text{Actual days of performance}} = \frac{\text{Allocable overhead}}{\text{contract per day}} = \frac{\text{Overhead allocable to}}{\text{contract per day}}$$

$$\text{Daily overhead} \times \text{Number of days of delay} = \text{Unabsorbed overhead}$$

In *R.W. Contracting, Inc.,*[17] the ASBCA provides an erudite discussion of when the Eichleay formula is appropriate for calculating unabsorbed overhead:

> The Eichleay formula furnishes a necessary surrogate for the normal accounting practice of applying an overhead rate to the appropriate direct cost base in situations where the contractor is delayed and direct costs that normally would have been incurred in the performance of the contract decreased or were eliminated during the period of delay. It is a practical and necessary expedient to compensate the contractor in situations where the direct cost base is eroded thus making use of the normal indirect cost allocation percentage rate inappropriate. Derivation of a daily overhead rate is merely a necessary substitute designed for such situations where achieving a more precise measurement is impracticable and/or use of the percentage rate on direct costs would be inequitable. The Eichleay formula is a time-honored means of approximating a "fair allocation" of unabsorbed indirect costs in situations where direct costs have been reduced during periods of compensable suspensions of work . . . .

Case law has established that three elements are necessary to recover Eichleay damages: the occurrence of a government-caused delay; the necessity to stand by during the delay; and the inability to take on other work during the delay.

The ASBCA concluded that a government-caused delay and disruption in the performance of a repair and overhaul contract did not entitle Oxwell, Inc.[18] to unabsorbed overhead because the contractor, in spite of the delay, maintained its direct labor base and relatively stable overhead rates. The Board noted the following:

> In short, appellant did not stand by . . . . Moreover, no other work was turned away.

> The fact that appellant was disrupted and delayed does not *ipso facto* mean that it is entitled to damages computed according to the Eichleay formula. Rather, appellant must present prima facie evidence establishing with reasonable certainty that it suffered some damages as a result of the disruption and delay. No such showing has been made.

The ASBCA also failed to sustain Interstate General Government Contractors, Inc.'s (IGGC) claim for unabsorbed overhead.[19] Although the CO delayed issuing the Notice to Proceed after contract award because of a pending bid protest, the board noted that IGGC was able to reassign its workers to other jobs during the delay period. In its decision, the Board reiterated:

> We have continually held that as a prerequisite to recovery under Eichleay "there must be a 'prima facie showing that [the contractor] had to stand by and that the delay somehow affected the contractor's operations so that it was not practical to undertake the performance of other work.'" . . . To undertake the performance of other work not only applies to new contract work but also work presently on hand which is used to keep a contractor's workforce busy. . . . Clearly, IGGC's work force was gainfully working at other jobs and not standing by awaiting the NTP.

Similarly, the Federal Circuit[20] affirmed that the Eichleay formula is not permitted when work has been extended because of additional work rather than a suspension, delay, or disruption of contract performance. The court concluded the following:

> Since delays are sudden, sporadic, and of uncertain duration, it is impractical for a contractor to take on other work. In contrast, the contractor in this case negotiated a change order which extended contract performance for a brief known period of time. The contractor experienced no suspension of work, no idle time and no uncertain periods of delay. Thus, computation of extended home office overhead using an estimated daily rate is an extraordinary remedy which is specifically limited to contracts affected by government-caused suspensions, disruptions, and delays of work.

In *Marvin C. Altmayer v. Johnson,*[21] the Federal Circuit concluded that the performance of minor tasks throughout the period of delay did not preclude the uses of the Eichleay formula to compute unabsorbed overhead. The court found as follows:

> The standby test does not require the contractor's work force to be idle. There is no requirement that a contract be suspended before a contractor is entitled to recover under Eichleay. Indeed in Eichleay itself, "performance of the contracts was at no time suspended. . . .
>
> Notwithstanding [Altmayer's subcontractor] Haas' continuous work on minor contract items, the fact remains that the overall project income was spread over an additional three month period. . . .
>
> That Haas may have bid on other contracts "at the very end" of the subject contract does not establish that it was able to reduce its overhead or take on other work during the delay. . . .

In *Mech-Con Corporation v. West*,[22] the Federal Circuit shifted the burden of proof on the third element—inability to take on work while standing by—required for recovery of Eichleay damages. The court concluded that after a contractor has established a prima facie case of entitlement by showing that the government required the contractor to stand by during a delay of uncertain duration, ". . . the burden shifts to the government to present rebuttal evidence or argument showing that the contractor did not suffer any loss because it was able to either reduce the overhead or take on other work during the delay."

In *Satellite Electric Co. v. Dalton*,[23] the Federal Circuit affirmed the Government had met its rebuttal requirement that the contractor was able to take on other work during the delay by showing that Satellite submitted bids on 49 jobs during the period. The court concluded: "If . . . the company was aggressively going after new work, it is reasonable to infer that it had the capacity to perform whatever work it could have obtained."

The question of what formula should be used to calculate unabsorbed overhead, at least with respect to construction contracts, was definitively answered in *Wickham Contracting Co. v. Fischer*,[24] wherein the Federal Circuit confirmed the following:

> Government contractors may use the Eichleay formula to calculate unabsorbed home office overhead when disruption, delay, or suspension caused by the government has made uncertain the length of the performance period of the contract. The uncertainty often precludes additional jobs. . . .
>
> The Eichleay formula . . . is the proper method, and the only proper method, for calculating unabsorbed home office overhead when a contractor otherwise satisfies the Eichleay requirements.

The ability to demonstrate that the company suffered damages as a result of the delay or disruption, however, remains key to a recovery of unabsorbed overhead.

The Eichleay formula has also been used successfully to calculate unabsorbed overhead in manufacturing contracts, although other methods have occasionally been accepted as well. One formula, established in *Allegheny Sportswear Co.*,[25] compares the overhead cost actually incurred on the delayed contract with the overhead cost that would have been incurred if there had been no delay. The "would have been incurred" scenario is constructed by shifting the delayed effort back to the period on which the work was originally scheduled. The formula is stated as:

$$\begin{array}{ccc} \text{Incurred overhead rate} & - & \text{Incurred overhead rate} & = & \text{Excess rate} \\ \text{during actual period} & & \text{for projected period} \end{array}$$

$$\text{Excess rate} \times \text{Contract base costs} = \text{Unabsorbed overhead}$$

The ASBCA, in its opinion on motion for reconsideration in *Entwistle Co.*,[26] calculated unabsorbed overhead using the burden fluctuation method which had been accepted in *Allied Materials & Equipment Co.*[27] Under this method, unabsorbed overhead is calculated for each cost pool according to the following formula:

$$\begin{array}{clcccc} 1. & \text{Actual overhead rate} & & \text{Overhead rate bid in} & & \text{Difference in} \\ & \text{incurred during contract} & - & \text{delayed contract} & = & \text{overhead rate} \\ & \text{performance} & & & & \\ 2. & \text{Actual total overhead base} & - & \text{Actual overhead base} & & \text{Residual} \\ & \text{cost incurred during} & & \text{cost incurred on} & = & \text{overhead base} \\ & \text{contract performance} & & \text{delayed contract} & & \text{cost} \\ 3. & \text{Difference in overhead rate} & \times & \text{Residual overhead} & = & \text{Unabsorbed} \\ & & & \text{base cost} & & \text{overhead} \end{array}$$

In *Essex Electro Engineers, Inc.*,[28] the contractor sought recovery of both unabsorbed overhead to compensate it for the contract delay, using the Eichleay formula, and burden fluctuation expense to compensate it for having to perform in a higher cost period than originally anticipated. The auditor considered the two burden claims to be duplicative, but ASBCA disagreed. In its decision, the Board stated the following:

> We are not persuaded that a claim for unabsorbed burden expense is duplicated by a claim for burden fluctuation. ... A claim for unabsorbed burden expense is really for a decrease in allocability to the other in-house work performed during the scheduled period of the original contract performance, which other work bore too great a portion of the plant's indirect costs because of the delay associated with the incurrence of direct labor and materials....
>
> Burden fluctuation is a claim based on the necessity to perform the original contract work in a later time period in which increased costs were incurred, a reasonable result of the government-caused delay.

The recovery of unabsorbed overhead in the context of delays involving manufacturing contracts became decidedly more complicated by the ASBCA's decision in *Do-Well Machine Shop, Inc.*[29] Even though the appeal before the ASBCA was for entitlement only, and both the contractor and the government acknowledged Eichleay as "the established formula for computing unabsorbed overhead," the opinion inferred that use of the Eichleay formula was inappropriate. In its decision, the ASBCA concluded the following:

> [T]he Eichleay formula was fashioned to deal with extended and unabsorbed home office overhead on construction contracts. Whereas the practice before this Board has been to apply the formula in construction cases where the Government delay precluded a contractor from taking other jobs to absorb the overhead, we have used different formulas in the case of manufacturing contracts. See for example, The Entwistle Company, ASBCA No. 14918, 75-2 BCA ¶11,420, aff'd and modified on recons., 76-2 BCA ¶12,108; Therm-Air Manufacturing Company, Inc., ASBCA No. 16453, 73-1 BCA ¶9983; Allegheny Sportswear Co., ASBCA No. 4163, 58-1 BCA ¶1684. Accordingly, appellant's quantum claims for unabsorbed overhead on these contracts should be recomputed in accordance with the guidance provided in these manufacturing contract cases.

This ASBCA decision is difficult to understand for two reasons:

- Unabsorbed overhead was calculated in *Therm-Air Manufacturing Co.*[30] on the basis of a modified Eichleay formula.
- The three decisions—*Entwistle Co.*,[31] *Therm-Air Manufacturing*,[32] and *Allegheny Sportswear Co.*[33]—all predate *Essex Electro Engineers*[34] in which unabsorbed overhead computed on the basis of Eichleay was accepted.

A year after *Do-Well*, the ASBCA accepted the Eichleay formula for calculating unabsorbed overhead with *So-Pak-Co.*,[35] but noted the following:

> Application of an "Eichleay formula recovery of unabsorbed overhead and G&A costs to a manufacturing contract like [So-Pak-Co.] contract 543 is rare but was employed in Therm-Air Manufacturing Co., Inc., ASBCA No. 16453, 73-1 BCA 9983. . . . Our findings support the elements of proof for application of the Eichleay formula explicated in Capital Electric Co. v. United States. . . . [A] compensable Government delay or suspension of work occurred . . . and the contractor could not have taken on any additional job during that delay or suspension period."

Guidance previously promulgated by the Defense Contract Audit Agency (DCAA) in Audit Guidance—Delay and Disruption Claims[36] generally concluded that a manufacturer was rarely harmed as a result of contract delay. The guidance expressed the following view:

> [I]f the work performed under a delayed contract has been performed, regardless of when, there cannot be any unabsorbed overhead unless 1) the total overhead costs has been increased or 2) other work had to be turned away, assuming there was work to be turned away.

This guidance was not only illogical but went well beyond the entitlement criteria established by the boards and courts. The DCAA guidance now incorporated in the DCAA *Contract Audit Manual* Section 12-800)[37] is decidedly more objective in its evaluation of unabsorbed overhead and, in particular, its acceptance of unabsorbed overhead calculated under the Eichleay method. Current guidance acknowledges that Eichleay has been accepted for use in both contractor and supply contracts and, with appropriate modifications, can be used in more complicated delay situations such as partial delays or partial replacement of delayed work.

Idle Labor and Equipment

When a contractor is faced with a government-caused contract delay, some direct costs can be incurred for nonproductive activities resulting from the delay. This can happen despite the contractor's best efforts to productively divert resources. It is especially likely in construction contracting because a remote work site or the very nature of the construction itself may not permit the transfer of resources to other work. It can also occur on supply or service contracts during delays of short duration. In such cases, when a contractor is not able to productively divert direct resources, the resulting costs may be recoverable in a request for equitable adjustment. The direct costs most frequently encountered are for idle labor and equipment.

Whenever disruptions in work flow occur, there is normally a question about the use of those employees assigned to the disrupted work. The effective use of employees in such situations is a management responsibility and is no different in the government contracting environment.

If the contractor cannot avoid those direct costs through good management, it may be appropriate to include them in an equitable adjustment request. This decision requires a good deal of management judgment and may require a contractor to try to forecast the length of the delay, since it may be the critical factor affecting the decision. For example, it may not be feasible to release an employee only to attempt to hire the employee back in a short time.

Delays may also result in idle equipment. If such equipment is used exclusively on one contract and cannot be used elsewhere, depreciation may continue to be allocated directly to a delayed contract if this was the prior practice. If equipment costs are included in overhead, idle equipment costs would be recovered through unabsorbed overhead. For construction contractors, the method of recovering idle equipment costs in equitable adjustments may be quite different. For equipment that is rented from third parties, the specific rental charges, on a daily or other periodic basis, will continue to be charged at the rental rates. For company-owned equipment, the method of calculating the cost of idle equipment will depend on the contractor's method of identifying equipment use cost by job.

If the company maintains records that segregate ownership and operating costs by individual pieces of equipment, those records will form the basis for calculating idle equipment costs. Generally, equipment ownership costs (depreciation, insurance, taxes, etc.) and certain maintenance costs are includable.

If the company does not maintain cost records by an individual piece of equipment, it may be appropriate to resort to industry-wide experience. Construction industry trade associations and equipment groups publish tables with the equipment usage rates that some contractors use. Some tables include rates for equipment in a standby status (assigned to a job but not being used). Federal Acquisition Regulation 31.105(d)(2)(i)(b) provides for the evaluating equipment usage rates based on predetermined schedules of construction equipment use rates, such as the construction ownership and operating schedule published by the U.S. Army Corps of Engineers.

A contractor claiming idle labor or equipment must by prepared to show that it has taken appropriate action to reduce the cost of the delay (similar to mitigating damages after a breach of contract). This will substantially aid in the ultimate recovery of claimed costs. The requirement to reduce the cost of the delay was established by the ASBCA in *Hardeman–Monier–Hutcherson*,[38] in which it stated "a contractor has the duty to minimize its cost in the execution of a change order in the same manner as he must mitigate his damages after a breach. Normally he would be required to transfer or discharge idle men, and find uses for his equipment pending the time that work can commence."

Loss of Efficiency

Even when labor is not totally idled by a government-caused delay, increased costs may result from the inefficient use of labor or equipment. Such inefficiencies may be the result of confusion, interruptions in the orderly progress of work, or increased start-ups.

To the extent that any of these losses of efficiency cause increased costs, they should be included in the calculation of costs associated with the delay. While it is clear that contractors are entitled to such adjustments from government-caused delays, determining the amount of adjustment is extremely difficult.

Normally, the amount of adjustment is calculated based on subjective judgments rather than segregated accounting data. Accounting data alone will not normally provide the needed information. Two methods used in determining the amount of loss of efficiency are (1) application of a percentage factor and (2) "estimated cost." The first method involves application of a percentage factor to labor hours or costs incurred during the disrupted period to compute the additional costs (hours) incurred as a result of the disruption. The estimated cost method measures the difference between actual labor costs incurred and an estimate of what labor costs would have been without the disruption.

Regardless of the method used, estimates are required. The boards and courts have accepted approximations because of the difficulty in proving exact amounts. Nevertheless, the estimate must have some underlying basis related to the specific circumstances of the delay. For example, a contractor could develop objective evidence comparing the amount of work accomplished during the period of disruption with the amount of work accomplished during normal operations. Without such an underlying basis, the amount of the calculated loss of efficiency may be denied or at least reduced. In court or board proceedings, it is usually advisable to have an expert witness, rather than a contractor employee, testify on the amount of lost efficiency. Such experts are looked upon as more objective. Again, however, the testimony of such expert witnesses should be backed up with objective evidence.

Performance in a Later Period

One of the consequences of a significant delay is usually an extension of the contract performance period. In some cases, the period of delay may be recovered by using additional labor or accelerated performance. However, when a contractor is required to perform the contract in a period later than originally planned because of a government-caused delay, it is entitled to recover any resulting increased costs in an equitable adjustment.

Such increased costs may occur because of increased labor rates or higher material costs than would have been incurred had performance occurred as originally planned. In these circumstances, the contractor must be able to show that actual labor rates and material prices increased, not just total labor or material costs. Increases in total labor or material costs may be due to inefficiencies or other causes not necessarily related to performance in a later period.

The inability of a contractor to prove the exact amount of labor rate increases applicable to a specific contract may not be a basis for complete denial of a claim. Although expressing a preference for actual labor cost data, the ASBCA in *Keco Industries, Inc.*[39] allowed the contractor to use plant-wide labor rates in calculating the equitable adjustment.

11-9. ACCELERATION

An equitable adjustment may also be required if the government, for whatever reason, decides to accelerate performance under a contract. This may be the result of a unilateral government decision that it needs the items sooner than originally contemplated. However, in most cases, it will result from a "constructive acceleration" related to a need to make up lost time due to delays. Equitable adjustments for constructive accelerations are limited to situations in which the contractor would be entitled to schedule extensions because of excusable delays.

Determining the existence of a constructive acceleration is no easy task. Based on an analysis of prior court and board cases, the ASBCA in *Fermont Division, Dynamics Corporation of America*[40] established the following conditions as a prerequisite to a successful acceleration claim based on a government failure to grant a time extension for an excusable delay:

(1) existence of a given period of excusable delay; and

(2) contractor notice to the Government of the excusable delay, and request for extension of time together with supporting information sufficient to allow the Government to make a reasonable determination.

EXCEPTIONS:

(a) such notice, request and information are not necessary if the Government's order (see (3) below) directs compliance with a given schedule expressly without regard to the existence of any excusable delay.

(b) the supporting information is unnecessary if it is already reasonably available to the Government;

(3) failure or refusal to grant the requested extension within a reasonable time; and

(4) a Government order, either express or implied from the circumstances, to (a) take steps to overcome the excusable delay, or (b) complete the work at the earliest possible date, or (c) complete the work by a given date earlier than that to which the contractor is entitled by reason of the excusable delay. Circumstances from which such an order may be implied include expressions of urgency by the government, especially if coupled with (i) a threat of default or liquidated damages for not meeting a given accelerated schedule, or (ii) actual assessment of liquidated damages for not meeting a given accelerated schedule;

(5) reasonable efforts by the contractor to accelerate the work, resulting in added costs, even if the efforts are not actually successful.

The notice to the CO of excusable delay and request for schedule extension should, like other communications to the government, be in writing. Contractors meeting the above conditions and strictly following the prescribed procedures should be able to prove an acceleration and negotiate an equitable adjustment.

Nevertheless, some of the conditions are generalizations that require interpretation. For example, one of the conditions is a "failure or refusal to grant the requested extension within a reasonable time." How long is a reasonable time? Undue delays in granting a request for schedule extension place a contractor in a precarious position. Does the contractor incur acceleration costs to make up lost time that may not be recoverable, or does it run the risk that not meeting delivery schedules will result in assessment of liquidated damages or a termination for default? In *Ashton Co.*,[41] the Department of Interior Board of Contract Appeals commented on government witness testimony that no action was taken, until the contract was completed, on requests for time extensions due to weather conditions. The Board stated that "the duty is upon the Government to obtain the climatological data without unnecessary delay. . . . To wait until the contract work is completed . . . could well force a contractor into acceleration." This example demonstrates a need for effective communications between the contracting parties.

Another problem in acceleration claims occurs when the contracting officer issues an acceleration order after the contractor experiences both excusable and contractor-caused delays. The question is whether the order is to make up the time of excusable or unexcusable delay. Unless the contract contains a special clause giving the CO the right to order the contractor to make up lost time for contractor-caused delays, the order could be assumed to be for excusable delays. When in doubt, a contractor should clarify the intent with the CO.

One of the most difficult questions involved in acceleration claims is what communications from the government constitute a constructive acceleration order. The boards and courts have held that "requests" to accelerate may be considered an order to accelerate if the request is firm. Threats to terminate for default or pressure to complete a schedule may also be construed as an acceleration order. Again, when in doubt, the matter should be clarified with the CO.

Acceleration Costs

Once a contractor is found to be entitled to an equitable adjustment for an acceleration, the next step is to determine which costs were incurred as a result of the acceleration order. Generally, a contractor is reimbursed only for costs incurred to make up for excusable delays. If a contractor can show that it was otherwise on schedule, except for the excusable delays, the only problem is identifying and proving the acceleration costs incurred. However, problems are encountered when a contractor has experienced both excusable and contractor-caused delays. In such cases, the contracting parties need to reach agreement on the costs related to the acceleration effort and a reasonable allocation of such costs to excusable and contractor-caused delays. The parties might agree to share all of the acceleration costs on a pro rata basis.

The most frequent types of costs encountered in acceleration-related equitable adjustments are discussed next.

Overtime and Shift Premiums

Overtime and shift premiums are the most common costs incurred in acceleration situations. The costs represent only the premium portion of pay for overtime or extra shift work. The basic labor costs are part of the normal costs of performing the work and are not included in an acceleration claim. Such premium costs are easily extracted from the accounting records and should be acceptable if the contractor can show that the work was performed as part of the acceleration.

Expedited Material Costs

Expedited material costs are incurred for efforts to acquire materials earlier than originally expected. For example, higher-priced transportation or higher prices paid to vendors or subcontractors for earlier deliveries may be recoverable. Also included might be the costs of extra internal expediters required to ensure prompt movement of materials through production.

Loss of Efficiency

Loss of efficiency or productivity is generally one of the most difficult costs to compute in an acceleration claim because of the inability to segregate such costs. In acceleration situations, loss of efficiency is the added cost involved because of the inability of workers to be as productive as they might be without the acceleration. For example, workers tend to be less productive when working long hours or when working in adverse weather. Also, accelerations may result in the need to hire new, untrained workers, who would be less productive than existing workers. The most effective way of calculating a loss of efficiency is to determine a factor representing the general decline in productivity as a result of the acceleration. This can be done by comparing the work accomplished per labor hour or dollar during the acceleration period with the work accomplished per labor hour or dollar in a normal period.

Other Costs

The list of significant other costs that may be attributed to an acceleration is almost limitless. The key is to identify all costs that can be reasonably attributed to the acceleration and that would not have been incurred otherwise. Applicable overhead and profit are normally included as part of acceleration claims.

11-10. DEFECTIVE SPECIFICATIONS

The need to reprice the contract may also occur when specifications provided in a government contract are defective. The identification and correction of these defective specifications may cause increases in the cost of contract performance. The impact of the delay caused by the defective specifications should be calculated as discussed earlier. Also, because defective specifications may not be discovered until sometime after the beginning of contract performance, the cost of wasted effort may be incurred. The boards of contract appeals and the courts have held that the cost of work performed in accordance with defective specifications is clearly to be included in the equitable adjustment. In *Hol-Gar Manufacturing Corp. v. U.S.*,[42] the Court of Claims stated the following:

> The Armed Services Board of Contract Appeals has recognized the correctness of the allowance of costs incident to an attempt to comply with defective specifications. See, e.g., J. W. Hurst & Son Awnings, Inc., 59-1 BCA 2095 at 8965 (1959), where the Board stated:

> Where, as here, the change is necessitated by defective specifications and drawings, the equitable adjustment to which a contractor is entitled must, if it is to be equitable, i.e., fair and just, include the costs which it incurred in attempting to perform in accordance with the defective specifications and drawings. Under these circumstances the equitable adjustment may be not be limited to costs incurred subsequent to the issuance of the change orders. [Citations omitted.]

> We hold that the [plaintiff] is entitled to an equitable adjustment which will compensate it for the costs which it incurred in trying to perform in accordance with the original specifications that turned out to be defective.

Costs may also be incurred to actually correct the defective specifications. The company may be required not only to identify the defective specifications but also to correct them to allow for continued contract performance. The costs directly related to this additional activity are to be included in the equitable adjustment.

Finally, correcting the defective specifications may entail the use of production techniques or the incurrence of costs for performance different from those that were originally anticipated. In this regard, the contract would require repricing to incorporate the costs associated with different production techniques or the use of different labor or materials.

11-11. TOTAL COST APPROACH

The method of calculating the costs of an equitable adjustment that is most favored by contractors and least favored by the government is the total cost approach. Essentially, this method determines the total cost of performance and deducts from that the total negotiated contract cost. It ascribes the difference as the measure of the cost portion of the equitable adjustment. As is apparent, the total responsibility for the cost impact is ascribed to the government. Under this method, no attempt is made to analyze the effect of the change. Because the connection between the government change and the cost impact is not presented, the boards and courts have traditionally not favored this approach. In *WRB Corp. of Texas*,[43] the Court of Claims stated the following:

This court has tolerated the use of the total cost method only when no other procedure was available and then only when the reliability of the supporting evidence was fully substantiated. There must be proof that (1) the nature of the particular losses make it impossible or highly impracticable to determine them with a reasonable degree of accuracy; (2) the plaintiff's bid or estimate was realistic; (3) its actual costs were reasonable; and (4) it was not responsible for the added expenses.

As a result, this approach should be used only when no other approach is appropriate and under the conditions for its use, as discussed in the above case, have been properly addressed.

11-12. JURY VERDICT APPROACH

When all else fails, the board or court must determine the proper amount of the equitable adjustment. This is referred to as a jury verdict. Once the contractor has proven entitlement to an adjustment and the only issue is determining the amount, a jury verdict may be used as a last resort. The responsibility of the board or court in this situation was stated as follows in *E. Arthur Higgins*:[44]

When a contractor has proven entitlement, but cannot define his costs with exact data, courts and appeals boards have been reluctant either to send the dispute back to the Contracting Officer for determination of excess costs or to send the contractor away empty handed when it is at all possible to make a fair and reasonable approximation of extra costs. ... It is not necessary that the amount be ascertainable with absolute exactness or mathematical precision. ... It is enough if the testimony and evidence adduced is sufficient to enable the court or board (acting as a jury) to make a fair and reasonable approximation....

The responsibility of the court or board to reach a jury verdict was emphasized in *S. W. Electronics & Manufacturing Corp.*[45] In this case, the Court of Claims stated that when entitlement was clear, the board or court is under a heavy obligation to provide some compensation and should render a jury verdict giving a fair and reasonable approximation of the damages.

Generally, in rendering a jury verdict decision, the board or court will announce only its determination of the amount. It will generally not explain or justify how the amount was obtained.

11-13. PROFIT

The appropriateness of applying profit to the amount of the cost portion of the equitable adjustment is usually not at issue. In *United States v. Callahan Walker Construction Co.*,[46] the U.S. Supreme Court stated that "an equitable adjustment of the [government's] additional payment for extra work involved merely the ascertainment of the cost of [the work added] and the addition to that cost of a reasonable and customary allowance for profit." Therefore, it is considered appropriate that profit be added to the changed effort for the same reasons that profit must be added to the cost estimates used to establish the original contract amount.

Because one objective of an equitable adjustment is not to change the profit or loss that would have been experienced on the unchanged portion of the contract, the use of the contract price or original bid price for the item(s) deleted may not be appropriate. If the profit on the deleted items is anticipated to vary from that contemplated in the original contract price, the estimated costs that would have been experienced may be a better measure of the appropriate adjustment. If the equitable adjustment is being calculated on a retroactive basis, the cost risk is less than it would be if the activity had not yet taken place. The regulations generally require that the structured approach to profit determination be used for contract changes in the same manner that it is used to determine the government's profit objective to negotiate contracts. This method recognizes the differing circumstances between the initial contract pricing activity and the activity related to pricing changes. (Methods of establishing profit objectives are discussed in Chapter 4.) If the changes are not significant in amount, it may be appropriate to apply the same profit rate reflected in the original contract. However, if the changes entail significantly different activities from those originally contemplated, it may be more appropriate to determine a rate that is either higher or lower than the originally contemplated profit rate.

In the case of deleted contract effort, there has been some debate on whether it is appropriate to reduce profit on the contract. While the issue has been handled both ways, the boards and courts have generally agreed that it is appropriate to add a factor for profit to contract reductions for deductive changes. The factors to be addressed in determining the amount of the reduced profit would be the same as those for adding profit to contract increases.

11-14. INTEREST

Interest is generally not includable in an equitable adjustment computation, as provided in the Pricing of Adjustments contract clause. The clause incorporates the cost principles in contracts, both cost-type and fixed-price, for which pricing actions are subject to cost analysis.

Inasmuch as the cost principles provide that interest is not an allowable cost (refer to Chapter 7), interest is includable in the contract price adjustment only if the contractor can demonstrate that it incurred an interest cost to finance changed effort for which the government was responsible. The allowability of such interest was addressed in *Automation Fabricators & Engineering Co.*[47] If the equitable adjustment becomes subject to a dispute and if any claim over $50,000 is certified pursuant to FAR 33.207, interest would also be included in any subsequent contract adjustment, as provided under the Disputes clause. Federal Acquisition Regulations 33.208 provides that simple interest at the rate fixed by the Secretary of the Treasury is due and payable from (1) the date of receipt of the certified claim by the CO, or (2) the date payment would have been due, whichever is later, to the date payment is received by the contractor. A more complete discussion is contained in Chapter 13.

11-15. SHIPBUILDING EQUITABLE ADJUSTMENT PROPOSALS

10 U.S.C. 2405(a) prohibited any price adjustment under a shipbuilding contract entered into after December 7, 1983, for an amount set forth in a claim, request for equitable adjustment, or demand for payment under the contract arising out of events occurring more than 18 months before submission of the claim, request, or demand.

The Court of Claims ruled in *Peterson Builders, Inc. v. United States*,[48] that the 18-month limitation started when the contractor begins performing the changed work, not when the work is authorized via a change notice. Because of the controversy over the certification of claims (see Chapter 13), shipbuilders were caught in the proverbial catch-22, where a claim originally submitted within the 18-month period was later dismissed because it was certified by the wrong corporate official. To remedy that situation, the Fiscal Year 1993 Defense Authorization Act[49] modified 10 U.S.C. 2405 to permit a contractor to resubmit the certification based on the contractor's knowledge and the supporting data that existed when the original certification was submitted. The Fiscal Year 1998 Defense Authorization Act[50] repealed 10 U.S.C. 2405.

11-16. SUMMARY

The key concept related to the amount of an equitable adjustment is the determination of reasonable costs. Whether the equitable adjustment is to be calculated before the change takes place or after, the key element is the measurement or estimation of the costs that have been or will be incurred to perform the changed activity. Accordingly, an accounting system should reasonably measure the cost of changes in all circumstances determined to be appropriate.

11-17. NOTES

1. General Builders Supply Co., Inc. v. United States, 187 Ct. Cl. 477, April 11, 1969, 409 F.2d 246.
2. Bruce Construction Corp. et al. v. United States, 163 Ct. Cl. 97, Nov. 15, 1963, 324 F.2d 516.
3. Pacific Architects and Engineers, Inc., a California Corporation and Advanced Maintenance Corp. v. United States, 203 Ct. Cl. 449, Jan. 23, 1974, 491 F.2d 734.
4. Celesco Industries, Inc., ASBCA No. 22251, Nov. 30, 1978, 79-1 BCA 13,604.
5. Montag–Halvorson–Cascade–Austin, July 6, 1958 CC 1121 (1958).
6. Nager Electric Co., Inc. and Keystone Engineering Corp. v. United States, 194 Ct. Cl. 835, May 14, 1971, 442 F.2d 936.
7. Ibid.
8. Contract Management, Inc., ASBCA No. 44885, Aug. 31, 1995, 95-2 BCA 27,886.
9. Pruitt Energy Source, Inc., ENGBCA No. 6134, July 6, 1995, 95-2 BCA 27,840.
10. Cen-Vi-Ro of Texas, Inc. v. United States, Ct. Cl. No. 334-73, June 24, 1975, 210 Ct. Cl. 684.
11. Nager Electric Co., Inc. and Keystone Engineering Corp. v. United States, April 30, 1970, 194 Ct. Cl. 835. (Note: Report of Trial Commissioner of the Court of Claims. For review by court, see Note 6.)
12. Bruce Construction Corp. et al. v. United States, supra, note 2.
13. Ibid.
14. Kemmons–Wilson, Inc. and South & Patton, Joint Venture, ASBCA No. 16167, Sept. 8, 1972, 72-2 BCA 9,689.
15. Aydin Corp. (West) v. Secretary of the Air Force., CAFC No. 94-1441, Aug. 10, 1995, 61 F.3d 1571.
16. Eichleay Corp., ASBCA No. 5183, July 29, 1960, 60-2 BCA 2,688; aff'd. on reconsideration, Dec. 17, 1960, 61-1 BCA 2,894.
17. R.W. Contracting, Inc., ASBCA No. 24627, April 4, 1984, 84-2 BCA 17,302.
18. Oxwell, Inc., ASBCA No. 39768, June 12, 1990, 90-3 BCA 23,069.
19. Interstate General Government Contractors, Inc., ASBCA No. 43369, March 17, 1992, 92-2 BCA 24,956.
20. C.B.C. Enterprises, Inc. v. United States, CAFC No. 91-5154, Oct. 20, 1992, 978 F.2d 669.
21. Marvin C. Altmayer v. Johnson, CAFC No. 95-1223, March 21, 1996, 79 F.3d 1129.
22. Mech-Con Corp. v. West, CAFC No. 95-1048, Aug. 4, 1995, 61 F.3d 883,886.
23. Satellite Electric Co. v. Dalton, CAFC No. 96-1135, Jan. 30, 1997, 105 F.3d 1418.
24. Wickham Contracting Co. v. Fischer, CAFC No. 93-1146, Jan. 6, 1994, 12 F.3d 1574.
25. Allegheny Sportswear Co., ASBCA No. 4163, March 25, 1958, 58-1 BCA 1,684.
26. Entwistle Co., ASBCA Nos. 14918, 15827, June 20, 1975, 75-2 BCA 11,420; aff'd. and modified on reconsideration, Aug. 31, 1976, 76-2 BCA 12,108.

27. Allied Materials & Equipment Co., ASBCA No. 17318, Feb. 28, 1975, 75-1 BCA 11,150.

28. Essex Electro Engineers, Inc., ASBCA No. 21066, Aug. 9, 1979, 79-2 BCA 14,035.

29. Do-Well Machine Shop, Inc., ASBCA No. 35867, Feb. 24, 1992, 92-2 BCA 24,843.

30. Therm-Air Manufacturing Co., ASBCA No. 16453, March 23, 1973, 73-1 BCA 9,983.

31. Entwistle Co., supra, note 26.

32. Therm-Air Manufacturing Co., supra, note 30.

33. Allegheny Sportswear Co., supra, note 25.

34. Essex Electro Engineers, Inc., supra, note 28.

35. So-Pak-Co., ASBCA No. 38906, July 8, 1993, 93-3 BCA 26,215.

36. Audit Guidance—Delay and Disruption Claims Defense Contract Audit Agency Pamphlet 7641.45, Aug. 1988 (canceled in Fall 1994).

37. Superintendent of Documents, Government Printing Office, Defense Contract Audit Agency Manual 7640.1, Washington, DC 20402. Catalog No. D-1, 47/2, 7640, 1/1283, 12-800 "Auditing Delay/Disruption Submissions."

38. Hardeman–Monier–Hutcherson, a Joint Venture, ASBCA No. 11785, March 13, 1967, 67-1 BCA 6,210.

39. Keco Industries, Inc., ASBCA Nos. 15184 and 15547, June 30, 1972, 62-2 BCA 9,576.

40. Fermont Division, Dynamics Corporation of America, ASBCA No. 15806, Feb. 20, 1975, 75-1 BCA 11,139.

41. Ashton Co., IBCA No. 1070-6-75, June 16, 1976, 76-2 BCA 11,934.

42. Hol-Gar Manufacturing Corp. v. United States, 175 Ct. Cl. 518, May 13, 1966, 360 F.2d 634.

43. WRB Corp. et al., a Joint Venture, dba Robertson Construction Co. v. United States, No. 67-621 April 19, 1968, 183 Ct. Cl. 409.

44. E. Arthur Higgins, AGBCA No. 76-128, Sept. 20, 1979, 79-2 BCA 14,050.

45. S.W. Electronics Manufacturing Corp. v. United States, Ct. Cl. 1981, 207-78, July 29, 1981, 655 F.2d 1078.

46. United States v. Callahan Walker Construction Co., Nov. 9, 1942 317 U.S. 56 (1942), 63 S. Ct. 113.

47. Automation Fabricators & Engineering Co., PSBCA No. 2701, May 2, 1990, 90-3 BCA 22,943.

48. Peterson Builders, Inc. v. United States, Ct. Cl. No. 91-1406C, May 5, 1992, 27 Fed. Cl. 443.

49. Fiscal Year 1993 Defense Authorization Act, 106 Stat. 2315, enacted Oct. 23, 1992, Pub. L. 102-484.

50. Fiscal Year 1998 Defense Authorization Act, 111 Stat. 1629, enacted Nov. 18, 1997, Pub. L. 105-85.

Chapter Twelve
Terminations

12-1. BACKGROUND

One of the major differences in contracting with the government, compared with contracting in the commercial environment, is the government's right to unilaterally terminate a contract.

Termination Authority

While the government normally reserves the right to terminate a contract by specific contract provision, its authority for such action is based on its role as a sovereign. Either by specific incorporation or by the "operation of law," termination clauses exist in almost all government contracts. In *United States v. Corliss Steam-Engine Co.*,[1] the U.S. Supreme Court ruled in 1876 that the government had the right to terminate a contract even though the contract lacked a provision to that effect. Incorporation by operation of law is perhaps best explained in *G.L. Christian and Associates v. United States*,[2] in which the Court of Claims found that: (1) the Armed Services Procurement Regulation (ASPR) governed the contract; (2) the ASPR was promulgated pursuant to law (the Armed Services Procurement Act of 1947, 10 U.S.C. 2301, et seq.), and therefore had the force and effect of law; (3) the ASPR required the termination clause; and (4) no authorized deviation was granted. The court basically ruled that if the procurement regulations require the inclusion of a clause, the clause exists in a contract whether physically incorporated in the contract or not.

Even though the courts have held that the government has the right to terminate without a contract clause providing for such action, the procurement regulations generally require insertion of such clauses. The termination clauses that are inserted in various types of contracts are contained in Federal Acquisition Regulation (FAR) 52.249-1 to 52.249-12. The government uses these clauses to implement termination procedures. Additionally, there are recommended modifications to the clauses for inclusion in subcontracts. Generally, a single clause for cost-type contracts covers both termination for convenience and termination for default, and separate clauses for convenience and default terminations are used in fixed-price contracts.

Types of Terminations

There are basically two types of terminations:

1.   Termination for convenience, which is related to the government's right to terminate a contract, either in whole or in part, for any reason deemed to be in the public's best interest.

2.   Termination for default, which occurs when a contractor either fails or refuses to deliver the required supplies or perform the required services or otherwise perform the contract or when the contractor's lack of progress endangers contract performance.

A contract is completely terminated when a contractor is directed to cease all work remaining to be performed, while partial termination requires that a portion of the contract effort continue. The work that is not completed at the termination's effective date and that the contractor must continue to perform is referred to as the "continued portion" of the contract. The work completed and accepted before the effective termination date is the "completed portion" of the contract. The "terminated portion" of the contract relates to work that is not completed and accepted before the effective termination date but that the contractor is to discontinue.

Notification

Once the government decides to terminate a contract, it must notify the contractor. Federal Acquisition Regulation 49.601 sets forth the approved forms of termination notices. Generally, the procedures involve mailing (via certified mail) or hand-delivering (with written acknowledgment) a written termination notice. Whatever the means used to convey the notice, it must specify the following:

- The type of termination (convenience versus default)
- The extent of the termination (partial or complete and, if partial, what part)
- The effective date of the termination (immediately upon receipt of notification, on a given future date, or on the date of completion of a particular item or the occurrence of a particular event)
- The steps to be taken to minimize the impact on personnel, if the termination is expected to result in a significant reduction in the workforce

After the initial notice of termination is issued, the termination contracting officer (TCO) should convene a conference with the contractor to develop a program for accomplishing an orderly settlement. The conference should address the following:

- The point at which the work is to be stopped
- The identification of subcontracts
- Obligation of the prime contractor to terminate subcontracts

- Status of any plans, drawings, and information that would have been delivered at contract completion
- Status of continuing work
- Arrangements for transfer of title and delivery to the government of any material required by the government
- Forms to be used to submit settlement proposals, accounting information, and requirements for partial payments
- Tentative time schedule for negotiation of the settlement
- Instructions, if any

12-2. TERMINATION FOR DEFAULT

If a company fails to deliver the supplies or services within the time specified in the contract and there are no excusable delays, the government has the right to terminate the contract immediately, regardless of how slight the delay may be. The government is not obligated to provide any prior notice. However, for failure to perform any other provision of the contract or failure to make progress, the government must provide an opportunity for a company to cure the defect. The contracting officer (CO) may notify the company that within 10 days after receipt of a notice, or within a longer period as the CO may authorize in writing, the company must cure the defect. After this period, if the problem is not remedied, the government may terminate the contract.

In *Composite Laminates, Inc. v. United States*,[3] the contractor argued that the government's cure notice was deficient because it did not specifically refer to the contract's inspection specification, even though the inspection deficiencies were the crux of the government's decision to terminate the contract. The Court of Federal Claims agreed that the cure notice appeared deficient but refused to grant Composite's motion for summary judgment, because the contractor was aware of the Navy's concern regarding compliance with the inspection specification through telephone calls, letters, and conversations. The court ruled that these forms of communication could be considered when determining the adequacy of a cure notice.

Boards of contract appeal have long held that failure of a subcontractor to make timely deliveries is not an excusable cause for nonperformance by the prime contractor, even when the subcontractor has declared bankruptcy.[4] Failure to comply with federal labor laws or labor reporting regulations has also been held to justify termination for default.[5] However, the Department of Labor must determine that a violation of labor laws or regulations has occurred prior to the action to terminate the contract for default.[6]

Basis for Settlement

Under cost-type contracts, the accounting procedures for default and convenience terminations are the same. The only real differences are that settlement expenses are not allowable costs on a termination for default, and fee is considered only for acceptable work.

Under fixed-price contracts, the contractor will be paid only for items completed and accepted, and payment will be at the contract price. The government is not liable for costs incurred on any undelivered work and is entitled to the repayment of any advance or progress payments applicable to the terminated portion of the contract. Settlement expenses are not allowable costs. The government may pay for and require a contractor to transfer title and deliver to the government any on-hand materials and supplies related to the terminated portion of the contract. The government may then turn these materials over to another contractor to reprocure the items terminated. If the cost of reprocuring the items from another supplier is greater than the cost that would have been incurred on the terminated contract, the government may recover the increased cost from the contractor whose contract was terminated.

Defenses against Termination for Default

A termination for default may be converted to a termination for convenience for actions and causes beyond the contractor's control or unreasonable acts by the government. While the government must prove that a default termination with respect to the unperformed work was proper, the contractor must establish that its failure to complete was either due to excusable causes beyond its fault or control or was caused by the government's material breach of contract.

- In *Melville Energy Systems, Inc. v. United States*[7] the Federal Circuit addressed the burden of proof required for either the government to obtain recovery of reprocurement costs or the terminated contractor to obtain recovery of excess costs incurred for acceptable work performed over amounts paid by the government. The court concluded that the decision to terminate for default was justified but denied the award of reprocurement costs because the government failed to provide "either a well supported summary figure or independent data from which the court could do a calculation." The court was left with the impression that the government "acted hastily in awarding the [reprocurement] contract ... or made more adjustments to the original scope of work than were necessary to complete the building." The court also denied the contractor any remuneration for excess work performed because its proof of the value of its work was equally inadequate. Rather than providing detailed support, Melville simply relied on a superficial analysis by a representative of Melville's surety.

- The Armed Services Board of Contract Appeals (ASBCA) converted *Technical Ordnance, Inc.*'s[8] termination for default to a termination for the convenience where the contractor followed all government specifications, yet the product failed. The Board held the following:

  > When a contract requires a contractor to build and test an item in accordance with detailed government specifications, the Government impliedly warrants that if those specifications are followed, the contractor will be able to produce an acceptable production. ... The appellant has met its burden of demonstrating that it complied with the specifications. It need not do more in this case.

- In *Defense Systems Corp. and Hi-Shear Technology Corp.*,[9] the ASBCA converted a termination for default to a termination for convenience because of commercial impracticability. The termination was converted in spite of the fact that the contractor stopped work on the contract because of the Navy's failure to deal with the defective technical data package (TDP). The Board concluded that a stringent zero defect requirement applied to the first article testing was impracticable to achieve because none of the prior contracts for MK 214 and 216 cartridges had "passed the contract prescribed contract performance tests under the zero defect acceptance criterion set forth in the appellant's contracts." The Board excused the contractor's decision to cease working on the contracts because:

> [W]hen the appellant "terminated" the contract by shutting down and stopping work on 29 March 1991, appellant was not fully aware of the impossibility of performance. Appellant only knew that it could no longer continue without additional funds from the Navy or indeed elsewhere and better TDPs. Its lack of awareness of the full implication of the defective TDPs and the zero defect performance requirement stemmed from appellant's being told by the Navy that other contractors were building to the TDPs and passing the contract performance tests.

In *McDonnell Douglas Corp. and General Dynamics Corp. v. United States*[10] the Court of Federal Claims converted the Navy's A-12 termination for default to a termination for convenience. After reviewing the evidence, the court concluded that neither the aircraft weight problem nor schedule delays were the real reasons that the contract was terminated for default. Rather, "It was terminated because the Office of the Secretary of Defense withdrew support and funding." In support of its decision, the court noted that the CO approved the termination memorandum after less than an hour of review and without reviewing any A-12 documents, consulting with technical personnel, or reviewing FAR provisions concerning terminations for default.

In converting terminations for default to terminations for convenience, legal fees incurred to convert the termination that are not part of the prosecution of a claim are recoverable as settlement costs. In *Alta Construction Co.*,[11] the Federal Circuit concluded that "the legal fees incurred in dealing with the surety and the Contracting Officer were not incurred in the prosecution of a claim against the Postal Service and were therefore recoverable above the maximum payment limitation that would otherwise apply."

The Court of Federal Claims ruled in *Alaska Pulp Corp.*[12] that a contractor can submit money claims for a government breach of contract prior to a court ruling on the propriety of the government's termination for breach of contract. While the FAR was not applicable to this Forest Service contract for timber harvesting and processing, the decision should have relevance to a contractor's submission of a termination settlement proposal prior to the adjudication of a contractor's appeal to convert a termination for default to a termination for convenience.

12-3. TERMINATION FOR CONVENIENCE

The Government's Right to Terminate

Although the government's right to terminate a contract for convenience has been broadly interpreted, some protection is accorded to contractors. In overruling *Colonial Metals Co. v. United States*,[13] the Court of Claims in *Torncello & Soledad Enterprises, Inc. v. United States*[14] concluded that the Termination for Convenience clause applies only when the circumstances of the bargain or the expectations of the parties have changed. However, the courts and the boards of contract appeals have been reluctant to apply the holding in *Torncello* beyond the scope of that case. In *Automated Services, Inc.*,[15] the Department of Transportation Board of Contract Appeals concluded that the validity of invoking the Termination for Convenience clause continues to be measured by the presence or absence of bad faith on the part of the government. This position was reaffirmed by the Federal Circuit in *Caldwell & Santmyer, Inc. v. Secretary of Agriculture*.[16] After award, it was discovered that the solicitation contained defective specifications and that corrective action would prejudice the other bidders. Caldwell claimed that the termination for convenience should be treated as a breach by the government. The court disagreed, holding that "... Torncello stands for the unremarkable proposition that when the government contracts with a party knowing full well that it will not honor the contract, it cannot avoid a breach claim by adverting to the convenience termination clause." The court found, "There is no evidence the Government intended before award to terminate the contract for any reason." In 1996, the Federal Circuit reversed an unpublished Court of Federal Claims decision that the Army Corps of Engineers improperly terminated a demolition contract with *Krygorski Construction Co., Inc.*[17] The Federal Circuit concluded that an increase in the cost of asbestos removal from 10% to 50% of the total price of the contract justified a termination for convenience and a competitive reprocurement.

Deadline for Submission of Settlement Proposal

The termination for convenience clauses required submission of the final termination settlement proposal no later than one year after the effective date of the termination, unless an extension is granted by the government. If the proposal is not submitted timely, the CO is authorized to unilaterally determine the amount, if any, due the contractor as a result of the termination. That unilateral determination is not subject to appeal.[18]

Basis for Settlement

Cost-Type Contracts

A contractor whose cost-type contract has been terminated can either (1) voucher out reimbursable costs, using Standard Form 1034, Public Voucher, for up to six months, then submit a settlement proposal using Standard Form 1437, as shown in Appendix 12.1, for the balance of unreimbursed costs and fees; or (2) submit a settlement proposal for the entire amount to be paid for unreimbursed costs and fees.

Fixed-Price Contracts

The settlement proposal generally must be prepared on either the inventory basis or the total cost basis. Settlement proposals may not be submitted on any other basis without prior approval of the chief of the contracting or contract administration office.

- *Inventory basis.* Under this method, the contractor lists only its costs relating or allocable to the terminated portion of the contract. The costs are broken down among raw materials, purchased parts, finished components, and work in process at the purchase price or manufactured cost. To this amount are added other costs, such as start-up costs, preproduction costs, allocable indirect expenses, profit on the work completed, the cost of settlements with any subcontractors, specific settlement expenses associated with the termination, and the price of finished items that were completed but had not yet been delivered at the time of the termination. Deducted from the foregoing are any disposal credits and any advance progress payments associated with the terminated portion of the contract. The form used to submit a settlement proposal on the inventory basis is Standard Form 1435, shown in Appendix 12.2. The forms used to support termination inventory items are included as Appendices 12.3 to 12.6. A short form (Standard Form 1438), included as Appendix 12.7, and an inventory schedule (Standard Form 1434), shown as Appendix 12.8 can be submitted for fixed-price settlement proposals of less than $10,000.

The government prefers the inventory basis because the settlement is related directly to the cost of the items actually terminated. Any remaining portion of the contract will continue, and unit prices will remain the same unless changed through an equitable adjustment. It may require considerable effort to identify incurred costs allocable to the various inventory items included in work in process and finished goods and to isolate start-up and contract preparatory costs and properly allocate these costs between terminated and remaining contract portions. Any continuing portion of the contract must be repriced through an equitable adjustment; otherwise, a contractor will earn a lower profit rate or may suffer a loss on the continuing portion, solely because of the termination.

- *Total cost basis.* When a complete termination occurs, all costs incurred before the termination date are calculated and an adjustment is made for profit or loss. These costs are added to the costs of any settlements with subcontractors and other settlement expenses. Amounts are deducted for items completed and delivered to the government, along with unliquidated advance and progress payments, and disposal and other known credits. When a partial termination occurs, the submission of the settlement proposal is deferred until the unterminated portion of the contract has been completed. The form used to submit a settlement proposal on a total cost basis is Standard Form 1436, shown in Appendix 12.9. The forms used to support special tooling and test equipment are shown in Appendix 12.6.

Use of the total cost basis normally requires advance approval by the CO. Such use will generally be authorized under a complete termination only if: (1) production has not commenced and accumulated costs represent planning and preproduction costs; (2) the accounting system will not lend itself to establishing unit costs for work in process; (3) the contract does not specify unit prices; or (4) the termination involves an undefinitized letter contract.

Termination of Lease Contracts

In recent years, the government has increasingly turned to lease instruments, rather than outright purchases, to obtain equipment. Such lease arrangements can take the typical forms of commercial leases, such as Lease to Ownership Plan (LTOP) and so forth. A contractor's ability to recover its investment if the government terminates the lease depends on the specific terms and conditions of the contract. Absent a specific contractual provision for termination liability, the government will not reimburse a contractor for costs that were intended to be recovered through options that are not exercised as a result of the termination.

In *Planning Research Corp., Inc.,*[19] the General Services Board of Contract Appeals (GSBCA) denied claims arising in connection with two equipment leases under a cost-reimbursement type contract for the development of an automated patent system. The contract solicitation required offerors to use five-year lease to ownership costs for hardware and software components required for contract performance. Planning Research entered into equipment lease agreements that provided for lease terms of 60 months "... if all options for renewal are exercised and subject to any termination rights." The initial term of each equipment lease was from the stated commencement date to the end of the then-current government fiscal year. Leases were renewable by written notice by the later of the start of the next government fiscal year or 30 days after government funding became available. In 1989, the CO notified Planning Research that the lease schedules would not be funded in 1990. Planning Research asserted that the Patent and Trademark Office's (PTO) failure to exercise the options constituted a breach of contract, an improper termination for convenience, and a deductive change. Planning Research claimed entitlement to full payment of the 60-month lease stream under LTOP. The GSBCA held that renewal of an LTOP is within the discretion of the leasing party, unless the LTOP specifically limits the circumstances under which the lessee may decline to exercise its option to renew and that no such restrictive language was included in the Planning Research lease agreements. Thus, the PTO was not deemed to be obligated to reimburse Planning Research for the cost of the remaining lease payments.

In contrast, the GSBCA concluded that the General Services Administration's (GSA) contract with *Pulsar Data Systems, Inc.*[20] was for a five-year operating lease plan, not a one-year operating lease plan with four one-year options. Consequently, when the GSA terminated the lease in the second year, the GSBCA noted the following:

> The whole arrangement makes no sense unless the contract has a five-year term. What contractor would agree to purchase expensive special-purpose equipment to lease to the Government, and then give the Government the "option" of not continuing the lease after the first year? The same applies to Pulsar's investors who gave money to Pulsar in return for an assignment of the lease payments. GSA's argument that the contract was a one-year contract, with four one-year options, is just plain wrong.

Equitable Adjustments

Because the total amount of the termination settlement is limited to the contract price of the items terminated, plus settlement expenses, the need for an equitable adjustment should be addressed in either partial or complete terminations. If the costs incurred on a completely or partially terminated contract have been increased because of government action or inaction, an equitable adjustment will result in (1) increasing the level at which a possible limitation on the termination settlement amount may apply, and (2) calculating a higher rate of profit earned to allow for a higher profit on the contract's remaining portion. Equitable adjustments are discussed in Chapter 11.

Payment

Contractors may submit Standard Form 1440, Request for Partial Payment (see Appendix 12.10.), which provides the basis for the government to make partial payments against costs incurred for the contract's terminated portion before a final settlement is reached. Partial payments are addressed in FAR 49.112. The amount of the partial payment to be made is at the discretion of the CO.

12-4. TERMINATION FOR CONVENIENCE ACCOUNTING PROBLEMS

Cost Principles

In calculating the costs to be included in termination settlement proposals, questions often arise about which cost principles govern. The FAR Part 49 termination provisions discuss a fairness concept in a broad sense, while the government has often used the precise tests found in the cost principles. The boards and courts have established that the answer is somewhere in between. In *Codex Corp. v. United States*,[21] the Court of Claims held that the application of the cost principles in Part 2 of Section 15 was subject to the general policies set forth in Section 8-301 because ASPR 8-214, by its express terms, mandated consideration of the fair compensation policies of Section 8-301. The ASBCA reiterated that premise in *General Electric Co.*[22] by citing "... reliance exclusively on strict accounting principles and the standards of ASPR Section XV ..." as a fatal flaw in the government's position.

Accounting Procedures

One of the difficulties in accounting for the cost of terminated contracts is the fact that accounting systems are normally designed to reflect an ongoing, continuous situation; most have not been designed to handle terminations. However, as a result of a termination, certain costs will be incurred that otherwise would not have been incurred. In addition, the premise upon which allocation procedures were established may no longer be valid. Unless accounting procedures are changed to reflect the change in circumstances, costs may not be properly allocated and proper recovery may not be obtained. It is highly unlikely that the cost accounting system for a fixed-price contract would identify, isolate, and report costs unique to a termination action. Indeed, this was concluded in *Algonac Manufacturing Co.*,[23] in which it was also concluded that the acquisition regulation does not require a fixed-price contractor to maintain elaborate cost accounting systems or follow prescribed accounting principles simply because the contract might be terminated.

This lack of a requirement to maintain specific accounting systems does not, however, shift the burden of proving the amounts of any entitlement to the government. In *Clary Corp.*,[24] the Board stated that "although it may have been legitimate for the appellant to have estimated its costs of performance where those costs were not shown on its accounting records, it was still necessary to demonstrate the bases and accuracy of those estimates." This case is consistent with other cases in which the burden of proof of costs incurred and entitlement fall to the contractor. The boards have permitted estimates when accounting records were unavailable through no fault of the contractor. In such cases, however, the contractor is still required to support its claim by the best available competent evidence.

The cost principle on termination costs (FAR 31.205-42) recognizes that contract terminations often give rise to the incurrence of costs or the need for special treatment of costs that would not have arisen had the contract not been terminated. It also addresses the need for revisions to normal accounting practices to reflect the unique environment created by a termination. This FAR provision covers certain areas that are unique to terminations:

- Common items
- Costs continuing after termination
- Initial costs
- Loss of useful value of special tooling, machinery, and equipment
- Rental costs under unexpired leases
- Alterations of leased property
- Settlement expenses
- Subcontractor claims

The cost principle reflects the following premises:

- The contractor will take all necessary action to minimize expenses, including the diversion of materials and supplies to any other contractor work.
- The government is not a guarantor of the company's business and therefore will not reimburse a company for indirect expenses that would have been allocated to the terminated portion of a completely terminated contract (i.e., unabsorbed overhead), which will be discussed in more detail later in this chapter.

Other cost principles that may be relevant in the event of contract termination are idle facilities and idle capacity costs (FAR 31.205-17), plant reconversion costs (FAR 31.205-31), and precontract costs (FAR 31.205-32).

In addition to submitting the settlement forms discussed earlier, contractors are generally required to submit Standard Form 1439, Schedule of Accounting Information (see Appendix 12.11), which contains general information about the accounting system and specific information about accounting methods used in preparing the settlement proposal.

Precontract Costs

Costs incurred before the contract's effective date directly pursuant to the negotiation and in anticipation of the award, when such costs are deemed necessary to comply with the proposed delivery schedule, are generally allowable to the extent that they would have been allowable if incurred after the award.

In *RHC Construction*,[25] the contractor was entitled to its precontract costs upon contract termination since it had prudently planned the work. The contract term was only eight weeks in length, and the required time to procure the appropriate material was four weeks. The Board ruled that the CO had incorrectly determined that the contractor was entitled to recover only those expenses incurred after the date of the formal contract award.

In *Bank of America*,[26] the Army entered into a contract for automated credit card systems for its open messes. After the pilot contract, the Army entered into a second contract for installing the system that the bank had developed. In submitting its proposed price, the bank advised the Army that the price included development costs and that the bank expected to recover such costs ($60,000) through profit earned on the contract. When the contract was terminated, the bank sought to recover its development costs as part of the termination settlement proposal. The Board's conclusion that the Army knew that the bank expected to recover its development costs and that such costs were in fact included in the contract price was key to its decision in favor of the bank. The board also noted that "absent the bank's pre-award disclosure that it expected to recover those costs, it [the board] would have considerable difficulty in finding pre-award costs recoverable."

In *General Electric*,[27] significant development labor costs were deemed reasonable, considering the advanced effort that had to be put forward toward the anticipated production order. The costs were allowed on the termination settlement proposal even though they were incurred before the effective contract date.

In *Kasler Electric Co.*,[28] the Department of Transportation Contract Appeals Board (DOTCAB) allowed the contractor to recover its pre-award proposal costs on the basis that "... the preaward solicitation analysis serves real functions closely related to fulfilling a contract schedule and is not merely a bid preparation exercise."

The ASBCA ruled in *Aislamientos y Construcciones Apache S.A.*[29] that fees paid to an architect to review building drawings for a roof repair contract during the study of the bid proposal were not precontract costs because they were not incurred in order to meet the contract delivery schedule.

Initial Costs

Typically, it costs a contractor a great deal more to produce the first unit contracted for than the last unit. During the initial stages of many contracts, especially production contracts, the contractor incurs abnormally high direct and indirect labor, material, and administrative costs. The regulations recognize essentially two types of such initial costs: starting-load and preparatory costs. Starting-load costs are the costs resulting from labor inefficiencies and excessive material losses due to inexperienced labor, employee training, changing processing methods, and so forth, during the early stages of a program. Preparatory costs are the costs incurred in preparing to perform the contract, including costs of plant rearrangement and alterations, management and personnel organization, and production planning.

In *Baifield Industries*,[30] the ASBCA decided that a supply contractor was entitled, upon a convenience termination, to recover as preparatory costs the cost of reasonable modifications necessary to outfit an existing facility for contract performance.

The basic issue with initial costs is not one of allocability but of identifiability. The regulations generally allow initial costs if they can be adequately identified and supported. The theory is that if the contract were completed, such costs would be spread over all units and recouped in the total contract price. If a contract is terminated, however, when such costs have been largely expended, they will be allocated only to completed units. As a result, the contractor would suffer a loss though no fault of its own. Therefore, identification and adequate support are the keys to recovering initial costs in a settlement proposal.

The regulations provide that if initial costs are claimed and have not been segregated in the contractor's books, segregation for settlement purposes is to be made from cost reports and schedules reflecting the high unit cost incurred during the early contract stages. Because contractors do not normally account for contract costs in anticipation of a termination and because of the difficulty of identification, contractors rarely segregate initial costs in their formal books of account. As a result, computations will normally be based on informal records, cost reports, budgetary and actual production data, and judgmental estimates.

The relative ease of identifying all allocable initial costs depends on the quality of supporting records, as well as the nature of the costs. Some initial costs should be relatively easy to identify; others will be very difficult.

The following are some initial costs and the records that can be used to support them:

- *Rate of production loss.* These can be based on scrap reports, efficiency reports, spoilage tickets, and the like. In proving excessive losses early in a program, the contractor could use trends and/or rely on historical experience.

- *Initial plant rearrangement and alterations.* These are usually based on a work order or service order, with costs accumulated against the order.

- *Management and personnel organization and production planning.* These are difficult to develop. They may have to be based on estimates using the assistance of technical personnel.

- *Idle time; subnormal production; employee training; and unfamiliarity with the product, materials, or processes.* As production continues, these costs should diminish due to "learning." This learning process may be expressed through the use of the "learning curve" theory. Additionally, many contractors maintain collective data on these factors in the form of efficiency reports, equivalent units produced, and so forth, which are often found to be acceptable support for starting-load costs.

After identifying initial costs, the problem then becomes one of allocating them to the terminated and continuing portions of the contract. Usually, this can be done on the basis of terminated and continuing units. For example, the improvement curve could be used to project total direct labor hours if the contract had been completed. Unit hours can then be determined and applied to the delivered units. The hours allocated could then be deducted from the total hours required to produce the delivered units. The difference could be costed using historical labor and overhead rates to determine the initial costs allocable to the terminated portion of the contract. Depending on the type of contract involved and the nature of the settlement proposal, it may be necessary to use the increased per-unit costs attributable to the nonterminated portion of the contract as a basis for an equitable adjustment.

Two important points should be remembered about initial costs. First, although segregating initial costs is not necessary for cost recovery, the better the accounting for these costs, the easier it will be to identify them and establish their validity in the event of a termination. The other point involves proving the nonrecurring nature of these costs. Unless nonrecurrence can be adequately shown, it may lead to the conclusion that the contract would have been performed at a loss, and the government will seek a loss adjustment to the termination settlement.

Indirect to Direct Reclassifications

Closely related to the issue of initial costs and sometimes involving the same types of costs (e.g., preparatory costs) is the reclassification of costs from indirect to direct. As previously stated, contractors' accounting systems are established to accurately determine costs on contracts expected to be completed, not terminated. Therefore, when a termination occurs, especially in the early stages of contract performance, normal costing procedures will not likely yield reasonable amounts of termination costs. As a result, it is frequently necessary to reclassify costs from an indirect to a direct charge to fairly and accurately represent the real cost allocable to the terminated contract. While such reallocations are specifically allowed for post-termination settlement expenses, they may also be appropriate for costs incurred before the termination notice.

Often, there is no relationship in terms of time between the incurrence of overhead and other indirect costs and their recoupment when allocated to contracts. Contractors must abandon their usual accounting methods for the allocating indirect expenses. They must directly identify all the cost elements concerned with the contract performance to ensure that they will recover all the expenses incurred as of the effective termination date. This applies to all categories of costs included in indirect expenses, such as engineering, purchasing, top management, plant management, production control, first-line supervisors, and so on.

In *Agrinautics*,[31] the Board allowed the reclassification of engineering labor from the engineering overhead and general and administrative (G&A) pools to direct labor. In the Board's view: "Not to allow the reclassification would result in a windfall to respondent and an unwarranted loss to appellant of cost incurred specifically for the contract."

Conventional accounting methods may not be suitable for preparing termination claims, since an allocation based on direct labor, or a similar base, often results in an inadequate recovery. For example, assume that a contractor received a production contract for which most of the required material was purchased and received in the early stages of performance. Also assume that purchasing and receiving expenses are normally charged to a manufacturing overhead pool that is allocated to contracts on the basis of direct labor hours. It is apparent that in the early stages of the contract, when few direct labor hours have been expended, an allocation of manufacturing overhead using direct labor hours will not produce equitable results. Therefore, direct costing of the purchasing and receiving expenses would be more appropriate in the circumstances.

Recognizing the problem, however, is considerably easier than implementing an acceptable solution. Once a contractor departs from its usual, accepted accounting practices, there is an implication of "double counting" (i.e., charging the same type of cost indirectly in one instance and directly in another). The regulations and cost accounting standards (CAS), however, provide an escape clause. Double counting may exist only for "costs incurred for the same purpose, in like circumstances." Therefore, inconsistent treatment of indirect costs in a termination claim may be justified as not "like circumstances." The CAS Steering Committee interim guidance W.G. 77-15 contains further details on this issue.

As can be seen from this discussion, it is very important to review terminated contracts to determine if any special situations require indirect to direct reclassification. Such reclassification can significantly affect the ultimate costs recovered in a termination settlement.

Common Items

Common items are materials that are common to both the terminated contract and the contractor's other work. The regulations state that the cost of common items that are reasonably usable on the contractor's other work is not allocable in a termination claim unless the contractor can show that it could not retain such items at cost without sustaining a loss. The items must be usable specifically by the contractor; it is not enough to show that the items are commonly used in the industry. It seems reasonable for the government to decline to accept and pay for materials that the contractor can reasonably use in its normal work without sustaining a loss. The key considerations involving common items are the phrases "reasonably usable" and "retain without sustaining a loss."

When materials are common to a contractor's other work but when the amount resulting from the termination would be largely in excess of the contractor's usual inventory, the retention of the material might adversely affect its cash or working capital position and result in a financial hardship. In such cases, common items need not be so classified. The contractor is not expected to retain common items acquired for the contract if the quantities on hand and on order exceed its reasonable requirements. To show this, a contractor must present convincing evidence that plans and production orders are insufficient to merit retention of the material. If the contractor has no other work and, despite sufficient efforts, is unable to obtain any work, it need not retain the common items, for doing so would result in a loss. This principle was affirmed by the ASBCA in *Southland Manufacturing Corp.*[32] It is clear that common items are not automatically unallowable, but, rather, their allowability is a factual matter.

The retention of a large inventory does not in itself entitle the contractor to claim an amount for excess inventory, however. When the inventory can be used within a reasonable period, regardless of size, the excess inventory claim will likely not be accepted. In *Symetrics Industries, Inc.*,[33] the ASBCA sustained the TCO's finding that 300 telemetry sets, which were transferred to a successor contract, met the definition of a "common item." Because the contractor was unable to prove that the items were transferred at a loss, the claim for recovery of an alleged lost quantity discount on the termination settlement proposal was denied.

Under FAR 45.605.2, contractors may return excess inventory to suppliers for full credit, less a normal restocking charge or 25% of cost, whichever is less. They may also seek reimbursement in the termination settlement proposal for transportation, handling, and restocking charges. Returning excess inventory to suppliers may represent a reasonable resolution of this problem.

In some cases, contractors may negotiate an allowance for reworking and rewarehousing to retain inventory items with the TCO's approval.

Production supplies are normally part of overhead; however, if unusually large quantities are purchased or are not the kind used in the contractor's unterminated business, it is acceptable to include these as well in a request for reimbursement of excess inventory.

Nonspecification Inventory

As the name implies, nonspecification inventory is the contract inventory on hand at termination that does not comply in all respects with specification requirements. Because the regulations are not specific, cost recoverability for nonspecification inventory has evolved through case law. The basic issues affecting allowability of these costs have been: (1) reasonableness; (2) whether due to contractor or government fault; (3) whether the items are reworkable; and (4) the government's right to assess the costs of correcting the deficiencies. Generally, the costs of nonspecification inventory are recoverable if they are reasonable, whether due to contractor or government fault, and whether the items are reworkable.

Reasonableness has been viewed in relation to the procurement's circumstances. Key considerations in determining reasonableness are the degree of difficulty in producing a product to specification and the stage of performance at which the contract is terminated. Obviously, the more complex or difficult the production process and the earlier in a contract's planned performance period that the contract is terminated, the more significant nonspecification material would be.

The boards of contract appeals have held that the costs of producing defective work are normally reimbursable under a cost-reimbursement contract, unless it is established that the defective production resulted from the contractor's careless work conduct. Moreover, although a fixed-price contractor is not entitled to be paid for items that do not comply with specification requirements, a termination for convenience deprives the contractor of the opportunity to recoup expenses associated with defective work incurred in the early stages of performance. Therefore, the general effect of a termination for convenience of a fixed-price contract is to convert the terminated portion into a cost-reimbursement contract.

The precedent that the government is barred from asserting offset claims for corrective work, as established in prior ASBCA decisions, such as *New York Shipbuilding*,[34] was indirectly repudiated in *Lisbon Contractors, Inc. v. United States*,[35] *Air Cool, Inc.*,[36] and *Aydin Corp.*[37] The ASBCA reaffirmed the principles of *New York Shipbuilding*, however, in *E.R. Mandocdoc Construction Co.*[38] in finding that the government's election to terminate the construction contract for convenience effectively converted the fixed-price contract to a cost-reimbursement-type contract, entitling E.R. Mandocdoc to recover allowable costs for the performance of the terminated work. The government lost whatever right it might have had to recover the cost of rust removal and refurbishment of the damaged materials when it prevented the performance of the uncompleted work by terminating the contract for convenience.

Continuing Costs/Loss of Useful Value

As a general rule, the termination clauses in government contracts require that all work be stopped for any portion of a terminated contract. While it is anticipated that all work will be stopped almost immediately, it is also recognized that not all activities, nor the incurrence of all costs, can be immediately halted. The incurrence of some costs will continue for a period after a contract is terminated. The nature of the costs and the actions taken to mitigate or prevent their incurrence will determine their acceptability as part of a termination settlement proposal. The government will resist payment of any costs that are attributed solely to a loss of business. This concept will be discussed later in this chapter under Unabsorbed Overhead.

The costs of idle facilities and idle capacity are not specifically addressed in the termination cost principle. However, FAR 31.205-17 recognizes that idle facilities and idle capacity may result from a contract termination and may be allowable. In *Celesco Industries, Inc.*,[39] the ASBCA allowed the costs of two buildings as idle facilities for five weeks following the contract termination. The buildings were assigned for the exclusive use of the project during contract performance and remained idle for four months after the termination. Because nothing in the record supported the four-month period of idleness as necessary or reasonable, the Board decided that five weeks was a reasonable period for dismantling the production line and making the buildings available for other purposes.

In *Lowell O. West Lumber Sales*,[40] the ASBCA ruled that costs may be recovered when it is impossible to discontinue those costs and expenses in spite of all reasonable efforts to stop work immediately. Included in this category, among other items allowed in this case, was depreciation expense from the termination date until the date the contract was originally anticipated to be completed.

In *Baifield Industries, Division of A-T-O, Inc.,*[41] the contractor was entitled to recover continuing costs, such as plant rent, security, depreciation, and maintenance, pending disposal of its plant equipment (rendered completely idle by the termination) and its termination inventory. The government contended that the costs did not bear a necessary relationship to the termination but rather to A-T-O's overall corporate needs. The Board responded with the following significant points:

> The government correctly states that neither the plant nor some of the equipment installed therein were acquired by A-T-O or appellant specifically for performance of the ... contract. However, that fact does not control the disposition of appellant's claim. The cost principles applicable to continuing contract costs do not condition allowability upon the acquisition of facilities, etc., solely for performance of the terminated contract. The relationship which must be shown is a clear connection between the costs claimed and the terminated contract and, further, that those costs could not have been reasonably shut off upon the termination.

The government also contended that the company, by delaying its disposition of inventory and equipment, did not obtain the best possible price. The Board's opinion was that the company exercised reasonable business judgment with regard to its disposition of termination inventory and equipment and that the government was not entitled to second guess the judgment. The amounts allowed were incurred over a 10-month period, which the Board concluded was reasonable and consistent with the additional time needed to complete the contract had it not been terminated.

In *Fiesta Leasing and Sales, Inc.,*[42] the ASBCA allowed the continuing costs of depreciation on buses used on a bus lease contract terminated by the government. The depreciation was allowed over the full 18-month lease period, even though the contract was terminated very early in contract performance. After termination, the company immediately attempted to mitigate the government's damages by advertising to sell some of the buses. When the buses could not be sold, the company began placing the buses under long-term leases and a daily rental program. All income from the lease and daily rental programs was credited to the government in the termination claim. In allowing the depreciation costs, the Board stated that "such depreciation costs are appropriately recoverable as continuing costs under Defense Acquisition Regulation (DAR) 15-205.42(b) where, as here, they could not be reasonably discontinued immediately upon termination. ... There is ... a clear connection between the costs claimed and the terminated contract and it is clear to us that these costs could not be discontinued immediately upon termination."

In *American Electric, Inc.,*[43] the Board held that production assets acquired by the contractor for contract performance had lost their useful value as a result of the termination. The Board concluded the following:

> The value of these assets is to be found in their ability to assist in the production of revenue in the future. Capital physical assets are, of course, ones of limited economic life and which are consumed (in an economic, not physical, sense) during the production of goods. The cost of this type of asset is amortized over the period of its useful life. The amortization for this type of asset is known, of course, as depreciation. Since the assets which we are discussing were obtained solely for one contract their utility or useful life was tied to and dependent upon that one contract. If that contract is terminated, the contractor has suffered a loss since the assets have lost their value, i.e., their ability to assist in the production of future revenue. That loss is what the ASPR cost principle was designated to compensate a contractor for. The termination gives rise to a need to treat the costs differently than they would normally be treated.

Finally, in *Essex Electro Engineers, Inc.*,[44] the Board ruled that the contractor could recover the full cost of residual equipment remaining at a plant when the contract was terminated for convenience. The government argued that a portion of the equipment constituted "common items" and, as such, would not be allowable since such equipment could be used on other contracts. However, the equipment was in excess of the contractor's current and future needs and, as such, no reasonable use of the equipment could be made without a loss to the contractor. Because the equipment was not judged to be "common items," the full amount claimed was allowed.

Unexpired Leases

Under the FAR termination cost principle, the costs for the unexpired portion of leases that were reasonably required for contract performance may be an allowable charge in the termination settlement. The contractor must show that all reasonable efforts were made to terminate, assign, settle, or otherwise reduce the costs of the lease.

- In *Sundstrand Turbo, a Division of Sundstrand Corp. v. United States*,[45] the Court of Claims allowed recovery of rental costs and idle space costs for 11 months following the date of termination; this period coincided with the scheduled contract completion date.
- In *Baifield Industries*,[46] the Board allowed the continuing rent on the unexpired lease until the sublessee took over the payments, concluding that the company's efforts to dispose of the plant after the termination were reasonable in the circumstances. When the contract was terminated, the company no longer needed its manufacturing plant where the contract was being performed; however, it needed to retain the plant until completing disposition of the inventory and equipment. The plant was being leased under a long-term lease arrangement with an unaffiliated lessor. Although the company diligently attempted to dispose of the plant on a timely basis, its attempts were unsuccessful. Attempts to interest other companies (including other divisions of Baifield Industries' parent A-T-O) in subleasing the plant were also unsuccessful, primarily because of the plant's relatively isolated location. The company finally located an interested sublessee, which assumed the rental obligation.
- The ASBCA reached a similar conclusion in *Southland Manufacturing Corp.*[47] The Board (1) concluded that Southland had made a reasonable effort to cancel or otherwise dispose of a building lease, and (2) allowed continuing lease costs after termination until the building was sublet to an outside party.

Severance Costs

Severance pay may be allowed for employees who would have worked on the terminated contract. Although the FAR does not expressly address the recovery of severance pay on terminated contracts, such costs have been addressed by the boards of contract appeals. For example, in *General Electric Co.*,[48] the Board concluded that severance pay costs were directly chargeable to the terminated contract as long as the costs met the general allowability and reasonableness criteria. However, cases have not specifically addressed the question of whether severance pay may be recovered for employees who had been working on a terminated contract but who were reassigned to other positions in the company, thereby displacing other employees who were terminated.

Settlement Expenses

The cost principles recognize that certain costs will be incurred, as a direct result of a termination, that would not have been incurred under normal contract performance. These costs are associated with stopping performance, terminating and settling subcontracts, and preparing and settling the termination proposal. Federal Acquisition Regulations 31.205-42(g) provides that the following costs are generally allowable:

- Accounting, legal, clerical, and similar costs reasonably necessary for preparing and presenting to TCOs settlement claims and supporting data on the terminated contract portion and for terminating and settling subcontracts.
- Reasonable costs for storage, transportation, protection, and disposition of property acquired for the contract.
- Indirect costs related to salaries and wages incurred as settlement expenses. Normally, such costs are limited to payroll taxes, fringe benefits, occupancy costs, and immediate supervision.

Federal Acquisition Regulation 31.205-42(g)(2) requires that settlement expenses, if significant, be separately identified and accumulated. This separation of settlement expenses from other expenses is the contractor's responsibility. One area that should be specifically considered is legal and accounting fees. Such fees incurred in connection with a termination settlement, including the preparation of the settlement proposal, are acceptable settlement expenses. Other legal fees are not. This was addressed in great detail in *A.C.E.S., Inc.*,[49] in which the ASBCA, in relying on prior cases, noted that "for recovery of legal fees as settlement expenses, claimants have been required to make a showing that the legal expenses claimed were incurred in 'settlement negotiations with the contracting officer'... as distinguished from litigation or other nonsettlement activities."

Accordingly, when a termination notice is received, a separate account or work order should be established to collect and separately identify legal and accounting fees associated with the termination.

The boards[50] and courts have generally allowed outside legal and accounting fees as settlement expenses under the following conditions:

- Both the rate per hour and the time charged are reasonable considering the complexity of the termination claim and the nature of the work performed.
- The contractor has limited experience in government contracts, in general, or in termination claims, in particular, and the outside legal and accounting advisors have the necessary expertise.
- Services performed are consistent with the level of expertise.
- Time charged is supported by records indicating specific descriptions of activities performed.

Other significant issues related to the allowability of settlement expenses should be kept in mind. Anyone involved in supporting a termination settlement proposal should keep a contemporaneous record of time charged to the termination and identify the specific activity performed. Any costs normally charged to overhead or G&A expenses should be excluded from such indirect expenses if the costs are charged directly as a settlement expense.

The government may attempt to disallow a portion of settlement expenses on the basis that such expenses represent an unreasonable percentage of a total claim. However, the boards have generally concluded that the reasonableness of settlement expenses is determined by analyzing the specific expenses claimed, not by an arbitrary percentage.

Profit

As previously noted, the settlement of a contract terminated for the government's convenience includes the negotiation of the profit on preparations made to perform the contract (e.g., initial costs) and the work that was actually performed (not including settlement expenses). Anticipatory profits and consequential damages are not allowed. Any reasonable method may be used to arrive at a fair settlement. Generally, the factors to be considered in determining the profit in a termination for convenience action are not unlike those considered in other pricing actions for contract changes. While many of these relate to the contract as a whole, special consideration should be given to the relative complexity of the tasks and risk performed in the early contract stages. Generally, management attention and financial investments are greater in the early periods of contract performance than in the later stages. The proposed profit settlement should reflect any such differences.

In *Lockley Manufacturing Co., Inc.*,[51] the ASBCA limited the profit rate for the terminated portion of the contract to the rate actually experienced by the contractor. The ASBCA stated that it "perceives no reason why the adjustment should provide the appellant more profit than it would have realized had the contract been completed on time." Determining the appropriate profit level does not necessarily follow this rule. Federal Acquisition Regulation 49.202(b) identifies nine factors that should be considered in negotiating an appropriate profit rate on work performed on the terminated portion of the contract.

1. Extent and difficulty of work performed compared to the total work required by the contract

2. Extent of engineering, production scheduling, planning, technical study, and supervision

3. Contractor efficiency, particularly relating to quantity and quality of production; cost reduction; use of materials, personnel, and facilities; and disposition of termination inventory

4. Amount and source of capital and extent of risk assumed

5. Inventive and developmental contributions and cooperation in providing technical assistance

6. Nature of the business

7. Rate of profit that would have been earned had the contract been completed

8. Rate of profit both parties contemplated at the time the contract was negotiated

9. Character and difficulty of subcontracting

In *Quality Seeding, Inc.*,[52] the Interior Board of Contract Appeals evaluated the first seven factors enumerated here (the last two factors did not apply because the contract was awarded pursuant to sealed bidding and had no subcontracts). The Board determined that had the contract been completed, the contractor would have earned a profit rate of 46.4%. In accepting that rate as the appropriate rate for application to costs incurred on the contract, the Board observed:

> All of the factors can be related to a contractor's excellence but particularly (2) (engineering other pre-production work), (3) (efficiency), and (5) (inventiveness). The underlying presumption is that the excellence and competence of the contractor, which promises a good result for the Government, should be rewarded even when the work is not completed as a result of the termination for convenience.

> The record makes clear, as discussed above, that the great bulk of the work ... had already been done.

In *Marathon Construction Corp.*,[53] the GSBCA denied recovery of profit on materials not delivered, based on the provisions of FAR 49.202(a), which provide that, [p]rofits shall not be allowed the contractor for material or services that, as of the effective date of termination, have not been delivered by a subcontractor, regardless of the percentage of completion."

Federal Acquisition Regulation 49.203 provides that if a contractor would have suffered a loss on a fixed-price contract if it were completed, that anticipated rate of loss should be reflected in the termination settlement. This is to ensure that the contractor does not use the contract termination as a "bail out" from a contract loss.

When a fixed-price contract is terminated during the early stages of contract performance, the government may have to assume that the contract, if performed to anticipated completion, would have resulted in a profit. However, if a substantial amount of the work has been performed or if substantial costs have been incurred, the government will likely attempt to estimate the total costs that would have been incurred had the contract been completed in order to determine whether or not a loss would have been experienced. While the government may request the contractor to prepare this estimate, there is no contractual obligation to do so. Whether it should be done depends on the specific circumstances of each case. If the government prepares an estimate to complete, consideration should be given to expected production efficiencies.[54] This has been interpreted to mean that, among other things, the application of the learning-curve theory should be considered.

If it is determined that a loss would have been experienced, the loss adjustment is developed by relating the total contract price to the total cost incurred before the termination, plus the estimated costs to complete the entire contract. The resulting percentage is applied to those costs accepted by the government (excluding settlement expenses) to determine the total termination costs allowed outside of settlement expenses. Profit will not be allowed.

Federal Acquisition Regulations 49.203(b) and (c) describe the methods for determining the maximum to be paid on inventory and total cost settlements. Simply stated, the loss formula is as follows:

$$\text{Proposed settlement} \times \frac{\text{Contract price}}{\text{Estimate at completion}}$$

The loss factor calculation is illustrated in Figure 12.1.

Contract Data	
Total contract price (50 units @ $24,000 each)	$1,200,000
Total amount invoiced for completed units (35 units @ $24,000 each)	$ 840,000
Total costs incurred under the contract	$1,350,000
Estimate of cost to complete contract	$ 150,000
Settlement with subcontractor	4 50,000
Settlement expenses	$ 10,000
Disposal credits	$ 50,000
Units completed and delivered before termination	35
Units completed and on hand and not to be delivered	5
Units terminated	10
Termination Settlement Basis—Inventory Basis (SF 1435)	

Contract Settlement			
Description	SF 1435 Line No.	Proposed Settlement	Adjusted for Loss (FAR 49.203)
Finished components	4	$ 70,000	
Work in progress	6	32,500	
Special tooling	7	20,000	
Other costs	8	30,000	
G&A expenses	9	10,000	
Settlements with subcontractors	14	50,000	
Total cost before settlement expense		212,500	170,000*
Settlement expenses	12	10,000	10,000
Profit		20,000	
Acceptable finished product		110,000	110,000
Less disposal credit		(50,000)	(50,000)
Net payment requested		$302,500	$240,000

$$\text{*Application of loss formula} \qquad \$212{,}500 \quad \frac{\$1{,}200{,}000}{\$1{,}500{,}000} = 170{,}000$$

Figure 12.1   Application of Loss Adjustment

The courts have consistently recognized that the application of a loss factor may be inappropriate when the cost overrun or loss is due to government action or inaction. Examples of government action or inaction include directed or constructive changes, government-caused delays, deficient specifications, or impossibility of performance. The existence of any of these conditions would entitle the contractor to an equitable adjustment that may remove the contract from its loss position.

In *Wolfe Construction Co.*,[55] the government was not entitled to apply a loss adjustment because the contract was not, in fact, in a loss position since the government was responsible for the cost increases the contractor experienced. The Board concluded that since "the government's pervasive maladministration of the contracts caused numerous claim events warranting upward adjustments of the contract prices … the government should not be permitted to benefit from a chaotic pricing situation it created."

In *M. E. Brown*,[56] the contractor was entitled to recover profit even though the contract was terminated before the CO issued the notice to proceed with the contract and no costs were incurred in performing actual contract requirements. Since costs were incurred (site visits and visits to the government office) as a result of the constructive suspension of work, the contractor was entitled to the application of profit on these costs.

If the contract can be shown to be impossible to perform, the loss adjustment would also not be appropriate. In *Scope Electronics, Inc.*,[57] the ASBCA stated that "the fact that the appellant performed unsuccessfully in a loss position has no effect on the termination allowance since we are convinced that performance of this contract was objectively impossible."

In *Astro-Dynamics, Inc.*,[58] the ASBCA concluded that the loss calculation did not apply to situations in which the government substantially contributed to the increased costs, and it was not possible to separate that portion of the loss from possible losses caused by the contractor. The Board's opinion stated:

> ... [T]he bases for our holding that the termination for default was improper and that the termination should be converted to one for the convenience of the government were that: the specifications and drawings were defective; the government's thread gauges were defective and that the rejection of the motor tubes was in part due to these defective gags; the government constructively changed the contract when it imposed a standard of acceptability higher than that required by the contract when it inspected the threads with an optical comparator; and the government constructively changed the contract when it reimposed the original tolerances specified in the contract.
>
> In view ... of the foregoing, all that was required of appellant was its submission of a total cost termination settlement proposal for settlement or determination by the contracting officer.

If directed and constructive changes have occurred before termination, FAR 49.114 provides for the TCO to "settle, as part of the final settlement, all unsettled contract changes." To assist in the settlement process, a request for equitable adjustment proposal identifying costs attributable to directed and constructive changes should be prepared and provided to the TCO, along with the termination settlement proposal. However, in unusual situations, such as when the contractor was provided defective specifications, it may be extremely difficult or even impossible to objectively identify and quantify the costs of the constructive changes. In such circumstances, the contractor may have no choice except to simply submit a total cost termination settlement proposal. This circumstance was addressed in *Astro-Dynamics, Inc.*,[59] in which the Board rejected the government's contentions that:

> ... the Board lacks jurisdiction because appellant has not submitted a separate claim for an equitable adjustment for costs relating to alleged constructive changes. ... [and that] each claim submitted to the contracting officer must contain sufficient detail to notify the contracting officer of the basic factual allegations upon which the claim is premised so as to allow the contracting officer to properly exercise discretion and make an informed decision on the claim. Without such information, the contracting officer has no obligation to issue a decision that can be appealed to the Board.

Unabsorbed Overhead

The subject of unabsorbed overhead warrants special attention. In the case of equitable price adjustments resulting from delays or disruptions, the courts and boards of contract appeals have defined "unabsorbed overhead" simply as the additional amount of overhead that ongoing contracts had to bear because the contractor could not continue working on a contract due to government action. Thus, the other contracts had to pick up overhead that would have otherwise been absorbed by the delayed or terminated contract.

The boards and courts generally have accepted unabsorbed overhead in the case of delays and disruptions, but not in the case of complete terminations. The rationale for these different conclusions are not found in statutes or regulations, which are silent on this issue, but rather in case law decisions.

Unabsorbed overhead was generally allowed on the mass terminations that occurred at the end of World War II. The first edition of ASPR, as well as subsequent revisions, did not specifically address this subject. In 1965, after experiencing problems with contract auditors and TCOs, industry requested the ASPR committee to address unabsorbed overhead. The Department of Defense (DOD) policy group concluded that such action was unnecessary but gave no indication whether it was for or against allowing unabsorbed overhead when contracts were completely terminated. In 1971, industry tried again in a recommendation to the Commission on Government Procurement. The Council of Defense and Space Industry Associations unsuccessfully requested that formal recognition be given to continuing costs under contracts terminated for the government's convenience, including "unabsorbed ongoing fixed overhead which would have to be unfairly absorbed against other business of the contractor, if not allowed on the termination claim." About that time, certain government officials took the initiative and proposed an ASPR revision to specifically cite unabsorbed overhead as unallowable under terminated contracts. The ASPR committee closed the case without a definitive decision.

Prior to 1993, the boards and courts were decidedly negative in decisions relating to the recovery of unabsorbed costs after the date of termination. For instance, in *Chamberlain Manufacturing Corp.*,[60] the ASBCA concluded the following:

> The continuing costs to which ASPR 15-205.42 refers clearly are only those costs directly related to the terminated contract which cannot reasonably be shut off immediately upon termination. It is obvious that appellant's overhead is a cost which will continue so long as appellant continues to exist as an ongoing organization and is thus not directly related to the terminated contract. ... Moreover, the continuation of overhead after a termination is a common occurrence and if the drafters of the regulation had intended to allow such costs they could have done so simply and clearly as they did for rental costs.

In *Pioneer Recovery Systems, Inc.*,[61] the ASBCA expanded on the above decision in observing the following:

> ... [T]he board recognizes that in individual instances the impact of a termination on overhead absorption may be practically indistinguishable from the impact of a comparable suspension of work, where unabsorbed overhead may be recoverable. But, in view of the innumerable circumstances in which delays or terminations may result in under absorption, or even "over absorption" (e.g., opportunity for more profitable business), and in view of the long standing precedent, construing ASPR 15-205.42, any change in the rule should be a matter for regulatory consideration.

However, the ASBCA concluded, in 1993 that *Industrial Pump & Compressor, Inc.*[62] was entitled to an equitable adjustment for unabsorbed overhead on a contract that experienced a government-caused delay and was subsequently terminated for convenience. The Board awarded Industrial Pump & Compressor the difference between the indirect costs that would have been allocated to the contract had the delay not occurred and the amount of indirect costs allocated to the contract as a result of the delay and subsequent termination, as shown below:

	Estimated Costs	Actual Costs	Difference (Unabsorbed Overhead)
Direct Labor	$ 464,437	$ 62,721	
Overhead Rate	78.4%	144.2%	
	$ 363,934	$ 90,458	$273,476
Total Cost Input	$1,750,336	$446,256	
G&A Exp. Rate	10.2%	16.2%	
	$ 178,534	$ 72,293	106,241
Total Unabsorbed Overhead			$379,717

The cost of the disruptive effects of partial termination can generally be adequately recovered through equitable price adjustments for the continuing portion. Without quite spelling it out, the boards of contract appeals and the courts have looked sympathetically at unabsorbed overhead in determining the cost of the continuing items, as they have in instances of delays and disruptions attributable to the government.

12-5. CASH FLOW

Terminated cost-type contracts remain eligible for uninterrupted cost recovery, via submission of public vouchers, for six months. Thus, major costs incurred during a protracted termination settlement process (subcontract settlements, severance pay, etc.) are eligible for immediate recovery. Such is not the case with terminated fixed-price contracts. Fixed-price contracts that are terminated for convenience experience immediate drains on cash flow. Partial payments on a terminated fixed-price contract can be requested only after an interim or final termination settlement proposal has been submitted. Large contract termination proposals can require months to prepare (the FAR permits prime contractors one year). During this intervening period, no cash flow mechanism is available, even though significant termination costs are being incurred. The National Security Industrial Association proposed a revision to FAR 49.209[63] that would permit interim cash flow recovery for fixed-price terminated contracts. Such relief is sorely needed.

12-6. SUMMARY

For companies contracting with the federal government, the possibility that the contract may be terminated is a "fact of life." While the results of a termination are usually less than desired, several actions must be taken to mitigate any adverse impact. Paramount among these is the need to evaluate the contractor's financial position at the time of the termination and the reasons for that position. This may entail redefining the appropriate accounting practices that must be used to measure the results of operations for the terminated work. After this, the process of negotiating a settlement can begin using the procedures appropriate to this unique environment.

12-7. NOTES

1. United States v. Corliss Steam-Engine Co., 91 U.S. 3211 (1876).
2. G.L. Christian and Associates v. United States, 160 Ct. Cl. 58, July 12, 1963, 320 F.2d 345; cert. denied, 375 U.S. 954 (1963, 9 CCF 72,180.)
3. Composite Laminates, Inc. v. United States, COFC No. 91-879C, Dec. 15, 1992, 27 Fed. Cl. 310 (1992).
4. Aerospace Engineering & Support, Inc., ASBCA No 47520, May 18, 1995, 95-2 BCA 27,702. See also Lafayette Coal Co., ASBCA No 32174, May 9, 1989, 89-3 BCA 21,963.
5. Kelso v. Kirk Bros. Mechanical Contractors, Inc., CAFC No. 92-1567, 93-1011, Jan. 13, 1994, 16 F.3d 1173.
6. National Interior Contractors, Inc., ASBCA 47131, July 31, 1996, 96-2 BCA 28,460.
7. Melville Energy Systems v. United States, CAFC No. 95-5150, Dec. 1, 1995, 33 Fed. Cl. 616.
8. Technical Ordnance, Inc., ASBCA No. 48086, June 13, 1995, 95-2 BCA 27,744.
9. Defense Systems Corp. and Hi-Shear Technology Corp., ASBCA Nos. 42,939, 42940, 43530, 43705, 44131, 44551 and 44835, May 24, 1995, 95-2 BCA 27,721.
10. McDonnell Douglas Corp. and General Dynamics Corp. v. United States, No. 91-1204C, April 8, 1996, 35 Fed. Cl. 358.
11. Alta Construction Co., PSBCA Nos. 1463 and 2920, Sept. 15, 1995, 96-1 BCA 27,961.
12. Alaska Pulp Corp. v. United States, Sept. 28, 1995, COFC No. 95-153C; 34 Fed. Cl. 100.
13. Colonial Metals Co. v. United States, 204 Ct. Cl. 320, April, 17, 1974, 494 F.2d 1355.
14. Ronald A. Torncello and Soledad Enterprises, Inc. v. United States, Ct. Cl. 1982, June 16, 1982, No. 486-80C, 681 F.2d 756.
15. Automated Services, Inc., DOTBCA No. 1753, Nov. 25, 1986, 87-1 BCA 19,459.
16. Caldwell & Santmyer, Inc. v. Secretary of Agriculture, CAFC No. 94-1314, June 8, 1995, 55 F.3d 1578.
17. Krygoski Construction Co., Inc., CAFC No. 53-5136, Aug. 1, 1996, 94 F.3d 1537.
18. Do-Well Machine Shop, Inc., ASBCA No. 36090, June 29, 1988, 88-3 BCA 20,994; aff'd. CAFC No. 88-1534, March 14, 1989, 870 F.2d 637.
19. Planning Research Corp., Inc., GSBCA No. 11286-COM, 96-1 BCA 27,954.
20. Pulsar Data Systems, Inc., GSBCA No. 13223, June 25, 1996, 96-2 BCA 28,407.
21. Codex Corp. v. United States, 226 Ct. Cl. 693, Feb. 24, 1981, 652 F.2d 69.
22. General Electric Co., ASBCA No. 24111, March 29, 1982, 82-1 BCA 15,725.
23. Algonac Manufacturing Co., ASBCA No. 10534, Aug. 1, 1966, 66-2 BCA 5,731.
24. Clary Corp., ASBCA No. 19274, Nov. 1, 1974, 74-2 BCA 10,947.
25. RHC Construction, IBCA No. 2083, July 26, 1988, 88-3 BCA 20,991.
26. Bank of America, ASBCA No. 1881, 1978, 78-2 BCA 13,365.
27. General Electric Co., supra, note 22.
28. Kasler Electric Co., DOTCAB No. 1425, 84-2 BCA 17,374.
29. Aislamientos y Construcciones Apache S.A., ASBCA No. 45,437, Oct. 31, 1996, 97-1 BCA 28,632.
30. Baifield Industries, Division of A-T-O, Inc., ASBCA No. 20006, Aug. 18, 1976, 76-2 BCA 12,096.
31. Agrinautics, ASBCA Nos. 21512, 21608, and 21609, Oct. 24, 1979, 79-2 BCA 14,149.
32. Southland Manufacturing Corp., ASBCA No. 16830, Nov. 29, 1974, 75-1 BCA 10,994.
33. Symetrics Industries, Inc., ASBCA No. 48529, April 8, 1996, 96-2 BCA 28,285.
34. New York Shipbuilding Co., A Division of Merritt–Chapman & Scott Corp., ASBCA No. 15443, Dec. 21, 1972, 73-1 BCA 9,852.
35. Lisbon Contractors, Inc. v. United States, CAFC No. 86-1461, Sept. 9, 1987, 828 F.2d 759.
36. Air Cool, Inc., ASBCA No. 32838, Dec. 3, 1987, 88-1 BCA 20,399.
37. Aydin Corp., EBCA No. 355-5-86, June 1, 1989, 89-3 BCA 22,044.
38. E.R. Mandocdoc Construction Co., ASBCA No. 43701, July 14, 1995, 95-2 BCA 27,800.
39. Celesco Industries, Inc., ASBCA No. 22460, March 30, 1984, 84-2 BCA 17,295.
40. Lowell O. West Lumber Sales, ASBCA No. 10879, Jan. 18, 1967, 67-1 BCA 6,101.
41. Baifield Industries, Division of A-T-O, Inc., supra, note 30.
42. Fiesta Leasing and Sales, Inc., ASBCA No. 29311, Jan. 30, 1987, 87-1 BCA 19,622., aff'd. Jan. 13, 1988, 88-1 BCA 20,499.
43. American Electric, Inc., ASBCA No. 16635, Sept. 27, 1976, 76-2 BCA 12,151, aff'd. in part, Oct. 5, 1977, 77-2 BCA 12,792.
44. Essex Electro Engineers, Inc., DOTCAB Nos. 1025 and 1119, Dec. 11, 1980, 81-1 BCA 14,838.
45. Sundstrand Turbo, a Division of Sundstrand Corp. v. United States, ASBCA No. 9112, Jan. 29, 1965, 65-1 BCA 4,653.
46. Baifield Industries, Division of A-T-O, Inc., supra, note 30.

47. Southland Manufacturing Corp., supra, note 32.

48. General Electric Co., supra, note 22.

49. A.C.E.S., Inc., ASBCA No. 21417, March 23, 1979, 79-1 BCA 13,809.

50. Fiesta Leasing and Sales, Inc., supra, note 42.

51. Lockley Manufacturing Co., Inc., ASBCA No. 21231, Jan. 26, 1978, 78-1 BCA 12,987.

52. Quality Seeding, Inc., IBCA No. 2297, Aug. 8, 1988, 88-3 BCA 21,020.

53. Marathon Construction Corp., GSBCA No. 13054-IWC, Sept. 11, 1995, 96-1 BCA 27,931.

54. Codex Corp. v. United States, supra, note 21.

55. Wolfe Construction Co., ENGBCA No. 5309, Sept. 9, 1988, BCA 88-3, 21,122.

56. M.E. Brown, ASBCA No. 40043, Aug. 28, 1990, BCA 91-1, 23,293.

57. Scope Electronics, Inc., ASBCA No. 20359, Feb. 16, 1977, 77-1 BCA 12,404.

58. Astro-Dynamics, Inc., ASBCA No. 41825, Feb. 27, 1991, 91-2 BCA 23,807.

59. Ibid.

60. Chamberlain Manufacturing Corp., ASBCA No. 16877, June 22, 1973, 73-2 BCA 10,139.

61. Pioneer Recovery Systems, Inc., ASBCA No. 24658, Feb. 20, 1981, 81-1 BCA 15,059.

62. Industrial Pump & Compressor, Inc., ASBCA No. 39003, Jan. 13, 1993, 93-1 BCA 25,757.

63. Letter from the President, National Security Industrial Association, dated April 17, 1992, to the Director of Defense Procurement, Department of Defense.

SETTLEMENT PROPOSAL FOR COST-REIMBURSEMENT TYPE CONTRACTS

FORM APPROVED OMB NO.
9000-0012

Public reporting burden for this collection of information is estimated to average 2.5 hours per response, including the time for reviewing instructions, searching existing data sources, gathering and maintaining the data needed, and completing and reviewing the collection of information. Send comments regarding this burden estimate or any other aspect of this collection of information, including suggestions for reducing this burden, to the FAR Secretariat (VRS), Office of Federal Acquisition and Regulatory Policy, GSA, Washington, D.C. 20405; and to the Office of Management and Budget, Paperwork Reduction Project (9000-0012), Washington, D.C. 20503.

To be used by prime contractors submitting settlement proposals on cost-reimbursement type contracts under Part 49 of the Federal Acquisition Regulation. Also suitable for use in connection with terminated cost-reimbursement type subcontracts.

COMPANY	PROPOSAL NUMBER	CHECK ONE □ PARTIAL □ FINAL
STREET ADDRESS	GOVERNMENT PRIME CONTRACT NO.	REFERENCE NO.
CITY AND STATE (Include ZIP Code)	EFFECTIVE DATE OF TERMINATION	

ITEM (a)	TOTAL PREVIOUSLY SUBMITTED (b)	INCREASE OR DECREASE BY THIS PROPOSAL (c)	TOTAL SUBMITTED TO DATE (d)
1. DIRECT MATERIAL	$	$	$
2. DIRECT LABOR			
3. INDIRECT FACTORY EXPENSE			
4. SPECIAL TOOLING AND SPECIAL TEST EQUIPMENT			
5. OTHER COSTS			
6. GENERAL AND ADMINISTRATIVE EXPENSE			
7. TOTAL COSTS (Items 1 thru 6)	$	$	$
8. FEE			
9. SETTLEMENT EXPENSES			
10. SETTLEMENTS WITH SUBCONTRACTORS			
11. GROSS PROPOSED SETTLEMENT (Items 7 thru 10)			
12. DISPOSAL AND OTHER CREDITS			
13. NET PROPOSED SETTLEMENT (Item 11 less 12)	$	$	$
14. PRIOR PAYMENTS TO CONTRACTOR	$	$	$
15. NET PAYMENT REQUESTED (Item 13 less 14)	$	$	$

CERTIFICATE

This is to certify that the undersigned, individually, and as an authorized representative of the Contractor, has examined this termination settlement proposal and that, to the best knowledge and belief of the undersigned:

(a) AS TO THE CONTRACTOR'S OWN CHARGES. The proposed settlement (exclusive of charges set forth in Item 10) and supporting schedules and explanations have been prepared from the books of account and records of the Contractor in accordance with recognized commercial accounting practices; they include only those charges allocable to the terminated portion of this contract; they have been prepared with knowledge that they will, or may, be used directly or indirectly as the basis of settlement of a termination settlement proposal or claim against an agency of the United States; and the charges as stated are fair and reasonable.

(b) AS TO THE SUBCONTRACTORS' CHARGES. (1) The Contractor has examined, or caused to be examined, to an extent it considered adequate in the circumstances, the termination settlement proposals of its immediate subcontractors (exclusive of proposals filed against these immediate subcontractors by their subcontractors); (2) The settlements on account of immediate subcontractors' own charges are fair and reasonable, the charges are allocable to the terminated portion of this contract, and the settlements were negotiated in good faith and are not more favorable to its immediate subcontractors than those that the Contractor would make if reimbursement by the Government were not involved; (3) The Contractor has received from all its immediate subcontractors appropriate certificates with respect to their termination settlement proposals, which certificates are substantially in the form of this certificate; and (4) The Contractor has no information leading it to doubt (i) the reasonableness of the settlements with more remote subcontractors or (ii) that the charges for them are allocable to this contract. Upon receipt by the Contractor of amounts covering settlements with its immediate subcontractors, the Contractor will pay or credit them promptly with the amounts so received, to the extent that it has not previously done so. The term "subcontractors," as used above, includes suppliers.

NOTE: The Contractor shall, under conditions stated in FAR 15.804-2, be required to submit a Certificate of Current Cost or Pricing Data (see FAR 15.804-2(a) and 15.804-6).

NAME OF CONTRACTOR	BY (Signature of authorized official)	
	TITLE	DATE
NAME OF SUPERVISORY ACCOUNTING OFFICIAL	TITLE	

AUTHORIZED FOR LOCAL REPRODUCTION
Previous edition is usable
J61233/10-09-96

EXPIRATION DATE: 4-30-92

1437-102

STANDARD FORM 1437 (REV. 7-89)
Prescribed by GSA - FAR (48 CFR) 53.249(a)(4)

Appendix 12.1 Standard Form 1437, Settlement Proposal for Cost-Reimbursement type Contracts

SETTLEMENT PROPOSAL (INVENTORY BASIS)

FORM APPROVED OMB NO. **9000-0012**

Public reporting burden for this collection of information is estimated to average 2.5 hours per response, including the time for reviewing instructions, searching existing data sources, gathering and maintaining the data needed, and completing and reviewing the collection of information. Send comments regarding this burden estimate or any other aspect of this collection of information, including suggestions for reducing this burden, to the FAR Secretariat (VRS), Office of Federal Acquisition and Regulatory Policy, GSA, Washington, D.C. 20405; and to the Office of Management and Budget, Paperwork Reduction Project (9000-0012), Washington, D.C. 20503.

FOR USE BY A FIXED-PRICE PRIME CONTRACTOR OR FIXED- PRICE SUBCONTRACTOR

THIS PROPOSAL APPLIES TO (Check one) ☐ A PRIME CONTRACT WITH THE GOVERNMENT ☐ SUBCONTRACT OR PURCHASE ORDER	COMPANY
SUBCONTRACT OR PURCHASE ORDER NO(S).	STREET ADDRESS
CONTRACTOR WHO SENT NOTICE OF TERMINATION	CITY AND STATE (Include ZIP Code)
NAME	NAME OF GOVERNMENT AGENCY
ADDRESS (Include ZIP Code)	GOVERNMENT PRIME CONTRACT NO. / CONTRACTOR'S REFERENCE NO.
If moneys payable under the contract have been assigned, give the following:	
NAME OF ASSIGNEE	EFFECTIVE DATE OF TERMINATION
ADDRESS (Include ZIP Code)	PROPOSAL NO. / CHECK ONE ☐ INTERIM ☐ FINAL

SF 1439, SCHEDULE OF ACCOUNTING INFORMATION ☐ IS ☐ IS NOT ATTACHED (If not, explain)

SECTION I - STATUS OF CONTRACT OR ORDER AT EFFECTIVE DATE OF TERMINATION

PRODUCTS COVERED BY TERMINATED CONTRACT OR PURCHASE ORDER (a)		FINISHED: PREVIOUSLY SHIPPED AND INVOICED (b)	FINISHED: ON HAND: PAYMENT TO BE RECEIVED THROUGH INVOICING (c)	FINISHED: ON HAND: INCLUDED IN THIS PROPOSAL (d)	UNFINISHED OR NOT COMMENCED: TO BE COMPLETED (Partial termination only) (e)	UNFINISHED OR NOT COMMENCED: NOT TO BE COMPLETED (f)	TOTAL COVERED BY CONTRACT OR ORDER (g)
	QUANTITY						
	$						
	QUANTITY						
	$						
	QUANTITY						
	$						

SECTION II - PROPOSED SETTLEMENT

(Use Columns (b) and (c) only where previous proposal has been filed)

NO.	ITEM (a)	TOTAL PREVIOUSLY PROPOSED (b)	INCREASE OR DECREASE BY THIS PROPOSAL (c)	TOTAL PROPOSED TO DATE (d)	FOR USE OF CONTRACTING AGENCY ONLY (e)
1	METALS				
2	RAW MATERIALS (other than metals)				
3	PURCHASED PARTS				
4	FINISHED COMPONENTS				
5	MISCELLANOUS INVENTORY				
6	WORK-IN-PROGRESS				
7	SPECIAL TOOLING AND SPECIAL TEST EQUIPMENT				
8	OTHER COSTS (from Schedule B)				
9	GENERAL AND ADMINISTRATIVE EXPENSES (from Schedule C)				
10	**TOTAL (Items 1 to 9 Inclusive)**				
11	PROFIT (explain in Schedule D)				
12	SETTLEMENT EXPENSES (from Schedule E)				
13	**TOTAL (Items 10 to 13 Inclusive)**				
14	SETTLEMENTS WITH SUBCONTRACTORS (from Schedule F)				
15	ACCEPTABLE FINISHED PRODUCT				
16	GROSS PROPOSED SETTLEMENT (Items 13 thru 15)				
17	DISPOSAL AND OTHER CREDITS (from Schedule G)				
18	NET PROPOSED SETTLEMENT (Item 16 less 17)				
19	ADVANCE, PROGRESS & PARTIAL PAYMENTS (from Schedule H)				
20	**NET PAYMENT REQUESTED (Item 18 less 19)**				

(When the space provided for any information is insufficient, continue on a separate sheet.)

AUTHORIZED FOR LOCAL REPRODUCTION
Previous edition is usable

EXPIRATION DATE: 4-30-92 1435-102

STANDARD FORM 1435 (REV. 7-89)
Prescribed by GSA - FAR (48 CFR) 53.249(a)(2)

J61225
10-09-96

Appendix 12.2 Standard Form 1435, Settlement Proposal (Inventory Basis)

SCHEDULE A - ANALYSIS OF INVENTORY COST (Items 4 and 6)

Furnish the following information (unless not reasonably available) for inventories of finished components and work-in-progress included in this proposal:

	TOTAL DIRECT LABOR	TOTAL DIRECT MATERIALS	TOTAL INDIRECT EXPENSES	TOTAL
FINISHED COMPONENTS				
WORK-IN-PROGRESS				

NOTE.-Individual items of small amounts may be grouped into a single entry in Schedules B, C, D, E, and G.

SCHEDULE B - OTHER COSTS (Item 8)

ITEM	EXPLANATION	AMOUNT	FOR USE OF CONTRACTING AGENCY ONLY

SCHEDULE C - GENERAL AND ADMINISTRATIVE EXPENSES (Item 9)

DETAIL OF EXPENSES	AMOUNT	FOR USE OF CONTRACTING AGENCY ONLY

SCHEDULE D - PROFIT (Item 11)

EXPLANATION	AMOUNT	FOR USE OF CONTRACTING AGENCY ONLY

(Where the space provided for any information is insufficient, continue on a separate sheet.)

STANDARD FORM 1435 (REV. 7-89) PAGE 2

J61226
10-09-96

Appendix 12.2   (Continued)

435

SCHEDULE E - SETTLEMENT EXPENSES (Item 12)			
ITEM	EXPLANATION	AMOUNT	FOR USE OF CONTRACTING AGENCY ONLY

SCHEDULE F - SETTLEMENTS WITH IMMEDIATE SUBCONTRACTORS AND SUPPLIERS (Item 14)			
NAME AND ADDRESS OF SUBCONTRACTOR	BRIEF DESCRIPTION OF PRODUCT CANCELED	AMOUNT OF SETTLEMENT	FOR USE OF CONTRACTING AGENCY ONLY

SCHEDULE G - DISPOSAL AND OTHER CREDITS (Item 17)		
DESCRIPTION	AMOUNT	FOR USE OF CONTRACTING AGENCY ONLY

(If praticable, show separately amount of disposal credits applicable to acceptable finished product included in Item 15.)

(Where the space provided for any information is insufficient, continue on a separate sheet.)

STANDARD FORM 1435 (REV. 7-89) PAGE 3

J61227
10-09-96

Appendix 12.2   (Continued)

DATE	TYPE OF PAYMENT	AMOUNT	FOR USE OF CONTRACTING AGENCY ONLY

(Where the space provided for any information is insufficient, continue on a separate sheet.)

CERTIFICATE

This is to certify that the undersigned, individually, and as an authorized representative of the Contractor, has examined this termination settlement proposal and that, to the best knowledge and belief of the undersigned:

(a) AS TO THE CONTRACTOR'S OWN CHARGES. The proposed settlement (exclusive of charges set forth in Item 14) and supporting schedules and explanations have been prepared from the books of account and records of the Contractor in accordance with recognized commercial accounting practices; they include only those charges allocable to the termination portion of this contract; they have been prepared with knowledge that they will, or may, be used directly or indirectly as the basis of settlement of a termination settlement proposal or claim against an agency of the United States; and the charges as stated are fair and reasonable.

(b) AS TO THE SUBCONTRACTORS' CHARGES. (1) The Contractor has examined, or caused to be examined, to an extent it considered adequate in the circumstances, the termination settlement proposals of its immediate subcontractors (exclusive of proposals filed against these immediate subcontractors by their subcontractors); (2) The settlements on account of immediate subcontractors' own charges are fair and reasonable, the charges are allocable to the terminated portion of this contract, and the settlements were negotiated in good faith and are not more favorable to its immediate subcontractors than those that the Contractor would make if reimbursement by the Government were not involved; (3) The Contractor has received from all its immediate subcontractors appropriate certificates with respect to their termination settlement proposals, which certificates are substantially in the form of this certificate; and (4) The Contractor has no information leading it to doubt (i) the reasonableness of the settlements with more remote subcontractors or (ii) that the charges for them are allocable to this contract. Upon receipt by the Contractor of amounts covering settlements with its immediate subcontractors, the Contractor will pay or credit them promptly with the amounts so received, to the extent that it has not previously done so. The term "subcontractors," as used above, includes suppliers.

NOTE: The Contractor shall, under conditions stated in FAR 15.804-2, be required to submit a Certificate of Current Cost or Pricing Data (see FAR 15.804-2(a) and 15.804-6).

NAME OF CONTRACTOR	BY (Signature of authorized official)	
	TITLE	DATE
NAME OF SUPERVISORY ACCOUNTING OFFICIAL	TITLE	

STANDARD FORM 1435 (REV. 7-89) **PAGE 4**

Appendix 12.2 (Continued)

INVENTORY SCHEDULE A
(METALS IN MILL PRODUCT FORM)
(See FAR Section 45.606 for instructions)

PARTIAL	FINAL

TYPE
- [ ] TERMINATION
- [ ] NONTERMINATION

DATE	TYPE OF CONTRACT	OMB No.: 9000-0015
		Expires: 05/31/98
	PROPERTY CLASSIFICATION	PAGE / NO. OF PAGES

Public reporting burden for this collection of information is estimated to average 1 hour per response, including the time for reviewing instructions, searching existing data sources, gathering and maintaining the data needed, and completing and reviewing the collection of information. Send comments regarding this burden estimate or any other aspect of this collection of information, including suggestions for reducing this burden, to the FAR Secretariat (MVR), Federal Acquisition Policy Division, GSA, Washington, DC 20405.

THIS SCHEDULE APPLIES TO (Check one)
- [ ] A PRIME CONTRACT WITH THE GOVERNMENT
- [ ] SUBCONTRACT(S) OR PURCHASE ORDER(S)

COMPANY PREPARING AND SUBMITTING SCHEDULE

GOVERNMENT PRIME CONTRACT NO.	SUBCONTRACT OR P.O. NO.	REFERENCE NO.

STREET ADDRESS

CONTRACTOR WHO SENT NOTICE OF TERMINATION

NAME		STATE ZIP CODE
STREET ADDRESS		
CITY	STATE ZIP CODE	CITY

LOCATION OF MATERIAL

PRODUCT COVERED BY CONTRACT OR ORDER

INVENTORY SCHEDULE

FOR USE OF CONTRACTING AGENCY ONLY	ITEM NO.	DESCRIPTION			DIMENSIONS						COST		FOR USE OF CONTRACTING AGENCY ONLY
		FORM, SHAPE, ROLLING TREATMENT (When applicable, type of edge. Example: HR coiled strip, CR flat sheets box rod, tubing in straight length, etc.)	HEAT TREATMENT, TEMPER, HARDNESS FINISH, ETC. (Example: Annealed and picked, 1/2 hard, polished, etc.)	SPECIFICATIONS, AND ALLOY OR OTHER VARIABLE DESIGNATION IN THE SPECIFICATION (Example: 00-T-951-D B16-42 Alloy 7 Grade B)	THICK-NESS (Wall for tubing, class for pipe, type for pipe, manufacturer's die no. for copper water-tube)	WIDTH (O.D. for tube diameter of rod, size for pipe, manufacturer's die no. for extruded shapes)	LENGTH		CONDITION (Use code)	QUANTITY	UNIT OF MEASURE	UNIT	TOTAL	CONTRACTOR'S OFFER
							FT/M	IN/CM						
(a)		(b)	(b1)	(b2)	(b3)	(b4)		(b5)	(c)	(d)		(d1)	(e)	(f)	(g)

This Inventory Schedule has been examined, and in the exercise of the signer's best judgement and to the best of the signer's knowledge, based upon information believed by the signer to be reliable, said Schedule has been prepared in accordance with applicable instructions; the inventory described is allocable to the designated contract and is located at the places specified; if the property reported is termination inventory, the quantities are not in excess of the reasonable quantitative requirements of the terminated portion of the contract; this Schedule does not include any items reasonably usable, without loss to the Contractor, on its other work; and the costs shown on this Schedule are in accordance with the Contractor's records and books of account.

The Contractor agrees to inform the Contracting Officer of any substantial change in the status of the inventory shown in this Schedule between the date hereof and the final disposition of such inventory.

Subject to any authorized prior disposition, title to the inventory listed in this Schedule is hereby tendered to the Government and is warranted to be free and clear of all liens and encumbrances.

NAME OF CONTRACTOR	BY (Signature of Authorized Official)	TITLE	DATE

NAME OF SUPERVISORY ACCOUNTING OFFICIAL | TITLE

AUTHORIZED FOR LOCAL REPRODUCTION
Previous edition not usable

J61291
01-17-97

STANDARD FORM 1426 (REV. 12-96)
Prescribed by GSA - FAR (48 CFR) 53.245 (f)

Appendix 12.3 Standard form 1426, Inventory Schedule A (Metals in Mill Product Form)

INVENTORY SCHEDULE A - CONTINUATION SHEET
(METALS IN MILL PRODUCT FORM)

TYPE: ☐ TERMINATION ☐ NONTERMINATION

DATE

FORM APPROVED OMB NO. 9000-0015

Public reporting burden for this collection of information is estimated to average 1 hour per response, including the time for reviewing instructions, searching existing data sources, gathering and maintaining the data needed, and completing and reviewing the collection of information. Send comments regarding this burden estimate or any other aspect of this collection of information, including suggestions for reducing this burden, to the FAR Secretariat (VRS), Office of Federal Acquisition and Regulatory Policy, GSA, Washington, D.C. 20405; and to the Office of Management and Budget, Paperwork Reduction Project (9000-0015), Washington, D.C. 20503.

GOVERNMENT PRIME CONTRACT NO.	SUBCONTRACT OR P.O. NO.	REFERENCE NO.	PROPERTY CLASSIFICATION	PAGE NO.	NO. OF PAGES

FOR USE OF CON-TRACT-ING AGENCY ONLY	ITEM NO.	DESCRIPTION					DIMENSIONS				CON-DITION (Use code)	QUAN-TITY	UNIT OF MEASURE	COST		CONTRACTOR'S OFFER	FOR USE OF CON-TRACT-ING AGENCY ONLY
		FORM, SHAPE, ROLLING TREATMENT	HEAT TREAT-MENT, TEMPER, HARDNESS, FINISH, ETC.	SPECIFICA-TIONS, AND ALLOY OR OTHER VARIA-BLE DESIGNA-TION IN THE SPECIFICATION	THICK-NESS	WIDTH	LENGTH							UNIT	TOTAL		
							FEET	INCHES									
(a)	(a)	(b)	(b1)	(b2)	(b3)	(b4)	(b5)		(c)	(d)	(d1)		(e)	(f)	(g)	

AUTHORIZED FOR LOCAL REPRODUCTION
Previous edition is usable
J61217
10-09-96

EXPIRATION DATE: 4-30-92

1427-102

STANDARD FORM 1427 (REV. 7-89)
Prescribed by GSA - FAR (48 CFR) 53.245(f)

Appendix 12.3 (Continued)

INVENTORY SCHEDULE B
(See FAR Section 45.606 for instructions)

TYPE			TYPE OF CONTRACT	DATE	OMB No.: 9000-0015
☐ PARTIAL	☐ FINAL	☐ TERMINATION ☐ NONTERMINATION			Expires: 05/31/98

Public reporting burden for this collection of information is estimated to average 1 hour per response, including the time for reviewing instructions, searching existing data sources, gathering and maintaining the data needed, and completing and reviewing the collection of information. Send comments regarding this burden estimate or any other aspect of this collection of information, including suggestions for reducing this burden, to the FAR Secretariat (MVR), Federal Acquisition Policy Division, GSA, Washington, DC 20405.

TYPE OF INVENTORY		PROPERTY CLASSIFICATION	PAGE NO.	NO. OF PAGES
☐ RAW MATERIALS (Other than metals)	☐ PURCHASED PARTS	☐ FINISHED COMPONENTS		
☐ FINISHED PRODUCT	☐ PLANT EQUIPMENT	☐ MISCELLANEOUS	COMPANY PREPARING AND SUBMITTING SCHEDULE	

THIS SCHEDULE APPLIES TO (Check one)

☐ A PRIME CONTRACT WITH THE GOVERNMENT   ☐ SUBCONTRACT OR PURCHASE ORDER

GOVERNMENT PRIME CONTRACT NO.   SUBCONTRACT OR P.O. NO.   REFERENCE NO.

STREET ADDRESS

CONTRACTOR WHO SENT NOTICE OF TERMINATION

NAME

CITY AND STATE (Include ZIP Code)

ADDRESS (Include ZIP Code)

LOCATION OF MATERIAL

PRODUCT COVERED BY CONTRACT OR ORDER

INVENTORY SCHEDULE

FOR USE OF CON- TRACT- ING AGENCY ONLY	ITEM NO. (a)	DESCRIPTION			CONDI- TION (Use code) (c)	TYPE OF PACKING (Bulk, bbls., crates, etc.) (b2)	QUAN- TITY (d)	UNIT OF MEASURE (d1)	COST (For finished product, show contract price instead of cost)		FOR USE OF CON- TRACT- ING AGENCY ONLY
		ITEM DESCRIPTION (b)	GOVERNMENT PART OR DRAWING NUMBER AND REVISION NUMBER (b1)						UNIT (e)	TOTAL (f)	CONTRACTOR'S OFFER (g)

The Contractor agrees to inform the Contracting Officer of any substantial change in the status of the inventory shown in this Schedule between the date hereof and the final disposition of such inventory.

Subject to any authorized prior disposition, title to the inventory listed in this Schedule is hereby tendered to the Government and is warranted to be free and clear of all liens and encumbrances.

This Inventory Schedule has been examined, and in the exercise of the signer's best judgment and to the best of the signer's knowledge, based upon information believed by the signer to be reliable, said Schedule has been prepared in accordance with applicable instructions; the inventory described is allocable to the designated contract and is located at the places specified; if the property reported is termination inventory, the quantities are not in excess of the reasonable quantitative requirements of the terminated portion of the contract; this Schedule does not include any items reasonably usable, without loss to the Contractor, on its other work; and the costs shown on this Schedule are in accordance with the Contractor's records and books of account.

NAME OF CONTRACTOR	BY (Signature of Authorized Official)	TITLE	

NAME OF SUPERVISORY ACCOUNTING OFFICIAL	TITLE	DATE

AUTHORIZED FOR LOCAL REPRODUCTION
Previous edition not usable   LHA

J61292 01-17-97

STANDARD FORM 1428 (Rev. 12-96)
Prescribed by GSA-FAR (48 CFR) 53.245(g)

Appendix 12.4   Standard Form 1428, Inventory Schedule B

INVENTORY SCHEDULE B - CONTINUATION SHEET

TYPE ☐ TERMINATION ☐ NONTERMINATION

FORM APPROVED OMB NO. 9000-0015

Public reporting burden for this collection of information is estimated to average 1 hour per response, including the time for reviewing instructions, searching existing data sources, gathering and maintaining the data needed, and completing and reviewing the collection of information. Send comments regarding this burden estimate or any other aspect of this collection of information, including suggestions for reducing this burden, to the FAR Secretariat (VRS), Office of Federal Acquisition and Regulatory Policy, GSA, Washington, D.C. 20405; and to the Office of Management and Budget, Paperwork Reduction Project (9000-0015), Washington, D.C. 20503.

TYPE OF INVENTORY
☐ RAW MATERIALS (Other than metals)
☐ PURCHASED PARTS
☐ FINISHED COMPONENTS
☐ FINISHED PRODUCTS
☐ PLANT EQUIPMENT
☐ MISCELLANEOUS

GOVERNMENT PRIME CONTRACT NO.	SUBCONTRACT OR P.O. NO.	REFERENCE NO.	PROPERTY CLASSIFICATION	DATE	PAGE NO.	NO. OF PAGES

FOR USE OF CON-TRACT-ING AGENCY ONLY	ITEM NO.	DESCRIPTION		TYPE OF PACKING (Bulk, bbls., crates, etc.)	CON-DITION (Use code)	QUAN-TITY	UNIT OF MEASURE	COST (For finished product, show contract price instead of cost)		CONTRACTOR'S OFFER	FOR USE OF CON-TRACT-ING AGENCY ONLY
		ITEM DESCRIPTION	GOVERNMENT PART OR DRAWING NUMBER AND REV. NUMBER					UNIT	TOTAL		
(a)		(b)	(b1)	(b2)	(c)	(d)	(d1)	(e)	(f)	(g)	

AUTHORIZED FOR LOCAL REPRODUCTION
Previous edition is usable
J61219
10-09-96

EXPIRATION DATE: 4-30-92

1429-102

STANDARD FORM 1429 (REV. 7-89)
Prescribed by GSA - FAR (48 CFR) 53.245(g)

Appendix 12.4 (Continued)

INVENTORY SCHEDULE C
(WORK-IN-PROCESS)
(See FAR Section 45.606 for instructions)

☐ PARTIAL ☐ FINAL

TYPE
☐ TERMINATION
☐ NONTERMINATION

TYPE OF CONTRACT

DATE

OMB No.: 9000-0015
Expires: 05/31/98

PAGE NO. | NO. OF PAGES

Public reporting burden for this collection of information is estimated to average 1 hour per response, including the time for reviewing instructions, searching existing data sources, gathering and maintaining the data needed, and completing and reviewing the collection of information. Send comments regarding this burden estimate or any other aspect of this collection of information, including suggestions for reducing this burden, to the FAR Secretariat (MVR), Federal Acquisition Policy Division, GSA, Washington, DC 20405.

THIS SCHEDULE APPLIES TO (Check one)

☐ A PRIME CONTRACT WITH THE GOVERNMENT

☐ SUBCONTRACT(S) OR PURCHASE ORDER(S)

COMPANY PREPARING AND SUBMITTING SCHEDULE

GOVERNMENT PRIME CONTRACT NO. | SUBCONTRACT OR P.O. NO. | REFERENCE NO.

STREET ADDRESS

CONTRACTOR WHO SENT NOTICE OF TERMINATION

NAME

CITY AND STATE (Include ZIP Code)

ADDRESS (Include ZIP Code)

LOCATION OF MATERIAL

PRODUCT COVERED BY CONTRACT OR ORDER

INVENTORY SCHEDULE

FOR USE OF CONTRACTING AGENCY ONLY	ITEM NO. (a)	DESCRIPTION		CONDITION (Use code) (c)	QUANTITY (d)	UNIT OF MEASURE (d1)	COST		CONTRACTOR'S OFFER (g)	FOR USE OF CONTRACTING AGENCY ONLY
		ITEM DESCRIPTION (b)	ESTIMATED WEIGHT (b1)				UNIT (e)	TOTAL (f)		

This Inventory Schedule has been examined, and in the exercise of the signer's best judgment and to the best of the signer's knowledge, based upon information believed by the signer to be reliable, said Schedule has been prepared in accordance with applicable instructions; the inventory described is allocable to the designated contract and is located at the places specified; if the property reported is termination inventory, the quantities are not in excess of the reasonable quantitative requirements of the terminated portion of the contract; this Schedule does not include any items reasonably usable, without loss to the Contractor, on its other work; and the costs shown on this Schedule are in accordance with the Contractor's records and books of account.

The Contractor agrees to inform the Contracting Officer of any substantial change in the status of the inventory shown in this Schedule between the date hereof and the final disposition of such inventory.

Subject to any authorized prior disposition, title to the inventory listed in this Schedule is hereby tendered to the Government and is warranted to be free and clear of all liens and encumbrances.

NAME OF CONTRACTOR | BY (Signature of Authorized Official) | TITLE

NAME OF SUPERVISORY ACCOUNTING OFFICIAL | TITLE | DATE

AUTHORIZED FOR LOCAL REPRODUCTION
Previous edition is not usable

J61293
01-17-97   LHA

STANDARD FORM 1430 (REV. 12-96)
Prescribed by GSA - FAR (48 CFR 53.245(h)

Appendix 12.5 Standard Form 1430, Inventory Schedule C (Work-In-Process)

INVENTORY SCHEDULE C - CONTINUATION SHEET (WORK-IN-PROCESS)

FORM APPROVED OMB NO. 9000-0015

TYPE

☐ TERMINATION ☐ NONTERMINATION

Public reporting burden for this collection of information is estimated to average 1 hour per response, including the time for reviewing instructions, searching existing data sources, gathering and maintaining the data needed, and completing and reviewing the collection of information. Send comments regarding this burden estimate or any other aspect of this collection of information, including suggestions for reducing this burden, to the FAR Secretariat (VRS), Office of Federal Acquisition and Regulatory Policy, GSA, Washington, D.C. 20405; and to the Office of Management and Budget, Paperwork Reduction Project (9000-0015), Washington, D.C. 20503.

GOVERNMENT PRIME CONTRACT NO.	SUBCONTRACT OR P.O. NO.	REFERENCE NO.	DATE	PAGE NO.	NO. OF PAGES

FOR USE OF CON-TRACT-ING AGENCY ONLY	ITEM NO.	DESCRIPTION		CON-DITION (Use code)	QUAN-TITY	UNIT OF MEASURE	COST		CONTRACTOR'S OFFER	FOR USE OF CON-TRACT-ING AGENCY ONLY
		ITEM DESCRIPTION	ESTIMATED WEIGHT				UNIT	TOTAL		
(a)		(b)	(b1)	(c)	(d)	(d1)	(e)	(f)	(g)	

AUTHORIZED FOR LOCAL REPRODUCTION
Previous edition is usable
J61221
10-09-96

EXPIRATION DATE: 4-30-92

1431-102

STANDARD FORM 1431 (REV. 7-89)
Prescribed by GSA - FAR (48 CFR) 53.245(n)

Appendix 12.5 (Continued)

INVENTORY SCHEDULE D
(SPECIAL TOOLING AND SPECIAL TEST EQUIPMENT)
(See FAR Section 45.606 for Instructions)

☐ PARTIAL ☐ FINAL

TYPE	TYPE OF CONTRACT	DATE	OMB No.: **9000-0015**
☐ TERMINATION ☐ NONTERMINATION	PROPERTY CLASSIFICATION		Expires: **05/31/98**
			PAGE NO. / NO. OF PAGES

Public reporting burden for this collection of information is estimated to average 1 hour per response, including the time for reviewing instructions, searching existing data sources, gathering and maintaining the data needed, and completing and reviewing the collection of information. Send comments regarding this burden estimate or any other aspect of this collection of information, including suggestions for reducing this burden, to the FAR Secretariat (MVR), Federal Acquisition Policy Division, GSA, Washington, DC 20405.

THIS SCHEDULE APPLIES TO (Check one)

☐ A PRIME CONTRACT WITH THE GOVERNMENT ☐ SUBCONTRACT(S) OR PURCHASE ORDER(S)

GOVERNMENT PRIME CONTRACT NO. SUBCONTRACT OR P.O. NO. REFERENCE NO.

CONTRACTOR WHO SENT NOTICE OF TERMINATION

NAME

ADDRESS (Include ZIP Code)

PRODUCT COVERED BY CONTRACT OR ORDER

COMPANY PREPARING AND SUBMITTING SCHEDULE

STREET ADDRESS

CITY AND STATE (Include ZIP Code)

LOCATION OF MATERIAL

INVENTORY SCHEDULE

FOR USE OF CONTRACTING AGENCY ONLY	ITEM NO. (a)	ITEM DESCRIPTION (b)	CONDITION (Use code) (c)	QUANTITY (d)	COST					CONTRACTOR'S OFFER (g)	FOR USE OF CONTRACTING AGENCY ONLY
					UNIT (e)	TOTAL (f)	APPLICABLE TO THIS CONTRACT				
							TO ENTIRE CONTRACT (11)	TO PORTION NOT TO BE COMPLETED (12)			

This Inventory Schedule has been examined, and in the exercise of the signer's best judgment and to the best of the signer's knowledge, based upon information believed by the signer to be reliable, said Schedule has been prepared in accordance with applicable instructions; the inventory described is allocable to the designated contract and is located at the places specified; if the property reported is termination inventory, the quantities are not in excess of the reasonable quantitative requirements of the terminated portion of the contract; this Schedule does not include any items reasonably usable, without loss to the Contractor, on its other work; and the costs shown on this Schedule are in accordance with the Contractor's records and books of account.

The Contractor agrees to inform the Contracting Officer of any substantial change in the status of the Inventory shown in this Schedule between the date hereof and the final disposition of such inventory.

Subject to any authorized prior disposition, title to the inventory listed in this Schedule is hereby tendered to the Government and is warranted to be free and clear of all liens and encumbrances.

NAME OF CONTRACTOR

BY (Signature of Authorized Official)   TITLE   DATE

NAME OF SUPERVISORY ACCOUNTING OFFICIAL   TITLE

AUTHORIZED FOR LOCAL REPRODUCTION
Previous edition is not usable

J61294
01-17-97   LHA

STANDARD FORM 1432 (REV. 12-96)
Prescribed by GSA - FAR (48 CFR) 53.2460)

Appendix 12.6 Standard Form 1432, Inventory Schedule D (Special Tooling and Special Test Equipment)

INVENTORY SCHEDULE D - CONTINUATION SHEET
(SPECIAL TOOLING AND SPECIAL TEST EQUIPMENT)

TYPE
☐ TERMINATION
☐ NONTERMINATION

DATE

FORM APPROVED OMB NO.
9000-0015

Public reporting burden for this collection of information is estimated to average 1 hour per response, including the time for reviewing instructions, searching existing data sources, gathering and maintaining the data needed, and completing and reviewing the collection of information. Send comments regarding this burden estimate or any other aspect of this collection of information, including suggestions for reducing this burden, to the FAR Secretariat (VRS), Office of Federal Acquisition and Regulatory Policy, GSA, Washington, D.C. 20405; and to the Office of Management and Budget, Paperwork Reduction Project (9000-0015), Washington, D.C. 20503.

GOVERNMENT PRIME CONTRACT NO.	SUBCONTRACT OR P.O. NO.	REFERENCE NO.	PROPERTY CLASSIFICATION	PAGE NO.	NO. OF PAGES

FOR USE OF CON-TRACT-ING AGENCY ONLY	ITEM NO.	ITEM DESCRIPTION	CON-DITION (Use code)	QUAN-TITY	UNIT	TOTAL	COST		CONTRACTOR'S OFFER	FOR USE OF CON-TRACT-ING AGENCY ONLY
							APPLICABLE TO THIS CONTRACT			
							TO ENTIRE CONTRACT	TO PORTION NOT TO BE COMPLETED		
(a)		(b)	(c)	(d)	(e)	(f)	(f1)	(f2)	(g)	

AUTHORIZED FOR LOCAL REPRODUCTION
Previous edition is usable

EXPIRATION DATE: 4-30-92

1433-102

STANDARD FORM 1433 (REV. 7-89)
Prescribed by GSA - FAR (48 CFR) 53.245(l)

J61223
10-09-96

Appendix 12.6 (Continued)

445

SETTLEMENT PROPOSAL (SHORT FORM)

FORM APPROVED OMB NO. 9000-0012

Public reporting burden for this collection of information is estimated to average 2.5 hours per response, including the time for reviewing instructions, searching existing data sources, gathering and maintaining the data needed, and completing and reviewing the collection of information. Send comments regarding this burden estimate or any other aspect of this collection of information, including suggestions for reducing this burden, to the FAR Secretariat (VRS), Office of Federal Acquisition and Regulatory Policy, GSA, Washington, D.C. 20405; and to the Office of Management and Budget, Paperwork Reduction Project (9000-0012), Washington, D.C. 20503.

For Use by a Prime Contractor or Subcontractor in Settlement of a Fixed Price Terminated Contract When Total Charges Claimed Are Less Than $10,000.

THIS PROPOSAL APPLIES TO (Check one)
☐ A PRIME CONTRACT WITH THE GOVERNMENT
☐ SUBCONTRACT OR PURCHASE ORDER

SUBCONTRACT OR PURCHASE ORDER NO.(S)

CONTRACTOR WHO SENT NOTICE OF TERMINATION

NAME

ADDRESS (Include ZIP Code)

If moneys payable under the contract have been assigned, give the following:

NAME OF ASSIGNEE

ADDRESS (Include ZIP Code)

COMPANY (Prime or Subcontractor)

STREET ADDRESS

CITY AND STATE (Include ZIP Code)

NAME OF GOVERNMENT AGENCY | GOVERNMENT PRIME CONTRACT NO.

CONTRACTOR'S REFERENCE NO. | EFFECTIVE DATE OF TERMINATION

SECTION I - STATUS OF CONTRACT OR ORDER AT EFFECTIVE DATE OF TERMINATION

PRODUCTS COVERED BY TERMINATED CONTRACT OR PURCHASE ORDER (a)		FINISHED			UNFINISHED OR NOT COMMENCED		TOTAL COVERED BY CONTRACT OR ORDER (g)
		PREVIOUSLY SHIPPED AND INVOICED (b)	ON HAND		TO BE COMPLETED (Partial termination only) (e)	NOT TO BE COMPLETED (f)	
			PAYMENT TO BE RECEIVED THROUGH INVOICING (c)	INCLUDED IN THIS PROPOSAL (d)			
	QUANTITY						
	$						
	QUANTITY						
	$						
	QUANTITY						
	$						

SECTION II - PROPOSED SETTLEMENT

NO.	ITEM (Include only items allocable to the terminated portion of contract)	AMOUNT OF CHARGE
1	CHARGE FOR ACCEPTABLE FINISHED PRODUCT NOT COVERED BY INVOICING (from SF 1434)	$
2	CHARGE FOR WORK-IN-PROGRESS, RAW MATERIAL, ETC., ON HAND (from SF 1434)	$
3	OTHER CHARGES INCLUDING PROFIT AND SETTLEMENT EXPENSES	$
4	CHARGES FOR SETTLEMENT(S) WITH SUBCONTRACTORS	$
5	GROSS PROPOSED SETTLEMENT (Sum of Items 1 thru 4)	$
6	DISPOSAL AND OTHER CREDITS (from SF 1434, Col. 2)	$
7	NET PROPOSED SETTLEMENT (Item 5 less 6)	$
8	ADVANCE, PROGRESS, AND PARTIAL PAYMENTS	$
9	NET PAYMENT REQUESTED (Item 7 less 8)	$

List your inventory on SF 1434 and attach a copy thereto. Retain for the applicable period specified in the prime contract all papers and records relating to this proposal for future examination.

GIVE A BRIEF EXPLANATION OF HOW YOU ARRIVED AT THE AMOUNTS SHOWN IN ITEMS 3, 4, 6, AND 7

I CERTIFY that the above proposed settlement includes only charges allocable to the terminated portion of the contract or purchase order. That the total charges (Item 5) and the disposal credits (Item 6) are fair and reasonable, and that this proposal has been prepared with knowledge that it will, or may, be used directly or indirectly as a basis for reimbursement under a settlement proposal(s) against agencies of the United States.

NAME OF YOUR COMPANY

BY (Signature of authorized official)

TITLE | DATE

(Where the space provided for any information is insufficient, continue on a separate sheet.)

AUTHORIZED FOR LOCAL REPRODUCTION
Previous edition is usable
J61234/10-09-96

EXPIRATION DATE: 4-30-92

1438-102

STANDARD FORM 1438 (REV. 7-89)
Prescribed by GSA · FAR (48 CFR) 53.249(a)(5)

Appendix 12.7 Standard Form 1438, Settlement Proposal (Short Form)

INSTRUCTIONS

1. This settlement proposal should be submitted to the contracting officer, if you are a prime contractor, or to your customer, if you are a subcontractor. The term contract as used hereinafter includes a subcontractor or a purchase order.

2. Proposals that would normally be included in a single settlement proposal, such as those based on a series of separate orders for the same Item under one contract should be consolidated wherever possible, and must not be divided in such a way as to bring them below $10,000.

3. You should review any aspects of your contract relating to termination and consult your customer or contracting officer for further information. Government regulations pertaining to the basis for determining a fair and reasonable termination settlement are contained in Part 49 of the Federal Acquisition Regulation. Your proposal for fair compensation should be prepared on the basis of the costs shown by your accounting records. Where your costs are not so shown, you may use any reasonable basis for estimating your costs which will provide for fair compensation for the preparations made and work done for the terminated portion of the contract, including a reasonable profit on such preparation and work.

4. Generally your settlement proposal may include under Items 2, 3, and 4, the following:

a. COSTS · Costs incurred which are reasonably necessary and are properly allocable to the terminated portion of your contract under recognized commercial accounting practices, including direct and indirect manufacturing, selling and distribution, administrative, and other costs and expenses incurred.

b. SETTLEMENTS WITH SUBCONTRACTORS · Reasonable settlements of proposals of subcontractors allocable to the terminated portion of the subcontract. Copies of such settlements will be attached hereto.

c. SETTLEMENT EXPENSES · Reasonable costs of protecting and preserving terminated inventory in your possession and preparing your proposal.

d. PROFIT · A reasonable profit with respect to the preparations you have made and work you have actually done for the terminated portion of your contract. No profit should be included for work which has not been done, nor shall profit be included for settlement expenses, or for settlement with subcontractors.

5. If you use this form, your total charges being proposed (line 5), must be less than $10,000. The Government has the right to examine your books and records relative to this proposal, and if you are a subcontractor your customer must be satisfied with your proposal.

STANDARD FORM 1438 (REV. 7-89) **PAGE 2**

J61235
10-09-96

Appendix 12.7   (Continued)

TERMINATION INVENTORY SCHEDULE E
(SHORT FORM FOR USE WITH SF 1438 ONLY)
(See FAR Section 45.606 for instructions)

☐ PARTIAL ☐ FINAL

DATE	PAGE NO.	NO. OF PAGES

OMB No.: 9000-0015
Expires: 05/31/98

Public reporting burden for this collection of information is estimated to average 1 hour per response, including the time for reviewing instructions, searching existing data sources, gathering and maintaining the data needed, and completing and reviewing the collection of information. Send comments regarding this burden estimate or any other aspect of this collection of information, including suggestions for reducing this burden, to the FAR Secretariat (MVR), Federal Acquisition Policy Division, GSA, Washington, DC 20405.

THIS SCHEDULE APPLIES TO (Check one)

☐ A PRIME CONTRACT WITH THE GOVERNMENT ☐ SUBCONTRACT(S) OR PURCHASE ORDER(S)

GOVERNMENT PRIME CONTRACT NO.	SUBCONTRACT OR P.O. NO.	REFERENCE NO.

CONTRACTOR WHO SENT NOTICE OF TERMINATION

COMPANY PREPARING AND SUBMITTING SCHEDULE

NAME

STREET ADDRESS

ADDRESS (Include ZIP Code)

CITY AND STATE (Include ZIP Code)

PRODUCT COVERED BY CONTRACT OR ORDER

LOCATION OF MATERIAL

TERMINATION INVENTORY

FOR USE OF CONTRACTING AGENCY ONLY	ITEM NO. (a)	DESCRIPTION			CONDITION (Use code) (c)	QUANTITY (d)	UNIT OF MEASURE (d1)	COST (For finished product, show contract price instead of cost)		CONTRACTOR'S OFFER (g)	FOR USE OF CONTRACTING AGENCY ONLY
		ITEM DESCRIPTION (b)	GOVERNMENT PART OR DRAWING NUMBER AND REVISION NUMBER (b1)	TYPE OF PACKING (Bulk, bbls., crates, etc.) (b2)				UNIT (e)	TOTAL (f)		

This Inventory Schedule has been examined, and in the exercise of the signer's best judgment and to the best of the signer's knowledge, based upon information believed by the signer to be reliable, said Schedule has been prepared in accordance with applicable instructions; the inventory described is allocable to the designated contract and is located at the places specified; if the property reported is termination inventory, the quantities are not in excess of the reasonable quantitative requirements of the terminated portion of the contract; this Schedule does not include any items reasonably usable, without loss to the Contractor, on its other work; and the costs shown on this Schedule are in accordance with the Contractor's records and books of account.

The Contractor agrees to inform the Contracting Officer of any substantial change in the status of the inventory shown in this Schedule between the date hereof and the final disposition of such inventory.

Subject to any authorized prior disposition, title to the inventory listed in this Schedule is hereby tendered to the Government and is warranted to be free and clear of all liens and encumbrances.

NAME OF CONTRACTOR	BY (Signature of Authorized Official)	TITLE	DATE

NAME OF SUPERVISORY ACCOUNTING OFFICIAL

TITLE

AUTHORIZED FOR LOCAL REPRODUCTION
Previous edition is not usable

J61295
01-17-97   LHA

STANDARD FORM 1434 (REV. 12-96)
Prescribed by GSA - FAR (48 CFR) 53.245(i)

Appendix 12.8   Standard Form 1434, Termination Inventory Schedule E (Short Form for Use With SF 1438 Only)

SETTLEMENT PROPOSAL (TOTAL COST BASIS)

FORM APPROVED OMB NO. 9000-0012

Public reporting burden for this collection of information is estimated to average 2.5 hours per response, including the time for reviewing instructions, searching existing data sources, gathering and maintaining the data needed, and completing and reviewing the collection of information. Send comments regarding this burden estimate or any other aspect of this collection of information, including suggestions for reducing this burden, to the FAR Secretariat (VRS), Office of Federal Acquisition and Regulatory Policy, GSA, Washington, D.C. 20405; and to the Office of Management and Budget, Paperwork Reduction Project (9000-0012), Washington, D.C. 20503.

FOR USE BY A FIXED-PRICE PRIME CONTRACTOR OR FIXED-PRICE SUBCONTRACTOR

THIS PROPOSAL APPLIES TO (Check one)
- ☐ A PRIME CONTRACT WITH THE GOVERNMENT
- ☐ SUBCONTRACT OR PURCHASE ORDER

SUBCONTRACT OR PURCHASE ORDER NO(S).

COMPANY

STREET ADDRESS

CONTRACTOR WHO SENT NOTICE OF TERMINATION

NAME

CITY AND STATE (Include ZIP Code)

ADDRESS (Include ZIP Code)

NAME OF GOVERNMENT AGENCY

GOVERNMENT PRIME CONTRACT NO. | CONTRACTOR'S REFERENCE NO.

If moneys payable under the contract have been assigned, give the following:

NAME OF ASSIGNEE

EFFECTIVE DATE OF TERMINATION

ADDRESS (Include ZIP Code)

PROPOSAL NO.

CHECK ONE
- ☐ INTERIM
- ☐ FINAL

SF 1439, SCHEDULE OF ACCOUNTING INFORMATION ☐ IS ☐ IS NOT ATTACHED (If not, explain)

SECTION I - STATUS OF CONTRACT OR ORDER AT EFFECTIVE DATE OF TERMINATION

PRODUCTS COVERED BY TERMINATED CONTRACT OR PURCHASE ORDER (a)		FINISHED PREVIOUSLY SHIPPED AND INVOICED (b)	ON HAND PAYMENT TO BE RECEIVED THROUGH INVOICING (c)	ON HAND PAYMENT NOT TO BE RECEIVED THROUGH INVOICING (d)	UNFINISHED OR NOT COMMENCED SUBSEQUENTLY COMPLETED AND INVOICED * (e)	UNFINISHED OR NOT COMMENCED NOT TO BE COMPLETED (f)	TOTAL COVERED BY CONTRACT OR ORDER (g)
	QUANTITY						
	$						
	QUANTITY						
	$						
	QUANTITY						
	$						

SECTION II - PROPOSED SETTLEMENT

NO.	ITEM (a)	(Use Columns (b) and (c) only where previous proposal has been filed) TOTAL PREVIOUSLY PROPOSED (b)	INCREASE OR DECREASE BY THIS PROPOSAL (c)	TOTAL PROPOSED TO DATE (d)	FOR USE OF CONTRACTING AGENCY ONLY (e)
1	DIRECT MATERIAL				
2	DIRECT LABOR				
3	INDIRECT FACTORY EXPENSE (from Schedule A)				
4	SPECIAL TOOLING AND SPECIAL TEST EQUIPMENT (SF 1432)				
5	OTHER COSTS (from Schedule B)				
6	GENERAL AND ADMINISTRATIVE EXPENSES (from Schedule C)				
7	TOTAL COSTS (Items 1 thru 6)				
8	PROFIT (Explain in Schedule D)				
9	TOTAL (Items 7 and 8)				
10	DEDUCT FINISHED PRODUCT INVOICED OR TO BE INVOICED *				
11	TOTAL (Item 9 less Item 10)				
12	SETTLEMENT EXPENSES (from Schedule E)				
13	TOTAL (Items 11 and 12)				
14	SETTLEMENTS WITH SUBCONTRACTORS (from Schedule F)				
15	GROSS PROPOSED SETTLEMENT (Items 13 thru 14)				
16	DISPOSAL AND OTHER CREDITS (from Schedule G)				
17	NET PROPOSED SETTLEMENT (Item 15 less 16)				
18	ADVANCE, PROGRESS & PARTIAL PAYMENTS (from Schedule H)				
19	NET PAYMENT REQUESTED (Item 18 less 19)				

* Column (e), Section I, should only be used in the event of a partial termination, in which the total cost reported in Section II should be accumulated to date of completion of the continued portion of the contract and the deduction for finished product (Item 10, Section II) should be the contract price of finished product in Column (b), (c) and (e), Section I.

NOTE. - File inventory schedules (SF 1426, 1428, 1430, and 1432) for allocable inventories on hand at date of termination (See 49.206).

(When the space provided for any information is insufficient, continue on a separate sheet.)

AUTHORIZED FOR LOCAL REPRODUCTION
Previous edition is usable

EXPIRATION DATE: 4-30-92

1436-103

STANDARD FORM 1436 (REV. 7-89)
Prescribed by GSA · FAR (48 CFR) 53.249(a)(3)

J61229
10-09-96

Appendix 12.9 Standard Form 1436, Settlement Proposal (Total Cost Basis)

SCHEDULE A - INDIRECT FACTORY EXPENSE (Item 3)

DETAIL OF EXPENSES	METHOD OF ALLOCATION	AMOUNT	FOR USE OF CONTRACTING AGENCY ONLY

NOTE. · Individual items of small amounts may be grouped into a single entry in Schedules B, C, D, E, and G.

SCHEDULE B - OTHER COSTS (Item 5)

ITEM	EXPLANATION	AMOUNT	FOR USE OF CONTRACTING AGENCY ONLY

SCHEDULE C - GENERAL AND ADMINISTRATIVE EXPENSES (Item 6)

DETAIL OF EXPENSES	METHOD OF ALLOCATION	AMOUNT	FOR USE OF CONTRACTING AGENCY ONLY

SCHEDULE D - PROFIT (Item 8)

EXPLANATION	AMOUNT	FOR USE OF CONTRACTING AGENCY ONLY

(Where the space provided for any information is insufficient, continue on a separate sheet.)

Appendix 12.9   (Continued)

SCHEDULE E - SETTLEMENT EXPENSES (Item 12)

ITEM	EXPLANATION	AMOUNT	FOR USE OF CONTRACTING AGENCY ONLY

SCHEDULE F - SETTLEMENTS WITH IMMEDIATE SUBCONTRACTORS AND SUPPLIERS (Item 14)

NAME AND ADDRESS OF SUBCONTRACTOR	BRIEF DESCRIPTION OF PRODUCT CANCELLED	AMOUNT OF SETTLEMENT	FOR USE OF CONTRACTING AGENCY ONLY

SCHEDULE G - DISPOSAL AND OTHER CREDITS (Item 16)

DESCRIPTION	AMOUNT	FOR USE OF CONTRACTING AGENCY ONLY

(If practicable, show separately amount of disposal credits applicable to acceptable finished product included on SF 1428.)

(Where the space provided for any information is insufficient, continue on a separate sheet.)

STANDARD FORM 1436 (REV. 7-89) **PAGE 3**

J61231
10-09-96

Appendix 12.9   (Continued)

SCHEDULE H - ADVANCE, PROGRESS AND PARTIAL PAYMENTS (Item 19)

DATE	TYPE OF PAYMENT	AMOUNT	FOR USE OF CONTRACTING AGENCY ONLY

(Where the space provided for any information is insufficient, continue on a separate sheet.)

CERTIFICATE

This is to certify that the undersigned, individually, and as an authorized representative of the Contractor, has examined this termination settlement proposal and that, to the best knowledge and belief of the undersigned:

(a) AS TO THE CONTRACTOR'S OWN CHARGES. The proposed settlement (exclusive of charges set forth in Item 14) and supporting schedules and explanations have been prepared from the books of account and records of the Contractor in accordance with recognized commercial accounting practices; they include only those charges allocable to the terminated portion of this contract; they have been prepared with knowledge that they will, or may, be used directly or indirectly as the basis of settlement of a termination settlement proposal or claim against an agency of the United States; and the charges as stated are fair and reasonable.

(b) AS TO THE SUBCONTRACTORS' CHARGES. (1) The Contractor has examined, or caused to be examined, to an extent it considered adequate in the circumstances, the termination settlement proposals of its immediate subcontractors (exclusive of proposals filed against these immediate subcontractors by their subcontractors); (2) The settlements on account of immediate subcontractors' own charges are fair and reasonable, the charges are allocable to the terminated portion of this contract, and the settlements were negotiated in good faith and are not more favorable to its immediate subcontractors than those that the Contractor would make if reimbursement by the Government were not involved; (3) The Contractor has received from all its immediate subcontractors appropriate certificates with respect to their termination settlement proposals, which certificates are substantially in the form of this certificate; and (4) The Contractor has no information leading it to doubt (i) the reasonableness of the settlements with more remote subcontractors or (ii) that the charges for them are allocable to this contract. Upon receipt by the Contractor of amounts covering settlements with its immediate subcontractors, the Contractor will pay or credit them promptly with the amounts so received, to the extent that it has not previously done so. The term "subcontractors," as used above, includes suppliers.

NOTE: The Contractor shall, under conditions stated in FAR 15.804-2, be required to submit a Certificate of Current Cost or Pricing Data (see FAR 15.804-2(a) and 15.804-6).

NAME OF CONTRACTOR	BY (Signature of authorized official)	
	TITLE	DATE
NAME OF SUPERVISORY ACCOUNTING OFFICIAL	TITLE	

J61232
10-09-96

Appendix 12.9   (Continued)

APPLICATION FOR PARTIAL PAYMENT

FORM APPROVED OMB NO.
9000-0012

Public reporting burden for this collection of information is estimated to average 2.5 hours per response, including the time for reviewing instructions, searching existing data sources, gathering and maintaining the data needed, and completing and reviewing the collection of information. Send comments regarding this burden estimate or any other aspect of this collection of information, including suggestions for reducing this burden, to the FAR Secretariat (VRS), Office of Federal Acquisition and Regulatory Policy, GSA, Washington, D.C. 20405; and to the Office of Management and Budget, Paperwork Reduction Project (9000-0012), Washington, D.C. 20503.

For use by Prime Contractor or Subcontractor under contracts terminated for the convenience of the Government.

THIS APPLICATION APPLIES TO (Check one) ☐ A PRIME CONTRACT WITH THE GOVERNMENT ☐ SUBCONTRACT OR PURCHASE ORDER SUBCONTRACT OR PURCHASE ORDER NUMBER(S).	APPLICANT
CONTRACTOR WHO SENT NOTICE OF TERMINATION NAME	STREET ADDRESS
	CITY AND STATE (Include ZIP Code)
ADDRESS (Include ZIP Code)	NAME OF GOVERNMENT AGENCY
IF CONTRACTOR HAS GUARANTEED LOANS OR HAS ASSIGNED MONEYS DUE UNDER THE CONTRACT, GIVE THE FOLLOWING:	GOVERNMENT PRIME CONTRACT NUMBER
NAME AND ADDRESS OF FINANCING INSTITUTION (Include ZIP Code)	CONTRACTOR'S REFERENCE NUMBER
NAME AND ADDRESS OF GUARANTOR (Include ZIP Code)	EFFECTIVE DATE OF TERMINATION / DATE OF THIS APPLICATION
NAME AND ADDRESS OF ASSIGNEE (Include ZIP Code)	AMOUNT REQUESTED $ / APPLICATION NUMBER UNDER THIS TERMINATION

SECTION I - STATUS OF CONTRACT OR ORDER AT EFFECTIVE DATE OF TERMINATION

PRODUCTS COVERED BY TERMINATED CONTRACT OR PURCHASE ORDER (a)		PREVIOUSLY SHIPPED AND INVOICED (b)	FINISHED ON HAND — PAYMENT TO BE RECEIVED THROUGH INVOICING (c)	FINISHED ON HAND — INCLUDED IN THIS APPLICATION (d)	UNFINISHED OR NOT COMMENCED — TO BE COMPLETED (e)	UNFINISHED OR NOT COMMENCED — NOT TO BE COMPLETED (f)	TOTAL COVERED BY CONTRACT OR ORDER (g)
	QUANTITY						
	$						
	QUANTITY						
	$						
	QUANTITY						
	$						

SECTION II - APPLICANT'S OWN TERMINATION CHARGES
(Exclusive of Its Subcontractors' Charges)

SETTLEMENT PROPOSAL
☐ ATTACHED
☐ PREVIOUSLY SUBMITTED

NO.	ITEM	CHARGES AS LISTED IN SETTLEMENT PROPOSAL
1	ACCEPTABLE FURNISHED PRODUCT (at contract price)	$
2	WORK-IN-PROGRESS	
3	RAW MATERIALS, PURCHASED PARTS, AND SUPPLIES	
4	GENERAL AND ADMINISTRATIVE EXPENSE	
5	**TOTAL (Sum of lines 1, 2, 3, and 4)**	$
6	SPECIAL TOOLING AND SPECIAL TEST EQUIPMENT	
7	OTHER COSTS	
8	SETTLEMENT EXPENSES	
9	**TOTAL (Sum of lines 5, 6, 7, and 8)**	$
10	SUBCONTRACTOR SETTLEMENTS APPROVED BY CONTRACTING OFFICER OR SETTLED UNDER A DELEGATION OF AUTHORITY AND PAID BY APPLICANT	$
	11. AMOUNTS RECEIVED	
a	UNLIQUIDATED PARTIAL, PROGRESS, AND ADVANCE PAYMENTS RECEIVED	$
b	DISPOSAL AND OTHER CREDITS	
c	**TOTAL (Sum of lines a and b)**	
d	AMOUNT OF PARTIAL PAYMENT REQUESTED	
e	**TOTAL (Sum of lines c and d)**	$

AUTHORIZED FOR LOCAL REPRODUCTION
Previous edition is usable
J61240/10-09-96

EXPIRATION DATE: 4-30-92   1440-102

STANDARD FORM 1440   (REV. 7-89)
Prescribed by GSA · FAR (48 CFR) 53.249(a)(7)

Appendix 12.10   Standard Form 1440, Application for Partial Payment

SECTION III - AGREEMENT OF APPLICANT

IN CONSIDERATION OF PARTIAL PAYMENT THAT MAY BE MADE, THE APPLICANT AGREES AS FOLLOWS:

(a) Repayment of Excess. If any partial payment made to the Contractor is in excess of the amount finally determined to be due on its termination settlement proposal or claim, the Contractor shall repay the excess to the Government upon demand together with interest at the rate established by the Secretary of the Treasury under 50 U.S.C. (App.) 1215(b)(2). Interest shall be computed for the period from the date of the excess payment to the date the excess is repaid. Interest shall not be charged however, for any (1) excess payment due to a reduction in the Contractor's proposal or claim because of retention or other disposition of termination inventory, until 10 days after the date of the retention or disposition, or any later date determined by the Contracting Officer because of the circumstances, or for (2) overpayment under cost-reimbursement research and development contracts (without profit or fee to the Contractor) if the overpayments are repaid to the Government within 30 days after demand.

(b) Prompt Settlement of Proposal. The applicant will make every effort to expedite final settlement of the termination settlement proposal and any proposals of its subcontractors.

(c) Disposal and Retention of Inventory. The applicant shall, within 10 days, notify the Contracting Officer whenever the proceeds received from the disposal of termination inventory, when added to the cost or agreed value of inventory retained by the applicant, exceeds the amount of its charges (Section II, Line 9) and the amount of such credits has not been included on Section II, Line b (Disposal and Other Credits).

SECTION IV - CERTIFICATE OF APPLICANT

I certify that the amount of charges (exclusive of subcontractors' charges) due as of the date of this application and allocable to the terminated portion of contract number _____ dated_____

with _____ , is not less than $ _____ : that, to the best of my knowledge,

(From Section II, Line 9)

the amounts received are set forth above: and that I have not assigned any moneys payable under this contract, except as set forth above.

NAME OF APPLICANT	BY (Signature of authorized official)	
	TITLE	DATE

SECTION V - RECOMMENDATIONS OF FIRST REVIEWING CONTRACTOR

The undersigned states that it has examined this application and has considered the applicant's general reputation. It has no reason to doubt the accuracy of the information contained in this application or that amount certified by the applicant as due will constitute a proper charge to be included in

the undersigned's termination settlement proposal against _____
it recommends that the requested partial payment be made.

The undersigned agrees that it will promptly pay over to the applicant or credit against amounts owing from the applicant any amount received for the benefit of the applicant under this application, and that it will repay to the Government on demand any amount not so paid or credited.

NAME OF CONTRACTOR	BY (Signature of authorized official)	
	TITLE	DATE

SECTION VI - RECOMMENDATIONS OF OTHER REVIEWING CONTRACTORS

Each of the undersigned states that it has no reason to doubt that the amount of the partial payment requested, and recommended above is due the applicant will constitute a proper charge in the termination settlement proposal of the undersigned.

Each of the undersigned agrees that it will promptly pay over to its immediate subcontractor or credit against amounts owing from such subcontractor any amount received for the benefit of the applicant under this application, and that it will repay to the Government on demand any amount not so paid or credited.

	CONTRACTOR	DATE	IDENTIFICATION OF YOUR CONTRACT	SIGNATURE OF OFFICER, PARTNER, OR OWNER
1				
2				
3				

(Where the space provided for any information is insufficient, continue on a separate sheet.)

J61241/10-09-96

STANDARD FORM 1440 (REV. 7-89) PAGE 2

Appendix 12.10 (Continued)

SCHEDULE OF ACCOUNTING INFORMATION

FORM APPROVED OMB NO.
9000-0012

Public reporting burden for this collection of information is estimated to average 2.5 hours per response, including the time for reviewing instructions, searching existing data sources, gathering and maintaining the data needed, and completing and reviewing the collection of information. Send comments regarding this burden estimate or any other aspect of this collection of information, including suggestions for reducing this burden, to the FAR Secretariat (VRS), Office of Federal Acquisition and Regulatory Policy, GSA, Washington, D.C. 20405; and to the Office of Management and Budget, Paperwork Reduction Project (9000-0012), Washington, D.C. 20503.

To be used by prime contractors submitting termination proposals under Part 49 of the Federal Acquisition Regulation. Also suitable for use by subcontractor in effecting subcontract settlements with prime contractor or immediate subcontractor.

THIS PROPOSAL APPLIES TO (Check one)	COMPANY (Prime or Subcontractor)
☐ A PRIME CONTRACT WITH THE GOVERNMENT ☐ SUBCONTRACT OR PURCHASE ORDER	
SUBCONTRACT OR PURCHASE ORDER NO.(S)	STREET ADDRESS

CONTRACTOR WHO SENT NOTICE OF TERMINATION	CITY AND STATE (Include ZIP Code)
NAME AND ADDRESS (Include ZIP Code)	
	NAME OF GOVERNMENT AGENCY

	GOVERNMENT PRIME CONTRACT NO.	CONTRACTOR'S REFERENCE NO.	EFFECTIVE DATE OF TERMINATION

1. INDIVIDUAL IN YOUR ORGANIZATION FROM WHOM ADDITIONAL INFORMATION MAY BE REQUESTED ON QUESTIONS RELATING TO:

ACCOUNTING MATTERS		PROPERTY DISPOSAL	
NAME		NAME	
TITLE	TELEPHONE NO.	TITLE	TELEPHONE NO.
ADDRESS (Include ZIP Code)		ADDRESS (Include ZIP Code)	

2. ARE THE ACCOUNTS OF THE CONTRACTOR SUBJECT TO REGULAR PERIODIC EXAMINATION BY INDEPENDENT PUBLIC ACCOUNTANTS?

☐ YES   ☐ NO   (Name and address of accountants)

3. INDEPENDENT ACCOUNTANTS, IF ANY, WHO HAVE REVIEWED OR ASSISTED IN THE PREPARATION OF THE ATTACHED PROPOSAL

NAME	ADDRESS (Include ZIP Code)

4. GOVERNMENTAL AGENCY(IES) WHICH HAVE REVIEWED YOUR ACCOUNTS IN CONNECTION WITH PRIOR SETTLEMENT PROPOSALS DURING THE CURRENT AND PRECEDING FISCAL YEAR

NAME	ADDRESS (Include ZIP Code)

5. HAVE THERE BEEN ANY SIGNIFICANT DEVIATIONS FROM YOUR REGULAR ACCOUNTING PROCEDURES AND POLICIES IN ARRIVING AT THE COSTS SET FORTH IN THE ATTACHED PROPOSAL? (If "Yes," explain briefly)

☐ YES   ☐ NO

6. WERE THE DETAILED COST RECORDS USED IN PREPARING THE PROPOSAL CONTROLLED BY AND IN AGREEMENT WITH YOUR GENERAL BOOKS OF ACCOUNT?   ☐ YES   ☐ NO

7. STATE METHOD OF ACCOUNTING FOR TRADE AND CASH DISCOUNTS EARNED, REBATES, ALLOWANCES, AND VOLUME PRICE ADJUSTMENTS. ARE SUCH ITEMS EXCLUDED FROM COSTS PROPOSED?   ☐ YES   ☐ NO

(Where the space provided for any information is insufficient, continue on a separate sheet.)

AUTHORIZED FOR LOCAL REPRODUCTION
Previous edition is usable
J61236/10-09-96

EXPIRATION DATE: 4-30-92   1439-102   **STANDARD FORM 1439**   (REV. 7-89)
Prescribed by GSA - FAR (48 CFR) 53.249(a)(6)

Appendix 12.11   Standard Form 1439, Schedule of Accounting Information

8. STATE METHOD OF RECORDING AND ABSORBING (1) GENERAL ENGINEERING AND GENERAL DEVELOPMENT EXPENSE AND (2) ENGINEERING AND DEVELOPMENT EXPENSE DIRECTLY APPLICABLE TO THE TERMINATED CONTRACT.

9. STATE TYPES AND SOURCE OF MISCELLANEOUS INCOME AND CREDITS AND MANNER OF RECORDING IN THE INCOME OR THE COST ACCOUNTS SUCH AS RENTAL OF YOUR FACILITIES TO OUTSIDE PARTIES, ETC.

10. METHOD OF ALLOCATING GENERAL AND ADMINISTRATIVE EXPENSE.

11. ARE COSTS AND INCOME FROM CHANGE ORDERS SEGREGATED FROM OTHER CONTRACT COSTS AND INCOME? (If "Yes," by what method?)
☐ YES   ☐ NO

12. METHOD OF COMPUTING PROFIT SHOWN IN THE ATTACHED PROPOSAL AND REASON FOR SELECTING THE METHOD USED. FURNISH ESTIMATE OF AMOUNT OR RATE OF PROFIT IN DOLLARS OR PERCENT ANTICIPATED HAD THE CONTRACT BEEN COMPLETED.

13. ARE SETTLEMENT EXPENSES APPLICABLE TO PREVIOUSLY TERMINATED CONTRACTS EXCLUDED FROM THE ATTACHED PROPOSALS? (If "NO," explain)
☐ YES   ☐ NO

14. DOES THIS PROPOSAL INCLUDE CHARGES FOR MAJOR INVENTORY ITEMS AND PROPOSALS OF SUBCONTRACTORS COMMON TO THIS TERMINATED CONTRACT AND OTHER WORK OF THE CONTRACTOR? (If "Yes," explain the method used in allocating amounts to the terminated portion of this contract.)
☐ YES   ☐ NO

15. EXPLAIN BRIEFLY YOUR METHOD OF PRICING INVENTORIES, INDICATING WHETHER MATERIAL HANDLING COST HAS BEEN INCLUDED IN CHARGES FOR MATERIALS.

16. ARE ANY PARTS, MATERIALS, OR FINISHED PRODUCT, KNOWN TO BE DEFECTIVE, INCLUDED IN THE INVENTORIES? (If "Yes," explain.)
☐ YES   ☐ NO

(Where the space provided for any information is insufficient, continue on a separate sheet.)

STANDARD FORM 1439 (REV. 7-89) **PAGE 2**

J61237
10-09-96

Appendix 12.11   (Continued)

456

17. WERE INVENTORY QUANTITIES BASED ON A PHYSICAL COUNT AS OF THE DATE OF TERMINATION? (If "NO," explain exceptions.)

☐ YES   ☐ NO

18. DESCRIBE BRIEFLY THE NATURE OF INDIRECT EXPENSE ITEMS INCLUDED IN INVENTORY COSTS (See Schedule A, SF 1435) AND EXPLAIN YOUR METHOD OF ALLOCATION USED IN PREPARING THIS PROPOSAL, INCLUDING IF PRACTICABLE, THE RATES USED AND THE PERIOD OF TIME UPON WHICH THEY ARE BASED.

19. STATE GENERAL POLICIES RELATING TO DEPRECIATION AND AMORTIZATION OF FIXED ASSETS, BASES, UNDERLYING POLICIES.

20. DO THE COSTS SET FORTH IN THE ATTACHED PROPOSAL INCLUDE PROVISIONS FOR ANY RESERVES OTHER THAN DEPRECIATION RESERVES?
(If "Yes," list such reserves)

☐ YES   ☐ NO

21. STATE POLICY OR PROCEDURE FOR RECORDING AND WRITING OFF STARTING LOAD.

22. STATE POLICIES FOR DISTINGUISHING BETWEEN CHARGES TO CAPITAL (FIXED) ASSET ACCOUNTS AND TO REPAIR AND MAINTENANCE ACCOUNTS.

23. ARE PERISHABLE TOOLS AND MANUFACTURING SUPPLIES CHARGED DIRECTLY TO CONTRACT COSTS OR INCLUDED IN INDIRECT EXPENSES?

(Where the space provided for any information is insufficient, continue on a separate sheet.)

STANDARD FORM 1439 (REV. 7-89) **PAGE 3**

J61238
10-09-96

Appendix 12.11 (Continued)

457

24. HAVE ANY CHARGES FOR SEVERANCE, DISMISSAL, OR SEPARATION PAY BEEN INCLUDED IN THIS PROPOSAL? (If "Yes," furnish brief explanation and estimates of amounts included.)

☐ YES   ☐ NO

25. STATE POLICIES RELATING TO RECORDING OF OVERTIME SHIFT PREMIUMS AND PRODUCTION BONUSES.

26. DOES CONTRACTOR HAVE A PENSION PLAN? (If "Yes," state method of funding and absorption of past and current pension service costs.)

☐ YES   ☐ NO

27. IS THIS SETTLEMENT PROPOSAL BASED ON STANDARD COSTS?

☐ YES (If "Yes," has adjustment to actual cost or adjustment for any significant variations been made?)   ☐ YES   ☐ NO (If "NO," explain.)
☐ NO

28. DOES THIS PROPOSAL INCLUDE ANY ELEMENT OF PROFIT TO THE CONTRACTOR OR RELATED ORGANIZATION, OTHER THAN (a) PROFIT SET FORTH SEPARATELY IN THE PROPOSAL OR (b) PROFIT INCLUDED IN THE CONTRACT PRICE AT WHICH ACCEPTABLE FINISHED PRODUCT, IF ANY, IS INCLUDED IN THE PROPOSAL? (If "Yes," explain briefly.)

☐ YES   ☐ NO

29. WHAT IS LENGTH OF TIME (PRODUCTION CYCLE) REQUIRED TO PRODUCE ONE OF THE END ITEMS FROM THE TIME THE MATERIAL ENTERS THE PRODUCTION LINE TO THE COMPLETION AS THE FINISHED PRODUCT?

30. STATE POLICY AND PROCEDURE FOR VERIFICATION AND NEGOTIATION OF SETTLEMENTS WITH SUBCONTRACTORS AND VENDORS.

CERTIFICATE

THIS CERTIFIES THAT, TO THE BEST KNOWLEDGE AND BELIEF OF THE UNDERSIGNED, THE ABOVE STATEMENTS ARE TRUE AND CORRECT.

NAME OF CONTRACTOR	BY (Signature of supervisory accounting official)	
	TITLE	DATE

(Where the space provided for any information is insufficient, continue on a separate sheet.)

STANDARD FORM 1439 (REV. 7-89) **PAGE 4**

J61239
10-09-96

Appendix 12.11   (Continued)

Chapter Thirteen

Disputes and Sanctions

13-1. BACKGROUND

Given the complexity and nature of the government contracting process, formal protests and disputes are bound to arise. As in commercial contracting, no matter how clearly the intentions are included in a solicitation or a contractual document and no matter how stable the environment, the diverse interests of the parties can easily create misunderstandings and disagreements. As examples, the parties may disagree on whether the government has followed the source selection evaluation criteria set forth in the solicitation notice; the amount of adjustment involved in a change order issued by the contracting officer (CO); the allowability of costs resulting from a contract termination; or the excess costs incurred because of government-caused delays.

Disagreements can be resolved through administrative or judicial processes; however, such resolution requires considerable time and expense. Often, such disagreements can be completely avoided through advance planning. Ambiguities about the source selection evaluation process to be followed by the government should be addressed in a prebidder's conference. Advance agreements can also be negotiated to avoid future disputes on the allowability of significant, special, or unusual costs that are not specifically addressed in the cost principles.

Protests and disputes can also be settled through negotiation. This method of resolution should not be taken lightly. Many bid protest and contracting issues involve "gray" areas in which both parties have valid arguments. The better the case a bidder or contractor can make for its position, the better are the chances of achieving a favorable settlement. Contractors may find it helpful to bring in an outside source with experience in the disputed area, to provide a fresh and perhaps more objective view of the issues, in addition to providing potential arguments not yet considered.

The lines of communication with the CO should be kept open as long as a favorable settlement is possible. Nevertheless, there may come a time when further discussion is clearly useless and the dispute must be resolved at another level. Contractors should not avoid the judicial or administrative disputes process if the issue is significant and if their representatives feel strongly about their position. Further, once the government is aware that a bidder or a contractor will resort to the formal resolution process if necessary, the government will be less likely to take an unreasonable position on future issues.

As an alternative to the judicial process of resolving formal disputes, an administrative process provides a simpler means of resolution. The authority for using an administrative board to resolve government contract disputes was approved by the Supreme Court in 1878.[1]

13-2. CONTRACT DISPUTES ACT OF 1978

The Contract Disputes Act of 1978[2] was enacted after a report by the Commission on Government Procurement called for sweeping reform in the system of legal and administrative remedies for resolving government contract disputes. The act implemented many of the Commission's recommendations and established a uniform statutory basis for settling contract disputes and claims. The Senate committee report on the proposed legislation provided a succinct description of its purpose:

> The Contract Disputes Act of 1978 provides a fair, balanced, and comprehensive statutory system of legal and administrative remedies in resolving Government contract claims. The Act's provisions help to induce resolution of more contract disputes by negotiation prior to litigation; equalize the bargaining power of the parties when a dispute exists; provide alternate forums suitable to handle the different types of disputes; and ensure fair and equitable treatment to contractors and Government agencies.[3]

This chapter describes the disputes process under the act and highlights the changes since the prior disputes resolution process.

Applicability

The act became applicable to new contracts awarded by executive agencies beginning on March 1, 1979. On contracts awarded before March 1, 1979, a contractor had the option of using the previous procedures in the Disputes clause of the contract or the procedures available under the act. However, to use this option, the contractor's claim must have been pending before a CO on March 1, 1979, or initiated later. The Court of Claims, in *Monroe M. Tapper and Associates v. United States*,[4] found that a claim is not "pending" once the CO issues a final decision.

With few exceptions, the act [Section 3(a)] applies to any express or implied contract entered into by an executive agency for the following reasons:

- Procurement of property, other than real property in being
- Procurement of services
- Procurement of construction, alteration, repair, or maintenance of real property
- Disposal of personal property

The act accords special treatment to Tennessee Valley Authority contracts and does not apply to contracts with foreign governments (or their agencies) or international organizations (or their subsidiary bodies) if the agency head determines that it would not be in the public interest.

Definition of a Claim

Prior to 1991, it had become a relatively common practice for contractors to submit termination settlement proposals and requests for equitable adjustments (REAs) as "claims" so that interest would run from the date of a proposal's submission. This practice was challenged, however, by a series of board and court decisions which held that a proposal does not normally meet the criteria for a claim under the Contract Disputes Act (CDA).

- The Armed Services Board of Contract Appeals (ASBCA) ruled in *James R. Roane Construction Co.*[5] that the contractor's termination settlement proposal was not a claim because no dispute existed between the parties when the proposal was submitted. In its opinion, the Board observed:

  > It is well settled that termination settlement proposals are generally not considered claims within the meaning of the Disputes clause and the CDA. The settlement proposal is merely part of the contractually designated procedure for administration of the contract. ... Here, petitioner has revised its settlement proposal substantially several times since its initial submission in December 1989. In response to the most recent proposal submitted in April 1991, the Government indicated its intention to conduct an audit and then enter into negotiations.

  > If, after negotiations have taken place, the parties reach an impasse, the contractor may file a claim and petition this Board for an order directing the contracting officer to issue a final decision if the contracting officer does not respond timely. ... That appellant attached a CDA certification to its settlement proposal does not transform it into a claim.

- In deciding whether Essex Electro Engineers, Inc.'s change order proposals were claims, the court of appeals iterated three requirements for a submission to constitute a claim: "(1) the demand or assertion must be in writing, (2) the money must be sought as a matter of right, and (3) the writing must set forth a sum certain."[6] The court concluded that Essex Electro's proposals for work to be performed were not claims because "neither of these submissions asserted anything as a matter of right."

- The Federal Circuit concluded that Dawco Construction, Inc.'s[7] proposal dated May 24, 1984, for increased costs incurred as a result of directed changes and differing site conditions encountered in the performance of its construction contract did not meet the CDA criteria for a claim because no request for payment was in dispute at the time. The court contrasted the May 24, 1984, proposal with later correspondence dated January 9, 1986, when it was clear that negotiations had been abandoned and the amount claimed was definitely in dispute. The Federal Circuit cited both the Defense Acquisition Regulation disputes clause that was incorporated into Dawco's contract as well as the Federal Acquisition Regulation (FAR) 33.201 definition of a claim that was written subsequent to the award of Dawco's contract. However, the language in these two citations is decidedly different. Dawco's disputes clause explicitly stated that "... a request for payment that is not in dispute when submitted is not a claim for purposes of the [Contract Disputes] Act." In contrast, FAR 33.201 defines a claim as follows:

  > [A] written demand or written assertion by one of the contracting parties seeking, as a matter of right, the payment of money in a sum certain, ... A voucher, invoice, or other routine request for payment that is not in dispute is not a claim.

- The ASBCA concluded in *Reflectone, Inc.*[8] that the contractor's certified request for equitable adjustment was not a claim because the amount was not in dispute when the REA was submitted. Although the CO on several occasions had denied government responsibility for contract delays, no amount was in dispute at the time of Reflectone's submission. The Board noted: "Dawco requires that the parties be in dispute over the amount requested. Clearly, in the appeal before us, RI had not quantified the impact of the delays on itself and communicated it to the Government prior to the 1 June 1990 REA." Although the Board's *Reflectone* decision was affirmed by the Federal Circuit,[9] the court later vacated its decision,[10] and reheard the case en banc. On rehearing en banc, the court reversed[11] and held as follows:

  > ... [P]roperly construed for its plain meaning the language of FAR 33.201 does not require that a payment contained in a purported CDA claim be in dispute before being submitted for decision to the CO unless that demand is a "voucher, invoice or other route request for payment." To the extent that Dawco and cases relying on Dawco can be read to suggest otherwise, they are overruled.

  With this Federal Circuit decision, the contentious issue of when is a claim a claim seems to have finally been resolved.

- The ASBCA[12] denied the recovery of costs incurred by an outside consultant, Excell, that were included in Bill Strong Enterprises, Inc.'s REA for delay and disruption caused by out-of-sequence work assignments. The ASBCA concluded that, at the time the REA was submitted on November 30, 1989, the government "disputed, in substantial part, the amount claimed by appellant." In reversing the ASBCA decision, the Federal Circuit held that the definition of a claim under FAR 31.205-33 is the same as the definition of a claim for purposes of establishing jurisdiction under the CDA and that Strong's proposal never ripened into a dispute.[13] The Federal Circuit remanded the appeal to the board with instructions to allow the costs to the extent they were reasonable and allocable. In a post-*Reflectone* decision,[14] the ASBCA on remand concluded that "... the status of a submittal as a claim under *Dawco* is not ipso facto determinative of allowability of costs associated herewith." In allowing Bill Strong's consultant costs, the ASBCA looked to the purpose for incurrence of the cost. If the cost was incurred for the purpose of furthering the negotiation process, it should be allowable, even if the negotiation ultimately fails and a claim is later submitted.

- The ASBCA denied a government motion to dismiss, for lack of jurisdiction, Jonathan Corporation's 150-page submission dated March 13, 1992, seeking reimbursement of corporate aircraft costs.[15] Although the CO had not rendered a final decision as of March 13, 1992, the Board concluded that the parties were in dispute over corporate aircraft expenses six months prior to Jonathan's submission. As support, the Board noted the following:
  - The CO's "failure to resolve clearly defined cost issues for five years is indicative of an impasse."
  - The CO had stated that the government agreed with the Defense Contract Audit Agency (DCAA) Form 1 and that he would make no further effort to reach agreement by negotiation before an appeal was taken.

  The Board also disagreed with the government's assertion that Jonathan's submission did not allege entitlement to a sum certain. The Board noted that Jonathan's submission tabulated, as disputed items, the sum certain amounts of corporate aircraft expense for which the DCAA had either issued a Form 1 or unilaterally eliminated 95% of the amounts proposed from Jonathan's provisional billing rates.

- In *World Computer Systems, Inc.*[16] the Department of Transportation Contract Appeals Board (DOTCAB) invalidated a final decision that incorporated cost disallowances from a DCAA audit report because the CO issued the final decision only one working day after receiving the audit report. The Board concluded that "there was simply insufficient time for a dispute over the Defense Contract Audit Agency findings to materialize."

Claims Relating to a Contract

The phrase *relating to a contract* includes breach of contract claims. Before the act, only disputes concerning a question of fact "arising under a contract" were subject to the administrative remedies process. Under the Tucker Act,[17] questions of law, such as breach of contract claims, were to be brought to a federal district court if the amount of the claim did not exceed $10,000 or to the Court of Claims for any amount. The Contract Disputes Act amended the Tucker Act to delete jurisdiction of the district courts over contract claims against the United States that are subject to jurisdiction of the Court of Claims.

Certification of Claims

Contractors must certify claims over $100,000. The threshold for certification was raised from $50,000 to $100,000 effective October 1, 1995. The certification requirement was added as a result of Admiral H. G. Rickover's testimony concerning "inflated" claims (i.e., unsupported claims inflated as a negotiation ploy to obtain a more favorable settlement). The act, as amended, provides that:

> For claims of more than $100,000, the contractor shall certify that the claim is made in good faith, that the supporting data are accurate and complete to the best of his knowledge and belief, and that the amount requested accurately reflects the contract adjustment for which the contractor believes the government is liable.[18]

Federal Acquisition Regulation 33.207 provides that a claim seeking the payment of money exceeding $100,000 is not a claim under the Act until certified. In *Harnischfeger*,[19] the ASBCA dismissed claims for lack of unqualified certification. The Board stated that the lack of a finite amount effectively precluded any meaningful consideration of the claim by the CO. In a related case, *Newell Clothing Co.*,[20] the contractor attempted to have the CO and ASBCA rule first on entitlement to a claim, reserving money damages for disposition by negotiation or further appeal. As such, Newell did not submit a certified claim. While there was a dissenting opinion, the majority opinion required a certified claim because it exceeded $50,000 and, therefore, dismissed the appeal as premature. In *Paul E. Lehman, Inc. v. United States*,[21] the Court of Claims held that a claim over $50,000 is not a valid claim unless it has been certified and dismissed a contractor's suit because of the lack of certification. The fact that a CO rendered a final decision on the claim was of no consequence because the court ruled that a contracting officer has no authority to waive a requirement imposed by statute. This ruling was affirmed in subsequent cases and should be considered firm. In *Skelly and Loy v. United States*,[22] the Court of Claims ruled that it did not have jurisdiction to hear an uncertified claim over $50,000. However, it stated that the contractor could correct the defect by resubmitting its claim with a proper certification.

Further, in *W.H. Moseley Co., Inc.*,[23] the ASBCA decided that it is not barred from ordering a CO to issue a new final decision when the contractor later submits a properly certified claim.

The issue of who should certify claims was litigated on numerous occasions. The government initially challenged certifications submitted under the Contract Disputes Act (CDA) for failure to comply with the FAR requirement that certification be made by "a senior company official in charge at the plant or location involved, or by an officer or general partner of the contractor having overall responsibility for conduct of the contractor's affairs." Among those companies challenging the certification requirements were Newport News Shipbuilding,[24] Emerson Electric Company,[25] and Grumman Aerospace Corporation.[26] In *Omega Services, Inc.*,[27] the ASBCA concluded that the company official signing the certification need not have the title of president but must essentially function as the chief executive officer. The Federal Circuit reversed the ASBCA decision in *Fischbach & Moore International Corp. v. Secretary of State*[28] and accepted the contractor's executive vice president's certification that the supporting data were accurate and complete to the best of his *understanding and belief* as opposed to his *knowledge and belief.*

Language clarifying who is the appropriate individual to execute the certificate was included in the Fiscal Year 1993 National Defense Authorization Act.[29] The act permits any individual who is authorized to bind the contractor and who has knowledge of (1) the basis of the claim or request and (2) the accuracy and completeness of the supporting data to sign the certificate. The Federal Courts Administration Act of 1992[30] amended the CDA to provide that a claim may be certified by "any person duly authorized to bind the contractor with respect to the claim." Furthermore, a key provision in the amendment states that "a defect in a certification of a claim shall not deprive a court or agency board of contract appeals of jurisdiction over the claim." However, a defective certification must be corrected before entering a final judgment.

The act has been interpreted to mean that when the government makes a claim against a contractor and withholds funds against a contract to obtain payment, the contractor does not have to certify its claim in order to get its money.[31]

Fraudulent Claims

If a contractor is unable to support any part of its claim and such inability is determined to be attributable to misrepresentation of fact or fraud, the contractor is liable to the government for an amount equal to the unsupported part of the claim in addition to the government's costs of reviewing the unsupported part of the claim.

The penalty provided under the act does not relieve the contractor from liability under the False Claims Act[32] (31 U.S.C. 231); also, liability under this provision can exist regardless of the size of the claim and whether or not it was certified.

Required Notices

Some contract clauses require notification to the CO of circumstances that may entitle the contractor to submit a claim. For example, under the "Changes—Fixed-Price" clause [FAR 52.243-1(c)], a contractor is required to assert a claim for an equitable adjustment within 30 days of receipt of the change notification unless waived by the contracting officer. Such notices or claims are usually prerequisites to the issuance of a final decision by the CO. If they are required but not presented, the contracting office may not make a final decision; therefore, there is no basis for appeal. Further, time restraints imposed may preclude further consideration of a claim. Some other clauses that contain such notification requirements are Differing Site Conditions, Economic Price Adjustment Standard Supplies, and Government Delay of Work.

Contracting Officer's Decision

The CO is the starting point for all claims relating to a contract, whether initiated by the contractor or the government. Contractor claims relating to a contract must be submitted to the CO for a decision. Government claims must also be formalized through a CO decision. However, claims assigned statutorily to another government agency are excluded. For example, in *Allied Painting & Decorating Co.*,[33] the ASBCA found that disputes falling under the Davis–Bacon Act are subject to a review and decision by the Secretary of Labor.

The CO's final decision is to be in writing, with a copy furnished to the contractor by mail or other means. Federal Acquisition Regulation 33.211 states that the decision must: (1) describe the claim or dispute; (2) refer to the pertinent contract terms; (3) state the factual area of agreement and disagreement; (4) present the final decision and the supporting rationale; and (5) inform the contractor of its rights to appeal to the applicable board of contract appeals or court of claims.

Not every letter, order, instruction, or communication issued by a contracting officer represents an appealable final decision. For example, in *R.G. Robbins Co., Inc.*,[34] a letter, which suggested a no-cost settlement in response to the contractor's proposed settlement of a partial termination for convenience, was not deemed final decision. The ASBCA stated that the standard for determining if a communication from a contracting officer represents a final decision is whether the "... communication manifested objectively that the contractor's claim cannot be satisfied or settled by agreement or, alternatively, that there has been a failure of the parties to agree upon the amount ...."

It is important to make a valid attempt to resolve disagreements before entering the dispute process, which can be costly as well as time-consuming. The ability to settle disputes in this manner depends on the government and contractor representatives' ability to maintain an open mind on the issues. The Office of Federal Procurement Policy (OFPP) regulatory coverage on the resolution of claims contains the following statement:

> In appropriate circumstances, before issuance of a contracting officer's decision on a claim, informal discussions between the parties, to the extent feasible by individuals who have not participated substantially in the matter in dispute, can aid in the resolution of differences by mutual agreement and should be considered.[35]

The CO's decision on any submitted claim of $100,000 or less must be issued within 60 days of receipt of the claim if requested by the contractor. On certified claims of more than $100,000, the CO is required to either issue a decision or notify the contractor when a decision is expected to be issued within 60 days of receipt of the claim. A key requirement is that the final decision must be issued within a reasonable time, considering the size of the claim, its complexity, and the adequacy of the contractor's support for the claim.

If the final decision is unreasonably delayed, a contractor may request the applicable board of contract appeals to direct the CO to issue a decision within a specified time. Further, the failure to issue a decision on a contract claim within the required period will be considered a denial of the claim. The contractor may then pursue the appeals process. In *SCM Corp. v. United States*,[36] the Court of Claims found that, since the CO neither issued a decision within 60 days after receiving SCM's certified claim nor formally notified SCM within that period that a specified time beyond 60 days would be required, he was deemed to have denied the claim. The claim had been pending before the contracting officer for almost two years before SCM obtained relief in the Court of Claims, and the CO never advised the contractor that he would need additional time to reach a decision. Similarly, in *Westclox Military Products*,[37] the ASBCA ruled that, notwithstanding the inadequacy of a submitted certified claim, the CO is not relieved of the statutory duty to issue (within 60 days) a final decision or notify the contractor when a decision can be expected. In the event a contractor appeals or files suit without the CO's final decision, the tribunal reviewing the claim may suspend its proceedings to obtain such a decision.

The Disputes clause (FAR 52.233-1) obligates a contractor to continue performance only if the dispute "arises under the contract." Nevertheless, in contracts that may be vital to security or the public health and welfare, procuring agencies are allowed to change the standard Disputes clause to obligate a contractor to continue performance even if a breach of contract dispute arises (FAR 33.214).

13-3. APPEALS PROCESS

Once the CO issues a final decision, a contractor has two options if it wants to contest the decision. It can appeal to the applicable agency contract appeals board, or it can file suit directly in the Court of Federal Claims. In either event, actions proceed de novo, which means that the CO's decision carries no presumption of correctness and that the court can either increase or decrease the award made in that decision.[38]

In a favorable disposition of a contractor's claim, interest on the amount found due the contractor is paid from the date the CO receives the claim from the contractor until payment. A favorable disposition could involve a final judgment by a board or by the Court of Federal Claims or a settlement between the government and the contractor before a board or court decision. The interest is paid at the rate established by the Secretary of the Treasury pursuant to Public Law 92-41.[39]

According to the House Judiciary Committee, the CDA "certification" requirement was intended only as a prerequisite to payment. However, in *Lehman*,[40] the Court of Claims held that without certification, there is no claim for the court to review. If there is no claim, there is nothing to which interest may be applied.

In *Brookfield Construction Co.*,[41] the Court of Claims held that, on claims pending as of the act's effective date, interest is payable only from that date (March 1, 1979) to the date of payment. In another case, *Fidelity Construction Co.*,[42] the DOTCAB decided, and the Court of Appeals affirmed, that a contractor's submission of an uncertified and grossly overstated claim did not start the "interest clock running." Instead, interest was determined from the time a certified and reasonable claim was submitted.

Simple interest is calculated using all of the Treasury rates in effect for the periods during which a claim remains unpaid.[43]

Court judgments and board monetary awards must be promptly paid to contractors. Payment is made from the U.S. Treasury and is backcharged to the procuring agency involved, to be paid out of available appropriated funds.

Agency Boards of Contract Appeals

An executive agency may establish a board of contract appeals if, after consulting with the Administrator of the OFPP, a workload study shows a need for at least three full-time board members. If the volume of claims is not enough to justify a board or if considered otherwise appropriate, the agency head may arrange for appeals to be decided by another agency board. Effective October 14, 1993, the National Aeronautics and Space Administration (NASA) discontinued the NASA Board of Contract Appeals and entered into an agreement with the Department of Defense (DOD) for NASA contract appeals to be decided by the ASBCA. Failing this, the agency head can submit the case to the Administrator of the OFPP for placement with an agency board.

The ASBCA, the largest of all boards, prepares an annual report of its activities after the end of each government fiscal year. The report provides such information as the number of appeals docketed and disposed of, average dollar amount of claims, types and nature of contracts involved, principal contract clauses involved, and average number of days from the docketing date to the decision date. Figure 13.1 presents the reported case workload for government fiscal years 1994, 1995, and 1996.

Members selected for agency boards must have at least five years experience in public contract law. The chair and vice chair of each board are selected from the board members by the agency head (or his/her designate). Board members are designated as administrative judges.

The boards have jurisdiction to decide any appeal of a CO's decision "relative to a contract," including breach of contract claims, which previously had to be decided judicially, and claims arising under implied contracts. Requests for relief under the Extraordinary Contractual Relief Act[44] (FAR, Part 50) are not considered claims under the act. In exercising their additional jurisdiction, the boards are authorized to grant any relief that would be available to a litigant asserting a contract claim in the Court of Federal Claims. While money damages are the usual form of relief available to the Court of Federal Claims, the boards have also been granted contract rescission[45] and reformation authority.[46] However, specific performance may not be ordered.[47]

The boards have the ability to administer oaths to witnesses, authorize depositions and discovery proceedings, and subpoena witnesses and production of books and papers. Subpoenas will be enforced in the federal district courts.

	FY 1994	FY 1995	FY 1996
On hand at beginning of year	2,027	1,977	1,822
Docketed during year	1,533	1,323	1,105
Total requiring disposition	3,560	3,300	2,927
Disposed of during year	1,583	1,478	1,384
On hand at year end	1,977	1,822	1,543

Figure 13.1   ASBCA Workload, Fiscal Years 1994–1996

Time Limitation for Filing an Appeal

Appeals must be filed within 90 days after receipt of the CO's decision. The time limit may be extended if the CO's final decision does not adequately inform the contractor of its rights and options.

The burden of proof is on the contractor to show that an appeal is timely. In *Policy Research, Inc.,*[48] the ASBCA reasserted that the act's 90-day provision was jurisdictional and that it had no authority to waive or excuse a contractor's failure to file within that period. This conclusion affirmed by the U.S. Court of Appeals for the Federal Circuit in *Cosmic Construction Co. v. United States.*[49]

The contractor must mail or otherwise furnish written notice of an appeal to the applicable board and must provide a copy to the CO. It is important that the notice (1) indicate that an appeal is being made, (2) identify the department and agency or bureau involved, (3) reference the CO's final decision, and (4) identify the contract involved in the dispute by number and the amount in dispute, if known. The contractor must leave no doubt that an appeal is intended.

Appeals Board Rules of Procedure

To achieve maximum uniformity in government contract appeals, the boards adopted OFPP guidelines, issued in June 1979,[50] except for minor variances due to a board's size or the nature of its docket. The following discussion highlights some of the more significant provisions of the guidelines; however, those involved in a dispute should refer to the applicable board's rules of procedure.

Docketing of Appeals.   When a notice of appeal is received by a board, it is docketed (placed on the board's docket). At that time, the appellant should receive written notice from the board, along with a copy of its rules of procedure.

Rule 4 File.   Within 30 days after receiving notice that an appeal has been filed, the CO should assemble and transmit to the board an appeal file (called the Rule 4 file), consisting of all documents pertinent to the appeal, and should furnish the appellant copies of these documents.

The appellant then has 30 days after receiving the file to transmit to the board any documents not contained in the file that are relevant to the appeal. Copies of such documents should be furnished to the government trial attorney. Since the Rule 4 file is considered part of the record upon which the board will make its decision, all relevant documents should be included and inappropriate documents excluded. In some cases, the board may not require a Rule 4 file if requested in the appeal or if stipulated later.

Complaint.   Within 30 days after receiving notice that the appeal has been docketed, the appellant is to file with the board a "complaint" setting forth simple, concise, and direct statements of each claim. The complaint should provide the basis for each claim, with references to the appropriate contract provisions, and the dollar amount claimed, if known. The rules allow for the complaint to be filed with the notice of appeal, or, alternatively, the notice of appeal may serve as the complaint if it contains the required information.

Answer to Complaint.   The government is required to prepare and submit to the board an "answer" to the complaint within 30 days after receiving the complaint. The government's answer is generally subject to the same requirements as the complaint. It should be simple, concise, direct, and preferably structured as a paragraph-by-paragraph admission or denial of corresponding paragraphs in the complaint. The appellant is provided a copy of the answer.

Amendments. Amendments to the complaint and to the answer are acceptable. Amendments may be made at the board's direction to either party to more definitively state the complaint or the answer or to reply to an answer. In addition, the board, at its discretion, may permit either party to amend its statements or "pleadings" under conditions fair to both parties.

Hearing Election. After the government's answer is filed, each party notifies the board whether it desires a hearing on the dispute or elects to have the case decided on the record without a hearing. Either party may elect to waive a hearing; however, this does not relieve the parties from the burden of proving the facts supporting their allegations or defenses. This may be accomplished through affidavits, depositions, answers to interrogatories (written questions), and stipulations to supplement other evidence in the record.

Prehearing Briefs. If a hearing is elected, the board may, at its discretion, require the parties to submit prehearing briefs to ensure the issues are adequately addressed. Either party may voluntarily submit a prehearing brief to the board provided it notifies the other party. All briefs must be received by the board at least 15 days before the hearing date, and a copy must be furnished to the other party.

Conferences. Whether or not a hearing is elected, the board may, at its discretion or by application of either party, arrange a conference (by telephone, if appropriate) to consider any matters that may aid in the appeal's disposition. Such matters may include (1) simplification, clarification, or severing of the issues; (2) agreements that will avoid unnecessary proof; and (3) the possibility of a settlement of any or all issues in dispute. The results of any such conferences, including rulings and orders, must be in writing and must be added to the board's record.

Discovery. To further document the record on which the board's decision will be based, the parties to the dispute are encouraged to engage in voluntary discovery procedures, including (1) taking depositions; (2) requesting issuance of subpoenas; (3) serving written interrogatories; and (4) requesting admissions and the production, inspection, and copying of documents. The board will intervene when necessary to protect the parties from undue requests or to order compliance with discovery requests.

Discovery, an important part of litigation, is critical to a successful prosecution, or possible settlement, of complex government contract cases. Discovery can identify weaknesses on the other side as well as its evidence. This information sometimes can be used as leverage in obtaining a favorable settlement. The boards generally look to the Federal Rules of Civil Procedure for guidance on discovery disputes (i.e., what is available versus what can be protected). Generally, the boards use the criterion of "good cause" in deciding what is or is not discoverable. For example, in *Airco, Inc.,*[51] the Department of the Interior Contract Appeals Board observed the following:

... [T]he touchstones of discovery are:

(1) probability that the discovery will lead to admissible evidence (but it is not a ground for objection that a document or other material involved in discovery is not admissible per se), and

(2) that the burden is commensurate with the need.

The objections to discovery are (1) privilege, but privilege is not absolute, especially when a competing concern overweighs the reason for the privilege, and (2) burden (i.e., the benefit likely to be derived from the discovery is clearly much smaller than the burden of compliance). If it can be shown that the requested information is relevant, needed, not subject to privilege, and not relatively burdensome to obtain, discovery is likely. However, if the requested information is privileged, is relatively burdensome to provide, and is not relevant or needed, discovery will likely be denied. These are extremes, however, and disputes in between these extremes must be viewed on a case-by-case basis.

The Freedom of Information Act (FOIA)[52] provides an important discovery tool for government contractors. This act provides for the right of access to information in the possession of most federal agencies. Before initiating litigation, the FOIA can be used to obtain information for deciding whether or not to litigate. It can be used to obtain information that is broader and more general than the scope of normal discovery. Further, information can often be obtained faster through the FOIA than through discovery. Of course, the act exempts documents from disclosure under nine exemptions. Exemptions most likely to be encountered by government contractors in requesting information for discovery purposes include Exemption 3, Specific Exemptions of Other Statutes; Exemption 4, Confidential Business Information, such as trade secrets and commercial or financial information; and Exemption 5, Agency Communications, which would be privileged and unavailable to a party in litigation with the agency. Since the FOIA can also be used to obtain contract information, government contractors need to understand their rights in preventing the disclosure of information submitted to the government. Normally, before information provided by a non-government source is released under the act, the source is notified of the intent to release and is given an opportunity to object to the release and to have its objections presented at a hearing.

Hearings and Representations.   Hearings are held at places and at times determined appropriate by the board. The board may adjust a hearing date if requested and if for good reason. The parties are to receive at least 15 days' notice of the time and place set for a hearing. In scheduling hearings, the board will consider the desires of the parties and the requirement for a just and inexpensive determination of appeals without unnecessary delay. Hearings are conducted informally and as deemed reasonable and appropriate in the circumstances. Evidence is offered in accordance with the federal rules of evidence, and witnesses are examined orally under oath or affirmation unless the presiding administrative judge or examiner orders otherwise. Because of the complex nature of many government contract issues, both contractors and the government rely on the testimony of expert witnesses to effectively present their cases. If scientific, accounting, or other specialized technical knowledge will assist the hearing officer in understanding the evidence presented or a fact at issue, the Federal Rules of Evidence allow expert witnesses to testify in the form of an opinion. Expert witnesses can be used effectively not only to support a position but also to rebut the testimony of an expert witness by the other side. An appellant may be represented before the board by an appropriate member of the appellant's organization or by a duly licensed attorney. In most cases, despite the relative informality of the proceedings, and especially if significant amounts are involved, the appellant should be represented by an attorney. At the conclusion of a hearing, and if agreed upon by all parties, posthearing briefs will be submitted.

Decisions and Motions for Reconsideration.   Board decisions on appeals are made in writing, with copies sent simultaneously to both parties. Generally, while hearings are conducted by a single administrative judge or examiner, decisions are made by a panel of administrative judges who decide the case by majority vote. The opinions of dissenting panel members are also provided. A motion for reconsideration of the decision may be filed within 30 days after receiving the decision. Such motions are not looked upon favorably by a board unless (1) newly discovered evidence is presented; (2) the decision contains a patent error, such as a math error; or (3) the decision needs clarification to be implemented. Rehashed arguments already on the record will be rejected.

Jurisdiction of Subcontractor Appeals.   The Contract Disputes Act has apparently had little, if any, effect on the rights of subcontractors in board proceedings. Normally, a subcontractor has no right of direct access to the boards because there is no "privity of contract" between the subcontractor and the government (i.e., the government is not a party to the subcontract). Nevertheless, there are exceptions to this general rule. Agency regulations or agreements may allow for direct access to the boards. Also, if the prime contractor is found to be acting as a purchasing agent for the government, a subcontractor may be found to have privity. Finally, a subcontractor may have its appeal brought to the board when the prime contractor agrees to sponsor an appeal on the subcontractor's behalf. In such cases, the prime contractor files the appeal and may either conduct the appeal or agree to have the subcontractor conduct it. When a contractor sponsors an appeal for a subcontractor in excess of the certification threshold, both the prime contractor and the subcontractor must certify the claim.[53] Because of potential problems concerning privity, the subcontractor should ensure that the subcontract includes provisions for the prime contractor to sponsor the subcontractor's appeal if the dispute is with the government. Furthermore, the subcontract should contain provisions for arbitration or other means for settling disputes between the contractor and the subcontractor.

Optional Accelerated and Small Claims Procedures.   One of the problems sought to be resolved by CDA was the inflexible board system that had evolved over the years. As a result, the act provided for accelerated and small claims appeals procedures, which are used at the sole election of the contractor. The election should be made in writing within 60 days after receiving notice that the appeal has been docketed. The rules of each agency board must include a procedure for the accelerated disposition of claims for $100,000 or less. The objective is to resolve such appeals within 180 days from the date the contractor elects to use the procedure. Although the conduct of accelerated cases is similar to the normal dispute process, time periods may be shortened, and pleadings, discovery, and other prehearing activities may be reduced or waived to enable the board to reach a decision within 180 days. The rules must also include a small claim procedure for the expedited disposition of claims for $50,000 or less. The objective is to resolve such appeals within 120 days from the date the contractor elects to use the procedure. Time periods of activities are shortened and rules are simplified to allow the board to reach a decision within the prescribed time. Decisions may be made by a single administrative judge and, unless fraudulent, are final and conclusive and may not be appealed. Such decisions have no precedential value for future cases (i.e., decisions in future cases may not be based on the findings in expedited cases). The dollar threshold for expedited procedures is reviewed by the Administrator of the OFPP every three years and adjusted based on selected economic indexes.

Judicial Review of Board Decisions.   A board's decision under regular or accelerated procedures is final unless (1) the contractor appeals the decision to the Court of Appeals for the Federal Circuit within 120 days after receiving the decision or (2) the agency head, after approval by the Attorney General, transmits the decision to the Court of Appeals for judicial review, again within 120 days. The 120-day period runs from receipt of the decision on the motion for reconsideration, not the original decision. Before the act, the government's ability to appeal board decisions to the Court of Claims was virtually impossible unless fraud or bad faith was found. In *S&E Contractors, Inc. v. United States,*[54] the Supreme Court decided that the Wunderlich Act was not intended to confer the same rights to contractors and the government regarding judicial review of board decisions. This decision was nullified by CDA Section 10(b), which states the following:

> [T]he decision of the agency board on any question of law shall not be final or conclusive, but the decision on any question of fact shall be final and conclusive and shall not be set aside unless the decision is fraudulent, or arbitrary, or capricious, or so grossly erroneous as to necessarily imply bad faith, or if such decision is not supported by substantial evidence.

The differentiation of questions of law and questions of fact is not always easily determined. Some cases involve mixed questions of law and fact.

Court of Federal Claims

Under the Federal Courts Administration Act of 1992,[55] the name of the United States Claims Court was changed to the United States Court of Federal Claims. (Before October 1982, the court was known as the U.S. Court of Claims Trial Division. It was changed to the U.S. Claims Court with the enactment of the Federal Courts Improvement Act.) In addition to its authority to decide monetary contract claims and disputes, the court's jurisdiction was expanded, under an amendment to the Tucker Act, to decide nonmonetary disputes, such as contract terminations for default and cost accounting standards compliance issues.

Appeals to the Court of Federal Claims must be filed within 12 months after receipt of the CO's decision.

Like decisions of the boards of contract appeals, decisions of the United States Court of Federal Claims can be appealed to the Court of Appeals for the Federal Circuit within 120 days.

Alternative Dispute Resolution

Contracting parties are increasingly turning to alternative dispute resolution (ADR) as a faster and less costly way to resolve disputes. Alternative dispute resolution is defined in FAR 33.201 as follows:

> [A]ny procedure or combination of procedures voluntarily used to resolve issues in controversy without the need to resort to litigation. These procedures include, but are not limited to, assisted

settlement negotiations, conciliation, facilitation, mediation, fact-finding, minitrials, and arbitration.

Congress permanently reauthorized the Administrative Dispute Resolution Act in 1996.[56] The act promotes the use of ADR by federal agencies to resolve disputes, and FAR 33.204 encourages agencies to use ADR procedures to the maximum extent possible. Executive Order 12988[57] issued in February 1996, requires government litigation counsel to be trained in ADR.

Department of Energy Acquisition Letter 94-22, effective January 22, 1995, states the agency's preference to use ADR in contract disputes if such an approach will facilitate resolution of the issue. The guidance particularly suggests that the parties consider ADR when only facts are in dispute and disputed amounts are less than $100,000. The guidance also suggests consideration of ADR if the responsible agency answers one or more of the following questions affirmatively:

1. Have settlement discussions reached an impasse?
2. Have ADR techniques been used successfully in similar situations?
3. Is there a significant disagreement over technical data, or is there a need for independent, expert analysis?
4. Does the claim have merit, but is its value overstated?
5. Are multiple parties, issues, and/or claims involved that can be resolved together?
6. Are there strong emotions that would benefit from the presence of a neutral?
7. Is there a continuing relationship between the parties that the dispute adversely affects?
8. Does formal resolution require more effort and time than the matter may merit?

Department of Defense Directive 5145.5, issued April 4, 1996, requires each DOD component to: implement ADR programs, use ADR techniques as an alternative to litigation or formal administrative proceedings whenever possible, review existing approaches to dispute resolution, and facilitate use of ADR where practical.

13-4. EXTRAORDINARY CONTRACTUAL RELIEF

The Extraordinary Contractual Relief Act,[58] as implemented by Executive Order 10789[59] and FAR, Part 50, permits certain executive departments and agencies to modify an existing contract without consideration when such action is in the national interest. The following federal executive departments and agencies are given such authority:

- Department of Defense
- U.S. Army
- U.S. Navy
- U.S. Air Force
- Department of the Treasury
- Department of the Interior

- Department of Agriculture
- Department of Commerce
- Department of Transportation
- Department of Energy
- National Aeronautics and Space Administration
- General Services Administration
- Government Printing Office
- Federal Emergency Management Agency
- Tennessee Valley Authority

Agency contract adjustment boards make the determinations and findings as to whether relief is to be granted. Decisions of these boards are not subject to appeal. The Senate and House Armed Services Committees have a period of 60 days of continuous sessions to veto any determinations that would obligate the government for amounts in excess of $25 million.

The incurrence of a contract loss is not a sufficient basis for exercising the authority conferred by the act. However, the act may be invoked when a loss on a defense contract will impair the ability of a contractor, whose viability is essential to the national defense, to continue contract performance. A contract may also be eligible for relief when the contract loss occurs because of government action. Contracts may also be amended to correct or mitigate the effect of mistakes, such as an ambiguity in the contract or an obvious mistake in an offeror's proposal.

Contractor requests for extraordinary contractual relief must provide the specific adjustment requested, a chronology of essential facts, and the basis for entitlement of relief. Requests for relief that exceed the simplified acquisition threshold require certification that the request is made in good faith and the supporting data are accurate and complete.

The Army Contract Adjustment Board[60] increased Remington Arms Company's contract by $75 million for recovery of health and life insurance benefits (HLIB), which were unfunded when Remington lost the recompetition for operating the Lake City Army Ammunition Plant (LCAAP). During its 45-year tenure as the plan operator, Remington had claimed reimbursement of its HLIB costs on a "pay-as-you-go" basis; as a result, the Army paid lower HLIB costs during those years than it would have paid if the costs had been accounted for on an accrual basis. In granting relief to Remington, the Board concluded the following:

> Remington's productive ability is not "essential to the national defense;" even if it were, the failure to award relief on the terms requested would be unlikely to plunge Remington into financial failure. But a denial of relief would clearly and substantially alter the bargain Remington struck with the Army in agreeing to operate LCAAP on a cost-reimbursement basis, if not place the company in a loss position with respect to those operations.

13-5. BID PROTESTS

Solicitations or awards affecting the economic interests of actual or potential offerors can be protested to the federal agency awarding the contract, the General Accounting Office, the Court of Federal Claims, and to a U.S. District Court.

Protests Filed with the Agency

A protest can be informally filed with the agency, as outlined in FAR 33.103. When the protest is filed before contract award, the award will normally be held in abeyance pending issuance of the agency decision on the protest; potential offerors will be informed of the protest and asked to extend the time for acceptance of offers. Award of the contract may proceed, in spite of the pending protest, if the product or service is urgently required, if delivery or performance will be severely affected by the delay, or if a prompt award is advantageous to the government. Protests received after contract award are processed in accordance with individual agency procedures. The CO is not required to suspend contract performance pending issuance of the agency decision unless it appears probable that the award will be invalidated.

Protests alleging apparent improprieties in the solicitation must be filed before the bid opening or the proposal receipt date. Protests for other reasons must be filed within 10 calendar days after the basis for the protest becomes (or should have become) known.

Protests Filed with the General Accounting Office

The Competition in Contracting Act (CICA)[61] significantly expanded the General Accounting Office's (GAO) role in bid protest resolution. Congress believed that a strong enforcement mechanism was necessary to ensure that its mandate for competition was enforced. Accordingly, the CICA provided, for the first time, an express statutory basis for the GAO to hear bid protest cases. Regulations implementing the CICA provisions are contained in Title 4 of the Code of Federal Regulations, Part 21, and in the FAR, Subpart 33.1. The GAO's bid protest regulations were revised in 1995 and 1996 to implement requirements of the Federal Acquisition Streamlining Act (FASA)[62] and the Clinger–Cohen Act.[63]

- Protests alleging improprieties in the solicitation notice must be filed before the bid opening or the closing date for receipt of proposals.
- Protests alleging improprieties in the award process must be filed within 10 calendar days after the basis of the protest is known or should have been known, except when a debriefing is requested. In that case, the protest must be filed no later than 5 days after the debriefing.
- The Comptroller General is required to issue a final decision on a protest within 100 calendar days from the date the protest is submitted but may, in certain circumstances, extend that time or use an "express option" for accelerated resolution of "suitable" protests within 65 calendar days.

Agencies are prohibited from awarding contracts after the CO has received notice of the protest unless the head of the procuring activity finds that urgent and compelling circumstances that significantly affect the government's interests will not permit delay. If award is made before the agency receives the notice of a protest but the protest is filed within 10 days of award, the agency must suspend contract performance while the protest is pending unless the head of the procuring activity authorizes such performance. If the head of the procuring agency finds that continued performance is merely in the "best interest" of the government but that no urgent or compelling reasons exist, the Comptroller

General's recommendation will be carried out without regard to any costs or disruption resulting from terminating, recompeting, or rewarding the contract.

If the protest is sustained, the Comptroller General is directed to recommend corrective action to the executive agency, and the agency must notify the Comptroller General if the recommendations are not implemented within 60 calendar days. Recommended actions may include contract termination, nonexercise of contract options, recompetition, reissuance of the solicitation, and contract award consistent with regulatory requirements. The Comptroller General may also "declare" a party entitled to the costs of bid or proposal preparation.

When signing Public Law 98-369, the President objected to those CICA provisions (award of attorney fees, stay of award, and suspension of performance) that appeared to delegate executive-level authority to the Comptroller General, an officer of Congress. These provisions were affirmed as constitutional by the Court of Appeals for the Third Circuit.[64] An appeal of this ruling to the Supreme Court was dropped in 1989, when the Fiscal Year 1989 Defense Appropriations Act limited the GAO's power to extend the stay of a procurement. The DOD again filed suit in District Court on June 26, 1991, in *United States v. Instruments, S.A., Inc.*, seeking a declaratory judgment that the CICA provisions are unconstitutional. The case was dismissed by the court on November 13, 1992.[65]

Protests Filed with the General Services Board of Contract Appeals

Prior to August 1996, the General Services Board of Contract Appeals (GSBCA) had jurisdiction over protests involving acquisition of automatic data processing equipment (ADPE) and services, with the following restrictions:

- The Brooks Act[66] defined a procurement as an ADPE procurement only if significant use of ADPE is required to perform specified services or to furnish specified products.

- The Warner Amendment to the Brooks Act precluded the GSBCA from deciding protests involving DOD procurements of ADPE that is integral to a weapons system.

Section 5101 of the Clinger–Cohen Act of 1996 repealed the Brooks Act and eliminated the GSBCA's jurisdiction to decide information technology protests, effective August 1996. Such protests are now heard before the GAO.

The Federal Circuit ruled that the GSBCA's jurisdiction to hear protests pre-Clinger–Cohen was limited to objections to the procurement process or the contract award itself; it did not extend to the reverse protest of a decision to terminate an awardee's contract following a protest of that award.[67]

Protests Filed with the Court of Federal Claims

The Court of Federal Claims is authorized under the Tucker Act[68] to rule on federal contract claims. The Federal Courts Improvement Act of 1982 granted the court express authority to grant equitable relief in bid protests filed before contract award. Protesters may seek equitable relief, as well as monetary relief for bid and proposal costs incurred. Legal fees are reimbursable only to the extent awarded under the Equal Access to Justice Act.[69]

Protests Filed with District Courts

District courts have jurisdiction over bid protests for nonmonetary relief pursuant to the Administrative Procedures Act.[70]

Protest Issues

Protests have frequently involved assertions that the government improperly evaluated a proposal in a negotiated procurement action, particularly that the government failed to follow the evaluation criteria in Section M of the solicitation notice. The CICA, as implemented in FAR 15.204-5 and 15.304(d), requires the solicitation notice to identify all factors and any significant subfactors that will be considered in awarding the contract, as well as their relative importance.

Solicitations for negotiated procurements include a standard FAR provision (FAR 52.215-1), which states in part:

(f)(1)   The Government intends to award a contract or contracts resulting from this solicitation to the responsible offeror(s) whose proposal(s) represents the best value after evaluation in accordance with the factors and subfactors in the solicitation. ...

(f)(4)   The Government intends to evaluate proposals and award a contract without offerors (except clarifications as described in FAR 15.306(a)). Therefore, the offeror's initial offer should contain the offeror's best terms from a cost or price and technical standpoint. ...

(f)(8)   The Government may determine that proposal is unacceptable if the prices proposed are materially unbalanced between line items or subline items. Unbalanced pricing exists when, despite an acceptable total evaluated price, the price of one or more contract line items is significantly overstated or understated as indicated by the application of cost or price analysis techniques.

(f)(10) A written award or acceptance of proposal mailed or otherwise furnished to the successful offeror within the time specified in the proposal shall result in a binding contract without further action by either party.

Cost Realism Analysis

Federal Acquisition Regulation 15.305(a)(1) requires the CO to, when appropriate, perform cost analysis in order to form an opinion on the degree to which the proposed costs represent the expected cost of performance, assuming reasonable economy and efficiency. As stated by the Comptroller General:

> ... [T]he purpose of cost realism analysis is not to determine what an offeror price's [sic] would be using a technical approach prescribed by the agency; rather, it is to determine what, in the government's view, it would realistically cost the offeror to perform given the offeror's own technical approach ...[71]

The procedures used by COs in cost analysis include the following:

- Verifying cost or pricing data and evaluating cost elements to assess the necessity for and reasonableness of proposed costs
- Evaluating the effect of the offeror's current practices on future costs
- Comparing costs proposed by the offeror for individual cost elements with historical actual costs and other relevant cost estimates
- Verifying that the offeror's cost submissions are in accordance with the contract cost principles and procedures in the FAR, Part 31, and Cost Accounting Standards (CAS) when applicable

- Determining whether any cost or pricing data necessary to make the contractor's proposal accurate, complete, and current have not been either submitted or identified in writing by the contractor

- Analyzing the results of make-or-buy program reviews, in evaluating subcontract costs

When an offeror proposes seemingly low cost estimates or fixed prices, consideration is given to factors such as the contractor's financial ability to perform and to satisfactorily provide the level of services, quality of services, and timeliness of delivery as promised in its technical proposal. For cost-type contracts, the government must ensure the contractor does not misrepresent the actual costs anticipated during contract performance. In doing so, it may need to make "cost realism adjustments" to an offeror's proposal.

The procuring agency bears the responsibility to defend its cost analysis under the circumstances as being reasonably based and not arbitrary.[72] Consequently, after performing an adequate cost analysis, the CO may exercise considerable judgment and discretion in the final scoring and evaluation.

The clause prescribed by FAR 52.237-10 requires an offeror responding to a solicitation for services to identify in its proposal uncompensated overtime hours and to estimate uncompensated overtime consistent with its cost accounting practices used to accumulate and report such hours. Since service contract solicitations generally require offerors to propose costs using an estimated number of hours, an offeror that can demonstrate that its salaried employees will work more than 40 hours per week without additional compensation can propose lower hourly labor costs. Solicitations often require rationale and justification supporting uncompensated overtime usage. In the increasingly competitive environment of contracting for professional services, substantiation of uncompensated overtime has become a key issue in several protests, as illustrated in the following bid protest decisions:

The GAO initially sustained Combat Systems Development Associates'[73] protest that the awardee's proposed uncompensated overtime should have been rejected. Although the awardee documented its proposed uncompensated overtime with certifications from employees promising that they would work the additional uncompensated hours, the agency failed to consider whether the employees' willingness to work those additional hours would be adversely impacted by an unannounced pay and benefit cut that management planned to expose on the day of contract award. On reconsideration,[74] the protest was denied after the Navy cost analysis panel recalculated the awardee's costs accepting only uncompensated overtime costs for employees whose salaries and benefits were not being cut. Because that analysis showed that the awardee's recalculated proposed costs were slightly less than the protester's, the awardee's proposal was deemed the greatest value to the government.

The GSBCA failed to sustain a protest by Martin Marietta Corporation,[75] alleging that the FAA did not reasonably evaluate the uncompensated overtime proposed by the awardee's subcontractors. The solicitation notice specifically advised offerors that uncompensated overtime "must be verifiable through the Defense Contract Audit Agency." Martin Marietta interpreted that requirement as precluding the institution of an uncompensated overtime program for the first time on this procurement. The GSBCA disagreed, accepting expert witness testimony that the DCAA can properly evaluate contractor accounting policies that have been instituted for the first time on a procurement.

Unbalanced Offers

An offer must be materially unbalanced before it is rejected under the auspices of FAR 52.215-16(g).

Large pricing differentials between base and option periods or significant front loading of first article units are indicators that an offer is unbalanced. The Comptroller General concluded[76] that unbalanced bidding existed with regards to unit prices proposed for first articles versus production units, because the solicitation involved firm production quantities with start-up costs properly allocable to the entire production and no risk associated with the nonexercise of an option. The Comptroller General contrasted that scenario with prior decisions that allowed full recovery of equipment start-up costs early in the contract period because the contractor would have no use for the equipment after the base period if the options were not exercised.

The Comptroller General similarly ruled in *Metal Trades, Inc.*[77] and *M&M Services, Inc.*[78] that basic quantity unit bid prices were not unbalanced in relation to option quantity bid prices where the bidder demonstrated that the lower option prices were due to exclusion of one-time costs. The Comptroller General concluded the following in *Metal Trades:*

> A bidder properly may allocate start-up and equipment costs to the base period where the bidder would have no use for the equipment at the end of the contract's basic term since, if these costs were allocated throughout the potential life of the contract and the options were not exercised, the bidder would never be able to recover its full cost of performance.

The Comptroller General found that an awardee's proposal for ship handling training services was not materially unbalanced.[79] The Request for Proposals (RFP) provided that the Navy would order a minimum of 1,500 and a maximum of 2,500 hours of training per year. Offerors could propose up to four per-hour training rates in varying increments. Although the awardee's rate for the first increment (1,500) was substantially higher than its rates for two remaining increments of 500 hours each, the Comptroller General concluded the following:

- The 1,500 hour rate did "not bear more than the actual cost to the offeror for these hours."
- Although the middle 500 hours appeared to carry a below-cost rate, "such pricing is unobjectionable; an offeror properly may decide to submit a price that is extremely low."

Best Value Analysis

"Best value" is defined in FAR 2.101 as the expected outcome of an acquisition that, in the Government's estimation, provides the greatest overall benefit in response to the requirement. While the best value procurement process permits award to other than a responsible offeror with the lowest price, a cost/technical trade-off analysis is required to ensure that the contract is awarded to the offeror providing the greatest value to the government. Of obvious concern is whether the government is paying too much for what it receives. A number of protests have challenged the evaluation process used by the government to select offers that provide the best value. As there is no exact method or process governing a best-value determination, the standard of reasonableness has been applied. If the award is consistent with the terms of the solicitation and the price premium is justified by specific technical enhancements, the award will stand. However, where a higher-cost, higher technically rated proposal is selected for award, the award decision must be supported by a rational explanation of why the technical superiority warrants the additional cost. In granting the protest in 1992 of an Air Force award, the GSBCA concluded the following:

> [T]he kind of superficial lip service which the Air Force paid to cost here is wholly unsatisfactory. ... [W]e conclude that even when technical is a more important factor than cost, the Government in performing a "best value" analysis, should examine and document whether the extent of technical superiority warrants a premium in price. Recognizing that there may be nonquantifiable elements involved in any such examination, the selection nevertheless must reflect an in-depth analysis of the circumstances which justify the trade-off. The Air Force violated the statutory mandate in 10 U.S.C. 2305(b)(4)(D) as well as the terms of the RFP by failing to consider price adequately, and in particular whether the price premium ... was warranted.[80]

In two decisions relating to the Internal Revenue Service (IRS) award of the Treasury MultiUser Acquisition Contract (TMAC), the GSBCA again focused on the process that must be followed in a successful best value procurement. In TMAC I 1, the Board concurred with protesters that the IRS failed to justify that benefits received were commensurate with the $500 million to $700 million price premium between the protestors and the contract awardee. In denying the IRS motion for reconsideration of the decision, the Board sought to distinguish between what is and what is not required in a successful best value analysis.

> The most important misconception exhibited in the IRS's motion is the notion that our opinion imposes some sort of formulaic requirement upon an agency making a cost/technical trade-off decision. For instance, the IRS asserts that our opinion: requires it to close the "price gap" through quantification of the technical differences ... ; prohibits it from relying on nonquantifiable factors in determining best value to the Government; establishes some sort of minimum cost ratio ... requires a more detailed price/technical analysis when the solicitation does not disclose relative weights for the two ... ; and requires the assignment of dollars to technical differences. ...

> The simple answers to these contentions are no, no, no, and no. The basis of our decision was and remains that the solicitation required price to be a factor, though not the most important one, in the award decision, and that the IRS's explanation of its decision indicates that price was not a factor in any significant way. We did not grant the protest because the IRS failed to follow any of the so-called "principles" outlined above. We granted it because the IRS's trade-off analysis fails to indicate that the Government will receive benefits commensurate with the price premium it proposes to pay. How such benefits might be demonstrated lies entirely within the IRS's discretion; the agency is assuredly not confined within any of the alleged parameters that it sets out in its motion.[81]

After the TMAC I decision, the IRS formed a working group to assess whether a price/technical trade-off analysis could be made. The group identified various discriminators among the proposals, divided the discriminators into two groups (quantified and nonquantified), and attempted to assess the impact of such discriminators on IRS operations. The Board concluded that this was a reasoned approach to deciding which offer represented the greatest value to the government. The Board noted the following in its TMAC II decision:

> All the agency was required to do was present a reasoned analysis showing that the Government expects to receive benefits commensurate with the price premium it will have to pay. ... Although the analysis that the Working Group undertook undoubtedly has numerous assumptions and some large margins of error, we do not lose sight of the basic principle that, in making its analysis, the agency is essentially exercising its business judgment, albeit one involving taxpayers' money, and not conducting a definitive or all-inclusive study. Absent some affirmative indication that the Group's method led to prejudicially incorrect results, we have no basis for overturning the award.

> In the first case, we had virtually nothing to support the award decision beyond the mere fact of AT&T's ... technical advantage. This by itself hardly explained a one-half to three-quarters

of a billion dollar price premium. On the current record, however, we can no longer conclude that the IRS is making award at a significantly higher cost to achieve slightly superior technical features, in contravention of the RFP.[82]

The Federal Circuit sustained the Board's decision, noting: "Government agencies are accorded a good deal of deference in awarding contracts. Here, the IRS has sufficiently demonstrated that price was a factor in the final decision to award the TMAC contract."[83]

In granting the protest of a single Desktop IV contract award, the GSBCA concluded that the Air Force had not seriously considered the solicitation provisions that an award could be made to one or two offerors based on an integrated assessment of the offerors' abilities to satisfy government requirements. In overturning the single award, the Board advised the Air Force that it could proceed with award provided it gave

> ... due considerations to combinations of proposals, which, given likely ordering patterns may lead to the best overall value to the Government, assuming no loss of technical advantages and the ability to save money.[84]

In *Systems Resources, Inc. v. Department of the Navy*,[85] the solicitation only mentioned "best value" and did not clearly indicate that the cost savings adjustment would be a significant factor in the evaluation process. The GSBCA's decision stated the following:

> Respondent must revise its solicitation to provide clear notice that it will be conducting a best value procurement in which technical enhancements over the Government's minimum requirements will permit a cost/technical tradeoff, if this is what respondent intends. Respondent shall then obtain revised proposals from all offerors.

The GSBCA denied Litton Systems, Inc.'s[86] protest of a best value award to Communication Systems Technology, Inc. (CSTI), concluding that projected cost savings related to CSTI's enhanced capabilities, unquantified additional features, and lower risk justified the award as the best value to the government.

The GSBCA sustained a protest filed by Unisys Corporation[87] because the protester's proposal was less costly than the awardee's proposal after adjustment for the cost/technical trade-off analysis. After concluding that the Source Selection Acquisition Council never performed a cost-benefit analysis of past performance, the GSBCA ruled that the Air Force should conduct a new best value analysis, appropriately considering past performance, and make another source selection decision based on the new best value analysis. On appeal, the Federal Circuit[88] reversed, concluding that the GSBCA did not have a sufficient basis to hold that the Service Selection was not grounded in reason. In concluding that the GSBCA impermissably substituted its judgment for that of the agency, the court concluded: "... the issue is not whether the Board disagrees with the agency's reasons, but whether the agency decision is wholly without reason."

The Federal Circuit similarly reversed a GSBCA decision to sustain B3H Corporation's protest of two Air Force contracts.[89] The court concluded that GSBCA inappropriately second-guessed the source selection authority's judgment in assigning weights to various nonquantified discriminators. In the court's view, the GSBCA "should have followed its clear line of precedent and deferred to the reasonable decision of the SSA."

The GAO denied Engineering and Professional Services, Inc.'s protest,[90] which alleged that the Air Force failed to disclose in the RFP its intention to consider discriminators in order to perform a technical/price tradeoff among competing proposals. The GAO concluded that identification and pricing of discriminators was an appropriate tool to help assess whether the awardee's technical superiority was worth the associated price premium. GAO concluded that the analysis related to the discriminators was considered consistent with the RFP, noting the following:

> "... since the proposal preparation instructions required offerors to submit a matrix detailing where their systems met or exceeded the RFP requirements and desirable features, and narratives describing where the offered system exceeded the stated requirements, the only reasonable interpretation of the RFP was that the agency intended to give evaluation credit where offerors proposed features that exceeded the RFP requirements."

The GAO sustained protests by Redstone Technical Services and Dynamic Science Inc.[91] of two awards by Redstone Arsenal on the basis that the CO failed to meet the standard for assuring that the cost/technical tradeoff is reasonable and consistent with the solicitation's evaluation criteria. The GAO concluded that the award decisions were not supported by rational explanations of why the technical superiority of the higher-cost offerors warranted the additional cost involved, even though cost was given less weight than the technical and management areas.

The U.S. District Court for the Northern District of California declined to issue a preliminary injunction requested by Delta Dental to bar performance of the Civilian Health and Medical Program of the Uniformed Services (CHAMPUS) dental contract.[92] The request for injunctive relief alleged, in part, that the government failed to provide appropriate credit for 16 technical enhancements that exceeded the minimum requirements. The court concluded that it would be inappropriate for the court to substitute its judgment for that of the government evaluators who appropriately reviewed Delta's Best and Final Offer (BAFO). In the court's opinion, "[t]he matrix of proffered technical enhancements that Delta claims were unrecognized by the Source Selection Evaluation Board (SSEB) evaluators and therefore, unrewarded by the agency represents nothing more than the exercise of sound discretion on the part of the agency."

Bid Protest Costs

After granting Sterling Federal Systems, Inc.'s protest of a NASA award, the GSBCA denied recovery of Sterling's expert consultant costs and in-house costs incurred by employees who participated in the protest.[93] In reversing its prior practice of allowing reimbursement for reasonable consultant costs and in-house employee costs, the GSBCA concluded that a 1991 Supreme Court decision[94] precluded award of such costs under federal fee-shifting statutes. The Federal Circuit vacated the GSBCA decision,[95] ruling that the Competition in Contracting Act[96] permitted a general allowance of litigation expense related to bid protests. The GSBCA's decision[97] on remand from the Federal Circuit concluded "... that our prior practice of allowing reimbursement of reasonable consultant fees and expenses and employee salaries and expenses, in appropriate circumstances, was a wise policy which should be continued."

13-6. EQUAL ACCESS TO JUSTICE ACT

The Equal Access to Justice Act (EAJA)[98] has substantial implications for small business concerns doing business with the government. This act provides that an agency conducting an "adversary adjudication" must award to a "prevailing party" other than the United States, reasonable fees and other expenses (in-house as well as outside assistance) incurred by that party during the proceedings unless the agency's position is found to be "substantially justified."

In simple terms, this means that eligible parties that prevail over the government in certain civil actions brought by or against the government may be awarded reasonable attorney fees and other expenses unless (1) the government acted reasonably during the conduct of a genuine dispute or (2) special circumstances make an award unjust. A "prevailing party" under the EAJA does not include (1) any individual whose net worth exceeds $1 million or (2) any sole owner of an unincorporated business or any partnership, corporation, association, or organization with a net worth exceeding $7 million or with more than 500 employees. In determining the eligibility of applicants, the net worth and number of employees for affiliated entities may be aggregated. The act's purpose is to provide to certain parties with limited resources the opportunity to seek review of, or defend against, unreasonable governmental action in situations when lack of financial capability would normally deter such action.

The EAJA was originally enacted on a three-year basis but was subsequently enacted permanently with several changes. First, the amended legislation expressly provides contract appeals boards with authority to award attorney fees and other expenses. Since the earlier EAJA did not expressly provide this authority, the court had held in *Fidelity Construction Co. v. United States*[99] that the EAJA did not permit the boards to award such fees. The act made this section retroactive, thus allowing recovery by contractors that previously sought, but were unable to obtain, relief from a board.

Second, the amended legislation attempts to clarify the standard for awarding attorney fees. The original act provided that fees would not be awarded if the government's position was "substantially justified." The act now provides that "whether or not the position of the agency was substantially justified shall be determined on the basis of the administrative record as a whole, which was made in the adversary adjudication for which fees and other expenses are sought." Although this change does not obviate all of the problems associated with recovering fees, it creates a less-subjective criterion.

The Department of Justice took the position that attorney fees generated before the EAJA's effective date are not recoverable, based on *Brookfield Construction Co., Inc.*,[100] in which the court held that the contractor was not entitled to interest on claims before the CDA's effective date, absent specific contract language to the contrary. However, the Court of Appeals confirmed in *Kay Manufacturing Co. v. United States*[101] that the EAJA allows recovery of fees and expenses incurred both before and after the effective date if the action was pending on the effective date or initiated thereafter.

13-7. PENALTIES AND SANCTIONS FOR NONCOMPLIANCE WITH REGULATORY REQUIREMENTS

The 1980s witnessed a significant expansion of legislation to combat alleged corporate crime and misconduct, which led to an increase in the regulatory requirements placed on government contractors. These requirements included penalties and sanctions for certain instances of noncompliance.

Sanctions are provisions for securing conformity to law by use of rewards or penalties or both. Another view would be that sanctions are enacted to make virtue morally obligatory or to furnish a motive for persons to seek it. If there is a general rule in the application of sanctions, it is that any sanction should bear some relevance to the offense and the offender. While debarment and suspension are sanctions that satisfy these objectives, other sanctions are imposed for false claims or statements, violations of agency regulations, and so forth. Remedies for alleged noncompliance that are frequently proved by the federal government range from administrative remedies, such as interruption of cash flow, downward price adjustments, and liquidated damages, to civil and criminal sanctions, such as those prescribed in the False Claims and False Statements Acts, Racketeer Influenced Corrupt Organizations Act, and suspensions and debarment.

Export Control Sanctions

Sanctions for violations of export controls are provided under the multilateral *Export Control Enhancement Act*.[102] For example, procurement sanctions were imposed by the U.S. government against Toshiba Corporation and its subsidiary, Toshiba Machine Company, as well as against Kongsberg Vaapenfabrikk and its subsidiary, Kongsberg Trading Company, for violating agreements that precluded those firms from providing U.S.-manufactured items to foreign nations.

Progress Payment Reduction or Suspension

Federal Acquisition Regulation 52.232-16(c) provides that the CO may reduce or suspend progress payments if the contractor fails to comply with any material requirement of the contract, such as failure to make progress or failure to make a good faith effort to comply with a subcontracting plan. DOD FAR Supplement 215.811-78(a)(7) specifically permits the administrative contracting officer to reduce or suspend progress payments if a contractor fails to correct significant estimating deficiencies. Also, DFARS 242.7208(b)(7) permits similar action with regard to contractor noncompliance with the material management and accounting system standards. DFARS 252.232-7006 was revised, effective January 15, 1992, to permit the agency head to reduce or suspend any contractor request for advance, partial, or progress payments that, based on substantial evidence, is believed to be fraudulent.

Downward Contract Price Adjustments, Including Penalties

A variety of contract provisions now require the payment of interest and penalties, as well as restitution for the amount of overpayment, due to noncompliance.

Defective Pricing

The Truth in Negotiations Act[103] provides for contract price reductions in the event that a contract price was increased due to the submission of defective cost or pricing data. Interest is computed on any overpayment at the current rate used by the IRS. If the defective submission is deemed to have been knowingly submitted, an additional penalty equal to the amount of the overpayment is imposed.

Cost Accounting Standards

Public Law 100-679[104] provides for downward price adjustments for any increased costs due to failure to comply with applicable cost accounting standards. Interest is applied to any overpayment at the interest rates prescribed by the IRS.

Unallowable Costs

The 1986 Defense Authorization Act[105] instituted penalties for including unallowable costs in proposals for settling indirect costs under defense contracts. The penalty was equal to the amount of disallowed cost, plus interest assessed on payments made for the disallowed items. If the unallowable cost was previously determined to be unallowable, the penalty was triple the amount of the disallowance (the basic penalty equal to the amount of the disallowed cost, plus an additional penalty equal to twice the amount of the disallowed cost), plus interest on the overpayment. Penalties of $10,000 for each proposal could also be imposed in addition to those described above.

A guidance issued by the DCAA in 1991[106] on applying unallowable cost penalties was quite controversial, particularly the conclusion that penalties apply to inadvertent inclusions of unallowable costs, even when the contractor discovers such errors and withdraws and corrects the rate proposals. The DCAA guidance, although endorsed by the DOD Director, Defense Procurement,[107] was mitigated by the Fiscal Year 1993 Defense Authorization Act,[108] which provides that penalties apply only to expressly unallowable costs and will be waived under one of the following conditions:

- A contractor withdraws its indirect cost rate proposal before the audit begins.
- The unallowable costs subject to the penalties are immaterial.
- The contractor demonstrates that (1) procedures, training, internal controls, and oversight reviews are in place to ensure that unallowable costs are not claimed; and (2) any unallowable costs subject to penalties were inadvertently claimed.

The 1993 act also (1) reduced the penalty for claiming a cost that was previously determined to be unallowable from triple the amount of the disallowed cost to double that amount and (2) deleted the additional $10,000 penalty.

Sections 2101 and 2151 of the FASA extended to all civilian agencies the same penalty provisions that previously applied only to defense contracts and raised the contract threshold for application of penalties from $100,000 to $500,000. Implementing regulations were effective October 1, 1995.

A DOD guidance[109] implementing the 1993 act established $10,000 as the materiality threshold. The guidance also established the following criteria for determining that an audit has begun:

- The DCAA notifies the contractor in writing that the audit has begun.
- The DCAA holds an audit entrance conference.
- The contractor is aware, based on other verifiable evidence, that the DCAA has begun the audit.

The Contract Audit Manual Section 6-608.5d. lists the initiation of field work related to the audit as an additional criterion.

A DCAA guidance issued in October 1992[110] concluded that the imposition of penalties is not contingent on the status of overhead resolution and that the DCAA should report penalty recommendations to the CO even for years in which final rates have been established.

Small and Small Disadvantaged Business Contracting Goals

The failure to exercise good faith efforts to comply with a subcontracting plan may subject a contractor to liquidated damages equal to the actual dollar amount by which the contractor failed to achieve its small business and small disadvantaged business subcontracting goals.

Civil and Criminal Sanctions

Noncompliance with statutory, regulatory, or contractual requirements may be shown to be fraudulent under at least three statutory sections: the False Statements Act[111] and two provisions known as the False Claims Act. A violation of the False Statements Act, a criminal statute, occurs when a contractor presents a statement knowing it to contain false information. The False Claims Act provisions include a criminal section[112] and a civil section.[113]

Additional statutes concerning civil and criminal sanctions are as follows:

- The False Claims Act Amendments of 1986[114] authorizes private individuals to bring civil enforcement actions, known as qui tam suits, on behalf of the United States.

- The Program Fraud Civil Remedies Act[115] provides an administrative remedy for contractors' false claims or statements.

- The Racketeer Influenced and Corrupt Organizations Act[116] imposes fines and penalties for committing two acts of racketeering, such as two acts of mail fraud or wire fraud, within 10 years. The basic penalties are fines and imprisonment, as well as mandatory forfeiture of the violator's interest in the company.

This brief recitation of sanctions and penalties clearly illustrates the risk that federal contractors face if they do not seriously address regulatory requirements throughout the procurement process. The fact that many of the remedies impose a far greater monetary liability than the harm suffered by the government as a result of the violation reflects the high priority that Congress and federal procurement executives have placed on administrative compliance. As further discussed in Chapters 14 and 15, the key to reducing contracting risk to a manageable level is incorporating compliance into the management systems for pricing, costing, and performing federal contracts.

Debarment and Suspension

Debarment and suspension are remedies available to the government to prohibit the award of contracts to a contractor that has committed, or is believed to have committed, an act indicating a serious lack of business integrity or honesty. Such lack of integrity would affect the contractor's present "responsibility" as a government contractor.

There are two types of debarment: statutory and administrative. Statutory, as the name implies, relates to willful violations of certain statutes, such as the Davis–Bacon and Walsh–Healey Acts. The period of a statutory debarment depends on the requirements of the applicable statute. Normally, contractors are to be accorded due process rights before debarment actions are taken.

The grounds for administrative debarment are set out in FAR 9.406-2 and in agency regulations. However, the decision to debar is discretionary. Normally, administrative debarment prevents a contractor from receiving a government contract or subcontract up to three years. If a contractor is suspended before being debarred, the suspension period should be considered in determining the debarment period. The grounds for administrative suspension are set out in FAR 9.407-2. A suspension is a temporary prohibition against the awarding of contracts to a contractor when there is probable cause that the contractor has committed an act that would justify debarment. The time of suspension varies, depending on the length of the investigations and any ensuing legal proceedings. Suspensions may be imposed without prior notice to the contractor. However, the contractor is normally given an opportunity to be heard after receiving notice, unless the notice is based on an indictment or other compelling reason.

In June 1982, the OFPP issued Policy Letter No. 82-1 (incorporated into FAR, Subpart 9.4) to provide uniform administrative debarment and suspension policies and procedures for the executive branch.[117] The letter made several changes in the former rules, including the following:

- Debarments and suspensions are normally imposed government-wide rather than agency-wide.
- Company-wide debarment and suspension is possible, rather than just the division or other organizational element involved.
- The agency head or an authorized designate is the "debarring and suspending official."
- A consolidated list of all debarred, suspended, and ineligible contractors is to be maintained by the GSA.
- More detailed criteria are established on the effect of the imputed actions of others in debarment proceedings. For example, fraudulent, criminal, or other seriously improper conduct of any officer, director, shareholder, partner, employee, or other individual associated with a contractor may be imputed to the contractor when it occurred in connection with the individual's duties for, or on behalf of, the contractor or with the contractor's knowledge, approval, or acquiescence. Acceptance of the benefits derived from the conduct is evidence of knowledge, approval, or acquiescence.

This policy represents just another step in the continuing attack on perceived fraud, waste, and abuse in government procurement. Within the statutory and regulatory framework of government contracting, it also represents a strong emphasis on the need for a complete understanding of the rules involved and the need for adequate accounting and internal control systems to ensure compliance with those rules.

13-8. SUMMARY

During the source selection process and during contract performance, disagreements that arise must be resolved through defined formal steps if they cannot be settled through negotiation. Although the negotiation of disagreements is the preferred approach and is used to resolve most disagreements, sometimes a third party may be needed to help resolve such issues.

The Contract Disputes Act of 1978, as amended, provides a statutory basis for an administrative alternative to the judicial process. It requires certification of claims over $100,000, institutes penalties for fraudulent claims, places time restraints on CO decisions, facilitates accelerated and expedited handling of appeals cases, and provides for the payment of interest on claims, which are ultimately decided in the contractor's favor.

Bid protests have often focused on whether the government properly evaluated the prospective offers.

Small businesses have been encouraged to challenge unreasonable government actions through the Equal Access to Justice Act. This act allows small businesses, as defined by the act, to recover reasonable attorney fees and other expenses when the government's position is not found to be "substantially justified." While the courts are authorized to make such awards in appropriate cases, contractors have not been very successful in recovering costs.

Finally, the government has an arsenal of sanctions, penalties, and criminal processes that can be imposed against a contractor. These "iron hand" government statutory and regulatory pronouncements are aimed at stamping out perceived fraud, waste, and abuse.

13-9. NOTES

1. Kihlberg v. United States, 97 U.S. 398 (1878).
2. Contract Disputes Act of 1978, 41 U.S.C. §§601–613, enacted Nov. 1, 1978, 92 Stat 2383, Pub. L. 95-563.
3. Report of the Committee on Government Affairs and the Committee on the Judiciary, U.S. Senate, to accompany S.3178, Senate Report 95-1118, Aug. 15, 1978, p. 1.
4. Monroe M. Tapper and Associates v. United States, Ct. Cl. 1979, Dec. 12, 1979, 611 F2.d 354.
5. James R. Roane Construction Co., ASBCA Nos. 43603–43608, Feb. 18, 1992, 92-2 BCA 24,802.
6. Essex Electro Engineers, Inc. v. United States, CAFC No. 91-5096, April 17, 1992, 960 F.2d 1576.
7. Dawco Construction, Inc. v. United States, CAFC No. 94-1013, March 2, 1995, 49 F.3d 1541.
8. Reflectone, Inc., ASBCA No. 43081, Oct. 19, 1992, 93-1 BCA 25,512; aff'd. April 2, 1993, 93-3 BCA 25,966.
9. Reflectone, Inc. v. United States, CAFC No. 93-1373, Sept. 1, 1994, 34 F.3d 1031.
10. Reflectone, Inc. v. Kelso, CAFC No. 93-1373, Dec. 5, 1994, 34 F.3d 1039.
11. Reflectone, Inc. v. Dalton, CAFC No. 93-1373, July 26, 1995, 34 F.3d 1572.
12. Bill Strong Enterprises, Inc., ASBCA Nos. 42946 and 43896, June 28, 1993, 93-3 BCA 25,961.
13. Bill Strong Enterprises, Inc. v. Shannon, CAFC No. 94-1013, March 2, 1995, 49 F.3d 1541.
14. Bill Strong Enterprises, Inc., ASBCA No. 42946, July 16, 1996, 96-2 BCA 28,428.
15. Jonathan Corp., ASBCA No. 47069, Dec. 16, 1994, 95-1 BCA 27,390.
16. World Computer Systems, Inc., DOTCAB No. 2802, Jan. 11, 1995, 95-1 BCA 27,399.
17. Tucker Act, 28 U.S.C. §1346(a)(2), 63 Stat 62, enacted April 25, 1949, Pub. L. 55, as amended.
18. Contract Disputes Act of 1978, §6(c)(2), supra, note 2.
19. Harnischfeger Corp., ASBCA Nos. 23918 and 24733, June 11, 1980, 80-2 BCA 14,541.
20. Newell Clothing Co., ASBCA No. 24482, Oct. 15, 1980, 80-2 BCA 14,744.
21. Paul E. Lehman, Inc. v. United States, Ct. Cl. 1982, Feb. 24, 1982, 673 F.2d 352.
22. Skelly and Loy v. United States, Ct. Cl. 1982, Aug. 11, 1982, 685 F.2d 414.
23. W.H. Moseley Co., Inc., ASBCA No. 27370-18, Jan. 13, 1983, 83-1 BCA 16,272.
24. Newport News Shipbuilding & Dry Dock Co., ASBCA No. 40747, March 4, 1991, 91-2 BCA 23,865.
25. Emerson Electric Co., ASBCA No. 37352, Dec. 5, 1990, 91-1 BCA 23,581.
26. Grumman Aerospace Corp. v. United States, CAFC No. 90-1217, Feb. 27, 1991, 927 F.2d 575.
27. Omega Services, Inc., ASBCA No. 38888, May 23, 1991, 91-2 BCA 24,043.
28. Fischbach & Moore International Corp. v. Secretary of State, CAFC 92-1092, March 3, 1993, 987 F.2d 759.
29. Fiscal Year 1993 Defense Authorization Act, 106 Stat. 2315, enacted Oct. 23, 1992, Pub. L. 102-484.

30. Federal Courts Administration Act of 1992, 28 U.S.C. §1491, Pub. L. 102-572.

31. Teton Construction Co., ASBCA Nos. 27700 and 28968, April 11, 1986, 86-2 BCA 18,971.

32. False Claims Act, 31 U.S.C. §3729, 96 Stat. 877, enacted Sept. 13, 1982, Pub. L. 97-258.

33. Allied Painting & Decorating Co., ASBCA No. 25099, Sept. 17, 1980, 80-2 BCA 14,710.

34. R.G Robbins Co., Inc., ASBCA No. 26521, Jan. 7, 1982, 82-1 BCA 15,643.

35. OFPP Policy Letter 80-3, dated Jan. 11, 1993, Subject: Regulatory Guidance on P.L. 95-563, the Contract Disputes Act, Para. I.1(c).

36. SCM Corp. v. United States, Ct. Cl. 1980, No. 576-79C, Oct. 10, 1980, 225 Ct. Cl. 647.

37. Westclox Miliary Products, ASBCA No. 25592, Aug. 4, 1981, 81-2 BCA 15,270.

38. Assurance Co. v. United States, CAFC 86-1350, 1987, March 10, 1987, 813 F.2d 1202.

39. Contract Disputes Act of 1978, §12, supra, note 2.

40. Paul E. Lehman, Inc. v. United States, supra, note 21.

41. Brookfield Construction Co. & Baylor Construction Corp., A Joint Venture v. United States, Ct. Cl. 1981, Sept. 23, 1981, 661 F.2d 159.

42. Fidelity Construction Co., DOTCAB Nos. 1213 and 1219, Feb. 11, 1982, 82-1 BCA 15,633, aff'd. CAFC 27-82, 1982, Feb. 18, 1983, 700 F.2d 1379.

43. Honeywell, Inc., GSBCA No. 5458, Sept. 30, 1981, 81-2 BCA 15,383; see also J.F. Shea Co., Inc. v. United States, CAFC No. 84-1166, Feb. 1, 1985, 32 CCF 73,224.

44. Extraordinary Contractual Relief Act, 50 U.S.C. 1431-1435, 72 Stat. 972, enacted Aug. 28, 1958, Pub. L. 85-804.

45. PAVCO, Inc., ASBCA No. 23783, April 8, 1980, 80-1 BCA 14,407.

46. Paragon Energy Corp. v. United States, Ct. Cl. 1981, April 8, 1981, 645 F.2d 966.

47. Arcon/Pacific Contractors, ASBCA No. 25057, Sept. 18, 1980, 80-2 BCA 14,709.

48. Policy Research, Inc., ASBCA No. 26144, Jan. 26, 1982, 82-1 BCA 15,618.

49. Cosmic Construction Co. v. United States, CAFC 23-82, 1982, Dec. 10, 1982, 697 F.2d 1389.

50. OFPP "Final Rules of Procedure for Boards of Contract Appeals Under the Contract Disputes Act of 1978," June 14, 1979, Government Contracts Reports, Commercial Clearing House, Paragraph 79,604.

51. Airco, Inc., IBCA No. 1074-8-75, Oct. 17, 1977, 77-2 BCA 12,809.

52. Freedom of Information Act., 5 U.S.C. §552, 81 Stat. 54, enacted June 5, 1967, Pub. L. 90-23, as amended.

53. Harrington Associates, Inc., GSBCA No. 6795, Oct. 15, 1982, 82-2 BCA 16,103.

54. S&E Contractors, Inc. v. United States, S. Ct. 1972, April 24, 1972, 31 L.Ed.2d 658.

55. Federal Courts Administration Act of 1992, 28 U.S.C. §171, enacted April 2, 1982, Pub. L. 97-164.

56. Administrative Dispute Resolution Act of 1996, 5 U.S.C. §571, enacted Oct. 19, 1996, Pub. L. 104-320.

57. Executive Order 12988, Civil Justice Reform, Feb. 2, 1996.

58. Extraordinary Contractual Relief Act, supra, note 44.

59. Executive Order 10789, Authorizing Agencies of the Government to Exercise Certain Contracting Authority in Connection with National Defense Functions and Prescribing Regulations Governing the Exercise of Such Authority, Nov. 14, 1958, as amended by E.O. 11051, Sept. 27, 1962; E.O. 11382, Nov. 28, 1967; E.O. 11610, July 22, 1971; and E.O. 12148, July 20, 1979.

60. Application of Remington Arms Co., Inc., ACAB No. 1238, May 8, 1991, 4 ECR P59.

61. Competition in Contracting Act of 1984, 40 U.S.C. §759(f)(5)(c), enacted July 18, 1984, Pub. L. No. 98-369.

62. Federal Acquisition Streamlining Act of 1994, enacted Oct. 13, 995, Pub. L. 103-355.

63. Clinger–Cohen Act of 1996 (formerly known as Federal Acquisition Reform Act of 1996), enacted Feb. 10, 1996, Pub. L. 104-106.

64. Ameron, Inc. v. U.S. Army Corps of Engineers, CA 3 Nos. 85-5226 and 85-5377, Dec. 31, 1986, 809 F.2d 979.

65. United States v. Instruments, S.A. Inc., and Fisons Instruments/VG Instruments, Comp. Gen. Intervenor, DCDC No. 91-1574, Nov. 13, 1992, 807 F. Supp. 811.

66. Brooks Automatic Data Processing Act, ch. 288, 40 U.S.C. §759, enacted June 30, 1949.

67. OAO Corp. v. Johnson, CAFC Nos. 94-1106, Feb. 17, 1995, 49 F.3d 721.

68. Tucker Act, supra note 17.

69. Equal Access to Justice Act, 5 U.S.C. §504, 28 U.S.C. §2412, Pub. L. 99-80.

70. Scanwell Laboratories, Inc. v. David D. Thomas, CA DC 1970, 424 F.2d 859.

71. SRS Technologies, Comp. Gen. No. B-238403, May 17, 1990, 5 CGEN 104,388. See also Gary Bailey Engineering Consultants, Comp. Gen. No. B-233438, March 10, 1989, Unpublished, 89-1 CPD P263.

72. Purvis Systems, Inc., Comp. Gen. Nos. B-245761 and B-245761.2, Jan. 31, 1992, 71 Comp. Gen. 203.

73. Combat Systems Development Associates Joint Venture, No. B-259920.2, June 13, 1995, 95-2 CPD P162.

74. Combat Systems Development Associates Joint Venture, Comp. Gen. Nos. B-259920.3 and B-259920.4, Sept. 8, 1995, 95-2 CPD P163.

75. Martin Marietta Corp., Management and Data Systems v. Department of Transportation and TRW, Inc., Systems Integration Group, Intervenor, GSBCA No. 13004-P, Jan. 13, 1995, 95-2 BCA 27,674.

76. Aluminum Castings, Inc., Comp. Gen. No. B-222476-2, Sept. 23, 1986, unpublished, 86-2 CPD P325.

77. Metal Trades, Inc., No. B-227915, Sept. 18, 1987, 87-2 CPD P277.

78. M&M Services, Inc., No. B-228717, Oct. 21, 1987, 87-2 CPD P382.

79. SIMSHIP Corp., No. B-253655.2, Dec. 2, 1993, 93-2 CPD P293.

80. Grumman Data Systems Corp. v. Department of Air Force, Contel Federal Systems, Inc. Intervenor, GSBCA No. 11635-P, March 19, 1992, 92-2 BCA 24,999.

81. International Business Machines Corp. and Lockheed Missiles & Space Co., GSBCA Nos. 11359-P-R and 11362-P-R, Oct. 25, 1991, 92-1 BCA 24,438.

82. Lockheed Missiles & Space Co. and International Business Machines Corp. v. Department of Treasury, AT&T Federal Systems, Intervenor, GSBCA Nos. 11766-P and 11777-P, June 2, 1992, 93-1 BCA 25,401.

83. Lockheed Missiles & Space Co. v. Bentsen, CAFC No. 92-1566, Aug. 30, 1993, 4 F.3d 955.

84. CompuAdd Corp. v. Department of Air Force, GSBCA Nos. 12021-P, 12028-P, 12041-P, and 12042-P, Dec. 23, 1992, 93-2 BCA 25,811.

85. Systems Resources, Inc. v. Department of the Navy, GSBCA No. 12536-P, Sept. 13, 1993, 94-1 BCA 26,388.

86. Litton Systems, Inc. v. Department of Transportation, GSBCA No. 12911-P, Sept. 26, 1994, 94-3 BCA 27,122.

87. Unisys Corp. v. Department of the Air Force, GSBCA No. 13129-P, March 3, 1995, 95-2 BCA 27,622.

88. TRW, Inc. and Widnall v. Unisys Corp., CAFC Nos. 95-1295, 95-1412, and 95-1416, Oct. 25, 1996, 98 F.3d 1325.

89. Secretary of the Air Force v. B3H Corp., CAFC Nos. 95-1042, 95-1043, and 95-1044, Feb. 8, 1996, 75 F.3d 1577.

90. Engineering and Professional Services, Inc., Comp. Gen. No. B-262179, Dec. 6, 1995, 95-2 CPD P266.

91. Redstone Technical Services and Dynamic Research, Inc., Comp. Gen. Nos. B-259222.2 and B-259224.2, March 17, 1995, 95-1 CPD P181.

92. Delta Dental Plan of California v. Perry, DC N Cal. No. C-95-2462 TEH, Feb. 20, 1996.

93. Sterling Federal Systems, Inc. v. NASA, GSBCA No. 10000-C(9835-P), May 22, 1992, 92-3 BCA 25,118.

94. West Virginia University Hospitals, Inc. v. Gay, 111 S. Ct. 1138 (1991).

95. Sterling Federal Systems Inc. v. Goldin, CAFC No. 92-1552, Jan. 28, 1994, 16 F.3d 1177.

96. Competition in Contracting Act of 1984, supra, note 61.

97. Sterling Federal Systems, Inc. v. NASA, GSBCA No. 10000-C (9835-P), March 10, 1995, 95-1 BCA 27,575.

98. Equal Access to Justice Act, supra note 69.

99. Fidelity Construction Co. v. United States, supra, note 42.

100. Brookfield Construction Co. & Baylor Construction Corp., supra, note 41.

101. Kay Manufacturing Co. v. United States, CAFC 478-73, 1983, Feb. 18, 1983, 699 F.2d 1376.

102. Multilateral Export Control Enhancement Amendment Act, enacted Aug. 23, 1988, Pub. L. 100-418.

103. Truth in Negotiations Act, 76 Stat. 528, 10 U.S.C. §2306(f), Pub. L. 87-653.

104. Office of Federal Procurement Policy Act Amendments of 1988, 41 U.S.C. §422(f)(3), Nov. 17, 1988, Pub. L. 100-679.

105. 1986 Defense Authorization Act, 99 Stat. 583, enacted Nov. 8, 1985, Pub. L. 99-145.

106. DCAA memorandum, dated Nov. 5, 1991, to Regional Directors, 91-PAD-197; subject: Audit Guidance on Penalties for Unallowable Costs, DFARS 231.70.

107. Letter from the Office of the Undersecretary of Defense, Director of Defense Procurement, dated April 29, 1992, to the President, National Security Industrial Association.

108. Fiscal Year 1993 Defense Authorization Act, supra note 29.

109. Director of Defense Procurement memorandum, dated Nov. 18, 1992, to the Directors of

Defense Agencies; Director, Procurement Policy, ASA (RD&A)/SARD-PP; Deputy for Acquisition Policy, Integrity, and Accountability, ASN (RD&A)/API&A; Deputy Assistant Secretary of the Air Force (Contracting), SAF/AQC; and Executive Director, Contract Management, DLA-A; subject: Penalties for Unallowable Costs.

110. DCAA memorandum, dated Oct. 8, 1992, to Regional Directors, DCAA, Director Field Detachment, 92-PAD-161(R); subject: Audit Guidance on Recommendation of Penalties on Closed Overhead Years.

111. False Statements Act, 18 U.S.C. §1001, 62 Stat. 683, enacted June 25, 1948, Pub. L. 772.

112. False Claims Act, 18 U.S.C. §287, 10 Stat. 3169, enacted Oct. 27, 1986, Pub. L. 99-562.

113. False Claims Act, 31 U.S.C. §3729, 96 Stat. 877, supra, note 32.

114. False Claims Act Amendments of 1986, 18 U.S.C. §3732, 100 Stat. 3158, enacted Oct. 27, 1986, Pub. L. 99-562.

115. Program Fraud Civil Remedies Act, 31 U.S.C. §§6101–6104, 100 Stat. 1874, enacted Oct. 21, 1986, Pub. L. 99-509.

116. Racketeer Influenced and Corrupt Organizations Act, 18 U.S.C. §1962.

117. OFPP Policy Letter No. 82-1, "Government-wide Debarment, Suspension and Eligibility," June 24, 1982.

Chapter Fourteen

Control and Management Systems

14-1. BACKGROUND

There is much more to a well-designed management information system than a ledger summarizing contract costs. To compete effectively in any market, management must receive the information necessary to plan and control its business. For a government contractor, the planning phase begins when a contract proposal is prepared. During that process, contracts are broken down into meaningful work packages with performance responsibility assigned to appropriate cost centers. Next, budgets of costs are prepared, along with a schedule containing key contract requirements and their estimated completion dates. This performance and cost plan is adjusted throughout the government award process. Ultimately, when a contract is obtained, management should use the proposed data to establish a performance and cost baseline as the basis for monitoring actual performance. Then, when comparisons of the actual result with the baseline reveal unfavorable variance, corrective action may be taken promptly.

For many government contractors, specific government requirements must be incorporated into their management information systems to adequately plan and monitor actual performance. These requirements affect key systems for estimating, monitoring, and recording cost.

The federal government places an emphasis on the adequacy of systems used to price, cost, and administer government contracts; alleged system deficiencies related to material requirements planning systems and estimating systems have resulted in Defense Federal Acquisition Regulation Supplement (DFARS) revisions as well as changes in the government's expectation of what constitutes adequate systems. In the complex federal acquisition environment, companies must have systems and controls that provide adequate accounting, estimating, and management information. That information often must be shared with the government. Our discussion will start with the general requirements of cost accounting systems, then will address key cost estimating, material management accounting, purchasing, project management, and property management systems.

14-2. COST ACCOUNTING SYSTEMS

The basic information required to be supplied by a government contractor's accounting system is that necessary to bill customers for costs incurred under flexibly priced contracts or to request progress payments under fixed-price contracts. Contractors also need subsidiary cost ledgers that collect costs for each cost objective. Cost ledgers can be designed in a variety of ways to permit efficient accumulation of costs for billing purposes. In practice, these records vary considerably, based on the individual company's need for information and the complexity of the contract terms.

Contractors performing contracts for which cost or pricing data were submitted before contract definitization must have cost accounting systems that comply with Federal Acquisition Regulation (FAR) [and perhaps Cost Accounting Standards (CAS)] requirements.

Basic attributes of an acceptable cost accounting system, as outlined on Standard Form 1408—Preaward Survey of Prospective Contractor Accounting System (See Appendix 3.11) include the following:

- Proper segregation of direct costs from indirect costs

- Identification and accumulation of costs by contract

- Logical and consistent methodologies for allocating indirect costs to intermediate and final cost objectives

- Accumulation of costs under general ledger control

- Charging of labor hours and costs to the appropriate cost objectives

- Interim (at least monthly) determination of costs charged to contracts through routine postings to books of account

- Exclusion from billings, claims, and proposals of costs that are unallowable pursuant to the federal contract cost principles (e.g., FAR, Part 31) or contract terms and conditions

- Identification of costs by contract line item if required by contract

- Segregation of preproduction costs from production costs

For flexibly priced contracts (cost-reimbursement, fixed-price-incentive, or fixed-price-determinable), allowable costs incurred form the basis for contract remuneration. Requests for progress payments under firm-fixed-price contracts must also reflect allowable costs incurred. Thus, accurate labor charging by contract is imperative. To ensure the reliability of recorded labor charges, a contractor must have an adequate internal control system for collecting and distributing labor costs. Accurate labor charging also encompasses consideration for all hours worked. If salaried employees work a significant number of hours in excess of the standard work week, a risk of labor mischarging to the government exists if all hours worked are not considered. Defense Contract Audit Agency (DCAA) auditors have long asserted that total time accounting is a basic requirement of FAR 31.201-4 and CAS 418, although no explicit regulatory provisions have mandated that practice. However, the Federal Acquisition (FAR) requires contractors and subcontractors, on cost-type contracts for services of $1 million or more, to document any uncompensated overtime hours to which an uncompensated overtime rate has been applied. Federal Acquisition Regulation 52.237-10 reads, in part:

(b) For any hours proposed against which an uncompensated overtime rate is applied, the offeror shall identify in its proposal the hours in excess of an average of 40 hours per week, by labor category at the same level of detail as compensated hours, and the uncompensated overtime rate per hour, whether at the prime or subcontract level. This includes uncompensated overtime hours that are in indirect cost pools for personnel whose regular hours are normally charged direct.

(c) The offeror's accounting practices used to estimate uncompensated overtime must be consistent with its cost accounting practices used to accumulate and report uncompensated overtime hours.

Most negotiated government contracts contain a clause similar to the one contained in FAR 52.215-2, which provides that "the contractor shall maintain ... all records and other evidence sufficient to reflect properly all costs claimed to have been incurred or anticipated to be incurred directly or indirectly in performance of this contract." The regulation does not specify that the contractor maintain any specific type of accounting system. Rather, FAR 31.201-1 states that "any generally accepted method of determining or estimating costs that is equitable and is consistently applied may be used, including standard costs properly adjusted for applicable variances."

In a job-order costing system, costs are collected using a work-order process. Such a process normally involves assigning a job or project number to final cost objectives (e.g., contracts) and certain indirect activities (e.g., independent research and development/bid and proposal [IR&D/B&P] projects and plant rearrangement projects). Contractors, particularly in a production environment, are not required by the regulations to account for costs by contract (e.g., maintain a job-order cost accounting system). A cost accounting system in a production environment is generally driven by the contractor's products and/or production processes. The cost accounting system should be deemed adequate if production costs are appropriately, equitably, and consistently allocated to all final cost objectives. This point was emphasized in *Texas Instruments, Inc.*,[1] in which the Armed Services Board of Contract Appeals (ASBCA) concluded that the contractor's process cost system, which was used to accumulate the costs of units to be delivered under both government and commercial orders, complied with CAS and applicable procurement regulations. A contractor's accounting system should enable an appropriate and equitable allocation of costs to cost objectives. The system should be (1) consistently applied, (2) nondiscriminatory against the government, (3) adequate, (4) efficient, (5) reliable, and (6) equitable.

For firm-fixed-price contracts, an adequate cost accounting system is required even though costs incurred on the contract do not affect the monies ultimately paid to the contractor upon contract completion. The cost accounting system is critical for providing data for follow-on contract pricing, tracking contract performance, and supporting cost-based progress payment requests.

To price follow-on contracts, information on the rate of improvement in performing repetitive tasks on subsequent production (i.e., learning curves) is important. Well-designed cost accounting systems should enable estimators to identify the costs or hours incurred on prior contracts or production lots. The ability to segregate nonrecurring costs from recurring costs is also critical for follow-on pricing. Clearly, the design of the accounting system is all-important in providing valuable input for the estimating and planning process.

With regard to using standard costs to project future performance, the DCAA *Contract Audit Manual*,[2] Section 9-314, provides that "The basic principle underlying the use of standard costs in estimating is that the standard cost plus the estimated variance must reasonably approximate the expected actual cost."

The obvious necessity is to capture and accumulate costs in a manner that reflects the cost of performance in individual government contracts. To do this, certain costs that can be identified specifically with contracts and/or products are treated as direct costs and are charged in that manner. Typically, direct costs include material, subcontracts, and labor, but they are by no means limited to these. Federal Acquisition Regulation 31.201-4 requires that costs charged directly to contracts be allocated "on a basis of the relative benefits received or other equitable relationship." In addition, to be allocated to a government contract, a cost must meet one of the following three conditions:

1. It must be incurred specifically for the contract.
2. It must benefit both the contract and other work and be distributed in reasonable proportion to the benefits received.
3. It must be necessary to the overall operation of the business, even if a direct relationship to any particular contract cannot be shown.

Indirect costs, or costs that benefit more than one contract, must be pooled and allocated to contracts on some equitable basis. According to FAR 31.203(b), the general criteria for establishing indirect cost pools are as follows:

> Indirect costs shall be accumulated by logical cost groupings with due consideration of the reasons for incurring such costs. Each grouping should be determined so as to permit the distribution of the grouping on the basis of the benefits accruing to the several cost objectives. Commonly, manufacturing overhead, selling expenses, and general and administrative (G&A) expenses are separately grouped. Similarly, the particular case may require subdivision of these groupings, e.g., building occupancy costs might be separable from those of personnel administration within the manufacturing overhead group. ... When substantially the same results can be achieved through less precise methods, the number and composition of cost groupings should be governed by practical considerations and should not unduly complicate the allocation.

Federal Acquisition Regulation 31.203(b) and (c) similarly provide flexibility in determining what allocation base to use in distributing costs from the indirect cost pools to contracts.

> This necessitates selecting a distribution base common to all cost objectives to which the grouping is to be allocated. The base should be selected so as to permit allocation of the grouping on the basis of the benefits accruing to the several cost objectives ... once an appropriate base for the distribution of indirect costs has been accepted, it shall not be fragmented by the removal of individual elements. All items properly includable in an indirect cost base should bear a pro-rata share of indirect costs irrespective of their acceptance as government contract costs. For example, when a cost input base is used for the distribution of general and administrative (G&A) costs, all items that would properly be part of the cost input base, whether allowable or unallowable, shall be included in the base and bear their pro-rata share of G&A costs.

Accounting for indirect costs presents a challenge to those uninitiated in government contracting. Through the acquisition regulations, and particularly through the cost accounting standards, the government has promulgated specific rules on the allocability of indirect costs. However, these rules still permit considerable flexibility in the number and types of pools that can be selected and the methods used for allocating indirect costs. An example of a simple indirect cost allocation structure for indirect costs is illustrated in Figure 14.1 for certain indirect pools and allocation bases.

Whichever methods are selected for classifying and allocating direct or indirect costs, a key requirement for satisfying government auditors is the existence of adequate audit trails. An accounting system provides satisfactory audit trails if: (1) transactions are traceable from origin to final posting in the books

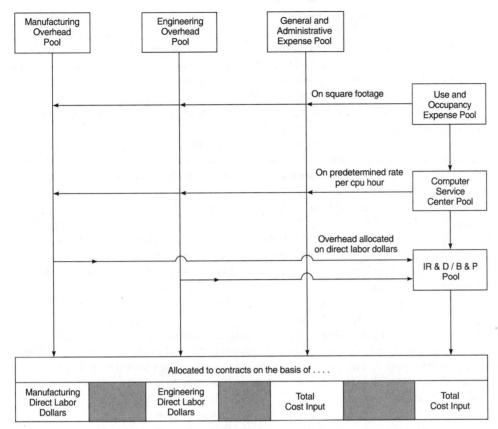

Figure 14.1 Indirect Cost Allocation System

of account, including the ledger summarizing costs by contract; (2) posting to accounts, including the ledger summarizing contract costs, is susceptible to breakdown into identifiable transactions; and (3) adequate documentation (e.g., time cards or vendors' invoices) is available and accessible to support the accuracy and validity of individual transactions.

The allocation of indirect costs in a highly automated environment or when management requires more precise measures presents an even greater challenge. Typical overhead allocation bases, such as direct labor, may not be representative of the indirect expense pools and management may need more precise costing. In the factory-of-the-future environment, the allocation of multiple cost pools over a variety of nonlabor bases, such as machine usage, may be more desirable. This need for new allocation methods is currently evident in the advanced cost management systems that are being implemented by a number of government contractors. Notwithstanding automation or diversity of allocation bases, requirements for audit trails still exist; and controls over input to the system and program logic are essential to validating the accuracy of such systems.

14-3. COST ESTIMATING SYSTEMS

In estimating the costs to be incurred on government contracts, contractors' cost estimating systems incorporate large amounts of data generated from a myriad of sources and departments. These data often include historical data, vendor quotations, projections based on changes in production methods, changes in technology, volume changes, management decisions, and price estimates of future costs. As such, the data obtained from the cost accounting systems must suit the needs of the cost estimating system. Federal Acquisition Regulation 15.407-5(a) stresses that the consistent preparation of proposals, using appropriate estimating methodologies, benefits both the government and the contractor by increasing the accuracy and reliability of individual proposals.

The accuracy of the contractor's cost estimating system cannot be stressed enough, since estimating mistakes can only harm the contractor. If the estimate has understated costs, the contractor may end up with a loss on the contract. If the proposed costs are overstated, the company may be vulnerable to a downward price adjustment as a result of defective pricing.

Defense Federal Acquisition Regulation Supplement 215.407-5 addresses this need for accuracy. As stated in DFARS 215.407-5-70, it is Department of Defense (DOD) policy that all defense contractors must have estimating systems that consistently produce well-supported proposals that are acceptable as a basis for negotiation of fair and reasonable prices. Defense contractors that receive $50 million or more in negotiated prime contracts and subcontracts for which certified cost or pricing data are required must comply with the requirements for (1) written disclosure of their cost estimating systems to the administrative contracting officer (ACO), (2) timely notification of changes in the systems, and (3) correction of potentially significant estimating deficiencies. Defense contractors that receive more than $10 million in contracts also may be subject to such requirements at the ACO's discretion.

The characteristics of an adequate estimating system and the indicators of potentially significant estimating deficiencies, as set forth in DFARS 215.407-5, are contained in Appendix 14.1.

Characteristics of an Adequate Estimating System

- Policies and Procedures

  Estimating policies and procedures should be in writing and established at a sufficient level within the organization to facilitate implementation. The policies and procedures should not only be comprehensive, but should also be continually updated to reflect current practices and management philosophy. Above all else, standardization of estimating methods should be encouraged whenever possible.

- Review and Approval

  The estimating system must establish clear responsibility for developing, reviewing, and approving cost estimates. This would include proper supervisory review at interim and completion points as well as appropriate management review. Flowcharts are an effective method of documenting the steps a proposal takes on its path through the estimating system. Organizational charts with lines of authority and responsibility within the estimating group(s) would also document the review and approval process.

- Historical Data

  There are many sources of data available for use in the estimating process. Consideration should always be given to historical data. An adequate estimating system provides for identification of the data's source and documents the estimating methods and rationale used to develop estimates.

Procedures should address the consistent use of estimating techniques and place emphasis on the use of the most current, accurate, and complete data.

- Management Information Systems

All effective pricing systems rely on a support system of good pricing data which comes from many organizations within the company (e.g., purchasing, accounting, production scheduling and control, and manufacturing). To be useful, the data must not only be current, accurate, and complete, but also be readily available in a usable format that is easy to understand and adaptable to current pricing requirements. Although the phrase *management information systems* has come to mean automated systems, both automated and manual systems can be effectively utilized.

Types of data these systems should collect include historical hours, labor rates, material costs, current material quotations, changes in make-buy decisions, indirect costs on an account by account basis, and fixed asset accounting. In addition, the accounting system must produce historical cost data that can be compared to previous cost estimates.

- Updating

The estimating system must contain procedures for timely updating of proposals as more current cost or pricing data becomes available, up to and including the certification date.

- Error Detection/Correction

The system should incorporate checks and balances to ensure timely detection and correction of errors and protection against cost duplications and omissions.

Management should review and verify the company's policies, procedures, and practices comply with regulations. Once in place, good procedures based on sound business policy and carried out by a knowledgeable staff can greatly reduce the risk of potential claims by the government for defective pricing. A checklist can help ensure that all applicable factors are properly considered.

Additionally, actual practices should be tested against established policies and procedures controlling the contract pricing activities. In most organizations, this testing can be adequately performed by an internal audit staff that is properly trained in the requirements of the Truth in Negotiation Act (TINA)

- Training

Personnel involved in preparing proposals should have sufficient training, experience, and guidance to perform their estimating tasks in accordance with the company's established policies and procedures. Furthermore, the ambiguities of the law and resulting disputes that have established the ground rules for defective pricing issues necessitate educating staff in the TINA requirements. Training can go a long way in achieving these goals, but only if the proper employees are included in the training sessions. The employees who require training will vary from one company to the next depending on the degree of sophistication of the estimating system; but at a minimum, all first-level negotiation and estimating personnel should be properly trained.

Estimating Procedures

An effective estimating manual is essential to a company's overall effort to comply with TINA and, in fact, is required by DFARS 215.811-75 for business units with annual DOD awards requiring cost or pricing data of $50 million or more. The major elements of an estimating manual should address the following:

- *Background.* Explains the requirements of the Truth in Negotiations Act, as well as the DFARS 215.407-5, which addresses estimating system contractual requirements.
- *Preproposal planning activities.* Discusses bid decision, pre-"kickoff" proposal activities, and the actual proposal kickoff.
- *Cost proposal submission requirements.* Distinguishes between certified cost or pricing data and information other than cost or pricing data and identified available exceptions so that certified cost or pricing data are submitted only when required, discusses the format used to claim an exception, and establishes internal procedures to review and approve the exception request.
- *Estimating responsibilities.* Depicts through a narrative summary or possibly a flowchart of who in the company is responsible for each activity in the estimating process.
- *Cost proposal preparation.* Includes procedures for estimating labor, materials, subcontracts, interdivisional work orders, other direct costs, and indirect cost rates, and addresses the review and approval cycle for cost proposals.
- *Proposal updates, negotiations, and certification.* Contains guidelines on when proposal updates should be prepared, as well as documentation requirements for memorandums of negotiations, and addresses the process for signing certificates of current cost or pricing data and the steps to be taken before signing the certificate.

Indicators of Potentially Significant Estimating Deficiencies

Some indicators of conditions that may produce or lead to significant estimating deficiencies are listed below. These indicators are not intended as a comprehensive checklist. They may, however, suggest the need for further analysis or evaluation. Since estimating is not an exact science and is partly based on judgment, differences between individual estimates and subsequent actual data are not necessarily indications of a system deficiency.

- Failure to assure that relevant historical experience is available and utilized by cost estimators as appropriate
- Continuing failure to analyze material costs or failure to perform subcontractor cost reviews as required
- Consistent absence of analytical support for significant proposed cost amounts
- Excessive reliance on individual personal judgment where historical experience or commonly utilized standards are available
- Recurring significant defective pricing findings within the same cost element(s)
- Failure to integrate relevant parts of other management systems (e.g., pro-

duction control or cost accounting) with the estimating system so that the ability to generate reliable cost estimates is impaired

- Failure to provide established policies, procedures, and practices to personnel responsible for preparing and supporting estimates

14-4. PURCHASING SYSTEMS

While the material management and accounting system (MMAS) addresses the need for accurate allocation of inventory costs, it does not address the reasonableness of cost. Therefore, the government requires that contractors exercise good judgment when they use government funds for subcontracts or material purchases. The FAR, Part 44, governs subcontracts under prime contracts.

Naturally, contractors do not have carte blanche for purchasing parts, materials, and supplies or for awarding subcontracts. While the government assigns to prime contractors the responsibility for managing their purchasing systems, it also places substantial controls on the contractors' activities in this area. The government wants to ensure that contractor purchasing systems efficiently and effectively spend government funds and comply with applicable rules and statutes. Therefore, the systems should have the following characteristics:

- Organizational placement of the purchasing function, which allows it to operate at maximum effectiveness.
- Adequate price competition for items purchased when multiple sources are available. Contractors are expected to use formal requests when time permits.
- Justification of directed sources when competition is not obtained. Such justifications may include (1) sole source, (2) production considerations, or (3) government-directed.
- Requirements for flow-down of specific government clauses to subcontractors. These requirements may be quite extensive, depending on the type of prime contract awarded. Some of the clauses flowed down may require modification because the government and the subcontractor have no contractual relationship.
- Adequate cost or price analysis of subcontractor proposals. Price analysis is required when the subcontractor is not required to provide cost or pricing data, and cost analysis is required otherwise. Such cost analysis includes technical assessment, preaward reviews, and updates of cost or pricing data.
- Subcontract negotiation documentation, including identification of data provided by the subcontractor; the subcontractor's certificate of current cost or pricing data, if applicable; and negotiation memoranda or minutes.
- Integration of procurement data with cost estimating data to ensure that current, accurate, and complete information is provided to the prime contract negotiators.
- Programs that are designed to ensure compliance with the Anti-Kickback Act of 1986 (41 U.S.C. 51-58, as implemented in FAR 3.502). Federal Acquisition Regulation 3.502-2(i) requires prime contractors to have programs in place that include the following:
  - Company ethics rules prohibiting kickbacks
  - Education programs for new employees and subcontractors

- Subcontractors' certifications that they have not paid kickbacks
- Procurement procedures that minimize the opportunity for kickbacks
- Periodic surveys of subcontractors to elicit information about kickbacks
- Procedures for reporting suspected kickbacks
- Annual declarations by employees concerning gifts or gratuities received from subcontractors and compliance with company ethics rules
- Personnel practices that document unethical or illegal behavior and that make such information available to prospective employers of former contractor employees

Policies and Procedures

Written purchasing policies and procedures should include the following:

- Delineation of the purchasing department's standards of ethical conduct, responsibility for contacting suppliers, making purchase commitments, and challenging requisition irregularities
- Keeping estimating organizations up to date with respect to vendor quotations and negotiated price data
- Review of designs, drawings, and specifications of subcontracted items
- Description of the make-or-buy program
- Method for developing and soliciting potential subcontractors
- Establishment of a formal source selection program
- Description of major and/or critical subcontractor reporting requirements for postaward management
- Identification of high-risk subsystems, components, and other items to be subcontracted
- Evaluation of suppliers and updating vendor historical data
- Timely preparation, appropriate review, approval, and transmission of accurate and compete technical data packages and/or purchase requisitions
- Current and comprehensive purchasing instructions for the preparation, processing, and issuance of purchase orders
- Methods of ensuring that purchasing personnel are complying with applicable government regulations and public laws
- Review of requisitions for the same or similar items for all purchasing requirements for consolidation to effect maximum economy, including the screening of available stocks and surpluses
- A system to ensure satisfactory flow-down of applicable prime contract terms and conditions in purchase orders and subcontracts
- The issuance of intracompany transactions
- Transactions between affiliates, subsidiaries, or parent company
- Requirements for adequate written justification of single/sole-source purchasing and split awards
- Cost-effective methods for processing the high volume of low-dollar-value orders and calls against blanket orders and open-end subcontracts
- Adequate preaward surveys of prospective suppliers
- Selection of the proper type of subcontracts

- Adequate cost and price analysis
- Documented justification of negotiation objectives and differences between negotiation objectives and negotiated prices
- Review and approval of requirements documents by appropriate technical and support functions before final acceptance by purchasing personnel
- Definitization of unpriced orders and changes in a timely manner
- Proper control of cost reimbursement, time and material, and labor-hour subcontracts
- Adequate visibility of the subcontracts in the areas of quality, cost, schedule, and performance
- Verification of performance before disbursing progress payments
- Control of the use of nonstandard parts and components by subcontractors
- Controls over the acquisition of special tools and special test equipment by subcontractors
- Establishment of material/inventory policy
- Acceptance or return of materials
- Use of government property
- Adequate review and processing of contract terminations
- Closing of subcontracts
- Administrative contracting officer advance notification and consent
- Adequate documentation of all aspects of the purchase order transactions
- Obtaining prompt payment discount terms from suppliers
- Effective systems for complying with the small and disadvantaged business and labor surplus area subcontracting program contract clause
- An effective system of qualifying suppliers and maintaining their quality and related performance history
- Supplier quality requirements

Purchase File Contents

The following list of purchase file contents represents the typical materials found in contractor's purchase order files. Traceability and cross-reference to files that are maintained on automated systems is considered acceptable practice.

- The purchase order
- The purchase requisition, along with all required approvals
- The request for quotations (RFQ), showing all bidders solicited
- Copies of the vendor's quotations
- A bid tabulation sheet that summarizes and compares vendor quotations
- Certificates for the rent-free use of government facilities
- Vendor surveys or facilities capability reports, including financial evaluations
- Source selection explanation
- Price or cost analysis data, such as analysis of previous prices paid, comparisons of vendor's price versus in-house estimate, analysis of the data submitted by a vendor in support of its proposed cost breakdown, and an analysis of a successful bidder's breakdown versus other bidder's breakdowns

- Negotiation summary, including current cost or pricing certificate, when appropriate
- Basis for selection of contract type
- Copies of technical data, such as engineer's technical evaluations, drawings, specifications, inspection requirements, and lists of special tooling or test equipment required
- Price redetermination or termination data, if appropriate
- Correspondence between the purchasing department and the bidders
- Evidence of small and disadvantaged business enterprise consideration
- Information concerning the use of special terms and conditions and approval thereof
- Departmental and management approvals, as required
- Administrative contracting officer notification and consent, if required

14-5. GOVERNMENT PROPERTY SYSTEMS

The FAR, Part 45, specifies how government property is to be provided, monitored, and controlled by the contractor. A contractor acquires government property in one of two ways. The first method is through the contract, which requires the government to furnish specified government-acquired property. The second method is through contractor purchases of property, such as special test equipment, materials, or components (referred to as contractor-acquired property), to which the government has title.

Although currently being rewritten and simplified, the current criteria established in the FAR, Subpart 45.5, apply to managing government property in the contractor's possession. These requirements are passed to the contractor through various contract clauses, depending on the contract type and the value of the government property. Some of the requirements have posed several problems for contractors in trying to implement material requirements planning systems. For example, multiple requirements are placed on property systems for different kinds of property (e.g., materials and plant equipment). However, the property control records must include the following information for every item of government property:

- The name, description, and national stock number (if furnished by the government or available in the property control system)
- Quantity received (or fabricated), issued, and on hand
- Unit price (and unit of measure)
- Contract number or equivalent code designation
- Location
- Disposition
- Posting reference and date of transaction

Other property system controls are required for the various kinds of property. For example, whether the property is furnished by the government or purchased under government contract, the contractor may be required to maintain various types of stock records, custodial records, and issue and receipt documents, and to meet conditions for multicontract cost and material controls (commingled inventories). There are also specific requirements for special tooling and special test equipment, plant real property, scrap or salvage, completed products, and others. The following are characteristics of an acceptable property administration system:

- Identification of government property through segregation or property tags
- Periodic physical inventories
- Appropriate care and maintenance of government property
- Restrictions and controls on limiting government property to authorized uses
- Monitoring and controls for the disposition of government property

Government property is to be reported on standard government forms, which may be required during contract performance. However, certain inventory forms are required as part of the contract closeout submission.

14-6. PROJECT MANAGEMENT SYSTEMS

The ability to monitor project costs on government contracts is of increasing importance to the government and independent certified public accountants (CPAs). The government is concerned about overpaying cost-based progress payments and not being forewarned about potential cost overruns. For the independent CPA, the concern is timely identification of potential losses and appropriate recognition of losses in the contractor's financial statements. While the information needed serves two distinct purposes and is calculated separately, it starts with the same underlying facts.

The preparation of a comprehensive contract cost and performance analysis and estimate of contract costs at completion is key to assessing progress and determining if problems exist. These estimates should be prepared at least quarterly to ensure the reliability of interim financial statements and to avoid surprises that come too late for effective corrective action. It is important that management be informed promptly and periodically of the key facts concerning contract performance. Sometimes, high-level summary reports, similar to the example in Appendix 14.2, are useful in providing an overview of the financial, schedule, and technical status and identifying the necessity for management action.

Many facts and judgmental data are inherent in project management systems. Also inherent in such systems is a configuration management function that tracks changes to the technical "baseline" of a product. With the complexity of such systems, it is difficult to design management reports that concisely present the key information needed, which includes:

- Actual cost to date
- Actual work performed
- Budgeted cost for work scheduled
- Budgeted cost for work performed (aka earned value)
- Estimated cost to complete
- Estimated cost at completion
- Contract amount (including changes)
- Projected overrun or underrun

- Contract schedule completion date
- Expected completion date

Graphical presentations, as shown in Appendix 14.3, are often useful in portraying this important information.

In the case of major procurements, the government takes a keen interest in the contractor's management information systems. To ensure that it can monitor the contractor's progress, the government inserts a clause, DFARS 252.234-7001, into contracts that requires the contractor maintain a cost/schedule control system (C/SCS). The criteria necessary to comply with this clause are quite involved and specific. Normally, the contractor's system will be subject to a validation review within 90 days after contract award, when the contract contains this clause. For smaller contractors, an alternate clause, DFARS 252.242-7005, requires a cost/schedule status report (C/SSR).

The C/SCS is frequently referred to as an earned value management system (EVMS). In December 1996, the Undersecretary of Defense (Acquisition & Technology)[3] established EVMS guidelines that should simplify system implementation and maintenance. The guidelines, which were jointly developed by government and industry, will be incorporated into the DFARS clause 252.234-7001. However, inasmuch as DFARS 252.234-7000, already references DOD Instruction (DODI) 5000.2, the guidelines have been implemented for all practical purposes. "The Earned Value Management Implementation Guide"[4] has replaced the "Cost/Schedule Control Systems Criteria Joint Implementation Guide,"[5] which was issued in 1976.

Previous management systems compared actual cost to budgeted cost. This management technique primarily measured the "burn rate"; that is, it addressed whether the contractor expended funds as planned, rather than determining how much work was actually accomplished (i.e., how much value was *earned* for the expended funds). In such systems an expenditure profile that was consistent with the plan would often obscure the fact that sufficient work had not been performed; the late identification of the potential overrun often precluded meaningful corrective action.

The earned value concept is fairly simple and may more easily be explained by an example. A contractor determines that a given subsystem can be designed for 540 hours over three months and subdivides the budget into the following subtasks:

Define requirements	40 Hours	Month 1
Preliminary design	60 Hours	Month 1
Preliminary design review	20 Hours	Month 1
Reliability study	80 Hours	Month 2
Detail design	160 Hours	Month 2
Critical design review	40 Hours	Month 3
Prepare drawings	100 Hours	Month 3
Drawing release	40 Hours	Month 3
	540 Hours	

The contractor expends 100 hours the first month as planned, but accomplishes only the definition of requirements and half of the preliminary design. A traditional comparison of a budget versus actuals approach would indicate budget underrun of 20 hours, with no indication that the contractor was experiencing problems. The earned value approach compares the 100 hours expended to the work accomplished. This example reflects a 30-hour unfavorable cost variance (70 hours earned, less 100 hours expended) and a 50-hour unfavorable schedule variance (70 hours earned, less 120 hours of work scheduled). This approach apprises management that there are problems with completing the design. Project management experience indicates that even when there is no cost variance, schedule variance is a reliable predictor of future cost variance, because additional costs must frequently be incurred to recover schedule. As can be seen from the above example, the earned value concept allows for earlier identification of potential problems in contract performance.

An effective project management system requires a complementary set of procedures and trained employees that ensure the system is meeting the defined objectives. Normally, a system description functions as an integrating document to focus attention on the project management task. The system description will leverage the existing investment in policies and procedures and show the relationship of existing controls to the project management task. Discussed below are some of the controls that are in place in healthy project management systems.

Work Breakdown Structure

Complex contracts must be subdivided into more manageable components. A work breakdown structure (WBS) is a hierarchical subdivision of the contractual effort. Traditionally, this subdivision has had a systems orientation. The weapon system is divided into the vehicle, ground support equipment, and so forth. The vehicle may then be subdivided into subsystems such as propulsion, guidance and control, and the like. The top levels of the WBS may be contractually specified and, in this case, is referred to as a contract work breakdown structure (CWBS). The contractor may then extend the CWBS to levels appropriate for internal management. No fixed number of levels is appropriate in all cases. Care should be exercised by the contractor in extending the WBS only to levels that add value to the management of the contract. An excessive level of detail increases cost unnecessarily. A rule of thumb: measuring the work should never become more important than accomplishing the work. It is common for WBS elements to have separate budgets and schedules.

Budget Baseline

Initially, the contract budget baseline is tied directly to the contract award value. Contractors normally remove the anticipated fee and establish a management reserve to be used for unforeseen circumstances that typically arise during performance of the contract. The contract award, less fee and management reserve, represents the funds available for budgeting and initially is referred to as undistributed budget. A contract budget baseline log should be established for tracking the assignment of undistributed budget to specific tasks. When additional funds are added to the contract for authorized changes, the fee, management reserve, and undistributed budget amounts may all be updated to reflect the change.

When undistributed budget is assigned to a specific task, the amount assigned is considered distributed budget. Management reserve is normally transferred initially to the undistributed budget and then released for specific tasks to a distributed budget. Thus, all distributed budget flows through the undistributed budget control. Distributed budget resides in control accounts (previously called cost accounts) where responsibility is assigned to a specific organization or cross-functional team. The organization responsible for the control account is normally responsible for planning and budgeting the task, performing the task, and explaining any significant variances that may occur.

Contract Schedule

The contract schedule, for most contractors, is a set of related schedules. The governing schedule is frequently referred to as the program master schedule, a schedule that normally identifies all contractual delivery requirements, critical program milestones, and important customer commitments. The program master schedule is the governing schedule for all subordinate schedules. In certain cases, the program master schedule may contain events from related contracts. Similar to the management reserve established in the budgeting process, a schedule reserve may be established by the contractor for internal milestones.

Subordinate schedules describe the schedule for performing specific parts of the contract in additional detail. Several types of subordinate schedules have been observed, and the type of subordinate schedules in use on a particular contract vary with the nature of the effort and contractor practices. Subordinate schedules must support the program master schedule for the management system to operate effectively. Subordinate schedules often include the following:

- A WBS schedule identifies the subtasks required to complete the contractual effort associated with the WBS element. The identified tasks are normally lower-level WBS elements or control accounts.

- At the operating level, control account schedules may exist. Sometimes called cost account plans, these schedules are normally constructed closer to the performance of the work, and usually contain schedules for specific work packages.

- Work that has not be planned discretely in specific work packages is kept with less detail in planning packages.

- Where multiple product deliveries are required in performance of the contract, a master production schedule (MPS) normally identifies all product deliveries associated with the contract (called independent requirements) and the internal schedule for producing the needed products (called MPS replenishments). The MPS is one of the primary inputs to a MMAS.

- Where a contractor is experiencing problems, recovery schedules facilitate the proper allocation of necessary resources to put the contract back on schedule.

Performance Baseline

The performance measurement baseline can be considered the product of contract budget baseline and contract schedule. In the performance measurement baseline, all distributed budget is time-phased. The level of time phasing should be sufficient enough to enable meaningful measurement of earned value.

Control Account and Variance Report

The control account is assigned to a single WBS element, has a budget and schedule, and is discrete enough in its definition to allow meaningful measurement of earned value. A single organization or team is responsible for performance of the effort being managed in the control account. It can be thought of as a "mini-contract." Periodically, usually monthly, performance on active control accounts is reported. These control account reports are the foundation for project management reporting at the CWBS and contract levels. Each month the responsible manager should evaluate earned value in relationship to expended costs and scheduled performance. In cases where actual performance is significantly different from planned performance, the responsible manager should document in writing the conditions causing the variation, the corrective action being taken, and any potential impact on the estimate at completion. Such documentation has traditionally been called a variance report.

These five controls provide reasonable assurance that deviations from the plan will be identified early, that meaningful corrective action can be taken, and that, where the estimate at completion must change, the change is communicated promptly.

14-7. MATERIAL MANAGEMENT AND ACCOUNTING SYSTEMS

Defense FAR Supplement 242.72, Contractor Material Management and Accounting Systems, applies not only to material requirements planning systems but also to all "systems for planning, controlling, and accounting for the acquisition, use and disposition of material." As stated in DFARS 242.7202, it is DOD policy that *all* defense contractors "have an MMAS that reasonably forecasts material requirements, ensures the costs of purchased and fabricated material charged or allocated to a contract are based on valid time-phased requirements and maintains a consistent, equitable and unbiased logic for costing material transactions." Ten standards (Appendix 14.4), referred to as the "10 key elements," are used in determining whether systems comply with DOD policy. The standards, developed jointly by the DOD and industry representatives, are rigorous.

For business units that receive defense awards of $70 million or more in the prior fiscal year or, subject to ACO direction, business units with defense awards over $30 million, the MMAS must be disclosed in writing and demonstrated to be adequate. Significant changes in the system must be disclosed to the ACO no later than 30 days after implementation. Subsequent written disclosure is not required unless the contractor's policies, procedures, or practices have changed. Once a contractor has demonstrated that its MMAS contains no significant deficiencies, demonstration requirements for subsequent reviews may be satisfied if internal audits are reasonably current and contain sufficient transaction tests to demonstrate MMAS compliance. The intent is that once an MMAS has been determined adequate, subsequent reviews, for the most part, will be an incremental assessment of areas in the MMAS system that have undergone change.

Costing of Material Transactions

The government's primary MMAS concern is the costing of material transactions, primarily the transfer of parts between contracts.

Material transaction costing must be based upon consistent, equitable, and unbiased logic [DFARS 252.242-7004(f)(7)]. Because transfers almost always directly affect progress billings, detailed descriptions must be provided as to circumstances that result in manual or system-generated transfers [DFARS 252.242-7004(f)(6)]. The contractor must also maintain and disclose a written policy describing the transfer methodologies [DFARS 252.242-7004(f)(7)].

Material is normally charged directly to a contract. For CAS-covered contractors, the regulatory basis for this costing methodology is CAS 411. As discussed in Chapter 8, CAS 411 provides for the direct allocation of the cost of units of a category of material, as long as the cost objective is identified at the time of purchase or production. This identification enables contractors to include the material cost of inventory in progress billings. Many defense contractor material requirements planning (MRP) systems enable such identification to minimize the amount of company-owned inventory.

Allocations of common inventory are covered by DFARS 252.242-7004(f)(8) and will be discussed later.

The expectation is that units charged directly to cost objectives at acquisition will continue to be charged to those same cost objectives through consumption and that the cost of the material charged will not change. Excessive transfer activity is an indicator that the MMAS system may not be functioning properly.

The DCAA *Contract Audit Manual*, Sections 5-712.3(d) and 6-305, cites a classic billing problem that occurs when parts are issued to spares requirements prior to acquisition of spares inventory and the contractor recovers part costs on the spares contract through delivery and on the production contract through progress billings. To avoid this problem, contractors should either adjust billings by the amount of inventory used to support spare contracts where the material for that requirement had not yet been received, or alternatively, move the cost from the production contract to the spares contract via transfer. The spares example can be generalized to any condition where material is assigned (issued) to a contractual requirement before the specific acquisition occurs to support that contractual requirement.

Subsequent to acquisition and payment for receipt, material cost will remain charged to the contract unless the material is transferred. The three most common reasons for transfers are:

1. The correction of mistaken charges
2. The redirection of previously acquired units when program requirements change
3. The disposition of residual inventory at contract closure

Unbiased Transfer Logic

The method for determining the contract from which to transfer material should be unbiased. The transferring contract will receive a credit and have its progress billings reduced. Therefore, the algorithm should not inadvertently be structured to favor company-owned, nongovernment, or fixed-priced inventory.

Some MRP systems enable the contractor to specify parameters that will control how the contract is selected. This type of logic enables contractors to specify families of related contracts. Typical examples are fiscal year contracts for the same production program and contracts for a particular customer (e.g., Navy, Air Force). Some companies use loan/payback logic in lieu of transfer/payback logic within a family of related contracts, especially when transfers within the family would not affect billings. Contractors using a family of contracts technique should be vigilant in maintaining the necessary control tables. Failure to do so jeopardizes the integrity of the family of contracts concept.

Consistent Transfer Valuation

Cost Accounting Standard 411 allows a contractor to use different valuation methods for different categories of material, and DFARS 242.72 allows a different costing method to be used for transfer charging than the method used for initial charging. However, the costing method used for transferring of a category of material must be consistent across all contract and customer types, and from accounting period to accounting period.

The valuation method to be used for manufactured part transfers is not addressed in the MMAS criteria. The DCAA *Contract Audit Manual*, Section 5-712.3(e), provides that any written, disclosed method for valuation of manufactured parts that provides a reasonable estimation of actual cost complies with MMAS standards.

The primary advantage of a standard cost system in an MMAS environment is that all transactions for a given part are valued the same, so issues associated with equitable treatment are avoided.

Overhead Application

The government prefers the application of overhead rates to value material transactions consistent with when the material was purchased or manufactured. The specific guidance in the DCAA *Contract Audit Manual* 6-305.3(d)(1) states the following:

> "As to indirect costs allocable to the prime costs, CAS 410.50(i) provides the proper accounting for allocating G&A costs and for transfers. In general, material transfers *should* be priced using the G&A (or overhead) rate derived when the material was purchased/ manufactured. The auditor should ascertain compliance with these standards." [Emphasis added]

Allocation from Common Inventory

Some contractors maintain all categories of material as common, for allocation to cost objectives. Other contractors maintain certain categories of material as common (e.g., raw material, as required material). Defense FAR Supplement 252.242-7004(f)(8) requires that reallocations, including credits to government contracts, be processed at least once each billing cycle. Inventories maintained for requirements not under contract are not to be allocated to contracts. Algorithms used for allocation must be based upon valid and current data.

If it is not cost effective to maintain specific requirement records for a category of material, material acquisition is usually determined from usage experience. Material acquired in this manner is sometimes called reorder point material. When inventory reaches the reorder point, an additional procurement is placed.

Other Material Transactions

Contractors must have a consistent, equitable, and unbiased method for costing other material transactions, particularly transactions associated with inventory loss and gain transactions. When an inventory loss occurs, it is normally necessary for the system to pick a contract to absorb the loss, even if losses are subsequently allocated. The chosen contract will need to reacquire inventory, which may result in an increase in contract cost. Therefore, the algorithm must be unbiased and not be based upon customer or contract type. Valuation of inventory gains actually present one of the more difficult challenges for contractors not using standard cost. Some contractors attempt to offset gains against prior losses, to the extent possible. However, sooner or later, the contractor must take a gain that cannot be offset by prior losses. A gain that cannot be offset by prior losses may be valued at the average cost of previous issues to open contracts.

Revaluation

Inventory (and work-in-process) revaluation can occur when purchase order prices are changed or late labor charges are recorded on shop orders subsequent to receipt of parts in the MRP system. When revaluation charges occur, to the extent practical, the contractor should identify the impact of the revaluation charges on previously booked material transactions, including transfers.

Control of Inventory

Contractors generally use one of two approaches to physically control contract inventory: physical segregation or commingling. Government-furnished property should always be physically segregated.

Physical Segregation

When material is purchased or manufactured for a particular contract, it can be physically stored separately from other contract inventories. This method ensures that material acquired for a contract is used on that contract. The primary disadvantage of the physical segregation method is increased operational cost. Physically segregated inventories may require more bins and warehouse space. Costs associated with receiving and kitting may be increased. Inventory and/or part shortages may also increase. A separate buffer normally must be established for each contract to avoid production problems.

Commingled Inventories

The contractor can physically commingle parts while keeping segregated records of contract identification within the system. This method avoids the operational inefficiencies associated with physical segregation, especially when used with the transfer/payback technique.

Commingling is expressly allowed under DFARS 252.242-7004(f)(9) [when approved in accordance with FAR 45.505-3(f)(3)], which states that the MMAS shall:

> "... have adequate controls to ensure that *physically commingled inventories that may include material for which costs are charged or allocated to fixed-price, cost-reimbursement, and commercial contracts* do not compromise requirements of any of the standards. ..." [Emphasis added.]

Valid Time-Phased Requirements and Accuracy Measurements

Before the MMAS standards were developed, existing American Production and Inventory Control Society (APICS) literature called for 95% master production schedule accuracy, 98% bill of material accuracy, and 95% inventory accuracy as standards to be met by companies successfully implementing an MRP system. An MRP system will generate time-phased requirements from the master production schedule, bills of material and lead times, then net those requirements against inventory and planned replenishments, resulting in the generation of purchase orders and shop orders. To the extent the inputs to the process (MPS, bills of material, and inventory) are accurate, the outputs from the process (purchase orders and shop orders) that result in costs being incurred will also be accurate. Hence the need for high accuracy levels as a control objective. The APICS standards were accepted without much analysis as to their applicability to the defense contracting environment, particularly the high rate of engineering change. Nevertheless, defense contractors made reasonable efforts to comply with the new standards, and the result has been a significant improvement in the material management control environment. Defense FAR Supplement MMAS clauses 242.252(f)(2) and 242.252(f)(5) require the contractor to demonstrate that there is no material harm to the government due to lower accuracy levels and that the cost to meet the accuracy goals is excessive in relation to the impact on the government.

The primary purpose of time-phased requirements from the DCAA perspective is the prevention of harm to the government, that is, ensuring that the government is not billed too early and is not billed for material that is not used on the contract.

Bill of Material Accuracy

The primary risk to the government with respect to bill of material (BOM) accuracy is that unnecessary parts will be ordered. Therefore, an accuracy measurement that focuses upon verifying part, quantity, and unit of measure as an integrated statement of need for high-value components is more important than verifying low value as required callouts. An inaccuracy that results from a related part (older/newer version) being called out can be less severe than an unnecessary part being called out. Measurements that give the same weight to the bill of material for a major subassembly as to the BOM for a fabrication detail appear to lack a materiality focus.

The government recognizes that the techniques for calculating the accuracy percentage for BOMs will vary from contractor to contractor (DCAM, Section 5-707.1.d). The overall guidance to auditors is that the BOM represents the actual material required to produce the product; BOMs that drive procurement and production are more appropriate than "as built" BOMs for accuracy measurement; contractors should have procedures and internal controls for ensuring accurate BOMs; and the method for calculating BOM accuracy should be reasonable.

The example formula in the *Manual* for BOM accuracy is as follows:

$$\text{BOM Accuracy} = \frac{\text{BOMs in Agreement}}{\text{Total BOMs Reviewed}} \times 100$$

This formula is not used by most contractors because it gives the same weight to a complex BOM as a simple BOM and disqualifies an entire BOM for a single error. Most contractors use some version of the following formula:

$$\text{BOM Accuracy} = \frac{\text{Measurement Points in Agreement}}{\text{Total Measurement Points}} \times 100$$

This formula is more reasonable in that complex BOMs are given more weight than simple BOMs and single errors do not disqualify an entire BOM. However, contractors should exercise care in selecting the measurement points so that items such as nomenclature and unit of measure do not skew the measurement pool to a higher percentage. The government might then conclude that the measurement is not reasonable.

An additional variation in the measurement formula which includes consideration for value is as follows:

$$\text{BOM Accuracy} = \frac{(\text{Measurement Point in Agreement} * \text{Dollar Value})}{(\text{Total Measurement Points} * \text{Dollar Value})} \times 100$$

By weighting the accuracy measurements by dollar value, emphasis is placed on those measures that have the greatest impact on possible harm to the government. The dollar-weighted method will also prevent the contractor from allocating resources unnecessarily to low value BOMs.

Master Production Schedule Accuracy

The MPS is a statement of high-level production that balances the need to support firm and forecasted independent product demand with available production capacity. In the commercial environment, it is also intended to level load production with capacity. It is neither a measure of performance nor the schedule for all shop orders. The reason the MPS accuracy metric is less than the BOM accuracy measurement primarily involves the capriciousness of forecasted demand. There is little, if any, forecasted demand for defense contractors.

Two acceptable methods for defining the MPS prior to measurement include the independent requirement approach and the MPS replenishment approach.

- Independent requirements identify when production and spares units will be issued to shipping in fulfillment of contractual requirements. From the perspective of most program managers, this is the MPS. The MPS is accurate if the independent requirements have been loaded with the right quantities, dates, and cost accumulation numbers. Overstatement of the MPS for production units is a significant deficiency.
- The MPS replenishment approach is more consistent with the traditional APICS approach to MPS. Initially, the MPS is defined as those replenishments that directly support the independent requirements. Within policy constraints (usually 90 to 120 days), the MPS replenishment dates are adjusted to more evenly level the load on production resources. The MPS is accurate if the MPS replenishments support the independent requirements, contain accurate quantities, specify dates that are within the policy window, and specify accurate cost accumulation numbers. This approach enables the most efficient use of manufacturing resources by ensuring stable production. The MPS should be reviewed and adjusted quarterly. This

MPS approach also enables the contractor to adjust where contract performance is behind schedule but a recovery plan is being implemented.

Techniques for calculating the accuracy percentage for MPS will also vary from contractor to contractor. The DCAA *Contract Audit Manual,* Section 5-707.2.b, recognizes that "although there are some common methods used for measuring MPS, no specific method is required," and that "each contractor should assess its own system and then identify the most appropriate method to demonstrate that the system generates realistic need dates for material."

Two examples of MPS accuracy are provided by the government. The first example formula in the *Manual* for MPS accuracy is as follows:

$$\text{Performance} = \frac{\text{Actual Production}}{\text{Planned Production}} \times 100$$

Clearly, this measurement is performance-oriented. If actual performance exceeds planned performance, accuracy amazingly exceeds 100%. This formula is not used by most contractors.

The second government example formula is as follows:

$$\text{MPS Accuracy} = \frac{\text{No. of End Items with Accurate Delivery Dates in Schedule}}{\text{No. of Contractually Deliverable End Items}} \times 100$$

This measurement is much more reasonable and, in fact, is identical to the independent requirement approach described earlier. A third variation in the measurement formula based in part on value is as follows:

$$\text{MPS Accuracy} = \frac{\text{Accurate MPS Replenishments} * \text{Dollar Value}}{\text{Contractual End Items} * \text{Dollar Value}} \times 100$$

This formula gives greater weight to high-value end items and lower weight to lower-value items and also considers the classic APICS interpretation of the MPS.

Inventory Accuracy

Inventory balances are used in the MRP netting algorithms and, as such, must be accurate by part to ensure the reasonableness of future order quantities. Inaccuracies may result in unnecessary material orders or shortages.

Because an error on an expensive item is more serious than an error on a low-value item, contractors frequently stratify inventory on annual dollar usage using a technique called ABC classification. Typically, the 20% of inventory items that constitute approximately 65% of annual dollar usage will be classified as A items, the 30% of inventory items that constitute the next 25% of annual dollar usage will be classified as B items, and the 50% of inventory items that constitute the last 10% of annual dollar usage will be classified as C items.

Typical cycle count programs count A parts monthly, B parts quarterly, and C parts annually. Some contractors have demonstrated that equivalent results are obtained by counting A parts quarterly, B parts annually, and C parts every three years. Other contractors have reduced the cost of cycle counts by reporting all zero-balance conditions when the last part is removed, reducing the total number of bin visitations.

APICS recognizes that a cycle count does not have to agree exactly with record inventory for the inventory to be accurate. An acceptable tolerance is usually established by ABC classification. Typical tolerances might be zero for A parts, 5% for B parts, and 10% for C parts.

Additionally, inventory location is important since parts must be physically located where the system believes them to be to facilitate their use. If parts have been mislaid, the contractor will incur additional expense in attempting to locate the parts. By maintaining high location accuracy, the contractor also demonstrates commitment to a strong control environment.

The government recognizes that the techniques for calculating the accuracy percentage for inventory, like MPS and BOM accuracy, will vary from contractor to contractor. The DCAA *Contract Audit Manual*, Section 5-710.3.c, states in part: "An inventory classification system may be used by a contractor to focus available resources on controlling those materials posing the greatest risk." The example formula provided in the *Manual* is as follows:

$$\text{Inventory Accuracy} = \frac{\text{No. of Parts Accurate}}{\text{No. of Part Counted}} \times 100$$

The above method is reasonable, especially when pre-established tolerances are considered. The only drawback is a lack of test for materiality. An additional formula which tests materiality is as follows:

$$\text{Inventory Accuracy} = \frac{\text{Accurate Parts Counts} * \text{Annual Dollar Usage}}{\text{Total Parts Counts} * \text{Annual Dollar Usage}} \times 100$$

A more aggressive formula, which can be used if harm must be calculated, is the following:

$$\text{Inventory Accuracy}$$
$$= \frac{\begin{array}{c}(\text{Accurate Parts Counts} * \text{Annual Dollar Usage}) \\ + \text{High Inventory Counts} * \text{Annual Dollar Usage})\end{array}}{\text{Total Parts Counts} * \text{Annual Dollar Usage})}$$

This last measurement reflects the fact that only low inventory counts (recorded inventory less than physical inventory) will result in unnecessary procurement or production.

Excess Inventory

If inventory in excess of time-phased requirements is included in progress billings to the harm of the government, the normal remedy sought is a decrease in progress billings. Therefore, the contractor should establish a control objective which ensures that lead times and ordering policies are reviewed periodically and that they are reasonable.

If the government causes excess to time-phased requirements by directing a postponement in the contract delivery schedule, the contractor should document the postponement's impact on time-phased requirements and seek specific relief, usually via a memorandum of agreement (MOA) from the ACO.

If excess in total is caused by contractor negligence, the reasonableness of the cost may be challenged. Excess in total can be caused by a variety of factors, such as minimum order size policies. The contractor should be more concerned with excess in total on high-value parts. Normally, this excess results from two primary sources: (1) cancellation of contract requirements and (2) obsolescence resulting from engineering changes.

Currently, most contractors do not have an audit trail on the creation, change, and deletion of dependent requirements. To maintain such an audit trail with existing technology has proven to be cost prohibitive. Nevertheless, since computing technology is improving rapidly, the contractor should periodically, perhaps on a biannual basis, review the cost–benefit equation to redetermine if maintenance of a dependent requirement audit trail is feasible.

The contractor has an obligation to disclose the existence of excess material in either inventory or on order, at the time that cost or pricing data is submitted. Some contractors use standard disclosure language. Others provide detailed listings to the government. The government prefers specific identification of excess material as soon as it is known to the contractor. Failure to attempt to identify excess material can be considered a serious control weakness.

Disclosure of excess material does not mean that the government is entitled to that inventory or the price of that inventory. The contractor cannot normally guarantee, at the time of proposal, that any excess in total will still be available for a particular contract. Determination of whether proposal values should be adjusted based upon available excess is a matter of negotiation.

Issue of Title

The issue of title to residual material at the end of a contract has been an area of discussion for a number of years. On cost plus contracts, the government retains title to residual inventory acquired during performance of the contract. On firm-fixed-priced contracts, the contractor obtains title to any remaining material upon completion of the contract, even if progress payments were made by the government during performance of the contract. The most complex title issue arises on fixed-price-incentive contracts, in which the contractor and the government share in any over/underruns. Fixed-priced-incentive contracts normally contain a price redetermination clause. The contractor can expect that the residual material will become an issue during price redetermination.

System Assurance

Because of all the issues associated with MRP I and MRP II implementations in the defense contracting environment, the MMAS regulations contain a number of controls intended to provide greater assurance to the government that MMAS systems are functioning properly.

Control Environment

Establishment of a strong MMAS control environment is the single most effective step that management can take to reduce risk associated with MMAS compliance. The MMAS compliance policy should be issued at the executive level of the business unit since MMAS compliance will require cooperative efforts that cross most organizations and disciplines within the business unit. Because the majority of transactions that are processed in an MMAS environment are performed by manufacturing operations, the manufacturing operations executive should issue a policy statement that unequivocally establishes MMAS compliance as a key objective for the manufacturing organization. At a minimum, the policy statement should specifically address the three key accuracy metrics. Annual MMAS compliance training sessions will further emphasize the importance of MMAS compliance to manufacturing personnel. In the training session, specific guidance should be given on higher-risk transactions (e.g., material gains to a specific contract).

Three other organizations may also be critical to successful MMAS implementation.

1. Engineering sometimes places demands on production resources. It is critical that such demands, especially production material consumption, are handled with sufficient discipline to ensure appropriate accounting.

2. The logistics organization will be an additional source of production material demand, especially for spares. Effective management of spares requirements and the associated replenishments is a prerequisite for complete system integrity.

3. The estimating function must be perceived as a customer of the MMAS system and provided accurate and complete data relative to excess inventory, contractual excess, and attrition on a timely basis. Policy statements from these organizations and specific interface procedures are an important element of the overall MMAS control environment.

System Description

The system description should be a comprehensive description of the formal system the contractor uses to ensure MMAS compliance. An MMAS disclosure is adequate when the contractor has provided the ACO with documentation that accurately describes the policies, procedures, and practices that the contractor *currently* uses in its MMAS and provides sufficient detail for the government to reasonably make an informed judgment regarding the adequacy of the MMAS. The system description should also include policies, procedures, and operating instructions that comply with FAR and DFARS. Typical sections in an MMAS system description are shown in Appendix 14.5.

When providing a system description under an initial MMAS disclosure, some level of modification may be required prior to obtaining ACO determination that the system description is adequate. The contractor should also anticipate possible requests for modification as a result of subsequent reviews.

A DFARS clause [242.7203(c)] that became effective September 1996 specifies that once an ACO determines that the contractor's MMAS is adequate, "written disclosure will not be required for the subsequent MMAS reviews unless the contractor's policies, procedures, or practices have changed in the interim period(s)." Contractors use judgment when considering changes that would impact their cost accounting disclosure statement. Similar judgment should be used prior to making changes to an MMAS that has been determined adequate.

Internal Audit

Contractors should subject their MMAS to periodic internal or external audits to ensure compliance with established policies and procedures.

As discussed further in Chapter 16, disclosure of internal audit reports can be a sensitive issue. The DCAA *Contract Audit Manual*, Section 5-715(c), states that "if the contractor contends that such reviews [as to meet the objective of Standard 10] have been performed but is unwilling to make them available to DCAA in any form, the auditor may be unable to determine if the contractor has complied with the standard."

In practice, contractors and the government have been able to find common ground. Some contractors use self-governance or compliance assessment resources independent of the internal audit staff to perform internal MMAS compliance audits. Others have used outside consultants. Still others provide abstracts of audit reports or remove company sensitive information. It is important that some level of documentation, including some work product, be disclosed as evidence of compliance with the internal audit requirement.

Finally, DCAA *Contract Audit Manual*, Section 5-715(d), states that "the contractor cannot comply to submission of an adequate demonstration if it does not provide the government 'sufficient evidence' of system compliance." If the internal auditor performs the self-assessment and demonstration, access to the detailed work products is a requirement in order to provide the necessary "sufficient evidence." Therefore, the contractor is cautioned to maintain an appropriate separation of duties between self-assessment and demonstration personnel.

Metrics and Diagnostics

At a minimum, the contractor must establish metrics that measure MPS, BOP, and inventory accuracy. Contractors should also have diagnostic tools that identify excess total inventory, inventory excess to contractual requirements, and inventory excess to time-phased requirements.

A strong diagnostic program facilitates MMAS compliance. Contractors should have tools that provide some or all of the following indicators of MMAS system health:

- Unsupported loans (loans in which the repayment has not been identified)
- Outstanding loan aging
- Identification of zero cost parts
- Unsupported contract requirements

Traditional MRP control practices and metrics, including the following, help demonstrate an adequate MMAS control environment:

- Total inventory
- Inventory/sales ratio
- Inventory shortage identification
- Obsolete and surplus activity
- Attrition activity
- Open shop order aging
- Dock to stock aging

Cost Accumulation Numbering Systems

In developing a strategy for MMAS compliance, contractors should give some attention to the nature of the cost accumulation numbering system. Almost without exception, contractor systems do not store the actual contract number in their database records, since this would be grossly inefficient and cumbersome. Instead, contractors store a charge number that translates to a specific contract number. These charge numbers typically range in size from four to sixteen characters, and frequently have imbedded subdivisions with specific meanings. Frequently, the primary subdivision is called a project, and generally relates to a specific contract.

For especially large contracts, a contract often consists of multiple projects. In other cases, such as spares contracts, a project can consist of multiple contracts. Because of the latter case, contractors sometimes match requirements and replenishments at an inappropriate level, that is, a level below the contract. This lower level matching can lead to unnecessary and undesirable transfer and loan activity.

Matching requirements and replenishments on a contract is all that MMAS requires. In some cases, it is helpful to add an additional field, separate from charge number and project, whose sole function is to ensure appropriate matching of requirements and replenishments by contract.

Earned-Value Management System Interface

Integration of the MMAS with the EVMS continues to be a concern for many contractors.

Point for Taking Material Earned Value

An earned-value system that records earned value at point of receipt will be degraded to the extent that issue based transfers occur. For this reason, earned value should be taken at issue, unless the contractor is exclusively using an ACO approved loan/payback technique, or a loan/payback system can be simulated. A hard transfer system generally cannot support earned value at receipt, since hard transfer systems can result in receipt activity in excess of contract requirements.

Subcontractor earned value should be taken at receipt or earlier. In fact, subcontractor performance can be measured prior to receipt using milestone methods and applied actual cost. A loan/payback technique, with approval from the ACO, should be considered when transfers occur on parts for which subcontractor progress payments are made.

Material Estimates at Completion

The EVMS guidelines place heavy reliance on open commitments. However, open commitments are a reliable predictor of material cost at completion only to the extent that the integrity of acquisition cost can be maintained.

Neither common inventory allocation systems, or standard cost systems nor hard transfer systems can preserve acquisition cost integrity. The only MMAS approaches that consistently demonstrate preservation of acquisition cost integrity are transfer/payback and loan/payback systems.

Standard cost systems can predict an estimate at completion (EAC) to the extent that the material price variance rate and material usage variance rate can accurately be predicted.

Common inventory allocation systems can predict an EAC to the extent that the allocated material cost for a program can be accurately predicted.

Work Breakdown Structure Identification

Integration of WBS identification into MMAS systems has sometimes been difficult. When the cost accumulation system has more than one charge number that can be used for the same part on the same contract, the potential risk of artificial mismatches is increased. Unless the MMAS system has logic to resolve minor differences in the cost accumulation numbers, additional unnecessary transfer activity may inadvertently be generated. Vigilant maintenance of the WBS structure within the MRP system is required to avoid artificial transfers when contract inventory is actually available. The use of a standard WBS format across all contracts for similar products sometimes helps to reduce problems.

Three techniques for assigning WBS numbers within an MRP system are typical. The first method assigns the WBS number based on the part number. The second method defaults the WBS number based on the part number, but allows an override of the part number at the BOM level. The third method defaults the WBS number for dependent requirements to the WBS number of the parent next assembly, unless an override is specified at the part or BOM level. The latter method provides the most flexibility and reduces the cost of WBS maintenance within the MMAS system.

Some contractors use a single material holding account per contract for the acquisition of material. If material is charged to a different WBS at issue, earned value should be taken at issue. Otherwise, earned value should be taken at receipt.

Material Budget Baseline

The time-phased requirements in the MMAS system provides an excellent source for establishing the budget baseline for material control accounts. Establishing multiple organizational responsibilities (with the possible exception of subcontracted items) adds no value. The number of material control accounts (previously cost accounts) should be exactly equal to the number of WBS elements for which material is procured.

The major problem with maintaining the material budget baseline is that the time-phased requirements established at the start of the program change as the MPS is adjusted, whereas the EVMS criteria seek a stable baseline. However, changes in the time-phased requirements for material and manufacturing due to MPS adjustments do not present the same inherent risk that schedule changes to engineering development tasks do. Normal adjustments to the MPS should not require the reporting and explanation of schedule variance. Schedule variance should be reported only when issues (or receipts) are not occurring to the time-phased requirements plan.

Cost of Compliance

A study was done in 1994 at the request of then Deputy Secretary of Defense William Perry to determine the regulatory cost of compliance. The study, sometimes referred to as the TASC study,[6] concluded that the regulatory cost of compliance for defense contractors for all government regulations was approximately 18% of each contractor's value added, defined as total expenditures less material incorporated into end products. The study also identified the 10 largest cost drivers and MMAS compliance ranked 8th, with an estimated compliance cost of 0.6% of total contract value added. It should be noted that this percentage is based on a contractor's total value added (including engineering), and thus may underestimate the compliance cost on the material management function. The study identified seven conditions that contributed unnecessarily to the regulatory cost of MMAS compliance.

An MMAS working group, established within the DOD Office of Acquisition Reform, concluded that "the cost of adopting and maintaining MMAS compliant systems is substantially outweighed by the potential savings." The seven conditions evaluated by the MMAS working group, and an eighth added for study by the group, are summarized as follows:

1. *Material management and accounting system application thresholds are too subjective and do not consider inflation.* The working group concluded that DFARS 242.7203 could be enhanced to reduce the cost of ongoing oversight without significantly increasing risk to the government. The working group recommended that DFARS 242.7203 be revised to provide an objective criterion for imposing MMAS disclosure, demonstration, and maintenance on contractors; to change threshold levels; and to distinguish between contractor actions required for initial disclosure and demonstration, and actions applicable only to subsequent system reviews.

2. *Physical segregation of material by contract significantly increases inventory control costs.* The working group concluded that DFARS 242.72 permits commingling except for government-furnished material and that contractors who segregate inventory do so for their own reasons. Therefore, the finding warranted no action. However, the working group observed that contractors that segregate inventory do so (among other reasons cited) "because it facilitates proper billing under progress payment requests and public vouchers."

3. *Recordkeeping for material routings are more extensive than for commercial operations.* The MMAS working group considered this finding a misunderstanding by the TASC study team, and therefore warranted no action.

4. *Obtaining government approval for material loan/payback involves delay.* The working group concluded that the existing DFARS language applies to a method, and not individual transactions. The group acknowledged that MMAS Standard 7, with respect to material transfers and the loan/payback rule, is susceptible to misinterpretation. The working group recommended revised language to clarify the standard.

5. *Government audit teams examine MMAS compliance redundantly on related reviews.* The working group observed that "critics apparently believe an MMAS compliance review is being performed whenever information related to an internal control of material functions or transactions is requested during an audit. The requested information, however, is typically needed ... [and] may be germane to other audit areas such as proposals or incurred cost, and which impacts functions such as estimating and purchasing." The working group concluded that "some aspects of material cost might be audited during an MMAS review while others

would be reviewed during other types of audit. To assess potential reductions in oversight, the Defense Contract Management Command (DCMC) established five reinvention laboratories that encompass MMAS oversight and audit."

6. *Material management and accounting system requirements inhibit purchase in commercial lot sizes.* The working group observed no instances in which MMAS standards precluded a contractor from combining all of its common part/component requirements into economic order quantities. The working group concluded that the issue was based on misunderstanding and that no further action was required.

7. *Material management and accounting system requirements necessitate use of expensive, advanced MRP systems.* The working group acknowledged that MMAS requirements may increase the cost of an integrated MRP system, but concluded they are good business practices that add value to the manufacturing process because of the unique nature and critical requirements related to products manufactured for national defense. No further action was considered.

8. *Internal MMAS audits should supplant government oversight.* The working group agreed that the concept of relying on the work of internal auditors was sound. Nevertheless, the working group concluded that the DOD goal of reduced oversight, however, does not mean an absence of oversight and the extent to which oversight may be reduced must be decided on a case-by-case basis. No action was considered.

The working group did not examine issues related to accuracy requirements since no accuracy issues were identified by either the TASC study or the industry members of the MMAS working group. The conclusion to be drawn is that industry has accepted the accuracy requirements.

Enterprise Resource Planning and Commercial Material Management and Accounting System

The application software industry, with few exceptions, abandoned the defense industry after disastrous results stemming from the 1987 congressional inquiries on MRP systems. At that time, application software was marketed via site licenses, an economic model that proved unprofitable unless a significant amount of post-sales consulting could also be obtained. Confusion stemming from the hearings, and potential inability for both contractors and software vendors poisoned the market.

In today's market, software license fees are determined by "seats," where each seat roughly corresponds to an employee that uses or may use the system. Software vendors are primarily motivated by the high seat counts found at many DOD contractors. Therefore, the software industry is again attempting to address the DOD business systems marketplace.

The primary offerings are next-generation enterprise resource planning (ERP) systems. These systems are based on new client–server and object-oriented techniques, and use process flow technology that has proven effective in other re-engineering efforts. The systems offer a high degree of integration between application modules and attractive features such as "drill-down" capability.

A key benefit claimed by commercial off-the-shelf (COTS) software products is that contractor investment in system maintenance can be minimized. The claimed benefit can appear very attractive to many information systems organizations. Whether the commercial software industry will be able to successfully develop such software products (i.e., a commercial MMAS compliant system), is yet to be determined. Enterprise resource planning systems compatible with DOD contracting will require a significant investment, access to knowledgeable experts, and industry input to successfully complete their goals.

Regardless of the software product employed by a contractor, the MMAS is still a formal system of procedural controls that requires a strong control environment; management involvement; and dedicated, trained employees. Companies that are considering replacing existing material management and accounting systems with ERP-based systems should move cautiously so the mistakes of the early 1980s are not repeated.

"Best Practice" Summary

The following twenty "Best Practices," while not appropriate in all circumstances, will generally enhance the usefulness of these systems in a government contracting environment and reduce compliance related risk.

Control Environment

- Establishment of a strong, proactive MMAS control environment
- Establishment of MMAS metric and diagnostic program (beyond BOM, MPS, and inventory accuracy)
- Inhibition of requirements based system generated transfers

Costing Material Transactions

- Transfer/payback system logic, with borrowing contract absorbing repayment cost
- Inventory valuation using moving average per contract methodology
- Manufactured part valuation based upon periodically updated catalog pricing
- Loan/payback system logic for subcontracted items (on which supplier progress payments are made)
- Storing only overhead and allocation rate reference data in MRP system

Physical Control of Material

- Physical segregation of government-furnished material
- Physical commingling of contractor-acquired material

Time-Phased Requirements and Accuracy Metrics

- MPS definition based upon MPS replenishments supporting independent requirements
- ABC inventory classification, with unit of measure/high-use adjustment

- Identification of excess inventory (valued)
- Identification of excess inventory to contractual requirements (valued)
- Consideration of material value in accuracy calculations

Earned-Value Management System Techniques

- Use of MRP time-phased requirements to establish material budget baseline
- Earned value at issue for material
- Earned value at receipt for subcontracted items
- Requirement WBS inferred from next higher assembly, with exception override
- Single organizational identification for material control accounts

Future Directions

More than 10 years have passed since the MMAS regulations were established. Considerable progress has been made by defense contractors in improving their material management control environment. The government has increased its understanding of contractor material management and accounting systems and the regulatory climate has improved somewhat. With the downsizing of the defense industry, the government has begun to realize that compliance dollars may be better spent on new weapon system development and hardware. Contractors may want to seek MMAS regulatory relief as an extension of the single process initiative (SPI) concept, despite current limitations. Self-certification and independent reviews can replace costly system demonstration. Publication of an MMAS implementation guide, similar to the Joint Implementation Guide (JIG) for earned-value management systems, would be advantageous to both the government and industry.

14-8. SUMMARY

A government's contractor's success depends largely on the adequacy of its systems for pricing, costing, and administering government contracts. In an environment where the treatment of costs so directly affects the amount of revenue to be received and the contractor's profitability, a highly developed cost accounting system is necessary. It is important that fully integrated systems and controls be maintained to ensure compliance with the unique requirements of government contracting.

Management information systems provide company executives with the tools required to monitor performance. Such systems must compare actual costs and schedule data with budgeted or planned data and identify variances. Also, proper internal controls are essential to protect a company's assets and to ensure that the accounting and management information system has integrity. Government contractors must address those aspects of internal controls unique to government contracting, particularly as they relate to contract administration, proposal preparation, estimating and bidding, purchasing, project administration, billing, contract cost accounting, income recognition, and job-site accounting.

Systems that provide the right information on a timely basis and comply with federal contracting requirements are key to successful contracting. Such systems do not just happen; they must be carefully planned to ensure that all relevant requirements have been considered.

14-9. NOTES

1. Texas Instruments, Inc., ASBCA No. 18621, March 10, 1979, 79-1 BCA 13,800.
2. Superintendent of Documents, Government Printing Office, Defense Contract Audit Manual 7640.1, Washington, DC 20402, Catalog No. D-1.46/2: 7640.1/1283.
3. Memorandum for Service Acquisition Executives, Assistant Secretary of the Air Force (Financial Management), Director, Ballistic Missile Defense Organization, Director, DCAA, Director, Defense Logistics Agency, Director, National Security Agency, Dec. 14, 1996; subject: Industry Standard Guide for Earned Value Management Systems.
4. Departments of the Air Force, Army, Navy, Headquarters; Ballistic Missile Defense Organization, National Security Agency, Headquarters; Defense Logistics Agency, Headquarters; DCAA, Earned Value Management Implementation Guide, Washington, DC, Dec. 11, 1996, SAF/AQ EVMS GUIDE.
5. Departments of the Air Force, Army, Navy, and the Defense Supply Agency, Cost/Schedule Control Systems Criteria Joint Implementation Guide, Washington, DC, Oct. 1, 1976, AFSCP/AFLCP 173-5.
6. The DOD Regulatory Cost Premium-Response to Secretary Perry's Follow-on Taskings (Sept. 1995), prepared jointly by Coopers & Lybrand LLC and TASC.

An adequate system should provide for the use of appropriate source data, utilize sound estimating techniques and appropriate judgment, maintain a consistent approach, and adhere to established policies and procedures.

In evaluating the adequacy of a contractor's estimating system, the ACO should consider whether the contractor's estimating system, for example:

- Establishes clear responsibility for preparation, review and approval of cost estimates;
- Provides a written description of the organization and duties of the personnel responsible for preparing, reviewing, and approving cost estimates;
- Assures that relevant personnel have sufficient training, experience and guidance to perform estimating tasks in accordance with the contractor's established procedures;
- Identifies the sources of data and the estimating methods and rationale used in developing cost estimates;
- Provides for appropriate supervision throughout the estimating process;
- Provides for consistent application of estimating techniques;
- Provides for detection and timely correction of errors;
- Protects against cost duplication and omissions;
- Provides for the use of historical experience, including historical vendor information, where appropriate;
- Requires use of appropriate analytical methods;
- Integrates information available from other management systems where appropriate;
- Requires management review including verification that the company's estimating policies, procedures and practices comply with this regulation;
- Provides for internal review of and accountability for the adequacy of the estimating system, including the comparison of projected results to actual results and an analysis of any differences;
- Provides procedures to update cost estimates in a timely manner throughout the negotiation process; and
- Addresses responsibility for review and analysis of the reasonableness of subcontract prices.

The following examples indicate conditions that may produce or lead to significant estimating deficiencies—

(a) Failure to ensure that relevant historical experience is available to and utilized by cost estimators, where appropriate.

(b) Continuing failure to analyze material costs or failure to perform subcontractor cost reviews as required.

(c) Consistent absence of analytical support for significant proposed cost amounts.

(d) Excessive reliance on individual personal judgment where historical experience or commonly utilized standards are available.

(e) Recurring significant defective pricing findings within the same cost element(s).

(f) Failure to integrate relevant parts of other management systems (e.g., production control or cost accounting) with the estimating system so that the ability to generate reliable cost estimates is impaired.

(g) Failure to provide established policies, procedures and practices to persons responsible for preparing and supporting estimates.

Appendix 14.1   Excerpts from DFARS 215.407-5-70

Summary of Contracts
($ in 000's)

| Contract Number | Financial | | | | | Schedule | | Technical Status | | Management Action Required |
| | Contract Amount | Cost Status to Date | | | Estimated Costs at Completion | Current | Estimated at Completion | Current | Predicted at Completion | |
		Budget	Actual	Variance						
82,330	9,000	6,200	6,600	400	9,800	60 days behind	30 days behind	Quality Control Problem	OK	Meeting with Customer 6/20
82,470	6,000	4,000	4,000	-0-	5,400	On time	On time	OK	OK	OK

Appendix 14.2 Summary of Contacts

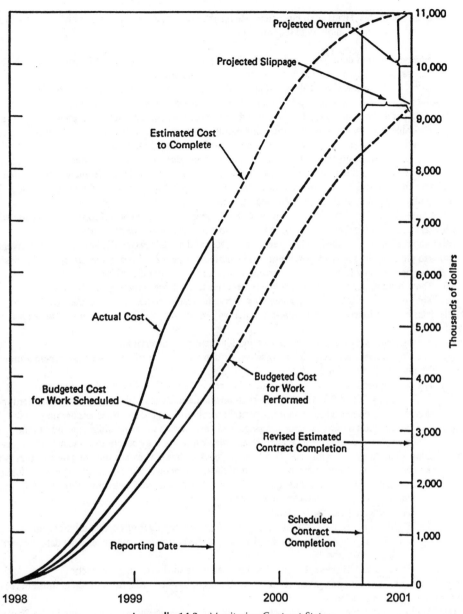

Appendix 14.3 Monitoring Contract Status

529

MMAS Standards. MMAS systems shall have adequate internal accounting and administrative controls to ensure system and data integrity, and comply with the following:

(1) Have an adequate system description including policies, procedures, and operating instructions which comply with the Federal Acquisition Regulation and Defense FAR Supplement;

(2) Ensure that costs of purchased and fabricated material charged or allocated to a contract are based on valid time-phased requirements as impacted by minimum/economic order quantity restrictions—

    (i) A 98 percent bill of material accuracy and a 95 percent master production schedule accuracy are desirable as a goal in order to ensure that requirements are both valid and appropriately time-phased.

    (ii) If systems have accuracy levels below these, the Contractor shall demonstrate that—

        (A) There is no material harm to the Government due to the lower accuracy levels; and

        (B) The cost to meet the accuracy goals is excessive in relation to the impact on the Government;

(3) Provide a mechanism to identify, report, and resolve system control weaknesses and manual override. Systems should identify excess/residual inventory as soon as known;

(4) Provide audit trails and maintain records (manual and those in machine readable form) necessary to evaluate system logic and to verify through transaction testing that the system is operating as desired;

(5) Establish and maintain adequate levels of record accuracy, and include reconciliation of recorded inventory quantities to physical inventory by part number on a periodic basis. A 95 percent accuracy level is desirable. If systems have an accuracy level below 95 percent, the Contractor shall demonstrate that –

    (i) There is no material harm to the Government due to the lower accuracy levels; and

    (ii) The cost to meet the accuracy goals is excessive in relation to the impact on the Government;

(6) Provide detailed descriptions of circumstances which will result in manual or system generated transfers of parts;

(7) Maintain a consistent, equitable, and unbiased logic for costing of material transactions –

    (i) The Contractor shall maintain and disclose written policies describing the transfer methodology and the loan/payback technique.

    (ii) The costing methodology may be standard or actual cost, or any of the inventory costing methods in 48 CFR 9904.411-50(b). Consistency shall be maintained across all contract and customer types, and from accounting period to accounting period for initial charging and transfer charging.

    (iii) The system should transfer parts and associated costs within the same billing period. In the few instances where this may not be appropriate, the Contractor may accomplish the material transaction using a loan/payback technique. The "loan/payback technique" means that the physical part is moved temporarily from the contract, but the cost of the part remains on the contract. The procedures for the loan/payback technique must be approved by the Administrative Contracting Officer. When the technique is used, the Contractor must have controls to ensure—

        (A) Parts are paid back expeditiously;

        (B) Procedures and controls are in place to correct any overbilling that might occur;

        (C) Monthly, at a minimum, identification of the borrowing contract and the date the part was borrowed; and

        (D) The cost of the replacement part is charged to the borrowing contract;

(8) Where allocations from common inventory accounts are used, have controls (in addition to those in (b) (2) and (7) of this clause) to ensure that—

    (i) Reallocations and any credit due are processed no less frequently than the routine billing cycle;

    (ii) Inventories retained for requirements that are not under contract are not allocated to contracts; and

    (iii) Algorithms are maintained based on valid and current data;

(9) Notwithstanding FAR 45.503-3 (f) (1) (ii), have adequate controls to ensure that physically commingled inventories that may include material for which costs are charged or allocated to fixed-price, cost-reimbursement, and commercial contracts do not compromise requirements of any of the standards in paragraphs (f) (1) through (8) of this clause. Government furnished material shall not be –

    (i) Physically commingled with other material; or

    (ii) Used on commercial work; and

(10) Be subjected to periodic internal audits to ensure compliance with established policies and procedures.

Appendix 14.4   Material Management and Accounting System Standards, DFARS 252.242-7004

Typical sections in an MMAS System Description are shown in Appendix 14.5.

Typical sections in an MMAS System Description include some or all of the following:

- MMAS Policy
    - Compliance Policy - Mission Statement   Standard 1
    - Policy/Procedure Cross-Reference   Standard 1
    - Operating Instruction Cross-Reference   Standard 1
- Control Environment and System Assurance
    - Description of Control Environment   Standard 2,3
    - Definition of Edits and Controls   Standard 2,3
    - Description of Exception Reports   DCAM 5-708(d)
    - Definition of Audit Trails and Records   Standard 4
    - Internal Audit
        - Self-Assessment   Standard 10
        - Independent Review   Standard 10
    - Accuracy
        - MPS Accuracy   Standard 2
        - BOM Accuracy   Standard 2
        - Inventory Accuracy (Cycle Count)   Standard 5
    - Transaction Testing   Standard 4
    - Training
        - Transaction Examples   Standard 4
- Physical Control
    - Government Furnished Material   Standard 9
    - Commingling Practices   Standard 9
    - Physical Segregation   Standard 9
- Contract Planning
    - Part Definition and Classification   Standard 2
    - Bill of Material Development and Maintenance   Standard 2
    - Independent Requirement Maintenance   Standard 2
    - Master Production Schedule   Standard 2
    - Lead Time
    - MRP Ordering Rule
    - WBS Incorporation
- Contract Execution
    - Contract Purchase Requisition Release/Approval
    - Contract Purchase Order Release/Approval
    - Receiving
    - Receiving Inspection
    - Stockroom Functions
        - Stockroom Receipt
        - Stockroom Issue (Requisition)
        - Location Change
        - Staging/Kitting
- Accounting System
    - Initial Charging   Standard 7
    - Inventory Valuation Methods   Standard 7
    - Loss/Gain Treatment   Standard 7
    - Scrap Treatment   Standard 7
    - Circumstances Causing Transfers   Standard 6
    - Transfer Methodology   Standard 7
    - Transfer/Payback Methodology   Standard 7
    - Loan/Payback Methodology   Standard 7
    - Common Inventory Allocation Techniques   Standard 8
    - Fabricated Part Valuation Technique   Standard 7
    - Obsolete and Surplus Disposition   Standard 3
    - Sensitive Transaction Methodology
- Contract Modification
    - Contract Change Incorporation   Standard 2
    - Contractual Excess Disposition   Standard 3
- Contract Completion/Termination
    - Contract Residual Disposition   Standard 3

Appendix 14.5   Typical sections in an MMAS System Description

Chapter Fifteen

Self-Governance

15-1. BACKGROUND

For years, the federal government and its suppliers, especially major contractors, shared a common culture in which working relationships were generally not confrontational. Compliance with federal laws and regulations was, for the most part, handled on an ad hoc basis. For example, a supplier might designate an individual within its organization to handle compliance responsibilities, such as (1) becoming involved in the business process when a cost representation was being prepared for submission to the government, and (2) responding to compliance issues raised by procurement officials as a result of their reviews.

The "old" system served the interests of both parties. The government received goods and services for which it contracted, and the suppliers enjoyed a steady flow of government business. A company was satisfied as long as it achieved its objectives—usually stated in terms of profitability or percentage of incurred cost recovered. The government was generally satisfied if the products worked and were reasonably priced. When violations of the procurement process were identified, they were almost always handled administratively; that is, the government would determine the dollar impact of the noncompliance and simply adjust the contract price accordingly. The criminal process was reserved for only the most flagrant cases of procurement fraud.

Driven in the mid-1980s by negative press reports of contract overpricing and a unified congressional drive to keep much closer tabs on federal expenditures, the government carefully scrutinized the contracting process and implemented a series of wide-ranging measures to unilaterally change the system. These measures included the following:

- Adopting severe noncompliance penalties and imposing them on contractors

- Enforcing new legislation that required contractors to establish cost accounting, quality assurance, and other financial management systems

- Demanding management certification of compliance to bolster corporate accountability
- Strengthening enforcement activities of inspectors general offices, whose missions were to oversee the procurement activities to ferret out "fraud, waste, and abuse"

These aggressive steps sent two clear signals. First, the contractor–government relationship was becoming more legalistic than in the past. Second, senior management would be held accountable for fulfillment of contractual obligations.

Senior executives of companies doing business with the government could no longer limit their focus to traditional measures of success, such as profitability, return on investment, and market share. A new imperative was now added to the list: government contract compliance.

To make certain that senior management expanded its focus to include compliance, procurement officials altered their approach in dealing with alleged violations. In making its analysis of whether administrative or criminal remedies should be pursued, the government asked two basic questions:

1. Did the noncompliance occur because of management direction?
2. Did the noncompliance occur because of management neglect; that is, did management fail to have in place effective systems to ensure compliance with procurement rules and regulations?

If the answer to either question was *yes*, the government resorted with increasing frequency to the criminal process. This approach was designed to let senior executives know that the government held them responsible for compliance. Allegations of labor mischarging, defective pricing, and quality assurance violations abounded. Long-time, reliable, and vital suppliers of defense systems were investigated for criminal violations. Where management direction was established as the basis for the improper activity, a company and officials involved were indicted. The government was also prone to indict where management failed to have a system in place that would provide reasonable assurance of compliance. While some charges of fraud were documented and justified, in far too many instances, government officials appeared to use the criminal process to remedy administrative contractual problems.

The new environment caught many contractors by surprise. Most companies had not dealt with compliance as a systems problem, as the government now required. Traditionally, a contractor's cost representation was not reviewed for compliance until it was prepared and submitted to the government. From that point, the contractor usually reacted to issues raised by the government auditors as a result of their reviews. Companies were not structured (or inclined) to directly involve senior management in compliance issues.

The government's criteria for determining when a noncompliance would be pursued as a legal matter were certainly unclear to contractors. As a result, contractors experienced great difficulty in predicting the outcome of reviews performed by procurement officials. Few who are knowledgeable about federal contracting would say that the procurement process did not suffer because of this diversion.

The government's intent was quite clear: Fix the level of responsibility for contract compliance at the highest corporate levels, thereby forcing suppliers to place a much greater emphasis on contract compliance. As a result, the contractor's response had to become just as clear: Implement the systems, procedures, and strategies that would ensure that everyone within the organization understood, followed, and complied with the contract rules.

This climate is still very much with us. Congress and the public continue to expect strong enforcement of complex regulatory requirements. To deal effectively with federal agencies and be in a position to define and manage settlement of contract questions, contractors must have some control over procurement and compliance processes. The government has urged contractors to establish (1) clearly stated compliance standards that are well documented and enforced; and (2) strategies, programs, and systems to exert control over procurement and compliance processes.

This control can be achieved by instituting a contract compliance program. Such a program involves (1) establishing and communicating a corporate commitment to compliance; (2) developing relevant written policies and procedures; (3) developing compliant financial management systems; (4) establishing compliance monitoring guidelines and corporate accountability; and (5) training all levels of employees within the organization.

This systematic approach to compliance minimizes allegations of noncompliance, helps management anticipate problems and take remedial steps before the government gets involved, and makes it easier to resolve allegations within existing administrative frameworks. Incorporating contract compliance into the corporate culture also enhances operational efficiency and integration of management and government information needs.

Compliance programs, appropriate for the size of the company and extent of government business, provide management with assurance that operating units have established the following:

- An environment of appropriate control awareness, attitude, and discipline
- Control systems that focus on areas of risk inherent in federal contracting, that achieve an appropriate balance between cost and benefits, and that operate effectively

While differing in specifics from company to company, these programs are referred to as "self-governance." Self-governance can be defined simply as the process a company undertakes to provide reasonable assurance that the company and its employees comply with applicable U.S. government procurement requirements.

15-2. SELF-GOVERNANCE VERSUS INTERNAL CONTROLS

Accounting and auditing literature for years has emphasized the importance of strong internal controls. Proper delegation of authority and differentiation of responsibilities are earmarks of a good internal control system. The responsibility for ensuring that an adequate control system exists rests on management. Boards of directors, as general overseers of all management functions, want to ensure themselves that management's responsibilities for the control system have been thoughtfully considered and met.

The way in which a company is controlled will vary, depending on such factors as size, dispersion of operating locations, complexity of the organization, and management philosophy. However, in any situation, management should establish an environment that creates the appropriate control awareness, attitude, and discipline. Management should also ascertain that each control system does the following:

- Fits the company's needs and management philosophy
- Focuses on areas of risk, particularly those that are inherent in government contracting
- Achieves a thoughtful balance between costs of controls and benefits

Management is accustomed to dealing with traditional internal accounting controls. Executives regularly make judgments about the quality of their employees and the accuracy and reliability of internal management reports. They have an intuitive sense, based on their familiarity with what is happening, of whether the system of internal accounting controls is operating effectively. The all-important feeling that "things are right" can be a real comfort to management.

In evaluating internal controls, some companies limit their consideration to those aspects of business management that are deemed to be significant to financial and accounting functions and activities. The wiser company evaluates the broad spectrum of management control, which includes, but is not limited to, accounting controls for a particular activity. In so doing, management's perspective is naturally broadened to consider how effectively and efficiently an activity is organized and how all the checks and balances ensure that employees effectively discharge their responsibilities.

Many factors should be considered in determining how a company is controlled, including the organization's degree of centralization and overall size. Senior executives of larger companies do not usually have the luxury of personal observation or inquiry to ensure that controls are operating as expected. Instead, they rely on administrative controls, internal auditors, or other monitoring groups to alert them on a timely basis to failures in the internal accounting control systems. Consequently, in larger companies, management and directors should be more sensitive to the actions they take to create the appropriate control environment. The people in the organization must "feel" senior management's interest in controls and its expectation that each member of the organization will adhere to prescribed control procedures.

In smaller companies, management may not have enough people to segregate duties as fully as might be desired. Control objectives may be achieved through the supervision of day-to-day activities by top management, who also are responsible for authorizing most business transactions. Members of management may assure themselves of adherence to their policies by personal observation and inquiry. Under these circumstances, documentation of policies and procedures may not be critical since management is otherwise assured that the people in the organization understand what is expected of them. Accordingly, an extensive internal audit function may not be needed.

Executives of smaller companies most likely approach the evaluation of their control systems with the confidence that they know their weaknesses and are comfortable with the risks inherent in them. Nevertheless, these executives should evaluate their internal accounting control system for the reasons suggested previously. Perhaps such an evaluation would emphasize those functions that rely more heavily on the control system than on management involvement; from management's perspective, these are the risk areas. Accordingly, it would be prudent to review any known weaknesses in the control system.

Directors of smaller companies must, of necessity, place greater reliance on top management for ensuring that internal accounting control objectives are achieved than directors of larger companies who can take comfort in sophisticated internal accounting control systems. Directors of smaller companies may therefore be particularly interested in re-evaluating the delegation of authority among the top management and the controls that restrain this group from exceeding that authority and overriding the control system. The directors may wish to request management to report to them on the evaluation of the control system, specifically on the following:

- Policies, including business ethics and practices, for areas of high business risk
- Weaknesses in the internal accounting control system
- Conflicts of interest, if any, of the top management group

Controls Unique to Government Contractors

Government contractors are not unlike other businesses when it comes to internal controls. Although the objectives are similar, the statutory, regulatory, and contractual requirements imposed on those dealing with the government are different from the requirements for those dealing with the private sector. These differences result in different risk assessments.

The functions inherent in government contracting, based on the risks unique to such contracting, and the control objectives necessary for such functions are listed in Appendix 15.1.

Specific internal controls that are necessary to achieve the control objectives are listed in Appendix 15.2 in the form of questions for each function. These questions relate specifically to government contracts and do not include all generalized controls necessary for a proper internal control system. Further, these questions are meant to apply to a broad spectrum of operations and may not apply to every size and type of government contractor. The questions are designed so that a "no" answer may indicate a control weakness.

Clearly, internal controls are a key element in a self-governance program. Companies with strong internal control systems will generally find effective self-governance programs easier to implement. The relationship between internal controls and self-governance may be best illustrated by the requirements of Audits of Federal Government Contractors.[1] While this guide covers numerous topics relating to accounting and auditing, it also addresses the internal control structure. It states that in addition to management philosophy and operating style, other elements of the control environment may include the following:

- Organizational structure
- Existence of an audit committee
- An ethics program
- Methods of assigning authority and responsibility

- Personnel policies and procedures
- External influences over the contractor (e.g., regulatory influences)
- Internal audit function

One could argue that self-governance encompasses all aspects of an effective internal control structure, as described in the guide. In fact, the term *self-governance* has become so widely accepted that we will use it throughout this chapter in referring to any broadly defined internal control structure.

15-3. SELF-GOVERNANCE INITIATIVES

Packard Commission

In June 1986, the President's Blue Ribbon Commission on Defense Management (i.e., the Packard Commission) issued its final report entitled "A Quest for Excellence."[2] The Commission found that most taxpayers were distrustful of the procurement process and of defense contractors specifically; Americans believed that half the defense budget was lost to waste and fraud. Both the government and industry agreed that something had to be done to improve not only the procurement process but also the public's perception of that process. Therefore, the report contained recommendations for both industry and the government. For industry, the recommendation's focused on three areas:

1. Codes of conduct addressing problems and procedures incident to defense procurement
2. Effective internal control systems to ensure compliance with those codes and the establishment of internal auditing capacity to monitor, among other things, compliance with codes and the efficacy of the control systems
3. Effective oversight of the entire process by an independent committee, such as an outside audit committee of the board of directors

For government, the recommendations also focused on three areas:

1. Coordinated oversight of defense contractors, elimination of undesirable duplication of official effort and, when appropriate, sharing of contractor data by audit agencies
2. Vigorous administration of military and civilian ethics regulations to assure that Department of Defense (DOD) employees comply with the same high standards expected of contractor personnel
3. Use of suspension and debarment only to protect the public interest where a contractor is found to lack "present responsibility" to contract with the federal government

The clear message to contractors was to develop an effective self-governance program. Companies used these recommendations, as well as the defense industry initiatives discussed below, to implement programs to address the concerns raised by the Commission. While these programs vary, the key elements of ethics statements, policies and procedures, control systems, compliance monitoring, and training are included in all self-governance programs.

Defense Industry Initiatives

In response to the Packard Commission, 18 defense contractors met and drafted six principles that became known as the Defense Industry Initiatives[3] on Business Ethics and Conduct. These six principles are as follows:

1. Code of ethics
2. Ethics training
3. Internal reporting of alleged misconduct
4. Self-governance through the establishment of systems to monitor compliance with federal procurement laws and the adoption of procedures for voluntary disclosure of violations to the appropriate authorities
5. Responsibility to the industry through attendance at best practices forums
6. Accountability to the public

To meet the requirements of Principle 6 (public accountability), a list of 18 questions, later expanded to 20 questions, was developed. (See Appendix 15.3.) Companies were to answer these questions, and their responses would be subject to independent review. The questions deal with codes of conduct, voluntary reporting procedures, and compliance reporting. Results of the audit are reported to the board of directors and are a means of monitoring a company's self-governance program.

The number of companies willing to become signatories to the defense industry initiative has not been overwhelming, primarily because of Principle 4, which deals with voluntary disclosure of suspected wrongdoing. Voluntary disclosure will be addressed later in this chapter.

Department of Defense Policy

The DOD Federal Acquisition Regulation Supplement (DFARS), Subpart 203.70, addresses standards of conduct. The DOD's policy regarding self-governance is contained in DFARS 203.7000. The policy, like the Packard Commission and the defense initiatives, focuses on the need for government contractors to conduct themselves with the highest degree of integrity and honesty and to have standards of conduct and internal control systems that

1. Are suitable to the size of the company and extent of their involvement in government contracting
2. Promote such standards
3. Facilitate timely discovery and disclosure of improper conduct in connection with government contracts
4. Ensure corrective measures are promptly instituted and carried out. For example, a contractor's system of management controls should provide for
   a. A written code of business ethics and conduct and an ethics training program for all employees
   b. Periodic reviews of company business practices, procedures, policies,

and internal controls for compliance with standards of conduct and the special requirements of government contracting

c. A mechanism, such as a hotline, by which employees may report suspected instances of improper conduct, and instructions that encourage employees to make such reports

d. Internal and/or external audits as appropriate

e. Disciplinary action for improper conduct

f. Timely reporting to appropriate government officials of any suspected or possible violation of law in connection with government contracts or any other irregularities in connection with such contracts

g. Full cooperation with any government agencies responsible for either investigation for corrective actions

Contractors that receive a DOD contract of $5,000,000 or more must either install an internal reporting mechanism and program or prominently display DOD hotline posters that encourage employees to report suspected misconduct.

The importance placed on the DOD policy is highlighted in DFARS 209.406-1, which addresses suspension and debarment. Guidance in this section advises the suspension/debarment official that the presence of a self-governance program is a mitigating factor in suspension/debarment proceedings. Clearly, it is in a company's best interest to implement a self-governance program that considers the elements outlined in DFARS 203.70.

Contractor Risk Assessment Guide

After the Packard Commission's call for self-governance, the DOD initiated a program to assess the strength of contractor internal control systems. The "Contractor Risk Assessment Guide,"[4] which came to be known as CRAG, was developed by a task force which included the Under Secretary of Defense for Acquisition, the DOD Inspector General, the Defense Contract Audit Agency (DCAA), and the defense industry. The DOD's primary objective for CRAG is succinctly contained in the first paragraph of the guide's overview:

> The DOD Contractor Risk Assessment Guide (CRAG) Program is designed to encourage Department of Defense (DOD) contractors to develop more effective contractor internal control systems and to improve the effectiveness and efficiency of DOD oversight. Contractors who can demonstrate the implementation of internal control systems that meet CRAG control objectives will receive less direct Government oversight. By assessing the effectiveness of contractor internal control systems, the extent of Government oversight can be reduced, thereby enabling DOD to concentrate its oversight resources on known problem areas.

Although a voluntary program, companies were strongly encouraged to participate. Whether a contractor should formally participate in CRAG is purely a management decision. However, the control objectives and procedures for each of the five areas covered by CRAG (indirect cost submissions, labor charging, material management and accounting systems, estimating systems, and purchasing) provide useful guidance on how to minimize risk of noncompliance.

While companies clearly acknowledge the need for good internal control systems, not everyone agrees that the benefits of CRAG are commensurate with the cost of obtaining formal acceptance of the CRAG area. This is especially true in light of existing similar DFARS requirements for estimating systems, material management and accounting system (MMAS) demonstrations, and contractor purchasing system reviews.

Voluntary Disclosure

The DOD voluntary disclosure program[5] was initiated to give contractors an opportunity to disclose information about potential wrongdoing. Disclosing such information and cooperating with the government is viewed favorably by the DOD as a strong indication of contractor integrity. Thus, the DOD will consider such cooperation before suspending or debarring a contractor.

To quality as a voluntary disclosure, four conditions must be met:

1. The disclosure must not be triggered by the contractor's recognition that the underlying facts are about to be discovered by the government through audit, investigation, or contract administration efforts or reported to the government by third parties.

2. The disclosure must be on behalf of the business entity, in contrast to admissions by individual officials or employees.

3. Prompt and complete corrective action, including disciplinary action and restitution to the government where appropriate, must be taken by the contractor in response to the matters disclosed.

4. After disclosure, the contractor must cooperate fully with the government in any ensuing investigation or audit.

If the DOD accepts a company into the voluntary disclosure program, the company signs a standard agreement acknowledging that (1) the government made no representations regarding the disposition of the matter; (2) the government decision to prosecute will, in part, reflect the extent of company cooperation; and (3) the Department of Justice retains its rights to take whatever action it deems appropriate. The agreement further gives the government access to any internal investigation the company undertakes.

A company should consult with legal counsel prior to any voluntary disclosure to ensure that its actions do not create undue legal exposure for the company. Questions have also been raised concerning employee constitutional rights when a company investigates suspected wrongdoing. Further, companies must be sure employee dismissals are in agreement with applicable laws, internal procedures, and collective-bargaining agreements to avoid wrongful terminations suits. Thus, while the voluntary disclosure program is a mechanism to demonstrate corporate integrity, caution must be exercised to protect all potentially affected parties.

15-4. ELEMENTS OF EFFECTIVE SELF-GOVERNANCE PROGRAMS

Establishing and Communicating Corporate Commitment

As with other critical corporate issues, responsibility for compliance rests with the chief executive officer (CEO). The most important component of an effective management program is a clear message from the highest level of the company, strongly stating management's commitment to compliance with applicable federal procurement laws and regulations.

Having identified the messenger (either the CEO or his/her agent), the company must determine how the message should be delivered. Some organizations have distributed a printed ethics statement from the CEO to employees, while others have used organization-wide meetings or videotapes, in conjunction with the printed statement, as the means of communication. Still others have utilized handbooks setting forth compliance objectives and performance expectations.

Each method has its benefits and drawbacks, and each has its place in the proper environment. No matter what communication vehicle is selected, the essential message—commitment to compliance—must be clear. It should address the special requirements of government contracting that apply to the company and clearly state that employees will be held accountable for actions inconsistent with the standards. It also should provide direction for employees on how to deal with specific employment-related situations.

Areas that an ethics statement should address include the following:

- Charges to government contracts
- Product substitution
- Quality assurance
- Unallowable costs
- Billing practices
- Certified cost or pricing data
- Marketing practices
- Subcontractor relationships
- Business courtesies—government and commercial customers
- Conflicts of interest
- Employment offers to government officials
- Handling of classified or company proprietary information
- Export requirements
- Record retention

Finally, the ethics statement should describe how to report possible violations. The statement should reassure employees that they will not be subject to retribution for reporting possible violations. An in-house "hotline" program and/or an ombudsman can expedite the reporting process of possible violations.

Because noncompliance with federal procurement laws and regulations can result in significant monetary and criminal exposure for the company and its officials, the ethics statement serves a critical function in alerting employees to the unique rules governing federal contracts and in holding them accountable for their actions.

Written Policies and Procedures

While a company's ethics statement may provide employees the principles under which they should operate, policies and procedures provide the detailed operating instructions to ensure adherence to the principles. Policies and procedures should give personnel the guidance needed to carry out their job responsibilities in a manner consistent with management's intentions. For example, an ethics statement might address the Truth in Negotiation Act's requirement for full disclosure of all relevant cost or pricing data before agreement on the price of a negotiated contract. To implement this requirement, a company should have written estimating procedures that identify the types of data that must be disclosed and assign responsibilities to specific functions to ensure that the data are disclosed before final price agreement.

Policies and procedures are needed for all major areas listed in the ethics statement, in addition to the normal policies and procedures a company should have as part of its internal control system.

In developing effective policies and procedures, companies must balance the need for sufficient detail to enable the employee to adequately perform his/her job against the possibility that too much detail may deter the employee from referring to the procedure on an ongoing basis. Having policies and procedures that people use and find helpful tends to result in consistent application for the area covered. If compliance policies and procedures are followed consistently, the risk of exposure to noncompliance with government procurement regulations is dramatically reduced.

Policies and procedures related to development of indirect cost rates, cost estimating, and access to records are discussed in Chapters 7, 14, and 16, respectively.

Systems

It should go without saying that companies need estimating/proposal pricing, cost accounting, material requirement planning, purchasing, property management, quality assurance, and other systems in place in order to manage and control operations. The systems must be designed to achieve compliance with government contracting requirements while optimizing cost recovery.

In the context of self-governance, *systems* refers to the automated or manual methods used to collect costs or provide information on a variety of areas, such as purchase orders, quotes, material usage, scrap, quality assurance, and government property. Systems capture transactions and provide the information needed for personnel to effectively carry out their job responsibilities. Chapter 14 explains in detail many of the more critical systems, but there are common elements in all systems that affect government procurements—namely, the information must be current, accurate, and complete.

Systems are an integral part of a company's internal control structure. In addition to maintaining generic business and shop floor systems required by any company, government contractors must maintain special systems to ensure compliance with government procurement regulations. The AICPA guide, "Audits of Federal Government Contractors," states:

The following factors, some of which are unique to government contractors, are particularly important elements of a contractor's internal control structure:

- Systems for monitoring compliance with government procurement regulations
- Estimating systems and proposal preparation practices
- Contract cost accounting practices
- Contract revenue recognition practices
- Billing procedures and controls
- Change order identification, pricing, and reporting
- Claims processing and reporting
- Inventory costing and control
- Government-furnished property
- Cost aspects of related-party and interorganizational transactions[6]

Compliance Monitoring

Establishing good accounting and internal control systems and then simply assuming that compliance has been achieved has inherent risk, because significant errors can occur even in the presence of effective internal controls. Since the government holds company management accountable for compliance with procurement rules, the longer a noncompliant practice goes undetected, the greater the potential financial risk to the company. Consequently, once a contractor has established and communicated its contract compliance policies and procedures, created the necessary systems, and trained its employees, it must take steps to ensure that established procedures are followed consistently throughout the organization. Since businesses are dynamic organizations, compliance procedures and systems can never be taken for granted. Operations must be monitored on a regular basis to ensure that procedures are being followed and that systems are not being bypassed. Perhaps most important, management must make periodic and routine reviews to ensure that existing procedures are still appropriate for required tasks.

Compliance monitoring serves as a kind of backbone for a good control program because it examines the whole process. It compares actual practices with policies, procedures, and regulatory requirements, and includes an analysis of the accounting system to ensure proper cost accumulation and strong internal controls.

Some companies that have established compliance review programs have done so as part of the internal audit function, while others have established separate compliance review groups. The Packard Commission's recommendations focused on internal auditing, but the same recommendations could be applied to any compliance review group.

> Defense contractors must individually develop and implement better systems of internal controls to ensure compliance with contractual commitments and procurement standards. To assist in this effort and to monitor its success, we recommend contractors take the following steps:
>
> 1. Establish internal auditing of compliance with government contracting procedures, corporate standards of conduct, and other requirements. Such auditing should review actual compliance as well as the effectiveness of internal control systems.
> 2. Design systems of internal control to ensure that they cover, among other things, compliance with the contractor's standards of ethical business conduct.
> 3. Establish internal audit staffs sufficient in numbers, professional background, and training to the volume, nature, and complexity of the company's government contracts business. ...[7]

Training

Self-governance cannot be effective without training. To avoid unacceptable or illegal conduct, contractors must determine what constitutes responsible compliance and must train their staffs to understand and abide by such determinations. Training must become an integral, ongoing element tailored to employee job responsibilities in every company dealing with the government. Various levels of training are necessary.

- Senior management must be made aware of specific new requirements that impact government contractors and consequences of noncompliance.
- All employees—particularly those in middle management—should be in-

formed of all relevant government regulations. Initial training on ethics statements and policies and procedures should be presented to all employees. As new employees are hired, this training should be incorporated into an orientation program to ensure that all employees are aware of what is expected of them in a government contracting environment.

- Employees should receive essential "how-to" information that relates government regulations to specific jobs in an organization. For a middle-level engineer, this may include information on how to control project costs, determine cost charges, and arrive at materials requirements. For the production-line worker, contract compliance training may demonstrate procedures for creating time-charge documents or filing materials receipts reports. For estimating personnel, there should be in-depth explanations about negotiating contracts with the government and responding to the government's audit process.

Companies should develop a formal training plan, by functional areas, for each employee. The plan should identify minimum training requirements, as well as desirable training enhancements to be provided if funds are available. These training objectives could be accomplished through formal courses conducted by universities or private firms; in-house training; or, in some cases, self-study.

15-5. MANAGEMENT AND PERFORMANCE OF THE COMPLIANCE FUNCTION

Audit Organization

An effective self-governance program requires some type of compliance-monitoring function to determine if the company is complying with applicable government procurement rules and regulations. This role is over and above that attributed to traditional internal audit organizations. As stated earlier, some companies have expanded the role of internal audit to include compliance auditing, while others have established a separate compliance function outside of internal audit. Organizationally, the contract compliance function would ideally report to the board of directors. This will ensure that the board fulfills its responsibility to monitor compliance with government procurement regulations and that the function is independent of management influence. The Packard Commission specifically recommended the following:

> Establish sufficient direct reporting channels from internal auditors to the independent audit committee of the contractor's board of directors to assure the independence and objectivity of the audit function. Auditors should *not* report to any management official with direct responsibility for the systems, practices, or transactions that are the subject of an audit. Such structure assures frank reporting of and prompt action on internal audit results. . . .[8]

Audit Planning

In deciding what compliance audits should be planned for the upcoming period, a number of factors must be considered. The absolute, as well as relative, dollars of sales resulting from negotiated procurements governed by the FAR versus total segment sales is an important factor in assessing noncompliance risk. Next, the type of contracts involved (i.e., fixed-price or cost-type) will determine the areas that are likely to be more sensitive. For example, with a preponderance of fixed-price contracts, emphasis should focus on the estimating process. In a cost-type contract environment, one would be more concerned with ensuring that unallowable costs are excluded from billings and that labor costs are properly charged. A contract mix of fixed-price, cost-type, and commercial would generally require focus on labor charging and accuracy of allocation methods. Each circumstance will be slightly different and requires careful evaluation of many risk factors.

When selecting specific areas to review, consideration should be given to how much time has passed since the last audit, changes that may have taken place, the results of any government reviews, and the sensitivity of the area. In addition to the company's perception of risk, consideration should also be given to the emphasis the government is placing on that area. The DCAA should share its audit plan and vulnerability risk assessments with the contractors it audits. This plan will give additional insight into areas that the government considers sensitive and, therefore, may affect the company's audit planning. Participation in CRAG requires an internal review of the area(s) of participation.

Some companies are participating in joint audits with the DCAA. Joint audits can be done under CRAG or outside of CRAG. In a joint audit, the DCAA maintains supervisory responsibility for its part of the work and usually issues its own report. To assess the adequacy of the contractor's audit work, the DCAA uses the documentation guidelines in the *Contract Audit Manual*[9] (Section 4-1000). An area of concern that may arise under a joint audit is how to handle disclosure of potential wrongdoing that may be uncovered during the audit. Defense Contract Audit Agency policy requires prompt reporting of suspected irregularities found during a joint audit. Such an action could preclude the company from having the issue treated as a voluntary disclosure.

Audit Performance

Successful compliance audits are performed by individuals who are knowledgeable about federal procurement rules and regulations. One of the conclusions in the Packard Commission report addressed the competency of internal audit staffs.

> Internal audit staffs—where they exist—generally have a satisfactory professional background. They need substantially more formal training, however, in the areas critical to compliance with federal procurement law, including Cost Accounting Standards, Federal Acquisition Regulations, Truth in Negotiations Act, and fraud detection.[10]

Regardless of the area being audited, certain common steps should be taken to focus on system validation (e.g., do the company's policies and procedures comply with federal procurement rules and regulations, and are they being followed?). The first step is to review the policies and procedures.

- Do they address the issues critical to that area?
- Are they written so that operating personnel have adequate guidance to perform their jobs?
- Do they address levels of review and approval?

- Do they address how employees should resolve questions that are not covered by the policy?

Next, the compliance audit must test the policies and procedures against actual transactions. The amount of testing will vary by sensitivity of the area and dollars involved. Likewise, the kind of transaction testing will vary by area. For example, testing invoices for exclusion of unallowable costs from final indirect cost submissions will differ from testing controls over government-furnished property. In either case, however, testing is necessary to determine if the proper controls are in place and operating effectively.

During a compliance audit, indications of potential wrongdoing may be uncovered. Such areas as labor mischarging, product substitution, defective pricing, and falsification or alterations of records are extremely serious. Before additional auditing is done, legal counsel should be consulted for a determination of whether any additional effort should be performed under the attorney–client or attorney work product privilege rule. Invoking such privilege is usually a prudent step, even if the work is eventually given to the government. By working through counsel, the remaining audit work can be closely monitored to protect the rights of the company, as well as those of individuals who may be potentially involved in the action.

Finally, a written report conveys the results of the audit. While the exact procedures may vary from company to company, the objective is to make sure that the report is accurate. Often, preliminary results are discussed with management in the audited area to verify the accuracy of the findings and to obtain any additional information that might be relevant. The written report is then reviewed by audit management before it is issued. Reports dealing with exceptions that may have an impact on costs charged to government contracts are especially sensitive and, depending on the issue and dollar impact of the findings, may also require coordination with legal counsel. Caution must be exercised when writing reports. Ambiguities can be misinterpreted and can cause significant problems when, in fact, no significant problems exist. For example, assume a labor charging audit finds an incorrect entry relating to a 12-digit charge code system, in which the first four digits indicate the contract, the next five digits indicate the work breakdown structure number, and the last three digits indicate the department number. If the error occurred in the last three digits, the charge number overall was not correct, but no final cost objective was incorrectly charged. Thus, labeling the error in the department number as mischarging would not accurately portray the situation.

For any audit exceptions, the impact on costs charged to contracts and reimbursed by the government should be quantified.

Audit Follow-Up

Company policies and procedures for the internal audit department typically include details on responses to audit reports. Generally, the response time frame and actions required by audited organization will depend on the sensitivity of the finding. Obviously, in responding to audit exceptions dealing with government compliance issues, timely corrective action is critical. In addition, for sensitive compliance issues, audit agreement on the corrective action plan is a good idea. Audit follow-up reviews should be scheduled to ensure the action plan was implemented within the agreed-to time frame. Companies that agree to share the results of compliance reviews with the government should include the corrective action plan in their discussion.

15-6. SUMMARY

Self-governance is clearly a process that responsible contractors and subcontractors should adopt to minimize the risk in performing contracts governed by the FAR. It is a proactive process that starts with a commitment by top management to do things right. Because the government holds contractors to high ethical standards, standards must be clearly and unequivocally communicated to all employees. Once ethical standards are established, policies and procedures that comply with applicable regulatory and statutory requirements must be in place and operating effectively, and employees must be adequately trained. Moreover, contract compliance monitoring must ensure that the policies and procedures are being followed as intended by management. It is this interaction of properly trained personnel, following fully compliant policies and procedures in an environment where top management demands adherence to high ethical standards, that permits companies to effectively operate as government contractors.

15-7. NOTES

1. Audits of Federal Government Contractors, with conforming changes as of May 1, 1996, prepared by the Government Contractors Guide Special Committee, American Institute of Certified Public Accountants, 1990.
2. A Quest for Excellence, a report to the President by the President's Blue Ribbon Commission on Defense Management, June 1986.
3. Defense Industry Initiatives on Business Ethics and Conduct, Appendix A, Conduct and Accountability, a report to the President by the President's Blue Ribbon Commission on Defense Management, June 1986.
4. The DOD Contractor Risk Assessment Guide, Oct. 1988, p.i.
5. Department of Defense Program for Voluntary Disclosures of Possible Fraud by Defense Contractors, July 24, 1986, Memorandum to Chief Executive Officers of Top 100 Department of Defense Contractors; reprinted in Federal Contracts Report, published by The Bureau of National Affairs, Inc., Aug. 11, 1986, Vol. 46, No. 6, p. 292.
6. Audits of Federal Government Contractors, §4.08, supra, note 1.
7. A Quest for Excellence, pp. 87–88, supra, note 2.
8. Ibid, p. 88.
9. Defense Contract Audit Agency Contract Audit Manual, Superintendent of Documents, P.O. Box 371954, Pittsburgh, PA 15250-7954, Government Printing Office (GPO), Catalog No. D-1.46/2.7640.1/1283.
10. A Quest for Excellence, p. 86, supra, note 2.

Function	Control Objective
Contract administration	To establish centralized responsibility for fulfilling contractual requirements and for ensuring that adequate safeguards for the commitment of company resources are established.
Proposal preparation, estimating, and bidding	To ensure that contracts are bid or negotiated in accordance with applicable regulatory requirements and management criteria on the basis of data carefully compiled in a manner that takes into account all factors that can be compared with subsequent performance.
Project administration and contract evaluation	To establish responsibility for monitoring performance (technical, cost, and schedule) to enable periodic evaluation of the contract status, progress, and profitability of each project.
Billing	To ensure that billings are adequately supported and reflect the requirements of contractual terms and acquisition regulations and to ensure that unbilled items are identified and periodically evaluated.
Project costing of labor, overhead, and material	To properly record all costs incurred to the correct project and to properly accumulate, classify, and summarize them in the accounts.
General accounting /contract revenues	To ensure that contract revenue and costs are recognized in accordance with management criteria and that all factors affecting profitability have been reflected in the amounts recorded.
Job site accounting	To provide adequate control over assets located, or under the responsibility of employees, at remote locations.
Quality assurance	To ensure that delivered products meet all product quality requirements included in applicable contracts.
Government furnished property	To ensure that the government-furnished property is properly obtained, used, and managed during contract performance.
Record retention	To ensure that records are retained pursuant to the government's retention requirements.
Export requirements	To ensure that no defense or nondefense articles are exported unless appropriate licenses have been obtained prior to the export.
Gratuities to government employees	To ensure that no gratuities are offered or given to government officials who are involved in the procurement or administration of contracts awarded to the company.
Marketing	To ensure that all employees are aware of and adhere to restrictions placed on the company under the Procurement Integrity Act.
Hiring current or former government employees	To ensure adherence to special restrictions and reporting requirements applicable to hiring or retaining certain former government employees.
Socioeconomic requirements	To ensure: (1) maximum subcontracting with small, small/disadvantaged businesses and small women-owned businesses; (2) nondiscrimination in employment; (3) compliance with Buy American Act requirements regarding domestic content of end products; and (4) compensation of employees consistent with applicable minimum wage, maximum hour, and overtime standards.

Appendix 15.1   Controls Unique to Government Contractors

Contract Administration

1. Is the contracts organization responsible to the president of the operating unit and separate and distinct from marketing? When contract administrators are assigned to contracts, do they have only indirect responsibility to the managers responsible for contract performance?

2. Are individuals assigned to the contracts organization experienced, and do they possess sound business judgment? Most importantly, are they familiar with government procurement regulations and contract clauses?

3. Has the company established a training program for contract administrators? Are administrators encouraged to join professional associations?

4. Is a senior contract administrator assigned to all significant and complex contracts?

5. Are all operational entities (manufacturing, engineering, etc.) clearly informed, through a policy manual or other formal means, of the restrictions placed on them in their dealings with the customer, particularly with respect to changes in the scope-of-work requirements set forth in the contract?

6. Is all contract-related correspondence between the company and the customer coordinated by the contract administrator responsible for the contract?

7. Are contract administrators required to attend all meetings between the company and the customer, and are minutes maintained of such meetings?

8. Are executed contracts required before the incurrence of costs? If not, is the contract administrator responsible for obtaining an advance agreement with the customer that such costs will be allowable?

9. Are contract files maintained in an orderly manner, and do they document the significant factors included in negotiations and other preliminary proceedings before contract award? Do they also contain the basic contract and amendments, all internal correspondence, all correspondence to and from the customer, billing invoices, and delivery documents?

10. Do company procedures outline how the tasks associated with a contract's performance are required to be identified, budgeted, and scheduled?

11. Does the internal audit staff conduct examinations of contract administration functions and summarize their findings in a report to the audit committee or president?

12. Are changes and other contract modifications coordinated with appropriate management and accounting personnel to ensure that adequate equitable adjustment claims can be submitted?

13. Are contract completion reviews made before closing a contract?

Proposal Preparation, Estimating, and Bidding

Proposal Presentation and Pricing Strategy

1. Are all solicited and unsolicited contract proposals (technical, management and cost) reviewed by a contract administrator (and in-house legal counsel where appropriate) before their submission to the customer? Is a formal memorandum on these reviews prepared and forwarded to appropriate contract and company management personnel?

−1−

Appendix 15.2   Internal Control Questionnaire

2. Are all firm-fixed-price and high-risk contract proposals reviewed by a committee, the majority of whose members are not responsible for performance, to ensure independence of thought and objectivity of pricing before their submission to the customer? Does the committee include representatives of finance, legal, and contracts? Is the committee involved in assessing significant proposal revisions until source selection?

3. Are all significant firm-fixed-price contracts properly approved before their execution? Do the formal minutes of a board or committee indicate such an approval where required?

4. Does the company have a formal policy on who may commit the company to the performance of a contract, and does such a policy differentiate by type and costs of contract?

5. Does the company generally refrain from, or have a policy against, "buying-in" on a contract?

6. Is every effort made by the company to assign to an awarded contract the contract administrator associated with the bid or proposal?

7. Is the proposed contract, before its execution by a designated officer of the company, reviewed by the contract administrator to determine that it is in total agreement with the proposal as amended in negotiations?

8. Are proposal efforts planned and the proposal managers selected generally on the understanding that they will also be the contract performance managers?

9. Is a record maintained of all contacts with the customer from the date of submission of the proposal to the completion of final negotiations?

10. Is the contracts organization responsible for ensuring that the company is maintained on the government's solicitation mailing list and not inadvertently removed?

11. Has the company established formal procedures for determining bid/no-bid decisions which incorporate pricing, financing, tooling, manufacturing, and delivery schedule considerations? Is a committee established for this purpose?

12. Are proposed prices for spare parts fair and reasonable?

13. Are budgets established and approved for proposal efforts, monitored for variances, and reviewed for the reasonableness of incurred costs?

14. Is the contracts organization responsible for controlling and monitoring the submission of all bids or proposals? Are records maintained on a current basis that indicate the date and other data relating to proposals submitted, anticipated dates of award, and awards received?

15. Does the contracts organization prepare a timely analysis on bids or proposals that were not awarded so that senior management will be informed and will have the opportunity to adjust policies or procedures if appropriate?

<u>Cost Estimating</u>

1. Is the estimating process formalized with written policies and procedures, preprinted forms, and specific instructions?

Appendix 15.2 (Continued)

2. Is the proposal based on detailed cost estimates prepared using formalized procedures?

3. Are estimating and costing practices consistent?

4. When factors are used to estimate costs for such efforts as quality assurance, inspection, and test, are they documented, current, and applied in a formal and consistent manner?

5. Are actual data on similar work used when appropriate to validate the quality of estimates?

6. Do cost estimates based on prior cost experience reflect differences in complexity, quantity, state of development of production methods, plant capacity, and make-buy factors between items previously produced and those for which estimates are being prepared?

7. Is the learning curve used when appropriate in estimating labor costs?

8. Are material estimates based on bills of material or other material listings current and adequately detailed?

9. Are projected cost levels and activity volumes considered in preparing cost estimates?

10. Are cost proposals reviewed and approved by management at interim points and upon completion to ensure that the proposal process is adequately documented?

11. Are procedures established, such as those identifying disclosure requirements, requiring proposal updates, and documenting data provided to the government, to ensure compliance with the Truth in Negotiations Act?

12. When applicable, is the certificate of current cost or pricing data signed by an individual involved in the negotiations?

Budgeting

1. Are material budgets established at the appropriate level based on defined quantities and estimated prices?

2. Are budgets established for all contract work with separate identification of cost elements (labor, material, etc.)?

3. Does the initial contract budget, including profit and management reserves, equal the negotiated contract value?

4. Are management reserves for contingencies provided only at the overall contract level? Are the reserves adequately controlled?

5. Is a time-phased budget established and maintained at an appropriate level against which contract performance can be measured?

6. Is the budget revised in a timely manner when the contract is amended and additional work agreed to that will result in added cost?

7. Does the contractor evaluate the effectiveness of the budgeting procedures through continuing comparisons of estimated costs with actual costs, particularly in relation to the original estimates if they are used for accounting purposes for any significant period during contract performance?

–3–

Appendix 15.2 (Continued)

Project Administration and Contract Evaluation

General

1. Is all contract work defined and structured before performance based on the final negotiated contract work statement at a level sufficient to monitor contract performance? Is this done before the assignment of organizational responsibilities?

2. Are work orders opened only with the formal written approval of designated officials?

3. Are work orders closed only upon evidence that established milestones have been completed?

4. Do work authorization policies and procedures clearly define and distinguish between:

   - IR&D and sponsored research.
   - IR&D and production engineering.
   - IR&D, B&P, and selling effort.
   - Similar statements of work on multiple contracts.

5. Are separate work orders required for the following types of projects:

   - Contracts.
   - IR&D projects.
   - Bids and proposals.
   - Maintenance and repair projects.
   - Self-constructed assets.
   - Plant betterment and rearrangements.

6. Are the individuals responsible for developing cost estimates also responsible for doing the work? If a central group is responsible, does it include representatives of the performing organizations?

7. Does the organizational structure clearly identify the performance (functional) organizations and subcontractors responsible for accomplishing the contract work? Are all tasks assigned to a performing organization?

8. For all significant contracts, are detailed work tasks defined for the planning and control of cost and schedule?

9. Are the start and completion dates of contract tasks adequately described and clearly defined? Are the tasks planned by cost element and assigned to a single organization?

10. Are subcontracted tasks clearly defined and identified to the appropriate prime contract tasks?

11. Does the company have procedures in effect to initially review and continually monitor the financial stability of major subcontractors so that the company will be aware on a timely basis of adverse financial situations and their impact on the contract? Does the company monitor the cost, technical progress, and delivery schedule of significant subcontractors?

12. Does the company have adequate methods for incorporating performance data from subcontractors into the reporting system being used? (This is particularly important when the subcontract is a cost-reimbursement and/or intercompany type.)

–4–

Appendix 15.2 (Continued)

13. Does the company analyze, on a monthly basis, the accounting for underabsorbed or overabsorbed indirect costs? Is it evident, when such differences are material, that consideration was given to using the actual rates for preparing estimates of costs at completion (see "Estimates to Complete" below) and for recording income or loss?

14. Are procedures in effect to alert the company when cost-type contracts are within 75% of the contract ceiling so that proper notice can be given in accordance with the "Limitation of Cost or Funds" clause?

Scheduling

1. Is contract work scheduled in a manner that describes the sequence of work and that identifies the significant task interdependencies?

2. Are such techniques as program evaluation and review or critical path method used when appropriate?

3. Are milestone events, technical performance goals, etc., identified at the appropriate contract task level?

4. Is a master milestone event schedule prepared and maintained?

5. Are intermediate milestone event schedules prepared and maintained that provide a logical sequence from the master milestone schedule to the detailed contract task level?

6. Do the company's procedures provide for comparing work accomplishment against the schedule plan? Are changes in the schedule adequately controlled?

Variance Analysis

1. Are cost and schedule performance measures carried out monthly by contract analysts in a consistent and systematic manner?

2. Does the company have variance analysis procedures and a demonstrated capability of identifying cost and schedule variances that:

   • Identify and isolate problems causing unfavorable cost or schedule variances?
   • Evaluate the impact of schedule changes?
   • Evaluate the performance of operating organizations?
   • Identify potential or actual overruns and underruns?

3. Are actual costs used for variance analysis reconcilable with data from the accounting system?

4. Are earned-value estimates made, and are they determined systematically and based on technical accomplishment versus cost?

5. Are significant variances between the contract budget, earned values, and actual cost and schedule traced to the lowest level necessary to establish the cause of each variance?

6. Are significant differences between planned and actual schedule accomplishments identified and reasons provided for the differences?

7. Are the data disseminated to contract management timely, accurate, and usable? Are the data presented so that problems may be readily identified?

–5–

Appendix 15.2 (Continued)

<u>Estimates to Complete</u>

1. Does the company periodically prepare (preferably at least quarterly) comprehensive estimates of contract profit or loss at contract completion, and are such estimates reviewed by senior management for reasonableness?

2. Are written policies and procedures adequate to ensure reasonably accurate estimates of costs at contract completion?

3. Do estimates of costs at completion consider the impact of existing variances?

4. In preparing comprehensive estimates of profit or loss at completion, does the company observe a physical inventory to determine the stage of work in process and, when appropriate, the pricing of quantities on hand?

5. Are estimates to complete developed in conjunction with the individuals responsible for performing the tasks?

6. Are learning-curve assumptions used for the estimate at completion based on historical company experience and modified to reflect current results on a timely basis?

7. Do the forecasted direct labor hourly rates used in the estimate at completion give effect to general increases and cost-of-living adjustments as required under negotiated union contracts? Is an appropriate measure of inflation used as the basis for the cost-of-living adjustment? If union contracts will be renegotiated during a contract, does the company use realistic measures, such as other recent union settlements, to forecast rates?

8. Are there procedures for estimating indirect rates for future years? Are accurate budgets prepared of indirect costs based on proper assumptions?

9. Does the company have procedures for the timely settlement of subcontractor proposals for design changes, and are reasonable estimates of the final negotiated amounts incorporated in contract costs?

Billing

1. Are expressly unallowable costs excluded from claimed direct and indirect costs?

2. Are fee retentions billed upon contract completion (closeout) to the maximum extent permitted by the contract, and not held back until audited or negotiated overhead rates are available?

3. Are contract costs incurred under cost-reimbursement or progress payment provisions billed at least monthly? Are costs claimed in accordance with applicable contract provisions [e.g., quarterly funding of pension costs, prior payment to vendors (if large business),]?

4. Are billed and unbilled receivables periodically segregated by agency and analyzed to determine if any adverse financing arrangement exists?

5. Is responsibility for delinquent accounts formalized, and are contract administrators and program managers notified when billed receivables are outstanding more than 30 days?

6. Is an aging analysis of unbilled accounts receivable periodically made so that billing may be expedited and the causes for the lack of billing identified and corrected?

-6-

Appendix 15.2 (Continued)

7. Is the accounting for unbilled receivables automated and integrated with the general ledger?

8. Are copies of invoices and supporting documents forwarded to the correspondence file maintained by the contract administrator?

9. Does the company periodically review cash remittance procedures to determine if deposits to its accounts can be expedited? Has the company considered whether it would be appropriate to establish several depositories throughout the United States?

10. Are prenumbered government receiving and inspection reports forwarded directly to the billing office from the shipping department to ensure that all goods delivered are billed?

Project Costing

Labor

1. Does the contractor have written policies and procedures in which it communicates to all employees the importance of charging the appropriate work order when completing time records? Is appropriate guidance given to employees to ensure against errors in labor charging?

2. Are employees informed about tasks and activities authorized by work orders to which they are charging? Can employees distinguish between similar activities on different projects? Does the company have a policy for recording uncompensated labor (mainly overtime of salaried employees) when it is considered material? (This may affect the amount of indirect expense allocated to contracts.)

3. Are time records required to be completed and signed by the employee and reviewed and approved by the supervisor?

4. Are floor checks performed and the charging of labor costs monitored?

5. Is compensated overtime properly authorized, including approval by the contracting officer when required?

6. With respect to labor transfer documents:

   • Are they numerically controlled?
   • Do they require the signatures of the employee and the employee's supervisor who approves the transfer before being processed?
   • Do they require an explanation of the transfer and appropriate supporting data?
   • Are documents required to be promptly processed?

7. Have procedures been established for coding and recording idle time?

8. Is there a written work authorization for all direct labor charged?

9. Is the classification and identification of employees (i.e., direct versus indirect) appropriate to the way in which they actually charge their time?

10. Is it possible to verify the integrity of labor charging through physical progress or documented evidence of work performed?

-7-

Appendix 15.2 (Continued)

556

<u>Indirect Costs</u>

1. Does the company evaluate, on an ongoing basis, the process of identifying and segregating unallowable costs and directly associated costs?

2. Has the company complied with the provisions of the "Allowable Cost and Payment" clauses and submitted its proposed final indirect rates based on actual cost experience, together with supporting data, within six months after its year end?

3. Is the annual indirect cost submission subject to appropriate review before execution of the indirect cost certificate?

4. Are annual budgets of indirect costs prepared and monitored monthly for significant fluctuations?

5. Has the company considered the applicability of the value-added (total cost input less materials and subcontracts) method of allocating G&A expense versus the total cost input method? [The value-added method prescribed under CAS 410 is particularly appropriate to service companies where certain contracts include major materials or subcontracts (e.g., computers) that, under the total cost input allocation method, would absorb a disproportionate amount of G&A expense.]

6. Does the company use off-site indirect rates which generally are lower than rates used for contracts performed in-house (e.g., a manufacturing company performing field service contracts)?

7. Does the company evaluate, for interim financial statement purposes, the effect of the difference in provisional and actual rates on the financial position of contracts in process? Does the company determine the financial position of contracts in process at actual rates at year end?

8. Does the company have a written policy for distinguishing between direct and indirect costs (CAS 418)? Is the policy consistently followed?

9. Does the company use its fiscal year as a basis for determining its indirect rates (CAS 406)?

10. Has the company considered the applicability of the cost on facilities capital and on assets under construction (CAS 414 and 417)?

11. Are adequate records maintained to support indirect costs claimed, and are procedures established to ensure that costs are charged to the correct cost pool?

Procurement

1. Does the company have a purchasing department and a formal policy and procedures manual that governs the department's activities? Are policies disseminated to an appropriate level?

2. Is senior management (e.g., vice president of finance, contract manager, and president) familiar with the policies and procedures of the purchasing organization and its major subcontractors and responsive to its operating policies?

3. Does the organizational structure and level of the purchasing department allow it to operate at maximum effectiveness?

–8–

Appendix 15.2 (Continued)

4. Has the purchasing department established standards governing the qualifications, training, and continuous evaluation of purchasing personnel? In particular, are personnel required to take part in company-sponsored training programs or to participate in outside seminars on a regular basis?

5. Has the company established the use of standardized purchasing forms that adequately support the procurement function?

6. Is a summary maintained of all purchase orders let during the year by vendor, including the dollar amount?

7. Does the internal audit department periodically review the purchasing department's procedures for adequacy and compliance with company policy?

8. Does the company have written policies prohibiting the acceptance of gifts, gratuities, or kickbacks from subcontractors and vendors?

9. Are conflict-of-interest statements required annually of all purchasing department employees? Is a statement required of employees who terminate before the annual circularization date?

10. Are vendors formally advised, on a periodic basis, that company policy prohibits the acceptance of gratuities by a purchasing representative?

11. Is there a requirement to maintain purchasing files that represent a complete and accurate history of purchasing transactions? Is each purchase file required to indicate why the award was made?

12. Are periodic reports of the purchasing function required so that management may monitor its performance?

13. Does the company have policies for letting purchase orders to small, small disadvantaged and small women-owned businesses in accordance with the acquisition regulations?

14. Are bills of materials reviewed by the company to determine which materials or items will be purchased and which will be made in-house?

15. Does the purchasing department have available a current copy of a priced bill of materials to ensure that:

    - Material specifications recorded in the purchase order and requisition match the specifications on the bill of materials?
    - All possible economies for ordering required materials, recognizing the total needs as reflected in the bill of materials and stock level requirements, are considered?
    - The price agreed to at the time of purchase is comparable to the price projected in the bill of materials?
    - Price increases are fully explained?

16. Are the company's make-or-buy policy and procedures documented in conformance with the acquisition regulations? Are make-or-buy decisions required to be adequately documented?

17. Do delivery dates of material required by the user organization generally allow adequate lead time to prevent excessive costs for expediting delivery?

18. Are follow-up procedures instituted to ensure delivery before the date production needs the item?

19. Is every effort made to incorporate in purchase orders the standard and applicable clauses of the prime contract, when appropriate?

–9–

Appendix 15.2 (Continued)

20. Does senior management periodically review all material single or sole-source procurements to determine that the procurements were justifiable?

21. Does the company have a continuing program of review and classification of single and sole-source items to determine whether they can be competitively bid?

22. Are sole-source procurements required to be: (1) conclusively and logically substantiated by the management of the department responsible for establishing the requirements in the requisition; (2) completely documented as to the facts and approved by the appropriate procurement management; and (3) reported, when material, at least quarterly to senior management?

23. Are vendors evaluated and rated on performance and financial criteria, and are such ratings kept current and used in supporting selections?

24. Is price or cost analysis performed on all quotations received?

25. Are certificates of current cost or pricing data obtained from subcontractors when appropriate?

26. Does the company support, lend direction to, and monitor the performance of subcontractors? Do company representatives visit subcontractors periodically or, if the subcontract is material, maintain a liaison office at the subcontractor site and require subcontractor progress reports that incorporate cost and schedule information when appropriate?

Physical Inventories

1. Does the contractor have written instructions and procedures on recording transfers of materials charged to a contract that are used on another contract?

2. Does the accounting department maintain detailed records on customer-furnished materials and equipment received, on hand, returned, or otherwise disposed of?

3. Are transfers of customer-furnished materials and equipment to and from various company locations properly documented?

4. Are detailed inventories of customer-furnished materials and equipment taken by persons independent of those charged with the physical custody of those inventories?

5. Has the contractor provided separate insurance coverage for customer-furnished materials or equipment when such requirement exists under the contract terms?

6. Has the contractor evaluated the need for any separate insurance coverage of government property for losses that might be sustained (excluding fire or stated casualty risks) for which it might become responsible, when no such insurance requirement exists under the "Government Property" contract clause?

General Accounting/Contract Revenues

1. Is the accounting department furnished with copies, or suitable summaries, of all pertinent contract terms, change orders, addendums, etc., of:

   • Prime contracts?

Appendix 15.2 (Continued)

- Subcontracts received?
- Subcontracts awarded?

2. Are direct costs accumulated by detailed task in a manner consistent with the budgets, using the cost accounting practices set forth in the disclosure statement and controlled by the general ledger?

3. Does the accounting system provide for determining unit or lot costs when appropriate?

4. Are material charges recorded at the point of usage or by another acceptable method?

5. Does the accounting system provide for material price and usage variances that are essential to the effective control of cost?

6. Is the material control system adequately explained and documented, including planning, requisitioning, and issuance to performing organizations?

7. Does inventory planning support the manufacturing schedule?

8. Does the company segregate, or can it otherwise identify within its accounting system, costs associated with change orders and claims that have not been negotiated?

9. Are company accounting policies on income recognition clearly outlined in an accounting manual or in some other formal manner?

10. Do company procedures provide for segregating (in the accounts or in work-sheet analyses) costs, including directly associated costs, that are not allowed by the acquisition regulations? Are appropriate provisions made for costs subject to a disallowance as a result of a government audit?

11. Does the company use provisional billing rates in the accumulation of unbilled costs? If so, do procedures adequately provide for adjusting the provisional rate or rates to actual at interim or year end?

12. Can costs be determined at interim points to provide data for repricing, for negotiating revised targets, or for determining progress payments?

Job-Site Accounting

Due to the size and location of some projects (particularly construction projects), a contractor may have to establish an accounting office at the job site, and all or part of the accounting functions relating to the project—including payrolls, purchasing, disbursements, equipment control, and billings—may be performed at the job site. Establishing an internal control system at job-site accounting offices may be difficult because home office direct supervision may be limited and because the offices may be staffed with a limited number of trained accounting personnel. Therefore, when off-site locations exist, the controls described above should be implemented as far as possible at those sites, and the following controls specifically related to field sites should also be implemented:

Cash

1. Is the practice of drawing checks to "cash" prohibited? If not, do the officials satisfy themselves that such checks have been cashed in reimbursement of petty cash or used for other proper purposes?

2. Are checks restrictively endorsed immediately upon receipt and promptly deposited?

-11-

Appendix 15.2   (Continued)

1. Is access and egress to the construction area gained only through check points?

2. Is a system used to account for the arrival and departure of employees?

3. Do procedures provide for the release of materials only upon receipt of a properly approved requisition?

4. Are there adequate controls to prevent theft or diversion of material?

5. Is material received delivered directly to the warehouse, storeroom, or production area via an inspection area?

Payroll

1. Concerning personnel:

   - Are requisitions for craft labor initiated by craft foremen?
   - Are these requisitions approved by supervisory personnel?
   - Are office staff positions approved by the resident construction manager?
   - Are referral slips from the local union halls required for all craft applicants?
   - Are notations on the referral slip relating to rates, subsistence, mileage allowance, reviewed to ascertain that they are based on the appropriate labor agreements?
   - Are tests made of distances traveled by employees when mileage and/or subsistence allowances are paid?
   - Are employees required to complete a personal history card and two copies of Form W-4?
   - Is one copy of Form W-4 forwarded to the home office?
   - Are badge numbers assigned to new employees consecutively by craft, and is a log maintained for badge assignments?
   - Are craft termination slips completed by the craft foremen?
   - Are these termination slips approved by supervisory personnel?
   - Is a copy of the termination slip routed directly to the payroll department?
   - Are the following documents maintained on file: (1) union referral slip, (2) employee personal history form, (3) field office copy of Form W-4, (4) termination slip, and (5) rate change authorization?

2. Concerning timekeeping:

   - Before badges are issued, is a check made to determine that all badges are accounted for?
   - Is the employee prevented from obtaining or returning more than one badge?
   - Do the timekeepers prepare an absentee report for all craft employees who have not reported to work when the badge shack is closed?
   - Is a log maintained of craft employees who arrive or depart at irregular times?
   - Is the log forwarded directly to the timekeeping department?
   - Does each craft foreman submit a daily time record indicating the hours worked, by task, for each crew member?
   - Are the foremen's daily time records approved by supervisory personnel?
   - Are the cost distribution accounts entered on the foremen's daily time records by the cost engineer?
   - Are the hours on the foremen's daily time records balanced in detail or in total, by craft, to the hours derived from the absentee and irregular hours reports?
   - Do the timekeepers or other appropriate personnel make daily head counts of the craft employees while they are at work on the job site?

-12-

Appendix 15.2 (Continued)

3. In preparing payroll:

    - Are the hours posted from the daily time records to the payroll register?
    - Are rates entered in the payroll register determined by reference to the appropriate labor agreements and to the daily time records for the tasks performed?
    - Are vacation payments made to union vacation funds included in the individual employee's gross earnings for the purpose of determining payroll taxes and withholding if required by Internal Revenue Service regulations?
    - Are the payroll calculations checked by employees who take no part in their preparation?
    - Is the completed payroll checked against the input data?
    - Before checks are signed, is the completed payroll reviewed and approved in writing by the field office manager and the resident construction manager?

4. In regard to job-site payments:

    - Are checks distributed so as to minimize fraud?
    - Is presentation of a badge or other identification required?
    - Is a list of undelivered payroll checks prepared in duplicate by the paymaster?
    - Does the paymaster return the undelivered checks, along with a copy of the above list, to the field office manager?
    - Is the other copy of the list initialed by the field office manager and retained by the paymaster?
    - Is identification required from employees subsequently claiming their checks from the field office manager?
    - Are employees required to sign the list of undelivered checks upon receipt of their checks?

Quality Assurance

1. Have work instructions been prepared that identify current quality assurance requirements at the operating department level?

2. Are quality assurance procedures distributed in a timely manner to all applicable organizations?

3. Do recordkeeping requirements detail inspection steps performed at various levels of operations?

4. Is the process for correcting defects adequately documented?

5. Is vendor/subcontractor quality adequately controlled?

Government-Furnished Property

1. Is government-furnished property properly segregated, secured, and maintained?

2. Is use of the property limited to the purposes intended and properly authorized before such use?

3. Do government property accounting records conform to the requirements of FAR 45.505?

4. Are physical inventories of government-furnished property periodically taken?

5. Is disposal of excess/unused government property properly authorized and reported?

Record Retention

Appendix 15.2   (Continued)

1. Do written procedures require retention of books, records, documents, and other supporting evidence to satisfy contract negotiation, administration, and audit requirements?

2. Do written procedures specify the specific retention period required for such source documents as purchase requisitions, purchase orders, paid checks, and labor distribution cards?

Export Requirements

1. Do written procedures require that licenses be obtained from the Office of Export Administration, Department of Commerce, before exporting nondefense articles and services?

2. Do written procedures require registration with the Office of Munitions Control, Department of State, before exporting defense articles or providing defense services?

3. Do written procedures require that a license be obtained from the Office of Munitions Control before the permanent export of any item on the U.S. munitions list?

Gratuities

1. Do company procedures prohibit extending offers or furnishing gratuities to government officials?

2. Are employees who regularly interact with government procurement personnel periodically provided with guidelines that preclude offering gratuities?

Marketing

1. Is asking for, giving, or receiving any proprietary data or source selection information prohibited?

2. Do policies define procurement officials, proprietary and source selection information, and other related terms?

3. Have marketing personnel been provided, and do they understand, restrictions under the Procurement Integrity Act? Is there periodic training on procurement integrity?

Hiring Current or Former Government Employees

1. Do personnel procedures require identification of a potential employee's or consultant's most recent functional responsibilities as a government official, if applicable?

2. Are potential employees or consultants requested to assert that no potential conflicts of interest resulting from government employment exist?

3. Is directly or indirectly offering employment to government personnel involved in an ongoing procurement prohibited?

Socioeconomic Requirements

1. Do written policies address subcontracting to small and small disadvantaged business concerns and to labor surplus area concerns?

2. Have required small, small disadvantaged and small women-owned business subcontracting plans been filed?

−14−

Appendix 15.2 (Continued)

3. Are subcontract awards to small, small disadvantaged and small women-owned business concerns monitored and required reports submitted?

4. Are programs in effect to identify potential small, small disadvantaged, and small women-owned vendors?

5. Has a written affirmative action plan been prepared?

6. Are notices required to be posted concerning equal opportunity in employment?

7. Are required Form EEO-1 (Standard Form 100) and other reports submitted as required?

8. Are records maintained to track the country of origin for parts, components, and raw materials incorporated into deliverable end items?

9. Do written procedures require review of contracts for applicable labor standards requirements?

-15-

Appendix 15.2 (Continued)

1. Does the company have a written code of business ethics and conduct?
2. Is the code distributed to all employees principally involved in defense work?
3. Are new employees provided any orientation to the code?
4. Does the code assign responsibility to operating management and others for compliance with the code?
5. Does the company conduct employee training programs regarding the code?
6. Does the code address standards that govern the conduct of employees in their dealings with suppliers, consultants and customers?
7. Is there a corporate review board, ombudsman, corporate compliance or ethics office or similar mechanism for employees to report suspected violations to someone other than their direct supervisor, if necessary?
8. Does the mechanism employed protect the confidentiality of employee reports?
9. Is there an appropriate mechanism to follow-up on reports of suspected violations to determine what occurred, who was responsible, and recommended corrective and other actions?
10. Is there an appropriate mechanism for letting employees know the result of any follow-up into their reported charges?
11. Is there an ongoing program of communication to employees, spelling out and re-emphasizing their obligations under the code of conduct?
12. What are the specifics of such a program?
    a. Written communication?
    b. One-on-one communication?
    c. Group meetings?
    d. Visual aids?
    e. Others?
13. Does the company have a procedure for voluntarily reporting violations of federal procurement laws to appropriate governmental agencies?
14. Is implementation of the code's provisions one of the standards by which all levels of supervision are expected to be measured in their performance?
15. Is there a program to monitor on a continuing basis adherence to the code of conduct and compliance with federal procurement laws?
16. Does the company participate in the industry's "Best Practices Forum"?
17. Are periodic reports on adherence to the principles made to the company's Board of Directors or to its audit or other appropriate committee?
18. Are the company's independent public accountants or a similar independent organization required to comment to the Board of Directors or a committee thereof on the efficacy of the company's internal procedures for implementing the company's code of conduct?
19. Does the company have a code of conduct provision or associated policy addressing marketing activities?
20. Does the company have a code of conduct provision or associated policy requiring that consultants are governed by, and oriented regarding, the company's code of conduct and relevant associated policies.

Appendix 15.3   Defense Industry Initiatives Questionnaire

Chapter Sixteen

Contract Audit Reviews

16-1. BACKGROUND

Government representatives, especially contracting officers (COs), are responsible for ensuring contractor compliance with all the terms and conditions of contracts. Because COs cannot possibly ensure such compliance themselves, various government agencies conduct a range of audits and reviews of contractor proposals and activities. The nature of the review varies with its intent. Typically, reviews either verify contractor assertions or provide government officials with some insight into the efficiency or effectiveness of contractor operations or the appropriateness of proposed costs.

The Defense Contract Audit Agency (DCAA) performs all contract auditing for the Department of Defense (DOD) and provides financial and accounting advice to COs. The DCAA also provides audit and advisory services to other agencies by interagency agreement. Consequently, the DCAA auditor is the key advisor to most COs in matters relating to cost and price. The contract auditor's activities include virtually every phase of the procurement process, from the preaward survey of contractor capability to the audit of final costs claimed on closure of cost-reimbursement contracts.

Government contractors may also be subject to the following audits or oversight reviews:

- The General Services Administration (GSA) Office of the Inspector General, Office of Audits, audits GSA multiple-award schedule (MAS) proposals and contracts, as well as GSA proposals and contracts for which cost or pricing data are required. The Department of Veterans Affairs (DVA) Office of the Inspector General performs similar audits of DVA MAS proposals and contracts.

- The Defense Contract Management Command (DCMC) conducts reviews of government property systems, quality assurance reviews, contractor purchasing system reviews, and system status reviews.

- Other agencies, including the General Accounting Office (GAO) and the various inspectors general organizations, review contractor records, frequently as part of reviews of the government contracting and auditing organizations.

Contract audits are generally performed in three broad situations.

1. The first situation involves the submission of a proposal before award of a contract. When a contractor submits cost or pricing data to support a proposal, the government generally requires that the contractor grant to the CO or authorized representatives the right to examine books, records, documents, and other data submitted, along with related computations and projections. Submission of a cost proposal automatically grants this right to review.

2. The second situation occurs once the contract is awarded. The Audit—Sealed Bidding clause (Federal Acquisition Regulation [FAR] 52.214-26) and Audit and Records—Negotiation clause (FAR 52.215-2) provide to the government the right to audit after contract award to determine the accuracy, completeness, and currency of cost or pricing data submitted. These audits may take place at any time after contract award until the expiration of three years from the date of final contract payment. The GSA audits of MAS proposals and contracts are based on the Examination of Record by GSA clause contained in General Services Acquisition Regulation (GSAR) 552.215-71.

3. The third general situation is when payments are to be based on incurred costs. The Audit and Records—Negotiation clause specifically addresses the government's right to audit a contractor's books and records to ensure that direct and indirect costs are properly claimed for reimbursement on flexibly priced contracts. When either interim or final payments are based on the incurrence of costs, such as progress payments on fixed-price contracts or reimbursement of cost on cost-reimbursement contracts, the government also establishes a contractual right to audit by including specific clauses to that effect, such as the Progress Payments clause (FAR 52.232-16) and the Allowable Cost and Payment clause (FAR 52.216-7).

16-2. ACCESS TO RECORDS

Contract Auditors' Right of Access

The Audit and Records—Negotiation clause gives the CO or an authorized representative "the right to examine and audit all records and other evidence sufficient to reflect properly all costs claimed to have been incurred or anticipated to be incurred in performance of this contract." In connection with the review of cost or pricing data, the clause gives the CO or an authorized representative the right to examine and audit all of the contractor's records, including computations and projects, related to the following:

1. The proposal for the contract, subcontract, or modification
2. Discussions conducted on the proposal(s) including those related to negotiation

3. Pricing of the contract, subcontractor, or modification

4. Performance of the contract, subcontract, or modification

The government's right of audit access to records has been defined to some extent by both the boards of contract appeals and the courts. In *Grumman Aircraft Engineering Corp.*,[1] the government disapproved certain costs because of the contractor's refusal to make franchise tax returns available. The tax returns directly supported the franchise tax expenses that were included in the indirect expense rates allocated to the contractor's cost-reimbursable contracts. The Armed Services Board of Contract Appeals (ASBCA) stated the following in its decision:

> When it entered into these cost-type contracts, appellant agreed "to maintain books, records, documents and other evidence pertaining to the costs and expenses of this contract (hereinafter collectively called the 'records') to the extent and in such detail as will properly reflect all net costs, direct and indirect, of labor, materials, equipment, supplies and services, and other costs and expenses of whatever nature for which reimbursement is claimed under the provisions of this contract." It is [*sic*] also agreed "to make available … any of the records for inspection, audit or reproduction by any authorized representative of the department or of the Comptroller General." That language is broadly inclusive. We would find it difficult to say that the Franchise Tax Return is not a "document" or "evidence pertaining to the costs and expenses of this contract."
>
> This is not a situation in which the government is asking that the contractor create new records or establish a new record keeping system. It is asking to see a document which is already in existence. The appellant, in essence, is responding that it will decide how much the Government auditor needs to see and which of the documents in its files are pertinent and proper for the auditor's perusal.
>
> At the same time the Government agrees to pay a contractor's cost of contract performance, it also reserves the right to satisfy itself with reasonable certainty what those costs truly are. When a contractor's obligation is to deliver the Government something for a competitively-arrived-at fixed price, it retains the right to keep its own counsel and strict privacy as to its cost of delivering that item. When, on the other hand, a contractor enters into a contract in which the Government agrees essentially to pay him what it costs him to perform, that contractor has also invited the Government into his office to determine what those costs are. Thereafter a Government auditor looks over his shoulder. The marriage of Government auditor and contractor is not easily dissoluble. The auditor certainly has no right to roam without restriction through all the contractor's business documents which have no connection with the government contract. But he has a right to satisfy himself as to items claimed to be part of the costs of performing the government contract. When the claim is as to an overhead or indirect cost, there may be some necessity to look at entries other than those of labor, material, and equipment used directly in the performance of the Government contract. We conceive of the audit function, when it applies, as a broad rather than a narrow one.

In *SCM Corporation v. United States*,[2] the Court of Claims upheld the government's right to refuse to reimburse the contractor for claimed costs incurred on a cost-reimbursable contract because of undue restrictions that the contractor placed on the audit's conduct. The contractor had refused to let the DCAA auditors:

- Note in their working papers such information as vendor names or employee names and compensation.
- Make copies of any company documents.
- Remove their working papers from the contractor's premises without the contractor's review and consent.

The court held that the contractor was not entitled to reimbursement of its costs until it allowed the government to properly audit its claim. The court concluded that the audit procedures used by the auditors were in accordance with generally accepted auditing standards and within the scope of the "audit" clause in the contract and that nothing in the contract entitled the contractor to payment for costs incurred without an unrestricted audit.

> As these cases show, the government does not have the right to roam unrestricted, but the right of access to records is fairly broad when the requested information directly or indirectly supports costs claimed for reimbursement on flexibly priced contracts.

Numerous controversies have surfaced over whether a literal interpretation of these words requires unlimited access to such records as contractor databases, board of directors' minutes, internal audit reports and working papers, management letters submitted by certified public accountant (CPA) firms, long-term business forecasts, and nonfinancial records pertinent to the performance of operations audits. In 1985, for instance, the court concluded that the DOD Inspector General (IG) had the right to access to Westinghouse Electric Corporation's internal audit reports. The IG had subpoenaed the reports after the DCAA's request for access to the documents had been denied. The court emphatically rejected the contractor's argument that the IG had issued the subpoena not for its own purpose but only to force the contractor to hand over the records to the DCAA. Concluding that the subpoena was issued as a tool of the IG, not a tool of the DCAA, the court relied on the IG's testimony that he had "taken over" the DCAA's audit and that an Assistant IG had been directed to report on the audit's progress. The decision notes the following:

> ... [E]ven if ... the DCAA is an independent component of the DOD, it is completely available for use when called upon by the IG both as a source of information and to carry out investigative delegations and assignment. ...

> Through the magical dexterity of Congress ... the nineteen thousand auditors and investigators in the scattered, disjointed DOD agencies were brought under the independent authority of the IG who could more effectively combat fraud, waste, abuse, and mismanagement ....

> While it may be that the IG should not have used the DCAA because the DCAA had reasons of its own for getting information about internal audit reports, it was nevertheless a discretionary right which Congress had given him, lacking his own personnel with which to act. ... Under such circumstances, it is not for this court to forbid the IG from using DCAA employees. ...[3]

Because the case involved an IG subpoena rather than a DCAA request for access to records, the decision did not address whether internal audit reports and work papers constituted records that must be furnished pursuant to the audit clause. The court clearly distinguished the IG's broader access rights from the DCAA's potentially more limited access rights by noting, "whether or not the DCAA itself has any rights to access of such records as demanded, which the respondent has refused, is of no concern to this enforcement proceeding."[4] The court decision was sustained on appeal.

Subsequent legislation granted the DCAA its own subpoena power. As a result, the DCAA served subpoenas on Newport News Shipbuilding and Dry Dock Company, demanding that the company produce the following:

- Internal audit reports, schedules of performed and planned audits, audit working papers, audit reports, follow-up actions on expense reports, and time-charging records of the internal auditors
- Federal tax returns, financial work papers, and supporting documentation

With regard to access to internal audit reports and work papers, the court concluded that the subpoena power granted to the DCAA did not expand the DCAA's access to records but merely provided subpoena authority for enforcing its existing access rights. The court distinguished this situation from that of West-inghouse, in which the DOD Inspector General, using the broad statutory sub-poena granted by the Inspector General Act, subpoenaed Westinghouse's inter-nal audit reports and chose to turn them over to the DCAA for review. The court agreed with the contractor that the DCAA lacks the authority to subpoena certain internal records. It concluded the following:

> ... [W]hen the DCAA's purpose under that statute and subpoena power are viewed alongside the Inspector General's statutory purpose and subpoena power, the Court must find that the DCAA is limited to what materials it can and cannot subpoena. Whereas the DCAA's access to contractor records, etc. is limited to pricing and cost data, the Inspector General's subpoena power is not so limited.[5]

Based on the legislative history and limiting language of the law and imple-menting regulations, the court determined that Newport News' internal audit reports were not cost or pricing data.

With regard to access to federal tax returns, financial work papers, and sup-porting documentation, the Fourth Circuit Court[6] overruled a previous district court decision by concluding that the DCAA did have access to "objective finan-cial and cost information, contained in a defense contractor's books, records, and other documents, that reflects upon the accuracy of cost charges submitted to the government." The court recognized the DCAA's rights to obtain corrobo-rative information and decided that federal tax returns, financial statements, and supporting schedules may be subpoenaed "to the extent that they assist DCAA in verifying costs charged under cost-type contracts." The court made a distinction between the objective and subjective information.

As an aftermath of that decision, Newport News again litigated the DCAA's access to labor and material cost projections that had been prepared for profit and loss analyses. The court concluded that such documents were within DCAA's subpoena authority because they:

> ... bear on the accuracy and reliability of the information submitted by [Newport News], and will be used by DCAA to corroborate the currency, accuracy and completeness of cost proposals, the costs incurred on current government contracts, and the estimates of total contract costs contained in various contract reports that are required to be submitted to the government.[7]

These decisions raise such questions as the following:

- Will the roles of the IG and DCAA become so blurred that it is difficult to say who is directing the contract audit function?
- Will the limitations on government access to records that are contained in the audit clause cease to be considered when the records are the subject of an IG subpoena?
- Will the use of subpoenas (either by the IG or DCAA) be confined to federal tax returns, and financial statement data or be expanded to cover corpo-rate board of director minutes, special studies performed by outside con-sultants, executive correspondence files, and other documents that may not be related either directly or indirectly to costs charged to government con-tracts?

In a separate but somewhat related matter, the ASBCA overruled the govern-ment's disallowance of the cost of Martin Marietta Corporation's internal audit department in response to the company's refusal to grant unlimited access to all internal audit reports and working papers. The company routinely provided to the DCAA, upon request, reports on government contracting areas. Its reservations about unlimited government access to all internal audit reports related to (1) the government's ability to protect sensitive company data from release under the Freedom of Information Act; and (2) Securities and Exchange Commission requirements concerning the release of inside information about potential acquisitions. In its decision, the Board concluded that the cost disallowance was unreasonable and arbitrary. In its view:

> ... [T]he internal audit documents were not necessary to determine if its costs were properly chargeable to the G&A of the contractor. Thus the suspension of the entire costs of appellant's internal audit function for three fiscal years has no reasonable relationship to the nature of the demand for access to the records or to the appellant's response. Where specific costs are questioned, the Government may suspend payment of such costs but the use of withholding payments, as a club to insure compliance with demands unrelated to the costs suspended must, at the very least, be exercised with discretion.[8]

Just as controversial is the issue of whether the clause grants to government officials the right to question contractor personnel and require them to respond to questionnaires.

The DCAA places a major emphasis on the use of interviews as an audit technique. Its *Contract Audit Manual* (CAM),[9] Section 2-306, states, "The auditor's work shall include the examination or development of sufficient evidence to afford a reasonable basis for the auditor's conclusions and recommendations regarding cost representations, management decisions influencing costs, financial statements, or any other matters requiring the auditor's opinion." Section 3-104.14i of the *Manual* further discusses the use of oral evidence, as follows:

> (1) Generally, oral evidence is useful in disclosing situations that may require examination or may corroborate other types of evidence already obtained by the auditor. Oral evidence can determine audit direction and, when appropriate, should be recorded and made part of the audit file.

> (2) Do not rely on this type of evidence to completely support an audit conclusion or opinion; use other confirming evidence, particularly where the matter is significant.

Section 6-404.9 of the *Manual* emphasizes that: "Effective interviews and a review of the labor system of internal controls (see CAM 5-900) can provide sufficient information to form an opinion on the adequacy of, and compliance with internal controls and the propriety of the recorded labor charge." Section 6-405.3i, which delineates specific procedures for physical observations (floor checks), instructs the auditor to:

> ... Determine whether the employee is performing in the proper capacity as direct or indirect labor and whether time is being charged correctly by discussing the nature of the work being performed with the employee and observing the actual work performance. If an employee's time for the prior period was charged to a cost code or work project other than the one he or she is working on during the floor check and the nature of his or her work is not such that it obviously entails frequent job changes, the employee should be queried regarding his or her work assignment in the prior period. This procedure may disclose errors, adjustments or alterations to the prior period labor distribution records which require further analysis.

Given the DCAA emphasis on interviews and floor checks, a carefully managed contractor program regarding government access to records and people becomes even more critical.

Examination of Records by the Comptroller General

The Examination of Records by the Comptroller General clause (formerly FAR 52.215-1) was eliminated on October 1, 1995. The Audit and Records—Sealed Bidding (FAR 52.214-26) and Audit and Records—Negotiation (FAR 52.215-2) were revised to provide for examination of records by the Comptroller General.

The GAO has continually expanded its activities and sought to review many aspects of a contractor's operations. Its efforts have been furthered by specific congressional requests encompassing government programs that extend beyond books and records. However, in two decisions,[10] the Supreme Court affirmed earlier Court of Appeals decisions that limited the GAO's access to directly pertinent contract data. The Supreme Court concluded that the Examination of Records clause did not require GAO access to data concerning a company's research, development, marketing, promotion, distribution, and administration costs.

16-3. DCAA AUDITS

The DCAA *Contract Audit Manual* (see Appendix 16.1 for the Table of Contents) contains guidance, techniques, standards, policies, and procedures to be followed by DCAA personnel in performing the contract audit function. The manual is a comprehensive document that provides valuable insight into the DCAA's reasons for performing various types of audits.

The need for audits may result from a variety of events, including the following:

- Audit requests from procurement or administrative agencies
- Contractual requirements
- Contract proposals or modifications to existing contracts
- Changes in contractor organization, operations, or systems
- Audit leads or other matters that lead the auditor to believe an audit is necessary to protect the government's interest

While certain audits may be predictable as the result of such events as submission of a cost proposal, a final indirect cost proposal, or a voucher, an audit may be internally initiated without a contractor's specific knowledge of the planned audit or the audit objectives. Once an audit assignment has been established, the audit is planned to determine its scope and the specific procedures to be applied.

Audit Approach

Contract auditors have a great deal of flexibility in planning audit activities for each audit planned.

How an auditor approaches a specific audit depends heavily on the auditor's professional judgment regarding the type of audit to be performed and the contractor being audited. For example, if the auditor perceives weaknesses or deficiencies in the contractor's systems or controls, either real or imagined, the extent of audit activity will likely be expanded significantly. The converse is also true. While the auditor's judgment figures significantly in the audit planning process, the DCAA guidelines also play a role. These guidelines call for a risk assessment, application of minimum annual audit requirements, and identification of audit leads for the various types of audits to be conducted.

Assessment of Internal Controls

Separate audit assignments are established to periodically review significant accounting and management systems and related controls. The results are summarized in the Internal Control Audit Planning Summary (ICAPS) (Appendix 16.2) and maintained in the permanent file for use in assessing control risk and the impact on related contract audit efforts.

Mandatory Annual Audit Requirements

The DCAA has established minimum annual audit requirements, which must be performed at each contractor location either as separate reviews or as integral components of routine audits. Internal controls affecting the mandatory annual audit requirements (MAARs) are summarized in the ICAPS for each related accounting and management system. The scope of transaction test and special purpose MAARs is impacted by the strengths of the contractor's internal controls and the currency of audit experience in the area. A more detailed discussion of the objectives and purposes of the requirements is contained in Appendix 16.3. The auditor must consider incorporating these requirements when planning assigned audits.

Audit Leads

Audit leads are reviewed and considered in the audit planning process to ensure that any matters of concern identified in prior audits are adequately considered in the scope of the assigned audit. These leads identify specific system deficiencies, internal control weaknesses, and other matters considered pertinent. They are maintained in a permanent file for audit planning purposes. Contractors can frequently anticipate these areas of concern and rectify any deficiencies or weaknesses based on auditor comments during audit exit conferences. However, specific matters relating to questioned costs on proposals cannot usually be anticipated.

Scope of Audit

The final step in the audit approach is establishing the scope of the audit. The audit may represent a "desk review," a review of specified elements, or a comprehensive review of a contractor's supporting documentation and books and records.

A desk review is generally limited to analyzing the documents submitted by the contractor. These reviews are typically limited to smaller proposals. In addition, the risk factors resulting from risk assessments must be relatively low, and the minimum annual audit requirements must be considered before performing a desk review. Desk reviews are generally performed when auditors understand the contractor's system and are confident that the government is at a minimum risk.

If the auditor feels that additional field work is required for any reason, the audit scope will be broader than a desk review. In some instances, the scope may be limited to evaluating specific cost items or elements. Such reviews may be performed as the result of a request from the procuring agency or as the result of the auditor's evaluation of existing circumstances.

Comprehensive audits are made when the audit values exceed the thresholds for a desk review, when the audit planning process indicates a potential risk to the government, or when the minimum annual audit requirements must be met. Standardized preprinted audit programs are used to the maximum extent possible to promote consistency and efficiency in audit performance. Various types of DCAA audits are discussed below.

Preaward Surveys

In a preaward survey, the procuring agency evaluates whether the prospective contractor is capable of performing the proposed contract. The survey may be accomplished by using data already in the agency files, data obtained from other government or commercial sources, on-site inspection of plants and facilities, or any combination of the above. A preaward survey is generally required when the information available to the CO is insufficient to determine a prospective contractor's responsibility. This is normally the case when the agency has had no previous experience with the offeror or when the anticipated level of activity with the company is to be significantly increased.

When a CO determines that a preaward survey is desirable, the appropriate technical and financial advisors are directed to make the necessary reviews. The technical personnel will evaluate the prospective contractor's performance capability and productive capacity, and the contract auditor will review the prospective contractor's financial capabilities and the adequacy of the estimating and accounting systems.

The objective of the financial capability survey, Standard Form 1407 (see Chapter 3, Appendix 3.10), is to determine whether the contractor's finances are adequate to perform the contract. In certain instances, a sound decision may be possible after a relatively simple review of a company's financial position and production commitments. In other circumstances, a more comprehensive review and analysis may be required. If private financing is needed, in addition to any government financing that may be provided, the auditor will normally verify the availability of such financing.

Auditors are admonished in the *Contract Audit Manual*, Section 14.301b, to be alert in all audit situations to conditions that may indicate contractor financial instability. The auditor considers various indicators, such as the Z score prediction model, bank line of credit requirements, current ratio, acid test ratio, liquidation of accounts payable, fund availability, and continued operating losses to assess whether the contractor's financing difficulties are unduly jeopardizing current and future contract performance.

A preaward accounting system survey, Standard Form 1408 (see Chapter 3, Appendix 3.11), is usually made to determine the adequacy and suitability of the contractor's accounting practices for accumulating costs under the type of contract to be awarded. Accordingly, the survey may emphasize the ability of the cost accounting system to provide specific information that the anticipated contract may require. Additionally, if the contemplated contract is a cost-based contract or a fixed-price contract with progress payment provisions, the auditor normally ensures that the accounting system has the capability to accumulate costs by contract on an interim basis.

Since the time available to complete the preaward survey is normally limited, the review may not be extensive in scope or depth. However, a major deficiency in a cost accounting system could preclude the award of a contract. Therefore, companies undergoing such a review should insist on knowing immediately any defects the government reviewers have noted. In anticipation of such a review, it may be well for management to conduct its own survey and correct any deficiencies.

Forward Pricing Audits

Forward pricing entails price estimating for specific products or services to be provided in the future. Forward pricing may include cost estimates for total contracts (proposals) or estimates for specific rates and factors (forward pricing rate agreements) to be used in all of a contractor's forward pricing efforts for an established period.

The objective of forward pricing proposal audits is to assist the procuring activity in determining a reasonable price for goods and services in accordance with procurement regulations and cost accounting standards (CAS). This objective provides the auditors with significant latitude in determining the scope of a particular proposal audit. Virtually every aspect of a contractor's operations that affects the price paid by the government is subject to audit scrutiny.

Proposal audits vary significantly from one contractor to another. These variations are principally due to the deviations in scope resulting from the specific needs of the procuring activity, the audit planning process and the unique characteristics of each procurement. The auditor will typically evaluate each element of cost for which audit evaluation has been requested. The procedures used in a comprehensive audit of the proposed cost elements may include the following:

- Review of the basis for the proposed cost (i.e., historical data, quotations, engineering, and estimates)
- Verification and analysis of relevant historical data
- Review and analysis of kinds and quantities proposed (i.e., labor hours by category and material)
- Analysis of current cost data (i.e., last year-end and year-to-date rates, factors, and contract costs)
- Analysis of proposed performance periods and economic adjustments proposed
- Analysis of forecasted business activities and their effects on rates and factors
- Comparison of proposed cost elements with the same or similar activities
- Comparison of estimating techniques with accumulation and reporting techniques (i.e., CAS 401 and 402)

Audits of forward pricing rates, such as labor, indirect expense, and scrap rates, are accomplished via the same objectives and procedures discussed above. The principal difference is that the audit scope is limited to the specific cost components of the proposed rates. In addition, procedures, internal controls, and/or methods of developing the rates are more extensively examined.

Incurred Cost Audits

Incurred costs constitute monies spent both directly and indirectly during contract performance. Incurred costs on flexibly priced contracts and subcontracts are subject to audit before contract settlement.

Indirect Cost Rate Proposals

Indirect cost rate proposals are submitted for audit under flexibly priced contracts (i.e., those contracts for which final remuneration is based on costs incurred during contract performance). The contractor's final indirect cost rate proposal is subsequently audited to some extent by the government. The objectives of the audit are to determine that (1) costs included in the indirect expense pools are allowable under applicable regulations and contract terms; (2) the indirect expenses have been homogeneously grouped for equitable allocation to contracts; (3) the bases used to distribute costs to contracts are appropriate given the types of expenses being distributed; and (4) the accumulation and distribution of indirect expenses have been consistently applied to all aspects of the contractor's operations, including government and nongovernment activities.

The audit procedures may vary significantly, depending on the results of the risk analysis as well as the materiality of the dollars allocated to flexibly priced contracts. However, as a minimum, the auditor will:

- Review account titles in each indirect expense pool to identify any obvious categories of unallowable expenses.
- Review the allocation bases to ensure the propriety of the allocation.
- Verify the mathematical accuracy of the proposed indirect expense pools, allocation bases, and indirect expense rates.

The minimum review is a desk audit of the contractor's final indirect cost rate proposal, without examination of any contractor records. More extensive indirect expense proposal audits, in addition to incorporating all of the steps above, include reviews of contractor accounting records and supporting documentation and detailed testing to determine the following:

- The adequacy of internal controls associated with the incurrence and recording of expenses
- The allowability of individual expenses within a variety of accounts
- The homogeneity of the indirect expense groupings (pools) to ensure equitable distribution of expenses to cost objectives
- The propriety of the bases used to apportion expenses to cost objectives to ensure cost allocations based on causal or beneficial relationships

Material Cost Audits

Material costs are usually reviewed through several distinct audits encompassing determination of requirements, accounting for material costs, purchasing and subcontracting, receipt of materials, and storing and issuing material.

Determination of Requirements. The audit steps will focus on assuring the following:

- Material requirements reflect timely buying practices at the most feasible economic order quantity.
- Future requirements projections are based on proposal activity and major programs.

- Material requirements are supported by a proper requisitioning system that reflects properly initiated and approved requisitions.

- Information generated by stock level requirements for standard items on bills of material are coordinated with production schedules.

- Controls that prevent (1) repetitive requisitioning of small quantities of the same item with substantial increases in cost or (2) requisitioning materials in excessive quantities or premature charging to government contracts, resulting in unnecessary costs and increased storage and handling.

Accounting (Payment) for Material Costs.   The basic audit objectives in the accounting for material costs includes verification of proper payments and distribution of material charges to contracts, accounts, and projects. Basic steps include verification of the following:

- Invoices are supported by authorized purchase orders.

- Invoice terms agree with the purchase order on price quantities, and other terms.

- Paperwork is matched—that is, invoices are supported by receiving and inspection reports, debit and credit memos, and so on.

- The arithmetic accuracy of extensions and discounts on invoices has been verified.

- Documents are properly marked to show proper account distribution and cancellation to avoid duplicate payments.

- Costs are paid before they are claimed on public vouchers or progress payments (not applicable to small business concerns).

Purchasing and Subcontracting.   At large contractor locations, purchasing and subcontracting systems are usually reviewed every three years in a team effort, consisting of representatives of the DCMC and the DCAA. The Contractor Purchasing System Review (CPSR) team's objective is to determine whether the purchasing system is effective and efficient in the expenditure of government funds and complies with public laws and contract requirements. These reviews are discussed in further detail later in this chapter. Special attention is given to the following:

- The degree of price competition obtained
- Pricing policies and techniques, including methods of obtaining accurate, complete, and current cost or pricing data and certification as required
- Methods of evaluating subcontractor responsibility, including the contractor's use of the List of Parties Excluded from Federal Procurement and Nonprocurement Programs and, if the contractor has subcontracts with parties on the list, the documentation, systems, and procedures the contractor has established to protect the government's interests
- Treatment accorded affiliates and other concerns having close working arrangements with the contractor
- Policies and procedures pertaining to small business concerns, including small disadvantaged and women-owned small business concerns
- Planning, award, and postaward management of major subcontract programs

- Compliance with Cost Accounting Standards in awarding subcontracts

- Appropriateness of types of contracts used

- Management control systems, including internal audit procedures, to administer progress payments to subcontractors

Material Management and Accounting Systems. All contractors are expected to conform to the 10 key elements for Material Management and Accounting Systems (MMAS), which are discussed in Chapter 14. However, contractors that received $70 million or more in defense prime contracts or subcontracts in the prior year are also subject to a formal program of government system reviews. The formal program requires contractors to disclose their MMAS practices and to demonstrate that their systems comply with the requirements. To determine whether a contractor adequately conforms to the required standards, the Administrative Contracting Officer (ACO) obtains the support and advice of the contract auditor.

Remedies available to the government when a contractor's MMAS is determined to be deficient include reduction or suspension of payments and, in severe cases, disapproval of contractor cost accounting and estimating systems. These risks can be effectively managed by maintaining a strong MMAS control environment that includes the establishment of appropriate policies and procedures, metrics and diagnostics to either demonstrate that the MMAS is functioning properly or to identify the need for corrective action if a potential contractor compliance problem is identified.

The preparation for, and the conduct of, an initial MMAS demonstration to the ACO can be a significant, nonrecurring cost. Therefore, the contractor should prepare extensively for the initial demonstration to avoid costs associated with redemonstration or a misunderstanding by the government regarding the operation of the system. The MMAS demonstration will be measured against the benchmark specified in DOD FAR Supplement (DFARS) 252.242-7004(3). An MMAS demonstration is adequate when the contractor has demonstrated the degree of compliance of its MMAS with the ten key elements, identified any significant deficiencies, provided the estimated cost impact of deficiencies, and prepared a comprehensive corrective action plan.

DOD FAR Supplement 242.7205 establishes review procedures for DOD contract administration and audit functions when evaluating the MMAS systems of contractors subject to disclosure, demonstration, and maintenance requirements. The evaluation team that reports significant MMAS deficiencies must also estimate the adverse impact on the government resulting from the deficiencies. The ACO must immediately provide a copy of the report citing such significant deficiencies to the contractor.

The contractor normally has 30 days to review and respond from the date of initial notification. If the contractor agrees with the report, the contractor has 60 days to correct the identified deficiencies or submit a corrective action plan. The corrective action plan must include milestones and actions to eliminate the identified deficiencies. If the contractor disagrees with the report, the contractor should provide written rationale within the same time period. The contractor should carefully review the government's basis for calculation of harm and submit its own estimate, when appropriate.

The government will review the contractor's response and determine whether the MMAS contains deficiencies that need correction. The government will also determine whether any contractor-proposed corrective actions are adequate to correct the deficiencies. If deficiencies are significant enough, progress payments or payments under public vouchers may be reduced or suspended. Therefore, the government has significant leverage toward obtaining contractor compliance.

Any reduction or suspension of payments will remain in effect until the ACO determines that the deficiencies are corrected or the amount of impact is immaterial. The maximum payment adjustment is the adverse material impact to the government, as specified in the evaluation report. The ACO is directed to use the maximum adjustment when the contractor either did not submit a corrective action plan or the corrective action plan is unacceptable. If an acceptable corrective action plan has been submitted, the ACO is directed to consider the quality of the contractor's self-assessment, demonstration, and corrective action plan in determining the appropriate adjustment percentage. Therefore, the contractor should make every effort to submit a responsive corrective plan, when applicable.

As the contractor implements the corrective action plan, the ACO should reinstate a portion of withheld amounts commensurate with the contractor's progress. The ACO and auditor will monitor the contractor's progress. If the contractor fails to make adequate progress, the ACO may elevate the issue to higher level management, further reduce or suspend progress payments, disapprove the contractor's estimating and/or cost accounting systems, and/or disallow charges as unreasonable.

Labor Cost Audits

Labor costs are reviewed in several distinct areas.

- Labor charging and allocation
- Payroll preparation and payment
- Personnel policies and procedures
- Overtime, extra pay shifts, and multishift work
- Uncompensated overtime
- Labor utilization
- Reasonableness of compensation
- Verification of labor costs

Three major audits cover a number of the areas listed above: compensation system reviews (CSR); floor checks; and audits of labor system internal controls.

CSR. This review is performed at least every three years at business segments with at least $50 million in negotiated federal awards for which such sales represent at least 10% of total sales. The purpose of the CSR is to determine the reasonableness of the total compensation paid to specific job classifications or categories for both direct and indirect employees. This includes determining (1) the adequacy of a contractor's compensation policies and procedures, and (2) whether the wage and salary structure provides a consistent basis for controlling and promoting the equity between internal and external factors.

Wage and salary surveys are used by the auditors to provide data relating to compensation levels for specific job classifications, and to evaluate compensation reasonableness. The surveys are used for matching a contractor's job classification to survey job classification based on position description. A specific match is called a benchmark. To evaluate reasonableness of compensation for each job classification, DCAA guidelines are used to calculate percentage variances between compensation paid by a contractor and the matching survey bench-mark.

Compensation levels above the established range of reasonableness (10% above the survey data average rates) are challenged. Similar procedures are used in evaluating fringe benefits, bonuses, and incentive compensation. Adjustments are usually on a prospective basis.

Floor Checks.   Defense Contract Audit Agency auditors make unannounced floor checks to determine the adequacy and accuracy of timekeeping systems for labor costs under cost-reimbursable contracts. During these reviews, the auditor:

- Determines whether the employees selected are at their assigned work sites
- Identifies the projects currently being performed by selected employees
- Reviews the adequacy of written documentation to identify the project to be charged
- Determines employee adherence to established time-reporting procedures (e.g., time report prepared daily in ink)
- Determines whether the subsequent labor distribution properly reflects the charges observed on employee time reports

Audits of Labor System Internal Controls.   This review focuses on the following:

- Employee awareness training
- Control and issuance of work authorizations
- Review of timekeeping
- Review of labor distribution
- Labor cost accounting
- Review of labor transfers and adjustments

Substantive testing in the audit of incurred labor costs is focused in high-risk areas. Auditors are admonished to be alert to conditions that support the existence of labor mischarging.

Billing Audits

Public vouchers submitted by a contractor under cost-type contracts are not routinely audited. Progress payments on fixed-price contracts may be audited at the request of the CO or when the auditor determines that an audit is necessary to protect the government's interest. As more contractors go on-line with electronic billing, the extent of the auditor's reliance on the contractor's cost accumulation, reporting, and billing systems and procedures becomes even more critical.

The objective of a billing audit is to verify that the amounts billed on the contract are in accordance with the contract terms and conditions, and are properly due the contractor. The audit generally determines that the amounts billed exclude unpaid or ineligible direct and indirect costs; are based on applicable provisional or actual indirect expense rates in effect; and that the request for payment is properly prepared and includes only those costs authorized under the contract terms. For cost-reimbursement type contracts, fees claimed are computed in accordance with contract terms and conditions.

Cost Accounting Standards Reviews

The CAS requirements imposed on contractors have added to the auditor's responsibilities as well. The auditor is required to perform CAS reviews and to render opinions on whether:

- The disclosure statement adequately describes actual or proposed cost accounting practices.
- Disclosed cost accounting practices comply with CAS.
- Failure to comply with CAS or to consistently follow disclosed cost accounting practices has resulted, or may result, in any increased cost to the government.
- Cost impact analyses submitted as a result of CAS noncompliance or changes in cost accounting practices are fair and reasonable.

Disclosure Statement Audits

As discussed in Chapter 8, certain contractors must submit disclosure statements that describe the cost accounting practices applied to contracts containing the CAS clause. Upon submission of a disclosure statement, government auditors perform a review to ascertain whether the statement adequately describes the cost accounting practices to be used in estimating, accumulating, and reporting costs on CAS-covered contracts. Either concurrent with or following this adequacy review, the auditor performs a compliance review to determine whether disclosed practices comply with CAS and FAR requirements.

To determine adequacy, the auditor validates the currency, accurateness, and completeness of the practices described in the statement. For contractors subject to continuous audit surveillance, the adequacy review may be performed largely by reviewing data in existing audit files. For contractors audited on a more limited basis, the volume of CAS-covered contracts is a major consideration in establishing the scope of the adequacy review.

The auditor compares the disclosed practices with the contractor's system, procedures, and practices to ensure that current and/or planned practices have been described. To be current, the statement must disclose current or planned practices that the contractor intends to follow in estimating, accumulating, and reporting costs on CAS-covered contracts.

The accuracy of the disclosure statement is determined by verifying that the practices have been clearly and distinctly disclosed. Vague, ambiguous, and contradictory descriptions of the contractor's cost accounting practices may cause disputes and litigation; therefore, the auditor carefully reviews the described practices for specificity and clarity. The auditor also verifies that the appropriate boxes are checked, the applicable code letters have been inserted, and all applicable questions have been answered on the disclosure statement. This verification may incorporate a review of policies, procedures, and internal controls, as well as specific attribute testing.

To be complete, the statement must disclose all significant cost accounting practices the contractor intends to use in estimating, accumulating, and reporting costs and must provide sufficient information to permit a full understanding of the accounting practices being described.

To determine compliance with CAS and acquisition regulations, the auditor compares the disclosed practices with those requirements and reports any noncompliances to the ACO. Initial compliance reviews are generally deferred until the adequacy review is completed because an adequacy statement is required before contract award. However, changes in disclosure statements as a result of accounting practice changes are reviewed concurrently for both adequacy and compliance.

Continuing Cost Accounting Standards Compliance Reviews

When a contractor is subject to CAS, the auditor is responsible for making periodic CAS compliance reviews of the contractor's cost accounting practices for estimating, accumulating, and reporting costs. Separate CAS compliance reviews may be performed when infrequent audit requirements exist or when specific requirements of a standard cannot be integrated into normal audits. For example, in a price proposal evaluation, the auditor will determine whether accounting practices used in pricing the proposal are consistent with the disclosure statement, if applicable, and/or established accounting practices for accumulating and reporting costs. In an incurred cost audit, such as a final indirect expense rate submission, the auditor's review will include an evaluation for compliance with applicable standards.

Cost Impact Analysis Reviews

Contractors and subcontractors subject to CAS are generally required to submit cost impact analyses to the government when a disclosed or established accounting practice is changed or when noncompliance with CAS or a disclosed or established accounting practice has been determined. The purpose of the analysis is to reflect the cost impact of the change or the noncompliance on all applicable CAS-covered contracts.

In a cost impact analysis review, the auditor is responsible for determining the following:

- All applicable CAS-covered contracts are included.
- The analysis has been properly prepared, and the method of presentation is adequate.
- The proposed amounts (cost impact) are fair and reasonable.

If a contractor does not submit the required cost impact analyses, the auditor assists the CO in estimating the cost impact.

Defective Pricing Audits

The DCAA gives postaward audits (reviews for compliance with the Truth in Negotiations Act[11]), a high priority. The criteria for selecting specific contracts for review are established by DCAA headquarters. Under these criteria, the DCAA selects pricing actions that exceed specified dollar amounts for specific contract types and samples contracts that do not meet the specific selection criteria. Generally all fixed-price and incentive contracts over $100 million are reviewed. Cost-type contracts (other than incentive) are generally not reviewed. In determining the number of fixed-price and incentive contracts under $100 million to be reviewed, the DCAA performs a risk assessment that considers hit rates (ratio of audits with findings of defective pricing to total postaward audits completed in the prior year), the amount of recommended postaward price adjustments in the prior year, and the results of estimating system and accounting system reviews.

Designated risk levels from low risk to high risk result in distinct differences in the number of pricing actions selected for postaward audit. The higher the risk assessment, the greater the number of selected contracts. If prior DCAA audits have disclosed little or no defective pricing and if the DCAA considers the estimating and accounting systems to be adequate, few contracts will be selected for review. Where the opposite is true, substantial number of contracts will be selected for review (e.g., all firm-fixed-price contracts over $10 million for high risk-rated contractors). Smaller contractors are automatically assigned high-risk levels.

The *Contract Audit Manual,* Section 14-102, requires the auditor to establish five points to prove the existence of defective pricing.

1. The information in question fits the definition of cost or pricing data.
2. Accurate, complete, and current data existed and were available to the contractor before agreement on price.
3. Accurate, complete, and current data were not submitted or disclosed to the CO or an authorized representative, and such individuals had no actual knowledge of such data or its significance to the proposal.
4. The government relied on the defective data in negotiating the contract price.
5. The government's reliance on the defective data caused an increase in the contract price.

Section 14-114 requires the auditor to use the agency's standard postaward audit program in performing defective pricing audits. The program lists preliminary, detailed, and concluding steps. The preliminary steps address the basic data that are needed to conduct the audit. Detailed steps address applicable to specific cost elements.

Examples of defective pricing indicators by cost element that are included as an attachment to the audit program are contained in Appendix 16.4.

Fraud Detection

While contract auditors generally are not responsible for detecting fraud, they are alert to any indications of fraud they may come across during their normal audit activity. To assist auditors in detecting fraud, the DOD Inspector General periodically issues guidance on transactions, events, or conditions that may be associated with fraudulent activities.

Auditors may make fraud referrals when they believe they have detected irregularities or indications of fraud. Under the referral process, the auditor is encouraged to prepare a draft, Suspected Irregularity Referral Form, DCAA Form 2000 (see Appendix 16.5), and discuss it with the audit supervisor. The supervisor or branch manager submits the form to the various investigative activities (e.g., local investigative offices, Defense Criminal Investigative Service, and Department of Justice Defense Procurement Fraud Unit) and to DCAA management.

To avoid referrals of fraud, contractors should work as closely as possible with the auditor. Communication with the auditor can eliminate the possibility of a referral resulting from a misunderstanding and can protect the company from extensive investigations and allegations of fraud.

16-4. AUDITS OF MULTIPLE-AWARD SCHEDULE CONTRACTS

The GSA Acquisition Regulation (GSAR) contains several provisions that give GSA or Department of Veterans Affairs (VA) auditors access to records and the right to conduct postaward audits. The objectives of postaward audits are to determine whether (1) the data submitted in the discount schedule and marketing data (DSMD) sheets required to be submitted prior to October 1, 1995, or the Commercial Sales Contract Formats, required to be submitted after October 1, 1995, were accurate, complete, and current; (2) the prices submitted were based on established catalog or market prices of items sold in substantial quantities to the general public (applies only to contracts awarded prior to October 1, 1995); and (3) the discounts and concessions to any customer, regardless of quantity and terms, exceed those offered to the government were fully disclosed and justified with supporting rationale and documentation. Additionally, the auditor is concerned with the contractor's or offeror's internal control system for properly preparing the schedule contract price list, accurately billing the government, promptly reporting price reductions, and reporting orders received under the schedule contract.

In determining the accuracy of the pricing and discount data supplied, the auditor reviews the marketing policies and discounts in effect during negotiations. During this review, the auditor usually requests complete lists of all customers having written pricing agreements and attempts to identify the circumstances and procedures where these prices can deviate from established policy. The objective is to test the accuracy and completeness of the discount disclosure by reviewing actual sales transaction prices. The sampling of commercial sales invoices (or equivalent computer data) is the main audit tool used to detect data that are not accurate, complete, or current.

The commerciality of the offered items was often a major audit issue prior to the revision of FAR 15.8 in October 1995. Offerors frequently certified to items' commerciality without adequate analysis of sales by model number at the catalog price (less published discounts) and at "other than catalog price." To verify commerciality, the auditor would review the company's analyses of sales information for all models offered in the proposal or, if no analyses were available, make an independent assessment of commerciality. Models that were not certified as commercial should have been listed and supported by cost or pricing data.

The postaward audit encompasses many of the same audit objectives and steps found in the preaward audit. The preaward audit of an offer does not preclude the postaward audit of the resulting contract. If the auditor determines that data were not accurate, complete, and current when price negotiations were concluded, the government will probably pursue a reduction in prices under the Price Reduction for Defective Pricing Data clause.

An additional postaward audit step involves the review of price reduction subsequent to contract award. Under the Price Reduction clause, the contractor is required to report to the CO all price reductions to commercial customers that occurred after contract award. In certain circumstances, such price reductions may trigger a reduction in prices to the government. Baker School Specialty Co., Inc.,[12] appealed a CO's final decision claiming a contract refund and a unit price reduction of items included on an schedule contract for display and communication boards. Prior to contract award, separate DSMDs were submitted for each of seven different special item numbers. The GSA audit report, which was the basis for the CO's final decision, identified instances in which discounts offered to certain of Baker's most favored customers were greater than those disclosed on the

DSMDs. Based on these identified greater discounts, the auditor projected the excess discounts to the entire contract. The audit also identified additional discounts that were provided to one of Baker's most favored customers subsequent to award of the MAS contract. The auditor reduced contract unit prices for the remainder of the contract to reflect this additional discount percentage. While the record clearly demonstrated that Baker submitted defective data and failed to comply with the requirements of the contract's price reduction provisions, the General Services Board of Contract Appeals (GSBCA) concluded that the audit report lacked sufficient detail to determine the appropriate price adjustment due to the government. The Board observed the following:

> Once GSA discovered the undisclosed discounts and concluded that failure to reveal them had led to a significant increase in the negotiated price, we would expect the auditors to review transactions involving the special item numbers presumably affected by the nondisclosures in question. There is no indication in the record that this was done. ... Whether these items correspond to the items actually affected by the nondisclosure remains unproven. In the absence of such proof, we are not prepared to uphold the Government' refund claim.

16-5. OTHER AUDITS AND REVIEWS

The government may make a variety of reviews in addition to those discussed earlier in this chapter. These reviews may be performed by auditors, technical personnel, or contract administration personnel, and may include such areas as (1) functional system reviews, (2) matters related to specific contract clauses, and (3) comprehensive system surveys. Most of these reviews, as discussed below, address the contractor's ability to comply with applicable regulations and specific contract terms and conditions.

Functional Reviews

Reviews of all functional areas involved in, or associated with, contract performance are performed by the DCMC. These functional audits reviews of written policies and procedures to determine that a contractor's operations are adequately documented and that the operations comply with applicable regulations. The contractor's management systems are critical for efficient and successful contract performance. A theoretical evaluation of these systems may provide the government with a high confidence level that the contractor will perform the contract on time; at the agreed price; and in compliance with contract specifications, requirements, and other terms and conditions of the contract. Any weaknesses detected in the systems are identified, and contractors are requested to take corrective actions to enhance the probability of successful contract performance.

The factors that determine which contractors will receive one of these comprehensive reviews include the dollar volume of the contractor's defense work, the criticality of the contractor's product, feedback from using organizations, and prevalence or repetitiveness of problems affecting contract performance.

Quality Assurance Reviews

Government agencies must ensure that contracts include appropriate inspection and other quality requirements. The extent of these requirements will vary, depending on the steps considered necessary to protect the government's interest. Contractors are responsible for controlling the quality of the product or service they sell. The government, however, takes an active role in assuring that products and services offered conform to contract requirements. It does this primarily through surveillance of contractor's quality control systems and programs. The quality assurance representative (QAR) is responsible for the government's quality assurance functions at each contractor location. The QAR plans and conducts reviews of contractor quality assurance systems. The extent of this surveillance is based on the classification of the item or service being acquired.

Generally, there are four levels of contract quality control.

1. *Government reliance on existing quality assurance systems.* This least restrictive level of contract quality control applies to the acquisition of commercial items.

2. *Government reliance and inspection by contractor.* This level of contract quality control provides for the contractor to do all the testing and inspection needed to ensure that supplies and services conform to contract requirements. This level is used for small purchases in which the potential loss from defects is low and the cost of government inspection exceeds the expected benefit.

3. *Standard inspection requirements.* In most procurements, contractors are required to provide and maintain an inspection system that is acceptable to the government and to maintain complete inspection records. The implementing clauses give the government the right to make its own inspections and to review inspection records. The contractor's inspection system is subject to periodic review by the government to determine its acceptability.

4. *Higher-level contract quality requirements.* Contracts for complex or critical items contain clauses requiring contractors to develop and maintain sophisticated quality assurance programs. These systems are subject to frequent review and evaluation by government personnel. The government solicitation notice will include the appropriate quality requirements.

Quality assurance reviews performed by the government will include an evaluation of the contractor's documented quality program/inspection system to ensure that it satisfies all required contract technical and quality requirements. The reviewer will evaluate the contractor's implementation of the written procedures. Independent inspection of product samples from selected areas is also performed to evaluate the effectiveness of the contractor's product inspection system of the process controls instituted to control the quality of product and services.

A comprehensive quality assurance review includes an evaluation of a contractor's system for the following:

- Handling and inspection of government-furnished material
- Final inspection and test of completed products
- Corrective action (prompt detection and correction of conditions adverse to quality)
- Cost of quality (maintaining cost data identifying cost of prevention and correction)
- Controlling drawings, documentation, and changes
- Providing for government inspection at subcontractor facilities

- Handling, storage, inspection, and delivery of products to protect the quality during storage, preservation, packing, and shipping
- Identification of the status of items inspected at various stages
- Receiving and inspection of purchased materials and supplies
- Calibration and maintenance of measuring and test equipment
- Handling nonconforming material
- Calibration and maintenance of production tooling
- Production processing and fabrication
- Incorporating quality requirements in purchasing documents
- Maintaining accuracy of documents (e.g., receiving inspections, in processing inspection)
- Maintaining statistical quality control analysis
- Maintaining effective quality work instructions

The DCAA *Contract Audit Manual*, Section 7-1909.1b.(2), advises auditors to be alert to violations of the government quality requirements. In those circumstances, auditors are directed to (1) comment in forward pricing audit reports that award should not be made until the deficiencies are corrected. Further, the auditors are directed to recommend advance agreements for limiting government liability for the costs of correcting quality control system deficiencies and to (2) recommend the use of advance agreements to limit government liability when quality deficiencies are noted on existing contracts.

Contractor Purchasing System Reviews

The FAR, Subpart 44.3, specifies that contractors expecting negotiated government sales in excess of $25 million are required to have a contractor purchasing system review. Such reviews are conducted at least every three years and may be required at levels below the $25 million threshold if considered necessary by the contracting agency.

The purchasing system review team includes several specialists, as considered necessary in the circumstances, assisted by an auditor. The team completely evaluates a company's purchasing system, and including a review of the following:

- The degree of price competition
- Subcontractor compliance with the Truth in Negotiations Act
- Policies and procedures for use of affiliates and related parties
- Policies and procedures pertaining to mandated socioeconomic programs
- Planning, award, and postaward management of major subcontract programs
- Compliance with CAS in awarding subcontracts
- Selection of appropriate subcontract types
- Management control systems, such as internal audit procedures to administer progress payments to subcontractors

The review team's objective is to determine whether the purchasing system is effective and efficient in the expenditure of government funds and complies with public laws and contract requirements. The review includes (1) an examination of the written policies and procedures, (2) evaluation of actual operating practices and methods through review of subcontract purchase order files, and (3) thorough discussions with the contractor's personnel. The key areas for review are the following:

- The existence and implementation of written purchasing policies and procedures
- The organizational independence of the purchasing department from other departments and the separation of the buying and receiving functions
- Numerical control and accounting for purchase requisitions and orders to avoid unauthorized purchases
- Consistent trends reflecting the negotiation of lower subcontract prices after award of the prime contract
- Adequacy of the competitive bid process and adherence to the FAR and contractual terms
- Independence of the receiving function from purchasing, accounting, and shipping
- Adequacy of the receiving report to identify the quantity and quality of materials and the acceptability of the items received
- Central control, inspection, and prompt distribution of incoming materials to storage or production
- Separate control and accountability of contractor-owned and government-owned materials
- Documentation control over the distribution of materials to stores and production areas
- Controls to prevent theft and diversion of materials, including special safeguards for high-value materials susceptible to personal use or sale
- Identification of stock levels and slow-moving materials
- Controls over materials returned to stock, noting appropriate credits and scrap material relative to disposition and credits

The ACO is officially designated to make final decisions on the review team's recommendations. If the review identifies major weaknesses, the ACO will notify the contractor and request corrective action. Failure to take corrective action could result in a disapproved system, which would increase government surveillance and could result in partial suspensions of progress payments and cost disallowances.

Government Property Audits

Government contractors are generally required to provide all property and equipment necessary to perform government contracts. It is common, however, for companies to possess government property—either provided by the government or acquired under the contract. Government agencies must ensure that companies having government property:

- Do not obtain a competitive advantage from having the property
- Use the property to the maximum extent in performing government contracts
- Allow its use only when authorized

- Pay rentals when its use is authorized on other than a rent-free basis
- Maintain adequate records on the property
- Provide justification for retaining government property when it is not in use
- Ensure maximum reutilization of the inventory within the government

Generally, negotiated government contracts do not hold contractors liable for loss of, or damage to, government property, provided contractor property control systems are adequate. These systems are audited by the government for compliance with the specific contract property clauses. Failure to maintain adequate systems could result in a disapproved system, which would make the contractor liable for loss or damage to the property. In these circumstances, the contractually determined presumption of contractor liability can be overcome only by proving with clear and substantiating evidence that the contractor was not at fault.

Property reviews performed by the government generally will address the following questions:

- Does the contractor currently have a satisfactory control system?
- Are items contractually authorized, and is consent or approval by internal and government sources obtained prior to acquisition?
- Is government property inspected, accurately documented on receiving reports, properly classified, and physically identified during the recovery process?
- Do property accounting records conform to FAR requirements, and are they accurate?
- Is government property properly segregated and adequately protected?
- Are quantities of government property reasonably consumed?
- Is government property utilized for the purpose intended?
- Is government property subject to scheduled and/or periodic maintenance?
- Does the contractor perform physical inventories as scheduled?
- Is there adequate backup documentation to support the inventory results posted to the property accounting records?
- Are inventory results properly submitted to the government property administrator?
- Does the contractor's property control system provide for control of government property in the possession of subcontractors or vendors?
- Does the contractor provide timely disclosure, reporting, and disposal of excess and/or residual government property through proper channels?
- Does the contractor prepare and submit required reports in a timely manner?
- Does the contractor report loss, damage, or destruction of government property to contractor property management and appropriate government representatives?
- Does the contractor have current written policies and procedures for controlling each classification of government property in their possession, and are these procedures available to all responsible contractor personnel?
- Does the contractor have a property administrator and/or adequate staff to properly control government property?

16-6. MANAGING THE AUDIT/REVIEW PROCESS

Audit Liaison

Obviously, companies that must undergo government audits want to minimize both the time required to conduct the audits and any negative financial impacts. To achieve these ends, companies should make a concerted effort to demonstrate a spirit of cooperation and a genuine desire to assist in the audit process. Such an effort should help to establish a working relationship with the auditors that minimizes conflicts, keeps the communication channels open, and provides a basis for resolving differences of opinion.

However, in today's complex federal procurement environment, a company must act prudently to protect its own interest during an audit. In recent years, more companies have developed policies and procedures to address the working relationships with government oversight personnel, such as government technical specialists and auditors, particularly with regard to responding to requests for information. Because the release of information that may be inappropriate, preliminary, or requested by inappropriate personnel, presents a risk to a company, a procedure should address the process for providing such information. Consistent application of the procedure can improve working relationships and can surface problems to the appropriate management level for prompt resolution. The key elements of the procedures should include the following:

- Overall guidance on responding to requests for information
- Designation of a liaison person or persons to handle all requests for information from the government
- A definition of what types of information are considered routine and what types are considered sensitive
- The form the government request should take (i.e., written or verbal)
- The company's position on release of routine information
- The company's position on release of sensitive information (e.g., who in the government should request the information and to whom it should be released)
- The company representative who will make the decision on releasing the sensitive information
- The company's position on access to computer databases
- The company representative who will decide on special requests for creation of data
- The company representatives who should provide verbal information to the government (e.g., department heads only, or only in the presence of a liaison person)
- Resolution of disagreements on whether the request for information is appropriate

A company should consider designating a key staff representative as the liaison with contract auditors. This person should:

- Be knowledgeable of the contract audit process, federal acquisition regulations, cost accounting standards, and contractual terms
- Possess a high degree of interpersonal skills

- Be knowledgeable of the accounting records and the internal control system
- Be familiar with the work performed under the contracts

Based on the auditor's entrance conference (discussed in the next section), the designated liaison should try to anticipate the purpose and scope of the audit and gather the books, records, and documents that, in the company's judgment, comprise all the support required to accomplish the audit objective. The contractor should advise the auditor to request any further information required for the audit from the designated liaison. It is important that responses to the auditor, even when negative, be reasonably prompt. The liaison should be responsible for making both requested data and personnel available to the auditor if management agrees that the request is appropriate. The liaison also should accompany the auditor whenever the auditor obtains oral information from other company personnel.

Data requested by the auditor, which are considered proprietary, require special effort to develop, or appear to be extraneous to the audit scope and objective should be identified as early as possible. If the right of government access is not reasonably clear, the auditor should be required to establish that the requested information is relevant to the audit scope and objectives.

Additionally, as the audit progresses, discussions between the auditor and the company's designated liaison should be encouraged. Discussing issues as they arise will help to ensure an appropriate understanding of the facts involved before the auditor makes any decision on audit recommendations.

Audit Conferences

Conferences regarding government audit activities should be conducted to protect both the contractor's and the government's interests. The contractor relies on the audit conference to monitor the government auditor's activities, and the government auditor uses the conferences to expedite the audit, enlist contractor support in obtaining the necessary records, and verify that conclusions are based on a proper understanding of all important facts.

Contractors should document discussions at both entrance and exit conferences to help resolve any issues that develop after the audit report. For example, the documentation could be used to support the contractor's position that certain cost or pricing data or other supporting data were provided to the auditor on a timely basis. Such documentation could then be used in a defense against an allegation of defective pricing.

Entrance Conferences

The DCAA's general policy, as outlined in the *Contract Audit Manual*, Section 4-302, requires the auditor to conduct an entrance conference with contractor personnel at the start of each audit. The objective of an entrance conference is to inform the contractor of the following:

- Purpose of the audit
- Audit plan and scope of audit
- Authority for the audit
- Types of contractor records required to perform the audit
- Duration of the audit

Contractors should insist on such conferences and should be satisfied that the authority for the audit is valid. The conference should also identify what the company can do to assist the auditor in the review.

Contractors should make every effort to understand the nature and extent of audit work to be performed, the types of records required to complete the audit, and how the audit results will be used. This understanding will generally enable the contractor to monitor the audit progress and to ensure that the auditor clearly comprehends the relevant data and systems associated with the audit issues. Ideally, the contractor should sufficiently understand the audit to ensure the following:

- Pertinent data can be assembled for audit review

- Points of contact with company officials or employees can be arranged on a timely basis to provide pertinent information

- Contractor records and systems can be discussed or explained to avoid misunderstandings or incorrect conclusions by the auditor

Exit Conferences

According to the *Contract Audit Manual*, Section 4-304, auditors are required to conduct exit conferences at the completion of each audit assignment. The objectives of the exit conference vary depending on the type of audit performed. With regard to price proposal audits, the auditor will not disclose the audit conclusions and recommendations on projected costs or rates that are to be negotiated by the CO unless specifically requested by the CO. However, the auditors are required to disclose factual matters observed during the audit, such as mistakes, system deficiencies, and failure to use specific historical data. The auditor is also required to advise the contractor of any costs to be reported as unsupported. Detailed discussions on these matters should provide insight into the basis for the auditor's findings. Contractors should take steps to ensure that auditors comply with this requirement. Generally, the auditor should fully discuss the results of defective pricing audits, incurred cost audits, system reviews, and most other audits in an attempt to rectify any problems, misunderstandings, or deficiencies. In addition, the auditor should discuss findings related to cost allowability/allocability that surface during incurred cost audits in an attempt to obtain the contractor's position on the findings before issuing the report.

The *Contract Audit Manual* requires the auditor to discuss any factual indication that cost or pricing data may have been defective and to offer the contractor an opportunity to review the findings and furnish any additional information for the auditor's consideration. The *Manual* also provides that a draft copy of the report exhibit(s) and accompanying footnotes may be provided to the contractor. Final determination as to the existence and the amount of defective pricing is the responsibility of the CO. In view of the serious financial consequences that can result from allegations of defective pricing, contractors should take special care to ensure that they are furnished the results of the review prior to the issuance of the audit report. Requests should be made for draft copies of the report, including exhibits and footnotes if they are not provided by the auditor at the exit conference.

16-7. AUDIT REPORTS

Government audit reports may have a significant impact on a contractor's ability to obtain new government business or to earn a reasonable profit on work performed or anticipated. Therefore, contractors should make every effort to minimize the potential negative effects of the audit report before it is released and should determine, to the extent practical, the basis for recommendations or findings contained in the report.

Auditors are generally not authorized to distribute copies of reports to the contractor; in most instances, contractors must obtain such copies from the cognizant CO. The CO normally releases reports relating to incurred cost, systems, compliance, and functional/operations audits. Release of these reports is generally in the government's best interest since it prompts resolution of the issues. However, as a general rule, contractors should not expect release of audit reports concerning projected costs or rates subject to future negotiation with the CO or allegations of unlawful activity. However, working closely with the auditor may reveal vital information that enables the contractor to prepare for and deal with the issues contained in the report.

The issuance of an adverse audit report will have various effects on the contractor. An adverse proposal report may affect a contractor's ability to negotiate a reasonable price, whereas a CAS noncompliance report or the withdrawal of a system approval may complicate the process of negotiating new business.

Given the variety of subjects reported on by government auditors and contract administration personnel, and the potential effects the reports may have, it is not practical to address each possibility in this book. However, a contractor should determine the potential effects of each government report pertaining to its operations. Discussing the nature of the report to be issued and the report's potential impact with the government representative should give a contractor some idea of what the future holds.

It is also extremely important that contractors promptly respond to audit report allegations, especially where they deal with system deficiencies, defective pricing, or cost-recovery issues. Failure to respond on a timely basis may lead to adverse actions being taken by the ACO or Procurement Contracting Officer (PCO) which can have serious financial consequences.

16-8. SUMMARY

Contract audits extend to virtually every stage of the procurement process. The scope of these audits is governed by specific provisions incorporated into solicitation documents, proposal forms, and resulting contracts.

Given the critical role of contract audits in the award, performance, and settlement of contracts, companies should carefully monitor the progress of such audits. The establishment of an audit liaison function and full utilization of entrance, interim and exit conferences are key elements in enhancing the contractor's position during contract audits.

16-9. NOTES

1. Grumman Aircraft Engineering Corp., ASBCA No. 10309, Sept. 15, 1966, 66-2 BCA 5,846.
2. SCM Corp. v. United States, Ct. Cl. 1981, No. 6-76, March 11, 1981, 645 F.2d 893.

3. U.S. v. Westinghouse Electric Corp., Misc. No. 11710, DC WD PA 1985, Aug. 14, 1985, 615 F. Supp. 1163, aff'd. CA-3 No. 85-3456, April 14, 1986, 778 F.2d 164.

4. Ibid.

5. Newport News Shipbuilding and Dry Dock Co. v. William H. Reed, Nos. Misc. 86-182NN and 86-5NN, DC Eva, March 20, 1987, 655F. Supp. 1408; aff'd. CA 4 No. 87-3832, Jan. 19, 1988.

6. Newport News Shipbuilding and Dry Dock Co. v. William H. Reed, No. Misc. 87-29NN, DC Eva, Dec. 21, 1987, 34CCF 75,460; rev'd. CA 4 No. 88-3520, Dec. 5, 1988, 862 F.2d 464.

7. Newport News Shipbuilding and Dry Dock Co. v. William H. Reed, No. Misc. 87-29NN, DC Eva, July 24, 1989, 737 F. Supp. 897; aff'd. CA 4 No. 89-1516, April 2, 1990, 900 F.2d 257.

8. Martin Marietta Corp., ASBCA Nos. 31248, 31255, and 31271, May 7, 1987, 87-2 BCA 19,875.

9. Available, by subscription, from the Superintendent of Documents, Government Printing Office, Defense Contract Audit Manual, 76401.1, P. O. Box 371954, Pittsburgh, PA 15250-7954.

10. Elmer B. Staats, Comptroller General of the United States et al. v. Bristol Laboratories, Division of Bristol-Myers Co., S. Ct. 1981, No. 80-264, April 29, 1981, 451 U.S. 400; 101 S. Ct. 2037; and Charles A. Bowsher, Comptroller General of the United States et al. v. Merck & Co., Inc.; Merck & Co., Inc. v. Charles A. Bowsher, Comptroller General of the United States, and the United States, S. Ct. 1983, Nos. 81-1273 and 81-1472, April 19, 1983, 460 U.S. 824; 103 S. Ct. 1587.

11. Truth in Negotiations Act.

12. Baker School Specialty Co., Inc., GSBCA No. 13101, Aug. 7, 1995, 95-2 BCA 27,866.

Appendix 16.1 DCAA Contract Audit Manual (DCAAM 7640.1)

Appendix 16.1 (Continued)

Appendix 16.1 (Continued)

Appendix 16.1 (Continued)

Assign No. _____
Report Date _____

DEFENSE CONTRACT AUDIT AGENCY
INTERNAL CONTROL AUDIT PLANNING SUMMARY
FOR THE _____ SYSTEM OF

_____

(Contract Name)

I. **MATERIAL AND SENSITIVITY**
  1. Materiality (For CFY Ending: _____)

	System	Contractor
Total Dollars	_____	_____
Gov't Flexibly Priced Dollars	_____	_____
Gov't Fixed Priced Dollars	_____	_____

  2. Sensitivity

  _____

  _____

II. **CONTRACT RISK ASSESSMENT**

	Control Risk			Reference to
	(System: Adequate/Inadequate)			Support Assessment
Control Objectives	Low	Mod	High	Report No./Date
1.				
2.				
3.				

Include working paper references or explanation to support all risk assessments. Briefly explain the reported system deficiencies which support all moderate or high control risk assessments (use continuation sheets as needed): _____

_____

III. **OVERALL SYSTEM**

Adequate _____	Inadequate:	Overall _____
		In Part _____

IV. **IMPACT ON THE SCOPE OF OTHER AUDITS**

	Required Substantive Testing			Describe General Scope of Required Substantive Testing (use continuation
Audit Areas	Min-imum	Increased	N/A	sheets as needed)
Contract Pricing				
Defective Pricing				
Incurred Material Costs				
Incurred Labor Costs				
Incurred Indirect/ODC Costs				
Contract Reporting				
Billings				
Closeouts				
Other _____				

Initials/Date:
  Auditor : _____
  Supervisor : _____
  FAO Manager : _____

Appendix 16.2 Pro-Forma ICAPS

Number and Title	Objectives	Purpose
1. Update Internal Control Survey	Prepare/update internal control audit planning summary and evaluate changes in contractor's internal controls.	Determining the extent of reliance that can be placed on the internal controls for contract costs and the need for and extent of substantive testing that may be required based on the observed strengths or weaknesses of contractor systems.
2. Contract Cost Analysis and Reconciliation to Books	Review summaries of the contractor's total annual contract costs by major cost element (material, subcontracts, intracompany charges and credits, etc.) and verify that the auditable contract costs reconcile to contractor accounting records by cost element (typically using work-in-process or other contract control accounts in the general ledger).	To provide an overview and order-of-magnitude frame of reference for direction of audit effort and other audit planning/performance considerations, and to verify that the auditable costs claimed or to be claimed on government contracts tie in to the amounts produced by the accounting system in the contractor's official books and records.
3. Permanent Files	Maintain/update permanent files for new or changed contractor organizations, operations, policies, procedures, internal controls, and accounting methods that influence the nature, level, and accounting treatment of costs being charged or to be charged to government contracts.	To provide an efficient and effective repository of current audit information. Permanent file maintenance should help identify the need for further audit reviews and analysis and help in determining the accounting methods that influence the nature, level, and extent of further testing required in specific cost accounts, functions, operations, and departments.
4. Tax Returns and Financial Statements	Review applicable tax returns and financial statements of the contractor.	To highlight possible areas requiring further attention and/or to reduce the extent of DCAA audit effort that might otherwise be required.
5. General Ledger, Trial Balance, Income and/or Credit Adjustments	Review the contractor's general ledger, trial balance, and other income/accounting adjustments (for example, unusual and/or sensitive journal entries).	To help identify any income and credits which the government may be entitled to obtain or share, and to evaluate the exclusion of any adjustments not reflected by the contractor in government contract costs.
6. Labor Floor Checks or Interviews	Perform floor checks, interviews, and/or other physical observations and related analyses of employee timekeeping.	To test the reliability of employee time records, that employees are actually at work, that they are performing in assigned job classifications, and that time is charged to the proper cost objective.
7. Changes in Direct/Indirect Charging	Review changes in procedures and practices for direct/indirect time charging of contractor employees for consistency with generally accepted accounting principles, the applicable cost principles per contracts, and any applicable Cost Accounting Standards requirements.	To verify that changes in direct/indirect charging practices charges do not have the effect of improperly shifting costs among cost objectives or circumventing cost targets or ceilings of certain contracts or other significant cost categories.
8. Comparative Analysis-Sensitive Labor Accounts	Perform comparative analysis of sensitive labor accounts.	To identify for further review any sensitive labor charges (for example, indirect charging by direct labor employees) that vary significantly from the prior period and/or budgetary estimates.
9. Payroll/Labor Distribution Reconciliation and Tracing	Review the contractor's labor cost distribution.	To test the overall integrity of labor cost records at the general ledger and cost ledger levels and to reconcile payroll accruals and disbursements, making sure that distribution entries trace to and from the cost accumulation records.
10. Labor Adjusting Entries and Exception Reports	Review adjusting journal entries and exception reports for labor costs.	To identify adjustments and/or exceptions that require further audit analysis and explanation.
11. Purchases Adjusting Entries and Exception Reports	Review adjusting journal entries and exception reports for costs of purchased services and material (including subcontract costs and intracompany charges).	To identify adjustments and/or exceptions that require further audit analysis and explanation.

Appendix 16.3   Schedule of Mandatory Annual Audit Requirements (MAARs), DCAA Control Audit Manual, Section 6-151 Supplement

Number and Title	Objectives	Purpose
12. Auditable Subcontracts/Assist Audits	Review auditable type subcontracts and intracompany orders issued by the contractor under auditable type government contracts and subcontracts, and arrange for any independent assist audits required.	To protect the government's interests concerning the ensuing costs.
13. Purchases Existence and Consumption	Make physical observations and/or inquiries in addition to documentation verification of contract charges for purchased materials and services.	To test that materials were in fact received (exist or were consumed) and that services were in fact performed.
14. Pools/Bases Reconciliation Books	Trace claimed pools and bases to accounting records.	To determine that the claimed indirect cost pools and allocation bases under government contracts reconcile to amounts in the contractor's official books and records.
15. Indirect Cost Comparison with Prior Years and Budgets	Review selected indirect cost accounts or transactions such as sensitive accounts, new accounts, accounts with large variances, etc.	To identify changes in cost accounting practices, reclassifications of costs, and areas with substantial increases or decreases in cost incurrence that require further audit analysis and/or explanation.
16. Indirect Account Analysis	Review selected indirect cost accounts or transactions such as sensitive accounts, new accounts, accounts with large variances, etc.	To obtain sufficient evidence to support an opinion on the allowability, allocability, and reasonableness of the costs.
17. IR&D/B&P Computations	Review the contractor's independent research and development and bid and proposal costs	To verify for proper classification and compliance with the terms of government contracts and any related agreements.
18. Indirect Allocation Bases	Review the contractor's indirect cost allocation bases for consistency with generally accepted accounting principles, the applicable cost principles per contracts, and any applicable Cost Accounting Standards requirements.	To assure that allocation bases are equitable for allocation of indirect costs to intermediate and final cost objectives.
19. Indirect Rate Computations	Review the accuracy of the contractor's rate computations for distributing interim and final indirect costs to intermediate and final cost objectives.	To confirm that contractor's rate computation are accurate for distributing indirect costs to government contracts.
20. Indirect Adjusting Entries	Review adjusting journal entries for indirect costs.	To identify adjustments that require further audit analysis and/or explanation.

Appendix 16.3 (Continued)

Description	Not Disclosed	Overstated/ Misstated	Inaccurate Data
All Elements			
1. An internal management report which contained significantly lower cost projections than costs proposed	x		
2. Fee and/or profit not properly stated		x	
3. Change in place of performance which affected proposed costs	x		
4. Cost impact of organization/accounting treatment change	x		
5. Mathematical errors			x
6. Reduction in specifications	x		
7. Error in computation of units produced in determining unit price		x	
Direct Labor			
1. Experienced labor costs	x		
2. Experienced labor hours	x		
3. Change in make or buy decision	x		
4. Change in manufacturing process	x		
5. Improvement curve application used to propose direct labor hours			x
6. Employee turnover and its historical effect on labor	x		
7. Manpower requirements		x	
8. Wrong department rates		x	
9. Elimination of supplementary assembly lines	x		
10. Preproduction development units were manufactured by slow and laborious manual methods used as basis for proposal		x	
11. Impact of new machinery on labor hours and on production-line methods	x		
Direct Material			
1. Purchase orders or quotation	x		
2. Experience direct material	x		
3. Material requirements		x	
4. Change in make or buy decision	x		
5. Data supporting material price contingency factor	x		
6. A proposed part was not acquired; proposal was in error or there was knowledge that part wouldn't be used		x	
7. Price breaks resulting from quantity purchases	x		
Other Direct Costs			
1. Experienced subcontract cost or pricing data	x		
2. Proposed costs recovered under prior government contract		x	
3. Agreement with another lessor or computer equipment	x		
4. Current tooling/testing	x		
5. Current computer data	x		
6. Introduction of special tooling/equipment	x		
Indirect Expenses			
1. Latest overhead rate	x		
2. Indirect material costs proposed as direct material costs		x	
3. Current G&A forecast	x		
4. Fringe benefit rate			x
5. Introduction of more effective material issuing and handling procedures	x		
6. Decrease in overhead expense	x		
7. Increase in labor base	x		

Appendix 16.4   Examples of Defective Pricing Indicators by Cost Element

SUSPECTED IRREGULARITY REFERRAL FORM

Name of DCAA Employee Submitting Referral (Print)	FAO Manager's Approval
	Name *(Print)*
Employee Location	Signature
	Date
	FAO's Name
	RORG Code
Phone No.	Phone No.

Instructions

Auditor - Information which suggests a reasonable basis for suspicion of fraud, corruption, or unlawful activity affecting Government contracts must be reported promptly. DCAA employees are encouraged to use this form.

This form is designed to identify the type of information typically needed by an investigator. Although you may not be able to supply all the information, be as thorough as possible in order to assist the investigator in understanding the possible irregularity.

You are required to discuss your suspicions and your written submission with your supervisor to assure that adequate information has been developed.

Supervisor/FAO Manager - Process the form in accordance with DCAA Instruction 7460.16. If there is any question as to whether or not this referral should be made, discuss it with the investigative office or your regional audit manager. The FAO manager should sign and date the form before forwarding it to Headquarters, DCAA (OAL), or making other required distributions. The FAO manager's signature indicates that the information contained in the Form 2000-0 is complete and accurate and that (s)he believes the facts presented raise a reasonable

Classification of Irregularity

To assist in the evaluation of the material presented, please check each type of irregularity you have reason to believe may have occurred. Check all that apply. Check the primary irregularity. For example, mischarging unallowable advertising costs into a supplies account in a certified overhead proposal would be described by checking 5c, identifying it as a false incurred cost certification, and checking 4a (FAR unallowables).

1. Defective Pricing
   ___ a. Pattern of Activity
   ___ b. Other: _____
2. Billing Irregularities
   ___ a. Progress Payments
   ___ b. Public Vouchers
   ___ c. Other : _____
3. Labor Irregularities
   ___ a. Timekeeping Irregularities
   ___ b. IR&D/B&P Mischarging
   ___ c. Other Mischarging: _____
4. Accounting Mischarging
   ___ a. FAR 31/CAS 405 Violations
   ___ b. Improper Transfer
   ___ c. Unallocable Costs
   ___ d. Other: _____
5. False Claims and Certifications
   ___ a. Equitable Adjustment Claims
   ___ b. Termination Settlements
   ___ c. Indirect Cost Certification
   ___ d. Other: _____

6. Consultants & Subcontractors
   ___ a. Consultant Irregularities
   ___ b. Subcontracting Irregularities
7. Materials
   ___ a. Product Substitution
   ___ b. MMAS
   ___ c. Other: _____
8. Ethical Violations
   ___ a. Kickbacks
   ___ b. Gratuities
   ___ c. Political Contributions
   ___ d. Foreign Corrupt Practices Act
   ___ e. Bribery
   ___ f. Restraints of Trade
   ___ g. Other: _____
9. Other irregular Activity
   ___ a. Conspiracy
   ___ b. Obstruction of an Audit
       (but see CAM 4-708)
   ___ c. Other: _____

NOTE: Certain types of irregularity should not be reported on the Form 2000.0. These include: matters already known to the Government such as suspected irregularities referred to DCAA for audit evaluation by another Government agency (e.g Hotline referrals); contractor voluntary disclosures (CAM 4-707); qui tam complaints (CAM 4-709); unsatisfactory conditions (CAM 4-800), especially 4-803, : "Serious Weaknesses on the Part of Contractor or Government Personnel;" and violations of DoD Standards of Conducts by DCAA employees (DCAAR 5500.2). Additionally, nothing contained on this form should be interpreted as requiring the referral of routine audit findings or disagreements with contractors or contracting officers for investigation.

DCAA FORM 2000.0 (EF)   Supersedes DCAAF 2000.0 dated September 1991   Page 1 of 4
April 1996

Appendix 16.5   DCAA Form 2000.0 (EF), Suspected Irregularity Referral Form

PART I - Contractor, Contracts, and Program Involved

a. Name of Contractor _____

Division _____

City, State, Zip _____

Location of Incident _____

b. Contracts Affected. Is contractor 8(a) business? Y ___ , N ___ . If specific contracts can be identified, please provide the information below on the largest of these:

Contract Number	Contract Type	Amount
_____	_____	_____
_____	_____	_____
_____	_____	_____
_____	_____	_____

If only general categories of contracts can be identified, provide whatever information is available on their type and value below:

c. Is there a pending contract modification, adjustment, claim resolution or agreement that relates in any way to the suspected irregularity?
Explain:

d. Name of affected major acquisition program, if any.

e. Organization and location which administers the (sub)contract(s).

f. Organization and location which awarded the (sub)contract(s).

PART II - Suspected Irregularity

Answer the following questions as fully as possible. Additional sheets of paper may be used to answer any of the questions if necessary.

a. Description of Irregularity-Provide a thorough description of the suspected irregularity or irregularities identified in the checklist on page 2, including reference, when known, to any regulatory provision(s) you believe may have been violated. Attach copies of any documents you believe are necessary to assist in understanding the irregular activity and why it is suspected. If documents are attached, be sure that they are referenced in your description.

b. What information suggests that the suspected irregularity was not accidental or inadvertent?

c. Identify the means by which the irregularity was accomplished (e.g., altered or falsified time cards, bogus invoices, deceit by suppression of the thruth, theft).

d. How was the irregularity identified (tip; overheard conversation, inference from audit evidence (describe), etc.)

e. Provide a full description of the books and records which are pertinent to the irregularity along with the contractor's nomenclature for these books and records.

f. Name, position, and location of individuals who provided information or who may have relevant information.

g. Estimate the loss or impact to known Government contracts with this contractor. If loss or impact can only be measured on one contract, then estimate that amount.

h. Describe the extent of the questionable practices, including the time span involved and whether it is an isolated incident or a pattern.

i. Position and name of person(s) involved.

j. Indicators of involvement of upper management.

k. If irregularity Category 9b (Obstruction of an Audit) was checked, briefly describe the difficulties experienced.

Appendix 16.5 (Continued)

PART III- Related Audit Activity

    a. Type of audit being performed when suspected irregularly was detected. (Also provide the audit assignment number.)

    b. Is continued audit effort planned for this audit assignment and/or does the FAO plan to extend, expand, or redirect audit effort in

    List the audit assignment number(s) for new audit effort.

    c. Are there any other in-process audits or completed audits related in any way to the suspected irregularity? List the audit assignment
       number(s)

PART IV - Distribution of Form 2000-0

    Please check all organizations to which distribution of this referral is being made.

  X DCAA Headquarters (ATTN: OAL)

____ Defense Criminal Investigation Service (DCIS)

____ Army Criminal Investigative Command (CID)

____ Naval Investigative Service (NIS)

____ Air Force Office of Special Investigations (AFOSI)

____ Administrative Contracting Officer (ACO) [unless advised to the contrary by the investigative organization]

       Identify: _____

____ Procurement Contracting Officer (PCO) [unless advised to the contrary by the investigative organization]

       Identity: _____

____ Other: _____

DCAA FORM 2000.0 (EF)   Supersedes DCAAF 2000.0 dated September 1991   Page 4 of 4
April 1996

Appendix 16.5 (Continued)

List of Acronyms

ABC	Activity Based Costing
ACO	Administrative Contracting Officer
ADPE	Automatic Data Processing Equipment
A–E	Architect–Engineer
AGBCA	Department of Agriculture Board of Contract Appeals
AICPA	American Institute of Certified Public Accountants
APB	Accounting Principles Board
APICS	American Production and Inventory Control Society
ASBCA	Armed Services Board of Contract Appeals
ASPM	Armed Services Procurement Manual for Contract Pricing
ASPR	Armed Services Procurement Regulation
B&P	Bid and Proposal
BAFO	Best and Final Offer
BCA	Board of Contract Appeals
BOM	Bill of Material
C/SCSC	Cost/Schedule Control Systems Criteria
CAFC	Court of Appeals for the Federal Circuit
CAM	Defense Contract Audit Agency Manual
CAS	Cost Accounting Standards
CASB	Cost Accounting Standards Board
CFR	Code of Federal Regulations
CICA	Competition in Contracting Act
Cl.Ct.	Claims Court
CLIN	Contract Line Item Number
CO	Contracting Officer
COFC	Court of Federal Claims
COTS	Commercial-off-the-Shelf
CPAF	Cost-Plus-Award-Fee
CPFF	Cost-Plus-Fixed-Fee
CPIF	Cost-Plus-Incentive-Fee
CPSR	Contractor Purchasing System Review

CRAG	Contractor Risk Assessment Guide
C/SCS	Cost/Schedule Control Systems
Ct. Cl.	Court of Claims
CWAS	Contractor Weighted Average Share in Cost Risk
DAC	Defense Acquisition Circular
DAR	Defense Acquisition Regulation (formerly ASPR)
DC D of C	District Court of the District of Columbia
DCAA	Defense Contract Audit Agency
DCAB	Department of Commerce Board of Contract Appeals
DCIS	Defense Criminal Investigative Service
DCMC	Defense Contract Management Command
DEAR	Department of Energy Acquisition Regulation
DFARS	Department of Defense FAR Supplement
DII	Defense Industry Initiatives
DLA	Defense Logistics Agency
DOD	Department of Defense
DODIG	Department of Defense Inspector General
DOE	Department of Energy
DOT	Department of Transportation
DOTCAB	Department of Transportation Contract Appeals Board
DSMD	Discount Schedule and Marketing Data
DVA	Department of Veterans Affairs
EAC	Estimate-at-Completion
EAJA	Equal Access to Justice Act
EBCA	Department of Energy Board of Contract Appeals
ECP	Engineering Change Proposal
EEO	Equal Employment Opportunity
ENGBCA	Corps of Engineers Board of Contract Appeals
EPA	Economic Price Adjustment
EPA	Environmental Protection Agency
ERISA	Employee Retirement Income Security Act
ESOP	Employee Stock Ownership Plan
ETC	Estimate-to-Complete
EVMS	Earned Value Management Systems
FAC	Federal Acquisition Circular
FAR	Federal Acquisition Regulation
FAS	Financial Accounting Standards
FASB	Financial Accounting Standards Board
FCCOM	Facilities Capital Cost of Money
FFP	Firm-Fixed-Price
FFRDC	Federally Funded Research and Development Center
FLSA	Federal Labor Standards Act
FMS	Foreign Military Sales
FOIA	Freedom of Information Act
FPI	Fixed-Price-Incentive
FPR	Federal Procurement Regulations
FPRA	Forward Pricing Rate Agreement
FSS	Federal Supply Schedule
FTR	Federal Travel Regulations
G&A	General and Administrative
GAAP	Generally Accepted Accounting Principles
GAO	General Accounting Office

GSA	General Services Administration
GSAR	General Services Acquisition Regulation
GSBCA	General Services Board of Contract Appeals
HUDBCA	Department of Housing and Urban Development Board of Contract Appeals
IBCA	Department of Interior Board of Contract Appeals
IFB	Invitation for Bids
IG	Inspector General
IRC	Internal Revenue Code
IRS	Internal Revenue Service
IR&D	Independent Research and Development
IRMS	Information Resources Management Service
JTR	Joint Travel Regulations
LBCA	Department of Labor Board of Contract Appeals
MAAR	Mandatory Annual Audit Requirement
MAS	Multiple Award Schedule
MMAS	Material Management Accounting System
MOA	Memorandum of Agreement
MOU	Memorandum of Understanding
MPS	Master Production Schedule
MRP	Material Requirements Planning
NASA	National Aeronautics and Space Administration
NASA PR	National Aeronautics and Space Administration Procurement Regulation
NASABCA	National Aeronautics and Space Administration Board of Contract Appeals
OEM	Original Equipment Manufacturer
OFPP	Office of Federal Procurement Policy
OMB	Office of Management and Budget
PCO	Procurement (or Procuring) Contracting Officer
PSBCA	Postal Service Board of Contract Appeals
QA	Quality Assurance
R&D	Research and Development
RFP	Request for Proposals
RFQ	Request for Quotations
S. Ct.	Supreme Court
SAR	Stock Appreciation Rights
SBA	Small Business Administration
SF	Standard Form
SIC	Standard Industrial Code
SIC	Suspected Irregular Conduct
TCO	Termination Contracting Officer
T&M	Time and Material
U.S.C.	United States Code
USAID	United States Agency for International Development
VE	Value Engineering
VECP	Value Engineering Change Proposal
WBS	Work Breakdown Structure

Glossary

ARMED SERVICES PROCUREMENT REGULATION: The uniform policies and procedures which governed the procurement of supplies, services, and research and development by the Department of Defense components until July 1978.

ACTUAL COST: An amount determined on the basis of cost incurred as distinguished from forecasted cost. Includes standard cost properly adjusted for applicable variance.

ADVANCE AGREEMENT: An agreement between the contractor and the government regarding the treatment of specified costs negotiated either before or during contract performance, but preferably before the cost covered by the agreement is incurred.

ADVANCE PAYMENT: Remittance by the government to a contractor prior to, in anticipation of, and for the purpose of performance under a contract or contracts.

ALLOCABLE COST: A cost that is assignable or chargeable to one or more cost objectives in accordance with the relative benefits received or other equitable relationship.

ALLOCATION: Assignment of an item of cost, or a group of items of cost, to one or more cost objectives. Includes both direct assignment of cost and the reassignment of a share from an indirect cost pool.

ALLOWABLE COST: A cost which meets the tests of reasonableness; allocability; compliance with standards promulgated by the Cost Accounting Standards Board, if applicable, otherwise generally accepted accounting principles, and practices appropriate in the circumstances; contractual terms; and limitations set forth in the acquisition regulations.

BASIC AGREEMENTS: A basic agreement is a written instrument of understanding, negotiated between an agency or contracting activity and a contractor that (1) contains contract clauses applying to future contracts, and (2) contemplates separate future contracts that will incorporate by reference the applicable clauses agreed upon in the basic agreement. A basic agreement is not a contract.

BASIC ORDERING AGREEMENT: A basic ordering agreement is a written instrument of understanding, negotiated between an agency, contracting activity, or contracting office and a contractor, which contains: (1) terms and clauses applying to future contract (orders); (2) description of supplies or services to be furnished; and (3) methods for pricing, issuing, and delivering future orders under the basic ordering agreement. A basic ordering agreement is not a contract.

BEST VALUE: The expected outcome of an acquisition that, in the government's estimation, provides the greatest overall benefit in response to the requirement.

BID AND PROPOSAL COST: Costs incurred in preparing, submitting, and supporting bids and proposal (solicited or unsolicited) on potential government and nongovernment contracts.

BUSINESS UNIT: Any segment of an organization, or an entire business organization which is not divided into segments.

COMMERCIAL ITEM: An item, including both supplies and services, of a class or kind which is used regularly for other-than-government purposes, and is sold or traded in the course of conducting normal business operations.

COMPENSATED PERSONAL ABSENCE: Any absence from work for reasons such as illness, vacation, holidays, jury duty or military training, or personal activities, for which an employer pays compensation directly to an employee in accordance with a plan or custom of the employer.

COMPETITIVE NEGOTIATION: A negotiated procurement that: is initiated by a request for proposals, which sets out the government's requirements and the criteria for evaluation of offers; contemplates the submission of timely proposals by the maximum number of possible offerors; and concludes with the award of a contract to the one offeror whose offer, price, and other factors considered, is most advantageous to the government.

CONSTRUCTIVE CHANGE: A contract change directed by an authorized representative of the government, other than a formal change order, or a change resulting from government action or inaction.

CONTINGENCY: A possible future event or condition arising from presently known or unknown causes, the cost outcome of which is indeterminable.

CONTRACT: A term used to describe a variety of agreements or orders for the procurement of supplies or services. An agreement, enforceable by law, between two or more competent parties, to do or not do something not prohibited by law, for a legal consideration.

CONTRACT AUDIT: The examination of books, records, documents, and other evidence and accounting procedures and practices pertaining to costs incurred or estimated to be incurred in the performance of one or more contracts. Includes providing advice on accounting and financial matters to assist in the negotiation, award, administration, repricing, and settlement of contracts.

CONTRACT FINANCING: Methods utilized by the government to provide financial assistance to contractors in advance of, or during, contract performance but prior to delivery and acceptance. In order of government preference, these methods are: progress payments (customary), guaranteed loans, progress payments (unusual), and advance payments.

CONTRACTING OFFICER: Any person who, either by virtue of his/her position or by appointment in accordance with prescribed regulations, is vested with the authority to enter into and administer contracts on behalf of the government and make determinations and findings with respect thereto, or with any part of such authority.

CONTRACT MODIFICATION: Any unilateral or bilateral written alteration in the specifications, delivery point, rates or delivery, contract period, price, quantity, or other provision of an existing contract resulting from a change order.

CONTRACT TYPE: Refers to specific pricing arrangements employed for the performance of work under contract. Specific pricing or remunerative arrangements, expressed as contract types, include firm-fixed-price, fixed-price-incentive, cost-plus-fixed-fee, cost-plus-incentive-fee, and several others. Among special arrangements that use fixed-price or cost-reimbursement pricing provisions are contract types called indefinite delivery contracts, basic ordering agreements, letter contracts, and others.

COST ACCOUNTING: A system of accounting and reporting the costs of producing goods or services, or of operating programs, activities, functions, or organizational units. The system may also embrace cost estimating and determining actual and standard costs for the purpose of aiding cost control.

COST ACCOUNTING STANDARDS: Standards promulgated by the Cost Accounting Standards Board under the authority of Public Laws 91-379 or 100-679 and with the objective of achieving uniformity and consistency in the cost accounting practices followed by defense contractors.

COST ANALYSIS: The review and evaluation of cost or pricing data and of the judgmental factors applied in projecting from the data to estimated costs. Includes appropriate verification of cost data, evaluation of specific elements of costs, and projection of these data to determine the effects on price factors like cost necessity, allowances for contingencies, and the basis used for allocation of overhead costs.

COST ESTIMATING: The process of forecasting a future result in terms of cost, based upon information available at the time.

COST INCURRED: A cost identified through the use of the accrual method of accounting and reporting, or otherwise actually paid. Cost of direct labor, direct materials, and direct services identified with, and necessary for, the performance of a contract, and all properly allocated and allowable indirect costs.

COST OBJECTIVE: A function, organizational subdivision, contract, or other work unit for which cost data are desired and for which provision is made to accumulate and measure the cost of processes, products, jobs, capitalized projects, etc.

COST OR PRICING DATA: Facts existing up to the time of agreement on price which prudent buyers and sellers would reasonably expect to have a significant effect on price negotiations.

COST REIMBURSEMENT: A family of pricing arrangements that provide for payment of allowable costs incurred in performing the contract. Under a cost-plus-fixed-fee arrangement, the dollar amount of fee is not subject to adjustment by reason of cost experience during contract performance.

DEFECTIVE COST OR PRICING DATA: Certified cost or pricing data, subsequently found to have been inaccurate, incomplete, or noncurrent as of the effective date of the certificate.

DEFENSE ACQUISITION REGULATION: The uniform policies and procedures which governed the procurement of supplies and services by the Department of Defense components from July 1978 to April 1, 1984.

DEFERRED COMPENSATION: An award made by an employer to compensate an employee in a future cost accounting period or periods for services rendered in one or more cost accounting periods prior to the date of the receipt of compensation by the employee. Does not include year-end accruals for salaries, wages, or bonuses that are to be paid within a reasonable period of time after the end of a cost accounting period.

DEPARTMENT OF DEFENSE FAR SUPPLEMENT: Policies and procedures issued by the Assistant Secretary of Defense for Production and Logistics by direction of the Secretary of Defense and in coordination with the Army, Navy, and Air Force and the director of the Defense Logistics Agency implementing and supplementing the Federal Acquisition Regulation.

DEPARTMENT OF ENERGY ACQUISITION REGULATION: Policies and procedures issued by the Department of Energy that implement and supplement the Federal Acquisition Regulations.

DIRECT COST: Any cost which is identified specifically with a particular final cost objective, but not limited to items which are incorporated in the endproduct as material or labor. Costs identified specifically with a contract are direct costs of that contract.

DISCLOSURE STATEMENT: The document (Form CASB-DS-1 or Form CASB-DS-2) designed to meet the requirements of Public Law 91-379 or Public 100-679 for describing contract cost accounting practices.

EQUITABLE ADJUSTMENT: An adjustment in the contract price and/or delivery schedule to compensate the contractor for changes in the contract.

ESTABLISHED CATALOG PRICE: A price included in a catalog, price list, schedule, or other form that is regularly maintained, published, or made available to customers and states prices at which sales are made to a significant number of buyers constituting the general public.

ESTABLISHED MARKET PRICE: A current price, established in the ordinary course of trade between buyers and sellers free to bargain, which can be independently substantiated.

EXPRESSLY UNALLOWABLE COST: A particular item or type of cost which, under the provisions of an applicable law, regulation, contract, or mutual agreement of the contracting parties, is specifically named and stated to be unallowable.

FACILITIES CAPITAL: The net book value of tangible capital assets and of those intangible capital assets that are subject to amortization.

FEDERAL ACQUISITION REGULATION: The policies and procedures which, effective April 1984, govern the procurement of supplies and services by federal agencies.

FEDERAL PROCUREMENT REGULATIONS: The policies and procedures issued by the General Services Administration under authority of the Federal Property & Administration Services Act which governed the procurement of supplies and services by federal agencies other than the Department of Defense prior to April 1, 1984.

FINAL COST OBJECTIVE: A cost objective which has allocated to it both direct and indirect costs, and, in the contractor's accumulation system, is one of the final accumulation points.

FIXED PRICE: A family of pricing arrangements whose common discipline is a ceiling beyond which the government bears no responsibility for payment in connection with performance under a contract. Under a firm-fixed-price arrangement, the negotiated price is not subject to any adjustment by reason of the contractor's cost experience in the performance of the contract.

FORMAL CHANGE ORDER: A written order signed by the contracting officer, or an authorized representative, directing the contractor to make changes in accordance with the Changes clause of the contract.

FORWARD-PRICING RATE AGREEMENT: A written understanding negotiated between a contractor and the government to make certain rates (e.g., labor, indirect) available for use during a specified period in preparing contract cost estimates or contract modifications.

GENERAL AND ADMINISTRATIVE (G&A) EXPENSE: Any management, financial, and other expense which is incurred by, or allocated to, a business unit and which is for the general management and administration of the business unit as a whole.

GENERAL SERVICES AGENCY ACQUISITION REGULATION: Policies and procedures issued by the General Services Administration that implement and supplement the Federal Acquisition Regulations.

GUARANTEED LOAN: A loan by a lending institution in which the government agrees to purchase a guaranteed portion or to share in a loss if requested by the lending institution.

HOME OFFICE: An office responsible for directing or managing two or more, but not necessarily all, segments of an organization. It typically establishes policy for, and provides guidance to, the segments in their operations; performs management, supervisory, or administrative functions; and may also perform service functions in support of the operations of the various segments. An organization which has intermediate levels, such as groups, may have several home offices which report to a common home office.

INCENTIVE ARRANGEMENT: A negotiated pricing arrangement which rewards a contractor for performance in accordance with contract-specified criteria.

INDEFINITE-DELIVERY CONTRACTS: Types of indefinite-delivery contracts (i.e., definite-quantity, requirements, and indefinite-quantity) for which the exact times and/or quantities of future deliveries are not known at the time of contract award. Such contracts may provide for firm-fixed prices, fixed prices with economic price adjustment, fixed prices with prospective redetermination, or prices based on catalog or market prices.

INDIRECT COST: Any cost not directly identified with (and to be allocated to) two or more cost objectives but not identified specifically with any final cost objective.

INDIRECT COST POOL: A grouping of incurred costs identified with (and to be allocated to) two or more cost objectives but not identified specifically with any final cost objective.

INTANGIBLE CAPITAL ASSET: An asset that has no physical substance, has more than minimal value, and is expected to be held by an enterprise for continued use or possession beyond the current accounting period for the benefits it yields.

INTERNAL CONTROLS: The organizational plan and all the methods and measures coordinated within a business to safeguard its assets, check the accuracy and reliability of accounting data, promote operational efficiency, and encourage adherence to prescribed management policies. Internal controls are subdivided into administrative controls and accounting controls.

INVITATION FOR BIDS: The solicitation document used in sealed bidding.

JOB-ORDER COSTING: A method of cost accounting whereby costs are accumulated for a specific quantity of products, equipment, repairs, or other services that move through the production process as a continuously identifiable unit; applicable material, direct labor, direct expense, and usually a calculated portion of overhead being charged to a job order; distinguished from process costing.

LETTER CONTRACT: A contractual instrument that authorizes the immediate commencement of activity under its terms and conditions, pending definitization of a fixed-price or cost-reimbursement pricing arrangement for the work to be done. Must specify the maximum liability of the government and be superseded by a definite contract within a specified time.

NASA PROCUREMENT REGULATION: The policies and procedures incorporated into the Federal Procurement Regulations Chapter 18 which, prior to April 1, 1984 governed the procurement of supplies and services by the NASA buying activities.

NATIONAL AERONAUTICS AND SPACE ADMINISTRATION FAR SUPPLEMENT: Policies and procedures issued by the National Aeronautics and Space Agency that implement and supplement the Federal Acquisition Regulations.

NEGOTIATING: One of the major methods of procurement, which is employed under certain permissive circumstances prescribed by statute when formal advertising is determined to be infeasible and impractical. In its more general context, a bargaining process between two or more parties, each with its own viewpoints and objectives, seeking to reach a mutually satisfactory agreement on, or settlement of, a matter of common concern.

OPERATING REVENUE: Amounts accrued or charged to customers, clients, and tenants for the sale of products manufactured or purchased for resale, for services, and for rentals or property held primarily for leasing to others. Includes reimbursable costs and fees under cost-type contracts and percentage-of-completion sales accruals, except that it includes only the fee for management contracts under which the contractor acts essentially as an agent of the government in the erection or operation of government-owned facilities. Excludes incidental interest, dividends, royalty and rental income, and proceeds from the sale of assets used in the business.

PENSION PLAN: A deferred compensation plan established and maintained by one or more employers to provide systematically for the payment of benefits to plan participants after their retirement; provided that the benefits are paid for life or are payable for life at the option of the employees.

PREPRODUCTION COSTS: Costs required to initiate production on particular orders.

PRICE ANALYSIS: The process of examining and evaluating a prospective price without evaluation of the separate cost elements and proposed profit.

PRICING: The process of establishing the amount or amounts to be paid in return for goods or services.

PROCESS COSTING: A method of cost accounting in which the costs incurred for a process are assigned to the units (both complete and incomplete) that have been produced or are in process during the cost accounting period.

PRODUCTION UNIT: A grouping of activities which either uses homogeneous inputs of direct material and direct labor or yields homogeneous outputs, such that costs or statistics related to these homogeneous inputs or outputs are appropriate as bases for allocating variances.

PROFIT CENTER: A discrete, organizationally independent segment of a company, which has been charged by management with profit and loss responsibilities.

PROGRESS PAYMENT: A payment made as work progresses under a contract on the basis of percentage of completion accomplished or costs incurred, or for work performed at a particular stage of completion.

PROPOSAL: Any offer or other submission used as a basis for pricing a contract, contract modification, or termination settlement, or for securing payments thereunder.

PROPRIETARY INFORMATION: Information contained in a bid or proposal or otherwise submitted to the government by a competing contractor in response to the conduct of a particular federal agency procurement, or in an unsolicited proposal, which has been marked by the competing contractor as proprietary information in accordance with applicable law and regulation.

PROSPECTIVE PRICING: A pricing decision made in advance of performance, based on analysis of comparative prices, cost estimates, past costs, or combinations of such considerations.

REASONABLE COST: A cost which, in its nature or amount, does not exceed what would be incurred by an ordinarily prudent person in the conduct of competitive business.

REPORTING COSTS: Selection of relevant cost data and its presentation in an intelligible manner for use by the recipient.

REQUEST FOR PROPOSALS: A solicitation document used in negotiated procurements in which the government reserves the right to award a contract based on initial offers received without any written or oral discussion with offerors.

REQUEST FOR QUOTATIONS: A solicitation document used in negotiated procurements which is a request for information. Since the document is not an offer, the government cannot initially accept it without confirmation or discussion with the offerors.

RESIDUAL VALUE: The net proceeds realized upon disposition of a tangible capital asset or the asset's fair value if it is traded in on another asset.

SEALED-BIDDING: One of the major methods of procurement, which employs competitive bids, public opening of bids, and award to the responsible bidder whose bid is most advantageous to the government, price and other factors considered.

SEGMENT: One of two or more divisions, product departments, plants, or other subdivisions of an organization reporting directly to a home office, usually identified with responsibility for profit and/or producing a product or service. The term includes government-owned contractor-operated (GOCO) facilities, and joint ventures and subsidiaries (domestic and foreign) in which the organization has a majority ownership or has less than a majority of ownership but over which it exercises control.

SERVICE CENTER: Departments or other functional units which perform specific technical and/or administrative services for the benefit of other units within a reporting unit.

SERVICE LIFE: The period of usefulness of a tangible capital asset (or group of assets) to its current owner, as expressed in units of time or output. The estimated service life of a tangible capital asset (or group of assets) is a forecast of its service life and is the period over which depreciation cost is to be assigned.

SMALL BUSINESS CONCERN: A concern, including its affiliates, that is independently owned and operated, not dominant in the field of operation in which it is bidding on government contracts, and qualified as a small business under the criteria and size standards in 13 CFR Part 121.

SMALL DISADVANTAGED BUSINESS CONCERN: A small business concern that is at least 51% unconditionally owned by one or more individuals who are both socially and economically disadvantaged, or a publicly owned business that has at least 51% of its stock unconditionally owned by one or more socially and economically disadvantaged individuals and that has its management and daily business controlled by one or more such individuals.

SOURCE SELECTION INFORMATION: Information, including information stored in electronic, magnetic, audio, or video formats, which is prepared or developed for use by the government to conduct a particular procurement, the disclosure of which to a competing contractor would jeopardize the integrity or successful completion of the procurement concerned.

STANDARD COST: Any cost computed with the use of pre-established measures.

TANGIBLE CAPITAL ASSET: An asset that has physical substance, more than minimal value, and is expected to be held by an enterprise for continued use or possession beyond the current accounting period for the services it yields.

TOTAL COST INPUT: The cost, except G&A expenses, which for contract costing purposes is allocable to the production of goods and services during a cost accounting period.

UNALLOWABLE COST: Any cost which, under the provisions of any pertinent law, regulation, or contract, cannot be included in prices, cost reimbursements, or settlements under a government contract.

WOMEN-OWNED SMALL BUSINESS CONCERN: A small business concern which is at least 5% owned by one or more women; or in the case of a publicly owned business, at least 51% of the stock is owned by one or more women.

Table of Cases

Lockheed-Georgia
ASBCA No. 27660
90-3 BCA 22,957

Taxes

Aerospace v. State Board of Equalization
State Board of Equalization No. B 036583
Sup. Ct., Nos. C-416134, C-578611
CA C of A 2d, Div. 7

U.S. v. Benton
DC WDMO, No. 89-0608-CV-W-3
1991 U.S. Dist. Lexis 4707

U.S. v. New Mexico et al.
CA-10 1980 No. 78-1755
624 F.2d 111
102 S. Ct. 1373
455 U.S. 720

Travel Costs

Big Three Industries
ASBCA Nos. 16949 and 17331
74-1 CA 10,483

General Dynamics
ASBCA No. 31359
92-1 BCA No. 24,698

United Technologies
ASBCA No. 25501
87-3 BCA 20,193

Assignment of Claims

Comp. Gen. No. B-159494
Comp. Gen. No. B-150528
Comp. Gen. No. B-194945
Comp. Gen. No. B-195629

Audit/Access to Records

Baker School Specialty
GSBCA No. 13101
95-2 BCA 27,866

Bristol Laboratories, Division of Bristol Myers
(S. Ct. 1981) No. 80-264
451 U.S. 400, 101 S. Ct. 2037

Grumman Aircraft Engineering
ASBCA No. 10309
66-2 BCA 5,846

Martin Marietta
ASBCA Nos. 31248, 31255, 31271
87-2 BCA 19,875

Merck
(S. Ct. 1983) Nos. 81-1273, 81-1472
460 U.S. 824; 103 S. Ct. 1587

Newport News Shipbuilding and Dry Dock v. Reed
Nos. Misc. 86-182-NN, 86-5-NN, DC EVA
655 F. Supp. 1408
CA 4 No. 87-3832

Newport News Shipbuilding and Dry Dock v. Reed
No. Misc. 87-29-NN DC EVA
34CCF 75,460
CA 4 No. 88-3520; CA 4 No. 89-1516
862 F.2d 464; 900 F.2d 257

SCM
Ct. Cl. 1981, No. 6-76
645 F.2d 893

U.S. v. Westinghouse Electric
Misc. 11710, DC WD PA 1985
615 F. Supp. 1163
CA-3 No. 85-3456
788 F.2d 164

Authority of Government Officials

Amis Construction and Consulting Services
LBCA No. 81-BCA-4
82-1 BCA 15,679

DBA Systems
NASABCA No. 481-5
82-1 BCA 15,468

DOT Systems
DOTCAB No. 1208
82-2 BCA 15,817

Federal Crop Insurance Corp. v. Merrill et al.
332 U.S. 380
68 S. Ct. 1

General Electric
ASBCA No. 11990
67-1 BCA 6,377

McDonnell Douglas
ASBCA No. 44637
93-2 BCA 25,700

Thompson Associates, Abbot W.
DOTCAB No. 1098
81-1 BCA 14,879

World Computer Systems
DOTCAB No. 2802
95-1 BCA 27,399

Bid Protests

Best Value Analysis

B3H
CAFC Nos. 95-1042, 95-1043, 95-1044
75 F.3d 1577

CompuAdd
GSBCA Nos. 12021-P, 12028-P, 12041-P, 12042-P
93-2 BCA 25,811

Delta Dental Plan of California
DC N Cal. No. C-95-2462 TEH

Engineering and Professional Services
Comp. Gen. No. B-262179
95-2 CPD P266

Grumman Data Systems
GSBCA No. 11635-P
92-2 BCA 24,999

International Business Machines and Lockheed Missiles & Space
GSBCA Nos. 11359-P-R, 11362-P-R
92-1 BCA 24,438

Litton Systems
GSBCA No. 12911-P
94-3 BCA 27,122

Lockheed Missiles & Space and International Business Machines
GSBCA Nos. 11766-P, 11777-P
93-1 BCA 25,401
CAFC No. 92-1566
4 F.3d 955

Redstone Technical Services and Dynamic Research
Comp. Gen. Nos. B-259222.2, B-259224.2
95-1 CPD P181

Systems Resources
GSBCA No. 12536-P
94-1 BCA 26388

Unisys
GSBCA No. 13129-P
95-2 BCA 27,622
CAFC Nos., 95-1295, 95-1412, 95-1416
98 F.3d 1325

Bid Protest Costs

Sterling Federal Systems v. NASA
GSBCA No. 10000-C (9835-P)
92-3 BCA 25,118; 95-1 BCA 27,575
CAFC No. 92-1552
16 F.3d 1177

West Virginia University Hospitals v. Gay
111 S. Ct. 1138 (1991)

Cost Realism

Bailey Engineering Consultants, Gary
Comp. Gen. No. B-233438
89-1 CPD P263

Combat Systems Development Associates Joint Venture
Comp. Gen. Nos. B-259920.2, B-259920.3, B-259920.4
95-2 CPD P162, 95-2 CPD P163

Martin Marietta, Management and Data Systems
GSBCA No. 13004-P
95-2 BCA 27,674

Purvis Systems
Comp. Gen. Nos. B-245761, B-245761.2
71 Comp. Gen. 203

SRS Technologies
Comp. Gen. No. B-238403
5 CGEN 104,388

District Court Authority

Scanwell Laboratories
CA DC 1970
424 F.2d 859

General Accounting Office Authority

Ameron v. U.S. Army Corps of Engineers
CA 3 Nos. 85-5226, 85-5377
809 F.2d 979

Instruments, S.A. and Fisons Instruments/VG Instruments
DC DC, No. 91-1574
807 F. Supp. 811

General Services Board of Contract Appeals Authority

Best Power Technology Sales
CAFC Nos. 92-118, -1254
984 F.2d 1172

OAO v. Johnson
CAFC Nos. 94-1106
49 F.3d 721

Multiple-Award Schedule Negotiation Policy

Baxter Healthcare
Comp. Gen. No. B-230580.5
5 CGEN 104,333

Defective Pricing

Baseline for Price Adjustment

Cost or Pricing Data

Teton Construction
ASBCA Nos. 27700, 28968
86-2 BCA 18,971

Contracting Officer's Final Decision

Allied Painting & Decorating
ASBCA No. 25099
80-2 BCA 14,710

Robbins, R.G.
ASBCA No. 26521
82-1 BCA 15,643

SCM v. U.S.
Ct. Cl. No. 576-79C
225 Ct. Cl. 647

Westclox Military Products
ASBCA No. 25592
81-2 BCA 15,270

Definition of a Claim

Dawco Construction v. U.S.
CAFC No. 94-1013
49 F.3d 1541

Essex Electro Engineers
CAFC No. 91-5096
960 F.2d 1576

Jonathan
ASBCA No. 47069
95-1 BCA 27,390

Reflectone
ASBCA No. 43081
93-1 BCA 25,512, 93-3 BCA 25,966
CAFC No. 93-1373
34 F.3d 1031; 34 F.3d 1039; 34 F.3d 1572

Roane Construction, James R.
ASBCA Nos. 43603-43608
92-2 BCA No. 24,802

Saco Defense
ASBCA Nos. 44,792, 45,171
93-3 BCA 26,029

Strong Enterprises, Bill
ASBCA No. 42946, 43896
93-3 BCA 25,961
CAFC No. 94-1013
49 F.3d 1541
ASBCA No. 42946
96-2 BCA 28,428

World Computer Systems
DOTCAB No. 2802
95-1 BCA 27,399

Discovery

Airco
IBCA No. 1074-8-75
77-2 BCA 12,809

Interest

Brookfield Construction & Baylor Construction, A Joint Venture
Ct. Cl. 1981
661 F.2d 159

Fidelity Construction
DOTCAB Nos. 1213, 1219
82-1 BCA 15,633
CAFC No. 27-82
700 F.2d 1379

Honeywell
GSBCA No. 5458
81-2 BCA 15,383

Lehman, Paul E.
Ct. Cl. 1982
693 F.2d 352

Shea, J.F. v. U.S.
CAFC No. 84-1166
32 CCF 73,224

Jurisdiction

Arcon/Pacific Contractors
ASBCA No. 25057
80-2 BCA 14,709

Assurance
CAFC No. 86-1350
813 F.2d 1202

Cosmic Construction
CAFC No. 23-82
697 F.2d 1389

Kihlberg v. U.S.
97 U. S. 398 (1878)

Paragon Energy
Ct. Cl. 1981
645 F.2d 966

PAVCO
ASBCA No. 23783
80-1 BCA 14,407

Policy Research
ASBCA No. 26144
82-1 BCA 15,618

S&E Contractors
S. Ct. 1972
31 L.Ed. 2d 658

Tapper & Associates, Monroe M.
Ct. Cl. 1979
611 F.2d 354

Equal Access to Justice

Brookfield Construction & Baylor Construction, A Joint Venture
Ct. Cl. 1981
661 F.2d 159

Fidelity Construction
DOTCAB Nos. 1213, 1219
82-1 BCA 15,633
CAFC 27-82
700 F.2d 1379

Kay Manufacturing v. U.S.
CAFC 478-73, 1983
699 F.2d 1376

Equitable Adjustments

Change in Cost Reporting

Aydin (West)
CAFC No. 94-1441
61 F.3d 1571

Contract Acceleration

Ashton
IBCA No. 1070-6-75
76-2 BCA 11,934

Dynamics Corporation of America, Fermont Division
ASBCA No. 15806
75-1 BCA 11,139

Contract Delay

Idle Labor
Hardeman–Monier–Mutcherson
ASBCA No. 11785
67-1 BCA 6,210

Interest

Automation Fabricators & Engineering
PSBCA No. 2701
90-3 BCA 22,943

Profit

U.S. v. Callahan Walker Construction
317 U. S. 56 (1942)
63 S. Ct. 113

Prospective versus Retroactive Pricing

Cen-Vi-Ro of Texas
Ct. Cl. No. 334-73
210 Ct. Cl. 684

Reasonable Costs

Bruce Construction et al
163 Ct. Cl. 197
324 F.2d 516

Nager Electric and Keystone Engineering
194 Ct. Cl. 835
442 F.2d 936

Requirements Contracts

Contract Management
ASBCA No. 44885
95-2 BCA 27,886

Pruitt Energy Sources
ENGBCA No. 6134
95-2 BCA 27,840

Shipbuilding Claims

Peterson Builders v. U.S.
Cl. Ct. No. 91-1406C
27 Fed. Cl. 443

Total Cost Approach

WRB et al., A Joint Venture, dba Robertson Construction v. U.S.
183 Ct. Cl. 409
12 CCF 81,781

Extraordinary Contractual Relief

Remington Arms
ACAB No. 1238
4 ECR P59

Fair Labor Standards Act

Malcolm Pirnie
758 F. Supp. 899
CA 2 No. 91-6138, 949 F.2d 611
U.S. S. Ct. No. 91-1748 cert. denied

Limitation of Costs

American Standard
ASBCA No. 15660
71-2 BCA 9,109

Clevite Ordnance
ASBCA No. 5859
1962 BCA 3,330

Dames & Moore
IBCA No. 2553
93-1 BCA 25,487

Datex
ASBCA No. 24794
81-1 BCA 15,060

DBA Systems
NASABCA No. 481-5
82-1 BCA 15,468

Defense Systems Concepts
ASBCA No. 44540
93-2 BCA 25,568

Dynamic Concepts
ASBCA No. 44738
93-2 BCA 25,689

ITT Defense Communications
ASBCA No. 14270
70-2 BCA 8,370

Metametrics
IBCA No. 1522-2-82
82-2 BCA 16,095

Research Applications
ASBCA No. 23834
79-2 BCA 14,120

SAI Comsystems
DOTCAB No. 1406
84-2 BCA 17,234

McDonnell Douglas and General Dynamics
No. 91-1294C
35 Fed. Cl. 358

Melville Energy Systems
CAFC No. 95-5150
33 Fed. Cl. 616

National Interior Contractors
ASBCA No. 47131
96-2 BCA 28,460

Technical Ordnance
ASBCA No. 48086
95-2 BCA 27,744

Leasing Contracts

Planning Research
GSBCA No. 11286-COM
96-1 BCA 27,954

Pulsar Data Systems
GSBCA No. 13223
96-2 BCA 28,407

Right to Terminate

Automated Services
DOTBCA No. 1753
87-1 BCA 19,459

Caldwell & Santmyer v. Secretary of Agriculture
CAFC No. 94-1314
55 F.3d 1578

Christian and Associates, G.L.
160 Ct. Cl. 58
320 F.2d 345
375 U.S. 954
9 CCF 72,180

Colonial Metals
204 Ct. Cl. 320
494 F.2d 1355

Corliss Steam Engine
1876 91 U.S. 321

Krygoski Construction
CAFC No. 53-5136
94 F.3d 1537

Torncello, Ronald A. & Soledad Enterprises v. U.S.
Ct. Cl. No. 486-80C
681 F.2d 756

Note: Page references to forms are in italic.

659

660